THE GUINNESS

WORLD

FACT BOOK

GUINNESS

ACKNOWLEDGEMENTS

Editor: Clive Carpenter

Editorial Assistant: Kathy Milligan

Layout: Rhoda and Robert Burns

Cover design: Jon Lucas

Artwork, maps and design: Eddie Botchway, Rhoda and Robert Burns

Index: Kathie Gill

Contributors: David Bradshaw, Bournemouth University; Dr Richard Brown, University of Sussex; Dr Stephen Burman, University of Sussex; Clive Carpenter; Kim Chesher; Dr David Dyker, University of Sussex; Dr Randolph Kent; Dr Christopher Pass, University of Bradford; Tina Persaud; Dr Andrew Robinson, University of Bradford; Dr Richard Tames; Dr John Walton, University College of Wales Aberystwyth.

Acknowledgements: We are indebted to the following for information - the diplomatic missions in London of Algeria, Argentina, Australia, Austria, Bangladesh, Belarus, Belgium, Brazil, Bulgaria, Canada, Chile, the People's Republic of China, Colombia, Croatia, Cuba, Cyprus, the Czech Republic, Denmark, Egypt, Estonia, Ethiopia, Finland, France, Germany, Greece, Hungary, Iceland, India, Indonesia, Ireland, Israel, Italy, Japan, Jordan, Kenya, the Republic of Korea, Latvia, Lebanon, Lesotho, Lithuania, Luxembourg, Malta, Malaysia, Mexico, Morocco, the Netherlands, New Zealand, Nigeria, Norway, Pakistan, Papua New Guinea, Peru, the Philippines, Poland, Portugal, the Russian Federation, Slovakia, Slovenia, South Africa, Spain, Sri Lanka, Sweden, Switzerland, Syria, Thailand, Tunisia, Turkey, the United States of America, Venezuela, Vietnam, and Zimbabwe, plus the Novosti News Agency, the Information Office of the European Union, and the United Nations Information Centre.

First edition
First published 1994
Reprint 10 9 8 7 6 5 4 3 2 1 0

© **Guinness Publishing Ltd, 1994**
Published in Great Britain by Guinness Publishing Ltd., 33 London Road, Enfield, Middlesex EN2 6DJ

Printed and bound by the Bath Press, Bath

'Guinness' is a registered trademark of Guinness Publishing Ltd.

British Library Cataloguing in Publication Data
The Guinness World Fact Book
1. World Statistics
910.21

ISBN 085112-798-3

CONTENTS

CONTENTS

CONTENTS

CONTENTS

▶ ▶ ▶ ▶ ▶ ▶ ▶ ▶ ▶ ▶ ▶ ▶

WORLD ECONOMY
AND
ORGANIZATIONS

A world of trading blocks. World recession. GATT. Leading GDPs -
The world's major economic powers. Production figures.
Population trends.The United Nations.
Other world bodies.

▶ ▶ ▶ ▶ ▶ ▶ ▶ ▶ ▶ ▶ ▶ ▶

A World of Trading Blocks

NAFTA, the European Union, the Far East . . . In the 1990s it has become increasingly common to talk in terms of regional, rather than national, economies. Indeed, it may appear that the world is dividing itself up into rival trading blocks.

The European Union covers 12 countries of Western Europe and, at the start of 1995, will expand with the addition of Austria and, if favourable results are obtained in national referenda, Finland, Sweden and Norway. Malta and Cyprus have been identified as the next candidates for entry to the Union, with the Czech Republic, Hungary, Poland and Slovakia close behind in the queue, probably achieving membership by the year 2000. These four Central European states have negotiated associate status of the EU, a standing that is also enjoyed by Bulgaria and Romania. EU trade agreements were concluded with the Baltic republics of Estonia, Latvia and Lithuania, which are likely to gain associate status in the short term. Slovenia will probably follow the same path. Finally, the European Economic Area agreement also brings Iceland and Liechtenstein, as well as the four states scheduled to join the EU in January 1995, within an ever-growing trading block. The EU, with its associates, looks set to form a European 'economic space', a market of some 470 million people.

The success of the European trading block spurred other countries into establishing blocks of their own. Canada negotiated a free-trade agreement with its giant neighbour, the USA. Mexico, an emerging economic power, proposed joining this pact, which, after some initial reluctance, became the North American Free Trade Agreement (NAFTA). Together, the three countries form the second-largest world trading block, with a market of over 365 million people. The importance of NAFTA can, though, be overestimated. Its effect upon the USA will not be great as the amount of trade liberalization involved is small compared with the EU.

In the Far East, both China and Japan have economies large enough to be considered trading blocks in their own right. Elsewhere, other blocks have been founded. ASEAN unites Brunei, Indonesia, Malaysia, the Philippines, Singapore and Thailand in a market of over 320 million people. Mercosur, a South American trade block comprising Argentina, Brazil, Paraguay and Uruguay, has a population of almost 200 million. Smaller blocks have emerged grouping the countries of the former Soviet Union (the CIS), of the Caribbean, the Andes, Central America, West Africa, Southern Africa, East Africa, and so on.

By 1994, the Pacific-rim conferences attended by the USA, Canada, Mexico, China, Japan, Australia, New Zealand, Chile and the emerging economic powers of Southeast Asia could be interpreted as the tentative foundations of a massive trading block uniting the economic powerhouses of North America and the Far East.

The GATT agreements (see pp. 10-11) have been about progress towards freer trade, but that progress has been held up by national vested interests. The establishment of large trading blocks is seen by some as a chance to escape the restraints of those national interests in favour of compromise. However, other observers are more pessimistic. The development of large and powerful trading blocks has also been interpreted as the replacement of national protectionism with regional protectionism.

There are signs of a 'fortress Europe' mentality that is mirrored by a 'fortress NAFTA' and, certainly, by a 'fortress Japan', whose protectionism is already legendary. There are fears of the growth of a small number of 'trade fortresses', each encompassing the countries of the developed world and turning their backs on the world economy. Already the countries of Southeast Europe and of the former Soviet Union are finding difficulty in breaching the tariff wall of the EU. Such protectionism could have devastating effects upon the economies of the developing world.

Regional trade blocks, however, have somewhat less substance than may be apparent. The imagery of regional integration is powerful - hence the opposition to NAFTA among American trade unions and in the US Congress, and in the continuing hostility among a broad range of public opinion in Norway to EU membership. The greatest effect upon world trade is likely to come not from regional bodies but rather from the general tariff reductions that have been achieved through the GATT.

World Recession

Although in the long term the world's leading nations do follow some general economic cycle, the so-called recession of the 1990s is different from all the preceding periods in certain key respects. First, the onset of recession and the duration of such recessions has varied between countries. Second, and most importantly, the onset of the 1990s recession was not brought about by some global external shock, such as the soaring oil prices in the 1970s, but instead by the need for some form of structural re-adjustment to counter the effects of the credit-driven growth of the 1980s. Finally, given the increasing interdependence of the world's leading economies, it is now easier for domestic situations to be transmitted onto the international scene.

The USA and the UK were the first of the leading nations to go into recession, in the middle of 1990 on the back of their debt-fuelled growth of the 1980s. In the case of the UK, much of the blame was put on the lowering of taxes and financial deregulation in the late 1980s, which resulted in inflationary pressures and an ever widening trade gap. The resultant tightening of monetary policy and high exchange rates resulted in a deep recession. The opportunity for fiscal regeneration was severely limited by an ever expanding public sector deficit.

Similarly, US economic policy was chiefly concerned with rectifying some of the excesses of the 1980s. Primarily this focused on limiting the degree of public sector interference in the economy with the emphasis on cutting the US budget deficit. At the same time there was a high level of corporate restructuring, the rationalization of many big US enterprises, especially in the defence sector, and concern at the depressed state of the world markets. Having sunk into recession first, these countries were likewise the first to recover. However, the length of their respective recessions and the strength of the recoveries stand in marked contrast. The USA experienced only a blip in its growth pattern in 1990/91 and has followed a strong path of recovery since. The UK on the other hand is still below its pre-recession level of GDP and its post-recession performance has been less than impressive.

Up until the second half of 1992 the economies of Germany, France, Italy and Japan had continued to expand. Aided by the investment surge, the impact of reunification helped push the German economy into a period of exceptional growth. However, by the second half of 1992, Germany was experiencing its worst recession since 1945. Paying the price of high interest rates (to attract foreign capital for reunification and stifle inflationary pressures at home), budget deficits and cost pressures, Germany increasingly lost its competitiveness with the rest of Europe. However, the deflationary impact of reunification was not confined to their domestic economy. Given the links between the European economies, especially through the Exchange Rate Mechanism (ERM) and trade in the European Union, its impact was transmitted to other European countries which had problems of their own. Italy was going through a period of profound economic and political reform with a move away from old state-owned industries and a huge public sector deficit. France similarly was moving towards more market-based policies while trying to deal with escalating unemployment and wage costs, and an increasing budget balance. In the case of both countries the transmission of Germany's problems into their own troubled economies was enough to pull them into recession.

Japan's economy began going sideways from early 1992, following a period of extraordinarily rapid money-driven growth in the late 1980s. While still out-performing its competitors, Japan has still been forced to take some corrective action to rectify this stalemate. Primarily Japan has suffered because of falling demand both domestically and internationally for its goods and services. The private sector is buffeted by poor corporate profits, asset prices have fallen dramatically, and industry is suffering from the strong yen and low consumer confidence due to weak personal income growth, rising job insecurity and high indebtedness.

Whatever its length and degree of severity, the so-called 1990s recession has been a process of correcting past excesses and restructuring. While the overall effect has been to dampen the level of world demand and thus exacerbate problems inherent within the economy of leading nations, it also stands in stark contrast to some of the newly industrializing countries (NICs), such as Taiwan, Singapore, Malaysia, Indonesia and Thailand. Their strong performance stands out against the problems which beset the developed nations.

9

World Trade Liberalization: The GATT and UNCTAD

In principle, most countries stand to gain from the establishment of 'free trade', that is, the removal of all restrictions on cross-frontier trade. Unrestricted international trade can bring both consumption and production gains to a country. Such trade enables countries to consume some goods and services more cheaply by importing them, and also to obtain some from other countries' resources and products that cannot be supplied by domestic producers. International trade promotes productive efficiency as it channels resources away from areas of the economy best served by imports and into industries where the country has production advantages over others and is thus able to establish itself as a major exporter. Since 1945 there has been a process of trade liberalization across the world, through the establishment of international organizations such as the General Agreement on Tariffs and Trade (GATT) and the United Nations Conference on Trade and Development (UNCTAD). Trade liberalization regionally has come about through the formation of several customs unions and free-trade areas such as the European Community (Union) and the European Free Trade Association.

THE GENERAL AGREEMENT ON TARIFFS AND TRADE (GATT)

The General Agreement on Tariffs and Trade was established in 1947 alongside the International Monetary Fund (IMF) and the World Bank to provide an international framework for promoting free trade as a means of increasing worldwide economic welfare. All the developed countries and a large number of developing countries (120) are members. They meet periodically to negotiate multilateral trade concessions under the supervision of the GATT secretariat, whose headquarters are in Geneva, Switzerland. The GATT not only coordinates the implementation of agreed tariff reductions but also operates a number of 'arbitration' panels to settle cases of dispute. GATT is particularly concerned to ensure that trade is conducted in a 'fair' way: GATT rules, for example, allow members to retaliate against imports that have been 'dumped' (that is, products sold in a foreign market at prices below the domestic ones).

GATT has two key operational principles, the first of which is reciprocity. This requires that where member A has agreed to lower its tariffs against member B's exports then member B will reciprocate by agreeing to introduce matching tariff reductions. The second principle, non-discrimination, prohibits members from granting preferential treatment to another country. This means that members must extend to each other the most favourable terms negotiated with any trading partner – the so-called 'most-favoured nation' principle. In practice, this principle has been waived in the case of regional free-trade alliances on certain conditions.

GATT has supervised eight major multilateral rounds of tariff negotiation (see box), which have resulted in a very substantial reduction in average tariff levels in the developed countries. On the whole tariff cuts have applied only to manufactured goods. Although the 'Uruguay Round' (1986-93) was concerned with manufactures it also emphasized the need to obtain major tariff reductions in agricultural produce and the liberalization of international trade in services. The 'Uruguay Round' was due to be completed in 1990 but encountered a number of negotiation problems. One main sticking point was the EC's subsidization of agricultural produce, which was resisted by the USA. In addition to agreeing to substantial cuts in industrial and agricultural tariffs and subsidies (see below), the Uruguay participants also agreed to various initiatives to liberalize trade in commercial services, gave a firmer commitment to enforce intellectual property rights and to open up government procurement contracts to greater international competition. It was also decided that GATT itself should be replaced by a new more formal body – the World Trade Organization (WTO, due to be established in 1995).

According to a 1993 study the Uruguay Round programme would add around $213bn (£138bn) a year to world income by the year 2002 if fully implemented. The study estimates the 'global price' of distortions due to protectionism at around $477bn. The Uruguay Round proposal to cut average tariffs and subsidies for agriculture would yield a gain of $190bn while an average 30% cut in remaining tariffs on industrial products would result in a gain of $23bn. In the present recessionary economic climate it is unlikely that all the Uruguay Round proposals will be implemented in full. For example, the USA and the EC have failed to make substantial progress on cutting agricultural and steel subsidies and the opening up of their public procurement business to international competition.

THE UNITED NATIONS CONFERENCE ON TRADE AND DEVELOPMENT (UNCTAD)

While the original GATT format advanced the interest of developed countries, developing countries felt that it did little to help them. Firstly, GATT tariff cuts in the 1950s and 1960s were applied almost exclusively to manufactured goods, which most developing countries did not produce to any great extent. Secondly, the reciprocity and non-discrimination principles were considered unfavourable to developing countries. In their case it was felt that some form of preferential treatment was desirable to assist their traditional industries and help newly established manufacturing industries. The developing countries' grievances led to the creation of the United Nations Conference on Trade and Development (UNCTAD) in 1964.

The major role of UNCTAD has been to 'lobby' for a more favourable trading environment for developing countries. As a result GATT adopted a 'special and differential treatment' provision, which waived the obligation on developing countries to reciprocate liberalization measures where this would be harmful to their development and trade needs. Pressure from UNCTAD also led to the adoption by GATT of a 'generalized' system of preferences (GSP), which gave developing countries' exports tariff-free or tariff-reduced access to the markets of developed countries. However, this promising development has been undermined by the use of non-tariff measures to exclude developing countries' exports, particularly competing agricultural products and low-technology manufactures. The Multi-Fibre Agreement, for example, was a quota system to restrict developing countries' textile exports entering developed countries' markets.

In addition to its work in obtaining tariff concessions, UNCTAD has promoted the extension of International Commodity Agreements, which are aimed at increasing and stabilizing the export prices of primary products as a means of raising developing countries' foreign-exchange earnings and producers' incomes.

GATT ROUNDS 1947-93

Rounds	Results
• 1947 Geneva (23 participants).	45,000 tariff cuts agreed, covering $10bn of trade in manufactures.
• 1949 Annecy, France (13 participants).	5,000 tariff cuts on manufactures.
• 1950-51 Torquay, England (38 participants).	8,700 tariff cuts on manufactures, equivalent to a 25% cut in 1948 tariff levels.
• 1956 Geneva (26 participants)	2,500 tariff cuts covering £2.5bn of trade in manufactures.
• 1960-62 'The Dillon Round' (26 participants).	4,400 tariff cuts covering $5bn of trade in manufactures.
• 1964-67 'The Kennedy Round' (62 participants).	Tariff cuts averaging 35%, covering $40bn of trade in manufactures.
• 1973-79 'The Tokyo Round' (99 participants).	Tariff cuts covering $30bn of trade in manufactures.
• 1986-93 'The Uruguay Round' (117 participants).	Tariffs on manufactures by the industrial economies to be lowered to an average of 3.9% from 6.3%, first concerted attempt to introduce major cuts in tariffs and subsidies on agricultural produce and liberalize trade in commercial services.

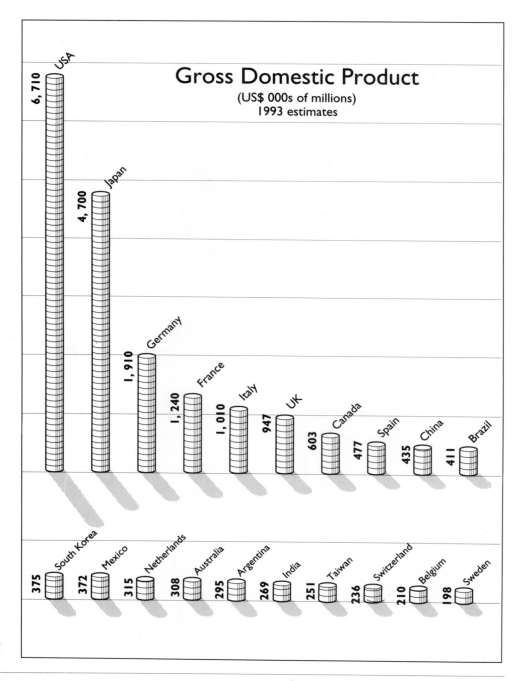

Gross Domestic Product

(US$ 000s of millions)
1993 estimates

USA — 6,710
Japan — 4,700
Germany — 1,910
France — 1,240
Italy — 1,010
UK — 947
Canada — 603
Spain — 477
China — 435
Brazil — 411

South Korea — 375
Mexico — 372
Netherlands — 315
Australia — 308
Argentina — 295
India — 269
Taiwan — 251
Switzerland — 236
Belgium — 210
Sweden — 198

Production Figures

Most of the annual production figures given below are for 1991-92. In some cases the latest comparable figures were for 1990, which are indicated with an *.

MAJOR MINERAL ORES

Bauxite *Production (in tonnes)*
Australia   39,900,000 p.a
Guinea   17,800,000 p.a
Brazil   10,800,000 p.a
Russia   5,800,000 p.a
India   4,840,000 p.a
Jamaica   4,150,000 p.a
Suriname   3,140,000 p.a

Copper ore *Production (in tonnes)*
Chile   1,920,000 p.a
USA   1,630,000 p.a
Canada   745,000 p.a
China   560,000 p.a
Russia*   550,000 p.a
Zambia   385,000 p.a
Peru   370,000 p.a

Diamonds *Production (in carats)*
Australia   35,000,000 p.a
Botswana   16,000 000 p.a
Zaïre   15,000,000 p.a
Russia*   15,000,000 p.a
South Africa 10,150,000 p.a

Gold *Production (in tonnes)*
South Africa   600 p.a
USA   300 p.a
Australia   240 p.a
Russia   240 p.a
Canada   180 p.a

Iron ore *Production (in tonnes)*
China   170,000,000 p.a
Brazil   150,000,000 p.a
Australia   115,000,000 p.a
Russia   97,300,000 p.a
Ukraine   75,700,000 p.a
USA   55,500,000 p.a
India   37,000,000 p.a
Canada   32,700,000 p.a
South Africa   28,900,000 p.a
Kazakhstan   22,000,000 p.a
Venezuela   20,000,000 p.a

Silver *Production (in tonnes)*
Mexico   2290 p.a

USA   1850 p.a
Peru   1770 p.a
Russia*   1500 p.a
Canada   1340 p.a

Tin ore *Production (in tonnes)*
Brazil 30,000 p.a
Indonesia   29,400 p.a
China   26,000 p.a
Malaysia   20,500 p.a
Thailand   11,500 p.a

Uranium *Production (in tonnes)*
Canada   9250 p.a
Russia 8200 p.a
Australia   3750 p.a
Niger   3000 p.a.
France   2100 p.a.
South Africa   1750 p.a
USA   1750 p.a
Namibia   1500 p.a

Zinc ore *Production (in tonnes)*
Canada   1,195,000 p.a
Australia   1,020,000 p.a
Russia   940,000 p.a
China   710,000 p.a
Peru   605,000 p.a
USA   545,000 p.a

MAJOR CROPS

Barley *Production (in tonnes)*
Russia   22,100,000 p.a
Germany 14,450,000 p.a
Ukraine   14,000,000 p.a
Canada   10,900,000 p.a
France   10,470,000 p.a
USA   10,110,000 p.a

Maize (Corn) *Production (in tonnes)*
USA   190,000,000 p.a
China   93,350,000 p.a
Brazil   30,600,000 p.a
France   14,600,000 p.a
Mexico   13,630,000 p.a
Kazakhstan   13,270,000 p.a
Romania   10,490,000 p.a
India   8,200,000 p.a

Rice *Production (in tonnes)*
China   187,450,000 p.a
India   110,945,000 p.a
Indonesia   47,770,000 p.a
Bangladesh   27,400,000 p.a
Vietnam   21,500,000 p.a

13

Thailand 18,500,000 p.a
Burma (Myanmar) 13,770,000 p.a
Japan 13,250,000 p.a
Brazil 9,960,000 p.a
Philippines 9,200,000 p.a

Cocoa beans *Production (in tonnes)*
Ivory Coast 700,000 p.a
Brazil 345,000 p.a
Ghana 280,000 p.a
Malaysia 225,000 p.a
Indonesia 215,000 p.a

Coffee *Production (in tonnes)*
Brazil 1,300,000 p.a
Colombia 1,050,000 p.a
Indonesia 405,000 p.a
Mexico 300,000 p.a
Vietnam 285,000 p.a
Côte d'Ivoire 240,000 p.a

Cotton lint *Production (in tonnes)*
China 5,700,000 p.a
Uzbekistan 4,000,000 p.a
USA 3,800,000 p.a
Pakistan 2,100,000 p.a
Brazil 1,880,000 p.a
India 1,700,000 p.a

Potatoes *Production (in tonnes)*
Russia 34,330,000 p.a
China 33,530,000 p.a
Poland 23,400,000 p.a
Ukraine 20,400,000 p.a
USA 18,970,000 p.a
India 15,250,000 p.a
Germany 10,230,000 p.a

Rubber *Production (in tonnes)*
Thailand 1,400,000 p.a
Indonesia 1,295,000 p.a
Malaysia 1,250,000 p.a

Sugar beet *Production (in tonnes)*
France 31,330,000 p.a
Ukraine 28,600,000 p.a
Germany 25,725,000 p.a
USA 25,265,000 p.a
Russia 24,300,000 p.a

Sugar cane *Production (in tonnes)*
Brazil 270,670,000 p.a
India 240,290,000 p.a
China 73,105,000 p.a
Cuba 58,000,000 p.a

Thailand 46,805,000 p.a

Tea *Production (in tonnes)*
India 730,000 p.a
China 565,000 p.a
Kenya 190,000 p.a
Sri Lanka 180,000 p.a

Tobacco *Production (in tonnes)*
China 3,120,000 p.a
USA 750,000 p.a
Brazil 585,000 p.a
India 560,000 p.a

Wheat *Production (in tonnes)*
China 95,005,000 p.a
India 54,520,000 p.a
USA 53,915,000 p.a
Russia 38,900,000 p.a
France 32,600,000 p.a
Canada 29,870,000 p.a
Turkey 20,400,000 p.a
Ukraine 19,500,000 p.a
Kazakhstan 18,500,000 p.a

LIVESTOCK
Cattle *Number*
India 198,400,000
Brazil 153,000,000
USA 99,560,000
China 81,410,000
Russia 54,700,000
Argentina 50,020,000

Sheep *Number*
Australia 148,205,000
China 112,820,000
New Zealand 52,570,000
India 55,740,000
Russia 52,200,000
Iran 45,000,000

Pigs *Number*
China 364,000,000
USA 57,685,000
Russia 35,400,000
Brazil 33,050,000
Poland 22,100,000

AGRICULTURAL AND ALLIED PRODUCTS
Beef and Veal *Production (in tonnes)*
USA 10,530,000 p.a
Russia 8,200,000 p.a
Brazil 2,800,000 p.a
Argentina 2,640,000 p.a
Germany 2,180,000 p.a

Beer *Production (hectolitres)*
USA 230,000,000 p.a
Germany 113,000,000 p.a
China 64,000,000 p.a
Japan 63,000,000 p.a
Russia 60,200,000 p.a
United Kingdom 54,900,000 p.a

Butter (and ghee) *Production (in tonnes)*
Russia 1,570,000 p.a
India 1,040,000 p.a
Germany 650,000 p.a
USA 635,000 p.a

Cow's milk *Production (in tonnes)*
USA 67,375,000 p.a
Russia 55,700,000 p.a
Germany 29,300,000 p.a
India 27,000,000 p.a
France 26,600,000 p.a

Eggs *Production (in tonnes)*
China 6,845,000 p.a
USA 4,005,000 p.a
Russia 2,230 ,000 p.a
Japan 2,465,000 p.a

Fishing catch (maritime/freshwater) *(in tonnes)*
China 12,095,000 p.a
Japan 9,310,000 p.a
Russia 6,965,000 p.a
Peru 6,945,000 p.a
Chile 6,165,000 p.a
USA 5,855,000 p.a
India 3,620,000 p.a.

Paper and paper board *Production (in tonnes)*
USA 72,700,000 p.a
Japan 29,100,000 p.a
China 18,500,000 p.a
Canada 16,600,000 p.a
Germany 13,500,000 p.a
Finland 8,500,000 p.a

Roundwood *Production (cu. metres)*
USA 495,000,000 p.a
India 279,800,000 p.a
China 277,000,000 p.a
Brazil 264,600,000 p.a
Canada 178,000,000 p.a
Indonesia 172,990,000 p.a
Nigeria 111,600,000 p.a
Russia 65,800,000 p.a

Sheep meat *Production (in tonnes)*

Australia 649,000 p.a
China 570,000 p.a
New Zealand 550,000 p.a
Russia 420,000 p.a
United Kingdom 382,000 p.a

Sugar
Production (in tonnes)
India 12,530,000 p.a
Brazil 8,675,000 p.a
China 7,835,000 p.a
Cuba 7,623,000 p.a
USA 6,531,000 p.a

Wine *Production (in tonnes)*
France 6,200,000 p.a
Italy 5,915,000 p.a
Spain 3,105,000 p.a
USA 1,490,000 p.a
Argentina 1,465,000 p.a
Germany 1,015,000 p.a

Wool *Production (in tonnes)*
Australia 548,000 p.a
New Zealand 226,000 p.a
China 123,000 p.a
Argentina 67,000 p.a
Uruguay 64,000 p.a

MANUFACTURED GOODS
Aluminium *Production (in tonnes)*
USA 6,460,000 p.a
Canada 1,900,000 p.a
Australia 1,265,000 p.a
Germany 1,230,000 p.a
Brazil 1,140,000 p.a
Japan 1,130,000 p.a

Cars *Production (thousands)*
Japan 7,450,000 p.a
USA 5,400,000 p.a
Germany 4,270,000 p.a
France 3,215,000 p.a
Spain 1,830,000 p.a
South Korea 1,300,000 p.a
United Kingdom 1,200,000 p.a
Belgium 1,065,000 p.a
Italy 775,000 p.a

Cement *Production (in tonnes)*
China 305,000,000 p.a
Japan 89,565,000 p.a
Russia 77,500,000 p.a
USA 65,050,000 p.a
India 51,660,000 p.a

South Korea 43,270,000 p.a
Italy 40,320,000 p.a

Crude steel *Production (tonnes)*
Japan 109,650,000 p.a
USA 91,600,000 p.a
China 82,000,000 p.a
Russia 77,100,000 p.a
Ukraine 45,000,000 p.a
Germany 38,875,000 p.a
South Korea 27,800,000 p.a
Canada 25,990,000 p.a
Italy 25,100,000 p.a
Brazil 23,900,000 p.a

Colour television sets *Production*
South Korea 16,175,000 p.a
China 13,150,000 p.a
USA 14,720,000 p.a
Japan 9,755,000 p.a
Russia 4,400,000 p.a

Shipping (merchant) *Launched (tonnes)*
Japan 5,245,000 p.a
South Korea 2,420,000 p.a
Romania 1,035,000 p.a
Germany 780,000 p.a
China (Taiwan) 740,000 p.a

ENERGY
Crude petroleum *Production (in barrels*)*
Russia 3,313,000,000 p.a
Saudi Arabia 2,965,000,000 p.a
USA 2,617,000,000 p.a
Iran 1,251,000,000 p.a
China 1,011,000,000 p.a
Mexico 975,000,000 p.a
United Arab Emirates 842,000,000 p.a
Venezuela 771,000,000 p.a
United Kingdom 656,000,000 p.a
Norway 622,000,000 p.a
Canada 567,000,000 p.a
Indonesia 532,000,000 p.a
Libya 526,000,000 p.a
* one barrel averages 159 litres.

Natural gas *Production (in cu. metres)*

Russia 645,000,000,000 p.a
USA 503,330,000,000 p.a
Canada 111,175,000,000 p.a
Netherlands 89,960,000 p.a
Turkmenistan 84,300,000 p.a
United Kingdom 53,900,000 p.a
Algeria 43,320,000 p.a
Mexico 42,000,000 p.a
Indonesia 40,450,000 p.a
Saudi Arabia 31,820,000 p.a

Coal (bituminous/lignite) *Production (tonnes)*
China 1,080,000,000 p.a
USA 907,400,000 p.a
Russia 353,300,000 p.a
India 229,000,000 p.a
Poland 215,000,000 p.a
Australia 214,000,000 p.a
Germany 183,000,000 p.a
South Africa 176,200,000 p.a
Ukraine 133,600,000 p.a
Kazakhstan 130,300,000 p.a
United Kingdom 87,000,000 p.a
Czech Republic 78,400,000 p.a
North Korea 67,000,000 p.a

Electricity *Production (in kW-hr)*
USA 2,797,000,000,000 p.a
Russia 1,068,000,000,000 p.a
Japan 888,086,000,000 p.a
China 618,000,000,000 p.a
Germany 573,752,000,000 p.a
Canada 507,913,000,000 p.a
France 454,702,000,000 p.a
United Kingdom 318,979,000,000 p.a
India 286,700,000,000 p.a
Ukraine 252,600,000,000 p.a
Brazil 234,366,000,000 p.a
Italy 222,041,000,000 p.a
South Africa 169,645,000,000 p.a
Australia 156,883,000,000 p.a
Spain 155,704,000,000 p.a
Sweden 146,535,000,000 p.a
Poland 136,337,000,000 p.a
Mexico 131,501,000,000 p.a
Norway 121,600,000,000 p.a
South Korea 118,738,000,000 p.a

Population and social trends

WORLD POPULATION

Somewhere between 24 June and 11 July 1987, the human population of the planet Earth reached 5 billion. Yet, two hundred years before that, when the world's population was barely more than one billion, political economists such as Thomas Malthus and David Ricardo were already predicting that the human species would breed itself into starvation. Nevertheless, despite their predictions, the human population keeps increasing - but so too does the food supply. Two contending views have emerged concerning the extent to which burgeoning populations affect food supply. The first is that population must be controlled if persistent malnutrition and starvation are not to become the inevitable lot for a substantial portion of the globe. The second is that, even with a projected global population of 10 billion by the year 2070, there is sufficient food to feed everyone.

In 1992, every day, the population of the world increased by an estimated 220,000 people - that is nearly an additional 80,000,000 people in one year. The rate of increase varies from an average of 0.75% per annum in Europe to 3.05% in Africa (see below).

LIFE EXPECTANCY
HIGHEST

Japan	79
Iceland	78
Sweden	78
Switzerland	78
Australia	77
Canada	77
France	77
Italy	77
Netherlands	77
Norway	77
San Marino	77

LOWEST

Guinea-Bissau	39
Afghanistan	42
Sierra Leone	42
Guinea	43
Gambia	44
Niger	45
Angola	46
Malawi	46
Burundi	47
Chad	47
Equatorial Guinea	47
Mauritania	47
Mozambique	47
Senegal	47
Uganda	47

Figures are the average life expectancy for 1990.

POPULATION OF MAJOR WORLD REGIONS (millions)

	1900	1950	1990	2025	2100
World	**1 622**	**2 518**	**5 292**	**8 504**	**11 186**
Asia*	1 070	1 558	3 402	5 265	6 385
Africa	110	222	642	1 597	2 931
Latin America	64	166	448	757	1 075
North America	81	166	276	332	314
Europe †	290	393	498	515	440
Oceania	7	13	26	38	41

* includes the populations of the states of the former USSR.

† excludes the populations of the states of the former USSR.

Population growth

Period	World population
Neolithic period	under 10 000 000
4000 BC	c. 50 000 000
AD 500	c. 100 000 000
AD 800	c. 200 000 000
c1550	c. 500 000 000
1805	1 000 000 000
1926	2 000 000 000
c1960	3 000 000 000
1974	4 000 000 000
1987	5 000 000 000
1998 (projected)	6 000 000 000
2010 (projected)	7 000 000 000
2023 (projected)	8 000 000 000
2040 (projected)	9 000 000 000
2070 (projected)	10 000 000 000

FERTILITY

In the following tables the crude birth rate measures the number of births per year per thousand. In the table listing territories with the highest crude birth rates, the figures given refer to the period 1985-90 (except for Mali and Malawi where earlier estimates are given).

Territories with the highest crude live birth rates

Country or territory	Births per thousand
Uganda	52.2
Rwanda	51.2
Zambia	51.1
Guinea	51.0
Tanzania	50.5
Somalia	50.1
Ivory Coast	49.9
Benin	49.2
Mali	48.7
Ethiopia	48.6
Botswana	48.5
Nigeria	48.5
Malawi	48.3
Sierra Leone	48.2

Territories with the lowest crude live birth rates

Country or territory*	Births per thousand
Falkland Islands	7.5 (1988)
Italy	9.7 (1989)
Japan	9.9 (1990)
Norfolk Island	10.0 (1981)
Greece	10.1 (1989)
San Marino	10.1 (1989)
Spain	10.7 (1988)
Austria	11.6 (1990)
Hungary	11.6 (1990)
Hong Kong	11.7 (1990)
Portugal	11.9 (1988)
Germany	11.4 (1989)
Belgium	12.0 (1988)
Isle of Man	12.1 (1989)
Andorra	12.2 (1990)

* non-sovereign territories are indicated in italics

POPULATION DENSITY

The least densely populated territories are to be found in high latitudes (e.g. Greenland and the Falkland Islands), in the major desert areas (e.g. Mongolia, Western Sahara, Mauritania and Namibia), or in parts of the world where tropical rain forests remain the dominant vegetation type. The most densely populated territories are mostly very small states or former colonial trading outposts with the character of city-states, or relatively small islands with diverse economies. Among the most populous states in the table is one low-income country that is heavily dependent on the productivity of its rich soils (Bangladesh), one middle-income country now rapidly industrializing (South Korea), and one major high-income country (The Netherlands).

Territories with the greatest density of population

Country or territory*	Population per km² (1990)
Macau	*29 962*
Monaco	28 500
Hong Kong	*5551*
Gibraltar	*5083*
Singapore	4859
Vatican City	1705
Gaza Strip	*1698*
Bermuda	*1144*
Malta	1120
Bangladesh	803
Guernsey	*760*
Bahrain	742
Maldives	722
Jersey	*714*
Barbados	594
Mauritius	531
Nauru	457
South Korea	432

Puerto Rico	405
San Marino	385
Tuvalu	373
The Netherlands	366

* non-sovereign territories are indicated in italics

Territories with the least density of population

Country or territory*	Population per km² (1990)
Greenland	*0.03*
Falkland Islands	*0.16*
Guyane (French Guiana	*1.10*
Mongolia	1.40
Western Sahara	*1.50*
Mauritania	1.97
Namibia	2.16
Australia	2.22
Botswana	2.22
Iceland	2.48
Libya	2.58
Suriname	2.58
Canada	2.66
Guyana	3.70
Gabon	4.38
Chad	4.42
Central African Republic	4.88

* non-sovereign territories are indicated in italics

POPULATION BY AGE
Third World countries with high birth rates tend to have young populations; developed countries with low birth rates tend to have more elderly populations.

Territories with the youngest population

Country	% of population under 25
Kenya	50
Uganda	50
Yemen	50
Botswana	49
Malawi	49
Rwanda	49
Tanzania	49
Zambia	49
Côte d'Ivoire	48
Niger	48
Nigeria	48

Territories with the oldest population

Country	% of population over 60
Sweden	23
Belgium	21
Norway	21

UK	21
Austria	20
Denmark	20
Greece	20
Italy	20

URBANIZATION
The increased migration of rural dwellers into cities - has been a particular feature of the second half of the 20th century. In 1950 under 30% of the population of the world lived in urban regions, but by 1990 almost 44% lived in cities, towns or their suburbs. The greatest proportion of urban dwellers is to be found in countries of the developed world. Some 97% of the population of Belgium, for example, is urban.

URBAN POPULATION
The definitions of 'urban' vary from country to country, often quite markedly, and these variations influence the positions of countries within the tables. Rapid urbanization is characteristic of the Third World. Conversely, in developed countries there is little scope for further growth in the level of urbanization. Indeed, in developed states the pattern of net population movement from country to town has been succeeded by a net movement from town to country.

Territories with the highest % of urban population

Country or territory*	
Gaza Strip	100.0
Macau	100.0
Monaco	100.0
Singapore	100.0
Vatican City	100.0
Belgium	97.0
Kuwait	96.0
Andorra	94.8
Hong Kong	*93.1*
Iceland	90.4

* non-sovereign territories are indicated in italics

Territories with the lowest % of urban population

Country or territory	
Bhutan	5.0
Burundi	5.0
Rwanda	8.0
Burkina Faso	9.0
Nepal	10.0
Ethiopia	12.1
Malawi	14.6

19

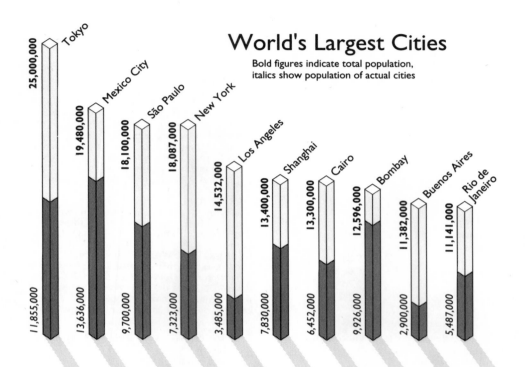

World's Largest Cities

Bold figures indicate total population,
italics show population of actual cities

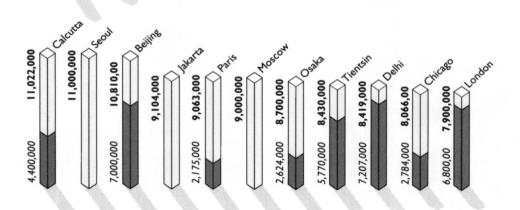

United Nations

Proposals to found 'a general organization . . . for the maintenance of international peace and security' were agreed between the four major unoccupied allied powers in World War II - China, the UK, the USA and the USSR - in 1944. At the United Nations Conference in San Francisco in April 1945, 50 participating countries signed the United Charter, which came into effect on 24 October 1945.

Of the world's sovereign states only the following are not members of the United Nations (UN): Taiwan (Republic of China), Switzerland, the Vatican City, Kiribati, Nauru, Tonga and Tuvalu. (However, Switzerland and the Vatican City have observer status at the UN, with the right to be present at sessions of the General Assembly, but without the right to participate.)

MEMBERS OF THE UN

Original members (October 1945): Argentina, Australia, Belgium, Bolivia, Brazil, Belarus (formerly the Byelorussian Soviet Republic which held UN membership 1945-91), Canada, Chile, China (which was represented from 1945 to 1971 by the Republic of China, which after 1949 was confined to Taiwan - in 1971 the UN withdrew recognition from Taiwan in favour of the People's Republic of China), Colombia, Costa Rica, Cuba, Czechoslovakia (since 1993 this seat has been held by the Czech Republic), Denmark, the Dominican Republic, Ecuador, Egypt, El Salvador, Ethiopia, France, Greece, Guatemala, Haiti, Honduras, India (although India did not gain independence until 1947, an Indian delegation signed the UN Charter in 1945), Iran, Iraq, Lebanon, Liberia, Luxembourg, Mexico, the Netherlands, New Zealand, Nicaragua, Norway, Panama, Paraguay, Peru, the Philippines, Poland, Saudi Arabia, South Africa, Syria, Turkey, Ukraine (formerly the Ukrainian Soviet Republic which held UN membership 1945-91), USSR (since 1992 this seat has been held by Russia), the UK, the USA, Uruguay, Venezuela, and Yugoslavia (which was suspended in 1992).

Members elected in 1946: Afghanistan, Iceland, Sweden, and Thailand. **In 1947:** Pakistan and Yemen. **In 1948:** Burma (officially known as Myanmar since 1989). **In 1949:** Israel. **In 1950:** Indonesia. **In 1955:** Albania, Austria, Bulgaria, Cambodia, Finland, Hungary, Ireland, Italy, Jordan, Laos, Libya, Nepal, Portugal, Romania, Spain, and Sri Lanka (which was elected as Ceylon). **In 1956:** Japan, Morocco, Sudan, and Tunisia. **In 1957:** Ghana and Malaysia (which was elected as Malaya). **In 1958:** Guinea. **In 1960:** Benin (which was elected as Dahomey), Burkina Faso (which was elected as Upper Volta), Cameroon, the Central African Republic, Chad, Congo, Côte d'Ivoire (which was elected as the Ivory Coast), Cyprus, Gabon, Madagascar, Mali, Niger, Nigeria, Senegal, Somalia, Togo, and Zaïre (which was elected as the Congolese Republic). **In 1961:** Mauritania, Mongolia, Sierra Leone, and Tanzania (which was elected as Tanganyika). **In 1962:** Algeria, Burundi, Jamaica, Rwanda, Trinidad and Tobago, and Uganda. **In 1963:** Kenya, Kuwait and Zanzibar (which ceased membership in 1964 upon its merger with Tanganyika to form Tanzania). **In 1964:** Malawi, Malta, and Zambia. **In 1965:** The Gambia, the Maldives, and Singapore. **In 1966:** Barbados, Botswana, Guyana, and Lesotho. **In 1967:** South Yemen (which ceased membership upon its merger with Yemen in 1990). **In 1968:** Equatorial Guinea, Mauritius, and Swaziland. **In 1970:** Fiji. **In 1971:** Bahrain, Bhutan, Oman, Qatar, and the United Arab Emirates. **In 1973:** The Bahamas, Germany (Federal Republic), German Democratic Republic (East Germany - which ceased membership upon its reunification with the Federal Republic of Germany in 1990). **In 1974:** Bangladesh, Grenada, and Guinea-Bissau. **In 1975:** Cape Verde, the Comoros, Mozambique, Papua New Guinea, São Tomé e Principe, and Suriname. **In 1976:** Angola, the Seychelles, and Western Samoa. **In 1977:** Djibouti and Vietnam. **In 1978:** Dominica and the Solomon Islands. **In 1979:** St Lucia. **In 1980:** St Vincent and the Grenadines, and Zimbabwe. **In 1981:** Antigua and Barbuda, Belize, and Vanuatu. **In 1983:** St Christopher and Nevis. **In 1984:** Brunei. **In 1990:** Liechtenstein and Namibia. **In 1991:** Estonia, Korea (People's Democratic Republic of - North Korea), Korea (Republic of - South Korea), Latvia, Lithuania, the Marshall Islands, and the Federated States of Micronesia. **In 1992:** Armenia, Azerbaijan, Bosnia-Herzegovina, Croatia, Georgia, Kazakhstan, Kyrgyzstan, Moldova, San Marino, Slovenia, Tajikistan, Turkmenistan, and Uzbekistan. **In 1993:** Andorra, Eritrea, Macedonia (elected as The Former Yugoslav Republic of Macedonia),

Monaco, and Slovakia.

THE ORGANIZATION OF THE UN

The UN has six principal organs (see below). All are based in New York, with the exception of the International Court of Justice, which is based in the Hague (in the Netherlands). The official languages of the UN are Arabic, Chinese, English, French, Spanish and Russian.

The General Assembly is composed of all the member-states. It can discuss anything within the scope of the Charter. Each member-state has up to five delegates but only one vote. A President is elected by the General Assembly each September for a single term. Decisions of the General Assembly are made by a qualified majority (two thirds) of those present on 'important' questions, and by a simple majority on other issues.

The Security Council is the main organ for maintaining international peace and security. It has five permanent members - China, France, Russia (from 1945 to 1992 this seat was held by the Soviet Union), the UK and the USA and 10 other members, who are elected by the General Assembly for a term of two years. (From 1949 to 1971, China was represented by the Republic of China, that is Taiwan. In 1993-94 the enlargement of the Security Council was widely discussed and there are suggestions that both Japan and Germany might become permanent members. Decisions of the Security Council are reached by a majority vote of at least nine of the 15 members. However, any one of the permanent members of the Security Council can exercise its right of veto.

The Economic and Social Council acts as a co-ordinating body for the numerous specialized agencies created by the UN. The Council - which has 54 members elected for a term of three years - aims to promote international co-operation in the economic, social and related fields.

The Trusteeship Council has effectively been wound up. All of the territories - mostly former German and Japanese colonies - placed under its supervision have achieved independence, with the exception of Palau (Belau).

The International Court of Justice The International Court of Justice, which is popularly known as the World Court, is available to offer legal rulings on any case brought before it

by UN members. (All UN members plus Switzerland are parties to the Statute of the Court.) In the event of a party failing to adhere to a judgement of the Court, the other party may have recourse to the Security Council. The World Court comprises 15 judges elected by the Security Council and the General Assembly for a term of nine years.

The Secretariat: The Secretariat performs the role of a civil service for the UN. Its head is the Secretary-General, who combines the task of chief administrative officer of the organization with that of international mediator. *Secretary-General*: Boutros Boutros Ghali (Egypt), since 1992.

SPECIALIZED AGENCIES OF THE UN

The 18 agencies of the UN are independent specialized bodies.

FAO (Food and Agriculture Organization of the United Nations) aims to improve levels of nutrition and standards of living and the production and distribution of food and all agricultural products, and, in so doing, to eliminate hunger. Headquarters: Rome, Italy.

GATT (General Agreement on Tariffs and Trade) was founded with the aim of laying down a common code of practice in international trade. Headquarters: Geneva, Switzerland. The GATT will cease to exist at the beginning of 1995 when it will be superseded by the new World Trade Organization. (See also pp. 10-11.)

IAEA (International Atomic Energy Agency) aims to encourage the use of atomic energy for peaceful means. Headquarters: Vienna, Austria.

ICAO (International Civil Aviation Organization) aims to encourage safety measures and co-ordinate facilities for international flight. Headquarters: Montreal, Canada.

IDA (International Development Association) aims to assist less developed countries by providing credits on special terms. The IDA is an affiliate of the World Bank (see below).

IFAD (International Fund for Agricultural Development) aims to generate grants or loans to increase food production in developing countries. Headquarters: Rome, Italy.

IFC (International Finance Corporation) aims to promote the flow of private capital internationally and to stimulate the capital markets. The IFC is an affiliate of the World Bank (see below).

ILO (International Labour Organization) aims to establish international labour standards and to improve social and economic well-being. Headquarters: Geneva, Switzerland.

IMF (International Monetary Fund) aims to promote international monetary co-operation. Headquarters: Washington, DC, USA.

IMO (International Maritime Organization) aims to co-ordinate safety at sea. Headquarters: London, UK.

ITU (International Telecommunications Union) aims to allocate telecommunications frequencies and to standardize telecommunications practices. Headquarters: Geneva, Switzerland.

UNESCO (United Nations Educational, Scientific and Cultural Organization) aims to stimulate popular education and the spread of culture. Headquarters: Paris, France.

UNIDO (United Nations Industrial Development Organization) aims to promote industrialization in developing countries. Headquarters: Vienna, Austria.

UPU (Universal Postal Union) aims to unite members in a single postal territory. Headquarters: Bern, Switzerland.

WHO (World Health Organization) aims to promote the attainment by all peoples of the highest possible standards of health. Headquarters: Geneva, Switzerland.

WIPO (World Intellectual Property Organization) aims to promote protection of intellectual property (inventions, copyright, etc.). Headquarters: Geneva, Switzerland.

WMO (World Meteorological Organization) aims to standardize meteorological observations and apply the information to the greatest international benefit, for shipping, agriculture, etc. Headquarters: Geneva, Switzerland.

World Bank (International Bank for Reconstruction and Development) aims to encourage development through capital investment (in particular, investment in poorer member nations). Headquarters: Washington, DC, USA.

WTO (World Trade Organization) begins operations in January 1995, when it replaces GATT.

It aims to lay down a common code of practice in international trade, to encourage tariff cuts and take other measures necessary to achieve world free trade. Headquarters: Geneva, Switzerland. (See also pp. 10-11.)

SUBSIDIARY ORGANS OF THE UN
The subsidiary organs of the UN are programmes or funds that are devoted to achieving economic and social progress in developing countries. These organs include:

UNDP (United Nations Development Programme) is the funding source of the technical assistance provided through the UN system. Headquarters: New York, USA.

UNFPA (United Nations Population Fund) aims to respond to needs in population and family planning. Headquarters: New York, USA.

UNHCR (United Nations High Commissioner for Refugees) aims to provide international protection for refugees. Headquarters: Geneva, Switzerland.

UNICEF (United Nations International Children's Emergency Fund) aims to meet the needs of children, particularly those in developing countries. Headquarters: New York, USA.

UNRWA (United Nations Relief and Works Agency) aims to provide relief and welfare services for Palestinian refugees. Headquarters: Vienna, Austria.

There are 24 other UN organs.

Other World Bodies

(Regional organizations, for example the EU, CIS, NAFTA and ASEAN, are dealt with in the appropriate regional chapter.)

THE BANK FOR INTERNATIONAL SETTLEMENTS (BIS)

The BIS is the central banks' bank. It was founded in 1930, originally to settle German reparations due after World War I. It aims to encourage co-operation between the central banks of different countries and to protect the facilities for international financial settlements and operations. The Board of Directors comprises two delegates from the central banks of Belgium, France, Germany, Italy, the United Kingdom and nine other states elected by the total membership. The USA also has the right to permanent representation but does not exercise this right.

Headquarters: Basel, Switzerland.

Membership: nearly 90 central banks.

THE COMMONWEALTH

The Commonwealth may be said to have its foundations in the 1926 Imperial Conference, which defined the position of the dominions of the British Empire as 'freely associated . . . members of the British Commonwealth of Nations'. The modern Commonwealth dates from 1949 when India became a republic but remained a member of the British Commonwealth recognizing 'the King as the symbol of the free association of . . . independent member nations'. The majority of Commonwealth members are republics and some have their own sovereign, but all recognize the British sovereign as Head of the Commonwealth.

The Commonwealth is an informal grouping of the UK and the majority of its former dependencies. It has no written constitution. It aims to encourage international, scientific and technical, educational and economic cooperation between members.

Secretary-General: Chief Emeka Anyaoku (Nigeria).

Headquarters: London, UK.

Membership: (dates of Commonwealth membership are given in brackets) Antigua and Barbuda (1981), Australia (founder member), the Bahamas (1973), Bangladesh (1972), Barbados (1966), Belize (1981), Botswana (1966), Brunei (1981), Canada (founder member), Cyprus (1961), Dominica (1978), The Gambia (1965), Ghana (1957), Grenada (1974), Guyana (1966), India (founder member), Jamaica (1962), Kenya (1963), Kiribati (1979), Lesotho (1966), Malawi (1964), Malaysia (joined as Malaya; 1957), the Maldives (1982), Malta (1964), Mauritius (1968), Namibia (1990), Nauru (special member; 1968), New Zealand (founder member), Nigeria (1960), Pakistan (founder member; withdrew 1972; readmitted 1989), Papua New Guinea (1975), St Christopher and Nevis (1983), St Lucia (1979), St Vincent and the Grenadines (1979), the Seychelles (1976), Sierra Leone (1961), Singapore (1965), Solomon Islands (1978), South Africa (founder member; withdrew 1961; readmitted 1994), Sri Lanka (founder member as Ceylon), Swaziland (1968), Tanzania (joined as Tanganyika; 1961), Tonga (1970), Trinidad and Tobago (1962), Tuvalu (special member; 1978), Uganda (1962), United Kingdom (founder member), Vanuatu (1980), Western Samoa (1970), Zambia (1964), and Zimbabwe (1980). Special members do not participate in ministerial meetings.

GROUP OF SEVEN (G7)

G7 is an informal grouping of the leading Western economic powers. Since 1975 the heads of government of these states have met for annual summits concerning major economic, monetary and political problems. The Group of Seven - originally the Group of Five, but enlarged when Canada and Italy joined - has neither constitution nor secretariat.

Membership: Canada, France, Germany, Italy, Japan, the United Kingdom, and the USA. The EU/EC has observer status; Russia has also been invited as an observer to recent G7 summits.

INTERNATIONAL CRIMINAL POLICE ORGANIZATION (INTERPOL)

Interpol was established in 1923 as the International Criminal Police Commission and was restructured and renamed in 1956. It aims to promote mutual assistance between criminal police authorities. The policy-making body of Interpol is the General Assembly, which meets annually.

Headquarters: Lyon, France.

Membership: over 165 states.

INTERNATIONAL ENERGY AGENCY (IEA)

The IEA is an autonomous agency of the OECD (see below). Founded in 1974, the Agency aims to improve energy supplies and to develop alternative sources of energy.

Headquarters: Paris, France.

Membership: Australia, Austria, Belgium, Canada, Denmark, Germany, Greece, Ireland, Italy, Japan, Luxembourg, the Netherlands, Norway, Portugal, Spain, Sweden, Switzerland, Turkey, the United Kingdom, and the USA.

THE INTERNATIONAL RED CROSS AND RED CRESCENT

The International Red Cross and Red Crescent movement is a neutral organization founded to negotiate between warring parties, to protect casualties of armed conflict, to develop the activities of individual societies, to protect prisoners of war (under the terms of the Geneva Convention), and to coordinate relief for the victims of natural and other disasters. The Conference of the International Red Cross and Red Crescent meets every four years.

Headquarters: Geneva, Switzerland.

Membership: The Red Cross or Red Crescent Societies of over 170 countries.

THE NON-ALIGNED MOVEMENT

The non-aligned movement is not a formal organization but a conference that usually meets every three years. The aims of the movement are to promote world peace, to reject any system of world power blocs and to help bring about a more-even distribution of the world's wealth. The end of the Cold War has reduced both the influence and the impetus of the movement.

Membership: Over 100 countries attended the last two conferences of the non-aligned movement, membership of which varies from one conference to another.

ORGANIZATION OF PETROLEUM EXPORTING COUNTRIES (OPEC)

OPEC was founded in Baghdad, Iraq, in 1960. It aims to coordinate the petroleum-producing and petroleum-exporting policies of members.

Headquarters: Vienna, Austria.

Membership: Algeria, Bahrain, Gabon, Indonesia, Iran, Iraq, Kuwait, Libya, Nigeria, Qatar, Saudi Arabia, the United Arab Emirates, and Venezuela.

ORGANIZATION FOR ECONOMIC CO-OPERATION AND DEVELOPMENT (OECD)

OECD was founded in September 1961 to replace the Organization for European Economic Co-operation, which had been established in connection with the Marshall Aid Plan in 1948. It aims to encourage and develop economic and social welfare in member-states and to stimulate aid to developing countries.

Headquarters: Paris, France.

Membership: Australia, Austria, Belgium, Canada, Denmark, Finland, France, Iceland, Germany, Greece, Ireland, Italy, Japan, Luxembourg, the Netherlands, Norway, Portugal, Spain, Sweden, Switzerland, Turkey, the United Kingdom, and the USA. Membership is by invitation rather than application. Mexico and Hungary are expected to gain membership in the near future. Yugoslavia (which was an observer) has been suspended.

WORLD COUNCIL OF CHURCHES

The World Council of Churches was established in 1948 in Amsterdam, the Netherlands. It unites Protestant (including Anglican), Orthodox, and Old Catholic Churches. Its governing body is the Assembly, which comprises delegates from members and which meets every seven or eight years. Its activities are categorized under four main headings: unity and renewal; life, education and mission; justice, peace and creation; and sharing and service.

Headquarters: Geneva, Switzerland.

Membership: over 330 Churches from over 110 countries.

OLYMPIC COMMITTEE

The first Olympic Games of the modern era took place in Athens, Greece, in 1896. The force behind their revival was Pierre de Fredi, Baron de Coubertin, born in Paris in 1863. The International Olympic Committee was formed in 1894.

Headquarters: Lausanne, Switzerland.

Membership: a record 169 nations took part in the 1992 Olympic Games.

AFRICA SOUTH OF THE SAHARA

Angola, Benin, Botswana, Burkina Faso, Burundi, Cameroon, Cape Verde, Central African Republic, Chad, Comoros, Congo, Côte d'Ivoire (Ivory Coast), Djibouti, Equatorial Guinea, Eritrea, Ethiopia, Gabon, Gambia, Ghana, Guinea, Guinea Bissau, Kenya, Lesotho, Liberia, Madagascar, Malawi, Mali, Mauritania, Mauritius, Mozambique, Namibia, Niger, Nigeria, Rwanda, São Tomé e Principe, Senegal, Seychelles, Sierra Leone, Somalia, South Africa, Sudan, Swaziland, Tanzania, Togo, Uganda, Zaïre, Zambia, Zimbabwe, Other territories.

The New South Africa

The apartheid political regime lasted from the election of the National Party in 1948 until its defeat in South Africa's first democratic election in 1994. The collapse was relatively swift and violent, the result of a complex interplay of internal and external factors. Chief among these were the increasing importance of manufacturing in the economy and the need for a more skilled and permanent black labour force; economic sanctions and growing opposition to apartheid from international investors; the end of the Cold War; and the state's inability to contain mounting popular protest except by repressive means. By the 1970s the regime was challenged by the rise of the Black Consciousness Movement associated with Steve Biko, by black workers' strikes, and by the revolt of black youth in the Soweto Uprising. From 1979 the government attempted to stabilize the situation by its 'total strategy' - reforms and repression at home and aggression abroad. This attempt to restructure apartheid failed because its constitutional changes made no provision for African participation in government. In the 1980s South Africa became increasingly ungovernable as rebellion in the black townships was supported by mass strikes. From 1986, the security forces were the virtual rulers of the country under a savagely administered State of Emergency. This did not prevent the influence of the exiled African National Congress (ANC) from once again becoming dominant among blacks. The ANC cause was supported by some Afrikaner intellectuals and prominent white businessmen who joined the call for the release of Nelson Mandela. Abroad, the 'total strategy' was no more successful. South Africa was unable to prevent black governments gaining power in Angola and Mozambique (1975), Zimbabwe (1980), and in Namibia (1989). The cynical policy of destabilizing neighbouring states became increasingly unpopular with the international community, especially when the collapse of the USSR reduced South Africa's strategic importance to the West.

In addition to uncontrolled state repression, there was fearful violence within the black community, largely between Chief Buthelezi's mainly Zulu Inkatha movement and supporters of the ANC. The rural-based and conservative Inkatha, secretly supported by elements within the security forces, was mainly to blame for the violence in Natal and in many urban areas. In the townships, there was often a virtual state of war between Zulu labour migrants, living in barrack-like, all-male hostels, and the rest of the community. Political stalemate was broken by the release of Mandela after 27 years of imprisonment and the unbanning of the ANC by the new State President, F.W. de Klerk, early in 1990. Amid continuing upheaval, the two men pursued their agreement to find a negotiated settlement to the country's political problems. Violence, including an urban bombing campaign by right-wing whites, continued up to the elections in 1994. Yet the attempts to sabotage the peace process failed because de Klerk succeeded in retaining the support of approximately two thirds of the whites and Mandela an equal proportion of support from the blacks. In 1993 they were jointly awarded the Nobel Peace Prize. As the undisputed leader of the majority of the country's inhabitants, however, Mandela's moral authority increasingly outweighed that of the existing President.

The ANC abandoned armed struggle and old-style Socialism and sought to reconcile the whites to their forthcoming loss of political power with constitutional guarantees. The party's economic policy was softened and it was accepted that South Africa should rejoin the Commonwealth. Meanwhile, the 'homelands' governments collapsed and the extremists of the white right-wing were physically routed. Buthelezi was forced into a last-minute decision to participate in the 1994 elections. His disputed victory in the KwaZulu/Natal province was diplomatically allowed to stand, and he was given the important post of Minister of Home Affairs in the new interim government of national unity (in which power-sharing is obligatory at both the national and provincial level). The National Party also retained a base with its electoral success in the Western Cape province, with de Klerk becoming a second deputy president, but the ANC swept to power nationally and also won in the other seven provinces. While years of turmoil may have brought about a new realism reversing the deprivations of apartheid in such major areas as housing and employment presents an enormous challenge.

Regional Organizations of Africa south of the Sahara

COMMUNAUTE FINANCIERE AFRICAINE (CFA)

The Communauté Financière Africaine is a monetary union founded to supply a common currency for former French African possessions. However, Guinea, Mauritania and Djibouti have left the Franc Zone and Equatorial Guinea, a former Spanish colony, has joined it. The CFA franc, which is pegged to the value of the French franc, was devalued in 1994.

Headquarters: Paris, France.

Membership: Benin, Burkina Faso, Cameroon, Central African Republic, Chad, Comoros, Congo, Côte d'Ivoire (Ivory Coast), Equatorial Guinea, Gabon, Mali, Niger, Senegal, and Togo.

ECONOMIC COMMUNITY OF WEST AFRICAN STATES (ECOWAS)

ECOWAS was founded in Lagos, Nigeria, in May 1975. It aims to promote trade and co-operation between members and to increase self-reliance within West Africa. Its most public achievement to date was the dispatch of an ECOWAS force to intervene in the Liberian civil war in 1990. The ECOWAS Assembly comprises heads of state and/or heads of government. The Assembly meets once a year and is chaired by each member in turn.

Headquarters: Abuja, Nigeria.

Members: Benin, Burkina Faso, Cape Verde, The Gambia, Ghana, Guinea, Guinea-Bissau, Liberia, Mali, Mauritania, Niger, Nigeria, Senegal, Sierra Leone, and Togo.

ORGANIZATION OF AFRICAN UNITY (OAU)

The OAU was founded in May 1963 in Addis Ababa, Ethiopia. It aims to promote African unity and collaboration in economic, social, cultural, political, defence, scientific, health and other matters, and to eliminate colonialism and apartheid from Africa. The OAU Assembly of heads of state and/or heads of government meets annually and is presided over by a chairman who is elected annually by the Assembly. The main administrative body of the Organization is the Secretariat.

Headquarters: Addis Ababa, Ethiopia.

Membership: Algeria, Angola, Benin, Botswana, Burkina Faso, Burundi, Cameroon, Cape Verde, Central African Republic, Chad, Comoros, Congo, Côte d'Ivoire (Ivory Coast), Djibouti, Egypt, Equatorial Guinea, Ethiopia, Gabon, The Gambia, Ghana, Guinea, Guinea-Bissau, Kenya, Lesotho, Liberia, Libya, Madagascar, Malawi, Mali, Mauritania, Mauritius, Mozambique, Namibia, Niger, Nigeria, Rwanda, São Tomé e Principe, Senegal, Seychelles, Sierra Leone, Somalia, South Africa, Sudan, Swaziland, Tanzania, Togo, Tunisia, Uganda, Zaïre, Zambia, and Zimbabwe. In 1982 the Sahrawi Democratic Republic (the disputed Western Sahara) was also admitted to membership; Morocco, which claims the Western Sahara, withdrew from the OAU in protest.

SOUTHERN AFRICA DEVELOPMENT COMMUNITY (SADC OR SADCC)

The SADC (which is also abbreviated as SADCC) was founded by the neighbours of South Africa with the aim of lessening the influence of that country upon their economies. Since the end of apartheid and the advent of majority rule to South Africa, the Community has changed its aims and now works to promote regional trade and development among the countries of Southern Africa, including South Africa.

Membership: Angola, Botswana, Lesotho, Malawi, Mozambique, Namibia, South Africa, Swaziland, Zambia, and Zimbabwe.

OTHER ORGANIZATIONS

The East African Common Market (EACM) – a trade and monetary pact formed by Kenya, Tanzania and Uganda – collapsed owing to distrust between the members arising from the continuing crises and unrest in Uganda and the opposing economic systems then adopted by Kenya and Tanzania. The former Belgian colonies of Burundi, Rwanda and Zaïre have attempted to set up a regional trading block.

African Trade

Angola Imports (kwanza million): 443 (1987). Exports ($ million): 3883 (1990 est). Main imports: raw materials. Main exports: mineral fuels. Principal trading partners: USA, Brazil, UK.

Benin Imports (francs million): 104,980 (1987). Exports (francs million): 34,266 (1987). Main imports: cereals. Main exports: raw cotton. Principal trading partners: France, Thailand, Portugal, USA.

Botswana Imports ($ million): 1780 (1990). Exports ($ million): 1779 (1990). Main imports: machinery and electrical goods. Main exports: diamonds. Principal trading partners: South Africa, UK.

Burkina Faso Imports ($ million): 322 (1989). Exports ($ million): 95 (1989). Main imports: manufactured goods. Main exports: raw cotton. Principal trading partners: France, Ivory Coast.

Burundi Imports (francs million): 46,154.2 (1991). Exports (francs million): 16,644.9 (1991). Main imports: machinery and transport equipment. Main exports: coffee. Principal trading partners: Belgium, Germany.

Cameroon Imports ($ million): 1271 (1988). Exports ($ million): 924 (1988). Main imports: machinery and transport equipment. Main exports: crude petroleum. Principal trading partners: France, Netherlands, Germany.

Cape Verde Imports ($ million): 112 (1991). Exports ($ million): 7 (1989). Main imports: foodstuffs and beverages. Main exports: bananas. Principal trading partners: Portugal, Netherlands, Japan.

Central African Republic Imports ($ million): 145 (1991). Exports ($ million): 74 (1991). Main imports: food. Main exports: coffee. Principal trading partners: France, Germany, Belgium.

Chad Imports ($ million): 419 (1988). Exports ($ million): 141 (1988). Main imports: petroleum products. Main exports: raw cotton. Principal trading partners: France, Cameroon, USA.

Comoros Imports ($ million): 43 (1989). Exports ($ million): 18 (1989). Main imports: rice. Main exports: vanilla. Principal trading partners: France, USA, Madagascar.

Congo Imports ($ million): 600 (1990). Exports ($ million): 976 (1990). Main imports: machinery 22.4%. Main exports: petroleum and petroleum products. Principal trading partners: USA, France, Spain.

Côte d'Ivoire (Ivory Coast) Imports ($ million): 2185 (1989). Exports ($ million): 2931 (1989).

Main imports: fuels and crude petroleum. Main exports: cocoa and cocoa products. Principal trading partner: France, Netherlands.

Djibouti Imports ($ million): 215.5 (1991). Exports ($ million): 17.4 (1991). Main imports: food and beverages 27.0%. Main exports: live animals. Principal trading partners: France, Ethiopia.

Equatorial Guinea Main imports: machinery and transport equipment. Main exports: cocoa. Principal trading partners: Spain, France.

Eritrea No figures available.

Ethiopia Imports ($ million): 1076 (1990). Exports ($ million): 294 (1990). Main imports: road transport machinery. Main exports: coffee. Principal trading partners: Italy, Germany, USA.

Gabon Imports ($ million): 767 (1989). Exports ($ million): 1288 (1987). Main imports: machinery and mechanical equipment. Main exports: crude petroleum and petroleum products. Principal trading partners: France, USA, Germany, Spain.

Gambia Imports ($ million): 200 (1990). Exports ($ million): 41 (1990). Main imports: food. Main exports: fish and fish preparations. Principal trading partners: France, UK, Switzerland.

Ghana Imports ($ million): 1275 (1991). Exports ($ million): 1024 (1991). Main imports: machinery and transport equipment. Main exports: cocoa. Principal trading partners: UK, USA, Germany.

Guinea Imports ($ million): 491 (1988). Exports ($ million): 548 (1988). Main imports: intermediate goods. Main exports: bauxite and alumina. Principal trading partners: France, Belgium.

Guinea-Bissau Imports ($ million): 39 (1984). Exports ($ million): 19 (1984). Main imports: transport equipment. Main exports: cashews. Principal trading partners: Portugal, France, Germany.

Kenya Imports (K£ million): 49,147 (1991). Exports (K£ million): 30,376 (1991). Main imports: machinery and transport equipment. Main exports: tea. Principal trading partners: UK, Germany, United Arab Emirates.

Lesotho Imports ($ million): 587 (1988). Exports ($ million): 64 (1988). Main imports: manufactured goods. Main exports: miscellaneous manufactured goods. Principal trading partners: South Africa, Switzerland, UK.

Liberia Imports ($ million): 129.91 (1988/89). Exports (Liberian $ million): 461.16 (1989). Main imports: machinery and transport equipment. Main exports: iron ore. Principal trading partners: Germany, USA.

29

Madagascar Imports ($ million): 426 (1991). Exports ($ million): 306 (1991). Main imports: mineral products. Main exports: vanilla. Principal trading partners: France, USA, Japan, Germany.

Malawi Imports ($ million): 705 (1991). Exports ($ million): 473 (1991). Main imports: basic manufactures 42.5%. Main exports: tobacco. Principal trading partners: UK, South Africa.

Mali Imports ($ million): 500 (1990). Exports ($ million): 271 (1989). Main imports: machinery and transport equipment. Main exports: raw cotton and cotton products. Principal trading partners: France, Ivory Coast.

Mauritania Imports ($ million): 351 (1989). Exports (ouguiya million): 18,231 (1991). Main imports: food. Main exports: fish. Principal trading partners: France, Japan, Spain.

Mauritius Imports ($ million): 1619 (1990). Exports ($ million): 1193 (1990). Main imports: textile fabrics, yarn and thread. Main exports: sugar. Principal trading partners: UK, France, USA, Germany, South Africa.

Mozambique Imports ($ million): 715 (1989). Exports ($ million): 101 (1989). Main imports: foodstuffs. Main exports: shrimps. Principal trading partners: Spain, USA, Japan, South Africa.

Namibia Imports ($ million): 861 (1988). Exports ($ million): 940 (1988). Main imports: food and other consumer goods. Main exports: minerals. Principal trading partner: South Africa.

Niger Imports ($ million): 345 (1985). Exports ($ million): 209 (1985). Main imports: raw materials and machinery. Main exports: uranium. Principal trading partners: France, Nigeria, USA.

Nigeria Imports (N million): 45,718 (1990). Exports (N million): 109,886 (1990). Main imports: machinery and transport equipment. Main exports: crude petroleum. Principal trading partners: USA, Germany, France, UK.

Rwanda Imports (R franc million): 38,474.5 (1991). Exports (R franc million): 11,971.2 (1991). Main imports: mineral fuels and lubricants. Main exports: coffee. Principal trading partners: Belgium-Luxembourg, Germany.

São Tomé e Princípe Imports ($ million): 13 (1987). Exports ($ million): 7 (1987). Main imports: food. Main exports: cocoa. Principal trading partners: Portugal, Germany, Netherlands.

Senegal Imports (franc million): 321,571 (1988). Exports (franc million): 176,083 (1988). Main imports: crude petroleum and products. Main exports: peanut oil. Principal trading partners: France, Italy, Spain.

Seychelles Imports ($ million): 173 (1991). Exports ($ million): 48 (1991). Main imports: machinery and transport equipment. Main exports: petroleum products. Principal trading partners: France, Kuwait, UK, South Africa.

Sierra Leone Imports (leone million): 65,176,599 (1992). Exports (leone million): 74,872,411 (1992). Main imports: food and live animals. Main exports: rutile. Principal trading partners: USA, UK, Netherlands, China, Germany.

Somalia Imports ($ million): 132 (1987). Exports ($ million): 104 (1987). Main imports: petroleum. Main exports: live animals. Principal trading partners: Italy, Saudi Arabia, Yemen.

South Africa Imports (rand million): 51,917.2 (1992). Exports (rand million): 67,456.8 (1992). Main imports: machinery and transport equipment. Main exports: gold. Principal trading partners: Germany, UK, Japan, USA, Netherlands.

Sudan Imports ($ million): 1060 (1988). Exports ($ million): 672 (1989). Main imports: machinery and transport equipment. Main exports: cotton. Principal trading partners: UK, USA, Japan.

Swaziland Imports ($ million): 590 (1989). Exports ($ million): 468 (1989). Main imports: machinery and transport equipment. Main exports: sugar. Principal trading partners: South Africa, UK.

Tanzania Imports (shilling million): 256,393 (1991). Exports (shilling million): 79,055 (1990). Main imports: machinery. Main exports: coffee. Principal trading partners: Germany, UK, Japan, Italy.

Togo Imports ($ million): 487 (1988). Exports ($ million): 242 (1988). Main imports: machinery. Main exports: phosphates. Principal trading partners: France, Netherlands.

Uganda Imports (new shilling million): 123,649 (1991). Exports (new shilling million): 146,661 (1991). Main imports: sugar. Main exports: unroasted coffee. Principal trading partners: Kenya, UK, Germany, USA.

Zaïre Imports ($ million): 886 (1990). Exports ($ million): 999 (1990). Main imports: mining equipment. Main exports: copper. Principal trading partners: Belgium, USA, France, Germany, Japan.

Zambia Imports ($ million): 1243 (1990). Exports ($ million): 899 (1990). Main imports: machinery and transport equipment. Main exports: copper. Principal trading partners: Japan, UK, USA.

Zimbabwe Imports ($ million): 1850 (1990). Exports ($ million): 1723 (1990). Main imports: machinery and transport equipment. Main exports: tobacco. Principal trading partners: South Africa, UK.

Angola

Official name: A República de Angola (The Republic of Angola).

Member of: UN, OAU, SADCC.

Area: 1,246,700 km² (481,354 sq mi).

Population: 10,609,000 (1992 est).

Capital: Luanda 1,200,000 (1988 est).

Other major cities: Huambo 203,000, Benguela 155,000, Lobito 150,000 (1982-83 est).

Languages: Portuguese (official), Kimbundu (27%), Umbundu (38%), Lunda (13%).

Religions: Roman Catholic (60%), animist (20%).

Education: Education is compulsory in theory between the ages of seven and 15. The literacy rate is 41.7% (1990 est). There is a university.

Defence: In 1992 government forces numbered 128,000. UNITA forces numbered 28,000 in 1992.

Transport: There are 72,000 km (45,000 mi) of roads and 2952 km (1845 mi) of railways. Luanda and Lobito are ports; Luanda has an airport.

Media: There are two daily newspapers and a state-run radio and television service.

GOVERNMENT
A 220-member Assembly is elected by universal adult suffrage for three years and a President for five years. The President appoints a Prime Minister and a Cabinet. Political parties include the (former Marxist) MPLA (People's Liberation Movement of Angola) and UNITA (the National Union for the Total Independence of Angola).

Party strength: (1992 election) MPLA129, UNITA 70 (most withdrew), others 21.

President: José Eduardo dos Santos (MPLA).

Premier: Marcolino José Carlos Moco (MPLA).

GEOGRAPHY
Inland from a coastal plain, plateaux, over 1000 m (3300 ft), cover 90% of Angola. Highest point: Serra Mòco 2610 m (8563 ft). Principal rivers: Kunene, Kwanza, Congo (Zaïre), Kwando. Climate: Angola is tropical, with

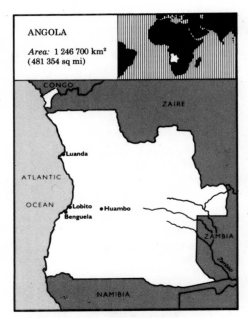

ANGOLA
Area: 1 246 700 km² (481 354 sq mi)

CONGO
ZAIRE
Luanda
ATLANTIC
OCEAN
Lobito • Huambo
Benguela
ZAMBIA
NAMIBIA

lower temperatures in the uplands.

ECONOMY
The economy has been wrecked by war. Angola is, however, rich in minerals (diamonds, iron ore and petroleum). Over half the labour force farms, mainly growing food crops. The main export crop is coffee.

Currency: New Kwanza (AOK); 1US$ = 71,033 AOK (May 1994).

GDP: US$6,010,000,000 (1990); US$620 per head.

RECENT HISTORY
Guerrilla wars against Portuguese colonial rule began in 1961. When independence was conceded (1975), rival guerrilla movements fought to control Angola. With Soviet and Cuban support, the MPLA, led by Agostinho Neto (1922-79), won and repulsed an invasion from South Africa. In the 1980s, Cuban troops supported the MPLA against Jonas Savimbi's South African-aided UNITA movement in the south. Foreign involvement in the civil war ended in 1990 and a ceasefire was negotiated (1991). MPLA and UNITA forces resumed fighting after UNITA refused to accept defeat in elections in 1992.

Benin

Official name: La République du Bénin (the Republic of Benin).

Member of: UN, OAU, ECOWAS.

Area: 112,622 km² (43,484 sq mi).

Population: 5,091,000 (1993 est).

Capital: Porto-Novo 208,000 (1983 est).

Other major cities: Cotonou 487,000, Parakou 66,000 (1983 est).

Languages: French (official), Fon (47%), Adja (12%).

Religions: Animist (61%), Sunni Islam (16%), various Christian Churches (22% - mainly Roman Catholic).

Education: Education is compulsory, in theory, between the ages of six and 13. In 1990 the literacy rate was 23.4%. There is a university.

Defence: In 1993 the total armed strength was 4300. There is selective military service.

Transport: There are 8435 km (5241 mi) of roads and 578 km (359 mi) of railways. Cotonou, the main port, has an international airport.

Media: There are two daily newspapers and a state-run radio and television service.

GOVERNMENT
An executive President and an 64-member National Assembly are elected by universal adult suffrage for four years. The main political parties include the Union for the Triumph of the Return of Democracy (UTRD), the (coalition) National Convention for Forces for Change (CNFC), and the Communist Party. After the election held in March 1991 a UTRD government was formed.

Party strength: UTRD 12, others (20 other parties) 52.

President: Nicephore Soglo (UTRD).

GEOGRAPHY
In the northwest lies the Atacora Massif; in the northeast, plains slope down to the Niger Valley. The plateaux of central Benin fall in the south to a low fertile region. A narrow coastal plain is backed by lagoons. Highest point: Atacora Massif 635 m (2083 ft). Principal rivers: Ouémé, Niger. Climate: The north is tropical; the south is equatorial.

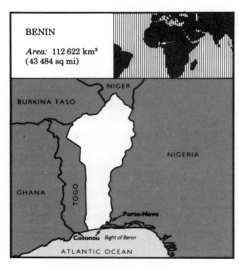

ECONOMY
The economy is based on agriculture, which occupies the majority of the labour force. The main food crops are cassava (manioc), yams and maize; the principal cash crop is palm oil. In the late 1980s, central planning was abandoned in favour of a market economy.

Currency: CFA Franc; 1US$ = 546.45 CFA Francs (June 1994).

GDP: US$2,061,000,000 (1992); US$410 per head.

RECENT HISTORY
Benin was known as Dahomey until 1975. Political turmoil followed independence from France in 1960, and five army coups took place between 1963 and 1972. The regime established by Colonel Kérékou in 1972 brought some stability, and after 1987, experiments with state socialism were moderated. In 1989 President Kérékou disavowed Marxist-Leninism, and appointed a civilian administration to guide Benin towards becoming a market economy. Kérékou was defeated in multi-party elections in 1991 and Benin achieved a peaceful transition from dictatorship to democracy. Benin has since sought Western assistance.

Botswana

Official name: The Republic of Botswana.

Member of: UN, OAU, Commonwealth, SADCC.

Area: 582,000 km² (224,711 sq mi).

Population: 1,325,000 (1991 est).

Capital: Gaborone 134.000 (1991 est).

Other main towns: Francistown 65,000, Selibi-Pikwe 38,000, Molepolole 37,000 (1990 est).

Languages: English (official language), Setswana (majority; national language).

Religions: Animist (over 50%), various Christian Churches - mainly Congregational, Anglican, Roman Catholic.

Education: Although education is not compulsory, over 80% of children attend seven years of primary schooling. In 1990 the literacy rate was estimated to be 86.7%. There is a university.

Defence: In 1993 the total armed strength was estimated to be 6100, of whom 6000 were in the army and 100 in the air force.

Transport: There are about 15,000 km (9375 mi) of roads and 888 km (555 mi) of railways. Gaborone has an international airport.

Media: There is a single daily newspaper and a single state-run radio station. South African television is transmitted.

GOVERNMENT

Thirty-four of the 40 members of the National Assembly are elected by universal adult suffrage for five years. Of the remainder, four are nominated by the President and specially elected; the Speaker and Attorney General are non-voting members. The President, who chairs and appoints a Cabinet, is elected for five years by the Assembly. (There is also a 15-member House of Chiefs whose sole brief is to deal with tribal, constitutional and chieftancy matters.) There are nine administrative districts. The main political parties are the Botswana Democratic Party (BDP) and the Botswana National Front (BNF).

Party strength: BDP 31, BNF 3, others 6.

President: Dr Quett Masire (BDP).

GEOGRAPHY

A central plateau divides a flat near-desert in the east of Botswana from the Kalahari Desert and Okavango Swamps in the west. Highest point: Tsodilo Hill 1375 m (4511 ft). Principal rivers: Chobe, Shashi. Climate: The climate is subtropical with extremes of heat. Most of the rainfall comes in the summer, but almost all of Botswana is periodically subject to drought.

ECONOMY

Nomadic cattle herding and the cultivation of subsistence crops occupies the majority of the labour force. The mainstay of the economy is mining for diamonds, copper-nickel and coal. Since 1980 Botswana has achieved high economic growth rates based upon the exploitation of mineral wealth.

Currency: Pula (BWP) of 100 thebe; 1US$ = 2.79 BWP (June 1994).

GDP: US$2,561,000,000 (1990); US$2040 per head.

BOTSWANA

Area: 582 000 km²
(224 711 sq mi)

ANGOLA   ZAMBIA

ZIMBABWE

NAMIBIA

Gaborone●

SOUTH AFRICA

RECENT HISTORY

The area became the British protectorate of Bechuanaland in 1885. Development was slow, and many Africans had to seek work in South Africa. Nationalism was late to develop, and independence - as Botswana - was granted without a struggle in 1966. Under the first president, Sir Seretse Khama, and his successor, Botswana has succeeded in remaining a democracy.

Burkina Faso

Official name: Burkina Faso or République de Burkina (previously Upper Volta).

Member of: UN, OAS, ECOWAS.

Area: 274,200 km² (105,869 sq mi).

Population: 9,780,000 (1993 est).

Capital: Ouagadougou 442,000 (1985 est).

Other major cities: Bobo-Dioulasso 229,000, Koudougou 52,000 (1985 est).

Languages: French (official), Mossi (48%), Fulani (10%).

Religions: Animist (49%), Sunni Islam (40%), Christian Churches (11% - mainly Catholic).

Education: Education is compulsory, in theory, between the ages of seven and 14. In 1990 the literacy rate was 18.2%. There is a university.

Defence: In 1993 the total armed strength was 7200. There is no military service.

Transport: There are 13,134 km (8161 mi) of roads and 495 km (308 mi) of railways.

Ouagadougou and Bobo-Dioulasso have international airports.

Media: There are eight daily newspapers, five radio stations and a state-run television service.

GOVERNMENT
Elections by universal adult suffrage are held every four years for a 107-member Assembly and every seven years for a President. The main political parties are the Organization for Popular Democracy Labour Movement (ODP-MT), the National Convention of Progressive Patriots-Social Democratic Party (CNPP-PSD), the African Democratic Assembly (ADA), the Alliance for Democracy and Freedom (ADL), and the Movement of Social Democrats (MDS). After the election in May 1992 a ODP-MT/CNPP-MT was formed.

Party strength: ODP-MT 78, CNPP-PSD 6, others 23.

President: Capt. Blaise Campoare (ODP-MT).

Prime Minister: Youssouf Ouedraogo (ODP-MT).

GEOGRAPHY
The country consists of plateaux about 500 m (1640 ft) high. Highest point: Mt Tema 749 m (2457 ft). Principal rivers: Mouhoun (Black Volta), Nakambe (White Volta), Nazinon (Red Volta). Climate: The country is hot and dry, with adequate rainfall - 1000 mm (40 in) - only in the savannah of the south. The north is semi-desert.

ECONOMY
Burkina Faso, one of the world's poorest states, has been severely stricken by drought in the last two decades. Nomadic herdsmen and subsistence farmers - producing mainly sorghum, sugar cane and millet - form the bulk of the population. Cotton, manganese and zinc are exported.

Currency: CFA Franc; 1US$ = 546.45 CFA Francs (June 1994).

GDP: US$2,863,000,000 (1992); US$300 per head.

RECENT HISTORY
Burkina Faso was the French colony of Upper Volta. During the colonial era, the country acted as a labour reservoir for more developed colonies to the south. Since independence in 1960, the country - which changed its name to Burkina Faso in 1984 - has had a turbulent political history, with a succession of military coups. A multi-party system was restored in 1992.

Burundi

Official name: La République du Burundi or Republika y'Uburundi (The Republic of Burundi).

Member of: UN, OAU.

Area: 27,834 km² (10,747 sq mi).

Population: 5,600,000 (1993 est).

Capital: Bujumbura 227,000 (1990 est).

Other major city: Gitega 95,000 (1990 est).

Languages: Kirundi (majority) and French - both official; Kiswahili.

Religion: Roman Catholic (65%), various Protestant Churches (mainly Anglican), animist.

Education: Education is compulsory, in theory, between the ages of sven and 12. In 1990 the literacy rate was 50%. There is a university.

Defence: In 1991 the total armed strength was 7200.

Transport: There are 6265 km (3893 mi) of roads. Bujumbura, which has an international airport, is a port on Lake Tanganyika.

Media: There is a single daily newspaper and a government-run radio and television service.

GOVERNMENT

A President - who appoints a Premier and a Cabinet - and an 81-member Assembly are elected by universal adult suffrage for four years. Political parties include the Front for Democracy in Burundi (Frodebu), the (former monopoly) Union for National Progress (Uprona), the Burundi People's Party (PPB), and the Party for Reconciliation of the People (PRP). After the election held in June 1993 a Frodebu government was formed.

Party strength: Frodebu 65, Uprona 16.

President (acting): Sylvestre Ntibantunganya.

Prime Minister (acting): Anatole Kanyakiko.

GEOGRAPHY

Burundi is a high plateau, rising from Lake Tanganyika in the west. Highest point: Mt Hela 2685 m (8809 ft). Principal rivers: Kagera, Ruzizi. Climate: The lowlands are hot and humid. Temperatures are cooler in the mountains.

ECONOMY

Farmers and farm labourers account for over 92% of the labour force. Agriculture produces

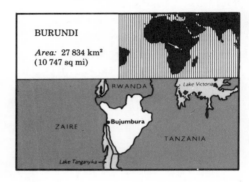

both subsistence crops and crops for export, such as coffee. The economy has been retarded by recurring tribal wars and was devastated by ethnic unrest and genocide in 1993-94.

Currency: Burundi franc (BIF) of 100 centimes; 1US$ = 249.6 BIF (June 1994).

GDP: US$1,210,000,000 (1991); US$210 per head.

RECENT HISTORY

Burundi was a semi-feudal kingdom in which the minority Tutsi tribe of pastoralists dominated the Hutu majority of agriculturalists. Colonized by Germany in 1890, it was taken over by Belgium after World War I under a League of Nations mandate. Independence came in 1962, after much conflict throughout the country. Following a military coup in 1966, a republic was established. The killing of the deposed king in 1972 led to a massacre of the Hutu. Burundi has been unstable ever since. Serious ethnic unrest in 1988 led to an exodus of Hutu refugees to Rwanda. The first multi-party elections in 1993 saw the defeat of the former monopoly party, but the victorious president and many of his government were slaughtered by Tutsi officers. A terrible wave of ethnic murders followed. The new president lost his life when the plane carrying the Rwandan and Burundian heads of state was shot down in 1994. Further ethnic violence erupted.

Cameroon

Official name: La République unie du Cameroun (The United Republic of Cameroon).

Member of: UN, OAU.

Area: 475,442 km² (183,569 sq mi).

Population: 13,100,000 (1993 est).

Capital: Yaoundé 712,000 (1987 est).

Other major cities: Douala 1,117,000, Nkongsamba 112,000 (1987 est).

Languages: French and English (both official), Fulani, Sao, Bamileke.

Religions: Animist (40%), Sunni Islam (20%), Roman Catholic (20%).

Education: Education is compulsory, in theory, between the ages of six and 12. In 1990 the literacy rate was 54.1%. There is a single university and five university colleges.

Defence: In 1993 the total armed strength was 8100 - 6600 in the army, 1200 in the navy and 300 in the air force.

Transport: There are 48,200 km (29,950 mi) of roads and 1104 km (686 mi) of railways. Douala is the principal seaport. Douala and Yaoundé have international airports.

GOVERNMENT
The 180 members of the National Assembly and a President are elected for a five-year term by universal adult suffrage. The President appoints a Council of Ministers and a PM. Political parties include the (former monopoly) Cameroon People's Democratic Movement (RDPC), the National Union for Democracy and Progress (UNDP), the Union for the Peoples of Cameroon (UPC), the Movement for the Defence of the Republic (MDR), and (the opposition coalition) Union for Change (UC). After the election held in March 1992 a RDPC-UNDP-UPC-MDR government was formed.

Party strength: RDPC-UNDP-UPC-MDR 94, UC 86.

President: Paul Biya (RDPC).

Prime Minister: Simon Achidi Achu (RDPC).

GEOGRAPHY
In the west, a chain of highlands rises to the volcanic Mont Cameroun. In the north, savan-

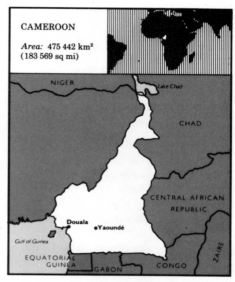

CAMEROON

Area: 475 442 km² (183 569 sq mi)

nah plains dip towards Lake Chad. Coastal plains and plateaux in the south and centre are covered with tropical forest. Highest point: Mont Cameroun 4069 m (13,353 ft). Principal rivers: Sanaga, Nyong. Climate: Cameroon is tropical, with hot, rainy conditions, but is drier inland.

ECONOMY
Cameroon is a major producer of cocoa, and other export crops include bananas, coffee, cotton, rubber and palm oil. The diversity of Cameroon's agriculture, and the rapid development of the petroleum industry, have given the country one of the highest standards of living in tropical Africa.

Currency: CFA Franc; 1US$ = 546.45 CFA Francs (June 1994).

GDP: US$10,036,000,000 (1991); US$820 per head.

RECENT HISTORY
After World War I, the German protectorate of Kamerun was divided between the UK and France. The French Cameroons became independent in 1960. After a plebiscite (1961), the northern British Cameroons merged with Nigeria; the south united with Cameroon. Multi-party elections were held in 1993, but the opposition alleged fraud.

Cape Verde

Official name: A República de Cabo Verde (The Republic of Cape Verde).

Member of: UN, OAU, ECOWAS.

Area: 4033 km² (1557 sq mi).

Population: 350,000 (1993 est).

Capital: Praia 62,000 (1990 est).

Other major cities: Mindelo 47,000, Sao Filipe 6000 (1990 est).

Languages: Portuguese (official), Crioulu (Creole; majority).

Religion: Roman Catholic (over 92%).

Education: Education is compulsory between the ages of seven and 13. In 1990 the literacy rate was 66.5%. There are no university-level institutions.

Defence: In 1992 the total armed strength was 1300 - 1000 in the army, 200 in the navy and 100 in the air force. There is selective military service.

Transport: There are 5615 km (3489 mi) of roads. The principal commercial shipping ports are Mindelo and Praia. There is an international airport at Espargos.

Media: There are four weekly newspapers, two state-run radio services and a single television channel.

GOVERNMENT
The 79 members of the National People's Assembly are elected for five years by universal adult suffrage. The Assembly elects a President - also for five years - who appoints a Council of Ministers and a Prime Minister. The main political parties are the (centre) Movement for Democracy (MPD) and the (socialist former monopoly) African Party for the Independence of Cape Verde (PAICV). After the election held in January 1991 a MPD government was formed.

Party strength: MPD 56, PAICV 23.

President: Antonio Mascarenhas (MPD).

Prime Minister: Carlos Veiga (MPD).

GEOGRAPHY
Cape Verde consists of ten volcanic, semi-arid islands, which are divided into two groups - the Barlavento (windward) and Sotavento (leeward) islands. There are no significant rivers and very little rain. Most of the moisture obtained by the islands comes from mist and sea-fog. Highest point: Monte Fogo 2829 m (9281 ft). Climate: Cooled by northeast winds, temperatures are sub-tropical rather than tropical. The climate is characterized by drought.

ECONOMY
Lack of surface water hinders agriculture, and over 90% of Cape Verde's food has to be imported. Foreign aid is being received to

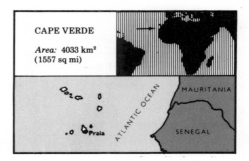

CAPE VERDE

Area: 4033 km² (1557 sq mi)

develop agriculture and to imrove the infrastructure of the islands. Money sent back by over 700,000 Cape Verdeans living abroad is vital to the economy, providing, on average, about 15% of Cape Verde's GDP. Fish, crustaceans and shellfish account for about one half of the country's export earnings.

Currency: Cape Verde escudo of 100 centavos; 1US$ = 84.4 escudos (June 1994).

GDP: US$331,000,000 (1991); US$850 per head.

RECENT HISTORY
Cape Verde - a former Portuguese colony - was linked with Guinea-Bissau in the struggle against colonial rule, but gained independence separately in 1975. The monopoly PAICV party offended Catholics by decriminalizing abortion and unrest grew in 1987-88. Social and political reforms were agreed in 1990, and in 1991 the PAICV was overwhelmingly defeated in elections by a newly legalized opposition group - the Movement for Democracy. Since then a free market economy has been introduced.

Central African Republic

Official name: La République Centrafricaine (The Central African Republic).

Member of: UN, OAU.

Area: 622,984 km² (240,535 sq mi).

Population: 2,999,000 (1993 est).

Capital: Bangui 598,000 (1988 est).

Other major cities: Bambari 52,000, Bouar 50,000 (1987 est).

Languages: French (official), Sangho (national).

Religions: Various Protestant Churches (48%), Roman Catholic (32%), animist (20%).

Education: Education is compulsory, in theory, between the ages of six and 14. In 1990 the literacy rate was 37.7%. There is a university.

Defence: In 1993 the total armed strength was 3800. There is selective military service.

Transport: There are 23,738 km (14,750 mi) of roads. Bangui is a river port and has an international airport.

Media: There is a single daily newspaper. There is a state-run radio and television service.

GOVERNMENT
The President - who appoints a Council of Ministers - is elected for a six-year term by universal adult suffrage. The 85-member National Assembly is elected directly for five years. The main political parties are the Central African People's Liberation Party (MPLC), the (former monopoly) Central African Democratic Rally (RDC), the Patriotic Front for Progress (FPP), the Liberal Democratic Party (PDL), the Alliance for Democracy and Progress (ADP) and the David Dacko Movement (MDD). After the election held in October 1993 a MPLC-PDL-ADP government was formed.

Party strength: MPLC 24, RDC 13, FPP 7, PDL 7, ADP 6, MDD 6, others 22.

President: Ange-Felix Patasse (MPLC).

Prime Minister: Jean-Luc Mandaba (MPLC).

GEOGRAPHY
The country is a low plateau, rising along the border with Sudan to the Bongos Mountains and in the west to the Monts Karre. Highest point: Mt Gaou 1420 m (4659 ft). Principal rivers: Oubangui, Zaïre, Chari. Climate: The north is savannah, with little rain between November and March. The south is equatorial with high temperatures and heavy rainfall.

ECONOMY
Subsistence farming dominates, although cotton and coffee are produced for export. Diamonds contribute over 25% of the country's foreign earnings. The country is poor, and - largely owing to mismanagement during Bokassa's rule - its economy has declined since independence.

Currency: CFA Franc; 1US$ = 546.45 CFA Francs (June 1994).

GDP: US$1,296,000,000 (1991); US$410 per head.

RECENT HISTORY
French influence began in 1889, and in 1903 the region became the French colony of Oubangi-Chari, which suffered greatly from the activities of companies that were granted exclusive rights to large areas. Independence, as the Central African Republic, was gained in 1960. Jean-Bédel Bokassa took power in a coup in 1965. In 1976 he declared himself emperor and was crowned in an extravagantly expensive ceremony. Revolts by students and schoolchildren helped to end his murderous regime in 1979. Multi-party elections were held in 1993.

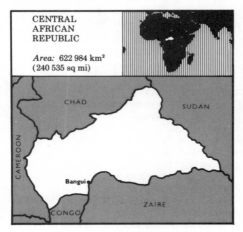

CENTRAL AFRICAN REPUBLIC

Area: 622 984 km²
(240 535 sq mi)

CHAD

SUDAN

CAMEROON

Bangui

ZAIRE

CONGO

Chad

Official name: La République du Tchad (The Republic of Chad).

Member of: UN, OAU.

Area: 1,284,000 km² (495,750 sq mi).

Population: 6,118,000 (1993 est).

Capital: N'Djamena 688,000 (1992 est).

Other major cities: Sarh 130,000, Moundou 118,000 (1992 est).

Languages: French and Arabic (both official), plus over 100 local languages.

Religions: Sunni Islam (50%), animist (25%), various Christian Churches - mainly Roman Catholic.

Education: Education is compulsory, in theory, between the ages of six and 14. In 1990 the literacy rate was 29.8%. There is a university.

Defence: In 1993 the total armed strength was over 25,000. There is selective military service.

Transport: There are 40,000 km (24,855 mi) of roads. N'Djamena has an international airport.

Media: There is a single daily newspaper. There are two state-run radio stations and a television service.

GOVERNMENT

Following a military coup in 1991, a transitional government system was established in 1993. A national conference has chosen a 57-member Higher Transitional Council. Although one-party rule was abandoned in 1993 the Council is dominated by the Patriotic Salvation Movement (MPS).

President: Idriss Deby (MPS).

Prime Minister: Delwa Kassire Koumakome (MPS).

GEOGRAPHY

Deserts in the north include the Tibesti Mountains, the highest part of the country. Savannah and semidesert in the centre slope down to Lake Chad. The Oubangui Plateau in the south is covered by tropical rain forest. Highest point: Emi Koussi 3415 m (11,204 ft). Principal river: Chari. Climate: Chad is hot and dry in the north, and tropical in the south.

Between November and April virtually no rain falls.

ECONOMY

Chad - one of the poorest countries in the world - has been wracked by civil war and drought. With few natural resources, it relies on subsistence farming, exports of cotton and on foreign aid.

Currency: CFA Franc; 1US\$ = 546.45 CFA Francs (June 1994).

GDP: US\$1,255,000,000 (1991); US\$210 per head.

RECENT HISTORY

The area around Lake Chad became French in the late 19th century. The French conquest of the north was not completed until 1916. Since independence in 1960, Chad has been torn apart by a bitter civil war between the Muslim Arab north and the Christian and animist Black

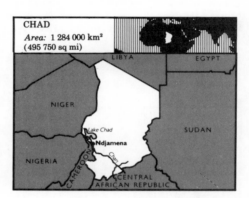

CHAD
Area: 1 284 000 km²
(495 750 sq mi)

African south. Various secessionist movements have also been active in Chad. Libya and France intervened forcefully on several occasions, but neither was able to achieve its aims. In October 1988, the civil war was formally ended. However, from March 1989 the former Chadian army chief, Idriss Deby, led a rebel force from bases in Sudan against the government in N'Djamena and took control of the whole country late in 1990. Unrest continues in the north. The territorial dispute with Libya concerning the Aozou strip was settled in Chad's favour in 1994 when Libya agreed to withdraw in accordance with a decision of the International Court.

Comoros

Official name: La République fédérale islamique des Comores (The Federal Islamic Republic of the Comoros).

Member of: UN, OAU.

Area: 1862 km² (719 sq mi; excluding Mayotte which is administered by France).

Population: 479,000 (1991 est; excluding Mayotte).

Capital: Moroni 60,000 (city 22,000; 1987 est).

Other main town: Mutsamudu 14,000 (1988 est).

Languages: French and Arabic - both official; Comoran (majority; a blend of Swahili and Arabic).

Religion: Sunni Islam (official; 99%).

Education: Education is compulsory, in theory, between the ages of seven and 15. In 1985 the literacy rate was 15%. There are no university-level institutes.

Defence: In 1990 the total armed strength was nearly 900 - about 700 in the army (which includes an air force unit) and 200 in the navy.

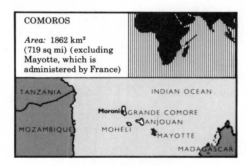

Transport: There are 605 km (376 mi) of roads. Moroni, the main port, has an international airport.

Media: There are two weekly newspapers and a state-run radio and television service.

GOVERNMENT
The President - who is elected for a six-year term by universal adult suffrage - appoints a Council of Ministers. The 42 members of the Federal Assembly are directly elected for five years. The main political parties are the Rally of Democrats for the Republic (RDR), the National Union for Democracy for the Comoros (UNDC), and the (former monopoly) Udzima party. After the election in December 1993 a RDR government was formed.

Party strength: RDR 24, UNDC 18.

President: Siad Mohamed Djohar (RDR).

Prime Minister: Mohamed Abdou Madi (RDR).

GEOGRAPHY
Ngazidja (Grande Comore) - the largest island - is dry and rocky, rising to an active volcano. Ndzouani (Anjouan) is a heavily eroded volcanic massif. Moili (Mohéli) is a forested plateau with fertile valleys. There are no significant rivers. Highest point: Mont Kartala (an active volcano; 2361 m/7746 ft). Climate: The tropical climate of the Comoros is dry from May to October, but with heavy rain for the rest of the year.

ECONOMY
Poor and eroded soils, overpopulation and few resources combine to make these underdeveloped islands one of the world's poorest countries. Subsistence farming occupies the majority of the population, although vanilla, cloves and ylang-ylang are produced for export.

Currency: Comorian franc of 100 centimes; 1US$ = 545.8 francs.

GDP: US$260,000,000 (1991); US$510 per head.

RECENT HISTORY
The four Comoran islands became a French colony in 1912. In a referendum in 1974, three islands voted to become independent, which they declared themselves without French agreement. The fourth island, Mayotte, voted against independence, and remains under French rule. Following a coup in 1978, an Islamic republic was proclaimed, and a single-party state established. In 1989, the third attempted coup in a decade resulted in the assassination of the president and a brief period of rule by European mercenaries. Multiparty rule was restored in 1990 and the former monopoly party lost all its seats in the Assembly in 1993.

Congo

Official name: La République du Congo (The Republic of the Congo).

Member of: UN, OAU.

Area: 342,000 km² (132,047 sq mi).

Population: 2,772,000 (1993 est).

Capital: Brazzaville 940,000 (1992 est).

Other major cities: Pointe-Noire 576,000, Loubomo 84,000 (1992 est).

Languages: French (official), Lingala patois (50%), Monokutuba patois (over 40%), Kongo (45%), Teke (20%).

Religions: Roman Catholic (53%), various Protestant Churches (22%), animist (25%).

Education: Education is compulsory, in theory, between the ages of six and 16. In 1990 the literacy rate was 56.6%. There is a university.

Defence: In 1993 the total armed strength was 10,800, plus 6100 paramilitary police.

Transport: There are 12,745 km (7920 mi) of roads and 795 km (494 mi) of railways. Pointe-Noire is the main seaport. Brazzaville and Pointe-Noire have international airports.

Media: There are four daily newspapers and a state-run radio and television service.

GOVERNMENT
The 125-member National Assembly, 60-member Senate and the President are elected for a five-year term by universal adult suffrage. The President appoints a Prime Minister and a Council of Ministers. Political parties include the Pan-African Union for Social Democracy (UPADS), the Rally for Democracy and Development (RDD), the Union for Democratic Renewal (URD), the (former monopoly ex-Communist) Congolese Party of Labour (PCT), and Rally for Democratic Social Progress (RDPS). After the elections held in June and October 1993, a UPADS-RDD coalition was formed.

Party strength: UPADS 47, URD 28, PCT 15, RDPS 10, RDD 6, others 19.

President: Pascal Lissouba (UPADS).

Prime Minister: Gen. Jacques-Joaquim Yhombi-Opango (RDD).

GEOGRAPHY
Behind a narrow coastal plain, the plateaux of the interior are covered by tropical rain forests and rise to over 700 m (2300 ft). Highest point: Mont de la Lékéti 1040 m (3412 ft). Principal rivers: Zaïre (Congo), Oubangui. Climate: Congo's tropical climate is hot and humid.

ECONOMY
Until 1991, Congo had a centrally planned economy. Privatization has begun but the country is crippled by the highest per capita external debt in Africa. Petroleum and timber are the main exports. Subsistence agriculture - chiefly for cassava - occupies over a third of the labour force.

Currency: CFA Franc; 1US$ = 546.45 CFA Francs (June 1994).

GDP: US$2,502,000,000 (1991); US$1,030 per head.

RECENT HISTORY
In the 1880s, the explorer Brazza placed the

kingdom of the Teke people under French protection, and in 1905 the region became the colony of Moyen-Congo. Independence was gained in 1960. In 1963, following industrial unrest, a Marxist-Leninist state was established. Since then, ethnic tensions have led to political unrest and military coups. A multi-party system was restored in 1991.

41

Côte d'Ivoire

Official name: La République de la Côte d'Ivoire (The Republic of the Ivory Coast). Since 1986 Côte d'Ivoire has been the only official name.

Member of: UN, OAU, ECOWAS.

Area: 322,462 km² (124,503 sq mi).

Population: 12,464,000 (1991 est).

Capitals: Yamoussoukro (de jure and administrative capital) 120,000, Abidjan (de facto and legislative capital) 1,850,000 (1987 est).

Other major city: Bouaké 220,000 (1987 est).

Languages: French (official), Bete (20%), Senufo (14%), Baoulé (12%).

Religions: Animist (60%), Christian, mainly Roman Catholic (20%), Sunni Islam (20%).

Education: Education is compulsory in theory between the ages of seven and 13. In 1990 the literacy rate was 53.8%. There is a university.

Defence: In 1993 the total armed strength was estimated to be 7100 - 5500 in the army, 700 in the navy and 900 in the ar force - plus 7800 paramilitary. There is selective military service.

Transport: There are about 55,000 km (34,370 mi) of roads and 638 km (399 mi) of railways. Abidjan has a commercial shipping port and an international airport.

Media: There are four daily newspapers. A state-run service broadcasts radio programmes and two television channels.

GOVERNMENT
The President - who is elected for a five-year term by universal adult suffrage - appoints a Premier and a Council of Ministers who are responsible to him. The 175-member National Assembly is also directly elected for five years. There are 49 local government units (départements). The main political parties are the (former monopoly) Democratic Party (PD), the Ivorian Popular Front (FPI) and the Workers' Party (PIT). Following the election in November 1990 a PD government was formed.

Party strength: PD 163, FP I9, PIT 1, others 2.

President: Henri Konan-Bédié (PD).

Prime Minister: Daniel Kablan Duncan (PD).

GEOGRAPHY
The north is a savannah-covered plateau. In the south, tropical rain forest - increasingly cleared for plantations - ends at the narrow coastal plain. Highest point: Mont Nimba 1752 m (5748 ft). Principal rivers: Sassandra, Bandama, Komoé. Climate: The south is equatorial with high temperatures and heavy rainfall; the north has similar temperatures but is drier.

ECONOMY
The country depends on exports of cocoa, coffee and timber, and has suffered since the 1980s as prices for these commodities have fallen. The devaluation of the CFA franc in 1994 added to the Ivory Coast's problems. Natural resources include petroleum, natural gas and iron ore. Political stability has helped economic growth.

Currency: CFA franc; 1US$ = 542.8 CFA francs (June 1994).

GDP: US$8,920,000,000 (1990); US$730 per head.

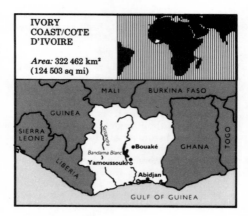

RECENT HISTORY
Colonized by France in the 19th century, the Ivory Coast became a relatively prosperous part of French West Africa. Independence was achieved in 1960 under the presidency of Félix Houphouët-Boigny (1905-94), who kept close links with France in return for aid and military assistance. Multi-party elections were held in 1990, but the opposition parties made claims of electoral fraud.

Djibouti

Official name: Jumhuriya Jibuti (The Republic of Djibouti).

Member of: UN, OAU, Arab League.

Area: 23,200 km² (8950 sq mi).

Population: 565,000 (1993 est), plus over 130,000 Somali refugees.

Capital: Djibouti 450,000 (1989 est).

Other main town: Ali Sabih 4000 (1989 est).

Languages: Arabic and French - both official; Somali (Issa; 37%).

Religion: Sunni Islam (96%; official), Roman Catholic (2%).

Education: Education is freely available between the ages of seven and 13 but is not compulsory. In 1987 the literacy rate was nearly 34%. There are no university-level institutions.

Defence In 1993 the total armed strength was 3300 plus a 600-member paramilitary police force and a 1200-member National Security force. There is no military service. About 4000 French troops are based in Djibouti.

Transport: There are 2897 km (1789 mi) of roads and 106 km (66 mi) of railways (which are part of the line connecting Addis Ababa with the sea). Djibouti, which has an international airport, is one of the two ports serving Ethiopia.

Media: There is a weekly newspaper and a state-controlled radio and television service.

GOVERNMENT
Every five years the 65-member Chamber of Deputies is elected by universal adult suffrage. The President - who is directly elected every six years - appoints a Prime Minister and a Council of Ministers who are responsible to him. Political parties include the (former monopoly) Popular Rally for Progress (RPP) and the New Democratic Party (PND). After the election in December 1992 the RPP retained power.

Party strength: RPP 65.

President: Hassan Gouled Aptidon (RPP).

Prime Minister: Barkat Gourad Hamadou (RPP).

GEOGRAPHY
Djibouti is a low-lying desert - below sea level in two basins, but rising to mountains in the north. There are no all-year rivers. Highest point: Musa Ali Terara 2062 m (6768 ft). Climate: Djibouti is extremely hot and dry, with rainfall under 125 mm (5 in) on the coast.

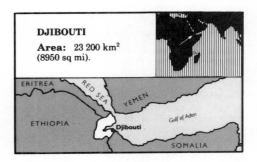

DJIBOUTI
Area: 23 200 km² (8950 sq mi).

ECONOMY
Lack of water largely restricts agriculture to grazing sheep and goats. The economy depends on the expanding seaport and railway, which both serve Ethiopia.

Currency: Djibouti franc of 100 centimes; 1US$ = 174.25 francs (June 1994).

GDP: US$216,600,000 (1986); US$475 per head.

RECENT HISTORY
France acquired a port in 1862 and established the colony of French Somaliland in 1888. In the 1950s and 1970s, the Afar tribe and Europeans voted to remain French, while the Issas (Somalis) opted for independence. In 1977, the territory became the Republic of Djibouti, but the new state has suffered ethnic unrest and drought. In 1981 Djibouti bcame a single-party state. In 1992, following the adoption of a new constitution, the single-party system was abandoned and multi-party elections were held, although the RPP retained all the parliamentary seats. Deep ethnic rivalry persists between the Issas and the (minority) Afars. The cabinet has a careful ethnic balance. In 1992-93 fighting erupted between government forces and the Afar FRUD guerrilla movement in the northeast.

Equatorial Guinea

Official name: La República de Guinea Ecuatorial (The Republic of Equatorial Guinea).

Member of: UN, OAU.

Area: 28,051 km² (10,831 sq mi).

Population: 377,000 (1993 est.).

Capital: Malabo 37,000 (1988 est.).

Other main city: Bata 24,000 (1988 est.).

Languages: Spanish (official), Fang, Bubi, Portuguese patois on Pagalu.

Religion: Roman Catholic majority.

Education: Education is compulsory, in theory, between the ages of six and 14. In 1983 the literacy rate was 62%. There are university-level institutions.

Defence: In 1993 the total armed strength was 3100 - 1100 in the army, 1000 in the navy and 1000 in the air force. There is also a 2000-member paramilitary force.

Transport: There are 2682 km (1667 mi) of roads. Malabo and Bata are the main ports. Malabo has an international airport; Bata has an airport that receives some international flights.

Media: There are two weekly newspapers, three state-run radio stations and a state-run television service.

GOVERNMENT

A President is elected for seven years and an 80-member National Assembly is elected for five years by universal adult suffrage. Political parties include the (former monopoly) Democratic Party of Equatorial Guinea (PDGE), the People's Social Democratic Convention (CPDS), the Social Democratic Union (UDS) and the Liberal Party (PL). After the election held in November 1993, which was boycotted by most of the opposition forces, the PDGE maintained power.

Party strength: PDGE 68, CPDS 6, UDS 5, PL 1.

President: Brig. Gen. Teodoro Obiang (Nguema Mbasogo) (PDGE).

GEOGRAPHY

The republic consists of the fertile island of Bioko (formerly known as Fernando Póo), the

much smaller islands of Pagalu (formerly known as Annobón) and the Corisco Group, and the district of Mbini (formerly known as Río Muni) on the African mainland. Highest

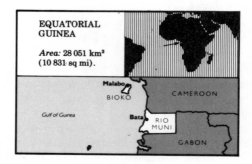

EQUATORIAL GUINEA

Area: 28 051 km² (10 831 sq mi).

point: Pico de Moca (Moka) 2850 m (9350 ft). Principal rivers: Campo, Benito, Muni. Climate: The tropical climate is hot and humid with heavy rainfall. The climate of the islands of Pagalu and Bioko is moderated by maritime influences.

ECONOMY

Mbini exports coffee and timber, but cocoa production on Bioko slumped after the departure of Nigerian workers (1976). The economy relies heavily upon foreign aid.

Currency: CFA Franc; 1US$ = 546.45 CFA Francs (June 1994).

GDP: US$144,000,000 (1992); US$330 per head.

RECENT HISTORY

The colony of Spanish Guinea was created in 1856. The harsh plantation system practised during the colonial era attracted much international criticism. Independence in 1968 began under the dictatorship of Francisco Nguema, who was overthrown by his nephew Teodoro Obiang in a military coup in 1979. One-party rule has been in force since 1987, but coups were attempted in 1981, 1983, 1986 and 1988. The return of political pluralism was allowed in 1993 but the first multi-party elections (November 1993) were condemned by US and Spanish observers as a 'paradox of democracy'. The UN has repeatedly criticized violations of human rights in Equatorial Guinea and the suppression of dissent on the island of Pagalu has been severe.

Eritrea

Official name: Eritrea.

Member of: UN, OAU.

Area: 117, 400 km² (45 300 sq mi).

Population: 3,670,000 (1993 est).

Capital: Asmara (Asmera) 344,000 (1991 est).

Other main towns: Massawa (Mitsiwa) 40,000, Assab 30,000 (1991 est).

Languages: Tigrinya (majority), Tigre, Arabic, Afar, Saho.

Religions: Sunni Islam (majority), Coptic Christian (minority).

Education: Education is not compulsory but schooling is free for up to 12 years from the age of six. There is no recent figure for the literacy rate. Eritrea has a single university.

Defence: The total armed strength in 1991 was estimated to be 60,000.

Transport: There are no figures available for road lengths. The 306 km (191 mi) railway from Massawa to Asmara is being reconstructed. Asmara has an international airport. Massawa and Assab are commercial shipping ports - the latter being the main port for Ethiopia.

Media: The daily press in Eritrea is being reestablished. There is a state-run broadcasting service.

GOVERNMENT
The Eritrean People's Liberation Front (EPLF) took control of Eritrea in May 1991 and forms the provisional government - for a transitional period not exceeding four years - pending the adoption of a constitution. Multi-party rule is scheduled to be introduced by 1995.

President (Head of state and of government): Issaias Afewerki.

GEOGRAPHY
Eritrea is physically an extension of the Ethiopian high plateau, although there are low coastal plains. The country includes the Dahlak Islands in the Red Sea. Principal river: Barka (seasonal). Highest point: Ramlo 2130 m (6986 ft). Climate: Eritrea has a dry tropical climate.

ECONOMY
A 30-year secessionist war has shattered the economy. The labour force is largely agricultural, growing sorghum and keeping livestock for hides (the major export). However, scarce and unreliable rainfall is a hazard. The main natural resource is salt. Before the armed struggle for independence began Eritrea was one of the most industrialized regions of Africa. Some industries, including footwear and textiles, remain but considerable foreign aid will be required to rescue the economy.

Currency: The Ethiopian birr is being used provisionally (see pp. 46-47).

GDP: US$393,415,000 (1993); US$115 per head.

RECENT HISTORY
The Italian colony of Eritrea was created out of coastal districts of Ethiopia and areas claimed by the (Turkish) Ottoman Empire in 1890. Used as the base for Italy's conquest of Ethiopia (1935-36), Eritrea came under British rule in 1941 when Italy was removed from East Africa. In 1952 the territory was federated as an autonomous state with Ethiopia but its incorporation as an Ethiopian province in 1962 sparked a rebellion against Ethiopia that lasted until 1991. In 1977 Eritrean guerrillas almost completely cleared the territory of Ethiopian forces, but the Marxist Ethiopian government of Col. Mengistu fought back with Soviet arms to reverse the position in the following year. The EPLF (see above) - with the Ethiopian Tigrayan Liberation Front - was finally instrumental in toppling Mengistu in 1991, when Eritrea effectively seceded from Ethiopia. A referendum in Eritrea in April 1993 produced an overwhelming majority in favour of independence and the territory assumed complete sovereignty on 24 May 1993.

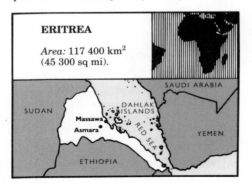

ERITREA

Area: 117 400 km²
(45 300 sq mi).

SAUDI ARABIA

SUDAN

DAHLAK ISLANDS

Massawa

Asmara

RED SEA

YEMEN

ETHIOPIA

Ethiopia

Official name: Ityopia (Ethiopia). (The designation The Federal Democratic Republic of Ethiopia has been adopted.) The country was previously known as Abyssinia.

Member of: UN, OAU.

Area: 1,106,200 km² (427,135 sq mi) excluding Eritrea.

Population: 51,830,000 (1993 est) excluding Eritrea.

Capital: Addis Ababa 1,739,000 (1991 est).

Other major cities: Dire Dawa 122,000, Gondar 95,000, Nazret 91,000, Dese (Dessie) 78,000, Harar 70,000 (1991 est).

Languages: Amharic (official), Arabic, Oromo (43%), Somali, Afar.

Religions: Ethiopian Orthodox (52%), Sunni Islam (31%), animist (11%).

Education: Education is freely available between the ages of six and 19 but it is not compulsory. In 1987 the literacy rate was estimated to be 71%. There are two universities.

Defence: In 1993 the total armed strength was about 100,000. Selective military service lasts between 12 and 18 months.

Transport: There are 27,972 km (17,385 mi) of roads and 782 km (486 mi) of railways. Since the secession of Eritrea, Ethiopia has no ports. Addis Ababa has an international airport.

Media: There are three daily newspapers, three radio stations and a state-run television service.

GOVERNMENT

An 87-member Council of Representatives was appointed in July 1991. Elections were held in June 1994 for a Constitutional Assembly, which will draft a new federal constitution. In 1991 a plan for a federal system of 14 autonomous regions (at that time including Eritrea) was announced. This was not fully introduced although four autonomous regions have been created, and 25 other regions, the result of the division of previous local government areas, are operating. The current system is to be replaced by 13 ethnic regions - Afar, Agau North, Agau South, Amhara, Beni Shangul,

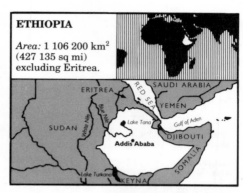

ETHIOPIA

Area: 1 106 200 km² (427 135 sq mi) excluding Eritrea.

Gambela, Gurage Kembatahadiya, Kaffa, Omo, Oromo, Sidama, Somali and Tigray - plus a federal capital district. The final nature of the new Ethiopian federation may not become clear until the newly elected constitutional assembly has produced its final proposals. The main political movement is the Ethiopian People's Revolutionary Democratic Front (EPRDF), which comprises the Ethiopian People's Democratic Movement (EPDM), the Tigray People's Liberation Front (TPLF), the Oromo People's Democratic Movement (OPDM), and the Afar Democratic Union, and is dominated by the TPLF. Other political movements include the Oromo Liberation Front, the Islamic Front for the Liberation of Oromia, the United Oromo People's Liberation Front, the Oromo Abo Liberation Front, the Afar Liberation Front and the All Amhara People's Organization.

Party strength: (Council of Representatives) EPRDF 32, others 55.

President: Meles Zenawi (EPRDF).

THE CABINET
includes

Prime Minister: Tamirat Layne (EPRDF).

Minister of Defence: Siye Abraha.

Minister of Finance: Alemayehu Dhaba.

Minister of Foreign Affairs: Seyoum Mesfin.

Minister of Internal Affairs: Kuma Demeksa.

Minister of Justice: Mehitema Solomon.

AUTONOMOUS REGIONS
Aseb (Asab) Area: 46,065 km² (17,786 sq mi).

Population: 246,000 (1993 est). Capital (provisional): Serdo. (The Aseb region was divided in May 1993 when part of the region, including the port-city of Aseb, became part of the newly independent state of Eritrea.)

Dire Dawa Area: 29,244 km² (11,291 sq mi). Population: 522,000 (1993 est). Capital: Dire Dawa.

Ogaden Area: 179,327 km² (69,239 sq mi). Population: 907,000 (1993 est). Capital: not yet designated.

Tigray Area: 53,498 km² (20,656 sq mi). Population: 3,000,000 (1993 est). Capital: Mekele.

GEOGRAPHY

The Western Highlands - including the Tigré Plateau and the Semien Mountains - are separated from the lower Eastern Highlands by a wide rift valley. Highest point: Ras Dashen 4620 m (15,158 ft). Principal rivers: Blue Nile (Abay Wenz), Tekeze, Awash, Omo, Sagan. Climate: Very hot and dry in the north and east, with a temperate climate in the highlands. There are many local climatic variations, ranging from the pleasant high plateaux to the hot lowlands.

ECONOMY

Secessionist wars have damaged an impoverished, underdeveloped economy. Most Ethiopians are involved in subsistence farming, but drought and overgrazing have led to desertification. Coffee is the main foreign-currency earner. The economy is in serious difficulties owing to the end of aid from the former Eastern bloc. However, rapid progress towards self-sufficiency has been made in the early 1990s and market-oriented reforms have encouraged the peasant farmers. Despite these advances over 4,000,000 Ethiopians still depend upon international food aid for their survival. The loss of Eritrea - and with it the country's only coast - is a problem. The railway line to Djibouti has assumed extra importance as Ethiopia's main access to international markets. The Red Sea Eritrean port of Aseb is still used by Ethiopia, which has concluded a free-trade agreement to export and import via Aseb.

Currency: Ethiopian birr of 100 cents; 1US$ = 5.48 birrs (June 1994).

GDP: US$5,958,000,000 (1992); US$110 per head.

RECENT HISTORY

Under Emperor Menelik II, Ethiopia survived the European scramble for empire and defeated an Italian invasion (1896). The ascent of the Emperor Haile Selassie (1892-1975) to the throne in 1930 marked a new dynasty and a new chapter in Ethiopia's history. Although, the Italians occupied Ethiopia from 1936 to 1941, Haile Selassie returned to lead his country to a prominent position in post-colonial Africa. He became the elder statesman of the continent, playing a prominent part in African affairs, and Addis Ababa became the headquarters of the Organization of African Unity. However, Haile Selassie failed to modernize Ethiopia or to overcome its extreme poverty. His reforms, when they came, were too little and too late for the army, which overthrew him in 1974. The former Italian colony of Eritrea was handed to Ethiopia in 1952 as an autonomous state within a federation of Ethiopia and Eritrea. In 1962, however, Eritrea's autonomy was revoked and Ethiopia was reorganized as a unitary state. This provoked the beginning of a guerrilla war by Eritrean separatists that lasted for three decades. After 1974, allied to the USSR, a left-wing military regime instituted revolutionary change, but, even with Cuban help, it was unable to overcome secessionist guerrilla movements in Eritrea and Tigray. Drought, soil erosion and civil war brought severe famine in the 1980s, and Ethiopia was the recipient of massive international humitarian aid. President Mengistu - who ruled a one-party Marxist-Leninist state from 1979 to 1991 - was toppled by an alliance of Tigrayan, Eritrean, Oromo and other forces in 1991. Multi-party rule was restored, but there has since been international concern about human rights violations. New constitutional arrangements to accommodate various regional secessionist movements are to be implemented. However, Eritrea effectively seceded in 1991 and - following a referendum in favour of independence - assumed internationally-recognized sovereignty in May 1993. The Oromo Liberation Front withdrew from the transitional government in 1992 and fighting erupted between Oromo forces and central government forces. The Oromo region is scheduled to achieve autonomy within Ethiopia's new federal structure, but some elements in the region are pressing for an independent state of Oromia.

Gabon

Official name: La République gabonaise (The Gabonese Republic).

Member of: UN, OAU, OPEC.

Area: 267,667 km² (103,347 sq mi).

Population: 1,280,000 (1993 est).

Capital: Libreville 352,000 (1988 est).

Other major cities: Port-Gentil 164,000, Masuku (formerly Franceville) 75,000 (1988 est).

Languages: French (official), 40 local languages including Fang (30%).

Religions: Roman Catholic (71%), animist (29%).

Education: Education is compulsory, in theory, between the ages of six and 16. In 1990 the literacy rate was 60.7%. There are two universities.

Defence: In 1993 the total armed strength was 4750 (plus the 2800-member paramilitary police and 2000 gendarmes).

GOVERNMENT
The President - who is elected by compulsory universal adult suffrage for a seven-year term -

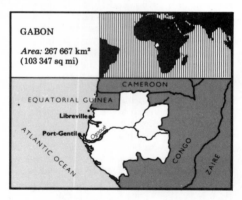

GABON

Area: 267 667 km²
(103 347 sq mi)

appoints a Council of Ministers (over which he presides) and a Prime Minister. The National Assembly has 120 members directly elected for five years. The main political parties include the (former monopoly) Gabonese Democratic Party (PDG), the National Rally of Woodcutters (RNB), the Gabonese Progress Party (PGP), the Union of Gabonese People (UPG), the Association for Socialism in Gabon (APSG), and the Gabonese Social Union (USG). After the election held in September 1990 the PDG retained power.

Party strength: PDG 66, PGP 19, RNB 17, others 18.

President: Omar Bongo (PDG).

Prime Minister: Casimir Oye Mba (PDG).

GEOGRAPHY
Apart from the narrow coastal plain, low plateaux make up most of the country. Highest point: Mont Iboundji 1580 m (5185 ft). Principal river: Ogooué. Climate: The equatorial climate is hot and humid with little seasonal variation.

ECONOMY
Petroleum, natural gas, manganese, uranium and iron ore - and a relatively small population - make Gabon the richest Black African country, although most Gabonese are subsistence farmers. There is a large, and increasing, number of (mainly) French workers in the oil and natural gas industries and in the service industries.

Currency: CFA Franc; 1US$ = 546.45 CFA Francs (June 1994).

GDP: US$5,380,000,000 (1992); US$4480 per head.

RECENT HISTORY
Gabon was colonized by the French in the late 19th century. Pro-French Léon M'Ba (1902-67) led the country to independence in 1960. Deposed in a coup (1964), he was restored to power by French troops. Under his successor, Omar Bongo, Gabon has continued its pro-Western policies. Pro-democracy demonstrations and strikes, followed by anti-government riots in 1990, prompted France to dispatch troops to Gabon to restore order. President Bongo appointed a transitional government and permitted the establishment of political pluralism. In 1990 multi-party legislative elections were held, followed by multi-party presidential elections in 1993 - upon both occasions the opposition parties alleged fraud. Social discontent is rising as the gap between rich and poor widens and a state of emergency has been imposed.

Gambia

Official name: The Republic of the Gambia.

Member of: UN, OAU, ECOWAS, Commonwealth.

Area: 11,295 km² (4361 sq mi).

Population: 1,033,000 (1993 est).

Capital: Banjul 171,000 (city 44,000; Serekunda-Kombo St Mary 103,000; Bakau 24,000; 1986 est).

Other main town: Brikama 24,000 (1986 est).

Language: English (official), local languages.

Religions: Sunni Islam (90%), various Protestant Churches (9%) - mainly Anglican.

Education: Education is freely available between the ages of eight and 14, but it is not compulsory. In 1990 the literacy rate was 27.2%. There are university-level institutions.

Defence: In 1992 the total armed strength was 800 (including an armed police force of over 600). Military service is normally voluntary, but is compulsory in certain circumstances.

Transport: There are 2386 km (1483 mi) of roads. The navigable River Gambia is the main communications link in the country. Banjul is a seaport and a river port. There is an international airport at Yundum.

Media: There are weekly and fortnightly papers, three radio stations (one of which is commercial) but no television station. There are plans to introduce a television service in the Gambia; in the meantime, Senegalese television is received throughout the country.

GOVERNMENT
The President and 36 of the 50 members of the House of Representatives are elected by universal adult suffrage every five years. The remaining 14 members of the House are appointed by either virtue of their office (nine members) or are elected by the traditional Assembly of Chiefs (five members). The President appoints a Vice-President - to lead the government in the House - and a Cabinet of Ministers. The main political parties are the People's Progressive Party (PPP), the National Convention Party (NCP) and the Gambia People's Party (GPP). After the election in April 1992 a PPP government remained in power until the coup in 1994.

Party strength: PPP 25, NCP 6, GPP 2, ind 3, ex-officio appointed members 9, representatives of the Assembly of Chiefs 5.

President: Lieut. Yayeh Jameh.

GEOGRAPHY
The Gambia is a narrow low-lying country on either bank of the River Gambia. Highest point: an unnamed point on the Senegalese border 43 m (141 ft). Principal river: Gambia. Climate: The climate is tropical, with a dry season from November to May.

ECONOMY
Until recent years the economy was largely based on the cultivation of groundnuts. Tourism is now the major foreign-currency earner and the country has suffered a consider-

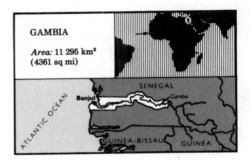

able fall in revenue as a result of the decline in the number of foreign tourists - mainly from the UK, Germany and Sweden - visiting the Gambia following the 1994 coup.

Currency: Dalasi of 100 butut; 1US$ = 9.71 dalasis (June 1994).

GDP: US$362,000,000 (1992); US$390 per head.

RECENT HISTORY
A British colony was established in 1843. The Gambia achieved independence in 1965 under Sir Dawda K. Jawara. In 1981 an attempted coup against his rule encouraged efforts to merge with the neighbouring French-speaking country of Senegal, but the confederation was dissolved in 1989. The Gambia was a multiparty democracy until the military seized power in July 1994.

Ghana

Official name: The Republic of Ghana.

Member of: UN, OAU, ECOWAS, Commonwealth.

Area: 238,537 km² (92,099 sq mi).

Population: 15,635,000 (1993 est).

Capital: Accra 1,580,000 (includes Tema 190,000; 1988 est).

Other major cities: Kumasi 490,000, Sekondi-Takoradi 175,000, Tamale 170,000 (1988 est).

Languages: English (official), Asante, Ewe, Ga.

Religions: Various Protestant Churches (30%), Sunni Islam (20%), Roman Catholic (over 25%), animist (17%).

Education: Education is compulsory, in theory, between the ages of six and 15. In 1990 the literacy rate was 60.3%. There are five universities.

Defence: In 1993 the total armed strength was 6850 - 5000 in the army, 850 in the navy, 1000 in the air force.

Transport: There are 36,700 km (22,800 mi) of roads and 953 km (592 mi) of state-run railways. Tema and Takoradi are the main ports. Accra has an international airport.

Media: There are three daily newspapers. A state corporation brodcasts radio and television programmes.

GOVERNMENT

The 200-member House of Parliament and a President are elected for four years by universal adult suffrage. A 25-member Council of State is appointed by the President. The main political parties include the National Democratic Congress (NDC), the (left-wing) National Convention Party (NCP), the Independence Party (IP), and the Egle Party (EP). After the election held in December 1992 the NDC remained in power.

Party strength: NDC 189, NCP 8, IP 2, EP 1.

President: Flight Lt. Jerry Rawlings (NDC).

GEOGRAPHY

Most of the country comprises low-lying plains and plateaux. In the centre, the Volta Basin - which ends in steep escarpments - contains the

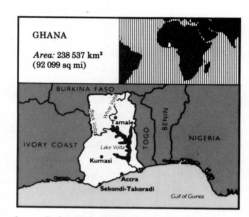

large Lake Volta reservoir. Highest point: Afadjato 872 m (2860 ft). Principal river: Volta. Climate: The climate is tropical with 2000 mm (80 in) of rainfall on the coast, decreasing markedly inland. The north is subject to the hot, dry Harmattan wind from the Sahara.

ECONOMY

Political instability and mismanagement damaged the economy of Ghana in the 1970s and 1980s. Agriculture occupies nearly 50% of the labour force, with cocoa being the main cash crop. Forestry and mining for bauxite, gold and manganese are also important activities.

Currency: Cedi of 100 pesewas; 1US$ = 941.6 cedis (June 1994).

GDP: US$6,176,000,000 (1992); US$400 per head.

RECENT HISTORY

Britain ousted the Danes (1850) and the Dutch (1872) to establish the Gold Coast colony in 1874. The great inland kingdom of Ashanti was not finally conquered until 1898. After World War II, the prosperity of the cocoa industry, increasing literacy and the dynamism of Dr Kwame Nkrumah (1909-72) helped the Gold Coast set the pace for decolonization in Black Africa. After independence in 1957 - as Ghana - Nkrumah's grandiose policies and increasingly dictatorial rule led to his overthrow in a military coup in 1966. Ghana has since struggled to overcome its economic and political problems. There were six coups in 20 years, including two by Flight Lieutenant Jerry Rawlings (1979 and 1982). A multi-party system was restored in 1992.

Guinea

Official name: La République de Guinée (The Republic of Guinea).

Member of: UN, OAU, ECOWAS.

Area: 245,857 km² (94,926 sq mi).

Population: 7,420,000 (1993 est).

Capital: Conakry 705,000 (1983 est).

Other major cities: Kankan 89,000, Kindia 56,000 (1983 est).

Languages: French (official), Soussou (11%), Fulani (40%).

Religions: Sunni Islam (85%), Roman Catholic and animist minorities.

Education: Education is compulsory, in theory, between the ages of seven and 13. In 1990 the literacy rate was estimated to be 24%. There are two universities.

Defence: In 1993 the total armed strength was 9700. There is also 9600-member paramilitary police force. Compulsory military service lasts for two years.

Transport: There are 28,400 km (17,600 mi) of roads and 662 km (411 mi) of state-run railways. Conakry has a commercial shipping port and an international airport.

Media: There are two weekly newspapers and a single state-run radio and television service.

GOVERNMENT
Power is exercised by the 15-member Military Committee for National Recovery, whose President is head of state and of government. Political pluralism is permitted and although multi-party presidential elections were held in 1993, no date has been set for multi-party elections for a new unicameral parliament. Political parties include the Party of Unity and Progress (PUP), the Rally for Guinean People (RPG) and the Union of the New Republic (UNR).

President: Gen. Lansana Conte (PUP).

GEOGRAPHY
Tropical rain forests cover the coastal plain. The interior highlands and plains are covered by grass and scrubland. There are mountains in the southwest. Highest point: Mont Nimba 1752 m (5748 ft). Principal rivers: Niger, Bafing,

Konkouré, Kogon. Climate: The climate is tropical with heavy rainfall. Temperatures are cooler in the highlands.

ECONOMY
Bauxite accounts for nearly 80% of Guinea's exports. However, agriculture involves over 75% of the labour force, producing bananas, oil

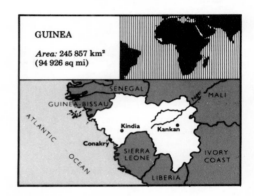

GUINEA

Area: 245 857 km²
(94 926 sq mi)

palm and citrus fruits for export, and maize, rice and cassava as subsistence crops. Despite mineral wealth, Guinea relies heavily on aid. The economy is susceptible to the rise and fall of the prices of two or three commodities on the international market.

Currency: Guinean franc; 1US$ = 977.91 francs.

GDP: US$3,083,000,000 (1992); US$510 per head.

RECENT HISTORY
Increasing French influence in the 19th century led to the establishment of the colony of French Guinea (1890). Unlike the rest of French Africa, Guinea voted for a complete separation from France in 1958, suffering severe French reprisals as a result. The authoritarian radical leader Sékou Touré (1922-84) isolated Guinea, but he became reconciled with France in 1978. The leaders of a military coup (1984) have achieved some economic reforms and in 1993 multi-party presidential elections were held, although the result was disputed by the opposition. Scheduled legislative elections were postponed and public demonstrations were banned. The country is troubled by continuing allegations of corruption.

Guinea-Bissau

Official name: Republica da Guiné-Bissau (Republic of Guinea-Bissau).

Member of: UN, OAU, ECOWAS.

Area: 36,125 km² (13,948 sq mi).

Population: 1,035,000 (1993 est).

Capital: Bissau 125,000 (1988 est).

Other major town: Bafatá 13,500 (1980 est).

Languages: Portuguese (official), Crioulo (Creole dialect; majority), plus minorities speaking various local languages.

Religions: Animist (55%), Sunni Islam (40%), Roman Catholic (5%)

Education: Education is compulsory, in theory, between the ages of seven and 12. In 1990 the literacy rate was 36.5%. There are no university-level institutions.

Defence: In 1993 the total armed strength was 7200. There is also a 2000-member paramilitary police. There is no military service.

Transport: There are 3500 km (2175 mi) of roads. Bissau is the main port. Bissalanca has an international airport.

Media: There are two daily newspapers and a state-run radio station.

GOVERNMENT

The 150-member National Assembly is elected for five years by universal adult suffrage. The Assembly elects a President, who appoints Ministers. The main political parties are the (former monopoly) African Party for the Independence of Guinea-Bissau and Cape Verde (PAIGC), the Guinea-Bissau Resistance-Bafata Movement (RGB-MB), and the Party for Renovation and Development (PRD). The results of the first multi-party elections, held in July 1994, were not available at the time of going to press.

President: Brig. Gen. João Bernardo Vieira (PAIGC).

Prime Minister: Carlos Correia (PAIGC).

GEOGRAPHY

Most of the country is low-lying, with swampy coastal lowlands and a flat forested interior

plain. The northeast is mountainous. Highest point: an unnamed point in the Fouta Djallon plateau 180 m (591 ft). Principal rivers: Cacheu, Mansôa, Géba, Corubel. Climate: The climate is tropical with a dry season from December to May.

ECONOMY

The country has one of the lowest standards of living in the world. Its subsistence economy is based mainly on rice. Palm kernels, groundnuts and cashew nuts are exported. Timber is exported. International agencies have attempted to relieve Guinea-Bissau's extreme financial

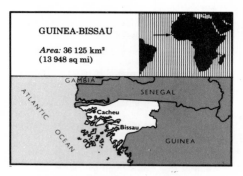

problems, which only tight accounting and austerity measures can hope to alleviate. Foreign aid has, however, helped to develop the infrastructure of the country and promoted the fishing industry - frozen fish are now exported.

Currency: Peso (GWP) of 100 centavos; 1US$ = 12,291.6 GWP (June 1994).

GDP: US$214,400,000 (1992); US$210 per head.

RECENT HISTORY

The colony of Portuguese Guinea was created in 1879. Failing to secure reform by peaceful means, the PAIGC movement mounted a liberation war (1961-1974). Independence was proclaimed in 1973 and recognized by Portugal in 1974. Following a military coup in 1980, the aim of union with Cape Verde was dropped. A multi-party system was introduced in 1991. An abortive coup in 1993 delayed the holding of the country's first multi-party elections, which were eventually held in the summer of 1994.

Kenya

Official name: Jamhuri ya Kenya (Republic of Kenya).

Member of: UN, OAU, Commonwealth.

Area: 580,367 km² (224,081 sq mi).

Population: 28,113,000 (1993 est).

Capital: Nairobi 1,505,000 (including suburbs) (1990 est).

Other major cities: Mombasa 426,000, Kisumu 167,000, Nakuru 102,000 (1985 est).

Languages: Swahili (official), English, Kikuyu (21%), Luhya (14%), Luo (11%), Kamba (11%).

Religions: Roman Catholic (27%), Independent African Churches (27%), Protestant Churches (19%), animist (19%), Sunni Islam (6%).

Education: Education is available at all levels but schooling is not compulsory. In 1990 the literacy rate was estimated to be 69%. There are four universities and a university college.

Defence: In 1993 the total armed strength was estimated to be 24,400 - 20,500 in the army, 1400 in the navy and a small number in the air force. Mombasa is the naval base. The paramilitary police has about 4000 personnel. There is no military service.

Transport: There are 62,573 km (38,881 mi) of roads and 3034 km (1885 mi) of railways. The main shipping port is Mombasa. Nairobi and Mombasa have international airports.

Media: There are five daily newspapers, three of which are published in English and two in Swahili. KBC, a state corporation, broadcasts three radio and four television channels.

GOVERNMENT

The President and the 200-member National Assembly are elected by universal adult suffrage for five years. The Vice President and the Cabinet of Ministers are appointed by the President. For local government purposes Kenya is divided into seven provinces and the city of Nairobi. The main political parties are (the former monopoly) Kenya African National Union (KANU), the Forum for the Restoration of Democracy - Kenya (FORD-K), the Forum for the Restoration of Democracy - Asili (FORD-A), the Democratic Party (DP), the Kenya National Congress (KC), Kenya Social Congress (KSC) and the Party of Independent Candidates of Kenya (PICK). Following multi-party elections in 1993 a KANU government was formed.

Party strength: (June 1994) KANU 115, FORD-K 29, FORD-A 24, DP 22, KNC 1, KSC 1, PICK 1, vacant seats 7.

President: Daniel arap Moi (KANU).

THE CABINET

Vice-President and Minister for Planning and National Development: Prof. George Saitoti (KANU).

Minister of Agriculture, Livestock Development and Marketing: Simon Nyachae (KANU).

Minister of Commerce and Industry: Kirugi M'Mukindia (KANU).

Minister of Cooperative Development: Kamwithi Munyi (KANU).

Minister of Culture and Social Services: Hussein Maalim Mohamed (KANU).

Minister of Education: Joseph Kamotho (KANU).

Minister of Energy: John Kyalo (KANU).

Minister of the Environment and Natural Resources: John Sambu (KANU).

Minister of Finance: Wycliffe Musalia Mudavadi (KANU).

Minister of Foreign Affairs: Stephen K. Musyoka (KANU).

Minister of Health: Joshua Angatia (KANU).

Minister of Home Affairs and National Heritage: Francis Lotodo (KANU).

Minister of Information and Broadcasting: Johnstone Makau (KANU).

Minister of Labour and Manpower: Philip Masinde (KANU).

Minister of Land Reclamation, Regional and Water Development: Darius Mbela (KANU).

Minister of Lands and Settlement: Jackson K. Mulinge (KANU).

Minister of Local Government: William Ole Ntimama (KANU).

Minister of Public Works and Housing: Jonathan N'Geno (KANU).

Minister of Research and Technical Training: Zachary Onyonka (KANU).

Minister of Tourism and Wildlife: Katana Ngala (KANU).

Minister of Transport and Communications: Dalmas Otieno (KANU).

Attorney-General: Amos Wako (KANU).

PROVINCES
Central Area: 13,175 km² (5087 sq mi). Population: 3,692,000 (1990 est). Capital: Nyeri.

Coastal Area: 83,603 km² (32,279 sq mi). Population: 2,150,000 (1990 est). Capital: Mombasa.

Eastern Area: 159,891 km² (61,734 sq mi). Population: 4,378,000 (1990 est). Capital: Embu.

Nairobi Area: 684 km² (264 sq mi). Population: 1,505,000 (1990 est). Capital: Nairobi.

North Eastern Area: 126,902 km² (48,997 sq mi). Population: 641,000 (1990 est). Capital: Garissa.

Nyanza Area: 16,162 km² (6240 sq mi). Population: 4,323,000 (1990 est). Capital: Kisumu.

Rift Valley Area: 173,868 km² (67,131 sq mi). Population: 5,357,000 (1990 est). Capital: Nakuru.

Western Area: 8360 km² (328 sq mi). Population: 2,837,000 (1990 est). Capital: Kakamega.

GEOGRAPHY
The steep-sided Rift Valley divides the high-

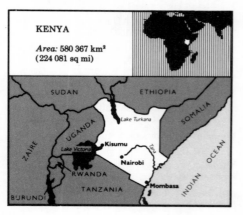

KENYA

Area: 580 367 km² (224 081 sq mi)

lands that run from north to south through central Kenya. Plateaux extend in the west to Lake Victoria and in the east to coastal lowlands. Highest point: Mount Kenya 5199 m (17,058 ft). Principal rivers: Tana, Umba, Athi, Mathioya. Climate: The coastal areas have a hot and humid equatorial climate. The highlands - which are cooler - experience high rainfall. The north is very hot and arid.

ECONOMY
Agriculture involves over 75% of the labour force. The main crops include wheat and maize for domestic consumption, and tea, coffee, sisal, sugar cane and cotton for export. Large numbers of beef cattle are reared, and Kenya is one of the few states in black Africa to have a major dairy industry. Tourism is an important source of foreign currency.

Currency: Kenya shilling of 100 cents; 1US$ = 56.16 shillings (June 1994).

GDP: US$8,543,000,000 (1992); US$330 per head.

RECENT HISTORY
The peoples of the area were forcibly brought under British rule in 1895 in the East African Protectorate, which became the colony of Kenya in 1920. White settlement in the highlands was bitterly resented by the Africans - particularly the Kikuyu - whose land was taken. Racial discrimination and attacks on African customs also created discontent. Black protest movements emerged in the 1920s, and after World War II these had developed into nationalism. From the 1920s, black protest was led by Jomo Kenyatta (c. 1893-1978), who in 1947 became the first president of the Kenya African Union. When the violent Mau Mau rising - which involved mainly Kikuyu people - broke out (1952-56), Kenyatta was held responsible and was imprisoned on doubtful evidence (1953-61). After the British had crushed the Mau Mau revolt in a bloody campaign, they negotiated with Kenyatta and the other African nationalists. Independence, under Kenyatta's KANU party, followed in 1963. His moderate leadership and pro-capitalist policies were continued by his successor, Daniel arap Moi, but considerable restrictions on political activity followed an attempted military coup in 1982. A campaign to end the one-party state included violent demonstrations in 1990. Multi-party elections in 1993 were won by KANU.

Lesotho

Official name: The Kingdom of Lesotho.

Member of: UN, Commonwealth, OAU, SADCC.

Area: 30,355 km² (11,720 sq mi).

Population: 1,903,000 (1993 est).

Capital: Maseru 130,000 (city 110,000, Maputsoe 20,000; 1988 est).

Other main towns: Teyateyaneng 14,000, Mafeteng 13,000 (1988 est).

Languages: Sesotho and English (official).

Religions: Roman Catholic (44%), various Protestant Churches (49% - mainly Lesotho Evangelical and Anglican).

Education: Education is compulsory, in theory, between the ages of six and 13. In 1990 the literacy rate was estimated to be over 75%. There is a single university.

Defence: In 1992 the total armed strength was 2000. There is no military service.

Transport: There are 4715 km (2930 mi) of roads and 2.6 km (1.6 mi) of railways. There is an international airport at Thota-Moli.

Media: There are three weekly newspapers, and a single (state-run) radio and television service.

GOVERNMENT

Lesotho is a constitutional monarchy in which elections are held by universal adult suffrage for a 65-member National Assembly to serve for five years. A Prime Minister and a Cabinet of Ministers are responsible to the Assembly. There is also a Senate composed of nominated members and traditional chiefs. The main political parties are the Basotho Congress Party (BCP) and the Basotho National Party (BNP). After the election in March 1993 a BCP government was formed.

Party strength: BCP 65.

King: HM King Letsie III (succeeded upon the exile and deposition of his father, 12 November 1990).

Prime Minister: Ntsu Mokhehle (BCP).

GEOGRAPHY

Most of Lesotho is mountainous. Highest point: Thabana Ntlenyana 3482 m (11,425 ft). Principal rivers: Orange, Caledon. Climate: Lesotho has a mild subtropical climate with lower temperatures in the highlands.

ECONOMY

Livestock - cattle, sheep and goats (for mohair) - are the mainstay of the economy. Natural resources include diamonds and abundant water, which is exported to South Africa. About one third of Lesotho's male labour force is employed in South Africa.

Currency: Loti (plural maloti) of 100 lisente; 1US$ = 3.65 maloti (June 1994).

GDP: US$1,053,000,000 (1991); US$580 per head.

RECENT HISTORY

Lesotho was founded in the 1820s by the Sotho leader, Moshoeshoe I (c. 1790-1870). The king-

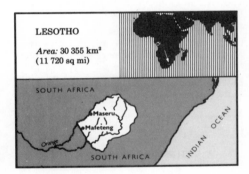

dom escaped incorporation into South Africa by becoming a British protectorate (known as Basutoland) in 1868. Although independence was achieved in 1966, the land-locked state remained dependent on South Africa. Chief Jonathan (Prime Minister 1966-86) - who curbed the monarchy's powers and attempted to limit South African influence - was deposed in a military coup. In 1990, the Military Council exiled King Moshoeshoe II and placed his son on the throne. Multi-party constitutional rule was restored in 1993.

55

Liberia

Official name: The Republic of Liberia.

Member of: UN, OAU, ECOWAS.

Area: 111,369 km² (43,000 sq mi).

Population: 2,884,000 (1993 est); in 1992 there were up to 700,000 Liberian refugees in neighbouring countries.

Capital: Monrovia 465,000 (1987 est).

Other main town: Buchanan 25,000 (1987 est).

Language: English (official).

Religions: Animist (50%), Sunni Islam (26%), various Christian Churches (24% - mainly Methodist, Baptist and Episcopalian).

Education: Education is compulsory, in theory, between the ages of six and 16. In 1985 the literacy rate was estimated to be 35%. There is a university.

Defence: As a result of the civil wars, the armed forces of Liberia have ceased to exist. The interim government is supported by an ECOWAS force of about 8000.

Transport: There are 8064 km (5011 mi) of roads and 490 km (304 mi) of railways. Monrovia has a shipping port and an international airport.

Media: There is a single daily newspaper. Five radio stations and a television station operate.

LIBERIA

Area: 111 369 km²
(43 000 sq mi)

SIERRA LEONE
GUINEA
St Paul
IVORY COAST
Monrovia
Buchanan
ATLANTIC OCEAN
GULF OF GUINEA

GOVERNMENT
The constitution provides for a President, Vice President, 26-member Senate and 64-member House of Representatives to be elected for six years by universal adult suffrage. The President appoints a Cabinet of Ministers. The Liberian political system broke down in 1990 owing to civil war. A five-member Council of State, which will appoint a 35-member transitional legislature, was appointed in 1993.

Head of state (acting president): Amos Sawyer.

GEOGRAPHY
A low swampy coastal belt borders a higher zone of tropical forest. Highest point: Mount Nimba 1380 m (4540 ft). Principal rivers: St Paul, St John, Cess. Climate: Liberia has a tropical climate with a wet season in the summer and a dry season in winter.

ECONOMY
Agriculture involves over 70% of the labour force. Cassava and rice are grown as subsistence crops, and rubber, coffee and cocoa for export. Liberia is a major exporter of iron ore, but the economy has been shattered by civil war.

Currency: Liberian dollar of 100 cents - US currency is also in circulation; 1US$ = 1 dollar (in theory).

GDP: US$975,200,000 (1988); US$400 per head.

RECENT HISTORY
Founded by the American Colonization Society in 1821-22 as a settlement for freed slaves, Liberia was declared a republic in 1847. Black American settlers dominated the local Africans and extended their control inland. From 1878 to 1980 power was held by presidents from the True Whig Party, including William Tubman (President 1944-71). His successor, William Tolbert, was assassinated during a military coup led by Samuel Doe, the first Liberian of local ancestry to rule. Doe was overthrown in a coup in 1990. Troops from several West African countries were dispatched by ECOWAS to restore order but civil war, initially involving two rebel forces, has continued beyond the official ceasefire in 1991. The NPFL (National Patriotic Front of Liberia), led by Charles Taylor, proved the most durable opposition to ECOWAS forces. A Council of State, drawn from the provisional government and the warring sides in the civil war, took office in 1993, but was unable to agree the appointment of ministers to a government of national unity.

Madagascar

Official name: Repoblika Demokratika n'i Madagaskar (The Democratic Republic of Madagascar).

Member of: UN, OAU.

Area: 587,041 km² (226,658 sq mi).

Population: 13,355,000 (1993 est).

Capital: Antananarivo (Tananarive) 802,000 (1990 est).

Other major cities: Toamasina 145,000, Fianarantsoa 125,000, Mahajanga 122,000 (1990 est).

Languages: Malagasy and French (both official).

Religions: Animist (47%), Roman Catholic (28%), Protestant Church of Jesus Christ in Madagascar (22%).

Education: Education is compulsory, in theory, between the ages of six and 13. In 1990 the literacy rate was 80.2%. There are six universities.

Defence: In 1993 the total armed strength was 23,000.

Transport: There are 54,200 km (33,700 mi) of roads and 1054 km (655 mi) of railways. Toamasina is the main port. Antananarivo has an international airport.

Media: There are five main daily newspapers, two radio stations and a televison service.

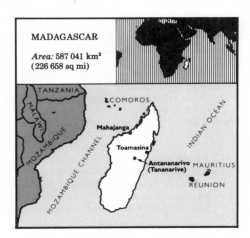

GOVERNMENT
The President is elected by universal adult suffrage for a seven-year term. He appoints a Prime Minister and a Council of Ministers. The 138-member National Assembly is directly elected for five years. Political parties include the Rasalama Active Forces Cartel (FVCR), Fihaonana, the National Union for Democracy and Development (UNDD), and the Congress Party for Malagasy Independence (AKFM) - which form the Committee of Active Forces - and the (former monopoly) Advanced Guard of the Malagasy Revolution (AREMA), Fanilo, Famima, and the Rally for Social Democracy (RDS). After the June 1993 election the Committee of Active Forces gained power.

Party strength: FVCR 46, MFM 15, Fanilo 13, Famima 11, RDS 8, Fihaonana 8, UNDD 7, AKFM 5.

President: Albert Zafy.

Prime Minister: Francisque Ravona.

GEOGRAPHY
Massifs form a spine running from north to south through the island. To the east is a narrow coastal plain; to the west are fertile plains. Highest point: Maromokotro Tsaratanana Massif 2885 m (9465 ft). Principal rivers: Ikopa, Mania, Mangoky. Climate: The climate is tropical, although the highlands are cooler.

ECONOMY
Agriculture employs three quarters of the labour force. The main crops are coffee and vanilla for export, and rice and cassava for domestic consumption. The island is an important producer of chromite. Drought adds to Madagascar's economic problems.

Currency: CFA Franc; 1US$ = 546.45 CFA Francs (June 1994).

GDP: US$2,884,000,000 (1992); US$230 per head.

RECENT HISTORY
In 1896 the island was annexed by France, although resistance continued until 1904. Strong nationalist feeling found expression in a major rising (1947-48) that was only suppressed with heavy loss of life. Independence was achieved in 1960. After a military coup in 1972, Madagascar had left-wing governments until multi-party presidential elections in 1993 resulted in a change of power.

Malawi

Official name: The Republic of Malawi.

Member of: UN, Commonwealth, OAU, SADCC.

Area: 118,484 km² (45,747 sq mi).

Population: 10,580,000 (1993 est), including about 1,000,000 refugees from Mozambique.

Capital: Lilongwe 220,000 (1987 census).

Other major cities: Blantyre 403,000, Mzuzu 115,000 (1987 census).

Languages: English (official), Chichewa (over 50%; official).

Religions: Various Protestant Churches (34%, mainly Presbyterian and Anglican), Roman Catholic (28%), animist (20%), Sunni Islam (16%).

Education: Education is compulsory, in theory, between the ages of six and 14. In 1987 the literacy rate was nearly 42%. There is a university.

Defence: In 1993 the total armed strength was 10,400 - 10,000 in the army.

Transport: There are 12,215 km (7590 mi) of roads and 797 km (495 mi) of state-run railways. Ferries on Lake Malawi are important. Lilongwe has an international airport.

Media: There is a daily newspaper and a state-run radio service.

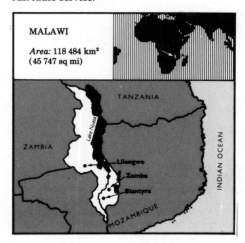

MALAWI

Area: 118 484 km²
(45 747 sq mi)

GOVERNMENT

An executive President - who appoints a Cabinet - and the 177-member National Assembly are elected for five years by universal adult suffrage. Political parties include the (former monopoly) Malawi Congress Party (MCP), the United Democratic Front (UDF), and the Alliance for Democracy (Aford). After the election in May 1994 a UDF government was formed.

Party strength: UDF 85, MCP 41, Aford 35, others 16.

President: Baliki Muluzi (UDF).

GEOGRAPHY

Plateaux cover the north and centre. The Rift Valley contains Lake Malawi and the Shire Valley. The Shire Highlands lie on the Mozambique border. Highest point: Mount Sapitawa 3002 m (9849 ft). Principal river: Shire. Climate: Malawi has an equatorial climate with heavy rainfall from November to April.

ECONOMY

Agriculture is the mainstay of the economy, providing most of Malawi's exports. Tobacco, maize, tea and sugar cane are the main crops. Malawi is one of the world's poorest nations.

Currency: Kwacha (MWK) of 100 tambala; 1US$ = 7.2 MWK (June 1994).

GDP: US$1,905,000,000 (1992); US$210 per head.

RECENT HISTORY

A British protectorate, later called Nyasaland, was declared in 1891. In 1915 the Rev. John Chilembwe led a violent rising in the fertile south where Africans had lost much land to white settlers. Dr Hastings Kamuzu Banda (c. 1902-) led the country's opposition to the resented union with the white-dominated Central African Federation (1953-63). From independence (as Malawi) in 1964 until 1994, Banda provided strong rule and - despite criticism - maintained close relations with South Africa. The country became a one-party state in 1966. In 1992-93, pressure for political reforms grew. Banda (who made himself Life President in 1971) was defeated in multi-party elections in 1994.

Mali

Official name: La République du Mali (The Republic of Mali).

Member of: UN, OAU, ECOWAS.

Area: 1,240,192 km² (478,841 sq mi).

Population: 8,646,000 (1991 est).

Capital: Bamako 650,000 (1987 census).

Other main cities: Ségou 89,000, Mopti 74,000 (1987 census).

Languages: French (official), Bambara (60%), Soninké, Fulani.

Religions: Sunni Islam (90%), animist (9%).

Education: Education is compulsory, in theory, between the ages of eight and 15. In 1990 the literacy rate was 32%. There are no universities.

Defence: In 1992 the total armed strength was 7400 - 7000 in the army, almost 400 in the air force. There is a 7800-member paramilitary police force. There is selective military service.

Transport: There are 18,000 km (11,185 mi) of roads and 646 km (401 mi) of railways. Bamako has an international airport.

Media: There are two daily newspapers and a state-run radio and television service.

GOVERNMENT
The 116-member National Assembly and a President are elected by universal adult suffrage to serve for three years and six years respectively. The President appoints a Premier and a Council of Ministers. The main political parties are the Alliance for Democracy in Mali (ADEMA), the National Council for Democracy (CNID), the Sudanese Union-African Democratic Rally (US-RDA), the Popular Movement for the Development of the Republic of West Africa (PMD), the Assembly for Democracy and Progress (RDP), and the Union for Democracy and Development (UDD). After the election held in March 1993 a ADEMA-CNID-RDP-led coalition was formed.

Party strength: Union for Democracy and Development (UDD) and the Sudanese Union (US-RDA).

President: Alpha Oumar Konare (ADEMA).

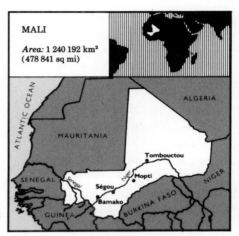

MALI

Area: 1 240 192 km² (478 841 sq mi)

Prime Minister: Abdoulaye Sekou Sow (ADEMA).

GEOGRAPHY
Mali comprises low-lying plains but rises in the Adrar des Iforas range in the northeast. The south is savannah; the Sahara Desert is in the north. Highest point: Hombori Tondo 1155 m (3789 ft). Principal rivers: Niger, Sénégal, Falémé. Climate: Mali is hot and largely dry, although the south has a wet season from June to October.

ECONOMY
Drought in the 1970s and 1980s devastated Mali's livestock herds. Only one fifth of Mali can be cultivated, producing mainly rice, millet and cassava for domestic use, and cotton for export.

Currency: CFA Franc; 1US$ = 546.45 CFA Francs (June 1994).

GDP: US$2,412,000,000 (1991); US$280 per head.

RECENT HISTORY
Conquered by France (1880-95), Mali became the territory of French Sudan. Mali became independent in 1960. A radical socialist government was toppled in 1968 by the military regime of General Moussa Traore, whose government faced severe economic problems. A single-party state operated from 1979 to 1992 when, after a popular uprising in 1991, a multiparty system was restored.

Mauritania

Official name: Jumhuriyat Muritaniya al-Islamiya (Islamic Republic of Mauritania).

Member of: UN, OAU, Arab League, ECOWAS.

Area: 1,030,700 km² (397,950 sq mi).

Population: 2,170,000 (1993 est).

Capital: Nouakchott 393,000 (1988 census).

Other major cities: Nouadhibou (Port Etienne) 59,000, Kaédi 31,000 (1988 census).

Languages: Arabic (official; 81%), French.

Religion: Sunni Islam (official; 99%).

Education: Education is freely available between the ages of six and 12 but is not compulsory. In 1990 the literacy rate was 34%. There is a single university.

Defence: In 1993 the total armed strength was 15,300 - 14,700 in the army. There is also a 5,700-member paramilitary force.

Transport: There are 7558 km (4696 mi) of roads and 689 km (428 mi) of railways. The main port is Point-Central (Noadhibou). Nouakchott and Nouadhibou have international airports.

Media: There are two daily newspapers and a state-run radio and television service.

GOVERNMENT
A President and a 79-member National Assembly are elected (for six years and five years respectively) by universal adult suffrage. A Senate (upper house) is indirectly elected. The President appoints a Prime Minister and a Council of Ministers. The main political parties are the (former monopoly) Social Democratic Republican Party (PRDS), the Union of Democratic Forces (UFD), the Mauritanian Renewal Party (PMR), and the Rally for Democracy and National Unity (RDUN). After the election held in March 1992 the PRDS retained power.

Party strength: PRDS 67, RDUN 1, PMR 1, ind 10.

President: Col. Maaouiya Sidi Mohammed Ould Taya (PRDS).

Prime Minister: Sidi Mohammed Ould Boubaker (PRDS).

GEOGRAPHY
Isolated peaks rise above the plateaux of the Sahara Desert that cover most of Mauritania. Highest point: Kediet Ijill 915 m (3050 ft). Principal river: Sénégal. Climate: The climate is hot and dry, with adequate rainfall only in the south.

ECONOMY
Persistent drought has devastated the nomads' herds of cattle and sheep. Fish from the Atlantic and iron ore are virtually the only exports.

Currency: Ouguiya of five khoums; 1US$ = 122.39 ouguiyas (June 1994).

GDP: US$1,083,000,000 (1992); US$520 per head.

RECENT HISTORY
All of Mauritania did not come under French rule until 1903. Mauritania became independent in 1960. When Spain withdrew from the Western Sahara in 1976, Morocco and Mauritania divided the territory between them, but Mauritania could not defeat the Polisario guerrillas fighting for West Saharan independence and gave up its claim (1979). Tension between the dominant Arab north and Black African south led to violence in 1989. The country was ruled by military governments after 1976 and became a one-party state in 1979. Multi-party elections were held in 1992, but were boycotted by the UFD, the principal opposition party.

MAURITANIA

Area: 1 030 700 km²
(397 950 sq mi)

MOROCCO

ALGERIA

WESTERN SAHARA

ATLANTIC OCEAN

Nouadhibou

Nouakchott

MALI

Senegal

SENEGAL

Mauritius

Official name: Republic of Mauritius.

Member of: OAU, Commonwealth.

Area: 2040 km² (788 sq mi).

Population: 1,105, 000 (1993 est).

Capital: Port Louis 143,000 (1991 est).

Other major cities: Beau Bassin/Rose Hill 96,000, Curepipe 67,000, Quatre Bornes 66,000 (1991 est).

Languages: English (official), Creole (French; nearly 30%), Hindi (over 20%), Bhojpuri, Chinese.

Religions: Hindu (51%), Roman Catholic (25%), Sunni Islam (17%), with Protestant, Buddhist and other minorities.

Education: Education is freely available between the ages of five and 18 but is not compulsory. Most children attend school between the ages of five and 11. In 1985 the literacy rate was 83%. There is a single university.

Defence: There are no armed forces but there is a 1300-member paramilitary police force.

Transport: There are 1831 km (1138 mi) of roads. Port Louis is the main port. There is an international airport at Plaisance.

Media: There are seven daily newspapers (in English, French and Chinese) and a single radio and television service, which is provided by a state-corporation.

GOVERNMENT
Elections are held by universal adult suffrage every five years for 62 members of the Assembly; up to 8 additional members may be appointed. The President - who is elected by the Assembly - appoints a Prime Minister who commands a majority in the Assembly. The PM, in turn, appoints a Cabinet responsible to the Assembly. The main political parties are the Mauritian Socialist Movement (MSM), the Mauritian Militant Movement (MMM), the Organization for the People of Rodrigues (OPR), the Movement of Democratic Workers (MTD), the Mauritius Labour Party (MLP), and the Mauritian Social Democratic Party (PMSD). After the election held in September 1991 the MSM-MMM-OPR-MTD coalition retained power.

Party strength: MSM-MMM-OPR-MTD 59, MLP-PMSD 3.

President: Cassam Uteem.

Prime Minister: Aneerood Jugnauth (MSM).

GEOGRAPHY
The central plateau of Mauritius is surrounded by mountains. Other islands in the group include Rodrigues and the Agalega Islands. Highest point: Piton de la Rivière Noire 826 m (2711 ft). Principal rivers: Grand River South East, Grand River North West. Climate: The climate is subtropical, although it can be very hot from December to April. Rainfall is high in the uplands.

ECONOMY
The export of sugar cane no longer dominates the economy as it used to, although sugar accounts for over one third of total exports. Other crops include tea and tobacco. Diversification is being encouraged, and light industry - in particular clothing - is of increas-

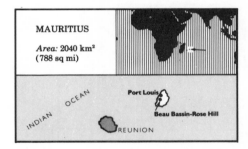

MAURITIUS

Area: 2040 km² (788 sq mi)

INDIAN OCEAN

Port Louis

Beau Bassin-Rose Hill

REUNION

ing importance. The principal source of foreign currency is now tourism, which expanded greatly during the late 1980s and early 1990s.

Currency: Mauritius rupee of 100 cents; 1US$ = 17.17 Mauritius rupees (June 1994).

GDP: US$3,011,000,000 (1992); US$2740 per head.

RECENT HISTORY
Mauritius was French from 1715 until 1814, when it became British. Black slaves were imported, followed in the 19th century by Indian labourers whose descendants are the majority community. Independence was gained in 1968 and a republic was proclaimed in 1992.

Mozambique

Official name: A República de Moçambique (Republic of Mozambique).

Member of: UN, OAU, SADCC.

Area: 799,380 km² (308,641 sq mi).

Population: 15,656,000 (1991 est).

Capital: Maputo 1,070,000 (1989 est).

Other main cities: Beira 290,000, Nampula 197,000 (1989 est).

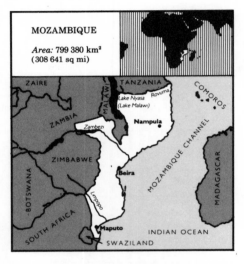

Languages: Portuguese (official), Makua-Lomwe (52%), Malawi (12%).

Religions: Animist (60%), Sunni Islam (15%), Roman Catholic (15%).

Education: Education is compulsory in theory between the ages of seven and 14. In 1990 the literacy rate was 32.9%. There is a university.

Defence: The total armed strength in 1993 was 52,000. There is selective military service of two years for men and women.

Transport: There are over 26,000 km (16,250 mi) of roads and 2988 km (1868 mi) of railways. Maputo and Beira are the main ports; Maputo has an international airport.

Media: There are two daily newspapers and a state-run radio and television service.

GOVERNMENT

The constitution provides for the election of a 250-member Assembly and a President by universal adult suffrage for five years. The President appoints a Cabinet and a Prime Minister. There are 11 provinces including the city of Maputo. Political parties include the (former Marxist) Frelimo, (right-wing) Renamo and the National Mozambican Union.

President: Joaquim Alberto Chissano (Frelimo).

Prime Minister: Mario da Graca Machungo (Frelimo).

GEOGRAPHY

The Zambezi River separates high plateaux in the north from lowlands in the south. Highest point: Mount Bingo 2436 m (7992 ft). Principal rivers: Limpopo, Zambezi, Shire. Climate: The climate is tropical with maximum rainfall and temperatures from November to March.

ECONOMY

Farming involves over 80% of the labour force, mainly growing cassava and maize as subsistence crops. Prawns and shrimps make up nearly one half of Mozambique's exports. The economy has been devastated by civil war and drought, and Mozambique is usually stated to be the poorest country in the world.

Currency: Metical (MZM); 1US$ = 5734.1 MZM (June 1994).

GDP: US$1,208,000,000 (1990); US$80 per head.

RECENT HISTORY

Forced labour and minimal development helped to fuel nationalist feelings against Portuguese colonial rule, and in 1964 the Frelimo movement launched a guerrilla war against the Portuguese. Independence was achieved in 1975, and a Marxist-Leninist state was established. The pressures of poverty and the destabilization of the state by South Africa, through support for Renamo guerrillas, led to renewed ties with the West, and Marxism was abandoned by Frelimo in 1989. In the 1990s the state has faced severe famine. A cease-fire - and a UN presence in Mozambique - were agreed in 1992. All armed groups are to be disbanded and elements of Renamo forces are to be integrated into the Mozambican army. Multi-party elections are to be held late in 1994.

Namibia

Official name: The Republic of Namibia or Republiek van Namibie.

Member of: UN, Commonwealth, SADCC, OAU.

Area: 824,292 km² (318,261 sq mi).

Population: 1,402,000 (1992 est).

Capital: Windhoek 115,000 (1988 est).

Other major cities: Walvis Bay 21,000, Swakopmund 16,000 (1988 est).

Languages: Afrikaans and English (both official), German, local languages.

Religions: Lutheran (30%), Roman Catholic (20%), other Christian Churches (30%).

Education: Education is compulsory between the ages of seven and 16. In 1985 the literacy rate was 72.5%. There is a single university.

Defence: In 1993 the total armed strength was estimated to be 7400 (all in the army).

Transport: There are 42,760 km (26,725 mi) of roads and 2382 km (1489 mi) of railways. Walvis Bay is the main port. Windhoek has an international airport.

Media: There are five daily newspapers. A single radio and television network broadcasts.

GOVERNMENT
A President and a 72-member Assembly are elected by universal adult suffrage for five years. The President appoints a Prime Minister and a Cabinet. Political parties include the (left wing) SWAPO (South West African People's Organization) and the (centre) Democratic Turnhalle Alliance (DTA).

Party strength: SWAPO 41, DTA 21, others 10.

President: Sam Nujoma (SWAPO).

Prime Minister: Hage Geingob (SWAPO).

GEOGRAPHY
The coastal Namib Desert stretches up to 160 km (100 mi) inland. Beyond the Central Plateau, the Kalahari Desert occupies the east. Highest point: Brandberg 2579 m (8461 ft). Principal river: Orange. Climate: Namibia has a hot dry tropical climate. Rainfall on the coast averages below 100 mm (4 in).

ECONOMY
Farming involves over 60% of the labour force, mainly raising cattle and sheep. The economy depends upon exports of diamonds and uranium, and is closely tied to South Africa.

Currency: Namibia uses South African currency.

GDP: US$1,350,000,000 (1989 est); US$1030 per head.

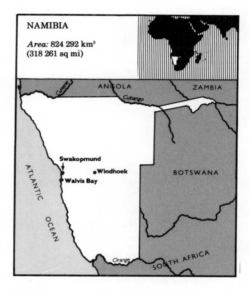

NAMIBIA

Area: 824 292 km² (318 261 sq mi)

RECENT HISTORY
A German protectorate of South West Africa (1884-1915) was established after great bloodshed - the Herero people were massacred (1903-04). South Africa conquered the area in World War I, and (after 1919) ruled it under a League of Nations mandate. The UN cancelled the mandate (1966), but South Africa, which refused to grant independence, ignored the ruling. SWAPO nationalist guerrillas began a campaign to free the territory. After a cease-fire agreement (1989), UN-supervised elections were held and independence, as Namibia, was gained in 1990. South Africa ceded the port and enclave of Walvis Bay, plus a string of small islands to the south of Walvis Bay, to Namibia in 1994.

Niger

Official name: La République du Niger (The Republic of Niger).

Member of: UN, OAU, ECOWAS.

Area: 1,267,000 km² (489,191 sq mi).

Population: 8,515,000 (1993 est).

Capital: Niamey 398,000 (1988 census).

Other main cities: Zinder 121,000, Maradi 113,000 (1988 census).

Languages: French (official), Hausa (85%).

Religion: Sunni Islam (85%).

Education: Education is compulsory, in theory, between the ages of seven and 15. In 1990 the literacy rate was over 28%. There are two universities.

Defence: In 1993 the total armed strength was 5300. There is selective military service lasting two years.

Transport: There are 11,258 km (6996 mi) of roads. The River Niger is navigable. Niamey and Agadez have international airports.

Media: There is a single daily newspaper. There is a state-run radio and television service.

GOVERNMENT

An 83-member National Assembly and a President are elected by universal adult suffrage. Parties include the (nine-party coalition) Alliance of Forces of Change (AFC, which includes the Social Democratic Convention-CDS, the Niger Party for Security and Democracy-PNDS and the Niger Alliance for Democracy and Progress-ANDP), and the (former monopoly) National Movement for a Development Society (MNSD). After the election in February 1993 an AFC government took office.

Party strength: MNSD 29, CDS 22, PNDS 13, ANDP 11, others 8.

President: Mahamane Ouamane (AFC).

Prime Minister: Mahamdou Issoufou (AFC).

GEOGRAPHY

Most of Niger lies in the Sahara Desert; the south and the Niger Valley are savannah. The central Aïr Mountains rise to just over 2000 m (6562 ft). Highest point: Mont Gréboun 2022 m

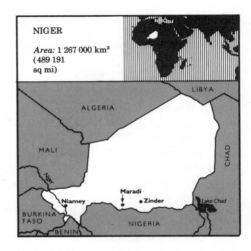

(6634 ft). Principal rivers: Niger, Dillia. Climate: Niger is dry and hot. The south has a rainy season from June to October.

ECONOMY

Livestock herds and harvests of subsistence crops - millet, sorghum, cassava and rice - have been reduced by desertification. Uranium, the main export, is mined, but falling prices for this commodity on the world market have added to Niger's many economic difficulties.

Currency: CFA Franc; 1US$ = 546.45 CFA Francs (June 1994).

GDP: US$2,537,000,000 (1992); US$310 per head.

RECENT HISTORY

The French territory of Niger was proclaimed in 1901, but much of the country was not brought under French control until 1920. Independence was achieved in 1960 under President Hamani Diori. After the economy was wracked by a prolonged drought, Diori was overthrown in a military coup (1974). Political pluralism was permitted in 1992 and in free elections for an assembly in February 1993 power changed hands peacefully. Tuareg secessionists in the north are a growing problem.

Nigeria

Official name: The Federal Republic of Nigeria.

Member of: UN, OAU, Commonwealth, OPEC, ECOWAS.

Area: 923,768 km² (356,669 sq mi).

Population: 88,514,000 (1991 census).

Capital: Abuja 379,000 (1991 census).

Other major cities: Lagos 5,686,000 (city 1,347,000), Ibadan 1,295,000, Kano 700,000, Ogbomosho 661,000, Oshogbo 442,000, Ilorin 431,000 (1991 census).

Languages: English (official), with over 150 local languages, including Hausa, Yoruba and Ibo.

Religions: Sunni Islam (48%), various Protestant Churches (17% - mainly Anglican, Methodist, Lutheran, Baptist and Presbyterian), Roman Catholic (17%).

Education: Education is compulsory, in theory, between the ages of six and 12. In 1990 the literacy rate was 50.7%. There are 30 universities and 24 polytechnics.

Defence: In 1993 the total armed strength was nearly 79,000 - 62,000 in the army, 7400 in the navy and 9500 in the air force.

Transport: There are nearly 125,000 km (77,700 mi) of roads and 3505 km (2178 mi) of railways. The main ports are Lagos, Port Harcourt, Calabar and Bonny - the latter specializes in oil. Lagos and Kano have international airports.

Media: There are 25 daily newspapers, most of which are regional. There is a government-owned radio authority and a similar television authority, which runs over 25 regional stations.

GOVERNMENT

A constitutional assembly was summoned in 1994. A Forces Ruling Council whose President is head of state and of government holds power following a coup in 1993. The 30 state administrations, the 450-member Federal Assembly and the two officially-sanctioned political parties were suspended in 1993.

President: Gen. Sani Abacha.

NIGERIAN STATES

Population figures are from the 1991 census. Areas of the states are estimates.

Abia Area: 4300 km² (1650 sq mi). Population: 2,298,000. Capital: Umuahia.

Adamawa Area: 44,800 km² (17,300 sq mi). Population: 2,124,000. Capital: Yola.

Akwa Ibom Area: 5100 km² (2000 sq mi). Population: 2,360,000. Capital: Uyo.

Anambra Area: 9700 km² (3750 sq mi). Population: 2,768,000. Capital: Akwa.

Bauchi Area: 64,600 km² (24,950 sq mi). Population: 4,294,000. Capital: Bauchi.

Benue Area: 33,900 km² (13,100 sq mi). Population: 2,780,000. Capital: Makurdi.

Borno Area: 32,500 km² (12,500 sq mi). Population: 2,597,000. Capital: Maiduguri.

Cross River Area: 12,600 km² (4900 sq mi). Population: 1,866,000. Capital: Calabar.

Delta Area: 9600 km² (370 sq mi). Population: 2,570,000. Capital: Asaba.

Edo Area: 25,600 km² (9900 sq mi). Population: 2,160,000. Capital: Benin City.

Enugu Area: 5300 km² (2050 sq mi). Population: 3,161,000. Capital: Enugu.

Imo Area: 11,850 km² (4,600 sq mi). Population: 2,486,000. Capital: Owerri.

Jigawa Area: 20,400 km² (7900 sq mi). Population: 2,830,00. Capital: Dutse.

Kaduna Area: 46,350 km² (17,900 sq mi). Population: 3,969,000. Capital: Kaduna.

Kano Area: 22,900 km² (8850 sq mi). Population: 5,632,000. Capital: Kano.

Katsina Area: 23,900 km² (9250 sq mi). Population: 3,878,000. Capital: Katsina.

Kebbi Area: 37,900 km² (14,600 sq mi). Population: 2,062,000. Capital: Birnin Kebbi.

Kogi Area: 10,300 km² (4000 sq mi). Population: 1,566,000. Capital: Ilorin.

Kwara Area: 66,900 km² (25,800 sq mi). Population: 2,099,000. Capital: Lokoja.

Lagos Area: 3345 km² (1292 sq mi). Population: 5,686,000. Capital: Ikeja.

Niger Area: 65,040 km² (25,110 sq mi). Population: 2,482,000. Capital: Minna.

Ogun Area: 16,760 km² (6470 sq mi). Population: 2,339,000. Capital: Abeokuta.

Ondo Area: 20,960 km² (8090 sq mi). Population: 3,884,000. Capital: Akure.

Osun Area: 15,100 km² (5830 sq mi). Population: 2,203,000. Capital: Oshogbo.

Oyo Area: 22,600 km² (8730 sq mi). Population: 3,489,000. Capital: Ibadan.

Plateau Area: 58,030 km² (22,400 sq mi). Population: 3,284,000. Capital: Jos.

Rivers Area: 21,850 km² (8440 sq mi). Population: 3,984,000. Capital: Port Harcourt.

Sokoto Area: 64,600 km² (24,900 sq mi). Population: 4,392,000. Capital: Sokoto.

Taraba Area: 46,600 km² (18,000 sq mi). Population: 1,481,000. Capital: Jalingo.

Yobe Area: 83,900 km² (32,600 sq mi). Population: 1,411,000. Capital: Damaturu.

Federal Capital Territory Area: 7315 km² (2824 sq mi). Population: 379,000. Capital: Abuja.

GEOGRAPHY
Inland from the swampy forest and tropical jungles of the coastal plains, Nigeria comprises a series of plateaux covered - for the most part - by open woodland or savannah. The far north is semi-desert. Isolated ranges of hills rise above the plateaux, the highest of which are the central Jos Plateau and the Biu Plateau in the northeast. Highest point: Vogel Peak (Dimlany) 2042 m (6700 ft). Principal rivers: Niger, Benue, Cross River, Yobe, Osse. Climate: The coastal areas are very humid and hot). Rainfall is heavy on the coast but decreases gradually inland - although there is a rainy season from April to October. The dry far north experiences the Harmattan, a hot wind blowing out of the Sahara.

ECONOMY
Nigeria is the major economic power in West Africa. The country depends upon revenue from petroleum exports, but a combination of falling petroleum prices and OPEC quotas has resulted in major economic problems, although it has also encouraged diversification. Natural gas is to be exported in liquid form to Europe. Major industries include petrochemicals, textiles and food processing. Over one half of the labour force is involved in agriculture, mainly producing maize, sorghum, cassava, yams and rice as subsistence crops. Cocoa is an important export.

Currency: Naira of 100 koba; 1US$ = 21.399 naira (June 1994).

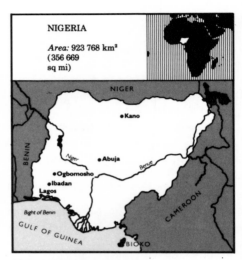

NIGERIA

Area: 923 768 km² (356 669 sq mi)

GDP: US$28,700,000,000 (1993 est); US$305 per head.

RECENT HISTORY
In 1914 the coast and the interior - which had been acquired by Britain between 1861 and 1886 - were united to form Britain's largest African colony. An unwieldy federal structure introduced in 1954 was unable to contain regional rivalries after independence (1960). In 1966, the first Prime Minister, Sir Abubakar Tafawa Balewa (1912-66), and other prominent politicians were assassinated in a military coup. After a counter-coup brought General Yakubu Gowon to power, a bitter civil war took place (1967-70) when the Eastern Region - the homeland of the Ibo - attempted to secede as Biafra. Although the East was quickly reintegrated once Biafra was defeated, Nigeria remained politically unstable. The number of states was gradually increased from 3 to 21 (and in 1991 to 30) in an attempt to prevent any one region becoming dominant. A military coup overthrew Gowon in 1975, and an attempt at civilian rule (1979-83) also ended in a coup. Another coup brought General Ibrahim Babangida to power in 1985. Following unrest, limited civilian rule was reintroduced in 1993, and two political parties were sanctioned. However, elections in the same year were overturned by a further military coup led by Gen. Sani Abacha. Chief Moshood Abiola, who is believed to have won the annulled presidential election, declared himself president in 1994 but was subsequently detained by the authorities.

Rwanda

Official name: La République rwandaise (French) or Republika y'u Rwanda (Kinyarwanda) (Republic of Rwanda).

Member of: UN, OAU.

Area: 26,338 km² (10,169 sq mi).

Population: 7,491,000 (1991 est); 5,500,000 (1994 est) after massacres and the flight of refugees

Capital: Kigali 300,000 (1990 est).

Other main towns: Ruhengeri 30,000, Butare 29,000 (1991 est).

Languages: French (12%; official) and Kinyarwanda (over 85%; official).

Religions: Roman Catholic (63%), animist (21%), Sunni Islam (8%), various Protestant Churches (8%).

Education: Education is compulsory in theory between the ages of seven and 15. The literacy rate was 50.2% in 1990. There is a university.

Defence: The total armed strength in 1991 was 5200, plus 1200 in the paramilitary militia.

Transport: There are 13,173 km (8185 mi) of roads. Kigali has an international airport.

Media: There are no daily newspapers. Radio is provided by a single state-run service.

GOVERNMENT
The constitution provides for the election of a President and a 70-member Assembly for five years by universal adult suffrage. The main political party is the (former monopoly) MRND (Mouvement Révolutionnaire National pour le Développement).

President: Pasteur Bizimungu. (FPR).

Prime Minister: Faustin Twagiramungu. (FPR).

GEOGRAPHY
Rwanda is a mountainous country whose highest peaks are in the volcanic Virunga Mountains. There are many lakes and most of the western boundary is formed by Lake Kivu. Highest point: Mont Karisimbi 4507 m (14,787 ft). Principal rivers: Kagera, Ruzizi. Climate: Rwanda is tropical but temperatures are cooled by high elevation.

ECONOMY
The economy was devastated by civil war in 1994. Subsistence farming occupies over 90% of the population; plantains and sweet potatoes are the main crops. Coffee and tin are the main exports. There are reserves of natural gas under Lake Kivu. Overpopulation is a major problem and Rwanda relies heavily upon foreign aid.

Currency: Rwanda franc (Franc rwandais) of 100 centimes. 1US$ = 142.6 Rwanda francs (May 1994).

GDP: US$1,818,000,000 (1992 est); US$250 per head.

RECENT HISTORY
The feudal kingdom of Rwanda - whose Tutsi minority dominated the majority Hutu tribe - was under German colonial rule from 1890 to 1916 and then Belgian rule until independence in 1962. The Tutsi monarchy was overthrown

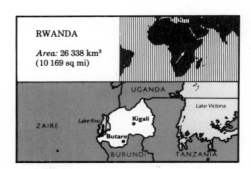

and many Tutsis fled into exile in 1961. From 1978 to 1991 Rwanda was a single-party state. Tribal violence followed a Tutsi attempt to regain power in 1983 and in 1990 the FPR (Front patriotique rwandais), an army of Tutsi refugees, invaded Rwanda, occupying much of the north. After the plane carrying President Habyarimana was shot down in 1994, government forces went on the rampage. In the ensuing ethnic violence, over 500,000 Tutsis were massacred by Hutu militias, over 2,000,000 refugees fled the country and the FPR took power. The UN agreed to send a French peacekeeping mission to Rwanda, and an international aid programme was organized to bring relief to Rwandan refugees in Zaire and Tanzania.

São Tomé e Príncipe

Official name: A República Democrática de São Tomé e Príncipe (The Democratic Republic of São Tomé and Príncipe).

Member of: UN, OAU.

Area: 964 km² (372 sq mi).

Population: 125,000 (1993 est).

Capital: São Tomé 43,000 (1991 est).

Other main town: Trindade 11,400 (1991 est).

Language: Portuguese (official), Fang (90%).

Religion: Roman Catholic (50%).

Education: Education is compulsory, in theory, for three years between the ages of six and 14. In 1981 the literacy rate was 57.4%. There are no university-level institutions.

Defence: In 1992 the total armed strength was 900 in the paramilitary gendarmerie.

Transport: There are 380 km (236 mi) of roads. São Tomé has a port and an international airport.

Media: There are two daily newspapers and a single radio and television service.

GOVERNMENT
The 55-member National People's Assembly is

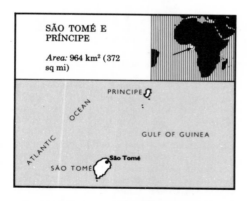

SÃO TOMÉ E PRÍNCIPE

Area: 964 km² (372 sq mi)

PRINCIPE

OCEAN

ATLANTIC

GULF OF GUINEA

São Tomé

SÃO TOMÉ

elected by universal adult suffrage for five years. The President - who appoints a Prime Minister and Council of Ministers - is also directly elected. Príncipe has internal autono-

my. Political parties include the (left-wing former monopoly) Movement for the Liberation of São Tomé e Príncipe (MLSTP), the (moderate) Democratic Convergence Party (PCD) and the Democratic Opposition Coalition (CDO). After the election in January 1991 a PCD government was formed.

Party strength: PCD 33, MLSTP 21, CDO 1.

President: Miguel Trovoada (PCD).

Prime Minister: Norberto Jose d'Alva Costa Alegre (PCD).

AUTONOMOUS ISLAND
Príncipe Area: 142 km² (55 sq mi). Population: 5600 (1991 census). Capital: Santo Antonio.

GEOGRAPHY
The republic consists of two mountainous islands about 144 km (90 mi) apart. There are no significant rivers. Highest point: Pico Gago Coutinho (Pico de São Tomé) 2024 m (6640 ft). Climate: The climate is tropical. A wet season - with heavy rainfall - lasts from October to May.

ECONOMY
Cocoa is the mainstay of a largely agricultural economy and the country is dependent upon international fluctuations in the price of this single commodity. Most of the land, in the smallest country in Africa, is nationalized. Fishing is increasing in importance.

Currency: Dobra of 100 centimos; 1US$ = 239.3 dobras.

GDP: US$42,000,000 (1991); US$350 per head.

HISTORY
The islands are former Portuguese colonies. Early in the 20th century, the islands' plantations were notorious for forced labour. Independence was gained in 1975 as a one-party socialist state. An invasion and coup attempt failed in 1988, but the Marxist government had to depend upon the presence of East European and Angolan troops to stay in office. Economic difficulties led the country to lessen its dependence on the Soviet bloc, and in 1990 the MLSTP abandoned Marxism. São Tomé e Príncipe became one of the first in Africa to adopt multi-party democracy after the collapse of Communism. The opposition PCD won multi-party elections in 1991.

Senegal

Official name: La République du Sénégal (The Republic of Senegal).

Member of: UN, OAU, ECOWAS.

Area: 196,722 km² (75,954 sq mi).

Population: 7,900,000 (1993 est).

Capital: Dakar 1,730,000 (1992 est).

Other major cities: Thies 201,000, Kaolack 180,000, Ziguinchor 149,000, St Louis 126,000 (1992 est).

Languages: French (official), Wolof (36%), Serer (19%), Fulani (13%).

Religions: Sunni Islam (94%), Roman Catholic.

Education: Education is compulsory, in theory, between the ages of seven and 13. In 1990 the literacy rate was 38%. There are three universities.

Defence: The total armed strength (1993) is 9700 - 8200 in the army, 700 in the navy, 800 in the air force. Selective military service lasts two years.

Transport: There are 14,117 km (8772 mi) of roads and 904 km (562 mi) of state-owned railways. Dakar, which has an international airport, is one of West Africa's largest commercial ports.

Media: There are three principal daily newspapers. There is a state-run and a private radio

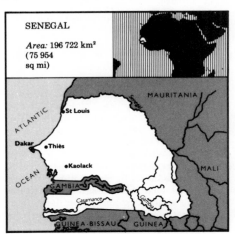

SENEGAL

Area: 196 722 km² (75 954 sq mi)

MAURITANIA

ATLANTIC

St Louis

Dakar •Thies

•Kaolack

OCEAN

MALI

GAMBIA

Casamance

GUINEA-BISSAU   GUINEA

station, and a government-owned and a commercial cable television station.

GOVERNMENT
The 120-member National Assembly is elected by universal adult suffrage for five years - 60 deputies are elected nationally by proportional representation; the remainder represent single-member constituencies. The President, who is directly elected for seven years, appoints and leads a Cabinet. Political parties include the Socialist Party (PS), the (liberal) Democratic Party (PDS), the (coalition) Jappoo Liggeenyal (JL), the Democratic League and Movement for the Labour Party (LD-MPT), the Independence and Labour Party (PIT), and the Senegalese Democratic Union (UDS). After the election in May 1993 the PS formed a government.

Party strength: PS 84, PDS 27, JL 3, LD/MPT 3, PIT 2, UDS 1.

President: Abdou Diouf (PS).

Prime Minister: Habib Thiam (PS).

GEOGRAPHY
Senegal is mostly low-lying and covered by savannah. The Fouta Djalon mountains are in the south. Highest point: Mont Gounou 1515 m (4970 ft). Principal rivers: Sénégal, Gambia, Casamance. Climate: Senegal has a tropical climate with a dry season from October to June.

ECONOMY
Agriculture involves over three quarters of the labour force. Groundnuts and cotton are grown as cash crops, and rice, maize, millet and sorghum as subsistence crops. The manufacturing sector is one of the largest in West Africa, but unemployment is high.

Currency: CFA franc; 1US$ = 546.45 CFA francs (June 1994).

GDP: US$6,110,000,000 (1992); US$780 per head.

RECENT HISTORY
A national political awareness developed after 1900, and Senegal contributed greatly to the nationalist awakening throughout French Africa. After independence in 1960, under the poet Léopold Sedar Senghor (1906-   ), Senegal maintained close relations with France, and received substantial aid. Attempted federations with Mali (1959-60) and Gambia (1981-89) were unsuccessful. Senghor retired in 1980, having re-introduced party politics.

69

Seychelles

Official name: The Republic of Seychelles.

Member of: UN, OAU, Commonwealth.

Area: 454 km² (173 sq mi).

Population: 71,000 (1992 est).

Capital: Victoria 24,000 (1987 est).

Languages: Creole (95%), English and French - all official.

Religion: Roman Catholic (92%), Anglican (6%).

Education: Education is compulsory between the ages of six and 15. In 1990 the literacy rate was 75%. There is a polytechnic.

Defence: In 1992 the total armed strength was 1300 - 1000 in the army, 200 in the navy and 100 in the air force. There is also a 800-member paramilitary force. Compulsory military service lasts for two years.

Transport: There are 319 km (198 mi) of roads. Victoria has a commercial shipping port and an international airport.

Media: There is a single daily newspaper. There is a government radio service and television service.

GOVERNMENT
The President - who appoints a Council of

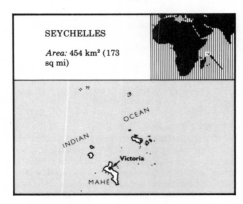

SEYCHELLES

Area: 454 km² (173 sq mi)

OCEAN

INDIAN

Victoria

MAHE

Ministers - and the 33-member National Assembly are elected for five years by universal adult suffrage. The Assembly comprises 22 members elected by constituencies and 11 members elected from a national list according to proportional representation. Political parties include the (former monopoly socialist) Seychelles People's Progressive Front (SPPF), the (conservative) Democratic Party (DP) and the (coalition) United Opposition. After the election held in July 1993 the SPPF retained power.

Party strength: SPPF 27, DP5, UO 1.

President: France Albert René (SPPF).

GEOGRAPHY
The Seychelles consist of 40 mountainous granitic islands and just over 50 smaller coral islands. There are no significant rivers. Highest point: Morne Seychellois 906 m (2972 ft) on the island of Mahé. Climate: The islands have a pleasant tropical maritime climate with heavy rainfall.

ECONOMY
The economy depends heavily on tourism, which employs about one third of the labour force. Fishing has expanded and tuna canning and the export of prawns have become important sources of foreign exchange. Coconuts are the principal cash crop. Industries include brewing, soft drinks and food processing. The government has attempted to diversify the economy but lack of resources has hampered the establishment of industries. Nevertheless, the islands have one of the highest standards of living in Africa.

Currency: Seychelles rupee of 100 cents; 1US$ = 4.967 rupees (June 1994).

GDP: US$376,000,000 (1992); US$5450 per head.

RECENT HISTORY
The islands became a French colony in the middle of the 18th century, were ceded to Britain in 1814 and gained independence in 1976. The Prime Minister - Albert René - led a coup against President James Mancham in 1977, and established a one-party socialist state seeking nonalignment. Attempts to overthrow René, including one involving South African mercenaries (1981), were unsuccessful. A new constitution was introduced and a multi-party system was restored in 1991. Free elections were held in 1993.

Sierra Leone

Official name: The Republic of Sierra Leone.

Member of: UN, OAU, ECOWAS, Commonwealth.

Area: 71,740 km² (27,699 sq mi).

Population: 4,491,000 (1993 est).

Capital: Freetown 550,000 (city 470,000, Koidu of 80,000; 1985 census).

Other main towns: Bo 26,000, Kenema 13,000 (1985 census).

Languages: English (official), Krio (Creole), Mende (34%), Temne (31%), Limba.

Religions: Animist (52%), Sunni Islam (39%), Anglican (6%).

Education: Education is available between the ages of five and 12 but it is not compulsory. In 1990 the literacy rate was 20.7%. There is a single university.

Defence: The total armed strength in 1993 was 6200, almost all of whom are in the army.

Transport: There are 7500 km (4660 mi) of roads and 84 km (52 mi) of railways, which are currently not used. Freetown is the main commercial shipping port. There is an international airport at Lungi.

Media: There is a single daily newspaper and a state-run radio and television service.

GOVERNMENT
There is constitutional provision for a President - who appoints a Cabinet - to be elected for seven years by universal adult suffrage, and for a 124-member House of Representatives to be elected for five years. Power is currently exercised by a military Supreme State Council and political parties have been suspended. A return to multi-party rule has been agreed in theory by the end of 1996.

Head of state (Chairman of the National Provisional Ruling Council): Capt. Valentine Strasser.

GEOGRAPHY
The savannah interior comprises plateaux and mountain ranges. The swampy coastal plain is forested. Highest point: Bintimani Peak 1948 m (6390 ft). Principal rivers: Siwa, Jong, Rokel.

Climate: The climate is tropical with a dry season from November to June.

ECONOMY
Subsistence farming - mainly rice - involves the majority of the labour force. The decline of diamond mining has added to economic problems. Unrest, which has in part been associated with the civil war in neighbouring Liberia, has damaged the economy and much of the infrastructure has been neglected. Corruption is a problem and a lack of qualified and experienced personnel hinders future development. Sierra Leone is one of the world's poorest nations. Foreign aid and investment almost dried up after the military seized power but has resumed, in part, now that an eventual return to civilian rule is envisaged.

Currency: Leone of 100 cents; 1US$ = 573.3 leones (June 1994).

GDP: US$740,000,000 (1992); US$170 per head.

RECENT HISTORY
Freetown was founded by British philanthropists (1787) as a settlement for former slaves, and became a British colony in 1808. The interior was added in 1896. Independence was gained in 1961. A disputed election led to army intervention (1967), and Dr Siaka Stevens - who came to power in a coup in 1968 - introduced a one-party state. An army junta seized power in 1992, replacing the previous military regime. The RUF (Revolutionary United Front) guerrilla movement is active in the southeast of the country. There have been a number of alleged coup plots and those accused of leading these attempts have been executed (1992-93).

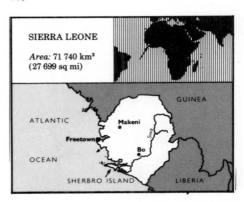

SIERRA LEONE

Area: 71 740 km²
(27 699 sq mi)

Somalia

Official name: Jamhuuriyadda Dimuqraadiga Soomaaliya (Somali Democratic Republic).

Member of: UN, Arab League, OAU.

Area: 637,657 km² (246,201 sq mi).

Population: 8,050,000 (1993 est). Up to 1,000,000 Somalis are refugees in surrounding countries.

Capital: Mogadishu 1,000,000 (1986 est).

Other major cities: Hargeisa 400,000, Baidoa 300,000, Burao 300,000 (1986 est).

Languages: Somali (national), Arabic (official).

Religion: Sunni Islam (official).

Education: Education is compulsory in theory between the ages of six and 14. In 1990 the literacy rate was estimated to be 24.1%. There is a single university.

Defence: Since 1991 there has been no national armed force.

Transport: There are over 22,200 km (13,800 mi) of roads. Mogadishu is an international airport and a commercial port.

Media: There is a single daily newspaper. There are several radio stations.

GOVERNMENT
The constitution provides for an Assembly comprising 171 members - 165 elected by universal adult suffrage for five years and 6 appointed by the President, who is elected by direct universal suffrage for a seven-year term. Since 1991 there has been no effective government.

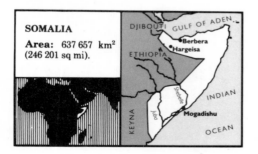

SOMALIA

Area: 637 657 km² (246 201 sq mi).

GEOGRAPHY
Somalia occupies the 'Horn of Africa'. Low-lying plains cover most of the south, while semi-arid mountains rise in the north. Highest point: Surud Ad 2408 m (7900 ft). Principal rivers: Juba, Shebelle. Climate: Somalia is hot and largely dry with rainfall totals in the north as low as 330 mm (13 in).

ECONOMY
Nearly two thirds of the labour force are nomadic herdsmen or subsistence farmers. Bananas are grown for export in the south, but much of the country suffers from drought. As a result of the civil war since 1991, much of the economic infrastructure of the country has been destroyed and famine is widespread.

Currency: Somali shilling of 100 cents; 1US$ = 2618 shillings (June 1994).

GDP: US$946,000,000 (1990); US$150 per head. The GDP has since declined drastically.

RECENT HISTORY
In 1886 Britain established a protectorate in the north of the region, while the Italians took the south. In World War II the Italians briefly occupied British Somaliland. In 1960 the British and Italian territories were united as an independent Somalia. In 1969 the president was assassinated and the army - under Major-Gen. Muhammad Siad Barre - seized control. Barre's socialist Islamic Somalia became an ally of the USSR. In 1977 Somali guerrillas, with Somali military support, drove the Ethiopians out of the largely Somali-inhabited Ogaden. Somalia's Soviet alliance was ended when the USSR supported Ethiopia to regain the Ogaden. In the late 1980s dissident groups within Somalia challenged Barre. In January 1991 they overran the capital and deposed Barre, but rival groups seized districts in the north and south. The infrastructure of Somalia collapsed in bitter civil war. In 1992 a UN US-led force intervened to relieve famine victims, but the foreign forces were unable to contain conflict between the 14 warring factions in Somalia, and most UN troops have been withdrawn. Insurgents in former British Somaliland have declared independence but their secessionist state (Somaliland) is unrecognized internationally. Despite signing a UN-sponsored peace pact the principal warring factions have not yet restored unity or government to Somalia.

South Africa

Official name: Republic of South Africa or Republiek van Suid-Afrika.

Member of: UN, OAU, Commonwealth.

Area: 2,346,537 km² (906,003 sq mi) - this excludes the Walvis Bay enclave which was ceded to Namibia in 1994..

Population: 40,716,000 (1993 est).

Capital: Pretoria (administrative capital) 823,000 (city 443,000), Cape Town (Kaapstadt) (legislative capital) 1,912,000 (city 777,000) (1985 census).

Other major cities: Johannesburg 4,000,000 (city proper 632,000; Greater Johannesburg 1,609,000, Soweto 915,000, Sasolburg 540,000,Vereeniging 540,000), Durban 982,000 (city 634,000), Port Elizabeth 652,000 (city 273,000), East London 194,000 (city 85,000), Bloemfontein (judicial capital) 233,000 (city 104,000) (1985 census).

Languages: Eleven official languages including Afrikaans, English, Xhosa (21%), Zulu (16%), Sesotho, Swazi, Ndebele, Venda and Tsonga.

Religions: Dutch Reformed Church, independent African Churches, with Anglican, Methodist, Roman Catholic, Hindu and Sunni Islam minorities.

Education: Education is to become compulsory for all South Africans between the ages of seven and 16. In 1990 the literacy rate was estimated to be over 80%. There are 24 universities including an open university.

Defence: In 1993 the total armed strength was 68,000 - 47,300 in the army, 4600 in the navy and 10,000 in the air force. The military wing of the ANC (see below) is to be incorporated into the South African armed forces. There is now no conscription.

Transport: There are 133,392 km (82,904 mi) of roads. The state-run railway system comprises 21,617 km (13,435 mi) of track. The principal commercial shipping ports are Cape Town, Mossel Bay, Port Elizabeth, East London and Durban. The main international airports are Johannesburg and Cape Town; Durban, Bloemfontein, East London and Port Elizabeth also have major airports.

GOVERNMENT
The Constitutional Assembly - which is scheduled to draft and agree a final constitution within two years - comprises a Senate (upper house) and a National Assembly (lower house). The 90-member Senate comprises ten senators appointed from each of the nine provinces in proportion to the number of votes each party receives in that province. The 400-member National Assembly comprises 200 members elected by universal adult suffrage from constituencies and 200 members elected by universal adult suffrage according to a system of proportional representation from the nine provinces that form the new quasi-federal system. A President and two Vice-Presidents are elected by the Assembly. A Cabinet of National Unity is responsible to the Assembly. The main political parties include the African National Congress (ANC), the (conservative, formerly white) National Party (NP), the (mainly Zulu) Inkatha Freedom Party (IFP), the (liberal) Democratic Party (DP), the (white right-wing) Freedom Front (FF), the (nationalist) Pan African Congress (PAC), the African Christian Democratic Party (ACDP) and the (white right-wing) Conservative Party (CP).

Party strength: ANC 252, NP 82, IFP 43, FF 9, DP 7, PAC 5, ACDP 2.

President: Nelson Mandela (ANC).

THE CABINET
First Vice-President: Thabo Mbeki (ANC).

Second Vice-President: Frederik Willem de Klerk (NP).

Minister of Agriculture: Dr A (Kraai) van Niekerk (NP).

Minister of Arts, Culture, Science and Technology: Ben Ngubane (IFP).

Minister of Correctional Services: Sipho Mzimela (IFP).

Minister of Defence: Joe Modise (ANC).

Minister of Education: Sibusiso Bhengu (ANC).

Minister of Environmental Affairs: Dr Dawie de Villiers (NP).

Minister of Finance: C. Liebenberg (NP).

Minister of Foreign Affairs: Alfred Nzo (ANC).

Minister of Health: Dr Nkosazana Dhlamini Zuma (ANC).

73

Minister of Home Affairs; Dr Mangosuthu Buthelezi (IFP).

Minister of Housing: Joe Slovo (ANC).

Minister of Justice: Dullah Omar (ANC).

Minister of Labour: Tito Mboweni (ANC).

Minister of Land Affairs: Derek Hanekom (ANC).

Minister of Energy Affairs: R.P. (Pik) Botha (NP).

Minister of Posts, Telecommunications and Broadcasting: Pallo Jordan (ANC).

Minister of Provincial Affairs and of Constitutional Development: Roelf Meyer (NP).

Minister of Public Enterprises: Princess Stella Sigcau (ANC).

Minister of Public Services and Administration: Zola Skweyiya (ANC).

Minister of Public Works: Jeff Radebe (ANC).

Minister of Safety and Security: Sydney Mufamadi (ANC).

Minister of Sport and Recreation: Steve Tshwete (ANC).

Minister of Trade, Industry and Tourism: Trevor Manuel (ANC).

Minister of Transport: Mac Maharaj (ANC).

Minister of Water Affairs and Forestry: Kadar Asmal (ANC).

Minister of Welfare and Population: Abe Williams (NP).

PROVINCES
Eastern Cape Area: 170,616 km² (65,875 sq mi). Population: 6,665,000 (1993 est). Capital: King William's Town.

Eastern Transvaal Area: 81,816 km² (39,736 sq mi). Population: 2,838,000 (1993 est). Capital: Nelspruit.

KwaZulu/Natal Area: 91,481 km² (35,321 sq mi). Population: 8,549,000 (1993 est). Capital: Pietermaritzburg. (Ulundi is co-capital.)

Northern Cape Area: 363,389 km² (140,305 sq mi). Population: 764,000 (1993 est). Capital: Kimberley.

Northern Transvaal Area: 119,606 km² (46,180

sq mi). Population: 5,121,000 (1993 est). Capital: Pietersburg.

North West Province Area: 118,710 km² (45,834 sq mi). Population: 3,507,000 (1993 est). Capital: Mmbatho.

Orange Free State Area: 129,437 km² (49,976 sq mi). Population: 2,805,000 (1993 est). Capital: Bloemfontein.

Pretoria-Witwatersrand Area Province (known as PWV) Area: 18,760 km² (7243 sq mi). Population: 6,847,000 (1993 est). Capital: Johannesburg. (Pretoria is co-capital.)

Western Cape Area: 129,386 km² (49,956 sq mi). Population: 3,620,000 (1993 est). Capital: Cape Town.

GEOGRAPHY
The Great Escarpment rises behind a discontinuous coastal plain and includes the Drakensberg Mountains. A vast plateau occupies the interior, undulating in the west and rising to over 2400 m (about 8000 ft) in the east. Much of the west is semi-desert, while the east is predominantly savannah grassland (veld). Highest point: Injasuti 3408 m (11,182 ft). Principal rivers: Orange (Oranje), Limpopo, Vaal. Climate: South Africa has a subtropical climate with considerable regional variations. The hottest period is between December and February. Rainfall is highest on the east coast, but much of the country is dry.

ECONOMY
The country is the world's leading exporter of

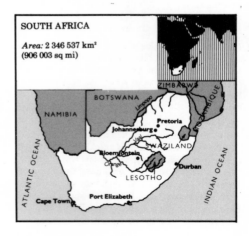

SOUTH AFRICA

Area: 2 346 537 km²
(906 003 sq mi)

gold - which normally forms about 40% of South African exports - and a major producer of uranium, diamonds, chromite, antimony, platinum and coal (which meets three quarters of the country's energy needs). Industry includes chemicals, food processing, textiles, motor vehicles and electrical engineering. Agriculture supplies one third of South Africa's exports, including fruit, wine, wool and maize. The highest standard of living in Africa is very unevenly distributed between whites and non-whites. The withdrawal of some foreign investors in the 1980s and early 1990s increased the drive towards self-sufficiency.

Currency: Rand of 100 cents; 1US$ = 3.622 rand (June 1994).

GDP: US$114,800,000,000 (1993 est); US$302 per head.

RECENT HISTORY

Black African peoples were long established in what is now South Africa when white settlement began in the Dutch colony of Cape Town (1652), but the conquest of the local African societies was only completed late in the 19th century. Britain acquired the Cape (1814), abolished slavery (1833), and annexed Natal (1843). The Boers (or Afrikaners) - of Dutch and French Huguenot descent - moved inland on the Great Trek (1835-37) to found the republics of the Transvaal and Orange Free State. After the discovery of diamonds (1867) and gold (1886), the Boers (Afrikaners) - led by Paul Kruger (1825-1904), president of the Transvaal - resisted British attempts to annex their republics, in which British settlers were denied political rights. This culminated in the Boer War (1899-1902). Although they lost the war, the Afrikaners were politically dominant when the Union of South Africa was formed (1910). The creation of the African National Congress (ANC) in 1912 was a protest against white supremacy, and by the 1920s black industrial protest was widespread. South Africa entered World War I as a British ally, taking German South West Africa (Namibia) after a short campaign (1914-15); after the war, the territory came under South African administration. Despite strong Afrikaner opposition, South Africa - under General Jan Christiaan Smuts (1870-1950; PM 1919-24 and 1939-48) - joined the Allied cause in World War II. After the Afrikaner National Party came to power (1948),

racial segregation was increased by the policy of apartheid ('separate development'), which deprived blacks of civil rights, segregated facilities and areas of residence by race, and confined black political rights to restricted homelands ('Bantustans'). Black opposition was crushed following a massacre of demonstrators at Sharpeville, and the ANC was banned (1960) by the government of Hendrik Verwoerd (1901-66; PM from 1958 to 1966, when he was assassinated). International pressure against apartheid increased. In 1961 South Africa left the Commonwealth, the majority of whose members pressed for economic sanctions against South Africa. In 1966 the UN cancelled South Africa's trusteeship of South West Africa (Namibia), but South Africa continued to block the territory's progress to independence. Black opposition revived in the 1970s and 1980s and found expression in strikes, the Soweto uprising of 1976, sabotage and the rise of the black consciousness movement. South African troops intervened in the Angolan civil war against the Marxist-Leninist government (1981) and were active in Namibia against SWAPO black nationalist guerrillas. P.W. Botha (1916- ; PM 1978-1984 and president 1984-89) granted political rights to the coloured and Indian communities, and implemented minor reforms for blacks. However, in 1986 - in the face of continuing unrest - Botha introduced a state of emergency, under which the press was strictly censored, the meetings of many organizations were banned and the number of political detainees - including children - rose sharply. His successor F.W. de Klerk released some ANC prisoners, and agreed to UN-supervised elections in Namibia leading to independence for that territory. In 1990 de Klerk lifted the ban on the ANC and released its imprisoned leader Nelson Mandela (1918-). In 1990-91, negotiations between the government and black leaders led to the dismantling of the legal structures of apartheid. Fighting between ANC and Inkatha supporters in black townships erupted resulting in many fatalities. In 1994 the first multi-racial elections were held in South Africa for a Constitutional Assembly. Nelson Mandela was elected as the country's first Black president and a multi-party government of National Unity was formed. South Africa has since joined the OAU and rejoined the Commonwealth, and, with all sanctions lifted, is once again a full member of the international community.

Sudan

Official name: Al Jumhuriyat al-Sudan (The Republic of Sudan).

Member of: UN, Arab League, OAU.

Area: 2,505,813 km² (967,500 sq mi).

Population: 25,000,000 (1993 est).

Capital: Khartoum 1,334,000 (city 476,000, Omdurman 526,000, Khartoum North 341,000; 1983 census).

Other main cities: Port Sudan (Bur Sudan) 207,000, Wadi Medani 141,000, El Obeid 140,000 (1983 census).

Language: Arabic (over 50%; official).

Religions: Sunni Islam (70%), animist (22%), various Christian Churches (8%).

Education: Education is freely available between the ages of seven and 12 but is not compulsory. The literacy rate was 27.1% in 1990. There are seven universities plus a polytechnic.

Defence: The total armed strength in 1993 was nearly 73,000 (plus over 40,000 Islamic paramilitary). Military service of three years is compulsory but effective only in the north.

Transport: There are 22,500 km (14,000 mi) of roads and 4874 km (3029 mi) of railways. Inland navigation on the Nile is important. Khartoum (on the Nile) and Port Sudan are the main ports. Khartoum has an international airport.

Media: There are ten daily papers and a state-run radio and television service.

GOVERNMENT

Sudan is ruled by the 15-member Command Council of the Revolution of National Salvation, whose chairman is head of state and of government. Political activity has been suspended, although a 300-member Transitional National Assembly has been appointed.

Head of state and government: Lt. Gen. Omar Hassan Ahmed al-Bashir.

GEOGRAPHY

The Sahara Desert covers much of the north and west, but is crossed by the fertile Nile Valley. The southern plains are swampy. Highlands are confined to hill country beside the Red Sea and mountains on the Ugandan border. Highest point: Kinyeti 3187 m (10,456 ft). Principal rivers: Nile (Nil), Nil el Azraq (Blue Nile), Nil el Abyad (White Nile). Climate: The south is equatorial, but the north is dry.

ECONOMY

Agriculture involves almost two thirds of the labour force, growing cotton for export, and sorghum, cassava and millet for domestic consumption. Since the early 1980s Sudan has been severely affected by drought and famine. The war in the south has damaged the economy.

Currency: Dinar; 1US$ = 35.05 dinars (June 1994).

GDP: US$10,107,000,000 (1992); US$400 per head.

RECENT HISTORY

From 1899 Sudan was administered jointly by Britain and Egypt. Independence was achieved in 1956. Sudan remains unstable, alternating between civilian and military regimes. The civil war between the Muslim north and the animist-Christian south that began in 1955 has intensified under the current Islamic fundamentalist military government. Sudan is increasingly isolated internationally owing to its backing for Iraq and Libya.

Swaziland

Official name: Umbuso Weswatini (The Kingdom of Swaziland).

Member of: UN, Commonwealth, OAU, SADCC.

Area: 17,363 km² (6704 sq mi).

Population: 814,000 (1993 est).

Capitals: Mbabane - administrative capital - 39,000, Lobamba - legislative and royal capital - 3000 (1986 census).

Other major towns: Manzini 52,000, Nhlang ano 4100, Piggs Peak 3200 (1986 census).

Languages: siSwati and English (both official).

Religions: Various Protestant Churches (37%; mainly Anglican and Methodist), Independent African Churches (28%), animist (21%), Roman Catholic (11%).

Education: Education is freely available between the ages of six and 13 but it is not compulsory. In 1985 the literacy rate was nearly 68%. There is a university and a university centre.

Defence: In 1990 the total armed strength was over 2700. There is also a paramilitary police force. Compulsory military service lasts for two years but is not universal.

Transport: There are over 2800 km (1740 mi) of roads and 525 km (326 mi) of railways. There is an international airport at Manzini.

Media: There are two English-language daily newspapers, two radio stations (one state-owned, the other commercial) and a state-run television service.

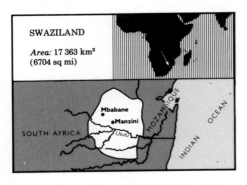

SWAZILAND

Area: 17 363 km²
(6704 sq mi)

GOVERNMENT
Swaziland is a monarchy in which the King appoints a Prime Minister and Cabinet. The King is advised by the 20-member Senate and the 65-member House of Assembly, and appoints 10 members to both. The 45 other members of the Assembly are directly elected; the 10 other members of the Senate are chosen by the Assembly. There are no political parties. The most recent election was in October 1993.

King: HM King Mswati III (succeeded upon the resignation of his mother as Queen Regent, 25 April 1986).

Prime Minister: Prince Jameson Mbilini Dlamini.

GEOGRAPHY
From the mountains of the west, Swaziland descends in steps of savannah (veld) towards hill country in the east. Highest point: Emlembe 1863 m (6113 ft). Principal rivers: Usutu, Komati, Umbuluzi, Ingwavuma. Climate: The veld is subtropical, while the highlands are temperate.

ECONOMY
Over two thirds of Swazis are subsistence farmers, growing crops and keeping cattle. Cash crops include sugar cane (the main export), cotton, citrus fruits, pineapples and maize. The country has important mineral reserves and exports diamonds, coal, gold and asbestos. High unemployment is reduced by Swazis taking work in South Africa.

Currency: Lilangeni (plural emalangeni) of 100 cents; 1US$ = 3.65 emalangeni (June 1994).

GDP: US$927,000,000 (1992); US$1080 per head.

RECENT HISTORY
The Swazi kingdom came under British rule in 1904. The country resisted annexation by the Boers in the 1890s and by South Africa during the colonial period. Following independence (1968), King Sobhuza II suspended the constitution in 1973 and restored much of the traditional royal authority. A bitter power struggle after his death (1982) lasted until King Mswati III was invested in 1986. Direct elections were reintroduced in 1993 but unlimited party politics have not yet been accepted.

Tanzania

Official name: Jamhuri ya Muungano wa Tanzania (Swahili) or The United Republic of Tanzania.

Member of: UN, Commonwealth, OAU.

Area: 945,087 km² (364,900 sq mi).

Population: 25,096,000 (1991 est).

Capitals: Dodoma (legislative and official capital) 204,000, Dar es Salaam (joint administrative capital) 1,361,000 (1988 census).

Other major cities: Mwanza 223,000, Tanga 188,000, Zanzibar 158,000 (1988 census).

Languages: English, Swahili (90%; 9% as a first language) - both official. There are about 120 local languages belonging to the Bantu, Nilotic and Cushitic groups. Arabic is spoken on the coast and various languages of the Indian sub-continent (Gujarati, Hindu and Punjabi) are spoken in Dar es Salaam.

Religions: Sunni Islam (33%), animist (40%), Roman Catholic (12%), Hindu, Anglican.

Education: Education is compulsory in theory between the ages of seven and 14. In 1990 the literacy rate was estimated to be over 94%. There are two universities.

Defence: In 1992 the total armed strength was nearly 46,000 - 45,000 in the army and nearly 1000 in the navy. There is a Citizen's Militia of 100,000. Military service lasts for two years.

Transport: There are over 82,000 km (50,960 mi) of roads and 3569 km (2218 mi) of railways. Dar es Salaam is the principal commercial shipping port and international airport. Other shipping ports include Tanga, Zanzibar and Mtwara, and Mwanza which is on Lake Victoria. Kilimanjaro and Zanzibar also have international airports.

Media: There are three national daily newspapers and a radio service with a separate channel operating in Zanzibar. There is a television service in Zanzibar but there is no service on the mainland.

GOVERNMENT

The President is elected by universal adult suffrage for a five-year term. The President appoints a Cabinet of Ministers and two Vice-Presidents - one President of Zanzibar, the other concurrently Prime Minister. The 244-member National Assembly comprises 119 members elected from the mainland, 50 members directly elected from Zanzibar, plus appointed and indirectly elected members. Zanzibar, which has its own legislature, is divided into five local government regions. For local government purposes the mainland is divided into 21 regions. The main political party is the (former monopoly) CCM (Chama Cha Mapinduzi - the Revolutionary Party). Other parties have been legalized since 1992 - they include the Civic Movement (Chama Cha Wananchi wa Tanzania), the National Convention for Construction and Reform, the Republic Party and two parties based in Zanzibar that seek a referendum on the continuation of the union of Zanzibar and mainland Tanzania - the Bismallah Party and the Movement for Democratic Alternative.

Party strength: CCM 244.

President: Ali Hassan Mwinyi (CCM).

THE CABINET

First Vice President and Prime Minister: John S. Malecela (CCM).

Second Vice President and President of Zanzibar: Dr Salim Amour (CCM).

Deputy Prime Minister and Minister for Home Affairs: Augustine L. Mrema (CCM).

Minister for Agriculture and Livestock Development: Jackson Makweta (CCM).

Minister for Communication, Transport and Works: Nalaila Kiula (CCM).

Minister for Community Development, for Women and Children: Anna Makinda (CCM).

Minister for Education and Culture: Phillemon Sarungi (CCM).

Minister for Finance: Prof. Kighoma Malima (CCM).

Minister for Foreign Affairs and International Cooperation: Joseph Rwegasira (CCM).

Minister for Health: Amran Mayagila (CCM).

Minister for Industry and Trade: Cleopa Msuya (CCM).

Minister for Information and Broadcasting: William Shija (CCM).

Minister of Justice and Constitutional Affairs: Samuel Sitta (CCM).

Minister for Labour and Youth: Ahmed Hassan Diria (CCM).

Minister for Lands, Housing and Urban Development: Edward Lowassa (CCM).

Minister for Science, Technology and Higher Education: Benjamin Mkapa (CCM).

Minister for Tourism, Natural Resources and the Environment: Juma Omar Juma (CCM).

Minister for Water, Energy and Minerals: Jakaya Kikwete (CCM).

AUTONOMOUS STATE
Zanzibar Area: 1660 km² (641 sq mi). Population: 376,000 (1988 census). Capital: Zanzibar.

GEOGRAPHY
Zanzibar comprises three small islands - Zanzibar, Pemba and Panza. The mainland - formerly Tanganyika - comprises savannah plateaux divided by rift valleys and a north-south mountain chain. Highest point: Kilimanjaro 5894 m (19,340 ft), the highest point in Africa. Principal rivers: Pangani (Ruvu), Rufiji, Rovuma. Climate: Tanzania has a tropical climate, although the mountains are cooler.

ECONOMY
Subsistence agriculture involves over 70% of the labour force and the development of agriculture, in particular the growing of food crops, has been a priority of the Tanzanian government. Cash crops include coffee, tea, cotton and tobacco. The large-scale cultivation of cloves for export is one of the mainstays of the economy of Zanzibar. Mineral resources include diamonds and gold, and coal is mined in the southwest of the country. Tanzania had a centrally planned economy, but more pragmatic policies have been implemented since 1985-87. The economy took a major downturn in the late 1970s and early 1980s when a costly intervention in the affairs of Uganda coincided with a fall in the price of the country's principal agricultural exports and a rise in the price of energy. Since then the situation has been exacerbated by recurring drought.

Currency: Tanzanian shilling of 100 cents; 1US$ = 515.65 shillings (June 1994).

GDP: US$2,780,000,000 (1990); US$120 per head.

RECENT HISTORY
In 1964 Tanganyika and Zanzibar united to form Tanzania. Zanzibar - formerly an Omani possession - became an independent sultanate in 1856 and then a British protectorate (1890-1963). After independence in 1963 the sultan of Zanzibar was deposed in a radical left-wing coup. The mainland became the colony of German East Africa in 1884 and the British trust territory of Tanganyika in 1919 when what are now Rwanda and Burundi were separated from the territory and placed under Belgian administration. Tanganyika became an independent state in 1961. President Julius Nyerere's policies of self-reliance and egalitarian socialism were widely admired internationally and initially received great support in Tanzania, but they proved difficult to implement and were largely abandoned by the time he retired as President in 1985. In 1979-81 Tanzanian forces intervened in Uganda to

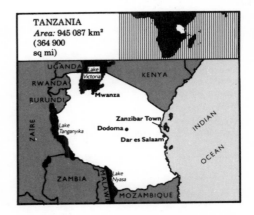

TANZANIA
Area: 945 087 km²
(364 900 sq mi)

help oust Idi Amin. In 1992 amendments to the constitution to legalize a multi-party political system were presented to the National Assembly. The first multi-party elections in Tanzania are scheduled to take place towards the end of 1995. In 1994 large numbers of refugees from the civil war in Rwanda entered northern Tanzania where refugee camps were established. and international agencies began relief work. The scale of the influx was a major problem for a poor country such as Tanzania - overnight the largest refugee camp became the second largest concentration of population in Tanzania.

Togo

Official name: La République togolaise (The Togolese Republic).

Member of: UN, OAU, ECOWAS.

Area: 56,785 km² (21,925 sq mi).

Population: 3,810,000 (1993 est).

Capital: Lomé 366,000 (1983 est).

Other main towns: Sokodé 34,000, Kpalimé 26,000 (1983 est).

Languages: French, Ewe (47%), Kabre (22%) - all official.

Religions: Animist (50%), Roman Catholic (26%), Sunni Islam (15%), various Protestant Churches (6%).

Education: Education is compulsory, in theory, between the ages of six and 12. In 1990 the literacy rate was 43.3%. There is a university.

Defence: In 1993 the total armed strength was 5300. There is also a 750-member force of paramilitary gendarmes. Military service, which lasts for two years, is selective.

Transport: Ther are 7545 km (4670 mi) of roads and 525 km (326 mi) of railways. Lomé has an international airport and a commercial port.

Media: There are two daily newspapers and a state-run radio and television service.

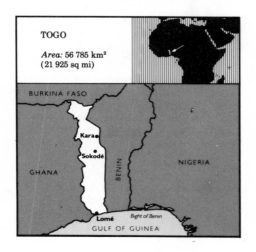

GOVERNMENT

The President - who appoints a Council of Ministers - is elected by universal adult suffrage for seven years. The 75-member National Assembly is elected for five years. Political parties include the (former monopoly) Rally for the Togolese People (RPT), the Action Committee for Renewal (CAR) and the Union of Justice and Democracy (UTD). After the election held in February 1994 a CAR-UTD government was formed.

Party strength: RPT 35, CAR 34, UTD 6.

President: Gen. Gnassingbe Eyadema (RPT).

Prime Minister: Edem Kodjo (UTD).

GEOGRAPHY

Inland from a narrow coastal plain is a series of plateaux rising in the north to the Chaine du Togo. Highest point: Pic Baumann 983 m (3225 ft). Principal rivers: Moni, Oti. Climate: Togo has a hot and humid tropical climate, although the north is drier.

ECONOMY

The majority of the labour force is involved in subsistence farming, with yams and millet as the principal crops. Phosphates are the main export.

Currency: CFA Franc; 1US$ = 546.45 CFA Francs (June 1994).

GDP: US$1,517,000,000 (1992); US$390 per head.

RECENT HISTORY

Colonized by Germany in 1884, Togoland was occupied by Franco-British forces in World War I, after which it was divided between them as trust territories. British Togoland became part of Ghana; the French section gained independence as Togo in 1960. Togo has experienced great political instability and several coups. Following anti-government protests, a multi-party system was restored in 1991. President Eyadema's real power was removed by the High Council of the Republic in 1991, but civil unrest has continued as the military has periodically intervened in the political life of the country. The presidential elections in 1993 were widely perceived to be flawed but multi-party legislative elections were held in 1994.

Uganda

Official name: The Republic of Uganda.

Member of: UN, Commonwealth, OAU.

Area: 241,139 km² (93,104 sq mi).

Population: 16,583,000 (1991 census).

Capital: Kampala 773,000 (1991 census).

Other main cities: Jinja 61,000, Mbale 54,000, Masaka 49,000, Entebbe 42,000 (1991 census).

Languages: English and Swahili (both official), with local languages including Luganda.

Religions: Roman Catholic (45%), various Protestant Churches (17%), animist (32%), Sunni Islam (6%).

Education: Education is not compulsory. In 1990 the literacy rate was 48.3 %. There are three universities (including an Islamic university) and a polytechnic.

Defence: In 1993 the total armed strength was estimated to be 70,000.

Transport: There are about 28,500 km (15,950 mi) of roads. About 1230 km (769 mi) of railways are in operation. A ferry service operates from Jinja to Mwanza in Tanzania. Uganda's international airport is at Entebbe.

Media: There are five daily newspapers published in English and two in Luganda. The state-run radio and television service broadcasts in English, Luganda and Swahili.

GOVERNMENT

Elections were held in 1994 for a 288-member Assembly comprising 214 members elected by universal adult suffrage, 10 members nominated by the President, 56 members nominated by special interest groups (trade unions, women's organizations, etc.) and eight members nominated by the four principal political parties in operation before parties were prohibited in 1986. There are 38 districts. The commander of the National Resistance Army - which took power in 1986 - is President. He appoints a Prime Minister and other Ministers.

President: Yoweri Museveni.

Prime Minister: George Adyebo.

GEOGRAPHY

Most of Uganda is a plateau that ends in the west at the Great Rift Valley and the Ruwenzori Mountains. Lake Victoria covers southeastern Uganda. Highest point: Ngaliema 5118 m (16,763 ft). Principal rivers: Nile, Semliki. Climate: The tropical climate is moderated by its altitude.

ECONOMY

Agriculture involves over three quarters of the labour force. Coffee normally accounts for 90% of Uganda's exports. Subsistence crops include plantains, cassava and sweet potatoes.

Currency: Uganda shilling (UGS); 1US$ = 944.6 UGS (June 1994).

GDP: US$3,814,000,000 (1990); US$220 per head.

RECENT HISTORY

The British protectorate of Uganda (established in 1894) was built around the powerful African kingdom of Buganda, whose continuing special status contributed to the disunity that has plagued Uganda since independence in 1962. Milton Obote, who suppressed the monarchies in 1966, was overthrown in a coup by Idi Amin in 1971. Under Amin political and human rights were curtailed, opponents of the regime were murdered and the Asian population was expelled. The army took over in 1979, supported by Tanzanian troops. Obote was restored but was ousted in a military coup in 1985, since when instability has continued. A constituent assembly was elected in 1994 and the traditional kingdoms of Uganda, including Buganda, were restored. In some rural areas AIDS has devastated the population.

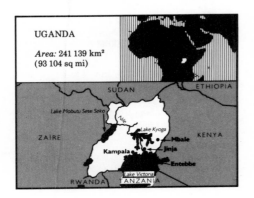

UGANDA

Area: 241 139 km²
(93 104 sq mi)

SUDAN · ETHIOPIA · Lake Mobutu Sese Seko · ZAIRE · Lake Kyoga · Mbale · KENYA · Kampala · Jinja · Entebbe · Lake Victoria · RWANDA · TANZANIA

Zaïre

Official name: La République du Zaïre (Republic of Zaïre).

Member of: UN, OAU.

Area: 2,344,885 km² (905,365 sq mi).

Population: 41,150,000 (1992 est).

Capital: Kinshasa 3,804,000 (1991 est).

Other major cities: Lubumbashi 740,000, Mbuji-Mayi 613,000, Kisangani 373,000, Kananga 372,000 (1991 est).

Languages: French (official); four national languages - Kiswahili, Tshiluba, Kikongo and Lingala; over 400 local languages.

Religions: Roman Catholic (48%), various Protestant Churches (28%), Kimbanguist (a Protestant African Church; 17%), animist (6%).

Education: Education is compulsory in theory between the ages of six and 12. In 1990 the literacy rate was 71.8%. There are three universities.

Defence: In 1991 the total armed strength was 29,700 - 27,000 in the army, 1300 in the navy and 1800 in the air force (plus 25,000 paramilitary gendarmes and 10,000 in the Civil Guard). In theory military service is compulsory; the length of service varies.

Transport: There are about 145,000 km (90,650 mi) of roads but increasingly few of these are passable owing to lack of maintenance. There are 4772 km (2983 mi) of railways, but few lines were functioning in 1994. Water transport is important and there are over 13,700 km (8560 mi) of inland waterways of which the Rivers Zaïre, Lualaba and Kasai are the most important. Matadi is the main seaport. There are international airports at Kinshasa, Lubumbashi, Goma, Kisangani and Bukavu.

Media: There are four daily newspapers. Two radio stations and a television station broadcast in five languages.

GOVERNMENT
The 222-member National Legislative Council is elected by compulsory universal suffrage for five years. The President - who is directly elected for seven years - appoints the National Executive Council of Commissioners (Ministers). The one-party state was abolished in 1991 when a national conference was convened to bring democracy to Zaïre. Some 160 political groups, including the (former monopoly) Mouvement populaire de la révolution, are active. Multi-party elections have yet to be held. The national conference nominated a 443-member High Council to act as a provisional government; the conference also appointed a Prime Minister. In most of the country effective government has ceased to exist. There are 10 regions, plus the national capital (Kinshasa), each of which is administered by a Regional Commissioner and six Councillors, all of whom are appointed by the President.

President: Marshal Mobutu Sese Seko.

Prime Minister: Kengo Wa Dondo. (The appointment of Kengo Wa Dondo in 1994 ended a period when Zaïre had rival PMs – one recognized by the national conference and one appointed by President Mobutu.

REGIONS
Bandundu Area: 295,658 km² (114,154 sq mi). Population: 4,617,000 (1991 est). Capital: Bandundu.

Bas-Zaïre Area: 54,078 km² (20,880 sq mi). Population: 2,485,000 (1991 est). Capital: Matadi.

Equateur Area: 403,292 km² (155,712 sq mi). Population: 4,312,000 (1991 est). Capital: Mbandaka.

Haute-Zaïre Area: 503,239 km² (194,302 sq mi). Population: 5,073,000 (1991 est). Capital: Kisangani.

Kasai-Occidental Area: 156,967 km² (60,605 sq mi). Population: 2,982,000 (1991 est). Capital: Kananga.

Kasai-Oriental Area: 168,216 km² (64,949 sq mi). Population: 3,338,000 (1991 est). Capital: Mbuji-Mayi.

Kinshasa Area: 9965 km² (3848 sq mi). Population: 3,804,000 (1991 est). Capital: Kinshasa.

Maniema Area: 131,871 km² (50,916 sq mi). Population: 2,690,000 (1991 est). Capital: Kindu.

Nord-Kivu Area: 60,057 km² (23,188 sq mi). Population: 1,210,000 (1991 est). Capital: Goma.

Shaba Area: 496,877 km² (191,845 sq mi).

Population: 5,207,000 (1991 est). Capital: Lubumbashi.

Sud-Kivu Area: 64,875 km² (25,048 sq mi). Population: 2,828,000 (1991 est). Capital: Bukavu.

GEOGRAPHY
Over 60% of the country comprises a basin of tropical rainforest drained by the River Zaïre (Congo) and its tributaries. Plateaux and mountain ranges surrounding the basin include the Ruwenzori Massif in the east. Highest point: Mont Ngaliema 5109 m (16,763 ft). Principal rivers: Zaïre, Lualaba, Lomami, Oubangui, Kasai. Climate: Zaïre has a humid, tropical climate with little seasonal variation, although the north is drier from December to February.

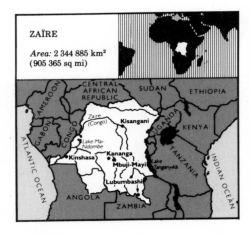

ECONOMY
Agriculture occupies over two thirds of the labour force. Although subsistence farming predominates, coffee, tea, cocoa, rubber and palm products are exported. Minerals are the mainstay of the economy, with copper, cobalt, zinc and diamonds normally accounting for about 60% of Zaïre's exports. However, the copper mines have flooded owing to lack of maintenance and there was no copper production in the first half of 1994. Diamonds are now the main export, but in 1993-94 the majority of diamonds exported from the country were smuggled. Zaïre suffers rampant inflation and one of the lowest standards of living in Africa.

Currency: The zaïre (ZRZ); 1US$ = 250.1 ZRZ.

GDP: US$8,117,000,000 (1991); US$230 per head.

RECENT HISTORY
The region - now Zaïre - was ravaged by the slave trade, and in 1885 became the personal possession of King Leopold II of the Belgians. However, international outrage at the brutality of the regime in the Congo Free State forced the king to grant the region to Belgium as a colony in 1908. As the Belgian Congo, the colony became a major exporter of minerals. The provision of social services, especially primary education, was relatively advanced, but the administration curbed almost all African political activity. As a result, the country was inadequately prepared when Belgium suddenly decolonized the Congo in 1960. Within days of independence, the army mutinied and the richest region - Katanga (now Shaba), under Moïse Tshombe - attempted to secede. The Congo invited the United Nations to intervene, but the UN force was only partly successful in overcoming continuing civil wars. Colonel Mobutu twice intervened and in 1965 made himself head of state. Pursuing 'authenticity', he renamed the country Zaïre and himself Mobuto Sése Séko. He gradually restored the authority of the central government and introduced a one-party state (1967). Mobutu's strong rule has attracted international criticism, but, until the early 1990s, he maintained support from Western states that value Zaïre as a source of strategic minerals. In 1990, popular discontent and pressure from Western countries won some reforms and - following the legal abolition of the one-party state - a national conference was summoned to bring democracy to Zaïre (1991). Since 1991 most Western governments have suspended assistance to the country. In 1992-93 conflicts developed between the national conference and the prime minister on one side and President Mobutu on the other. Sections of the armed forces became disaffected. Law and order has broken down in parts of the country and, except in isolated pockets, Zaïre as a nation state has practically ceased to exist. There is widespread ethnic unrest in Shaba, Kasai and in the former province of Kivu.

Zambia

Official name: The Republic of Zambia.

Member of: UN, Commonwealth, OAU, SADCC.

Area: 752,614 km² (290,586 sq mi).

Population: 7,818,000 (1990 census).

Capital: Lusaka 982,000 (1990 census).

Other major cities: Ndola 376,000, Kitwe 338,000, Mufulira 153,000 (1990 census).

Languages: English, Tonga (16%), Kaonda, Lunda, Luvale - all official; Bemba (34%).

Religions: Various Protestant Churches (50%), Roman Catholic (20%), animist.

Education: Education is compulsory, in theory, between the ages of seven and 14. In 1990 the literacy rate was 72.8%. There are two universities.

Defence: In 1993 the total armed strength was 21,600, of whom 20,000 are in the army.

Transport: There are 37,400 km (23,215 mi) of roads and 2164 km (1345 mi) of railways. Lusaka has an international airport.

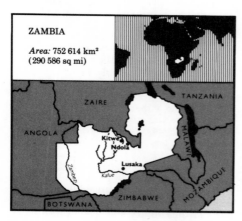

ZAMBIA

Area: 752 614 km²
(290 586 sq mi)

ZAIRE · TANZANIA · ANGOLA · MALAWI · Kitwe · Ndola · Lusaka · Zambezi · Kafue · MOZAMBIQUE · ZIMBABWE · BOTSWANA

Media: There are three daily newspapers and a state-run radio and television service.

GOVERNMENT
The 150-member National Assembly is elected by universal adult suffrage for five years. The President - who is directly elected for five years

- appoints a Cabinet. The 27-member House of Chiefs has advisory powers. The main political parties are the Movement for Multiparty Democracy (MMD), the (former monopoly) United National Independence Party (UNIP) and two splinter parties from the MMD - the National Party (NP) and the Caucus for National Unity (CNU). After the election held in November 1991 a MMD government was formed.

Party strength: MMD 99, UNIP 23, NP 17, CNU 5, others 1.

President: Frederick Chiluba (MMD).

GEOGRAPHY
Zambia comprises plateaux some 1000 to 1500 m (3300 to 5000 ft) high, above which rise the Muchinga Mountains and the Mufinga Hills. Highest point: an unnamed peak in the Muchinga Mountains, 2164 m (7100 ft). Principal rivers: Zambezi, Kafue, Luapula. Climate: Zambia has a tropical climate with a wet season from November to April.

ECONOMY
Zambia's economy depends upon the mining and processing of copper, lead, zinc and cobalt. Agriculture is underdeveloped and many basic foodstuffs have to be imported. Maize, groundnuts and tobacco are the main crops.

Currency: Kwacha of 100 ngwee; 1US$ = 697.9 kwachas (June 1994).

GDP: US$2,487,000,000 (1992); US$290 per head.

RECENT HISTORY
The area - which became known as Northern Rhodesia - was brought under the control of the British South Africa Company of Cecil Rhodes in the 1890s. In 1924 Britain took over the administration from the Company. Africans unsuccessfully opposed inclusion in the Central African Federation - with Nyasaland (Malawi) and Southern Rhodesia (Zimbabwe) - in 1953. Against strong opposition from white settlers, Kenneth Kaunda (1924-) led Northern Rhodesia, renamed Zambia, to independence in 1964. A one-party state was introduced in 1972-73. Popular discontent erupted in 1990 and free elections were held in 1991, when Kuanda was defeated in the first democratic change of government in English-speaking Black Africa.

Zimbabwe

Official name: The Republic of Zimbabwe.

Member of: UN, Commonwealth, OAU, SADCC.

Area: 390,759 km² (150,873 sq mi).

Population: 10,687,000 (1991 est).

Capital: Harare (formerly Salisbury) 1,184,000 (1992 est).

Other major cities: Bulawayo 621,000, Chitungwiza 274,000, Mutare (Umtali) 132,000, Gweru 125,000 (1989 est).

Languages: English (official), Chishona, Sindebele.

Religions: Animist (42%), Anglican (30%), Roman Catholic (15%), Presbyterian.

Education: Education is compulsory, in theory, between the ages of seven and 14. In 1990 the literacy rate was 66.9%. There is a single university.

Defence: In 1993 the total armed strength was 48,200 - 47,000 in the army, the remainder in the air force. Selective military service lasts for one year.

Transport: There are 85,237 km (52,964 mi) of roads and 2759 km (1714 mi) of railways. Harare, Bulawayo and the Victoria Falls all have international airports.

Media: There are two daily newspapers and a state corporation that supplies radio and television services.

GOVERNMENT

The 150-member House of Assembly comprises 120 members directly elected by universal adult suffrage for six years, 12 nominated members, 10 traditional chiefs and 8 appointed provincial governors. The House elects a President for a six-year term of office. For local government purposes, Zimbabwe is divided into eight provinces. Political parties include the Zimbabwe African National Union (ZANU-PF), the Zimbabwe Unity Movement (ZUM) and the Zimbabwe African National Union-Ndonga. After the election held in October 1990 a ZANU-PF government continued in office.

Party strength: ZANU-PF 148, ZUM 1, Ndonga 1.

President: Robert Mugabe (ZANU-PF).

THE CABINET
All members of ZANU-PF.

Vice-Presidents: Simon Vengayi Muzenda, Dr Joshua Mqabuko Nkomo.

Attorney-General: Patrick Anthony Chinamasa.

Minister of Defence: Moven Enock Mahachi.

Minister of Education and Culture: Dr Witness Pasichigare Magunda Mangwende.

Minister of the Environment and Tourism: Herbert Muchemwa Murerwa.

Minister of Finance: Dr Bernard Thomas Chidzero.

Minister of Foreign Affairs: Dr Nathan Marwirakuwa.

Minister of Health and Child Welfare: Dr Timothy Stamps.

Minister of Higher Education: Stanley Mudenge.

Minister of Home Affairs: Dumiso Dabengwa.

Minister of Industry and Commerce: vacant.

Minister of Information, Posts and Telecommunications: David Ishemunyoro Karimanzira.

Minister of Justice, Legal and Parliamentary Affairs: Emmerson Dambudzo Mnangagwa.

Minister of Lands, Agriculture and Water Development: Kumbirai Manyika Kangai.

Minister of Local Government, Rural and Urban Development: Joseph Msika.

Minister of Mines: Eddison Jonas Mudadirwa Zvobgo.

Minister of National Affairs, Employment Creation and Co-operatives: Didymus Noel Edwin Mutasa.

Minister of Public Construction and National Housing: Enos Chamunorwa Chikowore.

Minister of Public Service, Labour and Social Welfare: John Landa Nkomo.

Minister of State for Finance: Dr Tichaendepi Robert Masaya.

Minister of State for National Security: Dr Sydney Tigere Sekeramayi.

Minister of State for National Affairs, Employment Creation and Co-operatives: Gabriel Mharadze Machinga.

Minister of State for Women's Affairs: Thenjiwe Virginia Lesabe.

Minister of Transport and Energy: Dennis Norman.

Planning Commissioner: Richard Chemist Hove.

GEOGRAPHY
Central Zimbabwe comprises the ridge of the Highveld, rising to between 1200 and 1500 m (about 4000 to 5000 ft). The Highveld is bounded on the southwest and northeast by the Middle Veld and the Lowveld plateaux. Highest point: Mount Inyangani 2592 m (8504 ft). Principal rivers: Zambezi, Limpopo, Sabi.

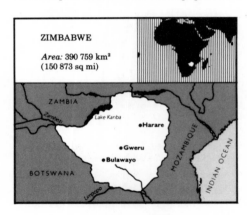

ZIMBABWE

Area: 390 759 km²
(150 873 sq mi)

ZAMBIA
Lake Kariba
●Harare
● Gweru
● Bulawayo
BOTSWANA
MOZAMBIQUE
INDIAN OCEAN

Climate: The climate is tropical in the lowlands and subtropical at altitude. There is a pronounced dry season from June to September.

ECONOMY
Agriculture - which involves about two thirds of the labour force - has been adversely affected by severe drought and lack of investment. Tobacco, sugar cane, cotton, wheat and maize are exported as well as being the basis of processing industries. Beef production is important. Natural resources include coal, gold, asbestos and nickel - the latter three being major exports. Tourism (particularly from South Africa and the UK) is increasingly important, with Great Zimbabwe and the Victoria Falls as the most popular tourist destinations. The principal Zimbabwean exports are tobacco, ferrochrome, gold, nickel, cotton, steel and textiles.

Currency: Zimbabwe dollar of 100 cents; 1US$ = 8.01 Zimbabwe dollars.

GDP: US$6,220,000,000 (1991); US$650 per head.

RECENT HISTORY
The area was gradually penetrated by British and Boer hunters, missionaries and prospectors from the 1830s, and was occupied by the British South Africa Company of Cecil Rhodes in the 1890s. The highlands of what became Southern Rhodesia were settled by white farmers, who deprived Africans of land and reduced them to a cheap labour force. Britain took over the administration from the Company in 1923 and granted self-government to the white colonists. Immigration from Britain and South Africa increased after World War II, but the whites remained outnumbered by the Africans by more than 20 to 1. Racial discrimination stimulated African nationalism, initially led by Joshua Nkomo (1917-). Southern Rhodesia - with Northern Rhodesia (Zambia) and Nyasaland (Malawi) - formed the Central African Federation in 1953. When the Federation was dissolved (1963), Britain refused the white Southern Rhodesian administration independence without progress to majority rule. The white government led by Ian Smith (1919-) unilaterally declared independence in 1965, renaming the country Rhodesia. Internal opposition was crushed and international economic sanctions were overcome, but guerrilla wars, mounted by African nationalists during the 1970s, became increasingly effective. In 1979 Smith had to accept majority rule, but the constitution he introduced was unacceptable either to the Zimbabwe African People's Union (ZAPU) of Joshua Nkomo or to the Zimbabwe African National Union (ZANU) of Robert Mugabe (1928-). All parties agreed to the brief reimposition of British rule to achieve a settlement. ZANU under Mugabe took the country to independence in 1980. In 1987 ZANU and ZAPU finally agreed to unite, effectively introducing a one-party state, although proposals for an official one-party system have been shelved.

Other territories

BRITISH INDIAN OCEAN TERRITORY
Status: a British territory.

Area: 60 km² (23 sq mi).

Population: 2900 military personnel (1991 est).

Geography: The five coral atolls of the Chagos archipelago lie northeast of Mauritius.

Recent History: The territory was created in 1965 to provide defence and communication facilities in the Indian Ocean for the UK and the USA.

MAYOTTE
Status: a French territorial collectivity.

Area: 376 km² (145 sq mi).

Population: 94,400 (1990 census).

Capital: Mamoudzou 12,000 (1990 census).

Geography: Mayotte is the most southeasterly island of the Comoros archipelago.

Economy: Mayotte depends upon the export of vanilla and ylang-ylang.

Recent History: The Comoros became French in 1843. France has administered Mayotte separately since 1975 when the three western islands unilaterally declared independence.

REUNION
Status: an overseas French département.

Area: 2512 km² (970 km²), plus dependencies 38.5 km² (15 sq mi).

Population: 597,000 (1990 census).

Capital: Saint-Denis 122,000 (1990 census).

Geography: Réunion is a rugged volcanic island east of Madagascar. Highest point: Piton des Neiges 3069 m (10,069 ft). The island has a tropical maritime climate with heavy rainfall.

Economy: The economy is dominated by sugar cane, which accounts for 90% of the exports.

Recent History: Réunion has been a French possession since 1638. It became an overseas département in 1974.

ST HELENA AND DEPENDENCIES
Status: British Crown colony.

Area: 411 km² (159 sq mi) - St Helena 122 km² (47 sq mi), Ascension 88 km² (34 sq mi), Tristan da Cunha group 201 km² (78 sq mi).

Population: 7100 (1992 est) - St Helena 5700, Ascension 1100, Tristan da Cunha 300 (1990 est).

Capital: Jamestown 1500 (1992 est) on St Helena.

Geography: St Helena is a mountainous island in the South Atlantic. Ascension is a barren, rocky island 1130 km (700 mi) northwest of St Helena. The Tristan da Cunha group of six bleak, mountainous islands lies 2120 km (1320 mi) southwest of St Helena.

Economy: St Helena relies on UK subsidies and fishing. Ascension is a communications base.

Recent History: St Helena became British in 1659; Ascension was annexed by Britain in 1815 when Napoleon I was exiled to St Helena. Tristan da Cunha was annexed in 1816, but was evacuated from 1961 to 1963 after a volcanic eruption.

WESTERN SAHARA
Status: a disputed territory under Moroccan administration.

Area: 266,000 km² (102,676 sq mi).

Population: 195,000 (1993 est).

Capital: El-Aaiun (Laayoune) 97,000 (1982 est).

Geography: The Western Sahara is a low, flat desert region with no permanent streams.

Economy: The economy is dominated by the production of phosphate at Bu Craa, the largest phosphate deposit in the world.

Recent History: The area became Spanish in 1884. In 1972-73 the Polisario liberation movement's fight against Spanish rule began. Spain withdrew, dividing the territory between Mauritania and Morocco (1976). Morocco absorbed the Mauritanian area when Mauritania withdrew (1979). In 1976 Polisario declared independence as the Sahrawi Arab Democratic Republic. A ceasefire, an agreement to hold a referendum on the territory's future and the deployment of a UN force were agreed (1991). The plebiscite has not yet been held.

AUSTRALASIA AND THE PACIFIC ISLANDS

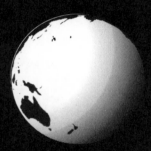

Australia, Fiji, Kiribati, Marshall Islands,
Micronesia (Federated States of), Nauru, New Zealand,
Papua New Guinea, Solomon Islands, Tonga, Tuvalu, Vanuatu,
Western Samoa, Other territories.

Australia comes of age

The participation of Australian troops in the Vietnam conflict alongside American forces just over a quarter of a century ago was one of the first, and most obvious, signs of a major change in Australia's chosen role in the world and in its perception of that role. During World War II, when Australia reinforced its traditional Commonwealth ties with Britain as an ally against the Axis powers, the north of the country was threatened by Japanese forces. This more immediate threat emphasized Australia's Pacific character and links were forged with the USA and New Zealand, leading to the formation of the ANZUS defence pact. Since 1945 migrants from all over Europe have gained assisted passage to Australia, thus diluting the British connection. When the UK joined the European Common Market in 1973, the links with Britain were further diminished. Since then Australia has looked for ever closer economic and other links with the new economic powers of East Asia - China, Japan, South Korea, Taiwan, Indonesia and Singapore - and with the USA, Canada and New Zealand. Over 27% of Australia's exports in 1991 went to Japan. Another 12% went to the ASEAN states (mainly Indonesia, Singapore and Malaysia), while the USA, South Korea and New Zealand respectively accounted for 11%, 6% and nearly 5% of Australia's exports. In the same year, over 23% of Australia's imports came from Taiwan, while Japan and the ASEAN countries accounted for 18% and 7% of Australia's imports respectively. Although Australia also numbers the UK and Germany among its more significant trading partners, Australia's major trading links are with Pacific nations.

AN AUSTRALIAN REPUBLIC

Australia's place in the world is as part of the booming Pacific Rim and, as such, the role of the British monarch as head of state of Australia is seen as a colonial anachronism. Although Australia effectively gained independence in 1901, its sovereignty did not receive legal status until it was defined under the terms of the Statute of Westminster in 1931. Confusion about Australia's status remained. The possession of a national flag that incorporates the British Union Flag in the canton (the upper left corner) and the position of a Governor General, now albeit always an Australian citizen, as the representative of the British sovereign as Queen of Australia are still thought of in some quarters as symbols of Australia's perceived lack of complete sovereignty. The Australian Prime Minister Paul Keating has pledged that, when Australia celebrates the centenary of national unity in 2001 it will do so with an Australian, rather than British, head of state. However, an Australian republic hosting the Olympic Games in Sydney in the year 2000 now also appears to be the goal.

THE NEW AUSTRALIANS

The rise of republicanism has been attributed to the influence of those descended from Irish Catholic immigrants. Before the Second World War Australia had a history of strained relations between its Protestant community (then largely of British origin) and Catholic community (mainly of Irish origin). Since 1945 immigration from continental Europe - mainly southern and eastern Europe - and East Asia has altered the nation's character.

The 1991 census revealed that about 20.8% of Australians were born outside the country - of those only 34% came from the UK, 33% from mainland Europe, 23% from Asia, and most of the remaining 10% from New Zealand or the islands of Oceania. Four out of five Australians were born and brought up in the country; among these, even those of wholly British ancestry are reported by opinion polls to feel more Australian than British. Immigrants to Australia from Italy, Croatia, Greece, Vietnam, Serbia, Poland, Hungary and Hong Kong have little or no natural affection for the British monarchy. If, and when, a referendum is held concerning Australia's constitutional future much will depend upon the timing of the plebiscite and the nature of the proposed changes. Opinion polls suggest that a figurehead presidency on the German model is more likely to win wide approval than an executive presidency of the American type. Australia's mood seems to be for change but, if those proposed include amendments to the governmental system that diminish the powers of the states in favour of Canberra, then there is every possibility that the republican movement will founder. Australian republicanism is in no way a mark of disrespect to the present monarch who is widely admired in the country. It is, nevertheless, possible that Australia's constitutional change will be misinterpreted by some people on the other side of the world, although republicanism in Australia is about Australia asserting its identity.

Regional Organizations of Australasia and of the Pacific Islands

ANZUS

ANZUS was set up in 1951 to form a collective defence policy for the preservation of peace in the Pacific region. Partners share in defence and technical intelligence, the supply of military and allied equipment, and undertake joint military and naval exercises. The Labour governments that ruled New Zealand from 1972 to 1975 and from 1984 to 1990 placed a ban on vessels powered by nuclear energy or carrying nuclear weapons in New Zealand. This clearly applied to US vessels and the ban raised a question mark over New Zealand's role as a full ANZUS member.

Headquarters: Canberra, Australia.

Membership: Australia, New Zealand, and the USA.

THE SOUTH PACIFIC BUREAU FOR ECONOMIC CO-OPERATION (SPEC)

The South Pacific Bureau for Economic Co-operation was founded in 1973. It aims to encourage regional trade, economic development and the expansion of transport links between members. The administration of the Bureau - including the Secretariat - is shared with that of the South Pacific Bureau (see below).

Headquarters: Suva, Fiji.

Membership: Australia, the Cook Islands (a self-governing territory of New Zealand), Fiji, Kiribati, the Marshall Islands, the Federated States of Micronesia, Nauru, New Zealand, Niue (a self-governing territory of New Zealand), Papua New Guinea, the Solomon Islands, Tonga, Tuvalu, Vanuatu, and Western Samoa.

THE SOUTH PACIFIC FORUM

The South Pacific Forum was founded in 1971 in Wellington, New Zealand. The Forum has no formal constitution but exists to further co-operation between members in a wide range of issues of mutual interest from environmental to social, from scientific to international. A particular concern is the status and development of those Pacific island territories that remain under colonial, or similar, administration. The Forum has a small permanent Secretariat, which is headed by a Secretary General. (See also the South Pacific Bureau for Economic Co-operation.)

Headquarters: Suva, Fiji.

Secretary General: Ieremia Tabai (Kiribati).

Membership: Australia, the Cook Islands (a self-governing territory of New Zealand), Fiji, Kiribati, the Marshall Islands, the Federated States of Micronesia, Nauru, New Zealand, Niue (a self-governing territory of New Zealand), Papua New Guinea, the Solomon Islands, Tonga, Tuvalu, Vanuatu, and Western Samoa.

OTHER ORGANIZATIONS

Ten Australasian and Pacific nations are members of the Commonwealth (see p. 24). Nauru and Tuvalu have special membership of the Commonwealth, that is they do not participate in Commonwealth meetings. Fiji was formerly a member but that membership lapsed following two coups and the declaration of a republic in 1987.

Four countries in the region are members of the Colombo Plan for Co-operative Economic and Social Development in Asia and the Pacific (see p. 305).

The greatest number of non-members of the United Nations is to be found in the Pacific, where the small island nations of Kiribati, Nauru, Tonga and Tuvalu have not applied to join the world body. These states do, however, belong to some of the specialized agencies of the UN.

The Compacts of Free Association, which the USA has concluded separately with the governments of the Marshall Islands and the Federated States of Micronesia, may be looked upon as a type of regional organization. Under these Compacts, the two republics gained sovereignty, able to conduct their own foreign affairs, but the USA retains complete responsibility for the republics' defence and security until the year 2001. (A similar Compact will be concluded with Palau once it has been approved by a referendum in that territory.)

Australasian and Pacific Trade

Australia Imports (Australian $ million): 48 911.6 (1991). Exports (Australian $ million): 52 447.2 (1991). Main imports: machinery and transport equipment 43% (1991/92), basic manufactures 15.4% (1991/92). Main exports: crude materials 24.7% (1991/92), food and live animals 17.6% (1991/92). Principal trading partners: Japan, USA, New Zealand, Germany, UK.

Fiji Imports ($ million): 652 (1991). Exports ($ million): 451 (1991). Main imports: machinery and transport equipment 22.4% (1991), basic durable manufactures 25.4% (1991). Main exports: sugar 32.7% (1991), gold 7% (1991). Principal trading partners: UK, Australia, New Zealand, Japan.

Kiribati Imports ($ million): 27 (1990). Exports ($ million): 3 (1990). Main imports: food 26.6% (1990), machinery and transport equipment 19.1% (1990). Main exports: copra 27.8% (1990), fish and fish preparations 27.1% (1990). Principal trading partners: Fiji, Australia, Japan.

Marshall Islands Imports ($ million): 34 (1988). Exports ($ million): 2 (1988). Main imports: food, agricultural raw materials, mineral ores, and concentrates 45.5% (1988), fuels and other energies 10.7% (1988). Main exports: food and agricultural raw materials 100% (1988). Principal trading partner: USA.

Micronesia Imports ($ million): 68 (1988). Exports ($ million): 2 (1988). Main imports: food, beverages and tobacco 41.4% (1988), manufactured goods 28.1% (1988). Main exports: copra 25.6% (1988), manufactured goods 12.8% (1988). Principal trading partners: Japan, USA.

Nauru Imports ($ million): 14 (1988). Exports ($ million): 74 (1988). Main exports: phosphates 99%. Principal trading partners: Australia, New Zealand.

New Zealand Imports ($NZ million): 14,215 (1991/2). Exports ($NZ million): 17,890.6 (1991/92). Main imports: machinery and transport equipment 38.5% (1991/92), chemicals and related products 31.1% (1991/92). Main exports: food and live animals 46.2% (1991/92), basic manufactures 13.9% (1991/92). Principal trading partners: Australia, Japan, USA, UK, South Korea.

Papua New Guinea Imports ($ million): 1403 (1991). Exports ($ million): 1283 (1991). Main imports: machinery and transport equipment 41.6% (1989), basic manufactures 20% (1989). Main exports: copper ore and concentrates 35.4% (1990), gold 35.3% (1990). Principal trading partners: Japan, Australia, Germany, USA.

Solomon Islands Imports ($ million): 92 (1990). Exports ($ million): 70 (1990). Main imports: machinery and transport equipment 24.8% (1990), manufactured goods 24.5% (1990). Main exports: timber products 34.1% (1990), fish products 29.9% (1990). Principal trading partners: Australia, Japan, UK.

Tonga Imports (T$ million): 76.8 (1991). Exports (T$ million): 20.6 (1991). Main imports: food and live animals 21.4% (1991), machinery and transport equipment 19% (1991). Main exports: squash 60% (1991), vanilla beans 14% (1991). Principal trading partners: Japan, Fiji, New Zealand, Australia.

Tuvalu Imports ($ million): 4 (1989). Exports ($ million): 0.06 (1989). Main imports : food and live animals 29.5% (1986), manufactured goods 25.2% (1986). Main exports: copra 86.4% (1986). Principal trading partners: Fiji, Australia, New Zealand.

Vanuatu Imports ($ million): 97 (1990). Exports ($ million): 19 (1990). Main imports: machinery and transport equipment 35.3% (1990), basic and miscellaneous manufactures 31.1% (1990). Main exports: copra 27.2% (1990), beef and veal 16.7% (1990). Principal trading partners: Netherlands, Japan, Australia, New Zealand.

Western Samoa Imports ($ million): 76 (1988). Exports ($ million): 15 (1988). Main imports: food 21.3% (1983), machinery 21.0% (1983). Main exports: coconut oil 37.2% (1988), taro 16.6% (1988). Principal trading partners: New Zealand, Australia, Japan, USA.

Australia

Official name: The Commonwealth of Australia.

Member of: UN, Commonwealth, ANZUS, OECD, South Pacific Forum.

Area: 7,682,300 km² (2 966 150 sq mi).

Population: 17,627,000 (1993 est).

Capital: Canberra 310,000 (including suburbs; 1991 census).

Other major cities: Sydney 3,699,000, Melbourne 3,154,000, Brisbane 1,327,000, Perth 1,193,000, Adelaide 1,050,000, Newcastle 433,000, Gold Coast 274,000, Wollongong 240,000, Hobart 184,000, Geelong 151,000, Townsville 114,000, Launceston 89,000, Cairns 76,000, Ballarat 75,000, Darwin 73,000, Bendigo 62,000, Rockhampton 61,000 (all including suburbs; 1991 census).

Language: English.

Religions: Anglican (26%), Roman Catholic (26%), Uniting Church in Australia (8%).

Education: Education is compulsory between the ages of six and 15. In 1990 the l iteracy rate was over 99.6%. There are 38 universities.

Defence: In 1992 the total armed strength was 63,200 - 28,600 in the army, 15,300 in the navy and 19,300 in the air force. The principal naval bases are Sydney, Cairns and Darwin.

Transport: There are 810,264 km (503,474 mi) of roads of which over 1200 km (745 mi) are motorways. There are six government-owned railway systems with a total track length of 37,295 km (23,174 mi). The main commercial shipping ports are Sydney, Newcastle, Melbourne, Port Kembla, Hay Point, Geelong, Port Hedland, Dampier, Brisbane, Gladstone, and Fremantle. The main international airports are Sydney, Melbourne, Perth, Brisbane, Adelaide, Hobart , Townsville, and Darwin.

Media: Because of the great distances between Australia's five main urban agglomerations, Australia's 71 daily newspapers are almost all regional. The government-funded ABC operates nationally providing one television and five radio networks. There are over 45 regional commercial television stations and 150 commercial radio stations.

GOVERNMENT

The Federal Parliament consists of two chambers elected by compulsory universal adult suffrage. The Senate has 76 members elected by proportional representation - 12 senators elected from each state for six years, 2 from both territories elected for three years. The House of Representatives has 148 members elected for three years. A Prime Minister, who commands a majority in the House of Representatives, is appointed by the Governor General, who is the representative of the British Queen as sovereign of Australia. The Prime Minister chairs the Federal Executive Council (or Cabinet), which is responsible to Parliament. Each state has its own government. The main political parties are the Australian Labor Party (ALP), the (conservative) Liberal Party of Australia (LP), the (conservative) National Party of Australia (NPA), the (liberal) Australian Democrat (AD)s, the Country Liberal Party (CLP) and the Greens (GWA). After the election held in 1994 a Labour (ALP) government was formed.

Party strength: ALP 80, LP 49, NPA 16, independent 2.

THE CABINET

Prime Minister: Paul Keating (ALP) .

Deputy Prime Minister, Minister for Housing and Regional Development: Brian Leslie Howe (ALP).

Minister for Aboriginal and Torres Strait Islander Affairs: Robert Edward Tickner (ALP).

Minister for Administrative Services: Francis Johh Walker (ALP).

Minister for Communications and the Arts, and Minister for Tourism: Michael John Lee (ALP).

Minister for Consumer Affairs: Jeannette McHugh (ALP).

Minister for Defence Science and Personnel: Gary Francis Punch (ALP).

Minister for Development Cooperation and Pacific Island Affairs: Gordon Neil Bilney (ALP).

Minister for Employment, Education and Training: Simon Crean (ALP).

Minister for Finance: Kim Christian Beazley (ALP).

Minister for Human Services and Health, and Minister assisting the PM for the Status of Women: Dr Carmen Mary Lawrence (ALP).

Minister for Industrial Relations and Minister for Transport: Laurence John Brereton (ALP).

Minister for Justice: Duncan Kerr (ALP).

Minister for Resources: David Peter Beddall (ALP).

Minister for Schools, Vocational Education and Training: Ross Vincent Free (ALP).

Minister for Social Security: Peter Jeremy Baldwin (ALP).

Minister for Veterans' Affairs: Con Sciacca (ALP).

Treasurer: Ralph Willis (ALP).

Assistant Treasurer: George Gear (ALP).

Attorney-General: Michael Hugh Lavarch (ALP).

Special Minister of State, Assistant Minister for Industrial Relations and Minister assisting the PM for Public Service Matters: Gary Thomas Johns (ALP).

STATES AND TERRITORIES

New South Wales Area: 801,600 km² (309,500 sq mi). Population: 6,000,000 (1993 est). Capital: Sydney.

Queensland Area: 1,727,200 km² (666,875 sq mi). Population: 3,095,000 (1993 est). Capital: Brisbane.

South Australia Area: 984,000 km² (379,925 sq mi). Population: 1,460,000 (1993 est). Capital: Adelaide.

Tasmania Area: 67,800 km² (26,175 sq mi). Population: 472,000 (1993 est). Capital: Hobart.

Victoria Area: 227,600 km² (87,875 sq mi). Population: 4,461,000 (1993 est). Capital: Melbourne.

Western Australia Area: 2,525,500 km² (975,100 sq mi). Population: 1,673,000 (1993 est). Capital: Perth.

Australian Capital Territory Area: 2400 km² (925 sq mi). Population: 298,000 (1993 est). Capital: Canberra. (The population given for Canberra above includes suburbs in New South Wales.)

Northern Territory Area: 1,346,200 km² (519,750 sq mi). Population: 168,000 (1993 est). Capital: Darwin.

GEOGRAPHY

Vast areas of desert cover most of the land in central and western Australia, a region of plateaux between 400 and 600 m (1300-2000 ft) with occasional higher regions, such as the Kimberley Plateau. In contrast to this arid, scarcely populated area - which covers more than 50% of the country - are the narrow coastal plains of the fertile, well-watered east coast where the majority of Australians live. Behind the plains - which range from temperate forest in the south, through subtropical woodland to tropical rain forest in Queensland - rise the Eastern Uplands, or Great Dividing Range. This is a line of ridges and plateaux, interrupted by basins, stretching from Cape York Peninsula in the north to the island of Tasmania. West of the uplands is the Great Artesian Basin extending from the Gulf of Carpentaria to the Murray River and Eyre Basins. Landforms in the basin include rolling plains, plateaux, salt lakes and river valleys. Between the Murray River and Eyre Basins are the Flinders and Mount Lofty Ranges. Many of Australia's rivers flow intermittently. Highest point: Mount Kosciusko 2230 m (7316 ft). Principal rivers: Murray, Darling, Lachlan, Flinders, Diamentina, Ashburton, Fitzroy. Climate: The north is tropical with wet summers (January to March) and dry winters. The north coast of Western Australia and the Northern Territory are subject to summer monsoons. The Queensland coast, which experiences tropical cyclones, has the heaviest rainfall, over 2500 mm (100 in) near Cairns. The interior is extremely hot and dry - over one third of Australia has less than 255 mm (10 in) of rain a year. The coastal fringes in the south are either temperate or subtropical, with winter rainfall, hot or warm summers and moderate winter temperatures. Winter snowfall is common in the highlands of the southeast and Tasmania.

ECONOMY

Since World War II, Australia's economy has been dominated by mining, and minerals now account for over 30% of the country's exports. Australia has major reserves of coal, petroleum and natural gas, uranium, iron ore, copper,

93

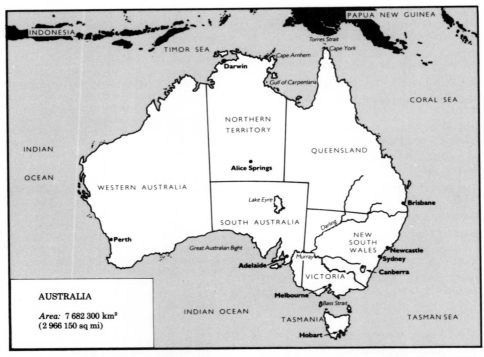

AUSTRALIA

Area: 7 682 300 km²
(2 966 150 sq mi)

nickel, bauxite, gold and diamonds. Manufacturing and processing are largely based upon these resources: iron and steel, construction, oil refining and petrochemicals, vehicle manufacturing and engineering are all prominent. The food-processing and textile industries are based upon agriculture. Australia's reliance on the agricultural sector has fallen considerably and in the 1990s there has been a planned reduction in the sheep population. However, the country is still the world's leading producer of wool. Major interests include sheep, cattle, cereals (in particular wheat), sugar (in Queensland) and fruit. A strong commercial sector, with banks and finance houses, adds to the diversity of the economy.

Currency: Australian dollar of 100 cents; 1US$ = 1.361 Australian dollars (June 1994).

GDP: US$308,000,000,000 (1993 est); US$17,303 per head.

RECENT HISTORY

In 1901, the Commonwealth of Australia was founded when the six British colonies of New South Wales, Queensland, South Australia, Tasmania, Victoria and Western Australia came together in a federation. Australia made an important contribution in World War I - one fifth of its servicemen were killed in action. The heroic landing at Gallipoli in the Dardanelles is commemorated with a day of remembrance in Australia. The Depression hit the country badly, but the interwar years did see international recognition of Australia's independence. World War II, during which the north was threatened by Japan, strengthened links with America. Australian troops fought in Vietnam and important trading partnerships have been formed with Asian countries. Since 1945, migrants from all over Europe have gained assisted passage to Australia, further diluting the British connection. Australia now has a close relationship with the USA and is a regional power in the South Pacific region. In the 1990s there was a marked growth in republicanism and the Labour Party leader, PM Paul Keating, came out in favour of an Australian republic by the year 2001.

Fiji

Official name: Matanitu Ko Viti (Republic of Fiji).

Member of: UN, South Pacific Forum.

Area: 18,376 km² (7095 sq mi).

Population: 762,000 (1993 est).

Capital: Suva 141,000 (city 70,000; 1988 census).

Other main town: Lautoka 29,000 (1988 census).

Languages: English (official), Fijian (48%), Hindi (46%).

Religions: Methodist (45%), Hindu (38%), Sunni Islam (7%).

Education: Education is freely available between the ages of six and 14 but is not compulsory. In 1986 the literacy rate was 87%. There is a university, which has centres in most Oceanian nations.

Defence: In 1992 the total armed strength was 5000. There is no military service.

Transport: There are 4821 km (2996 mi) of roads. Suva has a port and an international airport.

Media: There are two daily newspapers, a government-owned radio service (with five channels), two commercial radio stations and a television service.

GOVERNMENT
The 70-seat House of Representatives is elected for five years by universal adult suffrage - 37 members by Fijians (Melanesians), 27 by Indians, 1 by Rotumans, 5 by others. The 34-seat Senate comprises 24 members chosen by the 56-member traditional Council of Chiefs, 1 to represent Rotuma, and 9 appointed by the President. The Council appoints the President who, in turn, appoints a PM who commands a majority in the House. Political parties include the Fijian Political Party (FPP), the (multiracial) General Voters' Party (GUP), the (Indian) National Federation Party (NFP), the (right-wing nationalist) Fijian Nationalist United Front (FNUF), and the (largely Indian) Fiji Labour Party (FLP). After the election in February 1994 a FPP government was formed.

Party strength: FPP 31, NFP 20, FLP 7, GUP 4, others 8.

President: Kamisese Mara (FPP).

Prime Minister: Sitiveni Rabuka (FPP).

GEOGRAPHY
The mountainous larger islands are volcanic in origin. The smaller islands are mainly coral reefs. Highest point: Tomaniivi (Mount Victoria) 1323 m (4341 ft). Principal rivers: Rewa, Sigatoka, Navva, Nodi, Ba. Climate: Fiji experiences high temperatures and heavy rainfall with local variations.

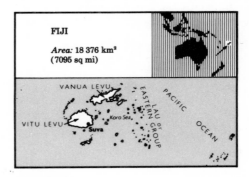

ECONOMY
Fiji's economy depends on agriculture, with sugar cane as the main cash crop. Copra, ginger, fish and timber are also exported. Tourism is increasing in importance.

Currency: Fiji dollar of 100 cents; 1US$ = 1.45 dollars (June 1994).

GDP: US$1,550,000,000 (1992); US$2070 per head.

RECENT HISTORY
Fiji became British in 1874. Indian labourers arrived to work on sugar plantations, reducing the Fijians, who retained ownership of most of the land, to a minority. Since independence (1970), racial tension and land disputes have brought instability. A military takeover in 1987 overthrew an Indian-led government and established a Fijian-dominated republic outside the Commonwealth. Fiji returned to civilian rule in 1990, with the resignation of the military officers from the cabinet. The new constitution guarantees political power for the native Melanese (Fijian) population.

Kiribati

Official name: Republic of Kiribati.

Member of: Commonwealth, South Pacific Forum.

Area: 717 km² (277 sq mi).

Population: 73,000 (1991 est).

Capital: Bairiki (on Tarawa) 25,000 (1990 census).

Languages: English (official), I-Kiribati.

Religions: Roman Catholic (over 50%), Kiribati Protestant (Congregational; over 40%).

Education: Education is compulsory between the ages of six and 14. In 1990 the literacy rate was estimated to be over 90%. There is no university but a higher education college offers degree-level courses.

Defence: Kiribati has no armed forces.

Transport: There are 640 km (398 mi) of roads. Tarawa is the main port. There are two international airports - one in South Tarawa; the other on Kiritimati Island.

Media: There are two weekly newspapers and a radio service which is run by a state corporation.

GOVERNMENT
The President and 39 members of the single-chamber Assembly (Maneaba ni Maungatabu) are elected by universal adult suffrage every four years. An additional member for Banaba is appointed to the Assembly, whose members nominate three or four of their number as presidential candidates. The President appoints a Cabinet of Ministers, which is responsible to the Assembly. All the members of the Assembly are independents, although a political party has been formed in opposition.

Acting President: Tekire Tameura (head of interim Council of State).

GEOGRAPHY
With the exception of the island of Banaba - which is composed of phosphate rock - Kiribati comprises three groups of small coral atolls which are widely scattered across about 5,000,000 km² (2,000,000 sq mi) of the Pacific Ocean. There are no significant rivers. Highest point: 81 m (265 ft) on Banaba. Climate: Kiribati has a maritime equatorial climate with high rainfall in the northern islands; the central and southern islands sometimes suffer from drought.

ECONOMY
Most islanders are involved in subsistence farming and fishing. The only significant export is copra. The sale of fishing licences to foreign fleets is an important source of foreign currency, but the islands remain one of the world's least developed territories. The government is encouraging the development of tourism. Kiribati is extremely low-lying and has been identified as one of the countries most vulnerable to any rise in sea-level that might occur as a result of global warming.

Currency: Kiribati uses Australian currency.

GDP: US$54,000,000 (1990); US$760 per head.

RECENT HISTORY
In the 18th century, the atolls were discovered by British sea captains, including Thomas Gilbert. The Gilbert Islands - which became British in 1892 - were occupied by Japan (1942-43). British nuclear weapons were tested on Christmas Island (1957-64). In 1979 the islands gained independence as Kiribati (pronounced Kiri-Bass).

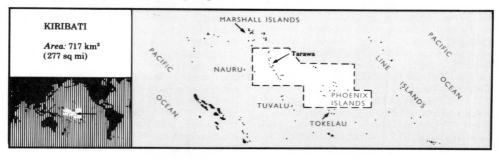

Marshall Islands

Official name: The Republic of the Marshall Islands.

Member of: UN, South Pacific Forum.

Area: 181 km² (70 sq mi).

Population: 52,000 (1993 est).

Capital: Dalap-Uliga-Darrit (on Majuro) 14,600 (1990 census).

Other main town: Ebeye 8000 (1990 census).

Languages: Marshallese and English (both official).

Religions: Various Protestant Churches (over 90%, including Assembly of God, Jehovah's Witnesses, Seventh-day Adventists, Church of Jesus Christ of Latter-day Saints), Roman Catholic minority.

Education: Education is compulsory between the ages of six and 14. In 1989 the literacy rate was estimated to be over 95%. There is a university centre of the University of the South Pacific.

Defence: The United States is responsible for the islands' defence.

Transport: There are no figures available for the length of roads in the Marshall Islands. There is an international airport on Majuro, which also has the main commercial shipping port.

Media: There are two weekly newspapers. There is a government-owned commercial radio station and US forces' television operates.

GOVERNMENT

The traditional 12-member Council of Chiefs (Iroij) has advisory and consultative powers in a limited range of matters. The 33-member Nitijela (Parliament) and the President are elected by universal adult suffrage for four years. The only political party is the (opposition) Ralik Ratak Democratic Party. The most recent election was in 1991.

President: Amata Kabua.

GEOGRAPHY

The Marshall Islands comprise two chains of about 870 principal reefs and small coral atolls and 34 main islands, with over 1150 islands

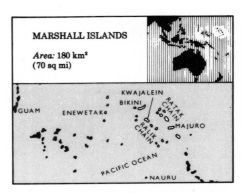

MARSHALL ISLANDS

Area: 180 km²
(70 sq mi)

and reefs in total. There are no significant rivers. Highest point: An unnamed point 6 m (20 ft) above sea-level. Climate: The climate is tropical with heavy rainfall.

ECONOMY

The islands have practically no resources and depend upon subsistence agriculture, tourism and US grants. The only significant export is copra. Fisheries are being developed. Since 1989 the Marshall Islands have had an international shipping register (a 'flag of convenience'), which has become a useful source of revenue. There is rising concern that the islands will not be economically viable when US aid, under the Compact of Free Association, runs out in 2001. Attempts to develop tourism have been hampered by a lack of communications.

Currency: The islands use US currency.

GDP: US$75,100,000 (1991); US$1577 per head.

RECENT HISTORY

The Marshall Islands were under Spanish (1875-85), German (1885-1914), and Japanese administration (1914-1945) before becoming part of the US Pacific Islands Trust Territory. They became internally self-governing in 1979. In 1986 US administration in the islands was formally terminated and the Marshall Islands became a sovereign republic, able to conduct its own foreign affairs, although under a Compact of Free Association the USA retains complete responsibility for the republic's defence and security until 2001. The UN did not recognize this new status of the Marshall Islands until December 1990, when the trusteeship was finally dissolved.

Micronesia, Federated States of

Official name: The Federated States of Micronesia.

Member of: UN, South Pacific Forum.

Area: 702 km² (271 sq mi).

Population: 103,000 (1993 est).

Capital: Palikir (on Pohnpei) 2000 (1990 est).

Other main towns: Wenn (formerly Moen) 10,400, Tol 6700, Kolonia 6300 (1990 est).

Languages: English, Trukese, Ponapean, Yapese, Kosraean. There are no official languages.

Religions: Various Protestant Churches (mainly Assembly of God, Jehovah's Witnesses and Seventh-day Adventists), Roman Catholic.

Education: Education is compulsory between the ages of six and 14. In 1989 the literacy rate was over 95%. There is no university.

Defence: The USA is responsible for defence.

Transport: There are 226 km (140 mi) of roads in the islands. Pohnpei and Chuuk have the main commercial shipping ports. There is an international airport in each of the four states.

Media: There are two weekly newspapers. There are four radio and three television stations.

GOVERNMENT
The President (who serves for four years) and the 14-member National Congress are elected by universal adult suffrage. The Congress comprises one senator elected from each of the four states for four years, and ten senators representing constituencies elected for two years. There are no political parties. The most recent election was in May 1991.

President: Bailey Olter.

MICRONESIAN STATES
Population figures are 1990 estimates.

Chuuk (formerly Truk) Area: 116 km² (45 sq mi). Population: 53,700. Capital: Wenn.

Kosrae Area: 109 km² (42 sq mi). Population: 7200. Capital: Kosrae.

Pohnpei (formerly Ponape) Area: 373 km² (144 sq mi). Population: 33,100. Capital: Kolonia.

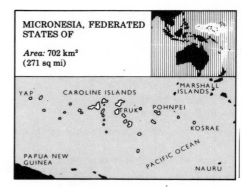

MICRONESIA, FEDERATED STATES OF

Area: 702 km² (271 sq mi)

Yap Area: 101 km² (39 sq mi). Population: 13,900. Capital: Colonia.

GEOGRAPHY
The Micronesian islands comprise over 600 islands in two main groups. The majority of the islands are low coral atolls, but Kosrae and Pohnpei are mountainous. Highest point: Mt Totolom 791 m (2595 ft). Climate: The climate is tropical with heavy rainfall.

ECONOMY
Apart from phosphate, the islands have practically no resources and depend upon subsistence agriculture, fishing, US grants and tourism.

Currency: Micronesia uses US currency.

GDP: US$157,400,000 (1989): US$1595 per head.

RECENT HISTORY
Previously known as the Caroline Islands, the islands were under Spanish (1874-99), German (1899-1914), and Japanese administration (1914-45) before becoming part of the US Pacific Islands Trust Territory. They became internally self-governing in 1979. In 1986 US administration in the islands was formally terminated and the Federated States became a sovereign republic, able to conduct its own foreign affairs, although under a Compact of Free Association the USA retains complete responsibility for the republic's defence and security until 2001. The UN did not recognize this new status of the Federated States until December 1990, when the trusteeship was finally dissolved.

Nauru

Official name: The Republic of Nauru.

Member of: Commonwealth (special member), South Pacific Forum.

Area: 21 km² (8 sq mi).

Population: 9400 (1990 est).

Capital: There is no official capital. Yaren - which is the largest settlement and the seat of all but one of the government ministries - is capital de facto. Domaneab is the other main settlement, but no population figure for either place is available.

Languages: Nauruan (official), English.

Religions: Nauruan Protestant Church (majority), Roman Catholic (minority).

Education: Education is compulsory between the ages of six and 16. The literacy rate was 99% in 1991. There is a university extension centre of the (Fijian-based) University of the South Pacific.

Defence: There are no armed forces; Australia is responsible for Nauru's defence.

Transport: There are about 20 km (13 mi) of roads. The island has a small airport, but the national airline (Air Nauru) operates a wide range of services throughout the Pacific. There is no shipping port on Nauru - goods have to be transferred to the shore by barge from ships moored offshore.

Media: Nauru has a weekly newspaper and a fortnightly newspaper. The island has a single radio station. The television service transmits (mainly) New Zealand programmes relayed by satellite.

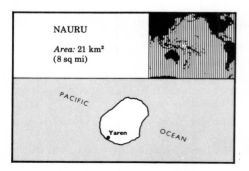

GOVERNMENT

The 18-member Parliament is elected by universal adult suffrage for three years. Parliament elects the President, who in turn appoints a Cabinet of Ministers. All of the members elected in 1992 are independents. There is only one formal political party, the (opposition) Democratic Party of Nauru.

President: Bernard Dowiyogo.

GEOGRAPHY

Nauru is a low-lying coral atoll. Most of the centre of the island has been turned into a 'lunar landscape' because of phosphate mining activities. There are no rivers. Highest point: an unnamed point 68 m (225 ft) on the central plateau. Climate: Nauru has a tropical climate which is tempered by maritime influences. Rainfall is heavy particularly between November and February.

ECONOMY

Nauru depends almost entirely upon the export of phosphate rock, stocks of which are expected to run out by 2010. Shipping and air services and 'tax haven' facilities are being developed to provide revenue when the phosphate is exhausted. The only settled and cultivated areas are in a narrow coastal strip between the beach and the 'lunar landscape' of the interior. Most of Nauru's drinking water has to be imported.

Currency: Nauru uses Australian currency (see pp. 92-94).

GDP: US$90,000,000 (1990 est); US$10,000 per head.

RECENT HISTORY

Germany annexed Nauru in 1888 following a request from German settlers on the island for protection during unrest between Nauru's 12 clans. Australia captured Nauru in 1914 and administered it - except for a period of Japanese occupation (1942-45) - until independence was granted in 1968. In the late 1980s Nauru increased its demands for the governments of Australia, New Zealand and the UK to pay for compensation towards the rehabilitation of areas that had been mined prior to independence. Nauru instituted legal proceedings when Australia refused compensation. In 1993 a settlement of the court case against Australia was achieved in favour of Nauru.

New Zealand

Official name: Dominion of New Zealand or Aotearoa (New Zealand in Maori).

Member of: UN, Commonwealth, ANZUS, South Pacific Forum, OECD.

Area: 269,057 km² (103,883 sq mi).

Population: 3,435,000 (1991 census).

Capital: Wellington 325,000 (city 150,000; 1991 census).

Other major cities: Auckland 885,000 (city 316,000), Manakau 227,000, North Shore 151,000), Christchurch 307,000 (city 293,000), Hamilton 149,000 (city 101,000), Napier with Hastings 110,000 (Napier city 52,000), Dunedin 109,000, Palmerston North 71,000, Rotorua 54,000, Invercargill 52,000, New Plymouth 49,000, Nelson 47,000, Whangarei 44,000, Wanganui 41,000 (all including suburbs; 1991 census).

Languages: English (official), Maori (1.5%).

Religions: Anglican (24%), Presbyterian (18%), Roman Catholic (15%), Methodist (5%).

Education: Education is compulsory between the ages of six and 15. The literacy rate was estimated to be virtually 100% in 1991. There are seven universities.

Defence: In 1993 the total armed strength was 10,900 - 4800 in the army, 2400 in the navy and 3700 in the air force. The main naval base is Auckland. There is no military service.

Transport: There are 146,655 km (56,624 mi) of roads and 4029 km (1556 mi) of privatized railways. Auckland, Wellington and Christchurch have international airports and the same cities are the main commercial shipping ports.

Media: There are 21 regional daily newspapers and no national press. Radio New Zealand operates three national and 35 community radio stations; Television New Zealand operates two national channels. There is also a commercial network plus satellite and cable networks.

GOVERNMENT

The 97-member House of Representatives is elected by universal adult suffrage (under a system of proportional representation) for three years to represent single-member constituencies, four of which have a Maori electorate and representative. The Governor General - the representative of the British Queen as sovereign of New Zealand - appoints a Prime Minister who commands a majority in the House. The PM, in turn, appoints a Cabinet, which is responsible to the House. For local government purposes New Zealand is divided into 16 regions, which are further divided into cities and districts. Chatham Islands, a separate district, are not included in any region. Tokelau is an autonomous island territory, which is legally part of the Dominion of New Zealand. The main political parties are the Labour Party (Lab), the (conservative) National Party (NP), the Alliance Party (All) and New Zealand First (NZF). Following the election held in November 1993 an NP government was formed.

Party strength: NP 50, Lab 45, All 2, NZF 2.

THE CABINET

Prime Minister: Jim Bolger (NP).

Deputy Prime Minister, Minister of Foreign Affairs and Trade and Minister of Pacific Island Affairs: Don McKinnon (NP).

Attorney-General, Minister of State Services, for Crown Health Enterprises and in charge of the Audit Department: Paul East (NP).

Minister of Accident Rehabilitation and of Compensation Insurance: Bruce Cliffe (NP).

Minister of Agriculture, of Forestry and of Racing: John Falloon (NP).

Minister of Commerce, of Industry, for Trade Negotiations, for State-Owned Enterprises, for Railways and of the Public Trust Office: Philip Burden (NP).

Minister for Conservation, of Lands, of Survey and Land Information, and in charge of the Valuation Department: Denis Marshall (NP).

Minister of Consumer Affairs: Katherine O'Regan (NP).

Minister of Defence, of Internal Affairs, of Civil Defence and in charge of War Pensions: Warren Cooper (NP).

Minister of Education: Dr Lockwood Smith (NP).

Minister of Employment and of Revenue: Wyatt Creech (NP).

Minister for the Environment, and for Research, Science and Technology: Simon Upton (NP).

Minister of Finance: W.F. Birch (NP).

Minister of Health and for Women's Affairs: Jenny Shipley (NP).

Minister of Housing and of Customs: Murray McCully (NP).

Minister of Immigration and of Business Development: Roger Maxwell (NP).

Minister of Justice, and Minister in charge of Treaty of Waitangi Negotiations, of Cultural Affairs and for Disarmament: Douglas Graham (NP).

Minister of Labour, of Fisheries and of Energy: Doug Kidd (NP).

Minister for Maori Affairs and Minister for the Police: John Luxton (NP).

Minister of Social Welfare and for Senior Citizens: Peter Gresham (NP).

Minister of State (Assistant Minister of Foreign Affairs and Trade): Robin Gray (NP).

Minister for Tourism, for Local Government and for Sport, Fitness and Leisure: John Danks (NP).

Minister of Transport, of Statistics, of Communication, of Information Technology, and of Broadcasting: Maurice Williamson (NP).

Minister of Youth Affairs: Roger McClay (NP).

REGIONS
Auckland Area: 5132 km² (1981 sq mi). Population: 954,000 (1991 census). Capital: Auckland.

Bay of Plenty Area: 12,473 km² (4816 sq mi). Population: 208,000 (1991 census). Capital: Whakatane.

Canterbury Area: 45,346 km² (17,508 sq mi). Population: 442,000 (1991 census). Capital: Christchurch.

Gisborne Area: 8352 km² (3225 sq mi). Population: 44,000 (1991 census). Capital: Gisborne.

Hawke's Bay Area: 14,164 km² (5469 sq mi). Population: 140,000 (1991 census). Capital: Napier.

Manuwatu-Wanganui Area: 22,215 km² (8577 sq mi). Population: 227,000 (1991 census). Capital: Palmerston North.

Marlborough Area: 10,520 km² (4062 sq mi). Population: 37,000 (1991 census). Capital: Blenheim.

Nelson Area: 442 km² (171 sq mi). Population: 47,000 (1991 census). Capital: Nelson.

Northland Area: 12,829 km² (4953 sq mi). Population: 132,000 (1991 census). Capital: Whangarei.

Otago Area: 31,991 km² (12,352 sq mi). Population: 186,000 (1991 census). Capital: Dunedin.

Southland Area: 32,676 km² (12,616 sq mi). Population: 103,000 (1991 census). Capital: Invercargill.

Taranaki Area: 7257 km² (2802 sq mi). Population: 107,000 (1991 census). Capital: New Plymouth.

Tasman Area: 10,458 km² (4038 sq mi). Population: 30,000 (1991 census). Capital: Westport.

Waikato Area: 24,653 km² (9519 sq mi). Population: 339,000 (1991 census). Capital: Hamilton.

Wellington Area: 8125 km² (3137 sq mi). Population: 403,000 (1991 census). Capital: Wellington.

West Coast Area: 23,336 km² (9010 sq mi). Population: 35,000 (1991 census). Capital: Greymouth.

Chatham Islands (not included in any region) Area: 963 km² (372 sq mi). Population: 800 (1991 census). Capital: Waitangi.

ISLAND TERRITORY
Tokelau Area: 13 km² (5 sq mi). Population: 1700 (1986 census). Capital: there is no capital; each atoll has its own administrative centre.

GEOGRAPHY
On South Island, the Southern Alps run from north to south, and in the southwest reach the sea in the deeply indented coast of Fjordland. The Canterbury Plains lie to the east of the mountains. North Island is mainly hilly with isolated mountains, including volcanoes - two of which are active. Lowlands on North Island are largely restricted to coastal areas and the Waikato Valley. Highest point: Mount Cook 3754 m (12,315 ft) - before a major rock slide

reduced the height of the mountain in December 1991, Mount Cook stood at 3764 m (12,349 ft). Principal rivers: Waikato, Clutha, Waihou, Rangitaiki, Mokau, Wanganui, Manawatu. Climate: The climate is temperate, although the north is warmer. Rainfall is abundant almost everywhere, but totals vary considerably with altitude and aspect, rising to over 6350 mm (250 in) on the west coast of South Island.

ECONOMY

The majority of New Zealand's export earnings come from agriculture, in particular meat, wool and dairy products. Forestry is expanding and supports an important pulp and paper industry. Apart from coal, lignite, natural gas and gold, the country has few natural resources, although its considerable hydroelectric-power potential has been exploited to produce plentiful cheap electricity - an important basis of New Zealand's manufacturing industry. Natural gas - from the Kapuni Field on North Island and the Maui Field off the Taranaki coast - is converted to liquid fuel. Despite having only a small domestic market and being remote from the world's major industrial powers, New Zealand has a high standard of living. In the early 1990s, inflation has fallen, economic growth is up and the country has come out of recession. In February 1994 unemployment stood at 9%.

Currency: New Zealand dollar (NZD) of 100 cents; 1US$ = 1.701 NZD (May 1994).

GDP: US$42,000,000,000 (1993 est); US$11,998 per head.

RECENT HISTORY

North Island was ceded to the British Crown by Maori chiefs under the Treaty of Waitangi (1840), while South Island was claimed by right of discovery. The 1840s were marked by fierce armed resistance to British settlement by the Maoris, the majority of whom live in North Island. Relations between the Maoris and the white settlers deteriorated further during the 1850s as the colonists sought more land and Maori chiefs increasingly refused to sell it. When troops were used to evict Maoris from disputed lands in Waitara, war broke out (1860). Fighting continued for most of the decade in North Island, and guerrilla action in the King Country was not suppressed until 1870. The Maori Wars retarded the European settlement of North Island, while from 1875 to

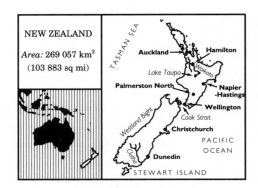

1900 the discovery of gold and the introduction of refrigerated ships to export meat and dairy products stimulated the colonization and economy of South Island. However, by the beginning of the 20th century, North Island was dominant again. By 1911 migrants from Britain had boosted the country's population to 1,000,000. Subsequent immigration has remained overwhelmingly British, although there are sizeable communities of Samoans, Cook Islanders, Croats and Dutch. Liberal governments (1891-1912) pioneered many reforms and social measures, including votes for women (1893) and the world's first old-age pensions (1898). Dominion status was granted in 1907, although the country did not formally acknowledge its independent status until 1947. In World War I, New Zealand fought as a British ally in Europe, achieving distinction in the disastrous Allied expedition to the Gallipoli peninsula during the campaign against Turkey (1915). When Japan entered World War II in 1941, New Zealand's more immediate security was threatened. The major role played by the USA in the Pacific War led to New Zealand's postwar alliance with Australia and America in the ANZUS pact, and the country sent troops to support the Americans in Vietnam. The entry of Britain into the EC in 1973 restricted the access of New Zealand's agricultural products to what had been their principal market. Since then New Zealand has been forced to seek new markets, particularly in the Far and Middle East. Under Labour governments (1972-75 and 1984-90), the country adopted an independent foreign and defence policy. Since 1990 the National (conservative) government has sharply restricted the welfare state.

Papua New Guinea

Official name: The Independent State of Papua New Guinea.

Member of: UN, Commonwealth, South Pacific Forum.

Area: 462,840 km² (178,704 sq mi).

Population: 3,918,000 (1993 est).

Capital: Port Moresby 193,000 (1990 census).

Other main cities: Lae 81,000, Madang 27,000, Wewak 23,000 (1990 census).

Languages: English (official), Pidgin English, Motu, and over 700 other local languages.

Religions: Roman Catholic (33%), various Protestant Churches (over 60%).

Education: Education is freely available between the ages of seven and 13, but it is not compulsory. In 1990 the literacy rate was 52%. There are two universities.

Defence: In 1993 the total armed strength was 3800 - 3200 in the army, 500 in the navy, 100 in the air force. There is no military service.

Transport: There are 19,736 km (12,263 mi) of roads. Port Moresby, the main port, has an international airport.

Media: There is a single daily newspaper. There are three radio services and a television channel.

GOVERNMENT

A 109-member Parliament is elected for five years by universal adult suffrage. The Governor General - the representative of the British Queen as sovereign of Papua New Guinea - appoints a Prime Minister who commands a majority in Parliament. The PM, in turn, appoints a Cabinet, which is responsible to Parliament. Each of the 20 provinces has its own government. The main political parties are the People's Democratic Movement (PDM), the Pangu Party, the National Party (NP), the (socialist) Melanesian Alliance (MA), the People's Action Party (PAP), the People's Progress Party (PPP), the Melanesian United Front (MUF), and the League for National Advancement (LNA). After the election held in June 1992 a PDM-PPP-LNA government was formed.

Party strength: Pangu 22, PDM 15, PAP 13, PPP 10, MA 9, others 9, ind 30.

THE CABINET

includes

Prime Minister: Paias Wingti (PDM).

Deputy Prime Minister and Minister for Foreign Affairs: Sir Julius Chan (PPP).

Minister for Agriculture and Livestock: Roy Evara (ind).

Minister for Commerce and Industry: David Mai (PPP).

Minister for Communications: Martin Thompson (LNA).

Minister for Correctional Institutions: John Kamb (PDM).

Minister for Defence: Paul Tohian (PPP).

Minister for Education: Andrew Baing (PPP).

Minister for Energy Development: Thomas Pelika (LNA).

Minister for the Environment: Parry Zeipi (ind).

Minister for Finance and Planning: Masket Iangalio (PDM).

Minister for Forests: Tim Neville (ind).

Minister of Health: Francis Koimanrea (ind).

Minister for Home Affairs: Andrew Psoai (PPP).

Minister for Housing: John Jaminan (PDM).

Minister for Justice and Attorney-General: Philemon Embel (PDM).

Minister for Labour and Employment: Castan Maibawa (ind).

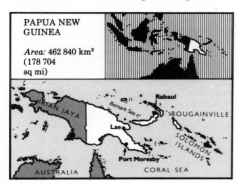

PAPUA NEW GUINEA

Area: 462 840 km² (178 704 sq mi)

Rabaul
Bismark Sea
BOUGAINVILLE
Lae
IRIAN JAYA
SOLOMON ISLANDS
Port Moresby
AUSTRALIA
CORAL SEA

Minister for Lands: Sir Albert Kipalan (ind).

Minister for Mining and Petroleum: John Kaputin (ind).

Minister for Public Service: John Orea (PAP).

Minister of State: Michael Ogio (PDM).

Minister for Tourism and Civil Aviation: Avusi Tanao (PDM).

Minister for Transport: Roy Yaki (PDM).

Minister for Works: Albert Karo (PDM).

PROVINCES
Population figures are 1990 estimates.

Central Province Area: 29,500 km² (11,400 sq mi). Population: 134,000. Capital: Port Moresby.

Eastern Highlands Area: 11,200 km² (4300 sq mi). Population: 333,000. Capital: Goroka.

East New Britain Area: 15,500 km² (6000 sq mi). Population: 151,000. Capital: Rabaul.

East Sepik Area: 42,800 km² (16,550 sq mi). Population: 276,000. Capital: Wewak.

Enga Area: 12,800 km² (4950 sq mi). Population: 194,000. Capital: Wabag.

Gulf Area: 34,500 km² (13,300 sq mi). Population: 74,000. Capital: Kerema.

Madang Area: 29,000 km² (11,200 sq mi). Population: 262,000. Capital: Madang.

Manus Area: 2100 km² (800 sq mi). Population: 30,000. Capital: Lorengau.

Milne Bay Area: 14,000 km² (5400 sq mi). Population: 155,000. Capital: Alotau (Samara).

Morobe Area: 34,500 km² (13,300 sq mi). Population: 404,000. Capital: Lae.

New Ireland Area: 9600 km² (3700 sq mi). Population: 80,000. Capital: Kavieng.

North Solomons (formerly Bougainville) Area: 9300 km² (3600 sq mi). Population: 160,000. Capital: Arawa (Buka).

Oro (formerly Northern Province) Area: 22,800 km² (8800 sq mi). Population: 96,000. Capital: Popondetta.

Sandaun (formerly West Sepik) Area: 36,300 km² (14,000 sq mi). Population: 131,000. Capital: Vanimo.

Simbu (formerly Chimbu) Area: 6100 km² (2350 sq mi). Population: 193,000. Capital: Kundiawa.

Southern Highlands Area: 23,800 km² (9200 sq mi). Population: 278,000. Capital: Mendi.

Western Province Area: 99,300 km² (38,350 sq mi). Population: 100,000. Capital: Daru.

Western Highlands Area: 8500 km² (3300 sq mi). Population: 330,000. Capital: Mount Hagen.

West New Britain Area: 21,000 km² (8100 sq mi). Population: 118,000. Capital: Kimbe.

National Capital District Area: 260 km² (100 sq mi). Population: 174,000. Capital: Port Moresby.

GEOGRAPHY
Broad swampy plains surround New Guinea's mountainous forested interior. In the east, the country includes the Bismarck archipelago (New Britain, New Ireland and the Admiralty Islands) and the northern Solomon Islands (including Bougainville). Highest point: Mount Wilhelm 4509 m (14,493 ft). Principal rivers: Fly (with Strickland), Sepik. Climate: The country experiences a tropical climate with high temperatures and heavy monsoonal rainfall.

ECONOMY
Agriculture occupies over 80% of the labour force. Most Papuans are subsistence farmers, although agricultural exports include palm oil, copra and cocoa. The mainstay of the economy is minerals, including large reserves of copper, gold, silver and petroleum.

Currency: Kina of 100 toea; 1US$ = 0.945 Kina (June 1994).

GDP: US$3,853,000,000; US$950 per head.

RECENT HISTORY
European colonization was not attempted until 1828 when the Dutch claimed western New Guinea. A British protectorate, established in the SE in 1884, was transferred to Australia (1906) and renamed Papua. Northeast New Guinea came under German administration in 1884, but was occupied by Australian forces in 1914. From 1942 to 1945 Japanese forces occupied New Guinea and part of Papua. In 1949 Australia combined the administration of the territories, which achieved independence as Papua New Guinea in 1975. Bougainville island - a major source of copper - attempted to secede (1990-92). Fighting on the island diminished in 1992 and peace talks began, but the dispute continues.

Solomon Islands

Member of: UN, Commonwealth, South Pacific Forum.

Area: 27,556 km² (10,639 sq mi).

Population: 349,000 (1993 est).

Capital: Honiara 37,000 (1991 est).

Other main town: Gizo 3700 (1991 est).

Languages: English (official), Pidgin English, over 85 local languages (85%).

Religions: Anglican (34%), Roman Catholic (19%), other Christian Churches.

Education: Education is not compulsory but is available between the ages of seven and 13. In 1985 the literacy rate was 60%. There is a university centre.

Defence: There are no armed forces.

Transport: There are 2100 km (1300 mi) of roads. Honiara, the main port, has an international airport.

Media: There are three weekly papers and a single (state-run) radio station.

GOVERNMENT
The 47-member National Parliament - which is elected by universal adult suffrage for four years - elects a Prime Minister who appoints a Cabinet. A Governor General is the representative of the British Queen as sovereign of the islands. The main political parties are the Group for National Unity (GNUR), the People's Alliance Party (PAP), the National Action Party (NAP), the Labour Party (Lab), the United Party (UP), the Christian Fellowship Group (CFG) and the National Front for Progress (NFP). The most recent election was in May 1993. A PAP-NAP-Lab-UP-CFG-NFP coalition was formed in 1993.

Party strength: Coalition 24, GNUR 23.

Prime Minister: Francis Billy Hilly (ind).

PROVINCES
Population figures are 1991 estimates.

Central Islands Area: 1286 km² (497 sq mi). Population: 21,000. Capital: Tulagi.

Guadalcanal Area: 5336 km² (2060 sq mi). Population: 61,000. Capital: Honiara.

Isabel Area: 4136 km² (1597 sq mi). Population: 16,500. Capital: Buala.

Makira Area: 3188 km² (1231 sq mi). Population: 25,000. Capital: Kira Kira.

Malaita Area: 4225 km² (1631 sq mi). Population: 87,000. Capital: Auki.

Temotu Area: 865 km² (334 sq mi). Population: 16,500. Capital: Santa Cruz.

Western Province Area: 9312 km² (3595 sq mi). Population: 65,000. Capital: Gizo.

Capital Territory Area: 22 km2 (8 sq mi). Population: 37,000. Capital: Honiara.

GEOGRAPHY
The mountainous volcanic Solomons comprise six main islands and several hundred small islands. There are no significant rivers. Highest point: Mount Makarakomburu 2447 m (8028 ft). Climate: It is tropical, with temperature and rainfall maxima from November to April.

ECONOMY
Subsistence farming occupies 30% of the labour force. Copra, cocoa and coconuts are exported. Lumbering is the main industry.

Currency: Solomon Islands dollar of 100 cents: 1US$ = 3.254 dollars (June 1994).

GDP: US$238,000,000 (1992); US$710 per head.

RECENT HISTORY
The Solomons became a British protectorate in 1893. Occupied by the Japanese (1942-45), the islands saw fierce fighting, including a major battle for Guadalcanal. Independence was gained in 1978.

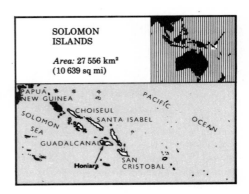

Tonga

Official name: Pule'anga Fakatu'i'o Tonga (The Kingdom of Tonga).

Member of: Commonwealth, South Pacific Forum.

Area: 748 km² (289 sq mi).

Population: 99,000 (1993 est).

Capital: Nuku'alofa 28,900 (1986 est).

Other major town: Mu'a 4000 (1986 est).

Languages: Tongan and English (both official).

Religions: Free Wesleyan Methodist (43%; offi-

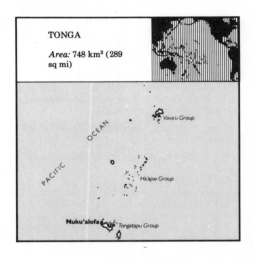

TONGA

Area: 748 km² (289 sq mi)

Vava'u Group

OCEAN

PACIFIC

Ha'apai Group

Nuku'alofa Tongatapu Group

cial), Roman Catholic (16%), Church of Jesus Christ of Latter-day Saints (12%), Free Church of Tonga (11%).

Education: Education is compulsory between the ages of six and 14. In 1985 the literacy rate was 90-95%. There is a university-level institute.

Defence: The national police (defence) force has 300 personnel.

Transport: There are 386 km (240 mi) of roads. Nuku'alofa is the main port and has an international airport.

Media: There are two weekly newspapers, a radio statio and a relayed television station.

GOVERNMENT

Tonga is a constitutional monarchy. The King appoints a Prime Minister and other Ministers to the Privy Council, which acts as a Cabinet. The 31-member Legislative Assembly comprises the King, the Privy Council, 9 hereditary nobles (chosen by their peers) and 9 representatives of the people elected for three years by universal adult suffrage. There is a single political party, the pro-reform People's Democratic Movement (PDM). The most recent election was in 1993.

Party strength: Non-party 22, PDM 6, independents 3.

King: King Taufa'ahau Tupou IV (succeeded upon the death of his mother, 15 December 1965).

Prime Minister: Baron Vaea.

GEOGRAPHY

The 172 Tongan islands - 36 of which are inhabited - comprise a low limestone chain in the east and a higher volcanic chain in the west. There are no significant rivers. Highest point: Kao 1030 m (3380 ft). Climate: The climate is warm with heavy rainfall.

ECONOMY

Agriculture involves most Tongans, with yams, cassava and taro being grown as subsistence crops. Coconut products are the main exports. Because of the system of land tenure and the increase in population, there is a shortage of farming land.

Currency: Pa'anga of 100 seniti; 1US$ = 1.372 pa'angas; the pa'anga is on a par with the Australian dollar.

GDP: US$136,000,000 (1992); US$1350 per head.

RECENT HISTORY

Civil war in the first half of the 19th century was ended by King George Tupou I (reigned 1845-93), who reunited Tonga, preserved its independence and gave it a modern constitution. From 1900 to 1970 Tonga was a British protectorate. Since 1987 pressure for constitutional reform has increased, particularly since the election of six pro-democracy commoners of the PDM in the 1993 election.

Tuvalu

Member of: Commonwealth (special member), South Pacific Forum.

Area: 26 km² (10 sq mi).

Population: 9500 (1993 est).

Capital: Fongafale (on Funafuti) 3400 (1990 est).

Languages: Tuvaluan and English.

Religion: (Congregational) Protestant Church of Tuvalu (97%), Seventh-day Adventist minority.

Education: Education is compulsory between the ages of six and 12. In 1990 the literacy rate was estimated to be 45%. There is a university extension centre of the (Fijian-based) University of the South Pacific.

Defence: There are no armed forces. (The 32-member police force is responsible for security.)

Transport: There are 8 km (5 mi) of roads in Tuvalu. Water transport between islands is the principal means of travel. There is a deep-water port and an international airport on the island of Funafuti.

Media: There is a fortnightly newspaper and a single radio station.

GOVERNMENT
The 12-member Parliament - which is elected by universal adult suffrage for four years - chooses a Prime Minister who appoints other Ministers. A Governor General represents the British Queen as sovereign of Tuvalu. There are no political parties. There were two elections in 1993.

Prime Minister: Kamuta Laatasi.

GEOGRAPHY
Tuvalu comprises nine small low-lying atolls, five of which enclose large lagoons. The islands are so low-lying that it has been suggested that Tuvalu would be one of the first countries at risk from inundation if a rise in sea level were to follow from global warming. There are no rivers. Highest point: an unnamed point, 6 m (20 ft). Climate: Tuvalu experiences high temperatures and heavy rainfall of 3000-4000 mm (120-160 in) per year.

ECONOMY
Subsistence farming - based on coconuts, pigs and poultry - involves the majority of the population. The only export is copra from coconuts and the country is vulnerable to frequent fluctuations in the price of this commodity on the

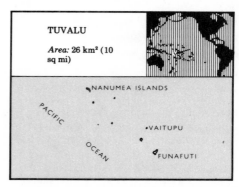

TUVALU

Area: 26 km² (10 sq mi)

NANUMEA ISLANDS

PACIFIC

VAITUPU

OCEAN

FUNAFUTI

international market. Tuvalu has a permanent trade deficit. Tuvalu has been identified by the UN as one of the world's least developed nations. It has a poor infrastructure, deficient communications, few resources, and a high rate of population growth. The migration of people from the outlying islands to the growing, and already overcrowded, urban area of Fongafale on Funafuti has added to the country's problems.

Currency: Tuvalu dollar of 100 cents; 1US$ = 1.37 Tuvalu dollars (June 1994); the Tuvalu dollar is pegged to the Australian dollar.

GDP: US$8,750,000 (1990); US$967 per head.

RECENT HISTORY
Tuvalu was claimed for Britain in 1892 as the Ellice Islands, which became linked administratively with the Gilbert Islands. A referendum in 1974 showed a majority of Polynesians in the Ellice Islands in favour of separation from the Micronesians of the Gilbert Islands (Kiribati). Independence was achieved as Tuvalu in 1978. In 1993 political turmoil between the supporters of two rival candidates for the premiership led to two general elections and the eventual election of a compromise candidate. The government of Tuvalu has publicized the country's vulnerability to any rise in sea level as a result of the 'greenhouse effect'.

107

Vanuatu

Official name: The Republic of Vanuatu or La République de Vanuatu.

Member of: UN, Commonwealth, South Pacific Forum.

Area: 12,189 km² (4706 sq mi).

Population: 160,000 (1993 est).

Capital: Port-Vila 19,000 (1991 est).

Other major town: Luganville 7000 (1991 est).

Languages: English (official; 60%), French (official; 40%), Bislama (national; 82% as a first language), and 130 other local dialects.

Religions: Presbyterian (33%), Anglican (30%), animist (20%), Roman Catholic (17%).

Education: Education is freely available between the ages of six and 11 but is not compulsory. In 1990 the literacy rate was estimated to be over 65%. There is a university centre of the University of the South Pacific.

Defence: There is a 300-strong paramilitary force.

Transport: There are 1062 km (660 mi) of roads. Port Vila and Luganville are the principal ports; there is an international airport at Bauerfield.

Media: There is a single weekly newspaper. A government-owned company provides a radio and television service.

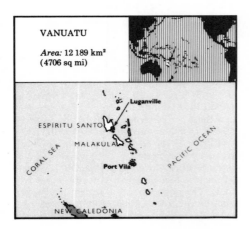

VANUATU
Area: 12 189 km²
(4706 sq mi)

Luganville

ESPIRITU SANTO

CORAL SEA

MALAKULA

PACIFIC OCEAN

Port Vila

NEW CALEDONIA

GOVERNMENT

The 46-member Parliament is elected for four years by universal adult suffrage. It elects a Prime Minister who appoints a Council of Ministers. The President is elected for five years by Parliament and the Presidents of Regional Councils. The main political parties include the (socialist) Vanuaaku Pati (VP), the (centre-right) Union of Moderate Parties (UMP), the (centre-right) National United Party (NUP), the Melanesian Progressive Party (MPP), the (socialist) Our Land Party (OLP) and a number of regional parties. After the election held in December 1991 a UMP-NUP coalition was formed.

Party strength: UMP 19, VP 12, NUP 10, others 5.

President: Jean-Marie Leye (UMP).

Prime Minister: Maxim Carlot (UMP).

GEOGRAPHY

Vanuatu comprises over 75 islands, some of which are mountainous and include active volcanoes. There are no significant rivers. Highest point: Mt Tabwebesana 1888 m (6195 ft). Climate: Vanuatu's tropical climate is moderated by southeast trade winds from May to October.

ECONOMY

Subsistence farming occupies the majority of the labour force. The main exports include copra, fish and cocoa. In 1993-94 the falling world price of copra led to economic difficulties. Tourism (in particular from Australia) is increasingly important and, along with agricultural diversification, features prominently in the government's development plans.

Currency: Vatu of 100 centimes; 1US$ = 113.59 vatus.

GDP: US$188,000,000 (1992); US$1210 per head.

RECENT HISTORY

British and French commercial interests in the 19th century resulted in joint control over the islands - then known as the New Hebrides - and the establishment of a condominium in 1906. The islands gained independence as Vanuatu in 1980, but have been troubled by attempted secession and political unrest.

Western Samoa

Official name: The Independent State of Western Samoa.

Member of: UN, Commonwealth, South Pacific Forum.

Area: 2831 km² (1093 sq mi).

Population: 163,000 (1993 est).

Capital: Apia 33,000 (1991 census).

Languages: English and Samoan (official).

Religions: Congregational (47%), Roman Catholic (22%), Methodist (15%).

Education: Education is compulsory between the ages of six and 15. In 1990 the literacy rate was 97%. There is a single university.

Defence: There are no armed forces. Defence remains the responsibility of New Zealand.

Transport: There are 2085 km (1296 mi) of roads. Apia has a port and an international airport.

Media: There are four weekly newspapers and a government-owned radio and television service.

GOVERNMENT
The 49-member Assembly (Fono) is elected for three years by universal adult suffrage. (The

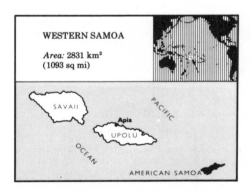

WESTERN SAMOA

Area: 2831 km²
(1093 sq mi)

SAVAII

PACIFIC

Apia

UPOLU

OCEAN

AMERICAN SAMOA

term of the current Assembly has been extended by two years.) Only members of the Matai - the elected clan leaders - are eligible to stand for election. The current head of state is analogous to a constitutional monarch, but future heads of state will be elected for a five-year term by the Assembly. The head of state appoints a Prime Minister who commands a majority in the Assembly. The PM, in turn, appoints a Council of Ministers, who are responsible to the Assembly. Political parties include the Human Rights Protection Party (HRPP), the Samoan National Development Party (SNDP) and the Samoan Democracy Party (SDP). After the election held in 1991 an HRPP government was formed.

Party strength: HRPP 26, SNDP 18, others 5.

Head of state: Malietoa Tanumafili II.

Prime Minister: Tofilau Eti Alesana (HRPP).

GEOGRAPHY
The country consists of seven small islands and two larger and higher volcanic islands. There are no significant rivers. Highest point: Mauga Silisli 1857 m (6094 ft). Climate: The islands have a tropical climate with high temperatures and very heavy rainfall.

ECONOMY
The majority of Samoans are involved in subsistence agriculture. Copra (from coconuts), cocoa and bananas are the main exports. The country - which is one of the poorest in the world - has suffered through fluctuations in the prices of its main exports. Large numbers of Samoans migrate to New Zealand to work.

Currency: Tala (WST) of 100 sene; 1US$ = 2.558 WST.

GDP: US$153,000,000 (1992); US$940 per head.

RECENT HISTORY
From the 1870s the USA, Britain and Germany became active in Samoa, and in 1899 the three rival powers divided the group, giving the nine western islands to Germany. New Zealand occupied the German islands in 1914, and administered Western Samoa until independence was granted in 1962. Major constitutional reforms in 1990 introduced universal adult suffrage and reduced the power of the Matai, the elected clan leaders. Relations with New Zealand have not always been easy since independence - immigration quotas have been a source of some problems, particularly as large numbers of Western Samoans have overstayed the duration of their working permits.

Other territories

AMERICAN SAMOA

Status: an unincorporated United States external territory.

Area: 197 km² (96 sq mi).

Population: 46,800 (1990 census).

Capital: Fagatogo (in Pago Pago urban area).

Main town: Pago Pago 4000 (1990 census).

Government: A Governor is elected by universal adult suffrage for four years and a 21-member House of Representatives for two years. The 18-member Senate is elected for four years according to Samoan tradition by chiefs. The islands return a non-voting member to the US Congress.

Geography: The territory comprises six main rocky tropical islands (of which Tutuila is the largest), plus Swain's Island to the north.

Economy: The main employers are tuna-canning and tourism. Most islanders are engaged in subsistence farming and fishing. Lack of resources and a rapidly increasing population have forced many islanders to migrate to the USA.

Recent History: The USA established a naval base at Pago Pago in 1878. The local chiefs ceded the islands to the USA in 1904. The islands became an unincorporated US territory in 1922 and received internal self-government in 1948.

ASHMORE AND CARTIER ISLANDS

Status: an Australian external territory.

Area: 5 km² (2 sq mi).

Population: uninhabited.

Geography: The tropical islands are sandy and coral reefs.

Economy: Indonesian fishermen fish in the territorial waters of the islands.

Recent History: The islands were annexed by Britain in 1878 (Ashmores) and 1931 (Cartier). They were transferred to Australia in 1931 and became an external territory in 1978.

COOK ISLANDS

Status: self-governing territory of New Zealand.

Area: 237 km² (92 sq mi).

Population: 19,000 (1991 est).

Capital: Avarua (on Rarotonga) 3000 (1991 est).

Government: The 24-member Parliament is elected for five years by universal adult suffrage. A Premier and six Ministers are responsible to Parliament. Prime Minister: Geoffrey Henry.

Geography: The 15 tropical Cook Islands comprise a northern group of mountainous volcanic islands and a southern group of coral atolls.

Economy: Papayas are the main export. Other sources of income include 'offshore' banking, postage stamps, and money sent home by over 20,000 Cook Islanders working in New Zealand.

Recent History: The Cook Islands became British in 1888 and were ceded to New Zealand in 1901. In 1965 the islands became self-governing in free association with New Zealand. They are empowered to gain independence unilaterally.

CORAL SEA ISLANDS TERRITORY

Status: an external territory of Australia.

Area: 8 km² (5 sq mi).

Population: no permanent inhabitants.

Geography: The tiny widely-scattered islands are very low-lying outcrops of sand and coral.

Recent History: The groups of atolls were constituted as the Coral Sea Islands Territory in 1969.

FRENCH POLYNESIA

Status: an overseas French territory.

Area: 4167 km² (1609 sq mi).

Population: 199,000 (1991 est).

Capital: Papeete 79,000 (1988 est).

Government: The 51-member Assembly is elected by universal adult suffrage for five years. A Council of Ministers is elected by the Assembly. The territory elects two deputies to the French Assembly and a senator to the Senate.

Geography: The territory has over 130 mainly mountainous tropical islands and coral atolls in five groups in the east Pacific - the

Windward Islands (including Tahiti), the Leeward Islands, and the Tuamotu, Austral and Marquesas Islands. The territory includes Clipperton Island to the south of Mexico.

Economy: Tourism is the main foreign-currency earner. Coconut oil and pearls are exported.

Recent History: The islands - which were annexed by France between 1791 and 1900 - became an overseas territory of the French Republic in 1958.

GUAM
Status: an unincorporated territory of the USA.

Area: 541 km² (209 sq mi).

Population: 133,000 (1990 census).

Capital: Agaña 4900 (city 1100; 1990 census).

Largest town: Dededo 32,000 (1990 census).

Government: Guam elects a Governor by universal adult suffrage for four years, a 21-member Legislature for two years and a non-voting member to the US House of Representatives.

Geography: Guam is a tropical island in the western Pacific. The north is a limestone plateau; the south comprises volcanic hills.

Economy: Guam, a duty-free port, attracts large numbers of Japanese tourists. US military bases are the major source of employment.

Recent History: After the Spanish-American War Guam was ceded by Spain to the USA (1898). Guam was occupied by the Japanese from 1941 to 1944, and became an unincorporated US territory in 1950.

HOWLAND, BAKER AND JARVIS ISLANDS
Status: unincorporated US territories.

Area: 5 km² (2 sq mi).

Population: uninhabited.

Government: The islands are the responsibility of the US Department of the Interior.

Geography: These three arid tropical coral islands are situated in the South Pacific.

Recent History: The islands were claimed by the USA in 1857. In 1936 the islands became unincorporated US territories.

JOHNSTON ATOLL
Status: an unincorporated territory of the USA.

Area: 1.3 km² (0.5 sq mi).

Population: no permanent population.

Government: Johnston Atoll is under the control of the US Department of Defense.

Geography: Johnston Atoll, a semi-circular reef, comprises four small tropical coral islands.

Recent History: The atoll was claimed by the USA in 1856 in order to exploit its guano deposits. A US air base was established in 1941. The atoll has since been used in association with nuclear-weapons testing.

KINGMAN REEF
Status: an unincorporated territory of the USA.

Area: 0.03 km² (0.01 sq mi).

Population: uninhabited.

Government: The reef is under the control of the US Department of Defense.

Geography: Only parts of Kingman Reef, a coral atoll, are permanently above sea level.

Recent History: Kingman Reef has been a US possession since 1922.

MIDWAY ISLANDS
Status: an unincorporated territory of the USA.

Area: 5 km² (2 sq mi).

Population: no permanent population. There is a US military establishment in the islands.

Government: The islands are administered by the US Department of Defense.

Geography: The subtropical Midway Islands, northwest of Hawaii, form a circular atoll.

Recent History: Midway - a US possession since 1867 - came under the control of the US Navy (1903). The Battle of Midway (1942) was a turning point in World War II in the Pacific.

NEW CALEDONIA
Status: a French overseas territory.

Area: 19,103 km² (7376 sq mi).

Population: 164,000 (1989 census).

Capital: Nouméa 65,000 (1989 census).

Government: Elections are held every six years for the assemblies of the three autonomous provinces - North, South and the Loyalty Islands. A provincial government is responsi-

111

ble to each Assembly. The three Assemblies sit together as the 54-member Congress. The territory is represented in the French National Assembly by two deputies and in the Senate by a senator.

Geography: New Caledonia island is a long, narrow, mountainous semi-tropical island 1500 km (900 mi) east of Queensland. The Loyalty Islands, Isle of Pines, the Beleep and Chesterfield Islands are all part of the the territory.

Economy: Tourism and the production of nickel, the main foreign-currency earners, were affected by political unrest in the 1980s.

Recent History: New Caledonia, which was annexed by France in 1853, became a French overseas territory in 1946. The Melanesian Kanaks, who form 43% of the population, increased pressure for independence in the 1980s, but were outvoted by people of European and Asian descent, who are concentrated around Nouméa. Rising political tension led to violence in 1984-85 and 1988. The territory was divided into three autonomous provinces in 1988. A referendum in 1987 rejected independence.

NIUE
Status: self-governing territory of New Zealand.

Area: 259 km² (100 sq mi).

Population: 2270 (1990 est).

Capital: Alofi 1000 (1989 est).

Government: The 20-member Assembly comprises one member elected by each of the 14 villages and six members elected from a single national constituency. A Cabinet, comprising a Premier and three Ministers, is responsible to the Assembly. Premier: Sir Robert Rex.

Geography: Subtropical Niue, east of Tonga, comprises a coral plateau ending in sea cliffs.

Economy: Niue lacks natural resources and has little water. Tourism is being developed. Unemployment is high and over 12,000 Niueans have migrated to work in New Zealand.

Recent History: Britain annexed Niue in 1900, but in 1901 transferred the territory to New Zealand. In 1974 Niue became a self-governing state in free association with New Zealand.

NORFOLK ISLAND
Status: an Australian external territory.

Area: 34.5 km² (13.3 sq mi).

Population: 1980 (1990 est).

Capital: Kingston 1980 (1990 est).

Government: A nine-member Legislative Assembly is elected by universal adult suffrage.

Geography: The island, which is fertile and hilly, lies about 1400 km (875 mi) east of Queensland.

Economy: The economy relies upon tourism and revenue from the issue of postage stamps.

Recent History: After being a penal settlement in the early 19th century, Norfolk Island was resettled from Pitcairn Island in 1856. Britain ceded the colony to New South Wales in 1897 but it was transferred to Australia as a territory in 1913.

NORTHERN MARIANA ISLANDS
Status: a US Commonwealth territory.

Area: 471 km² (184 sq mi).

Population: 43,300 (1990 census).

Capital: Chalan Kanoa (on Saipan) 39,000 (1990).

Government: A Governor and a nine-member Senate are elected by universal adult suffrage for four years; the 18-member House of Representatives is directly elected for two years.

Geography: The islands are a chain of 16 mountainous tropical islands in the western Pacific.

Economy: Farming, mainly in smallholdings, produces subsistence crops and vegetables for export. Tourism now dominates the economy.

Recent History: The islands were sold by Spain to Germany in 1899. Japan took the group in 1914 during World War I and received them as a League of Nations trusteeship in 1921. The islands saw fierce fighting during World War II. The group was included in the US United Nations Trust Territory of the Pacific Islands from 1947 until 1978 when they became a separate internally self-governing territory in free association with the USA.

PALAU (BELAU)

Status: a US-administered UN trust territory.

Area: 497 km² (192 sq mi).

Population: 15,500 (1991 est).

Capital: Koror 9500 (1990 census).

Government: Palau, a UN trust territory, is a non-sovereign republic. A President and Congress are elected by universal adult suffrage for four years. The Congress comprises a 16-member Senate, in which one member represents each of the 16 states, and a 18-member House of Delegates. President: Kuniwo Nakamura.

Geography: Palau comprises the volcanic hilly tropical island of Babelthuap, eight smaller hilly islands and nearly 350 small atolls.

Econony: Most Palauans are involved in subsistence farming and fishing. Tourism and the sale of fishing rights to foreign fleets are the main sources of foreign currency.

Recent History: Spain sold the islands to Germany in 1899. Occupied by Japanese forces in 1914, Palau remained Japanese until taken by the USA in 1944. In 1947 Palau became part of the UN Pacific Islands Trust Territory under US administration. Palau became an autonomous republic in 1981. However, Palau has repeatedly rejected the Compact of Free Association and independence because the Compact entitles the USA to base nuclear weapons in the islands.

PITCAIRN ISLANDS

Status: a British settlement.

Area: 44 km² (17 sq mi).

Population: 67 (1992 est).

Capital: Adamstown 67 (1992 est).

Government: The Island Magistrate is elected for three years by univeral adult suffrage. The Magistrate chairs the Island Council which comprises five members elected annually, three nominated members and an ex-officio member.

Geography: The group comprises four sub-tropical islands in the South Pacific about 4800 km (3000 mi) east of New Zealand. Pitcairn Island is volcanic in origin and rugged but fertile.

Economy: Pitcairn depends on subsistence farming, fishing and the sale of postage stamps.

Recent History: Populated by nine mutineers from the Bounty and their consorts (1790), Pitcairn became overpopulated by the middle of the 19th century and some of the islanders were removed to Norfolk Island.

WAKE ISLAND

Status: an unincorporated US territory.

Area: 8 km² (3 sq mi).

Population: 300 US service personnel (1990 est).

Government: The territory is administered by the US Department of Defense.

Geography: Wake comprises three small arid tropical islands around a lagoon west of Hawaii.

Recent History: The USA claimed Wake Island in 1899. After a major battle (1941), Japanese forces took Wake Island, occupying it until 1945.

WALLIS AND FUTUNA ISLANDS

Status: a French overseas territory.

Area: 274 km² (106 sq mi).

Population: 13,700 (1990 est).

Capital: Mata-Utu 810 (1990 est).

Government: The Territorial Council comprises three appointed members and the kings of Uvéa, Sigave and Alo. The 20-member Assembly is elected for five years by universal adult suffrage. The islands also return a deputy to the French National Asembly and a senator to the Senate.

Geography: The territory comprises two tropical archipelagos - Wallis (or Uvéa), a volcanic island, plus some coral reefs; Futuna, two mountainous islands divided between Sigave and Alo.

Economy: Large numbers of islanders have left owing to unemployment. The economy relies upon government employment and money sent back by islanders working abroad. Copra is the only significant export.

Recent History: France established a protectorate over Wallis in 1887 and Futuna in 1888. US forces took over the islands from 1942 to 1946 during World War II. The islands became a French overseas territory in 1961.

▶ ▶ ▶ ▶ ▶ ▶ ▶ ▶ ▶ ▶ ▶ ▶

THE
CARIBBEAN

Antigua and Barbuda, The Bahamas, Barbados, Cuba, Dominica,
Dominican Republic, Grenada, Haiti, Jamaica, St Christopher-Nevis
(St Kitts-Nevis), St Lucia, St Vincent and the Grenadines, Trinidad
and Tobago, Other territories.

Islands in the Sun

As a result of their separate historical and economic development, each of the island states and remaining dependent territories in the Caribbean has its own quite distinct character. There are, however, certain shared features.

EMIGRATION

With a very few exceptions, such as the US Virgin Islands, all of the Caribbean islands suffer emigration, often of the young, the best qualified and the most enterprising. Almost throughout the region unemployment is high, peaking at about 45% in St Vincent and the Grenadines and at least 20% in Haiti and the Dominican Republic. Emigration mitigates the effects of mass unemployment. Britain and France were formerly the principal destinations of those forced to leave the Caribbean, but the USA and Canada have long since become the magnets. Money sent back, for example, to the Antilles by islanders living and working abroad is an important source of revenue. The Caribbean islands, with their limited resources, have rapidly increasing populations, requiring unsustainably high economic growth rates in order to maintain the present standards of living. The population of the Dominican Republic, for instance, is increasing at a rate of 2.3% per annum. The larger islands tend to have greater economic problems. Haiti, for example, is the poorest state in the Western hemisphere. Its agricultural sector, the country's major employer, suffers shortages of equipment and investment and experiences severe ecological problems, largely as a result of overpopulation. Political instability and an economic embargo, leading to an energy crisis, have compounded the problems.

DIVERSIFICATION AND TOURISM

Many islands are characterized by over dependence upon a single commodity - sugar cane in the case of St Kitts-Nevis, bananas in St Vincent, St Lucia and Dominica, and bauxite in Jamaica. This makes their economies vulnerable to fluctuations in the international markets for these items. For this reason the governments of the Caribbean islands are actively encouraging diversification. Barbados has successfully attracted 'offshore' banking and broadened the island's industrial base as well as diversifying the agricultural sector. The government of St Lucia has, with assistance from Brazil, encouraged the cultivation of cashew nuts, while the revival of sea-island cotton has been undertaken in Antigua where the crop was formerly that island's main export. The priority in most islands, however, has been the encouragement of tourism, mainly from the USA and Canada but also from Western Europe. In Antigua, for example, tourism accounts for over 50% of total employment and contributes, both directly and indirectly, over two thirds of the island's GDP. Jamaica receives over 1,250,000 tourists a year - earnings from which are now equivalent to over three quarters of the value of total commodity exports. In some of the smaller islands, such as St Barthelémy (part of the French overseas département of Guadeloupe), the dependence upon tourism is almost total. In 1990-91 when recession coincided with the Gulf Crisis and War, fewer Americans took holidays abroad and in Barbados, for example, the number of stop-over tourists decreased by 7% (1990). On some islands tourist developments have caused environmental problems and an over-dependence upon catering for holidaymakers has led to a decline in agriculture in some Caribbean islands as tourism has attracted labour away from the land.

COOPERATION

Diversification is being undertaken with the assistance of other Western-hemisphere countries - and this increasingly includes Latin American countries such as Brazil and Venezuela, which is very active in Aruba, Barbados, the Netherlands Antilles and Trinidad. EC countries too are important sources of trade and aid in the region, in part through the Lomé Convention. French and Dutch investment are important in their dependencies - the French islands are part of both France and the EC. Britain is similarly involved in its former colonies and remaining small territories, while Puerto Rico benefits from continuing US aid and investment. However, neighbouring islands are seen as rivals rather than partners. The attempts to unite the former British islands in a West Indies Federation before independence were unsuccessful, but some inter-island co-operation has been achieved through the Organization of Eastern Caribbean Islands (OECS), the Caribbean Community and CARICOM (the Caribbean Common Market). St Lucia, in particular, has been an advocate of East Caribbean unity in a single state to strengthen the position of the small island communities in international trade, especially their dealings with the EC.

Regional Organizations of the Caribbean

THE CARIBBEAN COMMON MARKET (CARICOM)

The Caribbean Common Market was founded at the same time as its sister organization, the Caribbean Community (see below) - in 1973 in Chaguaramas, Trinidad and Tobago. The aims of the CARICOM are to promote economic cooperation between members. CARICOM shares its administration with the Caribbean Community.

Headquarters: Georgetown, Guyana.

Secretary General: Roderick Rainford (Jamaica).

Membership: Antigua and Barbuda, The Bahamas, Barbados, Belize, Dominica, the Dominican Republic, Grenada, Guyana, Haiti, Jamaica, St Christopher-Nevis (St Kitts-Nevis), St Lucia, St Vincent and the Grenadines, Trinidad and Tobago, Suriname, and Venezuela. Three non-sovereign territories are also in membership: the British Virgin Islands, Montserrat, and the Turks and Caicos Islands.

THE CARIBBEAN COMMUNITY

The Caribbean Community was founded in 1973 in Chaguaramas, Trinidad and Tobago. The aims of the Community are to promote cooperation in cultural, health, scientific and technological matters, and to coordinate foreign policy.

Caribbean Trade

Antigua and Barbuda Imports ($ million): 225 (1988). Exports ($ million): 22 (1988). Main imports: basic manufacture. Main exports: re-exports. Principal trading partners: Dominica, UK, Canada.

Bahamas Imports ($ million): 3001 (1989). Exports ($ million): 2786 (1989). Main imports: crude petroleum. Main exports: crude petroleum. Principal trading partners: USA, Saudi Arabia, Nigeria.

Barbados Imports ($ million): 695 (1991). Exports ($ million): 202 (1991). Main imports: machinery. Main exports: mineral fuels. Principal trading partners: UK, USA, Trinidad, Canada.

Cuba Imports (peso million): 8124.2 (1989). Exports ($ million): 5518 (1989). Main imports: minerals, fuels and lubricants. Main exports: sugar. Principal trading partners: Russia, Germany, China.

Dominica Imports ($ million): 118 (1990). Exports ($ million): 55 (1990). Main imports: basic manufactures. Main exports: food and live animals. Principal trading partners: UK, USA, Jamaica.

Dominican Republic Imports ($ million): 1721 (1991). Exports ($ million): 658,323 (1991). Main imports: crude petroleum and petroleum products. Main exports: ferronickel. Principal trading partners: USA, Netherlands, Venezuela, Japan.

Grenada Imports ($ million): 92 (1988). Exports ($ million): 32 (1987). Main imports: machinery and transport equipment. Main exports: nutmeg. Principal trading partners: USA, UK, Trinidad.

Haiti Imports ($ million): 374 (1991). Exports ($ million): 103 (1991). Main imports: mineral fuels. Main exports: local manufactures. Principal trading partners: USA, France, Japan, Canada, Italy.

Jamaica Imports ($ million): 1864 (1990). Exports ($ million): 1116 (1990). Main imports: fuels. Main exports: aluminium. Principal trading partners: USA, UK, Canada.

St Christopher and Nevis Imports (EC$ million): 168 (1990). Exports (EC$ million): 81 (1990). Main imports: machinery and transport equipment. Main exports: sugar. Principal trading partners: USA, UK, Trinidad.

St Lucia Imports (EC$ million): 732.4 (1990). Exports (EC$ million): 343.7 (1990). Main imports: food and live animals. Main exports: bananas. Principal trading partners: UK, USA, Trinidad.

St Vincent and the Grenadines Imports (EC$ million): 367,000 (1990). Exports (EC$ million): 210,000 (1990). Main imports: basic manufactures. Main exports: bananas. Principal trading partners: USA, UK, Trinidad.

Trinidad and Tobago Imports ($ million): 1222 (1990). Exports ($ million): 2049 (1990). Main imports: machinery. Main exports: crude petroleum and petroleum products. Principal trading partners: USA, UK, Jamaica, Barbados.

Antigua
and Barbuda

Member of: UN, Commonwealth, CARICOM, OAS.

Area: 442 km² (170.5 sq mi) - Antigua 280 km² (108 sq mi), Barbuda 161 km² (62 sq mi).

Population: 66,000 (1993 est).

Capital: St John's 36,000 (1986 est).

Language: English.

Religions: Anglican (44%), Moravian.

Education: Education is compulsory between the ages of five and 16. In 1990 the literacy rate was 90%. There is a university college which is part of the University of the West Indies.

Defence: In 1992 the defence force had a total strength of about 700.

Transport: There are 1165 km (724 mi) of roads. St John's has an international airport and a commercial shipping port.

Media: There are five weekly newspapers. A state-run radio service, a state-run television service, two independent radio stations and a cable television service operate.

GOVERNMENT
The 17-member House of Representatives is elected by universal adult suffrage for up to five years. The Senate, which also has 17 members, is appointed. Government is by a Cabinet of Ministers. A Prime Minister, commanding a majority in the lower house, is appointed by the Governor General, the representative of the British Queen as sovereign of Antigua. Barbuda has its own Council and some autonomy. The main political parties are the Antigua Labour Party (ALP) and the United National Democratic Party (UNDP). An ALP government was formed after the general election in 1994.

Party strength: ALP 11, UNDP 5, Barbudan representative 1.

Prime Minister: Lester Bird.

GEOGRAPHY
Antigua is a low limestone island, rising in the west. Barbuda - 45 km (28 mi) to the north - is a flat wooded coral island. Redonda is a rocky outcrop. There are no significant rivers. Highest point: Boggy Peak (on Antigua) 402 m (1319 ft). Climate: The tropical climate is moderated by sea breezes. Rainfall is low for the West Indies, and Antigua island suffers from drought.

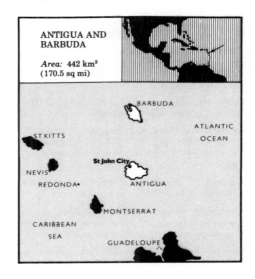

ANTIGUA AND BARBUDA

Area: 442 km² (170.5 sq mi)

BARBUDA

ATLANTIC OCEAN

ST KITTS

St John City

NEVIS

REDONDA•

ANTIGUA

MONTSERRAT

CARIBBEAN SEA

GUADELOUPE

ECONOMY
Tourism (mainly from the USA) is the mainstay of the country and employs over one half of the labour force. In an attempt to diversify the economy, the government has encouraged agriculture, but the lack of water on Antigua island is a problem.

Currency: East Caribbean dollar (XCD) of 100 cents; 1US$ = 2.7 XCD (May 1994).

GDP: US$363,000,000 (1990 est); US$4600 per head.

RECENT HISTORY
The British colonies of Antigua and Barbuda were united in 1860. Britain granted Antigua complete internal self-government in 1967. Since independence in 1981 the political life of the country has been dominated by the Bird family - Vere Bird was Prime Minister until 1994. Antigua has also been troubled by continuing allegations of corruption.

117

Bahamas

Official name: The Commonwealth of the Bahamas.

Member of: UN, Commonwealth, OAS, CARICOM (Community only).

Area: 13,939 km² (5382 sq mi).

Population: 266,000 (1993 est).

Capital: Nassau 169,000 (1990 census).

Other main city: Freeport 25,000 (1990 census).

Language: English.

Religions: Baptist (29%), Anglican (21%), Roman Catholic (26%), Methodist.

Education: Education is compulsory between the ages of five and 14. In 1990 the literacy rate was over 96%. There is a single university college.

Defence: In 1993 the total armed strength was estimated to be 2550.

Transport: There are 3370 km (2094 mi) of roads. Nassau and Freeport have commercial shipping ports and international airports.

Media: There are three daily newspapers. A government-owned corporation provides a radio and television service.

GOVERNMENT
The Senate (the upper house of Parliament) has 16 appointed members. The House of Assembly (the lower house) has 49 members elected by universal adult suffrage for five years. A Prime Minister, who commands a majority in the House, is appointed by the Governor General, who is the representative of the British Queen as sovereign of the Bahamas. The Prime Minister chairs the Cabinet, which is responsible to the House. The main political parties are the (centre right) Progressive Liberal Party (PLP) and the (centre) Free National Movement (FNM). After the election in August 1992 an FNM government took office.

Party strength: FNM 33, PLP 16.

Prime Minister: Hubert Alexander Ingraham (FNM).

GEOGRAPHY
The Bahamas comprises some 700 long, flat,

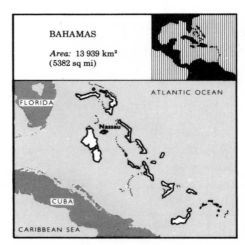

BAHAMAS

Area: 13 939 km² (5382 sq mi)

narrow islands, and over 2000 barren rocky islets. There are no significant rivers. Highest point: Mount Alvernia, Cat Island 63 m (206 ft). Climate: The climate is mild and subtropical, with no great seasonal variation in temperature. Rainfall averages just over 1000 mm (39 in). The islands are liable to hurricanes.

ECONOMY
Tourism - mainly from the USA - is the major source of income, and, with related industries, it employs the majority of the labour force. The islands have become a tax haven and financial centre. The Bahamas has established its own shipping registry and has become a 'flag of convenience' with one of the largest merchant shipping fleets in the world, most of them American-owned vessels. In 1993-94 economic problems were caused by the downturn in tourism as a result of the world recession.

Currency: The Bahamian dollar of 100 cents; 1US$ = 1 Bahamian dollar. (US currency is generally accepted in the Bahamas.)

GDP: US$3,165,000,000 (1991); US$11,990 per head.

RECENT HISTORY
Britain granted internal self-government to the Bahamas in 1964. Since independence in 1973, the Bahamas have developed close ties with the USA, but the relationship has been strained at times owing to an illegal drug trade through the islands. In the 1992 election Sir Lynden Pindling was ousted as PM after 25 years.

Barbados

Member of: UN, Commonwealth, CARICOM, OAS.

Area: 430 km² (166 sq mi).

Population: 260,000 (1993 est).

Capital: Bridgetown 102,000 (city 7500; 1990 census).

Other main towns: There are no other settlements that can be recognized as towns on the island of Barbados.

Language: English.

Religions: Anglican (40%), Pentecostalist (8%), Methodist (7%), Roman Catholic, plus small Hindu, Sunni Islam and Jewish minorities.

Education: Education is compulsory between the ages of five and 16. In 1990 the literacy rate was estimated to be over 99%. There is a university college (part of the University of the West Indies).

Defence: In 1991 the total armed strength was 154, plus volunteers and reserves. There is no military service.

Transport: There are 1573 km (977 mi) of roads. Barbados has no railways. Bridgetown has a commercial shipping port; there is an international airport at Seawell.

Media: There are two daily newspapers, three radio stations (one a government corporation and two commercial undertakings), a single television channel, plus three cable television services.

GOVERNMENT
The 21 members of the Senate are appointed; the 27 members of the House of Assembly are elected by universal adult suffrage for five years. The Governor General, the representative of the British Queen as sovereign of Barbados, appoints a Prime Minister who commands a majority in the House. The PM appoints a Cabinet responsible to the House. The main political parties are the (social democratic) Democratic Labour Party (DLP), the (social democratic) Barbados Labour Party (BLP) and the National Democratic Party (NDP). After the election in January 1991 a DLP government took office. (Parliament was dissolved and elections were called at the time of going to press.)

Prime Minister: L. Erskine Sandiford (DLP).

GEOGRAPHY
Barbados is generally flat and low, except in the north. There are no significant rivers. Highest point: Mount Hillaby 340 m (1115 ft). Climate: Barbados has a tropical climate. Rainfall is heavy, with totals everywhere above 1000 mm (40 in). The island is subject to hurricanes.

ECONOMY
Tourism - which employs about one third of the labour force - is the main source of income. The government has encouraged diversification, and there has been a growth in banking and insurance. Sugar - once the mainstay of Barbados - remains the main crop. In 1993-94 austerity measures were introduced as tourism declined with the world recession. At the same time, the production of sugar fell as world prices for that commodity decreased. By the end of 1993 unemployment in Barbados stood at over 25%.

Currency: Barbados dollar of 100 cents; 1US$ = 2.01 Barbados dollars (June 1994).

GDP: US$1,711,000,000 (1991); US$6630 per head.

RECENT HISTORY
In the British colony of Barbados in the 1930s, economic and social conditions for black Barbadians were miserable. Riots in 1937 led to reforms and also greatly increased black political consciousness. As a result, Barbadians, such as Grantley Adams and Errol Barrow, became prominent in Caribbean politics. Barbados gained independence in 1966 and has become an important influence among the smaller islands of the Lesser Antilles.

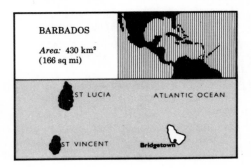

BARBADOS

Area: 430 km² (166 sq mi)

ST LUCIA

ATLANTIC OCEAN

ST VINCENT

Bridgetown

Cuba

Official name: La República de Cuba (The Republic of Cuba).

Member of: UN, OAS (suspended), ALADI (observer).

Area: 110,860 km² (42,803 sq mi).

Population: 10,700,000 (1991 est).

Capital: Havana (La Habana) 2,096,000 (including suburbs; 1990 est).

Other major cities: Santiago de Cuba 405,000, Camagüey 283,000, Holguín 228,000, Guantánamo 200,000, Santa Clara 194,000 (all including suburbs; 1990 est).

Language: Spanish.

Religion: Roman Catholic (39%), non-religious (over 40%).

Education: Education is compulsory between the ages of six and 12. In 1990 the literacy rate was estimated to be 94%. There are five universities (including a university college).

Defence: In 1992 the total armed strength was nearly 176,000 - 145,000 in the army, 13,500 in the navy and 17,000 in the air force. There are 135,000 reservists plus 119,000 paramilitary. The Cuban navy's main base is Cienfuegos. Military service, which lasts for three years, is compulsory. Conscripts also work on the land.

Transport: There are over 17,000 km (10,625 mi) of roads, of which 575 km (358 mi) are motorways. There are 4881 km (3050 mi) of public railways and 9638 km (6024 mi) of light railways used by the sugar plantations. Havana, the main commercial shipping port, handles two-thirds of Cuba's imports and exports. Havana has an international airport.

Media: Owing to austerity measures adopted in 1990 there is now only one daily national newspaper. Broadcasting is state-controlled. There are five national radio stations, over 40 provincial and municipal stations, plus two national television channels.

GOVERNMENT
The Communist Party is the only legal political party. A constitutional amendment in 1993 replaced the indirectly-elected parliamentary system with a directly-elected 589-member National Assembly. The Assembly elects 31 of its members to form the Council of State, whose President - as head of state and government - appoints a Council of Ministers.There are 14 provinces and a special territory.

President: Fidel Castro Ruz.

THE CABINET
The Cabinet comprises over 30 Ministers. They include:

First Vice-President and Minister of the Armed Forces : Gen. Raul Castro Ruz.

Minister of Foreign Affairs: Ricardo Alarcon de Quesada.

Minister of the Interior: Gen. Abelardo Colome.

Minister of Justice: Juan Escalona Reguera.

PROVINCES
Camagüey Area: 15,990 km² (6174 sq mi). Population: 732,000 (1989 est). Capital: Camagüey.

Ciego de Avila Area: 6910 km² (2668 sq mi). Population: 358,000 (1989 est). Capital: Ciego de Avila.

Cienfuegos Area: 4178 km² (1613 sq mi). Population: 359,000 (1989 est). Capital: Cienfuegos.

Granma Area: 8372 km² (3232 sq mi). Population: 781,000 (1989 est). Capital: Bayamo.

Guantánamo Area: 6186 km² (2388 sq mi). Population: 491,000 (1989 est). Capital: Guantánamo.

Havana (City) (Ciudad de la Habana) Area: 727 km² (281 sq mi). Population: 2,078,000 (1989 est). Capital: Havana.

Havana (Province) (La Havana) Area: 5731 km² (2213 sq mi). Population: 637,000 (1989 est).

Holguín Area: 9301 km² (3591 sq mi). Population: 983,000 (1989 est). Capital: Holguín.

Las Tunas Area: 6589 km² (2544 sq mi). Population: 485,000 (1989 est). Capital: Las Tunas.

Matanzas Area: 11,978 km² (4625 sq mi). Population: 603,000 (1989 est). Capital: Matanzas.

Pinar del Rio Area: 10,925 km² (4218 sq mi). Population: 685,000 (1989 est). Capital: Pinar del Rio.

Sancti Spiritus Area: 6744 km² (2604 sq mi). Population: 424,000 (1989 est). Capital: Sancti Spiritus.

Santiago de Cuba Area: 6170 km² (2382 sq mi). Population: 980,000 (1989 est). Capital: Santiago de Cuba.

Villa Clara Area: 8662 km² (3345 sq mi). Population: 801,000 (1989 est). Capital: Santa Clara.

Isla de la Juventud (special territory) Area: 2398 km² (926 sq mi). Population: 71,000 (1989 est). Capital: Nova Gerona.

GEOGRAPHY
Three ranges of hills and mountains run east to west across Cuba and occupy 25% of the country. The eastern system is the highest and most extensive; the central system comprises hills; the western system comprises rugged mountains. The rest of Cuba consists of plains which are largely covered in sugar cane plantations. Highest point: Pico Turquino 1971 m (6467 ft). Principal river: Cauto. Climate: The climate is semitropical. Temperatures average 26 C (78 F), and rainfall is heavy.

ECONOMY
Sugar (the leading export), tobacco and coffee are the main crops. State-controlled farms occupy most of the land but are unable to meet Cuba's food needs. Rationing is in force. Production of nickel - Cuba's second most

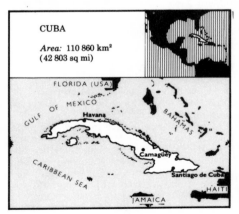

CUBA

Area: 110 860 km²
(42 803 sq mi)

FLORIDA (USA)
GULF OF MEXICO
Havana
BAHAMAS
Camagüey
CARIBBEAN SEA
Santiago de Cuba
HAITI
JAMAICA

important export - is increasing. The disruption of trading patterns that has followed the adoption of market economies in Eastern Europe and the end of Soviet subsidies have severely damaged the Cuban economy, which is on the verge of collapse. Severe fuel shortages have hit both transport and industry. The value of the peso is plummeting in real terms. Since 1993 Cubans have been allowed to hold dollars. This innovation, and the legalization of self-employment, have resulted in the emergence of a parallel dollar economy beyond state control. Moves are also being made to restrict the very large subsidies on basic products and to cut back on the extensive welfare state. Cuba continues to suffer the consequences of a US trade embargo.

Currency: Cuban peso (CUP) of 100 centavos; 1US$ = 0.759 CUP (official rate; May 1994). On the black market the exchange rate in May 1994 was 1US$ = 100 CUP (see above).

GDP: US$20,900,000,000 (1990); US$2000 per head.

RECENT HISTORY
The first war for independence from Spain (1868-78) was unsuccessful. The USA intervened in a second uprising (1895-98), forcing Spain to relinquish the island, but independence was not confirmed until after two periods of American administration (1899-1901 and 1906-09). Under a succession of corrupt governments, the majority of Cubans suffered abject poverty. In 1959, the dictatorship of Fulgencio Batista was overthrown by the guerrilla leader Fidel Castro (1926-), whose revolutionary movement merged with the Communist Party to remodel Cuba on Soviet lines. In 1961, US-backed Cuban exiles attempted to invade at the Bay of Pigs, and relations with America deteriorated further in 1962 when the installation of Soviet missiles on Cuba almost led to world war. Castro has encouraged revolutionary movements throughout Latin America, and his troops have bolstered Marxist governments in Ethiopia and Angola. At home, major advances in education and health care were achieved, but, owing to the lack of human rights, large numbers of Cubans have sought exile in Florida. Despite being a close ally of the USSR, Cuba became a leading Third World power, but the upheavals in the USSR and Eastern Europe in 1989-90 left the Cuban government increasingly isolated as a hard-line Marxist state.

Dominica

Official name: Commonwealth of Dominica.

Member of: UN, Commonwealth, CARICOM, OAS.

Area: 751 km² (290 sq mi).

Population: 71,200 (1990 census).

Capital: Roseau 16,000 (city 8000; 1990 census).

Other main town: Portsmouth 5000 (town 2200; 1990 census).

Languages: English (official), French patois.

Religion: Roman Catholic (77%), Anglican, Methodist, Pentecostal.

Education: Education is compulsory between the ages of five and 15. In 1986 the literacy rate was estimated to be 94.4%. There is a single university college (part of the University of the West Indies).

Defence: There are no armed forces.

Transport: There are 756 km (470 mi) of roads. Woodbridge Bay is the main commercial shipping port, while Meadow Hall is the international airport for the island.

Media: There are two weekly newspapers, one government-owned radio station, two independent radio stations and a commercial television station.

GOVERNMENT

Every five years, 21 members of the House of Assembly are elected by universal adult suffrage and nine are appointed by the President, who is elected for a five-year term by the House. The President appoints a Prime Minister and Cabinet. The main political parties are the (conservative) Dominica Freedom Party (DFP), the Dominican United Workers' Party (DUWP), and the (left-wing) Dominica Labour Party (LPD). After the election in May 1990 the DFP continued in office.

Party strength: DFP 11, DUWP 6, plus 9 appointed senators.

President: Crispin Sorhaindo.

Prime Minister: Eugenia Charles (DFP).

GEOGRAPHY

Dominica is surrounded by steep cliffs with a forested mountainous interior. Highest point: Morne Diablotin 1447 m (4747 ft). Principal river: Layou. Climate: Dominica has a tropical climate with little seasonal variation and very heavy rainfall. The island is subject to hurricanes.

ECONOMY

Dominica is a poor island. It produces bananas, timber and coconuts, and exports water to drier neighbours. Tourism is increasing in importance, but the island's economy still suffers from over dependence upon bananas. The restriction of trade in bananas to the European

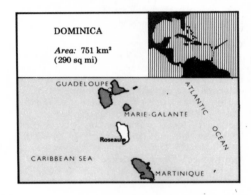

Comunity, which gives preference to bananas from French territories in the Caribbean, has become a major concern for Dominica.

Currency: East Caribbean dollar of 100 cents; 1US$ = 2.698 East Caribbean dollars (June 1994).

GDP: US$181,000,000 (1992); US$2510 per head.

RECENT HISTORY

A former British colony, Dominica was a member of the West Indies Federation from 1958 until 1962, when the federation collapsed. Dominica gained full internal autonomy in 1967 and independence in 1978. Eugenia Charles, the leader of the Dominica Freedom Party (DFP), has dominated the island's political scene for over 20 years. Following two coup attempts against the DFP - and suspected Defence Force involvement in drug trafficking - in the 1980s, the island's Defence Force was disarmed and disbanded.

Dominican Republic

Official name: República Dominicana (The Dominican Republic).

Member of: UN, OAS, ALADI (observer), CARICOM.

Area: 48,422 km² (18,696 sq mi).

Population: 7,635,000 (1993 est).

Capital: Santo Domingo 2,200,000 (including suburbs; 1989 est).

Other major cities: Santiago de los Caballeos 467,000, La Vega 189,000, San Pedro 137,000 (all including suburbs; 1989 est).

Language: Spanish (official).

Religion: Roman Catholic (over 90%).

Education: Education is compulsory between the ages of seven and 14. In 1990 the literacy rate was 83.3%. There are eight universities.

Defence: In 1992 the total armed strength was 22,000 - 15,000 in the army, 3000 in the navy, 4000 in the air force.

Transport: There are 17,000 km (10,656 mi) of roads and 1600 km (994 mi) of freight railways.

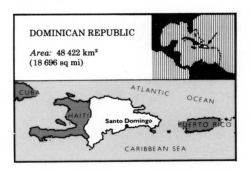

DOMINICAN REPUBLIC

Area: 48 422 km²
(18 696 sq mi)

CUBA

HAITI

ATLANTIC OCEAN

Santo Domingo

PUERTO RICO

CARIBBEAN SEA

Santo Domingo, the main port, has an international airport. Puerto Plata has the country's second international airport.

Media: There are 10 daily newspapers, 140 radio stations and 10 television stations, operating 13 channels.

GOVERNMENT
The President and the National Congress - a 30-member Senate and a 120-member Chamber of Deputies - are elected for four years by universal adult suffrage. The President appoints a Cabinet. Political parties include the (conservative) Social Christian Reform Party (PRSC), the (left-wing) Dominican Revolution Party (PRD), the (left-wing) Domincan Liberation Party (PLD), and the Independent Revolutionary Party (PRI). After the election in May 1994 the PRS retained power.

Party strength: PRSC 42, PLD 44, others 34.

President: Joaquin Balaguer (PRSC).

GEOGRAPHY
The republic consists of the eastern two thirds of the island of Hispaniola. The fertile Cibao Valley in the north is an important agricultural region. Most of the rest of the country is mountainous. Highest point: Pico Duarte 3175 m (10,417 ft). Principal river: Yaque del Norte. Climate: The climate is largely subtropical, but it is cooler in the mountains. Rainfall is heavy, but the west and southwest are arid. Hurricanes are a hazard.

ECONOMY
Sugar is the traditional mainstay of the economy, but nickel and iron ore have become the principal exports. Tourism is now the greatest foreign-currency earner.

Currency: Peso oro of 100 centavos; 1US$ = 13.05 pesos (June 1994).

GDP: US$7,613,000,000 (1992); US$1040 per head.

RECENT HISTORY
The 19th century witnessed a succession of tyrants, and by 1900 the republic was bankrupt and in chaos. The USA intervened (1916-24). Rafael Trujillo (1891-1961) became president in 1930 and ruthlessly suppressed opposition. He was assassinated in 1961. Civil war in 1965 ended after intervention by US and Latin American troops. Since then, an infant democracy has survived violent elections - the close election in 1994 was held to be irregular by the opposition, who claimed fraud. The country faces grave economic problems and has been criticized owing to the ease with which international sanctions against Haiti appear to have been breached over the land border between the two republics.

Grenada

Official name: The State of Grenada.

Member of: UN, OAS, Commonwealth, CARI-COM.

Area: 344 km² (133 sq mi).

Population: 91,000 (1991 census).

Capital: St George's 36,000 (city 4400; 1991 census).

Language: English (official); French-African patois.

Religions: Roman Catholic (82%), Anglican.

Education: Education is compulsory between the ages of six and 14 (in urban areas) and available in country areas. In 1990 the literacy rate was estimated to be over 85%. There is a university college plus a department of the University of the West Indies.

Defence: In 1993 there were no armed forces except for a small paramilitary Special Service Unit.

Transport: There are 1127 km (700 mi) of roads. St George's has a commercial shipping port. There is an international airport at Pointe Salines.

Media: There are six weekly newspapers. There is a radio station and three television channels.

GOVERNMENT

The Governor General - the representative of the British Queen as sovereign of Grenada - appoints a Prime Minister (who commands a majority in the House of Representatives), other members of the Cabinet and the 13-member Senate (the upper house of Parliament). The 15-member House of Representatives is elected for five years by universal adult suffrage. The main political parties include the (centrist) National Democratic Congress (NDC), the National Party (TNP), the (right-wing) Grenada United Labour Party (GULP) and the (centrist) New National Party (NNP). After the election held in 1990 an NDC government was formed.

Party strength: NDC 7, GULP 4, TNP 2, NNP 2.

Prime Minister: Nicholas Braithwaite (NDC).

GEOGRAPHY

A forested mountain ridge covers much of this well-watered island. The island of Carriacou forms part of Grenada. There are no significant rivers. Highest point: Mount St Catherine 840 m (2706 ft). Climate: Grenada has a tropical maritime climate with a dry season from January to May.

ECONOMY

The production of spices, in particular nutmeg, is the mainstay of a largely agricultural economy. Tourism is increasing in importance. The economy was severely disrupted by the political instability that Grenada suffered during the 1980s - repair and development of the island's infrastructure has been a priority.

Currency: East Caribbbean dollar of 100 cents; 1US$ = 2.698 East Caribbean dollars (June 1994).

GDP: US$210,000,000 (1992); US$2310 per head.

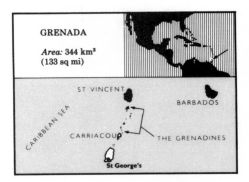

RECENT HISTORY

Grenada became British in 1783. Independence was gained in 1974. The left-wing New Jewel Movement seized power in a coup in 1979. In 1983 the PM Maurice Bishop was killed in a further coup in which more extreme members of the government seized power. Acting upon a request from East Caribbean islands to intervene, US and Caribbean forces landed in Grenada. A non-political interim council took power until elections were held in 1984. The last contingents of US and Caribbean forces left Grenada in 1985. After several days' fighting, the coup leaders were detained. Constitutional rule was restored in 1984.

Haiti

Official name: La République d'Haïti (Republic of Haiti).

Member of: UN, OAS, CARICOM.

Area: 27,750 km² (10,714 sq mi).

Population: 6,903,000 (1993 est).

Capital: Port-au-Prince 1,255,000 (city 753,000; Carrefour 241,000, Delmas 200,000, 1992 est).

Other major cities: Jacmel 217,000, Les Cayes 215,000 (including suburbs; 1988 est).

Languages: Creole (90%) and French - both official.

Religions: Roman Catholic (official; nominally 80%); the majority practises voodoo.

Education: Education is compulsory in theory between the ages of six and 12. In 1990 the literacy rate was 53%. There are two universities.

Defence: In 1992 the total armed strength was 7400. There is no military service.

Transport: There are 4000 km (2485 mi) of roads and 40 km (25 mi) of railways. Port-au-Prince has a commercial shipping port and an international airport.

Media: There are four daily newspapers. There are 29 radio stations and two television channels.

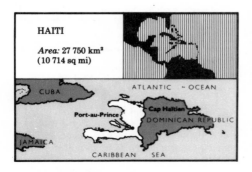

HAITI

Area: 27 750 km²
(10 714 sq mi)

CUBA

JAMAICA

ATLANTIC OCEAN

Port-au-Prince

Cap Haïtien

DOMINICAN REPUBLIC

CARIBBEAN SEA

GOVERNMENT
The constitution provides for elections by universal adult suffrage for a 27-member Senate, a 77-member Chamber of Deputies and a President, all to serve a five-year term. Constitutional rule was overturned by a mili-tary coup in 1991 and although there is a provisional President, government is effectively in the hands of the military leader Gen. Raoul Cedras.

Acting President and Prime Minister: Emil Jonassaint.

GEOGRAPHY
Haiti is the western part of the island of Hispaniola. Mountain ranges run from east to west, alternating with densely populated valleys and plains. Highest point: Pic La Selle 2680 m (8793 ft). Principal river: Artibonite. Climate: Haiti's tropical climate is moderated by altitude and by the sea.

ECONOMY
Agriculture involves some two thirds of the labour force, mainly growing crops for domestic consumption. Coffee is the principal cash crop. With few resources, overpopulated Haiti is the poorest country in the western hemisphere. A chronic fuel shortage has resulted from an international embargo on Haiti following the overthrow of constitutional rule.

Currency: Gourde of 100 centimes; 1US$ =11.99 gourdes (June 1994).

GDP: US$2,471,000,000 (1991); US$370 per head.

RECENT HISTORY
Coups, instability and tension between blacks and mulattos wracked 19th-century and early 20th-century Haiti until the USA intervened (1915-35). President François Duvalier ('Papa Doc'; in office 1956-71) and his son Jean-Claude ('Baby Doc'; 1971-86) cowed the country into submission by means of their infamous private militia, the Tontons Macoutes. The military took control after the younger Duvalier fled during a period of violent popular unrest. A period of unrest preceded Haiti's only democratic multi-party elections in 1991. However, the victor - a radical priest, Fr. Aristide - was toppled by the military within seven months. International pressure upon the military to return Fr. Aristide to power has included economic sanctions and the threat of possible American military intervention. Violence and intimidation remain endemic. Many thousands of Haitians attempt to enter the USA illegally every year.

Jamaica

Member of: UN, Commonwealth, CARICOM, OAS.

Area: 10,991 km² (4244 sq mi).

Population: 2,472,000 (1993 est).

Capital: Kingston 662,000 (city 104,000; 1991 est).

Other major cities: Spanish Town 92,000, Montego Bay 83, 000 (1991 est).

Language: English.

Religions: Church of God (17%), Anglican (10%), Baptist, Roman Catholic, Rastafarianism.

Education: Education is compulsory between the ages of six and 12, but only in some districts of the island. In 1990 the literacy rate was estimated to be 94.8%. There is a single university.

Defence: In 1993 the total armed strength was over 3350. There is no military service.

Transport: There are 16,435 km (10,212 mi) of roads and 208 km (120 mi) of railways. Kingston and Montego Bay have commercial shipping ports and international airports.

Media: There are three daily newspapers, a government-owned radio and television service and three other radio stations (two of them commercial).

JAMAICA

Area: 10 991 km²
(4244 sq mi)

CAYMAN ISLANDS

CUBA

Montego Bay

HAITI

CARIBBEAN SEA

Spanish Town

Kingston

GOVERNMENT
The 60-member House of Representatives (the lower house of Parliament) is elected for five years by universal adult suffrage. The 21-member Senate is appointed on the advice of the Prime Minister and the Leader of the Opposition. The Governor General - the representative of the British Queen as sovereign of Jamaica - appoints a Prime Minister who commands a majority in the House. The PM, in turn, appoints a Cabinet of Ministers who are responsible to the House. Jamaica is divided into 14 parishes. The main political parties are the (social democratic) People's National Party (PNP) and the (centre) Jamaican Labour Party (JLP). After the election held in March 1993 a PNP government was formed.

Party strength: PNP 52, JLP 8.

Prime Minister: Percival J. Patterson (PNP).

GEOGRAPHY
Coastal lowlands surround the interior limestone plateaux (the 'Cockpit Country') and mountains. Highest point: Blue Mountain Peak 2256 m (7402 ft). Principal river: Black River. Climate: The lowlands are tropical and rainy; the highlands are cooler and wetter. Jamaica is subject to hurricanes.

ECONOMY
Agriculture is the mainstay of the economy, with sugar cane and bananas as the main crops. Jamaica is one of the world's leading exporters of bauxite, which normally accounts for about two-thirds of the island's export earnings. Tourism - mainly from the USA - is the principal foreign-currency earner. Jamaica is troubled by persistant trade deficits, indebtedness and a shortage of foreign exchange. This has led to austerity measures, which have, in turn, increased social unrest. Unemployment is a major problem.

Currency: Jamaican dollar of 100 cents; 1US$ = 30.83 Jamaican dollars (June 1994).

GDP: US$3.365,000,000 (1991); US$1380 per head.

RECENT HISTORY
Jamaica became a British colony in the 17th century. By the 1930s, severe social and economic problems led to rioting and the birth of political awareness. Since independence in 1962, power has alternated between the radical People's National Party - led by Michael Manley - and the more conservative Jamaican Labour Party - whose leaders have included Sir Alexander Bustamente and Edward Seaga. The last decade has been characterized by rising social tension.

Saint Christopher and Nevis

(St Kitts-Nevis)

Official name: The Federation of Saint Christopher and Nevis. St Christopher is popularly known as St Kitts.

Member of: UN, Commonwealth, CARICOM, OAS.

Area: 262 km² (101 sq mi).

Population: 41,800 (1991 census).

Capital: Basseterre 15,000 (1991 census).

Other major town: Charlestown 1200 (1991 census).

Language: English (official).

Religion: Anglican (36%), Methodist (32%), Roman Catholic (11%).

Education: Education is compulsory between the ages of five and 17. In 1991 the literacy rate was over 98%. There is an extra-mural department of the University of the West Indies.

Defence: There are no armed forces.

Transport: There are 300 km (186 mi) of roads and 36 km (22 mi) of freight light railways. Baseterre has a shipping port and an international airport.

Media: There are two weekly papers, four radio stations and a government-owned television service.

GOVERNMENT
The National Assembly consists of 11 members elected by universal adult suffrage for five years and three or four appointed members. The Governor General - the representative of the British Queen as sovereign of St Kitts - appoints a Prime Minister who commands a majority in the Assembly. The PM appoints a Cabinet responsible to the Assembly. Nevis has its own legislature. Political parties include the People's Action Movement (PAM), the Labour Party (SKLP), the Nevis Reformation Party (NRP) and the (Nevis-based) Concerned Citizens Movement (CCM). After the election in November 1993 a PAM-NRP government was formed.

Party strength: PAM 4, SKLP 4, NRP 1, CCM 1.

Prime Minister: Kennedy Simmonds (PAM).

AUTONOMOUS ISLAND
Nevis Area: 93 km² (36 sq mi). Population: 9100 (1991 census). Capital: Charlestown.

GEOGRAPHY
St Kitts and Nevis are two well-watered mountainous islands, set 3 km (2 mi) apart. There are no significant rivers. Highest point: Nevis Peak 985 m (3232 ft). Climate: The moist tropical climate is cooled by sea breezes.

ECONOMY
The economy is based on agriculture (mainly sugar cane) and tourism.

Currency: East Caribbean dollar of 100 cents; 1US$ = 2.69 East Caribbean dollars (June 1994).

GDP: US$182,100,000 (1992); US$4670 per head.

RECENT HISTORY
St Kitts was united with Nevis and the more distant small island of Anguilla in a single British colony, which gained internal self-government in 1967. When Anguilla - a reluctant partner - proclaimed independence in 1967, the British intervened, eventually restoring Anguilla to colonial rule while St Kitts-Nevis progressed to independence in 1983.

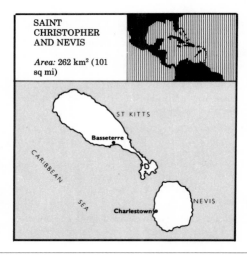

SAINT CHRISTOPHER AND NEVIS

Area: 262 km² (101 sq mi)

ST KITTS

Basseterre

CARIBBEAN SEA

NEVIS

Charlestown

127

Saint Lucia

Member of: UN, Commonwealth, CARICOM, OAS.

Area: 616 km² (238 sq mi).

Population: 136,000 (1993 est).

Capital: Castries 57,000 (city 11,000; 1990 census).

Other main town: Vieux Fort 23,000 (1990 census).

Languages: English (official), French patois (majority).

Religion: Roman Catholic (over 80%), with Anglican, Seventh-Day Adventist and Baptist minorities.

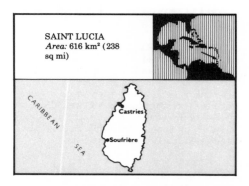

SAINT LUCIA
Area: 616 km² (238 sq mi)

Education: Education is compulsory between the ages of five and 15. In 1990 the literacy rate was over 80%. There is an extra-mural branch of the University of the West Indies.

Defence: There are no armed forces, although there is a paramilitary unit attached to the 300-member police force.

Transport: There are 805 km (500 mi) of roads. St Lucia has no railways. Castries and Vieux Fort have commercial shipping ports. Hewanorra is the main international airport; Vigie (Castries) airport also handles some international flights, catering for medium-range jets.

Media: There are two weekly newspapers, two radio stations (one of which is government-owned) and three television channels (two commercial and one cable).

GOVERNMENT

The 11-member Senate is appointed upon the advice of the Prime Minister and the Leader of the Opposition. The 17-member House of Assembly is elected by universal adult suffrage for a term of five years. The Governor General - as representative of the British Queen as sovereign of St Lucia - appoints a Prime Minister who commands a majority in the House. The PM, in turn, appoints a Cabinet which is responsible to the House. The main political parties are the United Workers' Party (UWP), the Labour Party (SLP), and the (left-wing) Progressive Labour Party (PLP). After the election in April 1992 a UWP government was formed.

Party strength: UWP 11, SLP 6.

Prime Minister: John Compton (UWP).

GEOGRAPHY

St Lucia is a forested mountainous island. There are no significant rivers. Highest point: Mount Gimie 959 m (3145 ft). Climate: St Lucia has a wet tropical climate. There is a dry season from January to April.

ECONOMY

The economy depends upon agriculture, with bananas and coconuts as the main crops, and upon tourism, which is increasingly important and is now the largest single employer in the island. The main economic problem is the price of bananas and the difficulties of obtaining free trade in this commodity because of the preference for fruit grown in French Caribbean territories that has been given by the European Community. Unemployment is high.

Currency: East Caribbean dollar of 100 cents; 1US$ = 2.69 East Caribbean dollars (June 1994).

GDP: US$454,000,000 (1992); US$2910 per head.

RECENT HISTORY

After being disputed by England and France, St Lucia finally became a British colony in 1814. Internal self-government was achieved in 1967 and independence in 1979. The low prices fetched by bananas led to unrest and strikes by farmers and agricultural workers in 1993.

Saint Vincent and the Grenadines

Member of: UN, OAS, CARICOM, Commonwealth.

Area: 389 km² (150 sq mi).

Population: 106,000 (1991 census).

Capital: Kingstown 26,000 (city 15,500; 1991 census).

Language: English (official).

Religions: Anglican (42%), Methodist (21%), Roman Catholic (12%).

Education: Education is not compulsory but is freely available between the ages of five and 12. In 1990 the literacy rate was estimated to be nearly 90%. There are no university level institutions.

Defence: There are no armed forces, but the 570-member police force includes a paramilitary element.

Transport: There are 943 km (586 mi) of roads. St Vincent has no railways. Kingstown has a commercial shipping port. There is an international airport at Arnos Vale on St Vincent; there is a smaller international airport on Bequia.

Media: There are three weekly newspapers, a single radio service and a television station. Barbadian television can also be received.

GOVERNMENT

The single-chamber House of Assembly consists of 6 nominated senators and 15 representatives elected for five years by universal adult suffrage. The Governor General - who is the representative of the British Queen as sovereign of St Vincent - appoints a Prime Minister who commands a majority of the representatives. The PM in turn appoints a Cabinet responsible to the House. The main political parties are the New Democratic Party (NDP), the St Vincent Labour Party (SVLP) and the Movement for National Unity (MNU). After the election held in February 1994 an NDP government continued in office.

Party strength: NDP 12, SVLP-MNU electoral alliance 3.

Prime Minister: James F. Mitchell (NDP).

GEOGRAPHY

St Vincent is a mountainous wooded island. The Grenadines - which include Bequia, Mustique, Canouan, Mayreau, Isle D'Quatre and Union Island - are a chain of 32 small islands and cays , which are situated to the south of St Vincent. There are no significant rivers. Highest point: Mount Soufrière, an active volcano, 1234 m (4048 ft). Climate: The country experiences a tropical climate with very heavy rainfall in the mountains.

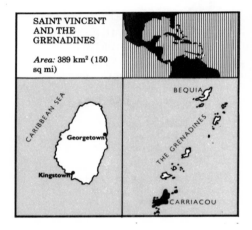

SAINT VINCENT AND THE GRENADINES

Area: 389 km² (150 sq mi)

BEQUIA

CARIBBEAN SEA

Georgetown

THE GRENADINES

Kingstown

CARRIACOU

ECONOMY

Bananas and arrowroot are the main crops of a largely agricultural economy. Bananas normally account for about 45% the country's exports and St Vincent is the world's leading producer of arrowroot. Up-market tourism in the Grenadines (particularly Bequia and Mustique) is being promoted.

Currency: East Caribbean dollar of 100 cents; 1US$ = 2.69 East Caribbean dollars.

GDP: US$187,000,000 (1991); US$1730 per head.

RECENT HISTORY

The island became a British colony in 1763, gained internal self-government in 1969, and achieved independence in 1979. St Vincent has been at the forefront of discussions concerning possible federation of the English-speaking Windward Islands.

129

Trinidad and Tobago

Official name: Republic of Trinidad and Tobago.

Member of: UN, Commonwealth, CARICOM, OAS.

Area: 5130 km² (1981 sq mi).

Population: 1,249,000 (1993 est).

Capital: Port of Spain 51,000 (1990 census).

Other main towns: San Fernando 30,000, Arima 30,000, Point Fortin 20,000 (1990 census).

Languages: English (official), Hindi (25%).

Religions: Roman Catholic (34%), Hinduism (25%), Anglican (15%), Sunni Islam (6%).

Education: Education is compulsory between the ages of five and 11. In 1990 the literacy rate was over 97%. There is a university.

Defence: In 1993 the total armed strength was 2650. There is a paramilitary police force.

Transport: There are 7895 km (4906 mi) of roads. Port of Spain has a commercial shipping port; Piarco is an international airport.

Media: There are four daily newspapers, a government-owned and a commercial radio station, and two commercial television channels (one state-owned).

GOVERNMENT
The 31-member Senate - the Upper House of Parliament - is appointed by the President, who is elected by a joint sitting of Parliament. The 36-member House of Representatives is elected for five years by universal adult suffrage. The President appoints a Prime Minister who commands a majority in the House. The PM appoints a Cabinet, which is responsible to the House. Tobago has autonomy. Political parties include the (centre) People's National Movement (PNM), the (Tobago-based) National Alliance for Reconstruction (NAR), and the (socialist) United National Congress (UNC). After the election held in December 1991 a PNM government was formed.

Party strength: PNM 21, UNC 13, NAR 2.

President: Noor Mohammed Hassanali.

Prime Minister: Patrick Manning (PNM).

AUTONOMOUS ISLAND
Tobago Area: 301 km² (116 sq mi). Population: 50,000 (1990 census). Capital: Scarborough.

GEOGRAPHY
Trinidad is generally undulating. Tobago is more mountainous. Highest point: Cerro Aripo 940 m (3085 ft) in Trinidad. Principal rivers: Caroni, Orotoire, Oropuche. Climate: Trinidad has a humid tropical climate, with a dry season from January to May.

ECONOMY
Petroleum and petrochemicals are the mainstay of the economy. Trinidad also has reserves of natural gas and asphalt. Tourism is a major foreign-currency earner and the development of tourism is seen as a priority.

Currency: Trinidad and Tobago dollar of 100 cents; 1US$ =5 .56 TT dollars (June 1994).

GDP: US$4,525,000,000 (1991); US$3620 per head.

RECENT HISTORY
Trinidad became British in 1797; Tobago was ceded to Britain in 1802. African slaves were imported to work sugar plantations, After the abolition of slavery in the 1830s, labourers came from India. The islands became a single colony in 1899 and gained independence in 1962 under Dr Eric Williams. His moderate policies brought economic benefits but provoked a Black Power revolt and an army mutiny in 1970. The country has been a republic since 1976. In July 1990, a small group of Islamic fundamentalists held the PM and several government ministers and parliamentarians hostage during an attempted coup.

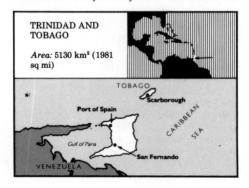

TRINIDAD AND TOBAGO

Area: 5130 km² (1981 sq mi)

TOBAGO
Scarborough
Port of Spain
CARIBBEAN SEA
Gulf of Paria
San Fernando
VENEZUELA

Other Territories

ANGUILLA
Status: a British Dependent Territory.

Area: 96 km² (37 sq mi) - Anguilla 91 km² (35 sq mi), Sombrero 5 km² (2 sq mi).

Population: 9000 (1992 est); Sombrero has no permanent population.

Capital: The Valley 500 (1988 est).

Government: The British sovereign is represented by a Governor who presides over the Executive Council, which comprises the Chief Minister, three other ministers and two ex-officio members. The 11-member House of Assembly comprises seven members elected by universal adult suffrage for five years, two ex-officio members and two members nominated by the Governor, who appoints the Chief Minister and a government enjoying a majority in the House. Chief Minister: Emile Gumbs.

Geography: Anguilla is a low-lying coral island in the eastern Caribbean. The colony includes the island of Sombrero, 48 km (30 mi) to the north. Highest point: Crocus Hill 65 m (213 ft). The climate is tropical and dry for most of the year.

Economy: Tourism is the dominant industry. Salt extraction and schooner-building are also of importance. Expatriot Anguillans working in the US Virgin Islands and the UK outnumber the island's resident population.

Recent History: British settlement began in the 17th century. After 1825 the island was administratively attached to St Kitts (St Christopher). Protests against this association began in the 19th century and culminated in a unilateral declaration of independence in 1967. British troops and police intervened in 1969 and the island reverted to direct British control in 1971, although the island was not formally separated from St Kitts-Nevis until 1980.

ARUBA
Status: an autonomous part of the Kingdom of the Netherlands.

Area: 193 km² (75 sq mi).

Population: 68,900 (1991 est).

Capital: Oranjestad 20,000 (1991 est).

Other main town: Sint Niclaas 17,000 (1991 est).

Government: The Dutch sovereign is represented by a Governor. The 21-member legislature (Staten) is elected by universal adult suffrage for four years. The Governor appoints a Prime Minister and a Cabinet. Prime Minister: Nelson Oduber.

Geography: Aruba is a relatively flat island 24 km (15 mi) north of the Venezuelan coast. Highest point: Jamanota 189 m (620 ft). Climate: The climate is tropical and dry - drinking water is desalinated.

Economy: Tourism is the major foreign-currency earner and financial services and data processing are of growing importance. The economy used to depend upon oil refining, which has now ceased. Lack of water restricts farming and most foodstuffs are imported.

Recent History: Aruba - claimed by the Dutch in 1634 - remained inhabited only by Arawak Indians until the 19th century when Spanish, Dutch and other settlers arrived. Part of the Dutch West Indies (later known as the Netherlands Antilles) until 1986, Aruba is now a separate autonomous part of the Kingdom of the Netherlands. Independence is scheduled for 1996 or 1997.

BRITISH VIRGIN ISLANDS
Status: a British Crown colony.

Area: 153 km² (59 sq mi).

Population: 16,700 (1991 census).

Capital: Road Town 2500 (1991 census).

Government: The British sovereign is represented by a Governor, who presides over the Executive Council, which comprises an ex-officio member and four members of the Legislative Council. The 11-member legislature comprises nine members elected by universal adult suffrage, an ex-officio member and the Speaker. The Governor appoints four ministers including a Chief Minister. Chief Minister: H. Lavity Stoutt.

Geography: The colony comprises three main mountainous volcanic islands (Tortola, Virgin Gorda, and Jost van Dyke), a flat coralline

131

island (Anegada) and more than 60 small islands and cays. They form the eastern part of the Virgin Islands group in the Caribbean. Highest point: Mt. Sage (on Tortola) 543 m (1781 ft). Climate: The climate is subtropical and pleasant.

Economy: The British Virgin Islands are totally overshadowed by their larger neighbour, the US Virgin Islands - in fact, American currency is used. Tourism and 'offshore' financial services dominate the economy, and money sent home by the considerable number of islanders working in the US Virgin Islands helps diminish a large trade deficit.

Recent History: The islands formally became English in 1672 and were part of the British Leeward Islands from 1872 to 1954, when they became a separate colony. Full internal self-government was granted in 1967. In recent years the illegal drugs trade through the islands has been a cause of concern.

CAYMAN ISLANDS
Status: a British Crown colony.

Area: 259 km² (100 sq mi).

Population: 27,000 (1991 est.)

Capital: George Town 12,900 (1989 census).

Government: The Governor presides over the Executive Council which comprises five ex-officio members and four members elected by and from the Legislative Assembly. The 18-member Assembly comprises 15 members elected by universal adult suffrage and three ex-officio members.

Geography: The three low-lying Cayman Islands are 290 km (180 mi) west of Jamaica. Highest point: Bluff 42 m (138 ft). The islands have a pleasant tropical maritime climate but are subject to hurricanes.

Economy: The islands' economy relies upon tourism - which employs nearly one third of the labour force - and upon financial services. Based upon its good communications with the nearby USA, its political stability and its bank secrecy laws, the colony is the largest 'offshore' financial centre in the world. As a result, the islands have one of the highest standards of living in the world.

Recent History: The islands were a dependency of Jamaica until 1959, when a separate colonial administration was established. Since then the Cayman Islanders have sought to restrict the electorate (to exclude immigrants) and to maintain the status quo, which is perceived to encourage 'offshore' finance and the very high standard of living.

GUADELOUPE
Status: a French overseas département, an integral part of the French Republic.

Area: 1705 km² (658 sq mi) - Basse-Terre 848 km² (327 sq mi), Grande-Terre 590 km² (228 sq mi), Marie-Galante 158 km² (61 sq mi), St Martin 54 km² (21 sq mi), St Barthélemy 21 km² (8 sq mi), La Désirade 20 km² (8 sq mi), Iles des Saintes 13 km² (5 sq mi).

Population: 378,000 (1990 census) - Basse-Terre 150,000, Grande-Terre 164,000, Marie-Galante 13,500, St Martin 28,500, St Barthélemy 5000, La Désirade 1600, Iles des Saintes 2000. .

Capital: Basse-Terre 14,100 (also capital of Basse-Terre; 1990 census).

Other island capitals: Pointe-à-Pitre (capital of Grande-Terre; city 26,100) 89,000, Grand-Bourg (capital of Marie-Galante) 6000, Marigot (capital of St Martin), Gustavia (capital of St Barthélemy), Grande-Anse (capital of La Désirade), Terre-de-Bas (capital of Iles des Saintes).

Languages: French (official), Creole (majority, except on St Martin), English (majority on St Martin).

Religion: Roman Catholic majority.

Education: Education is compulsory between the ages of six and 16. There is a university.

Transport: There are nearly 3600 km (2250 mi) of roads. There are airports on Grande-Terre, Marie-Galante, St Barthélemy and La Désirade. Pointe-à-Pitre is the main port.

Government: The 42-member General Council is elected by universal adult suffrage for six years. Guadeloupe is represented in the French National Assembly by four deputies and two senators.

Geography: Guadeloupe comprises a group of Caribbean islands: Grande-Terre and Basse Terre - which lie between Antigua and Dominica - are separated by a narrow channel; Marie-Galante, La Désirade and Iles des

Saintes are close by; St Martin is the northern half of a north Caribbean island whose southern half (Sint Maarten) is Dutch; St Barthélemy lies south of Sint Maarten. Highest point: La Soufrière (a volcano on Grande-Terre) 1467 m (4813 ft). Climate: The islands have a humid tropical climate.

Economy: Bananas and sugar cane are the main exports. Tourism is the principal foreign-currency earner.

Recent History: The islands have been French since the 17th century, although St Barthélemy - the last remaining Swedish colony - was purchased by France in 1877. In 1946 Guadeloupe became an overseas département.

MARTINIQUE
Status: a French overseas départment, an integral part of the French Republic.

Area: 1100 km² (425 sq mi).

Population: 360,000 (1990 census).

Capital: Fort-de-France 102,000 (1990 census).

Language: French (official), Creole (majority).

Religion: Roman Catholic (over 90%).

Education: Education is compulsory between the ages of six and 16. There is a university.

Transport: There are 1690 km (1056 mi) of roads. Fort-de-France has an international airport and a commercial shipping port.

Government: The 45-member General Council is elected by universal adult suffrage for six years. Martinique is represented in the French National Assembly by four deputies and in the Senate by two senators.

Geography: Martinique - which lies between St Lucia and Dominica - rises steeply from the sea to its mountainous interior. Highest point: Mt Pelée (a volcano) 1397 m (4583 ft). Climate: The tropical climate is moderated by the sea.

Economy: Agriculture produces bananas (the major export) and sugar cane (for rum). Tourism is increasingly important.

Recent History: Martinique - a French possession since 1635 - became an overseas département in 1946.

MONTSERRAT
Status: a British Crown colony.

Area: 98 km² (38 sq mi).

Population: 12,400 (1989 est).

Capital: Plymouth 1500 (1989 est).

Government: The Governor is the executive authority. The 12-member Legislative Council comprises seven members elected for four years by universal adult suffrage, two nominated members, two officials and the Speaker. The Governor presides over the seven-member Executive Council, to which he appoints four elected members of the legislature (including a Chief Minister) and the two official members of the legislature. Chief Minister: Reuben Meade.

Geography: Montserrat is a small mountainous island in the Leeward group in the eastern Caribbean. Highest point: Chance Peak 914 m (2999 ft). Climate: Montserrat has a tropical climate which is cooled by sea breezes.

Economy: The economy is dominated by tourism and services, particularly data-processing and the island is a computer centre of regional significance. The previously important 'off-shore' financial service sector was destroyed by a major banking scandal in 1989-90.

Recent History: Montserrat - a British possession since 1632 - did not become a separate colony until 1956. The island has enjoyed internal self-government since 1960 but resists independence.

NETHERLANDS ANTILLES OR THE ANTILLES OF THE FIVE
Status: an autonomous part of the Kingdom of the Netherlands.

Area: 800 km² (309 sq mi) - Curaçao 444 km² (171 sq mi), Bonaire 288 km² (111 sq mi), St Maarten 34 km² (13 sq mi), St Eustatius (popularly known as Statia) 21 km² (8 sq mi), Saba 13 km² (5 sq mi).

Population: 191,000 (1991 est) - Curaçao 144,000, Bonaire 11,100, St Maarten 33,500, St Eustatius 1100, Saba 1800.

Capital: Willemstad 125,000 (also capital of Curaçao; city 50,000; 1985 est).

Other island capitals: Philipsburg (capital of St Maarten) 6000, Kralendijk (capital of Bonaire) 1200, Oranjestad (capital of St Eustatius), The Bottom (capital of Saba).

Languages: Dutch (official), Papiemento (Creole; majority in Curaçao and Bonaire), English (majority in St Maarten, St Eustatius and Saba).

Religions: Roman Catholic (84%), various Protestant Churches (majority in St Maarten, St Eustatius and Saba).

Education: Education is not compulsory but is available between the ages of six and 17. There is a university in Curaçao.

Defence: Military service is now optional. There is a Dutch naval base at Willemstad.

Transport: There are 845 km (528 mi) of roads. The islands of Curaçao, Bonaire and St Maarten have international airports and shipping ports.

Government: The 22-member legislature (Staten) is elected by universal adult suffrage for four years - it comprises 14 members for Curaçao, three each for Bonaire and St Maarten, and one each for St Eustatius and Saba. The main political parties are the (social Christian) Partido Nashonal di Pueblo and the (left-wing) Frente Obrero i Liberashon/Social Independente - in Curaçao. The other islands have their own parties including Unión Patriótico Bonairiano. The Governor appoints a Prime Minister and a Cabinet. Prime Minister: Maria-Liberia Peters.

Geography: Curaçao and Bonaire lie off the coast of Venezuela; St Maarten is the southern half of the island shared by France in the Leeward Islands; St Eustatius and Saba are two very small islands north of St Kitts. The three northern islands are known as the Windward Islands although they are actually in the Leeward Islands. Highest point: Sint Christoffelberg (Curaçao) 372 m (1220 ft). Climate: The tropical climate is moderated by the sea.

Economy: Curaçao's economy depends upon refining Venezuelan oil and ship repairing. Bonaire produces textiles and salt. Tourism is important in all the islands.

Recent History: All five islands were claimed by the Dutch in the 17th century. With Aruba, they formed the Dutch West Indies, which were renamed the Netherlands Antilles in 1845. The islands were granted internal self-government in 1954. Aruba seceded in 1986.

PUERTO RICO

Official name: Estado Libre Asociado de Puerto Rico.

Status: a United States Commonwealth territory.

Area: 8959 km² (3459 sq mi).

Population: 3,522,000 (1990 census).

Capital: San Juan 963,000 (city 438,000; Bayamon 220,000, Carolina 178,000; 1990 census).

Other main towns: Ponce 188,000, Caguas 133,000 (1990 census).

Languages: Spanish (official; majority as a first language), English.

Religion: Roman Catholic (81%).

Education: Education is compulsory between the ages of six and 16. The state university is in three centres.

Defence: There is a Puerto Rican national guard and the US Navy has installations in the island. Puerto Rican males are subject to conscription in the US forces.

Transport: There are 21,737 km (13,585 mi) of roads. There are no passenger railways but there are 94 km (59 mi) of sugar cane railways. San Juan and Aguadilla have international airports; San Juan is the principal commercial shipping port.

Government: An executive Governor, a 27-member Senate and a 53-member House of Representatives are elected by universal adult suffrage for four years. The Governor appoints a Cabinet of 17 Secretaries. Puerto Rico returns a non-voting member to the US Congress. The principal political parties are the (pro-US statehood) New Progressive Party, the (pro-status quo) Popular Democratic Party and the (pro-independence) Puerto Rico Independence Party

Geography: Puerto Rico - the easternmost island of the Greater Antilles - is crossed from east to west by a mountainous chain. The islands of Vieques and Culebra are also included in the Commonwealth. Highest point: Cerro de Punta 1325 m (4347 ft). Climate: Puerto Rico has a humid maritime tropical climate.

Economy: Although Puerto Rico has no mineral resources, manufacturing industry dominates with pharmaceuticals, petrochemicals, electrical and electronic equipment, food processing and textiles as the major interests. Tourism from the USA is a major industry. The island is densely populated and there has been large-scale migration to the USA. US federal funds have developed the infrastructure and encouraged the service sector.

Recent History: Puerto Rico - a Spanish colony from 1509 - was ceded to the USA in 1898 following the Spanish-American War. The island gained internal self-government in 1952 when it became a Commonwealth and - despite periodic debates concerning its status - Puerto Rico has so far rejected either the option of independence or US statehood.

TURKS AND CAICOS ISLANDS
Status: a British Crown colony.

Area: 430 km² (166 sq mi).

Population: 12,400 (1990 census).

Capital: Cockburn Town 2500 (1990 census) on Grand Turk island.

Government: The British sovereign is represented by a Governor. The Legislative Council comprises 12 members elected by universal adult suffrage for four years, three nominated members, three ex-officio members and the Speaker. The Governor presides over the eight-member Executive Council, to which he appoints five elected members of the legislature (including a Chief Minister) and the three official members of the legislature. Chief Minister: Washington Misick.

Geography: The 30 Turks and Caicos Islands form two groups of low-lying islands to the southeast of the Bahamas. Highest point: an unnamed point 48 m (157 ft). Climate: The warm tropical climate is cooled by sea breezes.

Economy: The economy depends upon tourism (specializing in an 'upmarket' clientele) and 'offshore' banking and finance.

Recent History: The islands - which finally became British in 1766 - were linked administratively to Jamaica until 1959. They became a separate colony in 1962. The Turks and Caicos Islands were rocked by a major scandal in 1985-86 when the Chief Minister, another minister and a member of the legislature were arrested and later imprisoned in Florida on charges involving illicit drugs. The next Chief Minister and two of his ministers were subsequently found guilty of malpractice.

VIRGIN ISLANDS OF THE UNITED STATES
Status: an unincorporated US external territory.

Area: 352 km² (136 sq mi).

Population: 102,000 (1990 census).

Capital: Charlotte Amalie 12,300 (1990 census).

Languages: English (official), Creole, Spanish.

Religions: Episcopalian, Roman Catholic, Lutheran, Methodist.

Education: Education is compulsory between the ages of six and 16. There is a university.

Transport: There are over 1055 km (660 mi) of roads. Local ferries are important. St Thomas and St Croix have international airports.

Government: A Governor is elected by universal suffrage for four years and a 15-member Senate for two years. Political parties affiliated to the US Democratic and Republican parties operate. The islands return a non-voting member to the US Congress.

Geography: The territory comprises three main islands - St Croix, St Thomas and St John - and about 50 small cays. About 64 km (40 mi) east of Puerto Rico, the islands command the Anegada Passage, one of the principal shipping routes from the Atlantic Ocean to the Caribbean Sea. Highest point: Crown Mt (on St Thomas) 474 m (1772 ft). Climate: The tropical climate is tempered by trade winds.

Economy: The islands have no natural resorces. Tourism, which dominates the economy, is encouraged by the climate and the fact that the whole territory enjoys free port status. St Croix has one of the world's largest oil refineries. Almost one half of the population comprises workers from other Caribbean islands and wealthy (mainly retired) US residents.

Recent History: Denmark acquired St John and St Thomas in 1671 and St Croix in 1733. The USA purchased the islands from Denmark in 1917 because of their strategic position guarding the main shipping route to the Panana Canal. Since 1954 the islands have had a measure of self-government.

135

CENTRAL
AND
EASTERN EUROPE

Albania, Bosnia-Herzegovina, Bulgaria, Croatia, Czech Republic,
Estonia, Hungary, Latvia, Lithuania, Macedonia (The Former
Yugoslav Republic of), Poland, Romania, Slovakia, Slovenia,
Yugoslavia (Serbia and Montenegro).

The New Central Europe

Since the break-up of the Communist bloc in Eastern Europe, one part of the region has fared consistently better in economic terms than the rest. The Visegrad Group of Poland, the former Czechoslovakia and Hungary have done better in production terms, and have kept inflation down to lower levels, than almost all of the other East European Countries. They were the first to sign association agreements with the EC, and the first to come together to create a sub-regional free-trade area. While the record of the Visegrad countries on unemployment is mixed, living standards are generally substantially higher than in the other ex-Communist countries. The return of the left in recent elections in Poland and Hungary indicates that the populations of these countries have taken a critical view of the achievements of the last few years, but there can be little doubt that the Central-East European countries have been 'favoured'. To what extent does this reflect a more positive legacy from the late-Communist period, special treatment from the EU, or better management of the economy by national governments?

The New Economic Mechanism (NEM) established in Hungary in 1968 represented the first move towards market socialism within the Soviet bloc. In the early 1980s, during the period of martial law in Poland, President Jaruzelski set the Polish economy on a similar path of compromise between socialism and market principles. In neither case was market socialism a great success in itself. But it did allow the populations of these countries to get used to the categories of the market economy again, and it improved consumer-goods supplies in terms of quality and variety, paving the way for a shift of priorities back from intermediate production to the final consumer. In Poland the deep political and economic crisis of the late 1970s and early 1980s had the effect of 'clearing the decks' for the shock-therapy package of 1990, ensuring that restored capitalism could not be blamed for the (lagged) effects of the deficiencies of the old system. In Czechoslovakia, the military suppression of the Prague Spring of 1968 killed market socialism in one of its intellectual homelands. But the relative strength of the Czech economy, combined with a traditional Czech financial prudence, meant that the new regime of 1990 was not burdened with the fiscal deficits that have proved such an obstacle on the transition path elsewhere in the region.

THE ASSOCIATION AGREEMENTS WITH THE EC

In 1991 Poland, Czechoslovakia and Hungary negotiated agreements with the EC that promised free trade between the EC and these countries by 2001. Similar agreements were later signed between the EC and the Czech and Slovak republics. Over the ten-year transition period envisaged by the original agreements tariffs would gradually be lowered, and quantitative restrictions eliminated. A further agreement of June 1993 sped up the schedule for reducing tariffs, promising abolition of duties on a list of 'sensitive' industrial goods. But the agreements contain specific provisions for the imposition of emergency trade restrictions as and when the signatories see fit. In practice, the EC continues to impose such restrictions on such 'extra-sensitive' commodities as steel, while the CAP ensures that there will be no free trade in agricultural goods, even after 2001. The June 1993 agreement does nothing to protect the Visegrad countries from emergency trade restrictions, but it does state, that the co-signatories are on a path, not just to free trade, but to actual membership of the EU. Poland and Hungary both applied for full membership of the EU in April 1994; they are unlikely to receive a rapid positive response, but the applications in themselves represent one further stage in a historic process. The association agreements are clearly in practice less liberal than they look. The 'extra-sensitive' categories of goods on which the EC/EU is likely to continue to impose emergency trade restrictions in a number of cases correspond to major East European comparative advantages. On the other hand the EC/EU commitment to ultimate full membership of the Community for the Visegrad countries does, in itself, bring those countries into some kind of EC 'outer circle'. Signature of the association agreements created an anomaly in trade relations between the Visegrad countries themselves, inasmuch as EC firms would now have better access to Polish markets than, say, Hungarian firms. This was one of the factors lying behind the creation, in 1993, of the Central European Free Trade Area.

137

CEFTA

The CEFTA Agreement, which came into force in March 1993, originally foresaw an eight-year transition to free trade in industrial goods. Some 52% of Hungarian industrial exports to Poland already enter tariff-free, as does 50-55 per cent of Polish exports to Hungary. A further group of tariffs were scheduled to be reduced to zero by 1997. For the typically 'sensitive' categories of textiles, steel and vehicles zero tariffs would finally be achieved in 2001. (A supplementary protocol agreed on 29 April 1994 predicated an acceleration of the whole process, with free trade being finally achieved on 1 January 1998.) Finally, there are specific exemptions for the trade in auto parts, aimed at encouraging the development of micro-specialization within a sector in which the region has at least potential comparative advantage vis-à-vis the rest of the world. But not all dimensions of the CEFTA Agreement are so liberal. Signatories may maintain restrictions on exports of raw materials. As far as agriculture is concerned, there is simply no liberalization at all. The general-emergency trade restriction clauses of the Agreement are wide-ranging. In addition to the normal anti-dumping and safeguard measures sanctioned by GATT, the CEFTA Agreement permits emergency trade measures in cases where trading patterns are deemed to be injurious to competition, in the case of 'infant industries', and where restructuring is in progress. In East European conditions that last clause gives CEFTA governments carte blanche to impose emergency trade restrictions as they see fit. As with the association agreements, then, the CEFTA Agreement flatters to deceive. But if the efforts of the Visegrad countries are compared to the failures of the CIS countries in seeking to establish a CIS Economic Union, the achievement must be owned a considerable one. Again as with the association agreements, the ultimate commitment to free trade gives the Visegrad countries a goal that is lacking in most other parts of the East European region.

DOMESTIC ECONOMIC POLICY

Have the Visegrad countries, in their domestic economic policies, been models of shock therapy? Certainly, they have generally managed to hold their budget deficits to below 7% of GNP – elsewhere in the region the corresponding figure has been 10-40%, one of the main reasons for their above-average performance on inflation. But on privatization, commercialization, enforcement of bankruptcy, etc., policies have generally gone much more slowly, with the 'Thatcherite' Klaus government of the Czech Republic providing only a partial exception. While the pace of privatization has been constrained by factors outside government control, Visegrad governments have chosen to cut expenditure on education, training and R&D, albeit often in pursuit of the laudable goal of limiting fiscal imbalances. Against the background of continued decline or stagnation in labour productivity everywhere except Poland, this weakness of microeconomic policy may have serious medium-term implications. Of the four countries, Slovakia is perhaps least vulnerable to the charge of neglecting the microeconomy. But its attempts to restructure its defence-industry-dominated economy on a top-down basis smack more of Soviet-style dirigisme than of market-led structural policies.

The inflow of foreign direct investment into the Visegrad countries has been disappointing. Hungary has the best record in the region, with total FDI 1990–93 cumulating to over $6bn. The Czech Republic had an aggregate FDI figure in 1993 of nearly $1bn, but there has been little FDI into Slovakia. The Polish record is if anything worse than the Slovakian, though it started to improve from the end of 1993. The USA and Germany have been dominant within the pattern of FDI, with France also playing a significant role. But general levels of FDI have been very low by international standards.

Regional Organizations of Central and Eastern Europe

THE CENTRAL EUROPEAN FREE TRADE AGREEMENT (CEFTA)

The CEFTA (see pp. 137-38) was signed in December 1992 with the aim of setting up a free-trade area between members by the year 2001. This timetable has since been shortened (see the previous pages) and it is the ambition of the member-states of the CEFTA to achieve EU/EC membership before that date.

Slovenia has signed free-trade agreements with the CEFTA countries, but is not yet a member of the organization.

Membership: The Czech Republic, Hungary, Poland, and Slovakia.

THE DANUBE COMMISSION

The Danube Commission was established in 1949 to regularize the navigation of the River Danube and to ensure access to the shipping of all states.

Headquarters: Budapest, Hungary.

Membership: Austria, Bulgaria, Germany (consultative status), Hungary, Romania, Russia, Slovakia, Ukraine, and Yugoslavia (Serbia and Montenegro). Yugoslavia is effectively suspended from the organization.

EUROPEAN COMMUNITY (EU/EC)

Associate membership of the European Community (see pp. 347-49) has been achieved by a number of Central and East European countries. Associate status of the European Community implies eventual full membership of the EU, although such membership is a more immediate realistic prospect for the countries of the Visegrad Group - see below - than for Bulgaria and Romania. (The nature, and benefits of, associate membership are described on the preceding pages.)

Trade pacts, that are expected to lead to associate status of the European Community, have been concluded with the Baltic states.

Associate membership: Bulgaria, the Czech Republic, Hungary, Poland, Romania, and Slovakia.

Trade agreement status: Estonia, Latvia, and Lithuania.

THE VISEGRAD GROUP

The Visegrad group is not a formal organization but an informal grouping originally comprising Czechoslovakia, Hungary and Poland. The Visegrad Group gained formal existence upon the foundation of the Central European Free Trade Agreement (CEFTA) - see above.

Membership: The Czech Republic, Hungary, Poland, and Slovakia.

OTHER ORGANIZATIONS

The following states of Central and Eastern Europe have membership of the Council of Europe (see pp. 350-51): Bulgaria, the Czech Republic, Estonia, Hungary, Lithuania, Poland, Slovakia, and Slovenia. Membership of the Council is restricted to European democracies.

The following states of Central and Eastern Europe have signed NATO's Partnership for Peace Agreement (see pp. 350-51): Albania, Bulgaria, the Czech Republic, Estonia, Hungary, Latvia, Lithuania, Poland, Romania, Slovakia, and Slovenia.

The following states of Central and Eastern Europe are members of the Conference on Security and Co-operation in Europe (CSCE; see pp. 350-51): Albania, Bosnia-Herzegovina, Croatia, the Czech Republic, Estonia, Hungary, Latvia, Lithuania, The Former Yugoslav Republic of Macedonia, Poland, Romania, Slovakia, and Slovenia. Yugoslavia (that is, Serbia and Montenegro) was suspended in 1992.

Bulgaria and Romania are both members of the Black Sea Economic Co-operation Zone (see p. 207).

The Baltic States - Estonia, Latvia and Lithuania - have achieved a considerable degree of co-operation at government level, for example in defence and military matters. This co-operation does not, however, take the form of an established international organization. The Baltic States have, however, with Poland and the countries of the Nordic Council laid the foundations of an informal organization linking the countries bordering the Baltic Sea.

Central and Eastern European Trade

The trading patterns that existed before the fall of the Communist regimes of Central and Eastern Europe (1989-90) were determined by the Comecon pact, a trade organization that coordinated the economic development of the Soviet bloc (mainly for the benefit of the former Soviet Union). Comecon placed artificial restrictions upon international trade in the region, encouraging trade within the organization rather than with third parties. With the introduction of free market economies in Central and Eastern Europe, the organization was disbanded in March 1991.

The new trading patterns that have emerged since then are not always reflected in the following figures. For example, Russia, Ukraine and Belarus now take far fewer exports from Eastern and Central Europe, and supply the countries of the region with less goods.

Albania Imports ($ million): 446.5 (1990). Exports ($ million): 267.4 (1990). Main imports: machinery and equipment 25.2% (1990), fuels, minerals and metals 24.6% (1990). Main exports: crude minerals and metalliferous ores 46.8% (1990), food and food preparations 20% (1990). Principal trading partners (since 1991): Germany, Italy, Czech Republic, Bulgaria, Austria, Greece.

Bosnia-Herzegovina No recent figures are available. The principal imports are mineral fuels and other raw materials, and foodstuffs. Before the Bosnian war, chemicals and machinery were the principal exports. Croatia is the principal trading partner of the Muslim-Croat Bosnian federation. Before the border between Yugoslavia (Serbia and Montenegro) was sealed in 1994, Serbia was the principal trading partner of the self-proclaimed Bosnian Serb republic (the Republika Srpska).

Bulgaria Imports ($ million): 12,893 (1990). Exports ($ million): 13,347 (1990). Main imports: machinery and equipment 46.7% (1990), fuels, minerals, raw materials and metals 33.4% (1990). Main exports: machinery and equipment 59.0% (1990), beverages and food 12.1% (1990). Principal trading partners (since 1991): Russia, Germany, Italy, Greece, Turkey, Ukraine, Romania.

Croatia Imports ($ million): 3828 (1991). Exports ($ million): 3292 (1991). Main imports: minerals, fuels and lubricants 17.4% (1991), chemicals 13.4% (1991), food and live animals 10.6% (1991). Main exports: aluminium products, food and live animals. Principal trading partners (since 1991): Germany, Italy, the Czech Republic, Austria, Russia, the Netherlands.

Czech Republic Imports ($ million): 6970 (1990 est). Exports ($ million): 7600 (1990 est). Main imports: machinery and transport equipment 36.9%, minerals, fuels and lubricants 17.3% (1989). Main exports: specialized machinery and transport equipment 44.3% (1991), basic manufactures 22.4% (1989). Principal trading partners (since 1991): Germany, Austria, Slovakia, France, Italy, the Netherlands, UK, Poland, Hungary.

Estonia Imports (roubles million): 4454.5 (1991). Exports (roubles million): 5102.3 (1991). Main imports: textiles and textile articles 19% (1991), machinery 13.9% (1991). Main exports: textiles and textile articles 26.3% (1991), machinery 11.5% (1991), live animals and animal products 10% (1991). Principal trading partners (since 1991): Finland, Sweden, Germany, Russia, Latvia, Denmark, Ukraine, Belarus.

Hungary Imports (forints million): 878,500 (1992). Exports (forints million): 844,000 (1992). Main imports: basic manufactures 20.6% (1991), machinery and transport equipment 30.8 (1991). Total exports: machinery and transport equipment 22.4% (1991), food and live animals 22.1% (1991). Principal trading partners (since 1991): Germany, Austria, Italy, Czech Republic, Russia, Switzerland, France, Japan, the Netherlands.

Latvia Imports (roubles million): 6327 (1990). Exports (roubles million): 5283 (1990). Main imports: machinery and equipment, textiles. Main exports: food products, machinery and equipment. Principal trading partners (since 1991): Russia, Lithuania, Denmark, Germany, Ukraine, Belarus, Estonia, Sweden, Kazakhstan.

Lithuania Imports (roubles million): 5373. Exports (roubles million): 8495. Main imports: coal, fuel and petroleum products 20.7% (1991), chemicals, machinery. Main exports: food and food products 33.4% (1991), machinery.

Principal trading partners (since 1991): Russia, Germany, Ukraine, Belarus, Poland, Latvia, Sweden.

Macedonia (Former Yugoslav Republic of) Imports and exports: no recent figures are available. Main imports: fuel, machinery and transport equipment. Main exports: agricultural products. Principal trading partners: Bulgaria, Yugoslavia (Serbia and Montenegro). Before the imposition of UN sanctions in 1992, over 60% of Macedonia's trade was with Yugoslavia (Serbia and Montenegro.) The 1994 blockade imposed by Greece on trade with and through Macedonia has reduced Macedonia's imports and exports, which, in 1994, were increasingly 'sanctions busting' trade with Yugoslavia.

Poland Imports ($ million): 14,261 (1991). Exports ($ million): 14,460 (1991). Main imports: electro engineering products 37.6% (1991), chemicals 12.5% (1991), fuels and power 18.8% (1991), consumer goods. Main exports: electro engineering products 22.4% (1991), chemicals 11.5% (1991), iron and steel, machinery. Principal trading partners (since 1991): Germany, Russia, Austria, Netherlands, UK, the Czech Republic, Italy, Slovakia, Ukraine, Belarus, Switzerland.

Romania Imports ($ million): 5600 (1991). Exports ($ million): 4124 (1991). Main imports: mineral fuels 47.6% (1990), machinery and transport equipment 23.7% (1990). Main exports: fuels, mineral raw materials and metals 33.6% (1990), machinery and transport equipment 30.8% (1990). Principal trading partners (since 1991): Germany, USA, Italy, Russia, Ukraine, Saudi Arabia, Iran, Poland, the Czech Republic, Turkey.

Slovakia Imports (koruna million): 110,864 (1991). Exports (koruna million): 96,800 (1991). Main imports: mineral fuels, lubricants etc. 35.2% (1991), machinery and transport equipment 23.8% (1991). Main exports: basic manufactures 36.2% (1991), machinery and transport equipment 22.5% (1991). Principal trading partners (since 1991): Germany, the Czech Republic, Russia, Austria, Poland, Italy, Hungary, Ukraine.

Slovenia Imports (tolar million): 104,498 (1991). Exports (tolar million): 102,158 (1991). Main imports: machinery and transport equipment 34.5% (1991), basic manufactures 18.9%

(1991). Main exports: machinery and transport equipment 38% (1991), metals and metal goods 10.2% (1991). Principal trading partners (since 1991): Germany, Italy, France, Austria, Croatia, USA, Russia.

Yugoslavia (Serbia and Montenegro) Imports ($ million): n/a. Exports ($ million): n/a. Main imports: machinery and transport equipment 22.6% (1991), mineral fuels, lubricants etc. 18.9% (1991). Main exports: basic manufactures 27.1% (1991), machinery and transport equipment 19.6% (1991). Principal trading partners (before the imposition of United Nations sanctions in 1992 interrupted trade, except for foodstuffs and medicines): Russia, Germany, Italy. Principal trading partner (since the imposition of UN sanctions in 1992): The Former Yugoslav Republic of Macedonia (largely 'unofficial' trade).

Albania

Official name: Republika e Shqipërise (Republic of Albania).

Member of: UN, CSCE, NATO (partner for peace).

Area: 28,748 km² (11,100 sq mi).

Population: 3,422,000 (1993 est).

Capital: Tirana (Tiranë) 244,000 (1990 est).

Other major cities: Durrës 85,000, Elbasan 83,000, Shkodër 82,000, Vlorë 74,000, Korçë 65,000, Fier 45,000, Berat 44,000 (1990 est).

Languages: Albanian. (Gheg dialect in the north; Tosk dialect, the official language, in the south.)

Religions: Sunni Islam (20%), Greek Orthodox and Roman Catholic minorities. The practice of religion was banned from 1967 to 1990.

Education: Education is compulsory between the ages of seven and 15. There is a university.

Defence: In 1992 the total strength of Albania's armed forces was 40,000 (including 22,400 conscripts) - the army had a strength of 27,000, the air force 11,000 and the navy 2000. Conscription lasts for two years in the army and three years in the other services.

Transport: There are 6700 km (4188 mi) of main roads and 10,000 km (6250 mi) of other roads. The ownership of private cars was banned until 1991. There are 509 km (318 mi) of railway track. The single international airport in Albania is at Rinas, near Tirana.

Media: There are 41 daily newspapers, mostly regional. There is a single state-owned radio network (with regional stations) and one state-owned television station.

GOVERNMENT

A 140-member Assembly is elected under a system of proportional representation by universal adult suffrage for four years. The Assembly elects a President who appoints a Chairman (Prime Minister) and a Council of Ministers. Local government is in the hands of 26 districts (rreth). The principal political parties are the (centre) Democratic Party (DPA), the (former Communist) Socialist Party (SPA), the Social Democrat Party (SDP), the Union of Human Rights (UHR) and the Albanian Republican Party (ARP). After the general election held in March 1992 a coalition of DPA, SDP and ARP members and independents was formed.

Party strength: DPA 92, SPA 38, SDP 7, UHR 2, ARP 1.

President: Sali Berisha (DPA).

THE CABINET

Prime Minister (Chairman): Aleksandr Meksi (DPA).

Deputy Prime Minister (Deputy Chairman) and Minister for Public Order: Bashkim Kopliku (DPA).

Minister of Agriculture and Food: Rexhep Uka (DPA).

Minister of Construction, Housing and Land Distribution: Ilir Manushi (DPA).

Minister of Culture, Youth and Sport: Dhimitër Anagnosti (DPA).

Minister of Defence: Safet Xhulali (DPA).

Minister of Education: Ylli Vejsiu (DPA).

Minister of Finances and the Economy: Genc Ruli (DPA).

Minister of Foreign Affairs: Alfred Serreqi (DPA).

Minister of Foreign Economic Relations: Artan Hoxha (DPA).

Minister of Health and Environmental Protection: Tritan Shehu (DPA).

Minister of Industry, Mining and Energy Resources: Abdyl Xhaja (Independent).

Minister of Justice: Kudret Cela (Independent).

Minister of Labour, Emigration, Social Welfare and the Politically Persecuted: Dashamir Shehi (DPA).

Minister of Tourism: Osman Shehu (DPA).

Minister of Transport and Communication: Fatos Bitnicka (ARP).

Chairman of the State Control Commission: Blerim Cela (DPA).

Chairman of the Science and Technology Committee: Maksim Konomi (DPA).

General Secretary: Vullnet Ademi (SDP).

GEOGRAPHY

Coastal lowlands - including the basins of the rivers Drini (in the north) and Vjosa (in the south) - cover 25% of the country and support most of Albania's agriculture. Mountain ranges cover the rest of the country - the rugged limestone North Albanian Alps, the central uplands and the lower southern highlands. Highest point: Mount Korab 2751 m (9025 ft). Principal rivers: Semani, Drini, Vjosa. Climate: The Mediterranean coastal areas experience hot, dry summers and mild, wet winters. The mountainous interior is equally warm in the summer but has cold winters.

ALBANIA
Area: 28 748 km² (11 100 sq mi).

ECONOMY

Albania is poor by European standards. The economy is mainly based upon agriculture and the export of chromium (1,010,000 tonnes in 1990). By early 1992 most state-owned cooperative land had been redistributed into private hands. A National Privatization Agency for the privatization of state-owned industry was operating by 1992. In 1990 Albania ended self-imposed economic isolation and sought financial, technical and humanitarian assistance from the West. Nevertheless, the country has experienced short-term famine, continuing

emigration and, owing to a shortage of raw materials, a dramatic collapse in industrial output. These problems were added to by a government commitment to pay 80% of their previous salary to workers made redundant because of the raw materials shortage. Albania runs a large and increasing budget deficit. Revenues have fallen with declining production and severe social and economic problems mean that extra demands are being placed upon the state.

Currency: Lek of 100 qindarka (qindars or qintars); 1US$ = 109.97 leks (leke) (May 1994).

GDP: US$3,800,000,000 (1988); US$1300 per head.

RECENT HISTORY

Independence from the Ottoman (Turkish) Empire, to which it had belonged for 400 years, was declared in 1912 and a provisional government was formed. Albania was occupied in both the Balkan Wars (1912-13) and World War I, and a stable government within recognized frontiers did not exist until the 1920s. Interwar Albania was dominated by Ahmed Zogu (1895-1961), who made himself king (as Zog I) in 1928 and used Italian loans to develop his impoverished country. He fled when Mussolini invaded in 1939. Albania was annexed to Italy from 1939 to 1943 when it came under German occupation. Communist-led partisans took power when the Germans withdrew (1944). Under Enver Hoxha (1908-85; Communist Party leader 1943- 85) and Mehmet Shehu (PM 1954-81), the regime pursued rapid modernization on Stalinist lines, allied, in turn, to Yugoslavia, the USSR and China, before opting (in 1978) for self-sufficiency and isolation. In 1990, a power struggle within the ruling Communist Party was won by the more liberal wing led by President Alia, who instituted a programme of economic, political and social reforms. Emigration from Albania has been a feature since 1990. The Communist Party retained a majority in multi-party elections held in April 1991, but - as the Socialist Party - was defeated in 1992. Albania faces severe economic problems and the growing threat of major disorders in the Serbian province of Kosovo, where ethnic Albanians - who make up 90% of the population - are denied full civil rights by the minority Serbian community.

143

Bosnia-Herzegovina

Official name: Bosna i Hercegovina (Bosnia-Herzegovina).

Member of: UN, CSCE.

Area: 51,129 km² (19,741 sq mi) - in mid-1994 the (Bosnian Muslim-Bosnian Croat) Federation of Bosnia and Herzegovina controlled about 30% of the area, while the self-proclaimed Serb Republic controlled about 70% of the total area.

Population: 4,365,000 (1991 census); c. 3,500,000 (1993 est) - many refugees left Bosnia in 1992-93; over 200,000 people have been killed in the Bosnian war.

Capital: Sarajevo 526,000 (city 416,000; 1991 census); by 1994 the population of Sarajevo was c. 300,000.

Other major cities: Tuzla 130,000 (over 230,000 by 1994), Banja Luka 143,000, Mostar 110,000 (under 100,000 by 1994) (1991 census).

Languages: Serbo-Croat - a single language with two written forms.

Religions: Sunni Islam (44%), Serbian Orthodox (33%), Roman Catholic (17%) - pre-Bosnian war figures.

Education: In theory education is compulsory between the ages of seven and 15. Before the Bosnian war there were four universities.

Defence: By mid-1993 the forces controlled by the (Muslim-Croat) Bosnian government numbered about 90,000.

Transport: Transport in Bosnia has broken down. There are 21,168 km (13,153 mi) of roads, but many road routes are largely impassable. There are 1039 km (646 mi) of railways, none of which is still operating. Sarajevo airport is open intermittently.

Media: The Bosnian government retains control of a single radio and television network in Sarajevo where a daily newspaper continues publication.

GOVERNMENT
By 1993 government had broken down. Two separate assemblies - largely representing the previous nationally elected Assembly divided upon religio-linguistic lines - have evolved: the (internationally-recognized) government of the Federation of Bosnia-Herzegovina (largely Muslim and Croat), based in Sarajevo, and a (Bosnian Serb) government of the self-styled Republika Srpska, based in Pale. The city of Mostar was placed under EU administration in 1994. There are no recent figures for the party strength in the Bosnian parliament.

President (of the internationally-recognized government in Sarajevo): Alija Izetbegovic.

THE CABINET
includes

Prime Minister: Haris Silajdzic.

Deputy Prime Minister: Edib Bukvic.

Minister of Foreign Affairs: Irfan Llubijankic.

Minister of Internal Affairs: Bakir Alispalvic.

Minister of Justice: Sead Kveso.

GEOGRAPHY
Ridges of the Dinaric Mountains, rising to over 1800 m (6000 ft), occupy the greater part of the country and in places form arid karst limestone plateaux. The north comprises restricted lowlands in the valley of the River Sava. The combined length of two tiny coastlines on the Adriatic - now under Croat control - is less than 20 km (13 mi). Highest point: Maglic 2387 m (9118 ft). Principal rivers: Sava, Bosna, Drina. Climate: The north (Bosnia) has cold winters and warm summers; Herzegovina (the south) enjoys milder winters and warmer summers.

ECONOMY
The economy has been devastated by war since 1992. Central and east Bosnia is forested. Agriculture is a major employer and sheep, maize, olives, grapes and citrus fruit were important. Bosnia has little industry but possesses natural resources including coal, lignite, copper and asphalt.

Currency: The Yugoslav dinar is used in Serb-controlled areas; Croatian currency is used in Herzegovina. There is no Bosnian currency.

GDP: No reliable recent figures are available.

RECENT HISTORY
A major Bosnian revolt (1875-6) against Turkish rule attracted international concern, but the great powers overrode Bosnia's pan-Slavic aspirations at the Congress of Berlin

(1877-8) and assigned Bosnia-Herzegovina to Habsburg Austro-Hungarian rule. In Sarajevo in 1914, Gavrilo Princip, a Bosnian Serb student, assassinated Archduke Franz Ferdinand, the heir to the Austro-Hungarian Empire - an event that helped precipitate World War I. In 1918, Bosnia became part of the new Kingdom of Serbs, Croats and Slovenes, which was renamed Yugoslavia in 1929. Following the German invasion (1941), Bosnia was included in the Axis-controlled puppet state of Croatia. In 1945, when Yugoslavia was reorganized by Marshal Tito on Soviet lines, Bosnia-Herzegovina became a republic within the Communist federation. After the secession of Slovenia and Croatia and the beginning of the Yugoslav civil war (1991), tension grew between Serbs and Croats in Bosnia. The Muslim Bosnians reasserted their separate identity. In 1992, a referendum - which was boycotted by the Serbs - gave a majority in favour of Bosnian independence. International recognition of Bosnia-Herzegovina was gained in April 1992 but Bosnian Serbs, encouraged by Serbia, seized 70% of the country, killing or expelling Muslims and Croats in a campaign of 'ethnic cleansing'. The Bosnian Serbs, led by Radovan Karadzic, established an internationally-unrecognized republic based upon the resort of Pale. International peace and humanitarian efforts were attempted and, in an attempt to curb the Bosnian Serbs, strict UN sanctions were imposed on Serbia and Montenegro (Yugoslavia). By the autumn of 1993 the Bosnian government controlled only 10% of the country - central Bosnia, and enclaves including Bihac, Goradze and

Srbenica. Croat-Muslim fighting flared over control of central Bosnia. In September 1993 a plan for a Union of Republics of Bosnia and Herzegovina was rejected. By early 1994 the Bosnian army, which had been deprived of weapons with which to defend itself by an international arms embargo, was beginning to gain arms, confidence and territory. Following an inconclusive fierce fight to control Mostar, the Bosnian Muslims and the Bosnian Croats agreed to form a federation of ethnically-delineated cantons with Sarajevo as its neutral capital. The Bosnian Serbs refused to join this federation, but (in July 1994) were put under pressure to accept a new peace plan for Bosnia, which had been devised by the so-called 'Contact Group' (the USA, Russia, France, the UK and Germany). This envisages the partition of Bosnia into two states within a sovereign Bosnia-Herzegovina - a Muslim-Croat federation, with control of 51% of the land area of Bosnia-Herzegovia, and a Serb state occupying the remaining 49%. Sarajevo would be under UN administration for several years and Mostar would be administered by the EU. (An EU administrator took up residence in Mostar in July 1994.) Brcko and Doboj, towns which command the route between the two main parts of Serbian Bosnia, would also be under UN administration., while UN protection would be extended to the areas around the Muslim enclaves of Zepa, Gorazde and Srebrenica in eastern Bosnia. The Bosnian government would control the central part of Bosnia and most of Herzegovina, including access to the Adriatic Sea at Neum, as well as an enclave along the Croatian border at Orasje and a further enclave in the northwest around Bihac. The Muslim enclaves in eastern Bosnia would be detached 'islands' of the Muslim-Croat federation, but connected to Sarajevo by a swathe of UN-controlled territory. This plan - which has been presented to the belligerents on a 'take-it-or-leave-it' basis - was criticized by the Sarajevo government on the grounds that it rewarded ethnic cleansing and did not allow the Muslims to return to the towns from which they had been expelled by the Serbs. Eventually President Izetbegovic accepted the plan. The Serbian parliament hedged its 'acceptance' with so many qualifications that Pale is deemed to have rejected the plan. Following the Bosnian Serbs' rejection of the plan, Serbia's President Milosevic threatened to close his border with Serbian-controlled Bosnia.

BOSNIA-HERZEGOVINA

Area: 51 129 km² (19 741 sq mi).

CROATIA

Banja Luka

Sarajevo

Mostar

YUGOSLAVIA

Bulgaria

Official name: Republika Bulgariya (Republic of Bulgaria).

Member of: UN, CSCE, Council of Europe, NATO(partner for peace).

Area: 110,912 km² (42,823 sq mi).

Population: 8,473,000 (1992 census).

Capital: Sofia (Sofiya) 1,221,000 (including suburbs; 1990 est).

Other major cities: Plovdiv 379,000, Varna 315,000, Burgas 205,000, Ruse 192,000, Stara Zagora 165,000, Pleven 138,000, Dobrich (formerly Tolbukhin) 116,000, Sliven 112,000, Shumen 111,000 (including suburbs; 1990 est).

Languages: Bulgarian (official; 89%), Turkish (9%).

Religions: Orthodox (80%), Sunni Islam (8%), small Roman Catholic and Protestant minorities.

Education: Education is compulsory between the ages of six and 16. In 1990 the literacy rate was estimated to be over 97%. There are four universities and 16 other higher education institutions are regarded as having university status.

Defence: In 1992 the total armed strength was 107,000 - 75,000 in the army, 10,000 in the navy and 20,000 in the air force. Military service, which is compulsory, lasts 18 months. There is a voluntary militia of over 100,000.

Transport: There are 36,930 km (23,081 mi) of road including 276 km (173 mi) of motorway. There are 4299 km (2687 mi) of state-owned railways. Inland waterway traffic is important; Ruse and Lom are the principal ports on the River Danube. Varna and Burgas are the most important Bulgarian Black Sea ports. Sofia, Varna and Burgas have international airports.

Media: There are 24 principal daily newspapers (since 1990 including a number of mass circulation independent papers). There is a single state-owned radio and television network.

GOVERNMENT

The 240-member National Assembly is elected every five years by universal adult suffrage using a system of proportional representation.

The President - who is directly elected for five years - appoints a Chairman (Prime Minister) and a Council of Ministers that enjoy a majority in the Assembly. The main political parties are the (centre-liberal) Union of Democratic Forces (UDF), the (former Communist) Bulgarian Socialist Party (BSP), the (mainly Turkish and Pomak) Movement for Rights and Freedom (MRF)and the New Union for Democracy (NUD). The UDF is an alliance of various smaller parties and political groups. The most recent election was in October 1991. The coalition government formed in December 1992 comprises non-party experts.

Party strength: BSP 106, UDF 92, MRF 24, NUD 18.

President: Zhelo Zhelev (UDF).

THE CABINET

Prime Minister (Chairman): Lyuben Borov.

Minister of Agriculture: Georgi Tanev.

Minister of Culture: Ivailo Zhepolski.

Minister of Defence: Valentin Aleksandrov.

Minister of Finance: Stoyan Aleksandrov.

Minister of Foreign Affairs: Stanislav Daskalov.

Minister of Health: Tancho Gogalov.

Minister of Industry: Rumen Bikov.

Minister of Internal Affairs: Viktor Mikhailov.

Minister of Justice: Peter Korndzhev.

Minister of Science and Education: Marin Todorov.

Minister of Social Affairs: Yordan Hirstozkov.

Minister of Territorial Development, Housing Policy and Construction: Hristo Totev.

Minister of Trade: Kiril Bonev.

Minister of Transport and Communications: Kiril Ermenkov.

GEOGRAPHY

Despite possessing two major mountain chains Bulgaria largely consists of lowlands. The Balkan Mountains run from east to west across central Bulgaria. To the north, low-lying hills and fertile valleys slope down to the River Danube. The Danubian lowland occupies about one third of the country. To the south, another belt of lowland - the Upper Thracian lowland and the Tundzha lowland - separates the Balkan Mountains from the high, rugged Rhodope massif, which includes Bulgaria's highest peak. In the east, a third lowland adjoins the Black Sea. Highest point: Musala 2925 m (9596 ft). Principal rivers: Danube, Iskur, Maritsa. Climate: The continental north has warm summers and cold winters, while the southeast has a more Mediterranean climate. Except in the mountains, rainfall throughout Bulgaria is only moderate.

BULGARIA

Area: 110 912 km² (42 823 sq mi).

ECONOMY

With fertile soils, and few other natural resources, Bulgaria has a strong agricultural base. For nearly half a century, production was centred on large-scale, mechanized cooperatives, but privatization of land began in 1990. The principal crops include: cereals (wheat, maize, barley), fruit (grapes) and, increasingly, tobacco. Agricultural products are the basis of the food-processing, wine and tobacco industries. Eastern bloc grants helped develop industry including engineering, fertilizers and chemicals. Tourism is increasingly important - some 11,000,000 visitors a year are attracted by the Black Sea resorts in the summer and by winter sports facilities in the Balkan Mountains in the winter. Trade patterns have been disrupted in Central and Eastern Europe since 1990-91 when social, economic and political upheavals swept the region. Bulgaria - whose trade links with the USSR had been particular-

ly close - suffered more than most East European countries, with severe shortages of many commodities, particularly industrial raw materials and oil. Industrial production declined, and high rates of inflation (over 100% in 1992) and unemployment have been experienced. However, some progress has been made in the initial stages of the privatization of state-run industries and Bulgaria has moved towards an agreement of association with the European Community. However, Bulgaria's economic problems have not been helped by the lack of a stable government.

Currency: Lev (plural leva) of 100 stotinki; 1US$ = 54.19 leva (June 1994).

GDP: US$14,200,000,000 (1993 est); US$1687 per head.

RECENT HISTORY

Bulgaria was on the losing side in the final Balkan War (1913) and in World War I (in which Bulgaria was involved from 1915 to 1918) and forfeited territory to Greece and Romania. In World War II Bulgaria - under King Boris III - joined the Axis powers (1941-44), occupied part of Yugoslavia and annexed Greek Thrace (although these territorial gains were lost after the war). Boris III died under suspicious circumstances in 1943 - it was commonly believed that he was poisoned by order of Hitler. In 1944 a left-wing alliance seized power and the Soviet Red Army invaded. A Communist regime, tied closely to the USSR, was established and the king - Simeon II - was exiled (1946). During the next four and a half decades Bulgaria was the Soviet Union's most loyal ally in the Balkans. Following popular demonstrations in 1989, the hardline Communist leader Todor Zhivkov (1911-) was replaced by reformers who promised free elections and renounced the leading role of the Communist Party. Free elections were held in June 1990, when the Bulgarian Socialist Party (BSP) - formerly the Bulgarian Communist Party - was returned to power. Faced by severe economic problems, the BSP was unable to govern alone and a coalition government with a non-party prime minister took office in 1991. Short-lived coalitions involving various combinations of the three main parties - the BSP, the (centre-liberal) UDF and the (mainly ethnic Turkish and Pomak) MRF - and non-party independents have followed.

147

Croatia

Official name: Republika Hrvatska (The Republic of Croatia).

Member of: UN, CSCE.

Area: 56,538 km² (21,829 sq mi), including the area (about 30%) that is controlled by Serb forces.

Population: 4,821,000 (1993 est). Since 1992 Croatia has received over 600,000 Bosnian refugees.

Capital: Zagreb 934,000 (city 707,000; 1991 census).

Other major cities: Split 207,000 (city 189,000), Rijeka 206,000 (city 168,000), Osijek 165,000 (city 105,000), Zadar 76,000, Pula 62,000 (1991 census).

Languages: Croat (75%) - the form of Serbo-Croat written in the Latin alphabet, Serb (23%) - Serbo-Croat written in the Cyrillic alphabet.

Religions: Roman Catholic (77%), Orthodox (11%).

Education: Education is compulsory between the ages of six and 15. In 1990 the literacy rate was 97%. There are four universities.

Defence: In 1993 the total armed strength was nearly 110,000 - 105,000 in the army, 5000 in the air force, and under 1000 in the navy. Compulsory military service lasts 10 months.

Transport: There are 2425 km (1507 mi) of railways. There are 27,378 km (17,012 mi) of roads. Rijeka is the main port. Zagreb has an international airport.

Media: There are nine principal daily newspapers. There is a single (state-owned) radio and television network.

GOVERNMENT

The bicameral Assembly (Sabor) comprises a 138-member Chamber of Representatives (the lower house) elected by universal adult suffrage for four years and a 63-member Chamber of Municipalities (the upper house), comprising three members directly elected from each of the 21 counties into which the republic is divided. An executive President is directly elected for five years. The President appoints a Prime Minister and a Council of Ministers that enjoy a majority in the Chamber of Representatives. The main political parties are the (nationalist) Croatian Democratic Union (CDU), the Croatian Social-Liberal Party (CSLP), the (right-wing nationalist) Croatian Party of Rights (CPR), the Croatian People's Party (CPP), the (former Communist) Social Democratic Party-Party of Democratic Reform (SDP-PDRC), the Croatian Farmers' Party (CFP), Dalmatian Action (DA), the Istrian Democratic Assembly (IDA), the Rijeka Democratic Alliance (RDA), and the Serbian People's Party (SPP). After the election held in August 1992 a CDU government was formed.

Party strength: CDU 85, CSLP 14, SDP-PDRC 11, CPP 6, DA-IDS-RDA Alliance 6, CPR 5, CFP 3, SPP 3, ind 5.

President: Franjo Tudjman (CDU).

THE CABINET

Prime Minister: Nikica Valentic (CDU).

Deputy Prime Minister and Minister of Foreign Affairs: Mate Granic (CDU).

Deputy Prime Minister and Minister for Interior Policy: Vladimir Seks (CDU).

Deputy Prime Minister and Minister for the Economy: Borislav Skegro (CDU).

Deputy Prime Minister and Minister for Social Services: Dr Ivica Kostovic (CDU).

Minister of Agriculture and Forestry: Ivan Tarnaj (CDU).

Minister of Building and Environmental Protection: Zlatko Tomicic (CDU).

Minister of Defence: Gojko Susak (CDU).

Minister of Economic Affairs: Nadan Vidosevic (CDU).

Minister of Education and Culture: Vesna Gerardi-Jurkic (CDU).

Minister of Finance: T. Bozoprka (CDU).

Minister of Health: Andrija Hebrang (CDU).

Minister of the Interior: Ivan Jarnjak (CDU).

Minister of Justice: Ivica Crnic (CDU).

Minister of Labour and Social Welfare: Ivan Parac (CDU).

Minister of Maritime Affairs, Transport and Communications: Ivica Mudrinic (CDU).

Minister of Public Administration: Jurica Malcic (CDU).

Minister of Science and Technology: Dr Branko Jeren (CDU).

Minister of Tourism: Niko Bulic (CDU).

Ministers without portfolio: Dr Ivan Majdak (CDU), Zlatko Matesa (CDU), Cedomir Pavlovic (CDU), Dr Juraj Njavro (CDU).

GEOGRAPHY
Croatia is shaped like a crescent. The country comprises three distinct regions - Slavonia in

CROATIA

Area: 56 538 km^2 (21 829 sq mi) including the area (one third) controlled by Serb forces

the east is a fertile region of plains; central Croatia is a region of hills around Zagreb; Dalmatia is a coastal region separated from central Croatia by barren limestone (karst) ranges running parallel to the Adriatic coast. The Dubrovnik area is detached from the rest of Croatia by part of Bosnia. Serb occupation of the Krajina area means that north and south Croatia are now linked only by the Maslenica bridge. Highest point: Troglav 1913 m (6275 ft). Principal rivers: Sava, Danube, Drava. Climate: The interior is colder and drier than the Mediterranean coast.

ECONOMY
Croatia has important mineral resources including bauxite and oil. Slavonia grows cereals, potatoes and sugar beet. Manufacturing - aluminium, textiles and chemicals - dominates the economy. In 1991-3 the economy was damaged by the Yugoslav civil war, and the lucrative Dalmatian tourist industry collapsed. Many businesses have gone bankrupt and the country suffers high rates of inflation, severe unemployment, falling industrial and agricultural GNP, the cost of maintaining over 600,000 refugees and the expense of repairing war damage.

Currency: Croatian Kuna of 100 para; 1US$ = 5.75 Kunas (June 1994).

GDP: US$20,900,000,000 (1990) - this has declined considerably; US$4399 per head.

RECENT HISTORY
After World War I when the Habsburg Empire was dissolved (1918), the Croats joined the Serbs, Slovenes and Montenegrins in the state that was to become Yugoslavia in 1929. However, the Croats soon resented the highly centralized Serb-dominated kingdom and a Croat terrorist organization, the Utase, became active. In 1934 the Utase assassinated (the Serb) King Alexander I of Yugoslavia when he was on a state visit to France. Following the German invasion of Yugoslavia (1941), the occupying Axis powers set up an 'independent' Croat puppet state. Ante Pavelic, the head of the Croatian government from 1941 to 1945, had been the leader of the Utase terrorists before World War II. The Croat government adopted harsh anti-Serb policies including expulsions, massacres and forced conversions of Serbs to Roman Catholicism. In 1945 Croatia was reintegrated into a federal Communist Yugoslav state by Marshal Tito, but after Tito's death (1980), the Yugoslav experiment faltered in economic and nationalist crises. Separatists came to power in Croatia in free elections (1990) and declared independence (June 1991). Serb insurgents, backed by the Yugoslav federal army, occupied one third of Croatia including those areas with an ethnic Serb majority - Krajina and parts of Slavonia. The fierce Serbo-Croat war came to an uneasy halt in 1992 after Croatian independence had gained widespread diplomatic recognition and a UN peace-keeping force was agreed.

149

Czech Republic

Official name: Ceska Republika (The Czech Republic).

Member of: UN, CSCE, Council of Europe, CEFTA, NATO (partner for peace).

Area: 78,880 km^2 (30,456 sq mi).

Population: 10,302,000 (1991 census).

Capital: Prague (Praha) 1,212,000 (1991 census).

Other main cities: Brno 388,000, Ostrava 328,000, Olomouc 224,000, Zlin 197,000, Plzen 174,000, Ceské Budejovice 173,000, Hradec Kralové 163,000, Pardubice 162,000 (1991 census).

Languages: Czech (94%), Slovak (4%).

Religions: Roman Catholic (39%), non-religious (39%), various Protestant Churches (4%).

Education: Education is compulsory between the ages of six and 16. In 1992 the literacy rate was virtually 100%. There are 14 universities.

Defence: In 1993 the total armed strength was 107,000 - 71,000 in the army and 33,000 in the air force. Compulsory military service is being reduced from 18 months to 12 months.

Transport: There are 55,892 km (34,730 mi) of roads and 9453 km (5874 mi) of state-run railways. Prague has a metro system. Prague, Brno, Ostrava and Karlovy Vary have international airports.

Media: There are 22 principal daily newspapers, one half of which are printed in Prague. There is a single radio and television network.

GOVERNMENT

The bicameral Parliament comprises a 200-member Chamber of Deputies (the lower house) which is elected under a system of proportional representation by universal adult suffrage for four years and an 81-member Senate (the upper house) which is directly elected for six years. A President - whose role is largely ceremonial - is elected for a four-year term by an electoral college comprising the two houses of Parliament. The President appoints a Prime Minister who, in turn, appoints a Council of Ministers that commands a majority in the Chamber. The main political parties are the (conservative) Civic Democratic Party (ODS) which is in an electoral pact with the Christian Democratic Party (KDS), the Left Bloc (an electoral alliance including the Communist Party and the Democratic Left; KSCM-DL), the Social Democratic Party, the Liberal Social Union (an electoral alliance of the Socialist Party, the Agrarian Party and the Green Party; LSU), the (right-wing nationalist) Association for the Republic-Czech Republic Party (SPR-RCS), the Social Democratic Party (CSSD), the (Moravian and Silesian nationalist) Movement for Autonomous Democracy-Society for Moravia and Silesia (MADMS), the Civic Democratic Alliance (ODA), and the Christian Democratic Union-Czech People's Party (KDU-CSL). After the election held in June 1992 an ODS-KDU-CSL-ODA-KDS coalition was formed.

Party strength: ODS-KDU-CSL-ODA-KDS coalition 105, Left Bloc 35, CSSD 16, LSU 16, SPR-RCS 14, MADMS 14.

President: Vaclav Havel.

THE CABINET

Prime Minister: Dr Vaclav Klaus (ODS).

Deputy Prime Minister and Minister of Agriculture: Josef Lux (KDU-CSL).

Deputy Prime Minister: Jan Kalvoda (ODS).

Deputy Prime Minister and Minister of Finance: Ivan Kocarnik (ODS).

Minister of Culture: Pavel Tigrid (KDU-CSL).

Minister of Defence: Dr Antonin Baudys (KDU-CSL).

Minister of Economic Competition: Stanislav Belehradek (KDU-CSL).

Minister of the Economy: Karel Dyba (ODS).

Minister of Education: Ivan Pilip (KDS).

Minister of the Environment: Frantisek Benda (KDS).

Minister of Foreign Affairs: Dr Josef Zieleniec (ODS).

Minister of Health: Ludek Rubas (ODS).

Minister of Industry and Trade: Vladimir Dlouhy (ODA).

Minister of the Interior: Jan Ruml (ODS).

Minister of Justice: Jiri Novak (ODS).

Minister of Labour and Social Affairs: Jindrich Vodicka (ODS).

Minister of Privatization: Jiri Skalicky (ODA).

Minister of Transport: Jan Strasky (ODS).

Minister without portfolio: Igor Nemec.

GEOGRAPHY

The west - Bohemia - is an elevated basin drained by the rivers Elbe and Vlatava and their tributaries, and is surrounded by mountains - the uplands of the Bohemian Forest in the west and south, the Ore Mountains and Giant Mountains in the north, and the Bohemian-Moravian Highlands in the east. The east - Moravia - is a lowland that separates the Bohemian uplands from the Carpathian Mountains of neighbouring Slovakia. Highest point: Snezka 1603 m (5259 ft). Principal rivers: Elbe (Labe), Vlatava. Climate: The climate tends towards continental with warm sumers and cold winters, but there are many local variations owing to relief.

CZECH REPUBLIC

Area: 78 880 km² (30 456 sq mi).

ECONOMY

Apart from coal, there are few mineral resources, but the country is heavily industrialized and some areas have suffered from pollution. Manufactures include industrial machin-ery, motor vehicles, and consumer goods. Most of the older plant and uneconomic heavy industries of the former Czechoslovakia were situated in Slovakia, thus, when the federation was dissolved (1993), the Czech Republic was left with a healthier industrial base than its neighbour. The country is switching from a centrally planned to a free-market economy. Much of industry has been privatized, considerable foreign investment (80% German) has been attracted and the economy - the most stable in the former Soviet bloc - is increasingly tied to that of Germany.

Currency: Czech koruna of 100 haler; 1US$ = 28.46 koruna (June 1994).

GDP: US$31,500,000,000 (1993 est); US$3029 per head.

RECENT HISTORY

On the collapse of the Habsburg Empire, the Czechs and Slovaks united in an independent state (1918) - largely due to the efforts of Thomas Masaryk, who became Czechoslovakia's first president. In 1938, Hitler demanded that Germany be granted the Sudetenland, where ethnic Germans predominated. Lacking allies, Czechoslovakia was dismembered - Bohemia and Moravia became German 'protectorates'. Following liberation from Nazi occupation (1945), a coalition was formed, but the Communists staged a takeover in 1948. In 1968, moves by Party Secretary Alexander Dubcek to introduce political reforms met with Soviet disapproval, and invasion by Czechoslovakia's Warsaw Pact allies. The conservative wing of the Communist party regained control until 1989, when student demonstrations became a peaceful revolution led by the Civic Forum movement. Faced by overwhelming public opposition, the Communist Party renounced its leading role and hardline leaders were replaced by reformers. A new government, in which Communists were in a minority, was appointed and Civic Forum's leader - the playwright Vaclav Havel - was elected president. In 1990 free multi-party elections were held, Soviet troops were withdrawn and the foundations of a market economy were laid. Increased Slovak separatism led to the division of the country in 1993.

151

Estonia

Official name: Eesti Vabariik (Republic of Estonia).

Member of: UN, CSCE, Council of Europe, NATO (partner for peace).

Area: 45,226 km² (17,462 sq mi).

Population: 1,536,000 (1993 est).

Capital: Tallinn 505,000 (city 498,000) (1991 est).

Other major cities: Tartu 114,000, Narva 87,000, Kohtla-Järve 75,000, Pärnu 57,000 (1991 est).

Languages: Estonian (63%), Russian (31%), Ukrainian (3%), Belarussian (2%).

Religions: Lutheran (30%), Orthodox (10%).

Education: Education is compulsory between the ages of six and 17 in schools in which the Estonian language is the first language of instruction and the ages of seven and 17 in schools in which the Russian language is the first language of instruction. In 1991 the literacy rate was estimated to be virtually 100%. There are two universities.

Defence: In 1993 the total armed strength was 2500. Military service of 12 months is envisaged. Early in 1994 some 10,000 Russian troops were still stationed in Estonia. They are scheduled to be withdrawn by autumn 1994

Transport: There are 1026 km (641 mi) of state-owned railways and 14,811 km (9203 mi) of roads. Tallinn is a commercial shipping port and ferry port, and has Estonia's only international airport.

Media: There are six daily newspapers (most of which are published in Estonian) and a single (state-owned) radio and television service.

GOVERNMENT

A 101-member Assembly (Riigokogu) is elected for four years by universal adult suffrage. The President is elected by the Assembly for a five-year term. The President appoints a Prime Minister and a Council of Ministers who are responsible to the Assembly. The main political parties are the (nationalist) Pro Patria (PPNCP; known in Estonian as Isamaa), the Centre Faction (Centre), the Moderates (Mod), the Rural Centre Party (ERCP), the Union of the Coalition Party (UCP), the (nationalist) Estonian National Independence Party (ENIP), the Social Democratic Party (ESDP), the Liberals (Lib), the Independent Royalists, and independents and others including Greens, the former Communists and the Estonian Entrepreneurs' Party. After the election held in September 1992 - when only those Estonians, or their descendants, who were citizens of the country in 1940 were able to vote - a PPNCP-ERCP-ENIP-ESDP coalition was formed.

Party strength: PPNCP 22, Mod 12, Centre 10, ERCP 8, UCP 8, Royalists 8, ENIP 8, Lib 6, independents and others 19.

President: Lennart Meri.

THE CABINET Î
Prime Minister: Mart Laar (PPNCP).

Minister of Agriculture: Jaan Leetsaar (ERCP).

Minister of Culture and Education: Peeter Olesk (ENIP).

Minister of Defence: Enn Tupp (PPNCP).

Minister of the Economy: Toivo Jurgensen (PPNCP).

Minister of the Environment: Andres Tarand (ind).

Minister of Finance: Andres Lipstok (ind).

Minister of Foreign Affairs: Juri Luik (PPNCP).

Minister of the Interior: Heiki Arike (ind).

Minister of Justice: Urmas Arumae (PPNCP).

Minister of Social Affairs: Marju Lauristin (ESDP).

Minister of Transport and Communications: Andi Meister (ENIP).

Ministers without portfolio: Lila Hänni, Arvo Niitenberg.

GEOGRAPHY

Estonia comprises a low-lying gently undulating mainland which only rises above 300 m (984 ft) in the southeast. The north comprises a limestone plateau which ends on the Baltic coast in low cliffs. There are many rivers and lakes including Lake Peipus. Much of the country is forested. Estonia has many small and two larger offshore islands, Saaremaa and Hiiumaa, which together comprise 10% of the country.

Highest point: Munamägi 318 m (1042 ft). Principal rivers: Narva, Pärnu. Climate: Estonia has a moist temperate climate, characterized by mild summers and cold winters.

ECONOMY

Major industries include engineering and food processing. Progress towards the privatization of industry has been made. Gas for heating and industry is extracted from bituminous shale. The important agricultural sector is dominated by dairying but production declined by 25% in 1992. Over 600 farms have been privatized although over 150 large cooperatives remain in state hands. Since 1991 severe economic difficulties have resulted from Estonia's heavy dependency upon trade with Russia. Acute shortages of energy and raw materials have crippled the economy and Estonia's economy declined in tandem with Russia's until a new convertible Estonian currency, the kroon, was introduced in 1992. Since its introduction the kroon has been extremely stable, largely owing to the centre-right government's cautious monetary policies. Closer links with Scandinavian countries, in particular Finland, have been forged, and trade is increasingly with Scandinavian countries. Estonia is disadvantaged through not having many products for which there is a market in the European Community or EFTA. Efforts have been to exploit medieval Tallinn and the country's picturesque scenery to attract tourists from Germany and Scandinavia.

Currency: Kroon of 100 sents; 1US$ = 12.79 kroons (June 1994).

GDP: US$1,400,000,000 (1993 est); US$900 per head.

RECENT HISTORY

When the Communists took power in Russia (1917), Estonia (which had been ceded by Sweden to Russia in 1721) seceded. The late 19th century had witnessed a steady growth in Estonian nationalism, spurred by a period of intensive Russification in the 1880s and 1890s. Konstantin Päts, who had summoned an Estonian congress during the 1905 abortive Russian revolution, was declared premier in 1917 but a German occupation and two Russian invasions delayed independence until 1919. Estonia's fragile democracy was replaced by the dictatorship of Päts in 1934. The Non-Aggression Pact (1939) between Hitler and Stalin assigned Estonia to the USSR, which invaded and annexed the republic (1940). Estonia was occupied by Nazi Germany (1941-44). When Soviet rule was reimposed (1945), large-scale Russian settlement replaced over 120,000 Estonians who had been killed or deported to Siberia. In 1988, reforms in the USSR allowed Estonian nationalists to operate openly. Nationalists won a majority in the republic's parliament, gradually assumed greater autonomy and seceded following the failed coup by Communist hardliners in

ESTONIA

Area: 45 100 km^2 (17 413 sq mi).

Moscow (August 1991). The USSR recognized Estonia's independence in September 1991. The country faces a number of problems associated with the presence of a large Russian-speaking minority. In 1992 the introduction of strict Estonian citizenship laws that denied full rights to most Russian-speakers increased tension with Russia, which halted the withdrawal of troops from Estonia. Ethnic Russians make up 35% of the population of Tallinn and form an overwhelming majority in the eastern towns of Narva and Sillamäe. In the 1992 general election very few inhabitants of these eastern towns qualified to vote (see above). Narva and Sillamäe, near the Russian border, have unsuccessfully sought considerable autonomy and have held unofficial referenda on their status. In 1993 the citizenship law was eased to allow ethnic Russians with residential qualifications and fluency in Estonian to acquire full citizenship.

153

Hungary

Official name: Magyarország (Hungary) or Magyar Köztársáság (The Hungarian Republic).

Member of: UN, CSCE, Council of Europe, CEFTA, NATO (partner for peace).

Area: 93,036 km² (35,921 sq mi).

Population: 10,296,000 (1993 est).

Capital: Budapest 1,992,000 (1992 est).

Other major cities: Debrecen 215,000, Miskolc 192,000, Szeged 178,000, Pécs 170,000, Györ 130,000, Nyíregyháza 114,000, Székésfehérvár 109,000, Kecskemét 105,000, Szombathely 86,000, Szolnok 79,000, Tatabánya 73,000 (1992 est).

Language: Magyar (Hungarian; official) (97%), German (2%), Slovak (1%).

Religions: Roman Catholic (56%), (Presbyterian Calvinist) Reformed Church of Hungary and the Lutheran Church in Hungary (22%).

Education: Education is compulsory between the ages of six and 14. In 1991 the literacy rate was estimated to be virtually 100%. There are 19 universities.

Defence: In 1993 the total armed strength was 81,000 - 64,000 in the army and 17,000 in the air force. There is a border guard of some 20,000 personnel. Compulsory military conscription lasts for 12 months.

Transport: There are 7600 km (4722 mi) of state-run railways. Budapest has a metro system. There are 105,424 km (65,507 mi) of roads including 335 km (208 mi) of motorway. The Danube is a major inland waterway. Ferihegy (Budapest) is an international airport.

Media: There are over 30 principal daily newspapers, more than one half of which are published in provincial cities. Cable television competes with the (state-owned) television service. Commercial radio now operates alongside the state-owned radio service.

GOVERNMENT

The 386-member National Assembly is elected for four years by universal adult suffrage. It comprises 58 members elected from a national list under a system of proportional representation, 152 members elected on a county basis and 176 elected from single-member constituencies. The President - who is elected by the Assembly for a maximum of two four-year terms - appoints a Cabinet and a Prime Minister from the majority in the Assembly. Political parties include the (former Communist) Hungarian Socialist Party (MSzP), the (liberal) Alliance of Free Democrats (SzDSz), the (centre right) Hungarian Democratic Forum (MDF), the Independent Smallholders' Party (FKgP), the (centre right) Federation of Young Democrats (FIDESz), and the Christian Democratic People's Party (KDNP). After the election held in April 1994 a MSzP-SzDSz coalition government was formed.

Party strength: MSzP 209, SzDSz 69, MDF 38, FKgP 26, KDNP 22, FIDESz 20.

President: Arpad Goncz (SzDSz).

THE CABINET

Prime Minister (Chairman): Gyula Horn (MSzP).

Deputy Prime Minister and Minister of the Interior: Gábor Kuncze (SzDSz).

Minister of Agriculture: László Lakos (MSzP).

Minister of Culture and Education: Gábor Fodor (SzDSz).

Minister of Defence: György Keleti (MSzP).

Minister of the Environment and of Regional Policy: Ferenc Baja (MSzP).

Minister of Finance: László Bekesi (MSzP).

Minister of Foreign Affairs: László Kovacs (MSzP).

Minister of Industry and Trade: László Pál (MSzP).

Minister of Justice: Pál Vastagh (MSzP).

Minister of Labour: Magda Kósa (MSzP).

Minister of Transport and Telecommunications: Károly Lotz (SzDSz).

Minister of Welfare: Pál Kovacs (MSzP).

Minister without portfolio and Minister for the National Security Office: Bela Katona (MSzP).

GEOGRAPHY

The largest physical region in Hungary is the Great Alfold (or Great Hungarian Plain) which covers most of central and eastern Hungary.

The Great Alfold is divided by the valley of the River Tisza. West of the River Danube, a discontinuous belt of low mountains and hills - including the Bakony Mountains - runs from southwest to northeast across Hungary. These uplands, sometimes known as the Transdanubian Mountains, end in thickly wooded highlands in the northeast on the Slovak border. The Transdanubian uplands separate the Great Alfold from the Little Alfold, a more undulating plain than its larger namesake. The Little Alfold has better soils and is more densely populated than the Great Alfold. Highest point: Kékes 1015 m (3330 ft). Principal rivers: Danube (Duna), Tisza, Drava. Climate: The Hungarian climate is continental with long, hot dry summers and cold winters. Rainfall is moderate throughout the country.

HUNGARY

Area: 93 036 km² (35 921 sq mi).

ECONOMY
Nearly one seventh of the labour force is involved in agriculture. Major crops include cereals (maize, wheat and barley), sugar beet, fruit, and grapes for wine. Most of the land has been privatized. Despite considerable reserves of coal, Hungary imports more than half of its energy needs. Hungary also mines bauxite and brown coal. The steel, chemical fertilizer, pharmaceutical, machinery and vehicle industries are important. Since the early 1980s, private enterprise and foreign investment have been encouraged, and between 1989 and 1993 over one half of state-owned industry was privatized. Although Hungary has experienced economic difficulties including unemployment, falling GDP and inflation, Hungary's economic progress has been among the most impressive in Central and Eastern Europe. Hungary is

considered to be a prospective member of the OECD and has applied for membership of the EC.

Currency: Forint of 100 filler; 1US$ = 102.45 forints (June 1994).

GDP: US$38,800,000,000 (1993 est); US$3755 per head.

RECENT HISTORY
In 1867 Austria granted Hungary considerable autonomy within the Austro-Hungarian Empire (the Dual Monarchy). Hungary, in turn, granted some autonomy to Croatia. However, there was mounting friction between the governments in Vienna and Budapest and between the Hungarian authorities and various linguistic minorities. Defeat in World War I led to a brief period of Communist rule under Béla Kun (1919), then occupation by Romania. In the postwar settlement Hungary lost two thirds of its territory, mainly to Romania (Transylvania) and the new state of Czechoslovakia (Slovakia). After the deposition of the Habsburgs, Hungary remained a monarchy, without a monarch, until 1945. The Regent, Admiral Miklás Horthy (1868-1957), cooperated with Hitler during World War II in an attempt to regain territory, but defeat in 1945 resulted in occupation by the Red Army, and a Communist People's Republic was established in 1949. The Hungarian Uprising in 1956 was a heroic attempt to overthrow Communist rule, but was quickly suppressed by Soviet forces, and its leader, Imre Nagy, was executed. János Kadar - Communist Party Secretary 1956-88 - tried to win support with economic progress. However, in the late 1980s reformers in the Communist Party gained the upper hand, and talks with opposition groups led to agreement on a transition to a fully democratic, multi-party state. The (Communist) Hungarian Socialist Workers' Party transformed itself into the Socialist Party but was heavily defeated in the first free elections in May 1990 when conservative and liberal parties won most seats. Soviet troops left Hungary in 1990, and the country has joined Western European organizations and established a free-market economy. The status of over 3,000,000 Hungarians who are citizens of Slovakia, Romania and the former Yugoslavia has become an issue. In 1993 Hungary signed a treaty with Ukraine recognizing their present boundary which includes a Hungarian minority within Ukraine.

Latvia

Official name: Latvijas Republika (Republic of Latvia).

Member of: UN, CSCE, NATO (partner for peace).

Area: 64,589 km² (24,938 sq mi).

Population: 2,596,000 (1993 est).

Capital: Riga 897,000 (1992 est).

Other major cities: Daugavpils 127,000, Liepaja 114,000, Jelgava 74,000, Jūrmala 61,000, Ventspils 50,000 (1992 est).

Languages: Lettish (over 53%), Russian (34%), Belarussian (5%).

Religions: Lutheran (22%), Roman Catholic (7%), small Russian Orthodox minority.

Education: Education is compulsory between the ages of seven and 17. In 1992 the literacy rate was estimated to be 98%. There are two universities in Riga.

Defence: The total armed strength (in 1993) was 4900 including 270 in the navy and 53 in the air force. Compulsory military service lasts for 18 months. The 20,000 remaining Russian troops stationed in Latvia are scheduled to withdraw during 1994.

Transport: There are 3297 km (2061 mi) of railway track. There are 20,600 km (12,875 mi) of roads. Riga and Ventspils are important ports on the Baltic Sea; Riga has an international airport.

Media: There are eight main daily newspapers. The majority of these papers publish in Lettish and use the Latin script; a minority publish in Russian and use the Cyrillic script. Latvia has a single state-run radio and television network.

GOVERNMENT
A President - who appoints a Prime Minister and a Cabinet - and a 100-member Assembly (Saeima) are elected by universal adult suffrage for three years. The main political parties are the (right of centre) Latvia's Way (LC), Harmony for Latvia (SL), the Farmers' Union (LZS), the (former Communist) Equality Party, the (radical nationalist) For Fatherland and Freedom (TUB), the (centre-right) Democratic Centre Party (DCP), the (centre-right) Christian Democratic Union (LKDS), and the (radical nationalist) Latvian National Independence Movement (LNNK). After the election held in June 1993 an LC-LZS coalition government was formed.

Party strength: LC 36, LNNK 15, SL 13, LZS 12, Equality 7, TUB 6, LKDS 6, DCP 5.

President: Guntis Ulmanis (LZS).

THE CABINET
Prime Minister and Minister for Foreign Affairs: Valdis Birkavs (LC).

Deputy Prime Minister and Minister of State Reform: Māris Gailis (LC).

Deputy Prime Minister and Minister of Economics: Ojārs Kehris (LC).

Deputy Prime Minister and Minister of Justice: Egils Levit (LC).

Minister of Agriculture: Jānis Kinna (LZS).

Minister of Defence: Valdis Pavlovskis (LC).

Minister of Education, Culture and Science: Jānis Vaivads (LC).

Minister of Environmental and Regional Development: Girts Lūkins (LC).

Minister of Finance: Uldis Osis (LC).

Minister of the Interior: Girts Kristovskis (LC).

Minister of Transport and Communications: Andris Gūtmanis (LC).

Minister of Welfare: Jānis Ritenis (LZS).

Minister without portfolio: Edvins Inkens (LC).

GEOGRAPHY
Latvia comprises an undulating plain, lower in the west (traditionally known as Courland) than in the east (traditionally known as Livonia). Ridges of moraine cross the country, impeding drainage and creating widespread peat bogs. Latvia reaches the Baltic Sea and the large Gulf of Riga in a low sandy coastline. Highest point: Osveyskoye 311 m (1020 ft). Principal rivers: Daugava (Dvina or Western Dvina), Lielupe, Aiviekste. Climate: Latvia has a relatively mild climate with cool, rainy summers and cold winters. There are, on average, only 135 frost-free days per annum.

ECONOMY
Engineering dominates a heavily industrialized economy. Latvia has relied on Russian trade

and faces severe difficulties as it begins to introduce a free market. Severe shortages of raw materials - owing to the collapse of the former Soviet trade bloc - resulted in a dramatic decrease in industrial output and a consequent fall in exports. The government has given great importance to the establishment of the services sector of the economy, particularly banking. GNP decreased by 30% in 1992, and rapid inflation became a serious worry. However, cautious economic policies and the introduction of Latvia's own independent currency - the lat - marked a new chapter in the country's economic history. The lat achieved considerable stability and inflation, although still high by West European standards, had fallen to manageable limits by early 1993.

Currency: Lat of 100 santims; 1US$ = 0.562 lat (June 1994).

GDP: US$3,200,000,000 (1993 est); US$1200 per-head

RECENT HISTORY

Courland, the part of Latvia west of the River Daugava (Dvina), was an autonomous duchy until it was annexed by Russia in 1795; Livonia (or Vidzeme), the part of Latvia east of the River Daugava, was taken by Russia from Sweden in the 18th century. Under Russian rule, Latvian national consciousness grew throughout the 19th century. Riga became the third largest city in the Russian Empire. Following the Communist takeover in Russia (1917) and a brief German invasion of Latvia, Latvian nationalists - led by Karlis Ulmanis -

LATVIA

Area: 64 589 km²
(24 938 sq mi).

declared independence (1918). However, the infant republic was overrun by war when the Soviet Red Army invaded Livonia (1919) and the Latvian government was forced to take refuge in Courland, where German troops remained. An army of Baltic-German forces cleared Latvia of Soviet troops but attempted to assume control of the country as a base from which to fight the Red Army. Latvia, aided by a Franco-British naval force, eventually defeated the German forces and an independent internationally-recognized Latvian government took office in 1920. A democratic system lasted until 1936 when Karlis Ulmanis established a dictatorship. The Non-Aggression Pact (1939) between Hitler and Stalin assigned Latvia to the USSR, which invaded and annexed the republic (1940). After occupation by Nazi Germany (1941-44), Soviet rule was reimposed. Large-scale Russian settlement replaced over 200,000 Latvians, who were killed or deported to Siberia. Collective farming was forcibly introduced and the largely Russian-speaking northeast was annexed by Russia. In 1988, reforms in the USSR allowed Latvian nationalists to operate openly. Nationalists - led by Anatolijs Gorbunovs - won a majority in Latvia's parliament and declared that Latvia's independence had been restored (1990). Latvia refused to participate in the discussions called by Soviet President Mikhail Gorbachov to reform the Soviet Union and troops of the Soviet Ministry of Internal Affairs were deployed. Latvia finally seceded from the Soviet Union following the failed coup by Communist hardliners in Moscow (1991). The USSR recognized Latvia's independence in September 1991. Problems remain concerning the status of the large Russian minority - which includes many retired Russian military and civilian personnel - and the smaller Ukrainian and Belarussian minorities in Latvia. In the Latvian capital, Riga, ethnic Russians make up about 40% of the population. Although the last Russian forces in Latvia are scheduled to withdraw during 1994 the Russian government has stated that it will not complete withdrawal until it is satisfied that the rights of all ethnic Russians living in the country are fully protected. A new Latvian nationality law (June 1994), which would grant citizenship to non-Latvians born in the country but effectively exclude other minorities, increased Russo-Latvian tension. The first fully democratic Latvian elections since the 1930s were held in June 1993.

Lithuania

Official name: Lietuvos Respublika (Republic of Lithuania).

Member of: UN, CSCE, Council of Europe, NATO (partner for peace).

Area: 65,200 km² (25,174 sq mi).

Population: 3,760, 000 (1992 est).

Capital: Vilnius 597,000 (1992 est).

Other major cities: Kaunas 434,000, Klaipeda 208,000, Siauliai 149,000 (1992 est).

Languages: Lithuanian (81%), Russian (10%), Polish (7%), Belarussian (2%).

Religions: Roman Catholic (80%), Lutheran and Orthodox (Russian Orthodox and Lithuanian Old Believers) minorities.

Education: Education is compulsory between the ages of six and 15. The literacy rate is estimated to be over 98%. There are four universities.

Defence: The withdrawal of the last Russian soldiers from Lithuanian soil in September 1993 left the newly-formed Lithuanian forces as the only troops in the country. In 1993, the Lithuanian national defence force had a total armed strength of 7000. There is also a National Guard with about 12,500 personnel.

Transport: There are about 44,500 km (27,813 mi) of roads. There are 2007 km (1254 mi) of railway track. Klaipeda (once known as Memel) is a major commercial port on the Baltic Sea; river transport is important. Vilnius has an international airport.

Media: There are 16 principal daily newspapers. Over 90% of the country's press publishes in Lithuanian. Lithuania has a single (state-owned) radio and television network.

GOVERNMENT

The 141-member Parliament (Seimas) is elected for four years by universal adult suffrage under a system of proportional representation. The President is directly elected for five years. The President appoints a Prime Minister, who, in turn, appoints a Cabinet of Ministers. The principal political parties include the (former Communist) Lithuanian Democratic Labour Party (LDLP), the (nationalist) Citizens' Charter of Lithuania Movement (popularly known as Sajudis), the Lithuanian Social Democratic Party (SDP), the Christian Democratic Party of Lithuania (CDP), and the Polish Union (PU). Following the election held in October and November 1992 a coalition of LDLP members and independents was formed; this has subsequently been reshuffled.

Party strength: LDLP 73, Sajudis 30, CDP 16, SDP 8, PU 4, independents 10.

President: Algirdas Mykolas Brazauskas (LDLP).

THE CABINET

Prime Minister: Bronislovas Lubys.

Minister of Agriculture: Rimantas Karazija.

Minister of Communications and Information: Gintautas Zinteus.

Minister of Culture and Education: vacant at the time of going to press.

Minister of Defence: Linas Linkevicius.

Minister of the Economy: vacant at the time of going to press.

Minister of Energy: Algimantas Vladas Stasiukynas.

Minister of Finance: Eduardas Vilkelis.

Minister of Foreign Affairs: Povilas Gylys.

Minister of Forestry: vacant at the time of going to press.

Minister of Health: Jurgis Bredikis.

Minister of Housing and Urban Development: Julius Laiconas.

Minister of Industry and Trade: Kazimieras Klimasauskas.

Minister of the Interior: Romasis Vaitiekunas.

Minister of Justice: Jonas Prapiestis.

Minister of Social Security: Laurynas Mindaugas Stankevicius.

Minister of Transportation: Jonas Birziskis.

GEOGRAPHY

Central Lithuania comprises a low-lying plain crossed by ridges of glacial moraine that are covered with pine forests. A 100 km (60 mi) sandspit separates a large lagoon - the Kursiu Maries - from the Baltic Sea. Hills are confined to the low coastal Samogitian Hills and slightly higher land in the extreme east and southeast. There are over 3000 small lakes. Highest point: Juozapine 294 m (964 ft). Principal rivers: Nemunas (Neman), Vilnya. Climate: Winters are cold, summers are warm and rainfall is moderate.

ECONOMY

About 15% of the labour force is engaged in agriculture, principally cattle rearing and dairying in pastures reclaimed from marshes. As well as meat and milk, the main farming products are potatoes, flax and sugar beet. Much of the country is heavily forested. The engineering, timber, cement and food-processing industries are important. Ship-building is significant at Klaipeda. Lithuania - whose economy is weaker than that of the other two Baltic republics - faces an uncertain future as it dismantles state control and breaks away from the former Soviet trade system. Since 1991 the country's GDP has fallen by over 50%. This has been due to soaring inflation (over 1000% in 1992) and industrial decline - owing to a shortage of raw materials that used to be imported from other former Soviet republics. Lithuania is looking west but has few products that can find a ready market in the EC. By the beginning of 1993 about one third of Lithuania's state-owned industry had been privatized. However, the change of government in the autumn of 1992 signalled a slower pace of change towards a market economy. The adoption of a new Lithuanian currency, the litas, in

1993 brought the opportunity for a more independent economic policy.

Currency: Litas of 100 cents; 1US$ = 3.993 litas (June 1994).

GDP: US$7,000,000,000 (1993 est); US$1800 per head.

RECENT HISTORY

Consigned to Russian rule by the partitions of Poland at the end of the 18th century, Lithuania was subject to extensive Russification in every area of public life. When German forces invaded in 1915, they encouraged the establishment of a satellite Lithuanian state. Augustinas Voldemaras became Lithuania's first prime minister while the country was still under German occupation. After World War I, the new Lithuanian state became a republic but faced invasions by the Red Army from the east, attempting to reconquer Lithuania, and the Polish army from the west (1919-20) in a dispute over territory. Lithuania lost Vilnius - its traditional capital - in the war against Poland. Internationally recognized boundaries were not established until 1923, by which time the Lithuanian government had transferred to Kaunas. The dictatorship of Augustinas Voldemaras (1926-29) was followed by that of Antonas Smetona (1929-40). The Non-Aggression Pact (1939) between Hitler and Stalin assigned Lithuania to the USSR, which invaded and annexed the republic (1940). Lithuania was occupied by Nazi Germany (1941-44). When Soviet rule was reimposed (1945), large-scale Russian settlement replaced over 250,000 Lithuanians who had been killed or deported to Siberia. In 1988, reforms in the USSR allowed Lithuanian nationalists to operate openly. Sajudis - the nationalist movement led by a music professor, Vytautas Landsbergis - won a majority in the republic's parliament, but their declaration of independence (1990) brought a crackdown by Soviet forces in Lithuania. Following the failed coup by Communist hardliners in Moscow (in August 1991), the USSR recognized Lithuania's independence. Following the economic collapse of Lithuania (1992-93), Sajudis lost elections to the (former Communist) Lithuanian Democratic Labour Party. Since the advent to power of the former Communists the pace of privatization has slowed. However, the new government has pursued a vigorously nationalist path, securing the total withdrawal of Russian troops from Lithuania in 1993.

LITHUANIA

Area: 65 200 km² (25 174 sq mi)

LATVIA

BALTIC SEA

Klaipeda

Neman

Kaunas

RUSSIA

Vilnius

POLAND

BELARUS

159

Macedonia

(The Former Yugoslav Republic of Macedonia)

Official name: (internal) Republika Makedonija (Republic of Macedonia); (international) The Former Yugoslav Republic of Macedonia.

Member of: UN.

Area: 25,713 km² (9928 sq mi).

Population: 2,063,000 (1993 est).

Capital: Skopje (Skoplje) 563,000 (1991 census).

Other major cities: Tetovo 181,000, Kumanovo 136,000, Bitola (Bitolj) 122,000 (1991 census).

Languages: Macedonian (67%), Albanian (20%), Turkish (5%), Romanian (3%), Serb (2%). These percentages are disputed by Macedonia's ethnic Albanian population and by most of the republic's neighbours.

Religions: Macedonian Orthodox (over 60%), Sunni Islam (nearly 25%).

Education: Education is compulsory between the ages of seven and 15. In 1981 the literacy rate was 89%. There are two universities.

Defence: In 1993 the total armed strength was 10,400. This force was increased during 1993 and early 1994, and was estimated to be approaching nearly 20,000 personnel by the middle of 1994. Compulsory military service lasts for nine months.

Transport: There are 10,591 km (6582 mi) of roads and 693 km (431 mi) of railways. Skopje has an international airport. Macedonia's traditional links with the outside world have been north into Serbia and south into Greece. The former route has been largely cut owing to UN sanctions against Serbia; the latter route is cut owing to the Greek trade embargo upon Macedonia. Durres in Albania has now become the main port for Macedonia, but the cross-country route to that port is not easy. Work has started on a US-backed railway to Bulgaria.

Media: There are four main daily newspapers. There is a single state-owned radio and television service.

GOVERNMENT
The 120-member Assembly (Sobranje) and a President - who appoints a Cabinet and a Prime Minister - are directly elected for four years by universal adult suffrage. For administrative purposes the republic is divided into 30 districts. The main political parties include the (nationalist) Internal Macedonian Revolutionary Organization-Democratic Party for Macedonian National Unity (IMRO), the (former Communist) Social Democratic Alliance of Macedonia (SDSM), the Alliance of Reform Forces-Liberal Party (ALF-LP), and the (largely ethnic Albanian) Party of Democratic Prosperity-National Democratic Party (PDP). The most recent election was in November and December 1990. The government is led by the SDSM.

Party strength: IMRO 37, SDSM 31, PDP 25, ALF-LP 19, others 8.

President: Kiro Gligorov.

THE CABINET
includes

Prime Minister: Branko Crvenkovski (SDSM).

First Deputy Prime Minister: Stevo Crvenkovski.

Deputy Prime Minister: Becir Zuta.

Minister of Defence: Vlado Popovski.

Minister of the Economy: Petrus Stefanov.

Minister of Finance: Dzevdet Hajredini.

Minister of the Interior: Ljubomir Frckoski.

Minister of Justice: Tuse Gosev.

GEOGRAPHY
Macedonia is a plateau about 760 m (2500 ft) high, ringed by mountains including the Sar range. Most of the mountains in Macedonia are forested. The central Vardar valley is the main lowland. Highest point: Korab 2753 m (9032 ft). Principal rivers: Vardar, Strumica. Climate: The climate of Macedonia tends towards continental with heavy snowfall in the winter.

ECONOMY
Macedonia was the least developed part of the former Yugoslavia. The republic is largely agricultural, raising sheep and cattle and growing cereals and tobacco. The metallurgical, chemical and textile industries partly rely on local resources including iron ore. The economy has been severely damaged since its declaration of independence by an intermittent Greek economic blockade and the disruption of trade

**MACEDONIA
(FORMER YUGOSLAV
REPUBLIC)**
Area: 25 713 km²
(9928 sq mi).

with Serbia (owing to international sanctions against that state). The fruit and vegetable crops, and the products of the food processing industry (particularly wine and lamb), that would have been exported in 1994 were largely unable to find a market owing to the Greek blockade. There is a chronic fuel shortage owing to the inability to import fuel from traditional sources in Serbia or through Thessaloniki. International recognition (April 1993) brought membership of the IMF and some foreign investment. However, by the middle of 1994 the most lucrative economic activity in Macedonia was smuggling and sanctions busting. The republic's new currency, the Macedonian denar, is not yet widely quoted in exchange markets.

Currency: Macedonian denar; 1US$ = 751 denars (January 1994).

GDP: US$3,715,000,000 (1992); US$1812 per head.

RECENT HISTORY
After centuries of Turkish rule, Macedonia was partitioned following the First Balkan War (1912). Those areas with a Greek-speaking majority were assigned to Greece and the remainder was partitioned between Bulgaria and Serbia, the latter gaining the area comprising the present republic. Bulgaria continued to claim all Macedonia and occupied the region during World War I. In 1918 Serbian Macedonia was incorporated within the new

kingdom of Yugoslavia. When Yugoslavia was reorganized on Soviet lines by Marshal Tito in 1945 a separate Macedonian republic was formed within the Communist federation. After Tito's death (1980), the Yugoslav experiment faltered and local nationalist movements arose. Following the secession of Slovenia and Croatia, and the outbreak of the Yugoslav civil wars (1991), Macedonia declared its own sovereignty. The new state faced immediate fierce opposition from Greece, which objected to the use of the name 'Macedonia' and denied the existence of a 'Macedonian' people. Greece demands that Macedonia changes its name, its constitution (which contains a reference to speaking for 'all Macedonians') and its flag, which carries the Vergina Star of the Macedonian dynasty of Alexander the Great. Greece claims that all these show that the government in Skopje harbours territorial designs upon the northern Greek regions of Macedonia, a claim which the government of President Kiro Gligorov emphatically denies. The republic eventually gained international recognition in 1993 when it was admitted to the United Nations under the name The Former Yugoslav Republic of Macedonia, and is seated in the General Assembly next to Thailand because it is deemed to have a name beginning with T for The rather M for Macedonia. In February 1994 Greece imposed a total trade embargo on Macedonia (with the exception of food imports and medical supplies). This move - which has devastated the Macedonian economy - was condemned by all of Greece's EU partners. Before the embargo, the Macedonian economy had depended upon rail and road links with the northern Greek port of Thessaloniki. Before the dissolution of Yugoslavia over 80% of Macedonia's industrial exports were shipped through Thessaloniki. The stability and territorial integrity of Macedonia is threatened not only by its hostile neighbour to the south, but also by possible Serbian claims in the north and by the activities of ethnic Albanian nationalists within Macedonia, some of whom are seeking reunion with other Albanians in an enlarged state ruled from Tirana. In 1993 tension increased within Macedonia's ethnic Albanian population and several Albanian leaders were arrested and detained upon charges involving an alleged coup plot. Macedonia is seen by many international observers as a possible theatre for a major Balkan conflict that could involve Greece, Serbia, Albania, Turkey and Bulgaria.

161

Poland

Official name: Polska Rzecpospolita (Republic of Poland).

Member of: UN, CSCE, Council of Europe, CEFTA, NATO (partner for peace).

Area: 312,683 km² (120,727 sq mi).

Population: 38,273,000 (1991 est).

Capital: Warsaw (Warszawa) 1,656,000 (1990 est).

Other major cities: Katowice 1,604,000 (city 367,000; Sosnowiec 260,000; Bytom 230,000; Gliwice 222,000; Zabrze 203,000; Tychy 190,000; Chorzów 132,000), Lódz 848,000, Kraków 751,000, Wroclaw 643,000, Poznan 590,000, Gdansk 465,000, Szczecin 413,000, Bydgoszcz 382,000, Lublin 351,000, Bialystok 271,000, Czestochowa 258,000, Gdynia 252,000, Rydom 226,000, Kielce 213,000, (1990 est).

Languages: Polish (official; 99%); small Ukrainian and German minorities.

Religion: Roman Catholic (93%), Polish Orthodox (2%).

Education: Education is compulsory between the ages of seven and 14. There are 25 universities

Defence: In 1993 the army had a total strength of 194,000, the navy had 19,300 personnel and the air force had 83,000. Gdynia is the principal naval base. Conscription lasts for 18 months.

Transport: There are 363,000 km (227,000 mi) of roads of which 260 km (163 mi) are motorways. The state-owned railways have 26,228 km (16,393 mi) of track. The main seaports are Gdansk, Gdynia and Szczecin. Warsaw has Poland's sole international airport.

Media: There are over 60 daily newspapers. Poland has two state-run national TV channels, regional channels, a private commercial TV station and four national state-run radio channels.

GOVERNMENT

The 100-member Senate (Upper House) and the 460-member Sejm (Lower House) are elected for four years by universal adult suffrage. In the Sejm 391 seats are contested in constituencies and the remaining 69 are elected from party lists. The directly-elected President appoints a PM who commands a majority in the Sejm. The PM, in turn, appoints a Council of Ministers. Political parties are the (former Communist) Democratic Left Alliance (SLD), the (centre-left) Polish Peasant Party (PSL), the (centre) Democratic Union (UD), the (former Solidarity) Union of Labour (UP), the (conservative) Confederation for an Independent Poland (KPN), and the (independent) Non-Party Block to Support Reform (BBWR). After the election for the Sejm in September 1993 an SLD, PSL and UL coalition was formed.

Party strength: SLD 171, PSL 132, UD 74, UP 41, KPN 22, BBWR 16, German minority parties 4

President: Lech Walesa.

THE CABINET

Prime Minister: Waldemar Pawlak (PSL).

Deputy Prime Minister, Minister of the Economy and Minister for Finance: Prof. Grzegorz Kolodko (ind.).

Deputy Prime Minister, Minister of Social Policy and Minister for Justice: Wlodzimierz Cimoszewicz (ind.).

Deputy Prime Minister, Minister of State Administration and Minister of Education: Aleksander Luczak (SLD).

Minister of Agriculture: Andrzej Smietanko (PSL).

Minister of Communication: Andrzej Zielinski (ind.).

Minister of Culture: Kazimierz Dejmek (PSL).

Minister of Defence: Admiral Piotr Koloziejczyk (ind.).

Minister for Environmental Protection, Natural Resources and Forestry: Stanislaw Zelichowski (PSL).

Minister of Foreign Affairs: Andrzej Olechowski (ind.).

Minister of Foreign Economic Relations: Leslaw Podkanski (PSL).

Minister of Health: Prof. Jacek Zochowski (SLD).

Minister of Industry and Trade: Marek Pol (UP).

Minister of Internal Affairs: Andrzej Milczanowski (ind).

POLAND

Area: 312 683 km²
(120 727 sq mi).

Minister of Labour and Social Policy: Leszek Miller (SLD).

Minister for Ownership Transformation (Privatization): Wieslaw Kaczmarek (SLD).

Minister of Regional Planning and Construction: Barbara Blida (SLD).

Minister of Transport and Maritime Economy: Boguslaw Liberadzki (ind.).

GEOGRAPHY
Most of Poland consists of lowlands. In the north are the Baltic lowlands and the Pomeranian and Mazurian lake districts. Central Poland is a region of plains. In the south are the hills of Little Poland and the Tatra Mountains, part of the Carpathian chain. Highest point: Rysy 2499 m (8199 ft). Principal rivers: Vistula (Wisa), Oder (Odra), Narew. Climate: Poland's climate tends towards continental with short warm summers and longer cold winters.

ECONOMY
Polish agriculture is largely small-scale and privately owned. Over 25% of the labour force is involved in farming, growing potatoes, wheat, barley, sugar beet and fodder crops. The industrial sector is large-scale and, until the switch to a free-market economy began in 1990, centrally planned. Poland has major deposits of coal, and reserves of natural gas, copper and silver. Engineering, food processing, and the chemical, metallurgical and paper industries are important, but the economy has steadily deteriorated since the 1960s.

Privatization was accelerated after 1991, but although Poland made impressive economic reforms, and achieved higher growth rates than other East European countries, living standards have generally decreased.

Currency: Zloty; 1US$ = 22,715 zloty (June 1994).

GDP: US$72,500,000,000 (1993 est); US$1885 per head.

RECENT HISTORY
After World War I, Poland, which had been ruled by Russia, Austria and Prussia, was restored to statehood (1919), but the country was unstable. Marshal Józef Pilsudski (1867-1935) staged a coup in 1926, and became a virtual dictator. During the 1930s relations with Hitler's Germany - which made territorial claims on parts of Poland - became strained. An alliance with Britain did not deter Hitler from attacking Poland - thus precipitating World War II (1939). Poland was partitioned again, this time between Nazi Germany and the USSR. Occupied Poland lost one sixth of its population, including almost all the Jews, and casualties were high after the ill-fated Warsaw Rising (1944). Poland was liberated by the Red Army (1945), and a Communist state was established. The new Poland lost almost 50% of its territory in the east to the USSR, but was compensated in the north and west at the expense of Germany. A political crisis in 1956 led to the emergence of a Communist leader who enjoyed a measure of popular support, Wladyslaw Gomulka. In 1980, unrest following the downfall of Gomulka's successor, Edward Gierek, led to the birth of the independent trade union Solidarity (Solidarnosc), led by Lech Walesa (1943-). Martial law was declared by General Wojciech Jaruzelski in 1981 in an attempt to restore Communist authority. Solidarity was banned and its leaders were detained, but unrest and economic difficulties continued. In 1989 Solidarity was legalized and agreement was reached on political reform. Solidarity won free elections to the new Senate, and with the support of former allies of the Communists gained a majority in the Sejm. Disagreements concerning the speed at which market reforms were advancing and personality clashes split Solidarity. Walesa became president in 1990. Since multi-party elections in 1991 and 1993, several short-lived coalition governments have held office.

Romania

Official name: Rômania.

Member of: UN, CSCE, Council of Europe (guest), NATO (partner for peace).

Area: 237,500 km² (91,699 sq mi).

Population: 22,789,000 (1993 est.).

Capital: Bucharest (Bucuresti) 2,351,000 (1992 census).

Other major cities: Constanta 351,000, Iasi 343,000, Timisoara 334,000, Cluj-Napoca 328,000, Galati 326,000, Brasov 324,000, Craiova 304,000, Ploiesti 252,000, Braila 235,000, Oradea 221,000, Bacau 205,000 (1992 est.).

Languages: Romanian (official; 89%), Magyar (Hungarian) (10%), German (1%).

Religions: Romanian Orthodox (70%), Uniat (Greek Catholic) Church (3%), Roman Catholic (5%), Calvinist (2%).

Education: Education is compulsory between the ages of six and 16. In 1990 the literacy rate was over 94%. There are 15 universities.

Defence: In 1992 the total armed strength was 201,000 - 162,000 in the army, 19,000 in the navy, 20,000 in the air force. Compulsory military service lasts 12 months (18 months in the navy).

Transport: There are 11,127 km (6954 mi) of railways and 72,816 km (45,510 mi) of roads. Tulcea and Galati are river ports on the Danube; Constanta is the main Black Sea port. There are international airports at Bucharest, Arad, Constanta and Timisoara.

Media: There are 65 main daily newspapers. There is a single (state-owned) radio and television network.

GOVERNMENT

A President is directly elected by universal adult suffrage for five years. A 341-seat National Assembly (lower house) and a 143-seat Senate (upper house) are elected by proportional representation for four years; 13 seats are reserved for ethnic minorities. Political parties include the Party of Social Democracy of Romania (PSDR), the National Salvation Front (NSF), the (right-wing) Romanian National Unity Party (RNUF), the Hungarian Democratic Union of Romania (DUR), the (right-wing) Greater Romania Party (GRP), the (former Communist) Socialist Labour Party (SLP), the Agrarian Democratic Party of Romania (ADPR), and the Democratic Convention of Romania (DCR), an alliance of the Christian Democratic National Peasants' Party (CDNPP), the Party of the Civic Alliance (PCA), the New Liberal Party (NLP), the Romanian Social Democratic Party (RSDP) and the Romanian Ecology Party (REP). After the election held in September 1992 a PSDR-independent government took office.

Party strength: PSDR 117, NSF 43, CDNPP (DCR) 42, RNUF 30, DUR 27, GRP 16, PCA (DCR) 13, NLP (DCR) 13, SLP 13, RSDP (DCR) 10, REP (DCR) 4, ind 13.

President: Ion Iliescu (PDSR).

THE CABINET

Prime Minister: Nicolae Vacaroiou (PSDR).

Deputy Prime Minister and Chairman of the Council for Economic Strategy and Reform: Misu Negritoiu (ind).

Deputy Prime Minister and Minister of Employment and Social Security: Dan Mircea Popescu (PSDR).

Deputy Prime Minister and Minister of Finance: Florin Georgescu (ind).

Deputy Prime Minister and Minister of Foreign Affairs: Teodor Viorel Melescanu (ind).

Minister of Agriculture and Food: Ioan Oancea (PSDR).

Minister of Commerce: Constantin Teculescu (PSDR).

Minister of Communications: Andrei Chirica (ind).

Minister of Culture: Mihai Golu (PSDR).

Minister of Education: Liviu Maior (PSDR).

Minister of Health: Prof. Iulian Micu (PSDR).

Minister of Industry: Dumitru Popescu (PSDR).

Minister of the Interior: Gheorghe Ioan Danescu (ind).

Minister of Justice: Petre Ninosu (PSDR).

Minister of National Defence: Gen. Constantin Nicolae Spiroiu (ind).

Minister of Public Works and Planning: Marin Cristea (PSDR).

Minister of Research and Technology: Doru Dumitru Palade (ind).

Minister of Tourism: Matei Agaten Dan (PSDR).

Minister of Transport: Paul Teodoru (ind).

Minister of Waters, Forestry and Environmental Protection: Aurel Constantin Ilie (ind).

Minister of Youth and Sports: Gheorghe Anghelescu (PSDR).

GEOGRAPHY
The Carpathian Mountains run through the north, east and centre of Romania. To the west of the Carpathians is the tableland of Transylvania and the Banat lowland. In the south the Danube Plain ends in a delta on the Black Sea. Highest point: Moldoveanu 2544 m

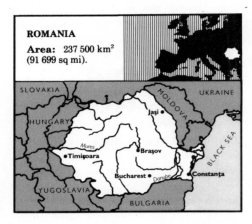

ROMANIA
Area: 237 500 km²
(91 699 sq mi).

(8346 ft). Principal rivers: Danube (Dunăria), Mures, Prut. Climate: Romania experiences cold snowy winters and hot summers. Rainfall is moderate in the lowlands and heavier in the Carpathians.

ECONOMY
State-owned industry - which employs nearly 40% of the labour force - includes mining, metallurgy, mechanical engineering and chemicals.

Natural resources include petroleum and natural gas. Considerable forests support a timber and furniture industry. Major crops include maize, sugar beet, wheat, potatoes and grapes for wine, but agriculture has been neglected, and - because of exports - food supplies have fallen short of the country's needs. Most of Romania's agricultural land has been privatized. Economic mismanagement under Ceausescu (see below) decreased already low living standards. Subsequent governments have faced appalling economic problems including high rates of inflation, sharp devaluation of the leu, drastic shortages of raw materials, and falling production and exports.

Currency: Leu of 100 bani; 1US$ = 1686.6 leus (June 1994).

GDP: US$21,100,000,000 (1993 est); US$915 per head.

RECENT HISTORY
Romania won territory with large Romanian populations from the Russian and Habsburg Empires at the end of World War I. Romania was forced by Germany to cede lands back to Hungary (1940), while the USSR retook Moldova. King Carol II fled. Romania, under Marshal Ion Antonescu, joined the Axis powers (1941), fighting the USSR to regain lost areas. King Michael dismissed Antonescu and declared war on Germany as the Red Army invaded (1944). A Soviet-dominated government was installed (1945) and the monarchy was abolished (1947). From 1952, under Gheorghe Gheorghiu-Dej (1901-65) and then under Nicolae Ceausescu (1918-89), Romania distanced itself from Soviet foreign policy but maintained strict Communist orthodoxy at home. Ceausescu, and his wife Elena, impoverished Romania by their harsh, corrupt, nepotistic rule. When the secret police put down demonstrations in Timisoara (1989), a national revolt (backed by the army) broke out. A National Salvation Front (NSF) was formed and a military tribunal executed Nicolae and Elena Ceausescu on charges of genocide and corruption. The Communist Party was dissolved; Ceausescu's oppressive social and economic legislation was annulled. In 1990, the NSF was reelected to power. An international team of monitors judged Romania's first postwar multi-party elections to be 'flawed' but not fraudulent. The NSF split in 1992 and the Party of Social Democracy - the larger offshoot - came to power.

Slovakia

Official name: Republika Slovenská (Slovak Republic).

Member of: UN, CSCE, Council of Europe, CEFTA, NATO (partner for peace).

Area: 49,025 km² (18,929 sq mi).

Population: 5,290,000 (1991 census).

Capital: Bratislava 444,000 (including suburbs; 1991 census).

Other major cities: Kosice 235,000, Nitra 90,000, Presov 88,000, Banská Bystrica 85,000, Zilina 84,000, Trnava 72,000, Martin 58,000, Trencín 57,000, Prievidza 53,000, Poprad 50,000 (1991 census).

Languages: Slovak (87%), Magyar (Hungarian) (12%), Czech (1%).

Religions: Roman Catholic (60%), Evangelical Churches (Slovak Evangelical Church of the Augsburg Confession, known as Slovak Lutherans, and Reformed Christian Church of Slovakia; 6%).

Education: Education is compulsory between the ages of six and 15. In 1990 the literacy rate was estimated to be virtually 100%. There are ten universities.

Defence: The total armed strength was estimated in 1993 to be 50,000. Compulsory military service lasts for 12 months.

Transport: There are 17,737 km (11,086 mi) of roads in Slovakia including 191 km (119 mi) of motorway. There are 3661 km (2288 mi) of railway track. A metro system is under construction in Bratislava. The Danube is an important inland waterway with ports at Bratislava and Komárno. International flights operate from Bratislava and Kosice airports.

Media: There are some 700 newspapers (both daily and weekly) including many new titles. About 30 papers are published in minority languages, mainly Magyar (Hungarian). There is a single (state-owned) radio and television network.

GOVERNMENT

The 150-member National Council is elected under a system of proportional representation by universal adult suffrage for four years. The Assembly elects a President for a five-year term. The President, whose role is largely ceremonial, appoints a Prime Minister and a Council of Ministers, responsible to the National Council. Slovakia is divided into four administrative regions. The main political parties are the (socialist nationalist) Movement for a Democratic Slovakia (HZDS), the (former Communist) Party of the Democratic Left (SDL), the (centre) Christian Democratic Movement (KDH), the National Democratic Party (NDS), the Slovak National Party (SNS), the Democratic Union (DU), and MKDH-ESWS, an electoral alliance of ethnic Hungarian parties. Following an election in June 1993, and a subsequent realignment of parties, a DU, SDL, KDH and NDS coalition government was formed in March 1994.

Party strength: HZDS 55, SDL 28, KDH 18, DU 16, MKDH-ESWS 14, SNS 9, NDS 6, independents 5.

President: Michal Kovác (HZDS).

THE CABINET

Prime Minister: Jozef Moravcik (DU).

Deputy Prime Minister: Brigita Schmognerova (SDL).

Deputy Prime Minister: Roman Kovác (DU).

Deputy Prime Minister: Ivan Simko (KDH).

Minister of Agriculture: Pavel Koncos (SDL).

Minister of Culture: Lubomir Roman (KDH).

Minister of Defence: Pavol Kanis (SDL).

Minister of Education and Science: Lubomir Harach (DU).

Minister of the Environment: Juraj Hrasko (SDL).

Minister of Finance: Rudolf Filkus (DU).

Minister of Foreign Affairs: Eduard Kukan (DU).

Minister of Health: Tibor Sagat (SDL).

Minister of Industry: Peter Magvasi (SDL).

Minister of the Interior: Ladislav Pittner (KDH).

Minister of Justice: Milan Hanzel (SDL).

Minister of Labour, Social and Family Affairs: Julius Brocka (KDH).

Minister of Privatization: Milan Janicina (NDS).

Minister of Transport, Communications and Public Works: Mikulas Dzurinda (KDH).

GEOGRAPHY

Slovakia mainly comprises mountain ranges including the Tatra Mountains on the Polish border. The only significant lowlands are in the south adjoining the River Danube and its tributaries. The relief means that the natural routes are mainly north-south, which is inconvenient in a country where most internal traffic is east to west. Highest Point: Gerlachovka 2655 m (8737 ft). Principal rivers: Danube, Vah, Hron. Climate: Slovakia has a continental climate characterized by warm summers and cold, snowy winters. There are many local climatic variations. The greatest differences are between the high cold Tatra Mountains and the sheltered Danube lowlands which have lower rainfall and much higher summer temperatures.

ECONOMY

Slovakia has a large agricultural sector. Wheat, maize, potatoes, barley and sheep are important. Heavy industry - particularly steel, chemicals and one of the largest arms industries in Europe - was introduced when the country was part of Communist Czechoslovakia. A drastic fall in international demand for arms added to Slovak unemployment and the government has actively sought to revive exports of arms. Other important industries include textiles, clothing, footwear, glass and leather.

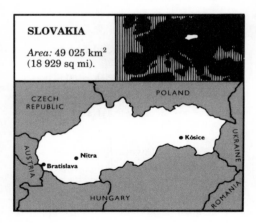

SLOVAKIA

Area: 49 025 km^2
(18 929 sq mi).

Varied natural resources include brown coal, copper, zinc and lead. At the dissolution of Czechoslovakia about two thirds of state-owned enterprises had been privatized but independent Slovakia has slowed the privatization of its uncompetitive out-of-date factories. Unemployment has increased, GDP has fallen and the loss of subsidies from Prague has damaged the economy.

Currency: Slovakian koruna of 100 halierov; 1US$ = 32.36 koruny (May 1994).

GDP: US$12,800,000 000 (1993 est); US$2420 per head.

RECENT HISTORY

At the beginning of the 20th century, what is now Slovakia had been under Habsburg rule since 1526. On the collapse of the Habsburg Empire (1918), the Slovaks seceded from Habsburg Hungary and joined the Czechs to form Czechoslovakia, a state that proved to be more centralized than the federalist Slovaks had expected. When Hitler's Germany dismembered Czechoslovakia in 1938, Slovakia became an Axis puppet state under the Slovak autonomist leader Jozef Tiso. Slovakia lost its Magyar (Hungarian) south to Hungary (1938). A popular revolt against German rule (the Slovak Uprising) took place in 1944. Following liberation (1945) Czechoslovakia was re-established. After the Communist takeover in 1948, heavy industry was introduced into rural Slovakia. In 1968, moves by Communist Party Secretary Alexander Dubcek (a Slovak) to introduce political reforms met with Soviet disapproval, and invasion by Czechoslovakia's Warsaw Pact allies. In 1969 the Slovak Republic became an equal partner with the Czech Republic under a new federal constitution. The conservative wing of the Communist Party regained control until 1989, when student demonstrations developed into a peaceful revolution. In 1990 free multi-party elections were held, Soviet troops were withdrawn and the foundations of a market economy were laid, but the pace of economic reform brought distress to Slovakia, whose old-fashioned industries were ill-equipped to face competition. Increased Slovak separatism led to the division of the country in 1993. Independent Slovakia faces severe economic difficulties as well as possible tension concerning the large Hungarian minority in the south.

Slovenia

Official name: Republika Slovenija (The Republic of Slovenia).

Member of: UN, CSCE, Council of Europe, NATO (partner for peace).

Area: 20,251 km² (7819 sq mi).

Population: 1,966,000 (1992 est).

Capital: Ljubljana 328,000 (city 276,000) (1991 census).

Other major cities: Maribor 189,000 (city 108,000), Celje 41,000, Kranj 37,000, Koper 25,000 (including suburbs; 1991 census).

Languages: Slovene (91%), Serbo-Croat (5%), with small Italian and Magyar (Hungarian) minorities.

Religions: Roman Catholic (over 90%), Slovene Old Catholic Church, Evangelical Lutheran Church of Slovenia.

Education: Education is compulsory between the ages of seven and 15. In 1990 the literacy rate was estimated to be virtually 100%. There are two universities and a university institute.

Defence: In 1992 the total strength of the Slovene army was 15,000, plus 85,000 reserves. There are plans to increase the size of the standing army to 20,000. A small coastal defence force has been founded. Compulsory military conscription lasts seven months.

Transport: There are 1196 km (748 mi) of railway track. There are almost 45,000 km (28,125 mi) of roads including 81 km (51 mi) of motorway. Koper (once known as Capodistria) is the only major port on Slovenia's short Adriatic coast. There are three international airports - Brnik (for Ljubljana), Maribor and Portoroz.

Media: There are six daily newspapers and nearly 200 other (mainly regional and local) papers. Slovenia has a single radio and television network.

GOVERNMENT

Under a new constitution, Slovenia has a unicameral Parliamen, the 90-member National Assembly. The Assembly serves for four years and comprises 38 members directly elected in constituencies by universal adult suffrage, 50 members indirectly elected by a national 'electoral college' according to a system of proportional representation and two nominated members - one each to represent Slovenia's small Italian and Hungarian minorities. The 40-member National Council is an advisory body, which may propose laws to the Assembly and demand that the Assembly review its decision on a law before promulgating it. The Council serves for five years and comprises 20 members directly elected to represent local interests and 20 members representing various social, economic, and professional interests. The President - whose role is largely a ceremonial one - is directly elected for five years. The Prime Minister (who is appointed by the President) appoints a Council of Ministers who enjoy a majority in the National Assembly. There are 62 local government districts. The main political parties are the (centrist) Liberal Democratic Party (LDP), the Slovenian Christian Democrats (SKD), the (right-wing) Slovenian National Party (SNS), the Associated List of Social Democrats (ZLSD), the (agrarian) Slovenian People's Party (SLS), the (centrist) Democratic Party (DS), the Independent SNS Deputy Group (a breakaway from the SNS; ISNS), the Greens - Ecological Social Party (Eco), and the Social Democratic Party of Slovenia (SDSS). Following the election held in December 1992 a coalition government of LDS, ZLSD, SKD, SDSS, and Eco members and independents was formed; the government has since been reshuffled.

Party strength: LDS 22, SKD 15, ZLSD 14, SLS 11, DS 5, ISNS 5, Eco 5, SNS 5, SDSS 4, others 4.

President: Milan Kucan.

THE CABINET

Prime Minister: Dr Janez Drnovsek (LDS).

Minister of Agriculture and Forestry: Joze Osterc (SKD).

Minister of Culture: Sergij Pelhan (ZLSD).

Minister of Defence: Jelko Kacin (SDSS).

Minister for Economic Affairs: Dr Maks Tajnikar (ZLSD).

Minister of Economic Relations and Development: Dr Davorin Kracun (LDS).

Minister of Education and Sport: Dr Slavko Gaber (LDS).

Minister of the Environment and Regional Planning: Dr Pavle Gantar (LDS).

SLOVENIA

Area: 20 251 km² (7819 sq mi).

Minister of Finance: Mitja Gaspari (ind.).

Minister of Foreign Affairs: Lojze Peterle (SKD).

Minister of Health: Dr Bozidar Voljc (Eco).

Minister of Interior Affairs: Ivan Bizjak (SKD).

Minister of Justice: Miha Kozinc (LDS).

Minister of Labour, Family and Social Affairs: Jozica Puhar (ZLSD).

Minister of Science and Technology: Dr Rado Bohinc (ZLSD).

Minister of Transport and Communications: Igor Umek (SKD).

Minister without Portfolio (responsible for legislation): Lojze Janko (ind.).

GEOGRAPHY
Most of Slovenia comprises mountains including the Karawanken Alps in the north and the Julian Alps in the centre. In the east, hill country adjoins the Drava valley. In the west, Slovenia has an Adriatic coastline of 30 km (19 mi), wedged between the Italian port of Trieste and the Croatian peninsula of Istria. Highest point: Triglav 2864 m (9396 ft). Principal rivers: Drava, Sava, Mura. Climate: Western Slovenia has a mild Mediterranean climate; eastern Slovenia tends to be more continental with colder winters. Rainfall is relatively heavy, particularly in the mountains, although the eastern lowlands adjoining the Hungarian border are drier.

ECONOMY
With a standard of living approaching that of West European countries, Slovenia was the most industrialized and economically developed part of the former Yugoslavia. Industries include iron and steel, textiles and coal mining.

Mass privatization is expected to be completed before the end of 1994. Agriculture specializes in livestock, fodder crops (particularly maize), potatoes, wheat and grapes (for wine). About 40% of the republic is wooded and forestry is an important industry. Before the Yugoslav civil wars Slovenia attracted many summer tourists to the Adriatic coast and winter skiers - tourism is reviving. The rest of former Yugoslavia was a major trading partner of Slovenia before 1991 and the country's economy has been disrupted by the loss of these markets. However, German, Italian and Austrian markets now play a much greater role and free-trade agreements have been concluded with the Czech Republic, Hungary and Slovakia. Slovenia experienced high inflation in the first period of independence but the rate of inflation decreased greatly after the government adopted tough monetarist policies and the republic adopted its own currency - the tolar. Slovenia has not suffered the severe economic decline that has characterized the other former Yugoslav republics.

Currency: Tolar of 100 stotins; 1US$ = 133.19 tolars (May 1994).

GDP: US$12,278,000,000 (1992); US$6133 per head.

RECENT HISTORY
At the turn of the 20th century, what is now Slovenia had been incorporated within the Habsburg (Austrian) province of Carniola for nearly six centuries. When the Habsburg Empire collapsed (1918), the Slovenes joined the Serbs, Croats and Montenegrins in the new state that was renamed Yugoslavia in 1929. However, a sizeable Slovene community remained under Italian rule until the border between Italy and Yugoslavia was redrawn after World War II. When Yugoslavia became a Communist federal state in 1945, the Slovene lands were reorganized as the republic of Slovenia. After the death of Yugoslav President Tito (1980), the federation faltered in nationalist crises. Slovenia, the wealthiest part of Yugoslavia, edged towards democracy. In free elections in 1990, nationalists gained a majority in the Slovene Assembly, which declared independence in June 1991. Following reverses in a short campaign, Yugoslav federal forces were withdrawn from Slovenia. The EC led the international community in recognizing Slovenia's independence in January 1992.

169

Yugoslavia (Serbia and Montenegro)

Official name: Federativna Republika Jugoslavija (The Federal Republic of Yugoslavia).

Member of: UN (suspended), CSCE (suspended).

Area: 102,173 km² (39,449 sq mi).

Population: 10,561,000 (1993 est).

MONTENEGRO (CRNA GORA)
Area: 13,812 km² (5333 sq mi).

Population: 615,000 (1991 census).

Capital: Podgorica (formerly known as Titograd) 130,000 (city 118,000; 1991 census).

Other main cities: Niksic 75,000, Bar 35,000, Kotor 23,000, Cetinje 15,000 (1991 census).

Languages: Serb (see Serbia, below) (93%), Albanian (7%).

Religions: Orthodox (both Serbian Orthodox and a revived Montenegrin Orthodox Church; nearly 80%), Sunni Islam (19%).

Education: Schooling is compulsory between the ages of seven and 15. In 1990 the literacy rate was over 89%. There is a university.

YUGOSLAVIA

Area: 102 173 km²
(39 449 sq mi)

Defence: See Serbia (below).

Transport: See Serbia (below). Bar is the principal port.

Media: There are three daily papers. A state-controlled company operates two radio and two TV networks.

GOVERNMENT
A 125-member Assembly and a President are elected by universal adult suffrage. The main political parties are the (former Communist) Democratic Party of Socialists of Montenegro (DPS), the Alliance of Reform Forces and the New Socialist Party of Montenegro.

President: Momir Bulatovic (DPS).

GEOGRAPHY
Ridges of mountains - rising to the Dinaric Alps in the east - occupy most of the country. The few cultivable lowlands include the area around Cetinje and the Zeta lowland. Montenegro's short Adriatic coastline is all that remains of Yugoslavia's coast. Highest point: Mt Durmitor 2522 m (8274 ft). Principal rivers: Piva, Zeta. Climate: Coastal Montenegro has a Mediterranean climate; the interior tends to be more continental with colder winters.

ECONOMY
Agriculture - especially raising livestock - dominates the economy. The land is poor and plots are small and fragmented. Under Yugoslav Communist rule the economy was diversified and iron and steel plants, HEP installations and shipbuilding were developed. The state's economy has been devastated by rampant inflation and international sanctions and Montenegro's lucrative tourist industry no longer exists. See also Economy of Yugoslavia, below.

SERBIA (SRBIJA)
Area: 88,361 km² (34,116 sq mi) including the formerly autonomous provinces of Kosovo (10,817 km²/4203 sq mi) and Vojvodina (21,508 km²/8304 sq mi).

Population: 9,791,000 (1991 census) including the formerly autonomous provinces of Kosovo (1,955,000; 1991 census) and Vojvodina (2,013,000; 1991 census). Since 1992, Serb refugees from Bosnia have increased this figure. No reliable figure for the number of refugees is available although most Bosnian Serb refugees in Serbia have resettled in and around Belgrade. The populations of Kosovo and Vojvodina have also been affected by population movements - many ethnic Hungarians have left Vojvodina, while ethnic Serbs have increasingly quit Kosovo.

Capital: Belgrade (Beograd) 1,555,000 (city 1,500,000; 1991 census).

Other major cities: Novi Sad 260,000 (city 179,000), Nis 230,000 (city 176,000), Pristina 210,000, Subotica 155,000 (city 100,000), Zrenjanin 81,000, Pancevo 73,000, Smederevo 64,000, Leskovac 62,000 (1991 census).

Languages: Serb - the version of Serbo-Croat written in the Cyrillic alphabet - (73%), Albanian (16%), Hungarian (4%). The number of Hungarian-speakers is diminishing owing to migration.

Religions: Orthodox (over 75%), Sunni Islam (over 12%), small Roman Catholic minority.

Education: Schooling is compulsory between the ages of seven and 15. In 1990 the literacy rate was estimated to be over 89%. There are six universities, one of which - in Kosovo - is effectively closed.

Defence: The Yugoslav federal forces have a total armed strength of 135,000 - 100,000 in the army, 29,000 in the air force and 6000 in the navy. (The Yugoslav navy is now based at Kotor in Montenegro.) Military service of one year is compulsory.

Transport: In Serbia and Montenegro combined there are about 46,020 km (28,595 mi) of roads. As not all of the railway lines in the two republics are still operating, no figure for the length of remaining track is available. The Danube in Serbia is a major navigable waterway. Belgrade has an international airport.

Media: There are nearly a dozen principal daily newspapers. A state-controlled company (RTS) broadcasts five radio and three TV networks.

GOVERNMENT
A 250-member National Assembly and a President are elected by universal adult suffrage. Under a new constitution (September 1992), Kosovo and Vojvodina no longer have autonomy. The main political party is the (former Communist) Socialist Party of Serbia (SPS). Other parties include the (right-wing) Serbian Radical Party (SRP), the (centrist) Serbian Democratic Movement, the Democratic Party, and the (Hungarian ethnic) Democratic Community (DC).

President: Slobodan Milosevic (SPS).

GEOGRAPHY
Ridges of mountains occupy the south and centre of the country. In the south the Sar Mountains form a high boundary between Serbia and Macedonia. The north (Vojvodina) is occupied by plains drained by the rivers Danube and Tisa. Highest point: Titov Vrh 2747 m (9012 ft). Principal rivers: Danube, Tisa, Morava, Drina. Climate: Serbia has a continental climate with warm summers and cold snowy winters.

ECONOMY
The economy of Serbia was devastated by international sanctions and rampant inflation in 1992-93. The situation was made worse by the fact that many of Serbia's industrial plants were old and inefficient compared with those in Slovenia and Croatia: before the secession of the latter two republics from Yugoslavia Serbia was effectively subsidized by her northern neighbours. The loss of foreign currency previously earned by the tourist industries of Croatia, Slovenia and Montenegro has also been damaging. See Economy of Yugoslavia, below.

GOVERNMENT OF YUGOSLAVIA
Under the terms of a new federal constitution (April 1992), Yugoslavia consists of two equal republics - Serbia and Montenegro. A Federal Assembly comprises a Chamber of the Republics, which has 40 members (20 elected by each of the two republican parliaments) and a 138-member Chamber of Citizens, which is elected by universal adult suffrage. A Federal President is elected by the Assembly. The President appoints a Prime Minister and a Council of Ministers but these federal authorities have, in practice, lesser powers than the two republics which have their own legislatures - the Serbian presidency in particular has assumed virtual sovereign powers.

President: Zoran Lilic.

Prime Minister: Radoje Kontic.

ECONOMY OF YUGOSLAVIA
Most of the land is privately owned. Major crops include maize, wheat, sugar beet, grapes, potatoes, citrus fruit and fodder crops for sheep. Industry - which is mainly concentrated

171

around Belgrade - includes food processing, textiles, metallurgy, motor vehicles and consumer goods. The country's economy was severely damaged by the wars in Croatia and Bosnia which began in 1991. The economy was then devastated by rampant inflation - over 20,000% in 1992 rising to 5% an hour in December 1993 - and by international sanctions imposed upon Serbia and Montenegro. The country's monetary and banking systems and its industrial sector virtually collapsed. International sanctions curbed Yugoslavia's trade and living standards have been reduced drastically. Late in 1993 a new currency, tied to the German D-mark, was introduced. This has not lost its value as rapidly as its predecessor, and, although the economy is but a shadow of its former state, a tentative recovery has begun.

Currency: Dinar; not quoted on the international market in June 1994.

GDP: No recent data for the Serb and Montenegrin economies are available.

RECENT HISTORY OF YUGOSLAVIA

Both Serbia and Montenegro were recognized as independent in 1878. By the start of the 20th century a Croat national revival within the Habsburg Empire looked increasingly to Serbia to create a South ('Yugo') Slav state. After Serbia gained Macedonia in the Balkan Wars (1912-13), Austria grew wary of Serbian ambitions. The assassination of the Habsburg heir (1914) by a Serb student in Sarajevo provided Austria with an excuse to try to quash Serbian independence. This led directly to World War I and the subsequent dissolution of the Habsburg Empire, whose South Slav peoples united with Serbia and Montenegro in 1918 to form the country known since 1929 as Yugoslavia. Yugoslavia was run as a highly centralized 'Greater Serbia'. The country was wracked by nationalist tensions, and Croat separatists murdered King Alexander in 1934. Attacked and dismembered by Hitler in 1941, Yugoslavs fought the Nazis and each other. The Communist-led partisans of Josip Broz Tito (1892-1980) emerged victorious in 1945, and re-formed Yugoslavia on Soviet lines. Expelled by Stalin from the Soviet bloc in 1948 for failing to toe the Moscow line, the Yugoslav Communists rejected the Soviet model, and pursued policies of decentralization, workers' self-management and non-alignment. After Tito's death in 1980, the Yugoslav experiment

faltered in economic and nationalist crises. The wealthier northern republics of Slovenia and Croatia led the movement towards democracy and Western Europe, while Serbia forcefully resisted the separatist aspirations of Albanian nationalists in Kosovo province. In 1990 the Communists conceded the principle of free elections. By the end of the year, the League of Communists of Yugoslavia had ceased to exist as a national entity, and elections were won by various centre-right, nationalist and regional socialist parties in all the republics except Serbia and Montenegro, where Communist parties won. Serbia exacerbated ethnic Albanian, and (to a much lesser extent) ethnic Hungarian, nationalism by the legal removal of most of the autonomous powers of Kosovo and Vojvodina. In June 1991 Slovenia and Croatia declared independence. Following reverses in a short campaign, Yugoslav federal forces were withdrawn from Slovenia, but Serb insurgents, backed by Yugoslav federal forces, occupied between one third and one quarter of Croatia including Krajina and parts of Slavonia, areas with an ethnic Serb majority. In 1992 the fierce Serbo-Croat war was halted and a UN peacekeeping force was agreed. The international community recognized the independence of Slovenia and Croatia. When Bosnia-Herzegovina received similar recognition, Bosnian Serbs, encouraged by Serbia, seized 70% of Bosnia, killing or expelling Muslims and Croats in a campaign of 'ethnic cleansing'. Serbia was widely blamed for the continuation of the conflict and - with Montenegro - was subjected to international trade and diplomatic sanctions. The Serb leadership, however, continued to promote the idea of a Greater Serbia which would join the rump Yugoslavia to Serb areas of Croatia (Krajina) and Bosnia-Herzegovina. Serbia and Montenegro formed a new Yugoslav federation but act as virtually independent countries. International peace efforts to end the Bosnian war were attempted in 1993 and tension increased in Kosovo. After the Bosnian Serbs rejected the Owen-Vance peace plan for Bosnia, international pressure upon Serbia to exert influence upon the Bosnian Serbs increased and sanctions upon Yugoslavia were tightened. Serbian pressure upon the Bosnian Serbs in 1994 failed to gain Serb agreement to the international 'Contact Group' plan to partition Bosnia-Herzegovina.

CENTRAL
AND
SOUTH AMERICA

Argentina, Belize, Bolivia, Brazil, Chile, Colombia, Costa Rica,
Ecuador, El Salvador, Guatemala, Guyana, Honduras, Nicaragua,
Panama, Paraguay, Peru, Suriname, Uruguay, Venezuela,
Other territories.

The resurgence of democracy in Central and South America

The shift away from authoritarian military and single-party regimes began in Latin America in 1982. Internal pressures for change were strengthened by Western, particularly US, encouragement - sometimes including economic coercion - and by the ending of the Cold War. The changes are dramatic and already show signs of being permanent.

THE ARMY RETREATS

In Latin America, democracy has vied with dictatorship since independence was achieved in the early 19th century. But by the 1970s the vast majority of the population lived under military or militarized regimes. Only three of the 20 Latin American countries could be regarded as democratic; the abuse of human rights was widespread, and was often tolerated by the West in the name of anti-Communism.

By 1990, for the first time, virtually the whole of mainland America enjoyed constitutional rule. Elections in 1982 in Brazil helped to establish the trend. Although Brazilian politics remain somewhat explosive, and the country's economy suffers continuing double-digit inflation, Brazil's democracy proved strong enough to take steps constitutionally to remove President Fernando Collor de Mello for impeachment in 1992.

Argentina's defeat by Britain in 1982 over the Falkland Islands (Islas Malvinas) discredited its military rulers. This allowed the return of civilian rule under President Raul Alfonsin in 1983. The subsequent democratic change of party and president in 1989, when Carlos Menem came to power, demonstrated that Argentine democracy had roots.

In 1990, popular opposition to General Pinochet's rule in Chile succeeded in returning the country to its long democratic tradition. Peaceful elections in 1994 confirmed Chile's democratic credentials and the country's political progress has been echoed by remarkable economic achievements with 6-7% real growth in 1993-94. Economically Chile appears to be stepping out of Latin America into the boom region of the Pacific Rim.

In Central America the hostility of the USA to left-wing governments (as in Nicaragua) and left-wing popular movements (as in El Salvador), complicated and delayed the process for change, and, in its invasion of Panama in 1989, the USA could claim to be on the side of reform. Nevertheless, political polarization remains a problem throughout the region, and in Nicaragua and El Salvador civil war persists. There are, however, signs of hope. In Guatemala, for example, the government coalition includes the extreme right-wing, Marxist trade unionists and liberal civil rights groups, and in 1994 Panama achieved its first really free democratic election.

In the 1990s Peru seemed to have contained the Maoist terrorist movement Sendero Luminoso, but, in 1992, pro-business President Alberto Fujimori suspended the constitution. Parliament was dismissed and opposition leaders were detained before elections were called for a constituent assembly, but these were boycotted by many of the traditional parties. The country has now returned to a multi-party system.

Colombia has been wracked by left-wing guerrillas, right-wing death squads and powerful drug-trafficking cartels since the 1980s, but the uncompromising stands taken by President Virgilio Barco and his successor Cesar Gaviria paid dividends. The 1994 elections were free and open, and a principal guerrilla group, the left-wing M-19 movement, has abandoned their armed struggle.

Venezuela has a tradition of civilian democracy stretching back to 1958, but a combination of economic problems and pressure for structural and social reforms has destabilized the country. There have been two abortive coup attempts by elements of the military in the 1990s but its democratic credentials were strengthened by the constitutional removal of President Carlos Andres Perez. Bolivia, long known for its instability, has enjoyed constitutional rule since 1982 and Paraguay saw the end of the Stroessner dictatorship in 1989. Throughout the region the military no longer plays the dominant role that it usurped for much of the 20th century and in 1994 every major Latin American country has had, or is scheduled to have, elections.

Regional Organizations of Central and South America

ANDEAN PACT
The Andean Pact was established in 1992 to create a free-trade area - with a common external tariff - in northern and western South America.

Headquarters: Lima, Peru.

Membership: Bolivia, Colombia, Ecuador, Peru, and Venezuela.

CENTRAL AMERICAN COMMON MARKET (CACM)
The Central American Common Market was founded in 1960, but lapsed in 1969. The organization was revived (1992-93) and is scheduled to establish a free-trade area in Central America by the end of 1994. CACM has a small secretariat.

Headquarters: Guatemala City, Guatemala.

Secretary General: Rafael Rodriguez Loucel (Guatemala).

LATIN AMERICAN INTEGRATION ASSOCIATION (ALADI)
ALADI (Asociación Latinoamericano de Integración) was established in December 1980 as a replacement for the Latin American Free Trade Area, which was formed in 1961. It aims to encourage trade and to remove tariffs between members. ALADI maintains a small secretariat.

Headquarters: Montevideo, Uruguay.

Secretary General: Jorge Luis Ordonez (Colombia).

Membership: Argentina, Bolivia, Brazil, Chile, Colombia, Ecuador, Mexico, Paraguay, Peru, Uruguay, and Venezuela.

Costa Rica, Cuba, the Dominican Republic, El Salvador, Guatemala, Honduras, Italy, Nicaragua, Panama, Portugal, and Spain have observer status.

MERCOSUR
Mercosur (Mercado del Sur - the Market of the South) originated in a free-trade pact between Argentina and Brazil in 1988. Mercosur is scheduled to become a free market in goods, services and labour at the beginning of 1995.

Membership: Argentina, Brazil, Paraguay, and Uruguay.

ORGANIZATION OF AMERICAN STATES (OAS)
The OAS was founded in Bogotá, Colombia, in 1948 as a successor to the International Union of American Republics (later the Pan American Union), which was founded in 1890. It aims to maintain the independence and territorial integrity of members, to achieve peace and justice on the American continent, and to encourage collaboration and inter-American solidarity.

Headquarters: Washington DC, USA.

Secretary General: João Clemente Baena Soares (Brazil).

Membership: Antigua and Barbuda, Argentina, The Bahamas, Barbados, Belize, Bolivia, Brazil, Canada, Chile, Colombia, Costa Rica, Cuba (which has been suspended since 1962), Dominica, the Dominican Republic, Ecuador, El Salvador, Grenada, Guatemala, Guyana, Haiti, Honduras, Jamaica, Mexico, Nicaragua, Panama, Paraguay, Peru, St Christopher and Nevis (St Kitts-Nevis), St Lucia, St Vincent and the Grenadines, Suriname, Trinidad and Tobago, the USA, Uruguay, and Venezuela.

OTHER ORGANIZATIONS
Belize and Guyana are members of the Commonwealth. French Guiana (Guyane) is an integral part of the French Republic and of the EU/EC.

Central and South American Trade

Argentina Imports ($ million): 4076 (1990). Exports ($ million): 12,353 (1990). Main imports: electrical machinery 25.7% (1989), minerals, fuels and oils, and bituminous substances 8.8% (1989), chemical products, basic manufactures. Main exports: iron, steel, base metal manufactures 22.9% (1989), animal fodder 13.9% (1989), prepared foodstuffs, beverages and tobacco 20.1% (1989), edible fruit, live animals and animal products. Principal trading partners: USA, Brazil, Germany, Italy, China, Netherlands, Chile.

Belize Imports ($ million): 211 (1990). Exports ($ million): 104.6 (1990). Main imports: manufactured goods 29.3% (1987), food 22.1% (1987). Main exports: sugar 40.9% (1990), orange concentrate 13.3% (1990), garments 14.5% (1990). Principal trading partners: USA, UK, Mexico.

Bolivia Imports ($ million): 992.3 (1991). Exports ($ million): 848.5 (1991). Main imports: raw materials for industry 33.7% (1991), capital goods for industry 30.0% (1991). Main exports: natural gas 27.4% (1991), metallic minerals (tin, zinc, silver, gold) 41.9% (1991), wood. Principal trading partners: Argentina, Brazil, USA, Chile, Germany, UK.

Brazil Imports ($ million): 21,004 (1991). Exports ($ million): 31,622 (1991). Main imports: machinery and electrical equipment 25% (1990), minerals 28.3% (1990), chemicals and chemical products, vegetable products. Main exports: prepared foodstuffs (including soya products, sugar, coffee, cocoa) 9.1% (1990), machinery and transport equipment (including boiler equipment) 7.9% (1990), mineral products (including haematite), vegetable products. Principal trading partners: USA, Germany, Netherlands, Japan, Argentina, Italy, Saudi Arabia, Belgium-Luxembourg.

Chile Imports ($ million): 7685.8 (1991). Exports ($ million): 9048.4 (1991). Total imports: intermediate goods 57.8% (1991), capital goods 23.9% (1991), consumer goods. Total exports: mining (mainly copper) 48.2% (1991), manufacturing (including foodstuffs, wine, etc.) 38% (1991). Principal trading partners: USA, Japan, Germany, Brazil, Argentina, France, Italy, UK, Taiwan, South Korea.

Colombia Imports ($ million): 4967 (1991). Exports ($ million): 7268.6 (1991). Main imports: mechanical and electrical equipment 5.2% (1991), chemical products 21.2% (1991), metals and mineral products. Main exports: agricultural, forestry and fishing products 32.6% (1991), coffee 18.3% (1991), minerals, textiles and textile products. Principal trading partners: USA, Germany, Japan, Venezuela, Netherlands, France, Chile, Canada, Brazil.

Costa Rica Imports ($ million): 1853 (1991). Exports ($ million): 1590.3 (1991). Main imports: basic manufactures for industry 35.1% (1991), non-durable consumer goods 16.3% (1991), machinery and equipment. Main exports: coffee 16.9% (1991), bananas 21.7% (1991), sugar, meat. Principal trading partners: USA, Germany, Japan, Venezuela.

Ecuador Imports ($ million): 2399 (1991). Exports ($ million): 2851 (1991). Main imports: industrial raw materials 41.2% (1991), industrial capital goods 22.1% (1991), transport equipment. Main exports: crude petroleum 37.1% (1991), bananas 25.1% (1990), seafood. coffee. Principal trading partner: USA, Japan, Germany, Brazil, Italy, Chile, Peru.

El Salvador Imports ($ million): 110 (1991). Exports ($ million): 420 (1991). Main imports: chemicals and chemical products 15.1% (1990), crude petroleum 9% (1991), machinery, plastics. Main exports: coffee 37.7% (1991), vegetable products 42.6% (1991), textiles and textile products. Principal trading partners: USA, Guatemala, Germany, Mexico.

Guatemala Imports ($ million): 1,851 (1991). Exports ($ million): 1,234 (1991). Main imports: primary and intermediate materials for industry 39.4% (1991), capital goods 18.9% (1991), chemicals and chemical products. Main exports: coffee 22.7% (1991), sugar 11.4% (1991). Principal trading partners: USA, Germany, Mexico, Japan, El Salvador, Venezuela, Netherlands.

Guyana Imports (G$ million): 34,274.9 (1991). Exports (G$ million): 28,397.7 (1991). Main imports: capital goods 40.6% (1991), fuels and lubricants 21.9% (1991). Main exports: bauxite 31.5% (1991), sugar 36.8% (1991). Principal trading partners: UK, USA, Venezuela, Trinidad.

Honduras Imports ($ million): 981 (1990). Exports ($ million): 912 (1990). Main imports: machinery and transport equipment 25.3% (1989), chemicals and chemical products 21.3% (1989), basic manufactures. Main exports: bananas 35.0% (1989), coffee 19.5% (1989), lead and zinc, shellfish. Principal trading partners: USA, Japan, Mexico, Germany, Venezuela.

Nicaragua Imports ($ million): 665 (1990). Exports ($ million): 321 (1990). Main imports: consumer goods 28.2% (1990), primary and intermediate goods for industry 16.3% (1990), crude petroleum and products 16.4% (1990). Main exports: coffee 21% (1990), meat 20.1% (1990), cotton 11.3% (1990). Principal trading partners: Germany, Japan, Mexico.

Panama Imports (balboa million): 2,018 (1992). Exports (balboa million): 474 (1992). Main imports: mineral products 15.3% (1992), chemicals and chemical products 10.7% (1992), transport equipment, electrical equipment. Main exports: bananas 43.4% (1992), shrimps 26.7% (1992), raw sugar. Principal trading partner: USA, Japan, Germany, Ecuador.

Paraguay Imports ($ million): 1275 (1991). Exports ($ million): 737 (1991). Main imports: machinery and transport equipment 12% (1991), fuels and lubricants 10% (1991), transport equipment. Main exports: cotton fibres 43.2% (1991), oilseeds 21.9% (1991), meat and meat products. Principal trading partners: Brazil, Argentina, USA, Netherlands, Japan, Switzerland, Belgium-Luxembourg.

Peru Imports ($ million): 3899 (1991). Exports ($ million): 3330 (1991). Main imports: raw and intermediate materials 40.9% (1991), wheat, rice. Main exports: copper 22.1 % (1991), zinc, fishmeal. Principal trading partners: USA, Germany, Japan, Brazil, Argentina, UK, Belgium-Luxembourg.

Suriname Imports (Sf million): 842.5 (1990). Exports (Sf million): 843 (1990). Main imports: materials and semi-manufactured goods 41% (1990), fuels and lubricants 15.6% (1990). Main exports: bauxite 73.9% (1990), aluminium 8% (1990), rice 5.3% (1990). Principal trading partners: Netherlands, USA, Norway.

Uruguay Imports ($ million): 1636 (1991). Exports ($ million): 1605 (1991). Main imports: machinery and appliances 21% (1991), mineral products 16.2% (1991), chemicals and chemical products. Main exports: textiles and products 26.8 (1991), live animals and animal products 23.4% (1991), hides and skins, miscellaneous vegetable products. Principal trading partners: Brazil, USA, Germany, Argentina, Mexico, Iran, France, Italy, UK.

Venezuela Imports ($ million): 9963 (1991). Exports ($ million): 17 586 (1991). Main imports: machinery and transport equipment 42.2% (1990), chemicals and chemical products 15.8% (1990), basic manufactures, crude materials. Main exports: crude petroleum and products 73.4% (1989), iron ore 2.1% (1989), basic manufactures, food and live animals. Principal trading partners: USA, Germany, Japan, Italy, Colombia, Brazil, France, Mexico.

Argentina

Official name: República Argentina (the Argentine Republic).

Member of: UN, OAS, ALADI, Mercosur.

Area: 2,766,889 km² (1,068,302 sq mi), excluding territories claimed by Argentina: the Falkland Islands (Islas Malvinas), South Georgia, South Sandwich Islands, and parts of the Antarctic.

Population: 33,500,000 (1993 est).

Capital: Buenos Aires 12,582,000 (city 2,961,000; 1991 census).

Other major cities: Córdoba 1,179,000, Rosario 1,096,000, Mendoza 729,000, La Plata 644,000, San Miguel de Tucumán 626,000, Mar del Plata 523,000, San Juan 358,000 (all including suburbs; 1991 census).

Languages: Spanish (95%; official), Guarani (3%).

Religion: Roman Catholic (92%), various Protestant Churches (7%).

Education: Education is compulsory between the ages of six and 14. In 1990 the literacy rate was 95.3%. There are 28 state and 20 private universities.

Defence: In 1993 the total armed strength was 71,000 - over 40,000 in the army, 21,500 in the navy and 9000 in the air force. Military service lasts 6-12 months in the army, 12 months in the air force, 14 months in the navy.

Transport: There are 211,370 km (131,339 mi) of roads and 34,115 km (21,185 mi) of railways. Buenos Aires has a metro. There is considerable traffic on inland waterways. The main shipping ports are Buenos Aires, Quen Quen and Rosario. Ezeiza (Buenos Aires) airport is one of the largest in Latin America. Argentina has nine other international airports.

Media: There are 15 daily Buenos Aires papers and another 30 daily papers published in the provinces. There are over 110 radio stations (40 of which are government-controlled) and nearly 100 television channels (28 of which are private). The majority of the radio and television stations are regional.

GOVERNMENT

The President and Vice-President are elected for a six-year term of office by an electoral college of 600 members who are chosen by universal adult suffrage. The lower house of Congress (the Chamber of Deputies) has 259 members elected by universal suffrage for four years, with one half of its members retiring every two years. The 48 members of the upper house (the Senate) are chosen by provincial legislatures - two from each province and two from the federal capital territory - to serve for nine years, with 18 members retiring every three years. There are 23 provinces and a federal territory; other territories - the Falkland Islands (Malvinas), South Georgia and South Sandwich Islands and certain Antarctic territories - are claimed. The main political parties are the Radical Civil Union (UCR), the (Peronist) Justicialista National Movement (PJ), the Union of the Democratic Centre (UCD), the (right-wing) Movement for Dignity and Independence (Modin) and various provincial parties. Partial elections were held in 1993. After the presidential election in May 1989 a Peronist government was formed.

Party strength: PJ 126, UCR 83, Modin 7, UCD 5, others 38.

President: Carlos Saul Menem (PJ).

THE CABINET

Minister of Defence: Dr Oscar Camillion.

Minister of the Economy and Public Works: Dr Domingo Cavallo.

Minister of Education and Culture: Jorge Alberto Rodriguez.

Minister of Foreign Affairs: Dr Guido Di Tella.

Minister of Health and Social Welfare: Dr Alberto Mazza.

Minister of the Interior: Dr Carlos Ruckauf.

Minister of Justice: Dr Rodolfo Barra.

Minister of Labour and Social Security: Dr Armando Caro Figueroa.

GEOGRAPHY

The Andes extend as a rugged barrier along the border with Chile. South of the Colorado River is Patagonia, an important pastureland - although much of it is semi desert. Over three-quarters of the population live in the pampas, whose prairies form one of the world's most productive agricultural regions. The subtropical plains of northeast Argentina contain part of the Gran Chaco prairie and rain forests. Highest point: Cerro Aconcagua 6960 m (22 834 ft).

Principal rivers: Paraná, Colorado, Negro, Salado, Chubut. Climate: Most of Argentina has a mild temperate climate, although the south is cooler and the northeast is subtropical. The higher parts of the Andes have a subpolar climate. Rainfall is heavy in the Andes and the far northeast, but generally decreases towards the dry south and southwest.

ECONOMY

Argentina is one of the world's leading producers of beef, wool, mutton, wheat and wine. The pampas produce cereals, while fruit and

ARGENTINA

Area: 2 766 889 km² (1 068 302 sq mi), excluding territories claimed by Argentina: the Falkland Islands (Islas Malvinas), S. Georgia, S. Sandwich Islands, and parts of the Antarctic

vines are important in the northwest. Pasturelands cover over 50% of Argentina - for beef cattle in the pampas and for sheep in Patagonia. However, manufacturing (including

chemicals, steel, cement, paper, pulp and textiles) now makes the greatest contribution to the economy. The country is rich in natural resources, including petroleum, natural gas, iron ore and precious metals, and has great potential for hydroelectric power. Argentina is remarkably self-sufficient, although its status as an economic power has declined owing to political instability and massive inflation. However, financial reforms and wide-scale privatization, in the 1990s improved the prospects of the economy. Inflation was down to 11% by May 1994, and the peso (which replaced the austral in 1992) was stable.

Curency: Peso; 1US$ = 0.98 pesos (June 1994).

GDP: US$295,000,000,000 (1993 est); US$8700 per head.

RECENT HISTORY

From 1880, large-scale European immigration and British investment helped Argentina, a former Spanish colony, to develop a flourishing economy. Prosperity was ended by the Depression, and, in 1930, the long period of constitutional rule was interrupted by a military coup. In 1946, a populist leader, Juan Perón (1895-1974), came to power with the support of the unions. His wife Eva was a powerful and popular figure, and after her death (1952), Perón was deposed (1955) because of his unsuccessful economic policies and his anticlericalism. Succeeding civilian governments were unable to conquer rampant inflation, and the military took power again (1966-73). An unstable period of civilian rule (1973-76) included Perón's brief second presidency. In the early 1970s, urban terrorism grew and the economic crisis deepened, prompting another coup. The military junta that seized control in 1976 received international condemnation when thousands of opponents of the regime were arrested or disappeared. In April 1982, President Galtieri ordered the invasion of the Falkland Islands and its dependencies, which had long been claimed by Argentina. A British task force recaptured the islands in June 1982, and Galtieri resigned. Constitutional rule was restored in 1983 under President Raul Alfonsin. In 1994 President Menem sought to change the constitution in order to be able to stand for a second term in office. For this purpose a constitutional assembly was called.

179

Belize

Member of: UN, Commonwealth, CARICOM, OAS.

Area: 22,965 km² (8867 sq mi).

Population: 204,000 (1993 est).

Capital: Belmopan 4000 (1992 est).

Other major towns: Belize City 45,000, Orange Walk 11,700, San Ignacio-Santa Elena 9500, Corozal 7000 (1992 est).

Languages: English (majority; official), Creole (33%), Spanish (32%), Garifuna (7%), Maya.

Religions: Roman Catholic (62%), various Protestant Churches (28% - mainly Anglican and Methodist).

Education: Education is compulsory between the ages of six and 14. In 1991 the literacy rate was 93%. There is a university college and a University of the West Indies department.

Defence: In 1993 the total armed strength was 650. British forces are stationed in Belize.

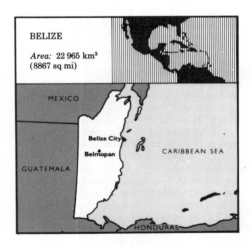

Transport: There are 2575 km (1600 mi) of roads. Belize City has a shipping port and an international airport.

Media: There are six weekly newspapers, a single state-run radio station and three television channels (two commercial).

180

GOVERNMENT

The eight members of the Senate (the upper house of the National Assembly) are appointed by the Governor General, the representative of the British Queen as sovereign of Belize. The 28 members of the House of Representatives (the lower house) are elected by universal adult suffrage for five years. The Governor General appoints a Prime Minister, who commands a majority in the House, and - on the PM's advice - a Cabinet, which is responsible to the House. The main political parties are the People's United Party (PUP) and the United Democratic Party (UDP). After the election in June 1993 a UDP government was formed.

Party strength: UDP 16, PUP 13.

Prime Minister: Manuel Esquivel (UDP).

GEOGRAPHY

Tropical jungle covers much of Belize. The south contains the Maya Mountains. The north is mainly swampy lowlands. Highest point: Victoria Peak 1122 m (3681 ft). Principal rivers: Hondo, Belize, New River. Climate: The subtropical climate is tempered by trade winds. Rainfall is heavy, but there is a dry season between February and May.

ECONOMY

The production of sugar, bananas and citrus fruit for export dominates the economy. Despite farming's major contribution to the economy, only 5% of Belize's total land area is cultivated. The illicit drug trade is an increasing problem.

Currency: Belize dollar (BZD) of 100 cents; 1US$ = 1.999 BZD (June 1994).

GDP: US$389,000,000 (1991); US$2050 per head.

RECENT HISTORY

The colony of British Honduras was renamed Belize in 1973 and gained independence in 1981. Following a severe hurricane in 1961, the capital was moved inland from Belize City to a purpose-built new town, Belmopan. Guatemala continued to claim Belize as part of her territory until 1991, when Guatemala recognized Belizean sovereignty. However, Belize suspended the territorial accord that had been agreed with Guatemala, claiming that the latter had received too many concessions in her maritime boundaries.

Bolivia

Official name: Républica de Bolivia (Republic of Bolivia).

Member of: UN, OAS, ALADI, Andean Pact.

Area: 1,098,581 km² (424,164 sq mi).

Population: 7,715,000 (1993 est).

Capital: La Paz (administrative capital) 1,050,000, Sucre (legal capital) 96,000 (1988 est).

Other major cities: Santa Cruz 615,000, Cochabamba 377,000, Oruro 195,000 (1988 est).

Languages: Spanish (official; 55%), Quéchua (5%), Aymara (22%).

Religion: Roman Catholic (official; 95%).

Education: Education is compulsory between the ages of six and 13. In 1990 the literacy rate was 77.5%. There are ten universities.

Defence: In 1992 the total armed strength was 31,500 - 23,000 in the army, 4500 navy, 4000 air force. Selective military service lasts a year.

Transport: There are 41,642 km (25,875 mi) of roads and 3643 km (2264 mi) of railways. La Paz and Santa Cruz have international airports.

Media: There are 13 daily (regional) newspapers, 160 radio stations and two TV stations.

GOVERNMENT
The President (who appoints a Cabinet), the 27-member Senate and the 130-member Chamber of Deputies are elected for four-year terms by universal adult suffrage. Political parties include the (right-wing) National Revolutionary Movement (MNR), the (centrist) Free Bolivia Movement (MBL), the (centrist) Civic Solidarity Union (UCS), the (centrist) Patriotic Accord (AP), and the Conscience of the Fatherland (Condepa). After the election in June 1993 a MNR-MBL-UCS government was formed.

Party strength: MNR 52, AP 35, UCS 20, Condepa 13, MBL 7, others 3.

President: Gonzalo Sanchez de Lozada (MNR).

GEOGRAPHY
The Andes divide into two parallel chains between which is an extensive undulating depression (the Altiplano), containing Lake Titicaca, the highest navigable lake in the

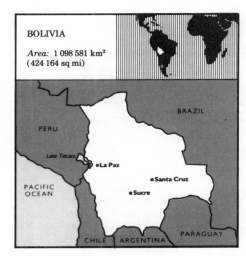

BOLIVIA
Area: 1 098 581 km²
(424 164 sq mi)

world. In the east and northeast, a vast lowland includes tropical rain forests (the Llanos), subtropical plains and semiarid grasslands (the Chaco). Highest point: Sajama 6542 m (21,463 ft). Principal rivers: Beni, Mamoré, Pilcomayo, Paraguay. Climate: Rainfall is negligible in the southwest, and heavy in the northeast. Temperature varies with altitude from the cold Andean summits to the tropical northeast.

ECONOMY
Bolivia is poor despite rich natural resources such as petroleum and tin. Lack of investment, political instability and the high cost of extraction have retarded development. Agriculture, which is labour intensive, produces domestic foodstuffs (potatoes and maize), and export crops (sugar cane and cotton). The illegal cultivation of coca is causing concern.

Currency: Boliviano of 100 centavos; 1US$ = 4.65 bolivianos (June 1994).

GDP: US$4,800,000,000 (1991); US$650 per head.

RECENT HISTORY
In the two devastating Chaco Wars against Paraguay (1928-30 and 1933-35) Bolivia sustained great human and territorial losses. For most of its independent history Bolivia has been characterized by political instability with a succession of military and civilian governments. Since 1982, however, Bolivia has had democratically elected governments.

181

Brazil

Official name: A República Federativa do Brasil (the Federative Republic of Brazil).

Member of: UN, OAS, ALADI, Mercosur.

Area: 8,511,965 km² (3,286,488 sq mi).

Population: 156,493,000 (1993 est).

Capital: Brasília 1,864,000 (city 1,841,000; 1991 est).

Other major cities: São Paulo 18,100,000 (city 9,700,000), Rio de Janeiro 11,141,000 (city 5,487,000, Nova Iguaçu 1,325,000), Belo Horizonte 3,446,000 (city 2,103,000), Recife 2,945,000 (city 1,336,000), Pôrto Alegre 2,924,000 (city 1,255,000), Salvador 2,362,000 (city 2,075,000), Fortaleza 2,169,000 (city 1,709,000), Curitiba 1,926,000 (city 1,248,000), Belém 1,296,000 (city 1,236,000), Goiânia 998,000, Manaus 997,000 (1991 est).

Language: Portuguese (official), various Amerindian languages (under 0.1%).

Religions: Roman Catholic (87%), various Protestant Churches (nearly 7%), Candomble (voodoo; 6%).

Education: Education is compulsory, in theory, between the ages of seven and 14. In 1989 the literacy rate was 81.2%. There are 74 universities.

Defence: In 1993 the total armed strength was 296,700 - 196,000 in the army, nearly 50,000 in the navy and over 50,000 in the air force. Compulsory military service lasts for one year.

Transport: There are over 1,671,000 (1,038,500 mi) of roads. There are 32,002 km (19,885 mi) of railways owned by the government, by individual states and privately-owned. Rio de Janeiro and São Paulo have metros. The Amazon and Parana and their tributaries are used for inland navigation. The main commercial shipping ports are Santos, Rio de Janeiro, Recife and Vitoria. Brazil has 21 international airports of which the two at Rio de Janeiro and the two at São Paulo are by far the largest.

Media: The size of Brazil - and the rivalry between Rio de Janeiro and São Paulo - have prevented the emergence of a national press. There are 288 daily papers, six main television networks, and 2970 radio stations.

GOVERNMENT

The President - who appoints and chairs a Cabinet - is elected for a five-year term by universal adult suffrage. The lower house of the National Congress (the Chamber of Deputies) has 503 members elected for four years by compulsory universal adult suffrage. The 91-

BRAZIL

Area: 8 511 965 km²
(3 286 488 sq mi)

member upper house (the Federal Senate) is elected directly for an eight-year term - one third and two thirds of the senators retiring alternately every four years. Each of the 26 states and the Federal District of Brasília has its own legislature. Political parties include the (moderate) Brazilian Democratic Movement (PMDB), the (moderate) Liberal Front (PFL), the (conservative) National Reconstruction Party (PRN), the (socialist) Worker's Party (PT), the Democratic Labour Party (PDT), the Social Democratic Party (PDS), the Social Democratic Party of Brazil (PSDB), the Workers' Party of Brazil (PTB), the Christian Democratic Party (PDC), the Liberal Party (PL), the Brazilian Socialist Party (PSB), the Communist Party of Brazil (PC do B), the Republican Socialist Party (PRS) and the Socialist Party (PCB). A referendum (1993) rejected a parliamentary system and a restoration of the monarchy in favour of the present system. The most recent election was in 1990. PMDB, PFL,

PSDB and PT support the government.

Party strength: PMDB 109, PFL 92, PDT 41, PRN 41, PDS 40, PSDB 37, PT 34, PTB 33, PDC 21, PL 15, PSB 12, PC do B 5, PRS 4, PCB 3, others 11.

President: Itamar Franco.

THE CABINET
Minister of Administration: Romildo Canhim (ind).

Minister of Agriculture, Supplies and Land Reform: Sinval S. Duarte Guazelli (PMDB).

Minister of the Air Force: Air Chief Marshal Lelio Viana Lobo (ind).

Minister of the Army: Gen. Zenildo Gonzaga Zoroastro de Lucena (ind).

Minister for the Civil Cabinet: Henrique Hargreaves (ind).

Minister/Chief of Staff of the Armed Forces: Admiral Arnaldo Leite Pereira (ind).

Minister of Communications: Djalma Bastos de Moraes (ind).

Minister of Culture: Luiz Roberto Nascimento e Silva (ind).

Minister of Education and Sports: Prof. Murilio de Avellar Hingel (ind).

Minister of the Environment and for Amazonia: Henrique Brandao Cavalcanti.

Minister of External Relations: Celsio Luiz Nunes Amorim (ind).

Minister of Finance: Rubens Ricupero (ind).

Minister of Health: Henrique Santillo (ind).

Minister of Industry, Trade and Tourism: Elcio Alvares (PFL).

Minister of Justice: Alexandre de Paula Dupeyrat Martins (ind).

Minister of Labour: Marcelo Pimentel (ind).

Minister for the Military Cabinet: Gen. Fernando Cardoso (ind).

Minister of Mining and Energy: Alexis Stepanenko (ind).

Minister of the Navy: Admiral Ivan da Silveira Serpa (ind).

Minister of Planning, the Budget and Coordination: Beni Veras (PSDB).

Minister of Rural Integration: Aluizio Alves (PMDB).

Minister of Science and Technology: Jose Israel Vargas (ind).

Minister of Social Security: Sergio Cutolo dos Santos (ind).

Minister of Social Welfare: Leonor Barreto Franco (ind).

Minister of Transport: Gen. Rubens Bayma Denys (ind).

BRAZILIAN STATES AND TERRITORIES
Population figures are 1991 estimates.

Acre Area: 152,589 km² (58,915 sq mi). Population: 428,000. Capital: Rio Branco.

Alagoas Area: 27,731 km² (10,707 sq mi). Population: 2,459,000. Capital: Maceió.

Amazonas Area: 1,564,445 km² (604,032 sq mi). Population: 2,055,000. Capital: Manaus.

Bahia Area: 561,026 km² (216,612 sq mi). Population: 11,953,000. Capital: Salvador.

Ceará Area: 150,630 km² (58,158 sq mi). Population: 6,587,000. Capital: Fortaleza.

Espirito Santo Area: 45,597 km² (17,605 sq mi). Population: 2,571,000. Capital: Vitória.

Goiás Area: 364,770 km² (140,838 sq mi). Population: 4,036,000. Capital: Goiânia.

Maranhão Area: 328,663 km² (126,897 sq mi). Population: 5,287,000. Capital: São Luis.

Mato Grosso Area: 881,001 km² (340,154 sq mi). Population: 1,776,000. Capital: Cuiaba.

Mato Grosso do Sul Area: 350,548 km² (135,347 sq mi). Population: 1,838,000. Capital: Campo Grande.

Minas Gerais Area: 587,172 km² (226,707 sq mi). Population: 16,071,000. Capital: Belo Horizonte.

Pará Area: 1,250,722 km² (482,904 sq mi). Population: 5,142,000. Capital: Belém.

Paraíba Area: 56,372 km² (21,765 sq mi). Population: 3,294,000. Capital: João Pessoa.

Paraná Area: 199,554 km² (77,048 sq mi). Population: 9,340,000. Capital: Curitiba.

Pernambuco Area: 98,281 km² (37,946 sq mi). Population: 7,482,000. Capital: Recife.

Piauí Area: 250,934 km² (96,886 sq mi). Population: 2,715,000. Capital: Teresina.

Rio de Janeiro Area: 44,268 km² (17,092 sq mi). Population: 14,420,000. Capital: Rio de Janeiro.

Rio Grande do Norte Area: 53,015 km² (20,469 sq mi). Population: 2,360,000. Capital: Natal.

Rio Grande do Sul Area: 282,184 km² (108,951 sq mi). Population: 9,298,000. Capital: Pôrto Alegre.

Rondônia Area: 243,044 km² (93,839 sq mi). Population: 1,135,000. Capital: Pôrto Velho.

Santa Catarina Area: 95,985 km² (37,060 sq mi). Population: 4,536,000. Capital: Florianópolis.

São Paulo Area: 247,898 km² (95,714 sq mi). Population: 33,777,000. Capital: São Paulo.

Sergipe Area: 21,994 km² (84,919 sq mi). Population: 1,440,000. Capital: Aracaju.

Tocantins Area: 277,322 km² (107,075 sq mi). Population: 1,009,000. Capital: Palmas.

Amapá (territory) Area: 140,276 km² (54,161 sq mi). Population: 264,000. Capital: Macapá.

Federal District (Distrito Federal) Area: 5814 km² (2245 sq mi). Population: 1,925,000. Capital: Brasília.

Fernando de Noronha (territory) Area: 26 km² (10 sq mi). Population: 1300. The island territory is administered from the mainland.

Roraima (territory) Area: 230,104 km² (88,843 sq mi). Population: 124,000. Capital: Boa Vista.

GEOGRAPHY

Nearly one half of Brazil is drained by the world's largest river system, the Amazon, whose wide, low-lying basin is still largely covered by tropical rain forest, although pressure on land has led to extensive deforestation. North of the Amazon Basin, the Guiana Highlands contain Brazil's highest peak. A central plateau of savannah grasslands lies south of the Basin. The east and south of the country contain the Brazilian Highlands - a vast plateau divided by fertile valleys and mountain ranges. A densely populated narrow coastal plain lies at the foot of the Highlands. Highest point: Pico da Neblina 3014 m (9888 ft). Principal rivers: Amazon, Paraná, São Francisco, Madeira, Juruá, Purus. Climate: The Amazon Basin and the southeast coast are tropical with heavy rainfall. The rest of Brazil is either sub-tropical or temperate (in the savannah). Only the northeast has inadequate rainfall.

ECONOMY

Agriculture employs about one quarter of the labour force. The principal agricultural exports include coffee, sugar cane, soyabeans, oranges, beef cattle and cocoa. Timber was important, but environmental concern is restricting its trade. Rapid industrialization since 1945 has made Brazil a major manufacturing country. While textiles, clothing and food processing are still the biggest industries, the iron and steel, chemical, petroleum-refining, cement, electrical, motor-vehicle and fertilizer industries have all attained international stature. Brazil has enormous - and, in part, unexploited - natural resources, including iron ore, phosphates, uranium, copper, manganese, bauxite, coal and vast hydroelectric-power potential. In the last two decades, rampant inflation has hindered development.

Currency: Cruzeiro Real; 1US$ = 2318.04 (June 1994).

GDP: US$411,000,000,000 (1993 est); US$2585 per head.

RECENT HISTORY

In 1889 a coup ended the long reign of the liberal Emperor Pedro II and established a republic. The republic was initially stable, but social unrest mounted and, in 1930, Getúlio Vargas seized power. Vargas attempted to model Brazil on Mussolini's Italy, but was overthrown by the military in 1945. In 1950, Vargas was elected president again, but he committed suicide rather than face impeachment (1954). Short-lived civilian governments preceded a further period of military rule (1964-85), during which the economy expanded rapidly, but political and social rights were restricted. Brazil returned to civilian rule in 1985 and in 1990 Brazilians were able to vote for a president for the first time in 29 years. In 1992 the strength of Brazil's new civilian democracy was shown by the peaceful removal of President Color de Mello for impeachment on charges of embezzlement. The country faces problems concerning the development of the Amazon Basin and in balancing the needs of developers and landless peasants on the one hand and the advice of conservationists and the interests of tribal peoples on the other.

Chile

Official name: República de Chile (The Republic of Chile).

Member of: UN, OAS, ALADI.

Area: 756,945 km² (292,258 sq mi). (Chile claims territories in the Antarctic, which are not included in this total.)

Population: 13,542,000 (1993 est).

Capital: Santiago 5,181,000 (1992 est). (The legislature meets in Valparaiso.)

Other major cities: Concepción 331,000, Viña del Mar 303,000, Valparaiso (legislative capital) 277,000, Talcahuano 247,000, Antofagasta 219,000, Temuco 212,000 (1992 est).

Languages: Spanish (official; over 94%), Araucanian (5%).

Religions: Roman Catholic (79%), various Protestant (mainly Evangelical) Churches (6%), non-religious (over 13%).

CHILE

Area: 756 945 km²
(292 258 sq mi)

Education: Education is compulsory between the ages of six and 13. In 1990 the literacy rate was 93.4%. There are 27 universities and institutes of university status.

Defence: In 1992 the total armed strength was 92,000 - 54,000 in the army, 25,000 in the navy, 13,000 in the air force. Compulsory military service lasts for two years.

Transport: There are 79,593 km (49,457 mi) of roads and 4470 km (2778 mi) of railways. Santiago has a metro. Valparaiso, Talcahuano and Antofagasta are the main commercial shipping ports. Santiago and Arica have international airports.

Media: There are 36 daily newspapers, one quarter of which are published in Santiago. There are over 350 radio stations and 11 television channels including one government-run station, an educational and regional station, and a single commercial station.

GOVERNMENT

Executive power is held by the President, who appoints a Cabinet of Ministers. The President is elected by universal adult suffrage for a single eight-year term. The National Congress has an upper chamber - of 38 senators directly elected for eight years and 10 senators appointed by the President - and a lower chamber of 120 deputies elected for a four-year term by universal adult suffrage. Since 1990 the National Congress has met in Valparaiso. Chile is divided into 13 regions. The main political parties include the (conservative) Christian Democrat Party (PDC), the (right-wing) National Renovation Party (RN), the Socialist Party (PAIS), and the (right-wing) Independent Democratic Union (UDI). The most recent election for the National Congress was held in December 1993.

Party strength: PDC 37, PAIS and allies 32, RN and allies 31, UDI 15, ind 5.

President: Eduardo Frei (PDC).

THE CABINET

Minister of Agriculture: Emiliano Ortega.

Minister of Central Planning: Luis Maira.

Minister of Defence: Edmundo Perez Yoma.

Minister of Education: Ernesto Schielfelbein.

Minister of Energy: Alejandro Jadresic.

Minister of Finance: Eduardo Aninat.

Minister of Foreign Affairs: Carlos Figueroa.

Minister of Housing: Dr Eduardo Hermosilla.

Minister of the Interior: German Correa.

Minister of Justice: Soledad Alvear.

Minister of Labour: Jorge Arrate.

Minister of Mining: Benjamin Teplisky.

Minister for the National Copper Corporation: Juan Villarzu Rohde.

Minister of National Properties: Adriana del Piano.

Minister of Public Health: Carlos Massad.

Minister of Promotion and Business: Felipe Sandoval.

Minister of Public Works: Ricardo Lagos.

Minister of Trade and Industry: Alvaro Garcia.

Minister of Transport: Narciso Irureta.

Minister of Women's Affairs: Josefina Bilbao.

General Secretary of the Government: Victor Manuel Reballado.

General Secretary of the Presidency: Genaro Arriagada.

GEOGRAPHY
For almost 4000 km (2500 mi), the Andes form the eastern boundary of Chile. Parallel to the Andes is a depression, in which lies the Atacama Desert in the north and fertile plains in the centre. A mountain chain runs between the depression and the coast, and, in the south, forms a string of islands. The 5337-km (3317-mi) long Pacific coastline is deeply indented in the south. The island of Tierra del Fuego is divided between Chile and Argentina. Principal rivers: Loa, Maule, Bio-Bio. Highest point: Ojos del Salado 6895 m (22,588 ft). Climate: The temperate climate is influenced by the cool Humboldt Current, but Chile's enormous range of latitude and its mountainous nature combine to produce a wide variety of local climates. Rainfall ranges from being negligible in the Atacama Desert in the north to heavy - over 2300 mm (90 in) - in the south. In parts, the climate is Mediterranean; elsewhere it ranges from hot desert to near tundra.

ECONOMY
The main agricultural region is the central plains, where cereals (mainly wheat and maize) and fruit (in particular grapes) are important. Excellent fishing grounds yield one of the world's largest catches of fish. There are considerable mineral resources and great hydroelectric-power potential. Chile is a leading exporter of copper, whose price on the international market is vital to the well-being of the Chilean economy. On average, copper accounts for about 45% of Chile's annual exports. The country also has major reserves of iron ore and coal, and important reserves of petroleum and natural gas have been found in the south. Chile has achieved high economic growth rates throughout the early 1990s and kept inflation under control. Chile remains outside the Andean Pact and Mercosur free-trade agreements but is expected to conclude pacts with Colombia and Venezuela. However, Chile's foreign trade is now with Pacific Rim rather than Latin American countries. Japan is now Chile's largest trading partner and ties are being made with other Asian countries as well as with Australia and New Zealand.

Currency: Chilean peso of 100 centavos; 1US$ = 422.4 pesos (June 1994).

GDP: US$45,000,000,000 (1993 est); US$3179 per head.

RECENT HISTORY
During the century following independence (1821), conservative landowners held power and Chile gained territory in two wars against Peru and Bolivia, including Bolivia's only access to the sea. Between the late 1920s and the 1940s, Chile was governed by liberal and radical regimes, but social and economic change was slow. The election of the Christian Democrats (1964) brought some reforms, but not until Salvador Allende's Marxist government was elected in 1970 were major changes - including land reform - realized. Chile was polarized between right and left, and political and economic chaos resulted in an American-backed military coup led by General Augusto Pinochet in 1973. Tens of thousands of leftists were killed, imprisoned or exiled by the junta. Pinochet reversed Allende's reforms, restructuring the economy in favour of landowners and exporters. Pressure on the dictatorship from within Chile and abroad encouraged the junta to return the country to democratic rule in 1990. Chile and Argentina have a long-running territorial dispute around the Beagle Channel. Both countries also claim sections of the Antarctic continent – claims which overlap.

Colombia

Official name: La República de Colombia (The Republic of Colombia).

Member of: UN, OAS, ALADI, Andean Pact.

Area: 1,141,748 km² (440,831 sq mi).

Population: 33,952,000 (1993 est).

Capital: Bogotá (officially known as Santa Fé de Bogotá DE; DE stands for Distrito Especial - Special District) 5,026,000 (including suburbs; 1992-93 est).

Other major cities: Medellin 2,121,000 (city 1,595,000), Cali 1,657,000, Barranquilla 1,034,000, Cartagena 707,000 (city 688,000), Cúcuta 450,000, Bucaramanga 364,000 (city 349,000), Ibagué 334,000 (1992 est).

Languages: Spanish (official; 99%), over 150 Amerindian languages (under 1%).

Religion: Roman Catholic (official; 93%).

Education: Education is compulsory in theory between the ages of six and 12. In 1990 the literacy rate was estimated to be 86.7%. There are 25 state universities, plus 24 private universities.

Defence: In 1993 the total armed strength was 140,000 - 120,000 in the army, 13,000 in the navy and 7000 in the air force. Military service is selective and lasts between one and two years.

Transport: There are over 129,200 km (80,300 mi) of roads of which only a fraction are paved. There are 3236 km (2011 mi) of railways. There is a metro in Caracas and one under construction in Medellin. The main commercial shipping ports are Barranquilla, Cartagena and de Portete. Bogota, Medellin, Cali and Barranquilla have international airports.

Media: There are over 30 daily newspapers, of which six are published in Bogota. There are nearly 520 radio stations, most of which cover only a small area. There are three national and three regional television stations.

GOVERNMENT

A President (who appoints a Cabinet of 13 members), a Senate of 102 members and a House of Representatives of 161 members are elected for a four-year term by universal adult suffrage. There are 32 local government depart-

ments plus the Capital District. The main political parties are the Liberal Party (PL), the Social Conservative Party (PSC), the (leftist) ADM-19 (April 19th Movement) and the (leftist) UP (Patriotic Union). Elections for the Senate were held in March 1994; elections for the House of Representatives were held in October 1991. A government of PL, PSC and independent members was formed. (A new Cabinet is to be appointed by President Samper at some time in August 1994.)

Party strength (Senate): PL 57, PSC 23, independents 18, others 4.

Party strength (House of Representatives): PL 86, PSC 15, ADM-19 15, UP 2, others 43.

President: Ernesto Samper (PL).

THE CABINET
(June 1994)

Minister of Agriculture: Dr Jose Antonio Ocampo (independent).

Minister of Communications: Dr William Jaramillo Gomez (PL).

Minister of Defence: Dr Rafael Pardo Rueda (PL).

Minister of Economic Development: Dr Mauricio Cardenas (PSC).

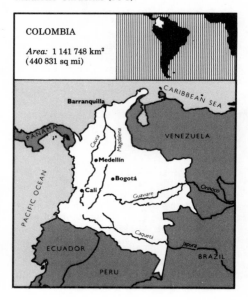

COLOMBIA

Area: 1 141 748 km²
(440 831 sq mi)

Minister of Education: Dr Maruja Pachon de Villamizar (PL).

Minister of the Environment: Dr Manuel Rodriguez Becerra (independent).

Minister of Finance and Public Credit: Dr Rudolf Hommes Rodriguez (PL).

Minister of Foreign Affairs: Dr Noemi Sanin de Rubio (PSC).

Minister of Foreign Trade: Dr Juan Manuel Santos Calderon (PL).

Minister of Health: Dr Juan Luis Londono (independent).

Minister of the Interior: Dr Fabio Villegas Ramirez (PL).

Minister of Justice: Dr Andres Gonzales (independent).

Minister of Labour and Social Security: Dr Jose Elias Melo Acosta (independent).

Minister of Mines and Energy: Dr Guido Nule Amin (independent).

Minister of Transport: Dr Jorge Bendeck Olivella (independent).

GEOGRAPHY
The Andes run north to south through Colombia with the greater part of the country lying to the east of the mountains in the mainly treeless grassland plains of the Llanos and the tropical Amazonian rain forest. A coastal plain lies to the west of the Andes. Highest point: Pico Cristóbal Colón 5775 m (18,947 ft). Principal rivers: Magdalena, Cauca, Amazon (Amazonas). Climate: The lower Andes are temperate; the mountains over 4000 m (13,100 ft) have perpetual snow. The rest of the country is tropical. The coasts and the Amazonian Basin are hot and humid. The Llanos have a savannah climate.

ECONOMY
Colombian coffee is the backbone of the country's exports; other cash crops include bananas, sugar cane, flowers and tobacco. However, profits from the illegal cultivation and export of marijuana and cocaine probably produce the greatest revenue. Mineral resources include iron ore, silver and platinum as well as coal, petroleum and natural gas, but the economy suffers as a result of a large illegal trade in gold and emeralds. The main industries are food processing, petroleum refining, fertilizers,

cement, textiles and clothing, and iron and steel. Diffficulties were caused in the 1980s by a sharp fall in the price of coffee on the international market. Economic problems include a general lack of law and order, great social and economic inequality and a high rate of inflation. However, the country has not suffered from the world recession and has continued to develop. Colombia has actively promoted trade pacts with neighbouring countries and has formed the 'Group of Three' free-trade area with Mexico and Venezuela, and negotiated free-trade deals with Chile, seven Central American states and a dozen small Caribbean island-states.

Currency: Colombian peso of 100 centavos; 1US$ = 824.48 pesos (June 1994).

GDP: US$63,200,000,000 (1993 est); US$2854 per head.

RECENT HISTORY
The struggle for independence from Spain (1809-1819) was fierce and bloody. Almost from Colombia's inception, the centralizing pro-clerical Conservatives and the federalizing anti-clerical Liberals have struggled for control, leading to civil wars (1899-1902 and 1948-1957) in which 400,000 people died. Since 1957 there have been agreements between the Liberals and Conservatives to protect a fragile democracy threatened by left-wing guerrillas, right-wing death squads and powerful drug-trafficking cartels. The 1990 presidential and legislative elections were disrupted by the assassination of several candidates, but the uncompromising stand taken against the drug cartels by President Virgilio Barco and his successor Cesar Gaviria paid some dividends. Violence decreased and a number of leading drug-traffickers were arrested. In a separate development, left-wing former guerrillas - such as ADM-19 - abandoned their armed struggle in favour of legitimate political activity. However, in spite of some political and economic progress, Colombia is still plagued by the activities of drug traders, other criminals and terrorists. Although the infamous Medillin drugs cartel was curtailed in the early 1990s, a new drugs cartel has risen to take its place in Cali. Despite these severe problems, Colombia has retained its democracy and the power-sharing agreement between the Liberals (PL) and Conservatives (PSC) continues, with coalition governments - although these parties contest presidential elections as opponents.

Costa Rica

Official name: República de Costa Rica (The Republic of Costa Rica).

Member of: UN, OAS, CACM.

Area: 51,100 km² (19,730 sq mi).

Population: 3,200,000 (1993 est).

Capital: San José 1,040,000 (city 303,000, Desamparados 55,000; 1990 est).

Other major cities: Limón 51,000, Alajuela 45,000, Puntarenas 38,000 (all including suburbs; 1990 est).

Language: Spanish (official).

Religion: Roman Catholic (official).

Education: Education is compulsory between the ages of six and 13. In 1990 the literacy rate was 92.8% - the highest in Central America. There are four universities.

Defence: There are no armed forces - the army was officially abolished in 1948. There is, however, a paramilitary police force, which in 1992 had 7500 personnel.

Transport: There are 35,536 km (22,081 mi) of roads and 700 km (435 mi) of railways. The main commercial shipping ports are Puntarenas (on the Pacific), Limón (on the Caribbean) and the new deep-water Pacific port of Caldera. San José has an international airport.

Media: There are six daily newspapers. There are five non-commercial and 40 commercial radio stations, plus one government-owned and five commercial television channels.

GOVERNMENT
Executive power is vested in the President, who is assisted by two Vice-Presidents and by a Cabinet of Ministers that he appoints. The President, Vice-Presidents and the 57-member Legislative Assembly are elected for four-year terms by compulsory universal adult suffrage. The main political parties are the (right-wing) Social Christian Unity Party (PUSC) and the (centre-left)National Liberation Party (PLN). Following the election held in February 1994 a PLN government took office.

Party strength: PLN 28, PUSC 25, others 4.

President: José Maria Figueras (PLN).

GEOGRAPHY
Between a narrow plain on the Pacific coast and a wider plain along the Caribbean coast rise a central plateau and mountain ranges. Highest point: Chirripó Grande 3820 m (12,533 ft). Principal river: Rio Grande. Climate: Rainfall is heavy along the Caribbean coast, but the Pacific coast is drier. Temperatures are warm in the lowlands, cooler in the highlands.

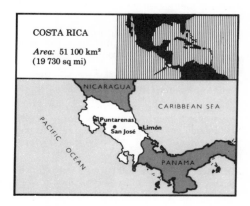

COSTA RICA

Area: 51 100 km²
(19 730 sq mi)

ECONOMY
Coffee is Costa Rica's major export. Bananas, sugar cane, beef cattle, cocoa and timber are also important. Despite Costa Rica's dependence upon international loans, the country has the highest standard of living in Central America.

Currency: Costa Rican colon of 100 centavos; US$ = 154.88 colons (June 1994).

GDP: US$6,299,000,000 (1992); US$2010 per head.

RECENT HISTORY
In the 19th century, Costa Rica developed largely in isolation from its neighbours. Dominated by small farms, Costa Rica prospered, attracted European immigrants, and developed a stable democracy. Following a brief civil war in 1948, the army was disbanded. Costa Rica has since adopted the role of peacemaker in Central America. In the 1990s Costa Rica has taken a lead in campaigning for free trade in bananas with the EC, which gives preference to bananas from French Caribbean territories.

189

Ecuador

Official name: República del Ecuador (The Republic of Ecuador).

Member of: UN, OAS, ALADI, Andean Pact.

Area: 270,670 km² (104,506 sq mi).

Population: 10,986,000 (1993 est).

Capital: Quito 1,388,000 (city 1,101,000; 1990 census).

Other major cities: Guayaquil 1,764,000 (city 1,531,000), Cuenca 272,000 (city 195,000), Ambato 229,000 (city 124,000) (1990 census).

Languages: Spanish (official; 93%), Quéchua.

Religion: Roman Catholic (93%).

Education: Education is compulsory for six years; pupils may start at age 6, 7 or 8. In 1990 the literacy rate was 85.8%. There are 18 technical universities and 3 polytechnics of university status.

Defence: In 1992 the total armed strength was 58,000. Selective military service lasts for one year.

Transport: There are over 37,635 km ((23,390 mi) of roads and 965 km (600 mi) of railways. Guayaquil is the main commercial port; Guayaquil and Quito have international airports.

Media: There are eight main daily newspapers, published in Quito and Guayaquil, and several regional papers. There are some 330 radio stations and over 10 television channels.

GOVERNMENT
The President is elected by compulsory universal adult suffrage for a single term of 4 years. The 77-member Chamber of Representatives is also directly elected; 12 members are elected for four years on a national basis and 65 members for a single term of two years on a provincial basis. The President appoints a Cabinet of Ministers. The main political parties include the (conservative coalition) Republican Unity Party (PUR), the Social Christian Party (PSC), the (right-wing) Roldosist Party (PRE), the Conservative Party (PCE), the Democratic Left (ID), the Popular Democracy Party (DP), the Popular Democracy Movement (MPD), the Socialist Party (PSE), and the Liberal Party

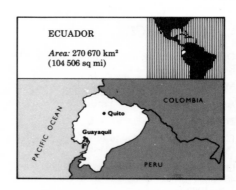

ECUADOR
Area: 270 670 km²
(104 506 sq mi)

COLOMBIA
Quito
Guayaquil
PACIFIC OCEAN
PERU

(PLR). After the election held in May 1992 a PUR-led government was formed.

Party strength: PSC 21, PRE 13, PUR 12, PCE 7, ID 7, DP 5, MPD 4, PSE 3, PLR 2, others 4.

President: Sixto Duran Ballo (PUR).

GEOGRAPHY
The Andes divide the Pacific coastal plain in the west from the Amazonian tropical rain forest in the east. Highest point: Chimborazo 6267 m (20,561 ft). Principal rivers: Napo, Pastaza, Curaray, Daule. Climate: The Amazonian Basin has a wet tropical climate. The tropical coastal plain is humid in the north, arid in the south. The highland valleys are mild, but the highest peaks have permanent snow.

ECONOMY
Agriculture is the largest single employer, and major export crops include cocoa, coffee and, in particular, bananas. Petroleum is the major foreign-currency earner. High inflation and foreign debt are severe problems.

Currency: Sucre of 100 centavos; 1US$ = 2061.7 sucres (June 1994).

GDP: US$11,790,000,000 (1992); US$1070 per head.

RECENT HISTORY
Throughout the 19th century there were struggles between liberals and conservatives. Relations with neighbouring Peru have long been tense - war broke out in 1941, when Ecuador lost most of its Amazonian territory, and there were border skirmishes in 1981. Since 1895 there have been long periods of military rule, but democratically elected governments have been in power since 1978.

El Salvador

Official name: La República de El Salvador (The Republic of El Salvador).

Member of: UN, OAS, CACM.

Area: 21,393 km² (8260 sq mi).

Population: 5,517,000 (1993 est).

Capital: San Salvador 1,522,000 (city 423,000; 1992 est).

Other major cities: Santa Ana 202,000 (city 145,000), San Miguel 183,000 (city 93,000), Mejicanos 118,000 (city 96,000) (1992 est).

Language: Spanish (official).

Religion: Roman Catholic (82%), various Evangelical Protestant Churches.

Education: Education is compulsory between the ages of seven and 16. In 1990 the literacy rate was 73%. There are six universities.

Defence: In 1993 the total armed strength was 30,500. Military service was abolished in 1992.

Transport: There are 12,495 km (7764 mi) of roads and 602 km (374 mi) of railways. San Salvador has an international airport.

Media: There are seven daily newspapers, two state-owned and 65 commercial radio stations and seven television channels.

GOVERNMENT
The President - who appoints a Cabinet of Ministers - is elected by universal adult suffrage for a single five-year term. Every three years, direct elections are also held for the 84-member National Assembly. The main political parties include (right-wing) the Nationalist Republican Alliance (ARENA), the Christian Democratic Party (PDC), the (left-wing coalition) Democratic Convergence-Farabundo Marti Liberation Front (CD-FMLN) and the (right-wing) National Conciliation Party (PCN). The most recent election to the Assembly was held in 1991; following presidential elections in 1994 an ARENA-led government was formed.

Party strength: ARENA 39, PDC 26, PCN 9, others 2.

President: Armando Calderon Sol (ARENA).

GEOGRAPHY
The country is mountainous, with ranges along the border with Honduras and a higher volcanic chain in the south. Highest point: Volcán de Santa Ana 2381 m (7812 ft). Principal rivers: Lempa, San Miguel. Climate: The tropical coast is hot and humid, while the interior is temperate.

ECONOMY
Agricultural products - in particular coffee and sugar cane - account for nearly two thirds of the country's exports. The economy has declined since the 1970s owing to the near civil war.

Currency: Colon of 100 centavos; 1US$ = 8.73 colons (June 1994).

GDP: US$5,697,000,000 (1991); US$1000 per head.

RECENT HISTORY
El Salvador was liberated from Spanish rule in 1821. The country has suffered frequent coups and political violence. In 1932 a peasant uprising - led by Agustín Farabundo Martí - was harshly suppressed. El Salvador's overpopulation has been partially relieved by migration to neighbouring countries. Following a football match between El Salvador and Honduras in 1969, war broke out because of illegal immigration by Salvadoreans into Honduras. Political and economic power is concentrated into the hands of a few families, and this has led to social tension. The country was in a state of virtual civil war from the late 1970s to 1992 with the US-backed military, assisted by extreme right-wing death squads, combating left-wing guerrillas - the FMLN-FDR (see above). A peace agreement between these forces was reached in 1992 and constitutional multi-party rule was restored.

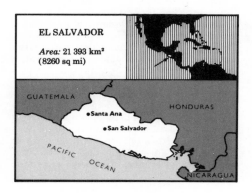

EL SALVADOR

Area: 21 393 km² (8260 sq mi)

GUATEMALA

HONDURAS

●Santa Ana

●San Salvador

PACIFIC OCEAN

NICARAGUA

191

Guatemala

Official name: República de Guatemala (Republic of Guatemala).

Member of: UN, OAS, CACM.

Area: 108,889 km² (42,042 sq mi).

Population: 9,713,000 (1993 est).

Capital: Guatemala City 2,074,000 (city 1,114,000, Mixco 369,000, Villa Nueva 134,000; 1992 est).

Other major cities: Puerto Barrios 338,000, Quezaltenango 246,000 (city 88,000) (1992 est).

Languages: Spanish (official; about 55% as a first language), over 20 Mayan languages (45%).

Religions: Roman Catholic (official; 65%), various Protestant Evangelical Churches (35%).

Education: Education is compulsory, in theory, between the ages of seven and 14 (in urban areas only). In 1990 the literacy rate was 55.1%. There are five universities.

Defence: In 1992 the total armed strength was 44,600. There are also 10,000 paramilitary. Compulsory military service lasts for two years or more.

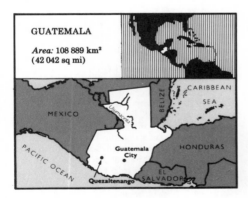

GUATEMALA

Area: 108 889 km²
(42 042 sq mi)

CARIBBEAN SEA

MEXICO

BELIZE

Usumacinta

Guatemala City

HONDURAS

PACIFIC OCEAN

Quezaltenango

EL SALVADOR

Transport: There are 13,352 km (8297 mi) of roads and 917 km (530 mi) of railways. Guatemala City has an international airport; the main port is Santo Tomas.

Media: There are eight daily newspapers, five government-owned and six cultural radio stations and five television channels.

GOVERNMENT

A President - who appoints a Cabinet - and a Vice President are elected for a five-year term by universal adult suffrage. The 116-member National Congress is also directly elected for five years - 87 members are directly elected; the remaining 29 members are returned under a system of proportional representation. Political parties include the (right-wing) Christian Democratic Party (PDGC), the (centre-right) Union of National Centre (UCN), and the (centre-right) Movement for Action and Solidarity (MAS). The most recent election was in 1990.

Party strength: UCN 41, PDGC 28, MAS 18, others 29.

President: Ramiro de Leon Carpio.

GEOGRAPHY

Pacific and Atlantic coastal lowlands are separated by a mountain chain containing over 30 volcanoes. Highest point: Tajumulco 4220 m (13,881 ft). Principal rivers: Usumacinta, Montagua. Climate: The coastal plains have a tropical climate; the mountains are more temperate.

ECONOMY

More than one half of the labour force is involved in agriculture. Coffee is the major export, while the other main crops include sugar cane and bananas.

Currency: Quetzal (CTQ) of 100 centavos; 1US$ = 5.744 CTQ (June 1994).

GDP: US$8,816,000,000 (1991); US$930 per head.

RECENT HISTORY

Since independence from Spain in 1821, Guatemala has mainly been ruled by dictators allied to landowners. However, in the 1950s President Jacobo Arbenz expropriated large estates, dividing them among the peasantry. Accused of being a Communist, he was deposed by the army with US military aid (1954). For over 30 years, the left was suppressed, leading to the emergence of guerrilla armies. Thousands of dissidents were killed or disappeared. Civilian government was restored in 1986. In 1993 President Serrano was deposed after attempting to impose a dictatorship, and a government of national unity took office.

Guyana

Official name: The Cooperative Republic of Guyana.

Member of: UN, Commonwealth, OAS, CARICOM.

Area: 214,969 km² (83,000 sq mi).

Population: 730,000 (1993 est).

Capital: Georgetown 195,000 (including suburbs; 1986 est).

Other major towns: Linden 30,000, New Amsterdam 20,000 (1986 est).

Languages: English (official), Hindu, Urdu.

Religions: Hinduism (34%), various Protestant Churches (34%) - mainly Anglican, Sunni Islam (9%), Roman Catholic (18%), Sunni Islam (10%).

Education: Education is compulsory between the ages of six and 14. The literacy rate in 1990 was 96.4%. There is a single university.

Defence: In 1993 the total armed strength was 1700, plus 3500 paramilitary. There is selective military service in the paramilitary.

Transport: There are 7200 km (4474 mi) of roads and 88 km (55 mi) of railways. Georgetown has a port and an international airport.

Media: There is a single daily paper and a state-run radio and television service.

GOVERNMENT

The 65-member National Assembly is elected for five years under a system of proportional representation by universal adult suffrage. The President - the leader of the majority in the Assembly - appoints a Cabinet led by the First Vice-President. Political parties include the (left-wing) People's Progressive Party (PPP), the (left-wing) People's National Congress (PNC), the (left-wing) Forum for Democracy (Forum), the (conservative) United Force (TUF), and the (left-wing) Working People's Alliance (WPA). After the election held in October 1992 a PPP government was formed.

Party strength: PPP 35, PNC 22, Forum 5, WPA 2, TUF 1.

President: Cheddi Jagan (PPP).

First Vice-President and Prime Minister: Samuel Hinds (PPP).

GEOGRAPHY

A coastal plain is protected from the sea by dykes. Tropical rain forest covers much of the interior. Highest point: Mt Roraima 2772 m (9094 ft). Principal rivers: Essequibo, Courantyne, Mazaruni, Demarara. Climate: The interior is tropical, while the coastal plain has a more moderate climate.

ECONOMY

Guyana depends on mining bauxite and growing sugar cane and rice. Nationalization and emigration have caused economic problems. Austerity measures have been in force since 1988.

Currency: Guyana dollar (GYD) of 100 cents; 1US$ = 134.11 GYD (June 1994).

GDP: US$266,000,000 (1991); US$330 per head.

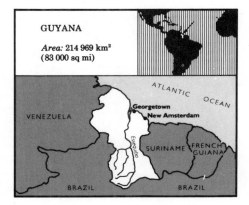

GUYANA

Area: 214 969 km² (83 000 sq mi)

RECENT HISTORY

Guyana is the former colony of British Guiana. From the 1840s large numbers of Indian and Chinese labourers were imported from Asia to work on sugar plantations. Racial tension between their descendants - now the majority - and the black community (descended from imported African slaves) led to violence in 1964 and 1978. Guyana has been independent since 1966. The first completely free elections in 20 years were held in 1992.

193

Honduras

Official name: La República de Honduras (Republic of Honduras).

Member of: UN, OAS, CACM.

Area: 112,088 km² (43,277 sq mi).

Population: 5,150,000 (1993 est).

Capital: Tegucigalpa 648,000 (including suburbs; 1988 census).

Other major cities: San Pedro Sula 301,000, La Ceiba 72,000, El Progreso 63,000, Choluteca 57,000 (including suburbs; 1988 census).

Language: Spanish (official).

Religions: Roman Catholic (85%), various Protestant Evangelical Churches (15%).

Education: Education is compulsory between the ages of seven and 13. In 1990 the literacy rate was 73.1%. There are two universities

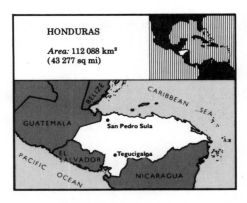

HONDURAS

Area: 112 088 km²
(43 277 sq mi)

Defence: In 1993 the total armed strength was 16,800 plus plus 5000 paramilitary. Military service lasts for eight months.

Transport: There are 11,375 km (7070 mi) of roads and 939 km (583 mi) of railways. Tegucigalpa has an international airport. Puerto Cortes is the main commercial port.

Media: There are seven daily newspapers, nine television stations and over 280 radio stations.

GOVERNMENT
The President and the 134-member National Assembly are elected by universal adult suf-

frage for four years. For local government purposes the country is divided into 18 departments. The main political parties are the Liberal Party of Honduras (PLH) and the (right-wing) National Party of Honduras (PNH). After the election in November 1993 a PLH government was formed.

Party strength: PLH 71, PNH 55, others 2.

President: Carlos Roberto Reina (PLH).

GEOGRAPHY
Mountains occupy about three quarters of Honduras; the remainder comprises small coastal plains. Highest point: Cerio las Minas 2849 m (9347 ft). Principal rivers: Patuca, Ulúa. Climate: The tropical lowlands experience high rainfall (1500-2000 mm/60-80 in). The more temperate highlands are drier.

ECONOMY
The majority of Hondurans work in agriculture, but despite agrarian reform, living standards remain low. Bananas and coffee are the leading exports, although meat is increasingly important. The over-dependence upon bananas and coffee have given cause for concern, particularly as the world market for both commodities have slumped in recent years. There are few natural resources.

Currency: Lempira of 100 centavos; 1US$ = 8.044 lempiras (June 1994).

GDP: US$2,980,000,000 (1991); US$550 per head.

RECENT HISTORY
Between independence from Spain (1821) and the early 20th century, Honduras experienced constant political upheaval and wars with neighbouring countries. US influence was immense, largely owing to the substantial investments of the powerful United Fruit Company in banana production. After a short civil war in 1925, a succession of military dictators governed Honduras until 1980. Since then the country has had democratically elected pro-US centre-right civilian governments although there have been allegations of abuses of human rights by the army. Following an attempted coup by part of the army in 1993 an investigation into these abuses has begun.

Nicaragua

Official name: República de Nicaragua (Republic of Nicaragua).

Member of: UN, OAS, CACM.

Area: 120,254 km² (46,430 sq mi).

Population: 4,265,000 (1993 est).

Capital: Managua 1,108,000 (city 682,000; 1988 est).

Other main cities: León 101,000, Granada 89,000 (1988 est).

Languages: Spanish (official), Amerindian languages (including Miskito; 4%).

Religion: Roman Catholic (90%).

Education: Education is compulsory between the ages of seven and 13. In 1990 the literacy rate was be 88%. There are four universities.

Defence: In 1993 the total armed strength was 15,200. Military service was abolished in 1990.

Transport: There are 15,000 km (9323 mi) of roads and 300 km (186 mi) of railways. Managua has an international airport. Corinto is the principal port.

Media: There are nine daily newspapers. There are nearly 60 radio stations and a single state-run television channel.

GOVERNMENT

A President and the 92-member National Assembly are elected by proportional representation for six years by universal adult suffrage. Political parties include the (coalition) National Opposition Union (UNO) and the (left-wing) Sandinista National Liberation Front (FSLN). UNO won the 1992 election but it has since lost its majority.

Party strength: UNO 43, FSLN 47, others 6.

President: Violetta Chamorro (UNO).

GEOGRAPHY

A fertile plain on the Pacific coast contains the majority of the population. Mountain ranges rise in the centre of the country. Tropical jungle covers the Atlantic coastal plain. Highest point: Pico Mogotón 2107 m (6913 ft). Principal rivers: Coco, Rio Grande, San Juan, Escondido. Climate: The climate is tropical and humid with a rainy season from May to October.

ECONOMY

A mainly farming economy was damaged in the 1980s by guerrilla warfare, a US trade embargo and hurricanes. Privatization and strict austerity programmes have been implemented. Coffee, cotton and sugar cane are the main export crops.

Currency: Cordoba oro of 100 centavos; 1US$ = 6.677 Cordobas oro (June 1994).

GDP: US$1,897,000,000 (1991); US$340 per head.

RECENT HISTORY

Since independence from Spain (1821),

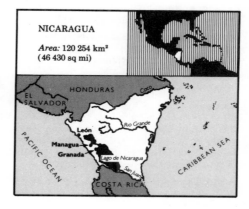

NICARAGUA

Area: 120 254 km² (46 430 sq mi)

Nicaragua has witnessed strife between conservatives and liberals. After 1900 the political situation deteriorated, provoking US intervention - US marines were based in Nicaragua from 1912 to 1925, and again from 1927 until 1933. General Anastasio Somoza became president in 1937. Employing dictatorial methods, members of the Somoza family, or their supporters, remained in power until overthrown by a popular uprising led by the Sandinista guerrilla army in 1979. Accusing the Sandinistas of introducing Communism, the USA imposed a trade embargo, making Nicaragua increasingly dependent on Cuba and the USSR. Right-wing US-financed Contra guerrillas fought the Sandinistas from bases in Honduras. A ceasefire was agreed in 1989. In free presidential elections in 1990, the Sandinista incumbent Daniel Ortega was defeated by Violetta Chamorro of UNO (see above).

195

Panama

Official name: La República de Panamá (The Republic of Panama).

Member of: UN, OAS.

Area: 77,082 km² (29,762 sq mi).

Population: 2,563,000 (1993 est).

Capital: Panama City 828,000 (city 585,000; San Miguelito 243,000; 1990 census).

Other main cities: Colón 141,000, David 103,000 (1990 census).

Language: Spanish (official).

Religions: Roman Catholic (85%), various Evangelical Protestant Churches (5%).

Education: Education is compulsory between the ages of six and 15. In 1990 the literacy rate was 88.1%. There are two universities.

Defence: In 1993 the total armed strength was 11,700, the majority in the paramilitary police.

Transport: There are just over 10,000 km (6214 mi) of roads and 583 km (362 mi) of railways. The Panama Canal is a major international waterway, linking the Pacific with the Atlantic. Balboa and Cristobal are the major ports. Panama City has an international airport.

Media: There are seven daily newspapers, 43 radio stations (most commercial), and seven television channels.

GOVERNMENT

A President, two Vice-Presidents and a 71-member Legislative Assembly are elected by universal adult suffrage for five years. The President appoints a Cabinet of Ministers. The main political parties include the (nationalist) Democratic Revolutionary Party (PRD), the (right-wing) Arnulfist Party (PA), the (centre-right) Papa Egoro Movement (MPE), and the (centre-right) Nationalist Republican Liberal Movement (MOLIRENA). After the election held in May 1994 a PRD-led government was formed.

Party strength: PRD 21, PA 12, MPE 6, MOLIRENA 5, others 27.

President: Ernesto Perez Balladreo (PRD).

GEOGRAPHY

Panama is a heavily forested mountainous isthmus joining Central America to South America. Highest point: Baru 3475 m (11,467 ft). Principal rivers: Tuira (with Chucunaque), Bayano, Santa Maria. Climate: Panama has a tropical climate with little seasonal change in temperature.

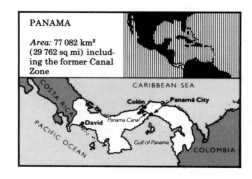

PANAMA

Area: 77 082 km² (29 762 sq mi) including the former Canal Zone

ECONOMY

Income from the Panama Canal is a major foreign-currency earner. Panama has a higher standard of living than its neighbours, although the political crisis of 1989 damaged the economy. Major exports include bananas, shrimps and mahogany.

Currency: Balboa of 100 centesimos; 1US$ = 1 balboa.

GDP: US$5,255,000,000 (1991); US$2180 per head.

RECENT HISTORY

Panama was part of Spanish New Granada (Colombia). In the 1880s a French attempt to construct a canal through Panama linking the Atlantic and Pacific Oceans proved unsuccessful. After Colombia rejected US proposals for completing the canal, Panama became independent (1903), sponsored by the USA. The canal eventually opened in 1914. The USA was given land extending 8 km (5 mi) on either side of the canal - the Canal Zone - complete control of which will be handed to Panama in 2000. From 1983 to 1989 effective power was in the hands of General Manuel Noriega, who was deposed by a US invasion and taken to stand trial in the USA, where he was found guilty of criminal activities. The first completely free elections in the state's history were held in 1994.

Paraguay

Official name: La República del Paraguay (The Republic of Paraguay).

Member of: UN, OAS, Mercosur, ALADI.

Area: 406,752 km² (157,048 sq mi).

Population: 4,613,000 (1993 est).

Capital: Asunción 732,000 (city 608,000; San Lorenzo 124,000; 1990 est).

Other major cities: Ciudad del Este 110,000, Pedro Juan Caballero 80,000, Concepción 63,000, Encarnación 44,000 (1990 est).

Languages: Spanish (official; 7%), Guaraní (official; 40%), bilingual Spanish-Guaraní (48%).

Religion: Roman Catholic (96%).

Education: Education is compulsory between the ages of seven and 13. In 1990 the literacy rate was 90.1%. There are two universities.

Defence: In 1992 the total armed strength was 16,500 - 12,500 in the army, 3000 in the (riverine) navy and 1000 in the air force. There are

PARAGUAY

Area: 406 752 km²
(157 048
sq mi)

BOLIVA

BRAZIL

ARGENTINA

Asunción

Paraguay

Paraná

Encarnación

8000 paramilitary police. Military service lasts 18 months in the army, 24 months in the navy.

Transport: There are 25,680 km (15,957 mi) of roads and 441 km (274 mi) of railways. The rivers Paraguay and Paraná are navigable. Asunción, a river port, has an international airport.

Media: There are six daily newspapers, one government-owned and 40 commercial radio stations, and four television stations.

GOVERNMENT
An 80-member Chamber of Deputies (lower house) and a 45-member Senate (upper house) are elected by universal adult suffrage for five years. Political parties include the Colorado Party (PC), the (left-centre) Authentic Radical Liberal Party (PLRA) and the National Encounter coalition (coalition). After the election held in May 1993 a PC government was formed.

Party strength: PC 38, PLRA 33, coalition 9.

President: Juan Carlos Wosmosy (PC).

GEOGRAPHY
The country west of the Paraguay River - the Chaco - is a flat semiarid plain. The region east of the river is a partly forested undulating plateau. Highest point: Cerro Tatug 700 m (2297 ft). Principal rivers: Paraguay, Paraná, Pilcomayo. Climate: Paraguay is subtropical, with much variation between the wet east and the dry west.

ECONOMY
Agriculture - the main economic activity - is dominated by cattle ranching, cotton and soyabeans. Cheap hydroelectric power installations on the Paraná River - including the Yacyreta-Agipe dam, the world's largest - have greatly stimulated industry. Electricity is exported.

Currency: Guarani; 1US$ = 1792.7 guaranis (June 1994).

GDP: US$5,374,000,000 (1991); US$ 1210 per head.

RECENT HISTORY
Since independence from Spain in 1811, Paraguay has suffered many dictators, including General José Francia, who totally isolated Paraguay (1814-40). War against Argentina, Brazil and Uruguay (1865-70) cost Paraguay over one half of its people and much territory. The Chaco Wars with Bolivia (1929-35) further weakened Paraguay. General Alfredo Stroessner gained power in 1954, ruling with increasing disregard for human rights until his overthrow in a military coup in 1989. Free multi-party elections were held in 1993.

197

Peru

Official name: República del Perú (Republic of Peru).

Member of: UN, OAS, ALADI, Andean Pact.

Area: 1,285,216 km² (496,225 sq mi).

Population: 22,916,000 (1993 est).

Capital: Lima 6,405,000 (city 5,494,000; Callao 515,000; 1990 est).

Other major cities: Arequipa 612,000, Trujillo 513,000, Chiclayo 410,000, Piura 310,000, Cuzco 275,000, Iquitos 270,000, Huancayo 210,000 (including suburbs; 1990 est).

Languages: Spanish (68% as a first language, but universally understood), Quechua (27% as a first language but spoken by over 47% of the population), Aymara (3% as a first language) - all official.

Religion: Roman Catholic (official; 91%), various Protestant Churches (2%).

Education: Education is compulsory, in theory, between the ages of six and 15. In 1990 the literacy rate was 85.1%. There are 35 universities (25 national and 10 private - two of which are Catholic).

Defence: In 1993 the total armed strength was 115,000 - 75,000 in the army, 25,000 in the navy and 15,000 in the air force. There is also a 70,000-member paramilitary police force. The navy is based at Callao. Selective military service lasts two years.

Transport: There are 69,942 km (43,460 mi) of roads and 3472 km (2157 mi) of railways. Callao is the main commercial shipping port. Lima is the principal international airport, while Cuzcu, Arequipa and Iquitos also have international airports.

Media: There are 30 daily newspapers, of which seven are published in Lima. There are about 300 radio stations, including a state-owned service, and one state-owned (cultural) television service and six commercial television networks.

GOVERNMENT

An 80-member Constitutional Congress was elected in November 1992. The Congress approved a renewal of the previous constitution which had provision for a President and a National Congress - comprising a 60-member Senate and a 180-member Chamber of Deputies - which were elected by universal adult suffrage for five years. Voting is compulsory, in theory, in Peru. The President appoints a Council of Ministers including a Prime Minister. Peru is divided into 11 regions, two departments and a constitutional province. The main political parties include Cambio 90, the Popular Christian Party (PPC), the Independent Moral Front (FIM), Renovation (R), the Democratic Movement of the Left (MDI), Democratic Coordination (CD), the National Front of Workers and Peasants (FNTC), the Popular Agricultural Front of Peru (FPAP), Solidarity and Democracy (SD), the (liberal) Popular Action (AP), and the (left-wing) APRA (American Popular Revolutionary Alliance). AP and APRA boycotted the 1992 elections, after which a largely non-party government was formed.

Party strength: Cambio 44, PPC 8, FIM 7, R 6, MDI 5, CD 4, FNTC 2, FPAP 2, SD 2.

President: Alberto Fujimori (Cambio).

THE CABINET

Prime Minister and Minister of Foreign Affairs: Efrain Goldenberg Schreiber.

Minister of Agriculture: Absalon Vasquez Villanueva.

Minister of Defence: Gen. Victor Malca Villanueva.

Minister of the Economy and Finance: Jorge Camet Dickman.

Minister of Education: Jorge Trelles Montero.

Minister of Energy and Mines: Daniel Hokama Tokashiki.

Minister of Fisheries: Jaime Sobero Taira.

Minister of Health: Jaime Freundt-Thurne Oyanguren.

Minister of Industry, Commerce, Tourism, Integration and International Commercial Negotiations: Liliana Canale Novella.

Minister of the Interior: Gen. Juan Briones Davila.

Minister of Justice: Dr Fernando Vega Santa Gadea.

Minister of Labour and Social Promotion: Augusto Antoniolli Vasquez.

Minister of Transport, Comunications, Housing and Construction: Dr Dante Cordova Blanco.

Minister of the Presidency: Raul Vittor Alfaro.

GEOGRAPHY
The coastal plain is narrow and arid. The Andes - which are prone to earthquakes - run in three high parallel ridges from north to south. Nearly two thirds of Peru is tropical for-

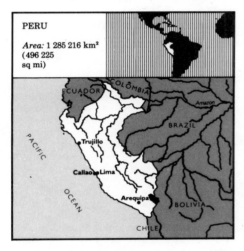

PERU

Area: 1 285 216 km² (496 225 sq mi)

est (the Selva) in the Amazon Basin. Highest point: Huascarán 6768 m (22,205 ft). Principal rivers: Amazon, Ucayali, Napo, Marañón. Climate: A wide climatic variety includes semi-tropical desert - cooled by the Humboldt Current - on the coast, the very cold Alpine High Andes, and the tropical Selva with heavy rainfall.

ECONOMY
About one third of the labour force is involved in agriculture. Subsistence farming dominates in the interior; crops for export are more important near the coast, where irrigation using water from Andean rivers, is becoming increasingly important. Major crops include coffee, sugar cane, cotton and potatoes, as well

as coca for cocaine. Sheep, llamas, vicuñas and alpacas are kept for wool. Rich natural resources include silver, copper, coal, gold, iron ore, petroleum and phosphates. The fishing industry - once the world's largest - has declined since 1971. A combination of natural disasters, a very high birth rate, guerrilla warfare and the declining value of exports have severely damaged the economy. After rampant inflation the New Sol was introduced to replace the Sol, which had become of little value.

Currency: New Sol of 100 centavos; 1US$ = 2.19 New Sols (June 1994).

GDP: US$21,250,000,000 (1991); US$950 per head.

RECENT HISTORY
Much of South America was governed from Lima as the Spanish Viceroyalty of Peru. Independence was proclaimed in 1821 after the Argentine San Martín took Lima, but Spanish forces did not leave until 1824. Independent Peru saw political domination by large landowners. Progress was made under General Ramon Castilla (1844-62) and civilian constitutional governments at the beginning of the 20th century, but instability and military coups have been common. War (1879-83) in alliance with Bolivia against Chile resulted in the loss of nitrate deposits in the south, while victory against Ecuador (1941) added Amazonian territory. From 1968 a reformist military government instituted a programme of land reform, attempting to benefit workers and the Indians. Faced with mounting economic problems the military swung to the right in 1975 when Gen. Juan Velazco and his government of army officers was ousted in a bloodless coup. After 1980 elections were held regularly, but owing to the economic crisis and the growth of an extreme left-wing guerrilla movement - the Sendero Luminoso ('Shining Path') - Peru's democracy remained fragile. In 1992, President Alberto Fujimori effected a coup, suspending the constitution and detaining opposition leaders. These actions were widely condemned by the USA and other members of the OAS. Subsequent elections were boycotted by the principal opposition parties. Guerrilla activity lessened after the capture of Abimael Guzman, the leader of the Sendero Luminoso in 1992.

199

Suriname

Official name: Republiek Suriname (Republic of Suriname).

Member of: UN, OAS.

Area: 163,265 km² (63,037 sq mi).

Population: 405,000 (1993 est).

Capital: Paramaribo 246,000 (city 68,000; 1988 est).

Other main town: Nieuw Amsterdam 6000 (1988 est).

Languages: Dutch (official; 30%), Sranang Togo (Creole; 31%), Hindi (30%), Javanese (15%), Chinese, English, Spanish (official - designate).

Religions: Hinduism (28%), Roman Catholic (22%), Sunni Islam (20%), Moravian (15%).

Education: Education is compulsory between the ages of six and 12. In 1990 the literacy rate was 94.9%. There is a university.

Defence: In 1993 the total armed strength was 1800 - 1400 in the army, 240 in the navy and 160 in the air force. Military service was abolished in 1993.

Transport: There are 9153 km (5688 mi) of roads and 301 km (187 mi) of private freight railways. Paramaribo has a commercial port and an international airport.

Media: There are two daily newspapers, two television stations (one commercial, the other government-owned) and ten radio stations.

GOVERNMENT

A 51-member National Assembly is elected for five years by universal adult suffrage. A President and a Vice-President - who is also the Prime Minister - are elected by the Assembly, and a Cabinet is appointed by the President. The main political parties are the (coalition of socialist and ethnic parties) New Front for Democracy and Development (NFDD), the (military-backed) New Democratic Party (NDP) and the (coalition anti-military) Democratic Alternative '91 (DA). After the election in May 1991 the NF formed a government.

Party strength: NFDD 30, NDP 12, DA 9.

President: Ronald Venetiaan (NFDD).

Prime Minister: Jules Ajodhia (NFDD).

GEOGRAPHY

Suriname comprises a swampy coastal plain, a forested central plateau, and southern mountains. Highest point: Julianatop 1286 m (4218 ft). Principal rivers: Corantijn, Nickerie, Coppename, Saramacca, Suriname, Commewijne, Maroni. Climate: Suriname has a tropical climate with heavy rainfall.

ECONOMY

The extraction and refining of bauxite is the mainstay of the economy. Other exports include shrimps, sugar and oranges. Economic development has been hampered by political instability and emigration.

Currency: Suriname guilder of 100 cents; 1US$ = 1.784 guilders (June 1994).

GDP: US$1,727,000,000 (1992); US$3690 per head.

RECENT HISTORY

Dutch settlement began in 1602 and the area was confirmed as a Dutch colony in 1667. Suriname has a mixed population, including American Indians, and the descendants of African slaves and of Javanese, Chinese and Indian plantation workers. Since independence in 1975, racial tension has contributed to instability, and there have been several coups in which Col. Desi Bouterse played an important role. Constitutional rule was restored in 1991.

SURINAME

Area: 163 265 km²
(63 037 sq mi)

GUYANA — Corantijn — Paramaribo — Maroni — ATLANTIC OCEAN — FRENCH GUIANA — BRAZIL

Uruguay

Official name: La República Oriental del Uruguay (The Eastern Republic of Uruguay).

Member of: UN, OAS, ALADI, Mercosur.

Area: 176,215 km² (68,037 sq mi).

Population: 3,150,000 (1993 est).

Capital: Montevideo 1,370,000 (city 1,312,000; Las Piedras 58,000; 1985 census).

Other major cities: Salto 80,000, Paysandú 76,000, Rivera 57,000 (1985 census).

Language: Spanish (official).

Religions: Roman Catholic (58%), various Protestant Churches.

Education: Between the ages of six and 14, six years of education are compulsory. In 1990 the literacy rate was 96.2%. There are two universities.

Defence: In 1992 the total armed strength was 24,700 - 17,200 in the army, 4500 in the navy and 3000 in the air force. There is no military service.

Transport: There are 52,000 km (32,300 mi) of roads and 3002 km (1866 mi) of railways. Montevideo, the main port, has an international airport.

Media: There are 13 daily newspapers, 105 radio stations and 20 television stations.

GOVERNMENT

The President, the 31-member Senate and 99-member Chamber of Deputies are elected for four years by universal adult suffrage. The President appoints a Council of Ministers. Political parties include the (conservative) National Party (the Blancos; PN), the (centre) Colorado Party (PC), the (left-wing coalition) Broad Front (FA), and the (social democratic) New Space (EN). After the election held in November 1989 a PN government was formed.

Party strength: PN 39, PC 30, RA 21, EN 9.

President: Luis Alberto Lacalle (PN).

GEOGRAPHY

Uruguay consists mainly of low undulating plains and plateaux. The only significant ranges of hills are in the southeast. Highest point: Cerro de las Animas 500 m (1643 ft). Principal rivers: Río Negro, Uruguay, Yi. Climate: Uruguay has a temperate climate with warm summers and mild winters.

ECONOMY

Pastureland - for sheep and beef cattle - covers about 80% of the land. Meat, wool and hides are the leading exports. Despite a lack of natural resources, Uruguay has a high standard of living. The country faces economic difficulties including high inflation and the financial demands of a large public sector and social security system.

Currency: Peso of 100 centesimos; 1US$ = 4.95 pesos (June 1994).

GDP: US$8,895,000,000 (1991); US$2860 per head.

RECENT HISTORY

From independence in 1808 until 1903 Uruguay was ruled by dictators and wracked

by civil war. However, prosperity from cattle and wool, and the presidencies of the reformer José Battle (1903-7 and 1911-15), turned Uruguay into a democracy and an advanced welfare state. A military dictatorship held power during the Depression. By 1970 severe economic problems had ushered in a period of social and political turmoil, and urban guerrillas became active. In 1973 a coup installed a military dictatorship that made Uruguay notorious for abuses of human rights. In 1985 the country returned to democratic rule.

201

Venezuela

Official name: La República de Venezuela (Republic of Venezuela).

Member of: UN, OAS, ALADI, Andean Pact.

Area: 912,050 km² (352,144 sq mi).

Population: 20,662,000 (1993 est).

Capital: Caracas 3,436,000 (city 1,290,000; 1990 census).

Other major cities: Maracaibo 1,401,000 (city 1,207,000), Valencia 1,274,000 (city 955,000), Maracay 957,000 (city 538,000), Barquisimeto 787,000 (city 724,000), Cuidad Guayana 543,000 (1990 census).

Languages: Spanish (official; 98%), various Amerindian languages.

Religion: Roman Catholic (92%).

Education: Education is compulsory between the ages of five and 14. In 1990 the literacy rate was 88.1%. There are 22 universities including two polytechnics of university status.

Defence: In 1993 the total armed strength was 75,000 - 34,000 in the army, 11,000 in the navy, 7000 in the air force and 22,000 in the paramilitary National Guard. Military service, which is selective, lasts for two years.

Transport: There are 77,529 km (48,174 mi) of roads and 363 km (226 mi) of railways. Caracas has a metro. Lake Maracaibo is the most important inland waterway. The main ports are La Guaira, Maracaibo, Puerto Ordaz and Puerto Cabello. Caracas has an international airport; seven regional airports, the most important of which is Maracaibo, also receive international flights.

Media: There are 25 daily newspapers, eight of which are published in Caracas. There are eight state-run, four cultural and over 160 commercial radio stations, plus two state-run and three commercial television channels.

GOVERNMENT
The President and both Houses of the National Congress are elected for five years by universal adult suffrage. The Senate - the upper House - comprises 49 elected senators, plus former Presidents. The Chamber of the Deputies has 205 directly elected members. Each of the 20 states has its own governments. The President appoints a Council of Ministers. The main political parties are (left of centre) Democratic Action (AD), the Social Christian Party (COPEI), the (centre right) Convergence (Convergencia), the (left-wing) Radical Cause Party (Causa R), and the Socialist Movement (MAS). After the election in December 1993 a Convergencia-independent government was formed.

Party strength (Chamber): AD 56, COPEI 54, Causa R 40, Convergencia 26, MAS 26, others 3.

President: Rafael Caldera (Convergencia).

THE CABINET
includes

Minister of Defence: Rafael Angel Montero.

Minister of Finance: Julio Sosa Rodriguez.

Minister of Foreign Affairs: Miguel Angel Burelli.

Minister of Home Affairs: Ramon Escobar Salom.

Minister of Justice: Ruben Creixems.

VENEZUELAN STATES
Population figures are from the 1990 census.

Anzoátegui Area: 43,300 km² (16,700 sq mi). Population: 924,000. Capital: Barcelona.

Apure Area: 76,500 km² (29,500 sq mi). Population: 305,000. Capital: San Fernando de Apure.

Aragua Area: 7014 km² (2700 sq mi). Population: 1,195,000 Capital: Maracay.

Barinas Area: 35,200 km² (13,600 sq mi). Population: 456,000. Capital: Barinas.

Bolivar Area: 238,000 km² (91,900 sq mi). Population: 969, 000. Capital: Ciudad Bolivar.

Caraboto Area: 4650 km² (1795 sq mi). Population: 1,559,000. Capital: Valencia.

Cojedes Area: 14,800 km² (5700 sq mi). Population: 197,000. Capital: San Carlos.

Falcón Area: 24,800 km² (9600 sq mi). Population: 633 ,000. Capital: Coro.

Guárico Area: 64,985 km² (25,090 sq mi). Population: 526,000. Capital: San Juan de Los Morros.

Lara Area: 19,800 km² (7600 sq mi). Population: 1,270,000. Capital: Barquisimeto.

Mérida Area: 11,300 km² (4400 sq mi). Population: 615,000. Capital: Mérida.

Miranda Area: 7950 km² (3070 sq mi). Population: 2,026,000. Capital: Los Teques.

Monagas Area: 28,900 km² (11,200 sq mi). Population: 503,000. Capital: Maturin.

Nueva Esparta Area: 1150 km² (440 sq mi). Population: 281,000. Capital: La Asunción.

Portuguesa Area: 15,200 km² (5900 sq mi). Population: 626,000. Capital: Guanare.

Sucre Area: 11,800 km² (4600 sq mi). Population: 723,000. Capital: Cumaná.

Táchira Area: 11,100 km² (4300 sq mi). Population: 860,000. Capital: San Cristóbal.

Trujillo Area: 7400 km² (2900 sq mi). Population: 520,000. Capital: Trujillo.

Yaracuy Area: 7100 km² (2700 sq mi). Population: 412,000. Capital: San Felipe.

Zulia Area: 63,100 km² (24,400 sq mi). Population: 2,387,000. Capital: Maracaibo.

Amazonas (territory) Area: 175,750 km² (67,900 sq mi). Population: 60,000. Capital: Puerto Ayacucho.

Delta Amacuro (territory) Area: 40,200 km² (15,500 sq mi). Population: 91,000. Capital: Tucupita.

Federal Dependencies (Dependencias Federales) (the islands of San Andres and Providencia) Area: 120 km² (50 sq mi). Population: 2200. Capital: no capital; the islands are administered by the federal government.

Federal District (Distrito Federal) Area: 1930 km² (745 sq mi). Population: 2,266,000. Capital: Caracas.

GEOGRAPHY

Mountains in the north include the north-south Eastern Andes and the Maritime Andes, which run parallel to the Caribbean coast. Central Venezuela comprises low-lying grassland plains (the Llanos). The Guiana Highlands in the southeast include many high steep-sided plateaux. Highest point: Pico Bolivar 5007 m (16,423 ft). Principal rivers: Orinoco, Rio Meta, Coroni, Apure. Climate: The tropical coast is arid. The cooler mountains and the tropical Llanos are wet, although the latter has a dry season from December to March.

ECONOMY

Petroleum and natural gas normally account for over 80% of export earnings. Agriculture is mainly concerned with raising beef cattle, and growing sugar cane and coffee for export; bananas, maize and rice are grown as subsistence crops.

Currency: Bolivar of 100 centimos; 1US$ = 170.74 bolivars (June 1994).

GDP: US$64,000,000,000 (1993 est); US$3050 per head.

RECENT HISTORY

Spain began to develop Venezuela in the 17th century. In 1806 Francisco Miranda (1752-1816) led a war of independence that was successfully concluded by Simon Bolívar (1783-1830) in 1823. Initially united with Colombia and Ecuador, Venezuela seceded in 1830. Independence was followed by a series of military coups, revolts and dictators, including Juan Vicente Gómez, whose harsh rule lasted from 1909 to 1935. Since General Marcos Peréz Jiménez was overthrown in 1958, Venezuela has been a civilian democracy. There have, however, been two abortive coup attempts in the 1990s, partly as a result of economic uncertainty, corruption and austerity.

Other territories

FALKLAND ISLANDS
Status: a British Crown colony.

Area: 12,170 km² (4698 sq mi).

Population: 2120 (excluding military personnel; 1991 census).

Capital: Port Stanley 1560 (1991 census).

Government: The 10-member legislature comprises eight members elected by universal adult suffrage and two ex-officio members.

Geography: The Falklands consist of two main and over 100 small bleak islands in the southern Atlantic, about 770 km (480 mi) northeast of Cape Horn. Highest point: Mt Adam 704 m (2310 ft). Climate: The climate is mild in summer and cold in winter, with the strong winds all year.

Economy: The barren interior is used as pasture for sheep and wool is the only major export. Fishing is growing in importance.

Recent History: The islands were claimed and (briefly) settled by Britain in the 18th century. Argentina claimed and settled the uninhabited islands in 1820 but was expelled from the Falklands by the USA in 1831. Britain resumed its occupation in 1833 and a British community was established in the islands. Argentina continued to claim the islands, initially through diplomatic activity. Britain maintained that ceding the islands to Argentina would be contrary to the principle of self-determination of the islands' inhabitants. In April 1982 Argentine troops invaded and occupied the Falklands, but were defeated and expelled in June by British forces.

FRENCH GUYANA (GUYANE)
Status: an overseas French département.

Area: 90,000 km² (34,750 sq mi).

Population: 115,000 (1990 census).

Capital: Cayenne 42,000 (1990 census).

Government: The 19-member General Council and the 31-member Regional Council are both elected for six years by universal adult suffrage. Guyane also elects two deputies to the French National Assembly and a senator to the Senate.

Geography: The département is a tropical lowland mainly covered in jungle. Principal river: Moroni. Highest point: Mont St Marcel 635 m (2083 ft). Climate: The climate is hot and humid with heavy rainfall.

Economy: The economy depends upon timber and upon subsidies from metropolitan France. Very little land is cultivated and mineral ores, including bauxite, are not widely exploited.

Recent History: The area finally became French in 1819 and - including the notorious Devil's Island - was used as a penal colony from 1798 to 1935. It became an overseas département of the French Republic in 1946.

SOUTH GEORGIA
AND SOUTH SANDWICH ISLANDS
Status: British Territories.

Area: 4091 km² (1580 sq mi) - South Georgia 3755 km² (1450 sq mi); South Sandwich Islands 336 km² (130 sq mi).

Population: no permanent population, although there is a small military garrison and a scientific station at Grytviken in South Georgia.

Capital: Grytviken.

Geography: South Georgia is a bleak, mountainous island 1290 km (800 mi) east of the Falkland Islands. Much of the island has permanent snow-cover. The South Sandwich Islands - which are 760 km (470 mi) southeast of South Georgia - are active volcanoes which are covered by glaciers. Highest point: Mount Paget 2934 m (9625 ft) on South Georgia. Climate: The climate is harsh, cold and windy.

Recent History: Both groups of islands - which were annexed by Britain in 1775 - are claimed by Argentina. In 1955 Argentina refused a British referral of the dispute to the International Court of Justice. Argentine personnel occupied some of the South Sandwich Islands in 1976 and Argentine forces invaded South Georgia in 1982. Britain retook both groups in 1982 and in 1985 separated them from the Falkland Islands, to which they had been attached as dependencies in 1908.

COMMONWEALTH OF INDEPENDENT STATES

Armenia, Azerbaijan, Belarus, Georgia, Kazakhstan, Kyrgyzstan, Moldova, Russia, Tajikistan, Turkmenistan, Ukraine, Uzbekistan.

Russia and the 'near abroad'

Russia regards as the 'near abroad' those countries whose independence many, if not most, Russians cannot take seriously - the other former Union republics of the USSR. The collapse of the Soviet Union in December 1991 left some 25 million ethnic Russians stranded as citizens of one of the 14 other former Union republics. The fate of the Russians in the 'near abroad' has become a more prominent item on the Moscow agenda since the rise of extreme nationalism and the rebirth of a powerful Communist Party as witnessed in the elections to the Russian Duma in December 1993.

The case of the ethnic Russians in the Baltic states of Estonia, Latvia and Lithuania has a high profile, in part because they form such a large percentage of the population in Estonia and Latvia. The majority of the ethnic Russians are descendants of a large-scale Russian settlement imposed on the region by Stalin in 1945 when the three republics were reannexed to the Soviet Union following their occupation by Nazi Germany during World War II. This settlement continues to be deeply resented by the Balts, particularly as newcomers from Russia were brought in to replace nearly 600,000 Balts who had either been killed or exiled to Siberia by Stalin. In Latvia, the Letts are only just in the majority; in Estonia, ethnic Russians form a majority in much of the east of the country. The nervousness of the Baltic states concerning the presence of a large minority whose allegiance to their newly independent homeland is perceived as suspect is compounded by the utterances of right-wing nationalists in Moscow, such as Vladimir Zhirinovsky, who deny the right to sovereignty of the Baltic states.

In Ukraine over one fifth of the population is either intensely Russified or ethnic Russian. The presidential election in Ukraine in July 1994 highlighted a deep division that could eventually lead to strife and the break-up of Ukraine. Leonid Kuchma, the victor who advocated closer ties with Moscow, won almost unanimous support in the southern and eastern parts of Ukraine and in Crimea, where Russian-speakers are in the majority. Leonid Kravchuk, the defeated incumbent (nationalist), won a similarly crushing victory in the

west and central regions of Ukraine where Ukrainian national consciousness is greatest. Kazakhs form the majority in the south of Kazakhstan; Russians dominate in the north where talk of secession is growing. Ethnic Russians are quitting Alma-Ata and other cities of the south to return to Russia, leaving their compatriots in the north increasingly uneasy and militant. None of the other former Soviet republics of Central Asia has such a large ethnic Russian minority as Kazakhstan, but in all of them that minority is diminishing because of emigration to Russia. Even in Turkmenistan and Uzbekistan, which have the closest relationships with Moscow, the ethnic Russian population is decreasing.

Nowhere did the Russian retreat seem so striking as in the Caucasus. The Azeri-Armenian conflict over Nagorno-Karabakh, the secessionist war of the Abkhazians against the Georgian authorities and the growth of nationalism among various Islamic minorities within Russia itself reduced Russia's influence and interest in the region. The troubled Chechenya republic declared itself independent, claiming to have seceded from the Russian Federation, and Russia did not persevere with its attempts to reclaim the rogue state. But Russia's retreat was more apparent than real. Moscow has tried to broker peace between Armenia and Azerbaijan, and has forced Georgia to join the CIS as its price for containing the Abkhazian conflict. The Caucasus is still very much a Russian sphere of influence.

The CIS itself has withered. It is no longer a monetary union and, with the growth of independent forces in the other former Union republics, it has less significance as a military pact. Russia's influence over the 'near abroad' is growing in other ways, in particular with agreements with individual republics, for example a defence pact with Tajikistan and a monetary agreement with Belarus.

The CIS has not proved to be a means for Russia to maintain its influence over the now independent states of the former Soviet Union. However, after an initial period of rejection of all things Russian in the former Union republics, Moscow's influence over its former empire is increasing as economic and geopolitical realities dictate. This influence is strongest in Ukraine and Belarus, which many Russians view as junior partners in a Slavic Orthodox family.

Regional Organizations of the Countries of the Commonwealth of Independent States

BLACK SEA ECONOMIC CO-OPERATION ZONE

Founded in 1992, the Black Sea Economic Zone aims to promote trade and economic co-operation between members and to control pollution of the Black Sea.

Membership: Armenia, Azerbaijan, Bulgaria, Georgia, Moldova, Romania, Russia, Turkey, and Ukraine.

COMMONWEALTH OF INDEPENDENT STATES (CIS)

The CIS is sometimes, quite erroneously, described in the popular press as if it were a country. The CIS is merely a regional organization of independent countries, in much the same way that the EU, NATO, and the OAS are international organizations. Following the dissolution of the Soviet Union in December 1991, representatives of Belarus, the Russian Federation and Ukraine met at Minsk, Belarus, to conclude an agreement to found an organization that is, in some respects, the successor to the USSR in economic, military and political co-ordination. Membership was declared open to other former Soviet republics, and to similar states that had not formed part of the USSR. Eight further states joined the CIS at a meeting at Alma-Ata, Kazakhstan.

The principal objective of the CIS is to provide for unitary control of strategic armed forces, including nuclear weapons, that formerly belonged to the USSR. The CIS aims to create a 'single economic space', but this objective has been largely abandoned as individual members have adopted their own economic policies and agreements as well as their own currencies. Only Russia and Tajikistan have a common currency, although Belarus is also scheduled to readopt the rouble. CIS peace-keeping forces have been in operation in Moldova, Azerbaijan and Tajikistan.

In January 1993, some members of the CIS signed a defence alliance and established an economic co-ordination committee and a Commonwealth bank.

There are few institutions of the CIS: the affairs of the organization are dealt with on a direct inter-state basis rather than by central institutions.

Headquarters: Minsk, Belarus.

Membership: Armenia, Azerbaijan, Belarus, Georgia, Kazakhstan, Kyrgyzstan, Russia, Tajikistan, Turkmenistan, Moldova, Ukraine, and Uzbekistan.

Membership of the CIS defence alliance and economic co-ordination committee: Armenia, Belarus, Kazakhstan, Kyrgyzstan, Russia, Tajikistan, and Uzbekistan.

ECONOMIC CO-OPERATION ORGANIZATION (ECO)

The Economic Co-operation Organization was founded in 1965 to promote trade in southwest Asia. The organization lapsed but was revived and expanded in 1992 to aid the development of Central Asia.

Membership: Azerbaijan, Iran, Kyrgyzstan, Pakistan, Tajikistan, Turkmenistan, Turkey, and Uzbekistan.

OTHER ORGANIZATIONS

The following countries of the CIS are members of the CSCE: Armenia, Azerbaijan, Belarus, Georgia, Kazakhstan, Kyrgyzstan, Moldova, Russia, Tajikistan, Turkmenistan, Ukraine, and Uzbekistan.

Some CIS countries are also members of NATO's Partnership for Peace (see pp. 350-51).

CIS Trade

Armenia Imports ($ million): n/a. Exports ($ million): n/a. Main imports: food products; coal and natural gas. Main exports: processed food, chemicals. Principal trading partners: Georgia, Russia.

Azerbaijan Imports (roubles million): 8836 (1991 est). Exports (roubles million): 11,456. Main imports: industrial products, food and live animals. Main exports: petroleum and petroleum products. Principal trading partners: Russia, Georgia.

Belarus Imports ($ million): n/a. Exports ($ million): n/a. Main imports: food-processing and consumer goods 21.4% (1990), machine building and metal work 35% (1990). Main exports: vehicles, machines and other metal workings 46% (1990), consumer goods 17.8% (1990). Principal trading partners: Russia, Ukraine, Germany.

Georgia Imports (roubles million): 6839 (1990). Exports (roubles million): 5983 (1990). Main imports: industry chemical fuel 8.4% (1990), agriculture 7.2% (1990). Main exports: food 39.8% (1990), light industry 21% (1990). Principal trading partners: Russia, Azerbaijan.

Kazakhstan Imports ($ million): n/a. Exports ($ million): n/a. Main imports: food and live animals. Main exports: natural gas, food and live animals. Principal trading partners: Russia, Uzbekistan.

Kyrgyzstan Imports ($ million): 443 (1991). Exports ($ million): 20 (1991). Main imports: food and agriculture products. Main exports: industrial products 65% (1991). Principal trading partners: Russia, Kazakhstan.

Moldova Imports (roubles million): 6461.4 (1990). Exports (roubles million): 6176.7 (1990). Main imports: industrial products 91.6% (1990). Main exports: food and agricultural products 41.5% (1990). Principal trading partners: Ukraine, Romania.

Russia Imports (roubles million): 75,280 (1990). Exports (roubles million): 106,795 (1990). Main imports: light industry 20.4% (1990), food industry 16.7% (1990). Main exports: machine building industry 34.9% (1990), petroleum and natural gas 14.6% (1990). Principal trading partners: Germany, Ukraine, Kazakhstan, Poland, Bulgaria.

Tajikistan Imports (roubles million): 3,359 (1990). Exports (roubles million): 2,377 (1990). Main imports: machine building 27% (1990), light industry 25.4% (1990). Main exports: light industry 44.1% (1990), non-ferrous metallurgy 17.3% (1990). Principal trading partners: Uzbekistan, Russia.

Turkmenistan Imports ($ million): n/a. Exports ($ million): n/a. Main imports: food and food products. Main exports: natural gas, food products. Main trading partners: Russia, Uzbekistan, Iran.

Ukraine Imports (roubles million): 38,989 (1990). Exports (roubles million): 38,319 (1990). Main imports: machine building 48% (1990), light industry 24.9% (1990). Main exports: machine building 46.6% (1990), iron and steel 19.8% (1990). Main trading partners: Russia, Poland, Germany, Iran.

Uzbekistan Imports (roubles million): 14,662 (1990). Exports (roubles million): 9351 (1990). Main imports: machine building 24.7% (1990), light industry 20.2% (1990). Main exports: light industry 45.3% (1990), food and agricultural products 13.5% (1990). Principal trading partners: Russia, Kazakhstan, Turkmenistan.

Armenia

Official name: Hayastani Hanrapeut'yun (Republic of Armenia).

Member of: UN, CIS, CSCE.

Area: 29,800 km² (11,500 sq mi).

Population: 3,550,000 (1993 est).

Capital: Yerevan 1,283,000 (1991 est).

Other major city: Kumayri (Gyumri; formerly Leninakan) 163,000 (1991 est).

Languages: Armenian (official; 93%), Azeri (3%), Kurdish (2%).

Religion: Armenian Apostolic (Orthodox) majority, Sunni Islam (minority).

Education: Education is compulsory between the ages of six and 15. There are no available figures regarding the literacy rate. There is a university and a polytechnic.

Defence: In 1993 the total armed strength was 20,000. Military service lasts for two years.

Transport: There are 7700 km (4785 mi) of roads and 823 km (511 mi) of railways. Yerevan has an international airport and a metro.

Media: There are three daily papers and a state-run radio and television service.

GOVERNMENT
A 185-member State Council and a President are elected by universal adult suffrage for four years. Political parties include the Pan-Armenian National Movement (HHSh), the Armenian National Movement, the (ultra-nationalist) Union for National Self-Determination (NUSD), National Unity (NU) and the Armenian Revolutionary Federation (ARF). The government is supported by HHSh (the majority party), NUSD and ARF.

President: Levon Ter-Petrosyan (HHSh).

Prime Minister: Hrand Bagratyan (HHSh).

GEOGRAPHY
All of Armenia is mountainous - only 10% of the country is under 1000 m (3300 ft). Highest point: Mt Aragats 4090 m (13,418 ft). Principal rivers: Araks, Zanga. Climate Armenia has a dry continental climate with considerable local variations owing to altitude and aspect.

ECONOMY
The industrial sector includes chemicals, metallurgy, textiles, precision goods and food processing. Major projects have provided hydro-electric power and irrigation water for farming. Privatization has begun, but the war against Azerbaijan has devastated the economy and resulted in an energy shortage.

Currency: Dram; which is not yet quoted.

GDP: US$7,349,000,000 (1992); US$2150 per head. The GDP has since declined drastically.

RECENT HISTORY
Russia took east Armenia between 1813 and 1828. The west Armenians under Turkish rule suffered persecution and, in 1896 and 1915, large-scale massacres. During World War I Turkey deported nearly 2,000,000 Armenians (suspected of pro-Russian sympathies) to Syria and Mesopotamia. The survivors contributed to an Armenian diaspora in Europe and the USA. Following the collapse of Tsarist Russia, an independent Armenian state emerged briefly (1918-22). Armenia was annexed by the USSR in 1922. After the abortive coup by Communist hardliners in Moscow (September 1991), Armenia declared independence and received international recognition when the USSR was dissolved (December 1991). Since 1990 Azeri and Armenian forces have been involved in a violent dispute concerning the status of Nagorno Karabakh, an enclave of Orthodox Christian Armenians surrounded by Muslim Azeris. By early 1994 Armenia had overrun 20% of Azerbaijan. Russia is promoting a ceasefire.

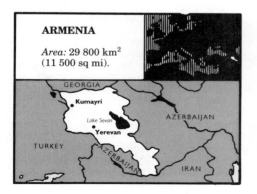

ARMENIA

Area: 29 800 km² (11 500 sq mi).

GEORGIA

Kumayri

Lake Sevan

AZERBAIJAN

Yerevan

TURKEY

IRAN

Azerbaijan

Official name: Azarbayjan Respublikasy (Azerbaijani Republic).

Member of: UN, CSCE, CIS, NATO (partner for peace).

Area: 86,600 km² (33,400 sq mi).

Population: 7,283,000 (1993 est).

Capital: Baku 1,757,000 (1989 census).

Other major cities: Gyanzha (Gäncä; formerly Kirovabad) 270,000, Sumgait (Sumqayit) 234,000 (1989 census).

Languages: Azeri (official; 83%), Russian (6%), Armenian (2%).

Religion: Shia Islam majority, Orthodox Christian minorities.

Education: Education is compulsory between the ages of six and 15. There is no recent figure for the literacy rate. There are two universities.

Defence: In 1994 estimates of the total armed strength were from 30,000 upwards. Military service lasts two years.

Transport: There are 36,700 km (22,800 mi) of roads and 2090 km (1299 mi) of railways. Baku, which is a port on the Caspian Sea, has a metro and an international airport.

Media: There are several daily newspapers. There is a single state-run radio and television service.

GOVERNMENT
A President and a 350-member Parliament (Milli Majlis) are elected by universal adult suffrage for four years. Party politics parties include New Azerbaijan (YA), the Popular Front of Azerbaijan (KJ), the Party for National Independence (Istiklal), the Social Democratic Party (SDP), and the National Front (MJ). The YA forms the government.

President: Geidar Aliyev (YA).

Prime Minister: Col. Surat Guseynov.

GEOGRAPHY
Azerbaijan comprises lowlands beside the Caspian Sea, part of the Caucasus Mountains in the north and the Little Caucasus in the south. Azerbaijan includes the Nakhichevan enclave to the west of Armenia. Highest point: Bazar-Dyuzi 4480 m (14,694 ft). Principal rivers: Kura, Araks. Climate: A wide climatic range includes dry and humid subtropical conditions beside the Caspian Sea and continental conditions in the mountains.

ECONOMY
Important reserves of oil and natural gas are the mainstay of the economy and the basis of heavy industries. Agricultural exports include cotton and tobacco. Sturgeon are caught in the Caspian Sea for the important caviar industry. The war with Armenia has damaged the economy and Azerbaijan suffers a very high rate of inflation.

Currency: Manat, which is not fully convertible.

GDP: US$6,290,000,000 (1992); US$870 per head.

RECENT HISTORY
Russia conquered the region early in the 19th century. During World War I, an independent Azeri state was founded with Turkish assistance (1918), but was invaded by the Soviet Red Army in 1920. Azerbaijan became part of the USSR in 1922. Independence was declared after the abortive coup in Moscow by Communist hardliners (September 1991) and was internationally recognized when the USSR collapsed (December 1991). Since 1990 Azeri and Armenian forces have fought over Nagorno Karabakh, an enclave of Orthodox Christian Armenians surrounded by the Shiite Muslim Azeris. By 1993 Armenian forces occupied 20% of Azerbaijan - this disastrous defeat led to the coup by Col. Guseynov and Geidar Aliyev.

AZERBAIJAN

Area: 86 600 km² (33 400 sq mi).

GEORGIA

RUSSIA

CASPIAN SEA

ARMENIA

Gyandzha

Kura

Baku

TURKEY

Nakhichevan

IRAN

Belarus (Byelorussia)

Official name: Respublika Belarus. Formerly known as Byelorussia. (There seems to be little agreement upon the English language transliteration of the name of the republic. Belarus, Bielarus, Bielorussia and Byelorussia are all used. However, the government in Minsk, the United Nations and HM Foreign and Commonwealth Office in London all favour Belarus as the correct English language version of the name of the country.)

Member of: UN, CIS, CSCE.

Area: 207,546 km² (80,134 sq mi).

Population: 10,353,000 (1993 est).

Capital: Minsk (Mensk) 1,643,000 (including suburbs; 1991 est).

Other major cities: Gomel (Homel) 503,000, Vitebsk (Vitsyebsk) 369,000, Mogilev (Mahilyou) 363,000, Grodno (Hrodno) 285,000, Brest 269,000, Bobruysk (Bobrujsk) 223,000 (1991 est).

Languages: Belarussian (also known as Belorussian) (80%), Russian (13%), Polish (4%), with small Ukrainian, Lithuanian and other minorities.

Religions: Belarussian Orthodox majority, Roman Catholic (5%). (The Belarussian Orthodox Church gained independence within the Russian Orthodox Church in 1990.)

Education: Education is compulsory between the ages of seven and 17. In 1990 the literacy rate was estimated to be over 98%. There are three universities and four polytechnics.

Defence: In 1993 the total strength of the armed forces was 103,000 (which is to be reduced to 90,000) - 89,000 in the army and 14,000 in the air force. Compulsory military service lasts for 18 months. The last Russian troops are scheduled to be withdrawn from Belarus by 1999. At independence, there were 54 former-Soviet nuclear warheads based on Belarussian soil. These are now under the control of the CIS and are unable to be used unilaterally.

Transport: There are over 265,600 km (166,000 mi) of roads in Belarus. There are 5590 km (3494 mi) of rail track. Minsk has a metro and an international airport.

Media: There are 12 principal (state-owned) daily newspapers and over 190 regional and local papers that appear daily or more than once a week. There is a single (state-owned) radio and television network.

GOVERNMENT
Under new constitutional arrangements a 160-member Assembly (Sejm) and a President - who will appoint a Chairman (Prime Minister) and a Council of Ministers - is elected by universal adult suffrage for four years. The current legislature is the Supreme Soviet which was elected in March 1990. The principal political groupings are the former Communists (Comm), the (former Communist) Belarus for Democracy group (BFD) and the Belarussian Popular Front (BPF). A number of smaller political parties and groups are active. After the breakaway from the former Communists of the Belarus for Democracy group in 1991, the Assembly elected in March 1990 is as follows.

Party strength: Comm 300, BFD 33, BPF 27.

President: Alexander Lukashenko.

THE CABINET
A new government was about to be appointed as this book went to press.

GEOGRAPHY
Belarus - formerly spelt Byelorussia (meaning White Russia) - comprises lowlands covered with glacial debris in the north, fertile well-drained tablelands and ridges in the centre, and the low-lying Pripet Marshes in the south and east. Much of the country is flat. Forests cover large stretches of Belarus, in particular in the west. Highest point: Dzyarzhynskaya Mountain 346 m (1135 ft). Principal rivers: Dnepr, Pripyat, Dvina, Neman. Climate: The continental climate is moderated by the proximity of the Baltic Sea. Belarussian winters are considerably milder than those in European Russia to the east.

ECONOMY
Although Belarus has few natural resources, its economy is overwhelmingly industrial. Major heavy engineering, chemical, fertilizer, oil refining and synthetic fibre industries were established as part of the centrally-planned

Soviet economy, but output has declined since 1991. Belarus is dependent upon trade with other former Soviet republics from which it imports the raw materials for its industries and upon which it relies as a market for its industrial goods. Problems in maintaining supplies from other former Soviet republics, high rates of inflation and severe cuts in demand for military equipment (which was formerly a major industry) have contributed to the country's severe economic problems. However, the first steps towards establishing a market economy have been made. Contamination from the Chernobyl accident (see below) affected about 20% of Belarus, causing areas to be sealed off and necessitating the eventual resettlement of up to 2,000,000 people. As well as incurring enormous economic costs in clearing-up operations, resettling, health care, etc., the Chernobyl disaster has also had a profound effect upon farming in the new republic. The disaster has reduced the acreage available to Belarussian agriculture and expenditure to repair the damage caused by Chernobyl represents over 10% of the Belarussian budget. Agriculture is dominated by raising fodder crops for beef cattle, pigs and poultry. Flax is grown for export and the local linen industry. Extensive forests supply important woodworking and paper industries. In 1992 Belarus introduced a new currency, the Belarussian rubel (which unofficially became known as the zaichik). The Belarussian rubel rapidly lost its value and is to be replaced.

Belarus is within the Rouble Zone and has, consequently, been hit by high rates of inflation. In 1994, therefore, Belarus concluded an agreement with Moscow by which the Belarussian rubel is to be abandoned and the Russian rouble is to be reintroduced.

Belarussian economic policy will thus become subject to the decisions of the Russian government and the Russian central bank. Critics maintain that this will effectively relegate Belarus to the status of a Russian economic province.

Currency: Belarussian rubel (or zaichik) of 100 kopecks; the Belarussian rubel is not quoted on the international currency market. (The rubel is to be replaced by the reintroduced Russian rouble - see above.)

GDP: US$30,200,000,000 (1992); US$920 per head. (The Belarussian GDP has since decreased sharply.)

RECENT HISTORY

The Belarussians came under Russian rule as a result of the three partitions of Poland (1772, 1793 and 1795). The region suffered some of the fiercest fighting between Russia and Germany during World War I. Following the Russian Revolution, a Byelorussian Soviet republic was proclaimed (1919). The republic was invaded by the Poles in the same year and divided between Poland and the Soviet Union in 1921. Byelorussia was devastated during World War II. In 1945 the Belarussians were reunited in a single Soviet republic. A perceived lack of Soviet concern for the republic at the time of the accident at the Chernobyl nuclear power station (just over the Ukrainian border; see also above) strengthened a reawakening Belarussian national identity. Byelorussia declared independence following the abortive coup by Communist hardliners in Moscow (September 1991) and - as Belarus (pronounced 'By-ella-roose') - received international recognition when the USSR was dissolved (December 1991). In 1993-94 Belarus negotiated a close economic and monetary link with Russia. This arrangement - which could result in the virtual end of Belarussian economic independence - has been criticized by many nationalists as likely to return the country to Russian domination. In the first Belarussian presidential elections in July 1994 a populist outspoken critic of corruption, Alexander Lukashenko, defeated the conservative prime minister, Vyacheslav Kebich. President Lukashenko has advocated a return to Soviet-style economics and the formation of a Slavic 'brotherhood' of Belarus, Russia and Ukraine. A closer relationship with Russia seems to be certain for Belarus.

BELARUS

Area: 207 600 km^2
(80 200 sq mi).

LITHUANIA
RUSSIA
Vitebsk
RUSSIA
Minsk
POLAND
Mogilev
Brest
Gomel
UKRAINE

Georgia

Official name: Sakartvelos Respublica (The Republic of Georgia).

Member of: UN, CSCE, CIS.

Area: 69,700 km² (26,900 sq mi).

Population: 5,493,000 (1993 est).

Capital: Tbilisi 1,283,000 (1991 est).

Other major cities: Kutaisi 238,000, Rustavi 162,000, Batumi 138,000 (1991 est).

Languages: Georgian (70%), Armenian (8%), Russian (6%), Azeri (3%), Ossetian (2%), Greek (2%), Abkhazian (2%).

Religions: Georgian Orthodox majority.

Education: Education is compulsory between the ages of seven and 17. There is no recent figure for the literacy rate. There are three universities and a polytechnic.

Defence: In 1993 the total armed strength was 20,000. Military service lasts two years.

Transport: There are 33,900 km (21,000 mi) of roads and 1570 km (976 mi) of railways. Tbilisi, has a metro and an international airport. Batumi is the main commercial shipping port.

Media: There are several daily papers and a single state-run radio and television service.

GOVERNMENT

The constitution provides for the election for four years by universal adult suffrage of a 234-member legislature and a President, who appoints a Council of Ministers. In 1993 the legislature dissolved itself, having granted emergency powers to the President. Political parties include the Citizen's Union of Georgia (CUG), (coalition nationalist) Round Table-Free Georgia, Mshvidoba (Peace), the National Independence Party and the Georgian Popular Front.

President: Eduard Shevardnadze (CUG).

Prime Minister: Otar Patsatsia (CUG).

GEOGRAPHY

The spine of the Caucasus Mountains forms the northern border of Georgia. A lower range, Little Caucasus, occupies the south. Central Georgia comprises the Kolkhida lowlands. Highest point: Elbrus (on the Russian border)

GEORGIA

Area: 69 700 km² (26 900 sq mi).

5642 m (18,510 ft). Principal rivers: Kura, Rioni. Climate: Coastal and central Georgia has a moist Mediterranean climate. The rest of the country is drier but the climate varies considerably with altitude and aspect.

ECONOMY

Despite a shortage of cultivable land, Georgia has a diversified agricultural sector including tea, citrus fruit, tobacco, cereals, vines, livestock and vegetables. Machine building, food processing and chemicals are major industries. The economy was damaged by civil war (1991-92).

Currency: Georgan coupon, which is not yet convertible.

GDP: US$4,670,000,000 (1992); US$850 per head.

RECENT HISTORY

Russia annexed Georgia by degrees early in the 19th century. Following the Russian Revolution (1918), a Georgian republic briefly existed but it was invaded by the Soviet Red Army (1921). Georgia became part of the USSR in 1922. Following the abortive coup by Communist hardliners in Moscow (September 1991), Georgia declared independence. Locked into a fierce civil war, Georgia remained outside the CIS until 1993 when the republic was obliged to join as a price for military support in Abkhazia. A state council - led by Eduard Shevardnadze, the former Soviet Foreign Minister - replaced a military council in 1992. War erupted in the north when Abkhazian Muslims attempted secession in 1992. A Russian-brokered ceasefire came into force in 1994.

213

Kazakhstan

Official name: Qazaqstan Respublikasi (The Republic of Kazakhstan).

Member of: UN, CSCE, CIS.

Area: 2,717,300 km² (1,049,200 sq mi).

Population: 17,186,000 (1993 est).

Capital: Alma-Ata (Almaty) 1,156,000 (1991 est).

Other major cities: Karaganda (Qaraghandy) 609,000, Chimkent (Shymkent) 439,000, Semipalatinsk (Semey) 345,000, Pavlodar 343,000 (1991 est).

Languages: Kazakh (40%), Russian (38%), German (6%), Ukrainian (5%), Uzbek (2%).

Religions: Sunni Islam majority, Russian Orthodox minority, various Protestant Churches.

Education: Education is compulsory between the ages of seven and 17. There are no recent figures for the literacy rate. There are three universities and two polytechnics of university status.

Defence: In 1993 the total armed strength was 44,000 - army and air force. CIS (mainly Russian) forces are also based on Kazakh soil.

Transport: There are 164,900 km (102,464 mi) of roads and 21,200 km (13,173 km) of state-run railways. The large rivers in the north of the country are important inland waterways. Alma-Ata has an international airport.

Media: There are seven principal daily newspapers. There is a single state-run radio and television service; a private radio station was closed early in 1994.

GOVERNMENT
An executive President and 135 members of the 177-member Parliament (Kenges) are elected for four years by universal adult suffrage. The Kenges comprises 135 directly-elected members representing single-member constituencies (see above) and 42 members elected from a 'state list' by national and regional government officials (who are government appointees). The President appoints a Prime Minister and a Cabinet of Ministers. For local government purposes, there are 19 provinces. The main political parties are the Congress of People's Unity of Kazakhstan (SNEK), the (SNEK ally) Trades Union Federation (TUF), the (progressive coalition) People's Congress of Kazakhstan (NKK), the Socialist Party (SP), the Peasants' Union (PU), and the (mainly ethnic Slav) Lad (Harmony) movement. Following the election held in March 1994 a government of SNEK members and independents allied to SNEK was formed.

Party strength: SNEK 30, mainly SNEK appointees 42, SNEK-allied independents 59, TUF11, NKK 9, SP 8, PU 4, Lad 4.

President: Nursultan Nazarbayev (SNEK).

THE CABINET
includes

Prime Minister: Sergei Tereshchenko.

First Deputy Prime Minister: Kazhageldin Akezhan Magzhan.

Deputy Prime Minister and Minister for Science and Technology: Galym Abilsiitov.

Deputy Prime Minister and Minister for Foreign Economic Relations: Sydyk Abishev.

Deputy Prime Minister: Tulegen Zhukeyev.

Deputy Prime Minister: Asygat Zhabagin.

Deputy Prime Minister: Zhanibek Haribzhanov.

Deputy Prime Minister: Sergey Kulagin.

Minister of Agriculture: Baltash Moldabayevich Tursumbayev.

Minister of Defence: Col-Gen. Sagadat Nurmabagambetov.

Minister of the Economy: Beysenbay Izteleuov.

Minister of Foreign Affairs: Kanat Saudabayev.

Minister of the Interior: Vladimir Shumov.

Minister of Justice: Nagashibay Amangaliyevich Shaykenov.

Minister for the National Bank: Daulet Sembayen.

GEOGRAPHY
Kazakhstan comprises a vast expanse of low tablelands (steppes) in the middle of Central Asia. In the west, plains descend below sea level beside the Caspian Sea. Uplands include ranges of hills in the north and mountain chains, including the Tien Shan, in the south

214

and east. Kazakhstan has several salt lakes, including the Aral Sea, which is shrinking because of excessive extraction of irrigation water from its tributaries. Deserts include the Kyzylkum in the south, the Kara Kum in the centre, and the Barsuki in the north. Highest point: Khan Tengri 6398 m (20,991 ft). Principal rivers: Syrdarya, Irtysh, Chu, Illi, Tobol, Ural, Ishim, Emba. Climate: The Kazkah climate is characterized by bitterly cold winters and hot summers. Rainfall is low, ranging between 200 mm (8 in) in the north to 500 mm (20 in) or more in the southeast, and precipitation is negligible in the deserts.

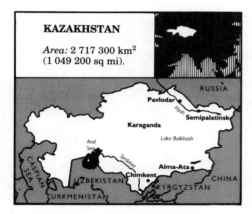

KAZAKHSTAN

Area: 2 717 300 km²
(1 049 200 sq mi).

ECONOMY
Kazakhstan is a major supplier of food and raw materials for industry to other former Soviet republics, particularly Russia. The transition to a market economy was not embarked upon in earnest until 1994 when a mass privatization campaign began. It is hoped that by mid-1995 up to 30% of the economy will have been privatized. Agriculture employs almost one half of the labour force. Large collective farms on the steppes in the north contributed one third of the cereal crop of the former USSR. Other major farming interests include sheep, fodder crops, fruit, vegetables and rice. Kazakhstan is rich in natural resources including coal, tin, copper, lead, zinc, gold, chromite, oil and nickel. Industry is represented by iron and steel (in the Karaganda coalfield), pharmaceuticals, food processing and cement. Kazakhstan has campaigned actively to attract Western (mainly US and German) investment, and has succeeeded in gaining funds for the exploitation of

the country's very considerable oil and natural gas resources. Kazakhstan had hoped to remain within the Russian rouble zone, but an assertive Russian monetary policy forced the Kazakh government to withdraw.

Currency: Tenge; 1US\$ = 8.96 tenge (January 1994) - the tenge is not yet fully convertible on the international money market.

GDP: US\$34,200,000,000 (1993 est); US\$2000 per head.

RECENT HISTORY
Russia completed conquest of the Kazakh lands in 1822 and 1848. During the Tsarist period there was large-scale Russian peasant settlement on the steppes, but Russian rule was resented and there was a major Kazakh revolt during World War I. After the Russian revolution, Kazakh nationalists formed a local government and demanded autonomy (1917). The Soviet Red Army invaded in 1920 and established an Autonomous Soviet Republic. Kazakhstan did not become a full Union Republic within the USSR until 1936. Widespread immigration from other parts of the USSR became a flood in 1954-56 when the 'Virgin Lands' of north Kazakhstan were opened up for farming. By the time Kazakhstan declared independence - following the abortive coup by Communist hardliners in Moscow (September 1991) - the Kazakhs formed a minority within their own republic. When the USSR was dissolved (December 1991), Kazakhstan was internationally recognized as an independent republic. The vast new Kazakh state - in theory, a nuclear power because of former Soviet nuclear weapons on its territory - occupies a pivotal position within Central Asia, but co-operation between the Central Asian states has been limited as the republics see one another as rivals, producing similar commodities for export. President Nursultan Nazarbayev has been a leading advocate of closer association with other former Soviet republics, particularly Russia, within the CIS. In 1994 the first multi-party elections were held in Kazakhstan but these were criticized by international observers who cited irregularities. The elections - which returned 105 ethnic Kazakhs to the 177-member legislature - marked a further step in advancing the interests and power of ethnic Kazakhs. However, there is some tension in northern Kazakhstan where separatist sentiments are growing among ethnic Russians, who form a majority in that part of the country.

215

Kyrgyzstan

Official name: Kyrgyzstan Respublikasy (Republic of Kyrgyzstan). Formerly known as Kirghizia.

Member of: UN, CSCE, CIS.

Area: 198,500 km² (76,600 sq mi).

Population: 4,422,000 (1991 est).

Capital: Bishkek (formerly Frunze) 642,000 (1991 est).

Other major cities: Osh 219 000, Dzhalal-Abad 74,000, Tokmak 71,000 (1991 est).

Languages: Kyrgyz (53%), Russian (21%), Uzbek (13%), Ukrainian (3%), German (2%).

Religions: Sunni Islam majority, Russian Orthodox minority.

Education: Education is compulsory between the ages of six and 17. There are no figures available concerning the literacy rate. There are two universities and a polytechnic.

Defence: In 1993 the total armed strength was 12,000. There is no military service. CIS (mainly Russian) forces are also based in Kyrgyzstan.

Transport: There are 19,100 km (11,900 mi) of roads and 789 km (490 mi) of state-run railways. Bishkek has an international airport.

Media: There are four daily newspapers, a single state-run radio and television service.

GOVERNMENT
Under a new constitution, a 350-member legislature (the Uluk Kenesh) and a President are elected for five years by universal adult suffrage. The President appoints a Prime Minister and a Council of Ministers. For local government purposes there are seven provinces. The main political parties are the Kyrgyzstan Democratic Movement, the Communist Party, and the Kyrgyz Social Democratic Party. Elections under the new constitution are scheduled - the existing legislature has a majority of nationalist and Communist members.

President: Askar Akayev.

Prime Minister: Apas Jumagulov.

GEOGRAPHY
Most of Kyrgyzstan lies within the Tien Shan mountains. Restricted lowlands - including the Chu valley and part of the Fergana valley - contain most of the population. Highest point: Pik Pobedy 7439 m (24,406 ft). Principal rivers: Sarydzhaz, Naryn, Kyzylsu. Climate: The country's altitude and position deep within the interior of Asia combine to produce an extreme continental climate. Precipitation is low in many areas.

ECONOMY
Agriculture is dominated by large collectivized farms that specialize in growing fodder crops for sheep and goats, and cotton under irrigation. Natural resources include coal, lead, zinc and considerable hydroelectric-power potential. Food processing and light industry are expanding. The privatization of the economy has begun. However, economic problems include a lack of investment, high inflation and a 'brain drain' of qualified Russians.

Currency: Som of 100 cents; 1US$ = 5.80 som (Jan 1994).

GDP: US$3,653,000,000 (1992); US$826 per head.

RECENT HISTORY
The Kyrgyz - a Turkic people - retained their independence until after 1850 when the area was annexed by Russia. Opposition to the Russians - who were given most of the best land - found expression in a major revolt in 1916 and continuing guerrilla activity after the Russian Revolution. A Kirghiz Soviet Republic was founded in 1926 and became a full Union Republic within the USSR in 1936. After the abortive coup by Communist hardliners (September 1991), Kirghizia declared independence and - under its new name, Kyrgyzstan - received international recognition when the Soviet Union was dissolved (December 1991).

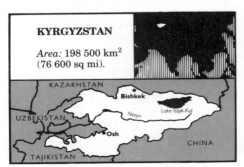

KYRGYZSTAN

Area: 198 500 km²
(76 600 sq mi).

KAZAKHSTAN

Bishkek

Naryn

Lake Issyk-Kul

UZBEKISTAN

Osh

CHINA

TAJIKISTAN

Moldova

Official name: Republica Moldoveneasca (Republic of Moldova).

Member of: UN, CIS, CSCE, NATO (partner for peace).

Area: 33,702 km² (13,012 sq mi).

Population: 4,373,000 (1991 est).

Capital: Chisinau (formerly Kishinev) 754,000 (city 676,000) (1991 est).

Other major city: Tiraspol 186,000 (1991 est).

Languages: Moldovan (Romanian; 67%), Ukrainian (13%), Russian (13%), Gagauz (4%).

Religions: Orthodox majority - both Russian Orthodox and Romanian Orthodox Churches.

Education: Education is compulsory between the ages on seven and 17. In 1990 the literacy rate was 95%. There is a university.

Defence: The total armed strength is 14,000 (1993). There are Russian troops in Trans-Dnestr.

Transport: There are over 20,300 km (12,616 mi) of road and 1150 km (715 mi) of railways. Chisinau has an international airport.

Media: There are four daily newspapers and a state-owned radio and television network.

GOVERNMENT
A President and a 104-member Parliament are elected for four years by universal adult suffrage. The President appoints a PM and a Council of Ministers. Political parties include the (nationalist centrist) Agrarian Democratic Party (ADP), the (former Communist) Socialist Party (SP), the (pro-Russian) Yedinstvo (Unity) Party, the (pro-Romanian) Peasants and Intellectuals Bloc (PI) and the (pro-Romanian) Christian Democratic People's Front (CDPF). After the election held in 1994 a mainly ADP government was formed.

Party strength: ADP 56, SP-Unity and allies 28, PI 11, CDPF9.

President: Mircea Snegur.

Prime Minister: Andrei Sangheli.

GEOGRAPHY
Central hills separate northern and southern plains between the River Prut and the Dnestr valley. Highest point: Balaneshty 430 m (1409 ft). Principal rivers: Dnestr, Prut. Climate: Moldova is mild and slightly continental.

ECONOMY
Large collective farms produce fruit (particularly grapes), vegetables, cereals and tobacco. Industries include food processing, machine building, and footwear and clothing. Little progress has been made to privatize farming or industry. The collapse of the Soviet trade system (1991) and civil war in Trans-Dnestr have damaged the economy.

Currency: Moldovan leu of 100 bani; the leu is not yet fully convertible.

GDP: US$5,493,000,000 (1992); US$1260 per head.

RECENT HISTORY
Known as Bessarabia, the area declared independence from Russia in 1917 but became part of Romania in 1918. When Romania entered World War II as a German ally, the USSR reoccupied Bessarabia, which became the Moldavian Soviet Republic (1944). Following the abortive coup by Communist hardliners in Moscow (September 1991), Moldavia declared independence and, as Moldova, received international recognition when the USSR was dissolved (December 1991). Conflict broke out in 1992 when Russian and Ukrainian minorities, fearing a reunion of Moldova with Romania, proclaimed the republic of Trans-Dnestr. The intervention of CIS (mainly Russian) forces brought an uneasy peace, but Moldovan authorities no longer control Trans-Dnestr. In 1994 a referendum in Moldova rejected union with Romania and pro-Romanian parties lost multi-party elections.

MOLDOVA

Area: 33 702 km² (13 012 sq mi).

UKRAINE

Chisinau

ROMANIA

Tiraspol

BLACK SEA

217

Russia

Official name: Rossiyskaya Federativnaya Respublika (Republic of the Russian Federation) or Rossiya (Russia).

Member of: UN, CIS, CSCE.

Area: 17,075,400 km² (6.592.800 sq mi).

Population: 148,000,000 (1993 est).

Capital: Moscow (Moskva) 8,967,000 (city 8,769,000; 1989 census).

Other major cities: St Petersburg (Sankt-Peterburg; formerly Leningrad) 5,020,000 (city 4,456,000), Nizhny Novgorod (formerly Gorky) 1,438,000, Novosibirsk 1,436,000, Yekaterinburg (formerly Sverdlovsk) 1,367,000, Samara (formerly Kuybyshev) 1,257,000, Omsk 1,148,000, Chelyabinsk 1,143,000, Kazan 1,094,000, Perm 1,091,000, Ufa 1,083,000, Rostov 1,020,000, Volgograd 999,000, Krasnoyarsk 912,000, Saratov 905,000, Voronezh 887,000, Vladivostok 648,000, Izhevsk (formerly Ustinov) 635,000, Yaroslavl 633,000, Tol'yatti 630,000, Irkutsk 626,000, Simbirsk (formerly Ulyanovsk) 625,000, Krasnodar 620,000, Barnaul 602,000, Khabarovsk 601,000, Novokuznetsk 600,000, Orenburg 547,000, Penza 543,000, Tula 540,000, Kemerovo 520,000, Ryazan 515,000, Astrakhan 509,000, Tomsk 502,000, Naberezhniye Chelny (formerly Brezhnev) 501,000, Lipetsk 499,000, Tyumen 494,000, Vyatka (formerly Kirov) 491,000, Ivanovo 482,000, Murmansk 473,000, Bryansk 459,000, Tver (formerly Kalinin) 455,000, Cheboksary 449,000, Magnitogorsk 446,000, Nizhny Tagil 439,000, Kursk 433,000, Arkhangelsk 428,000, Kaliningrad 408,000, Grozny 401,000, Chita 377,000, Vladimir 376,000, Kurgan 370,000, Kaluga 366,000, Ulan-Ude 362,000, Saransk 347,000, Oryol 345,000, Sochi 342,000, Tambov 334,000 (all including suburbs; 1989 est).

Languages: Russian (83%), Tatar (4%), Ukrainian (3%), Chuvash (1%), Bashkir (1%), Belarussian (1%), Chechen (1%). Over 0.5% of the population speak one of the following languages as a first language: Mordovian, German, Udmurt, Mari, Kazakh, Avar and Armenian. There are over 100 other languages spoken in Russia.

Religions: Orthodox (27%), with Sunni Muslim, Jewish, Baptist, Roman Catholic, the revived Russian 'Greek Catholic' (Uniat) Church, and other minorities.

Education: Education is compulsory between the ages of seven and 15. There are 42 universities, 32 polytechnics of university status and over 100 other institutes offering courses of degree level.

Defence: Russia has a total armed strength of 2,720,000 (some of whom are part of CIS joint forces) - 1,757,000 in the army, 318,000 in the navy and 300,000 in the air force. The Russian navy has 1730 vessels including submarines while the Russian air force has 3700 combat aircraft. In 1992 Russia had 2968 nuclear warheads. (The remainder of the former Soviet nuclear arsenal was divided between three republics - Ukraine 176 warheads, Belarus 54 warheads and Kazakhstan 104 warheads. However, these warheads are under joint CIS control and, in theory, cannot be used unilaterally.) All Russian males are subject to 18 months' military conscription.

Transport: Russia has 87,090 km (54,430 mi) of railways operating both passenger and freight services. Metro and/or rapid light transit systems operate in Moscow, St Petersburg, Nizhny Novgorod, Novosibirsk, Samara and Yekaterinburg. There are about 855,000 km (534,000 mi) of roads. The most important Russian ports include St Petersburg and Kaliningrad on the Baltic Sea, Murmansk on the Barents Sea, Novorossiysk and Sochi on the Black Sea, and Vladivostok, Magadan, Nakhodka and Petropavlovsk on the Pacific coast. Inland navigation is important on Russia's many major rivers. International air services only operate from a limited number of centres and are concentrated on Moscow and St Petersburg.

Media: The press in Russia is undergoing drastic restructuring. Some titles are now published intermittently and several new titles, including 'tabloids' have appeared. Nearly 4800 newspapers are published (most of them on a weekly basis) but there are only about one dozen major daily titles. Broadcasting is in the hands of the All-Russian State Television Radio Broadcasting Company, but there are now some commercial stations.

GOVERNMENT

Russia is a federation of 21 republics and 68 other regions which have similar powers under the terms of the new Russian constitution of 1993. (Chechenya has not ratified the new treaty between the republics and has unilaterally declared independence, but has not gained any international recognition of its claims.) An executive President - who appoints a Council of Ministers including a Prime Minister - is directly elected for a maximum of two five-year terms. The new Russian Parliament is the Federal Assembly whose two houses are elected for four years by universal adult suffrage. The lower house, the State Duma, comprises 450 members, 225 of whom are elected by single-member constituencies while the remaining 225 are elected from party lists on a system of proportional representation. The upper house, the Federal Council, comprises two members elected from each of the 21 republics and 68 other regions. Political parties include the (liberal reformist) Russia's Choice, the (liberal reformist) Party of Unity and Accord (Unity), the (liberal reformist) Yavlinsky-Boldyrev-Lukin bloc (Yabloko), the (liberal reformist) Russian Movement for Democratic Reforms, the (centrist) Democratic Party of Russia, the (centrist) Civic Union, the (centrist) Future of Russia-New Names Party, the (corporatist) Constructive Ecological Movement of Russia, the (corporatist) Women of Russia Movement, the (corporatist) Dignity and Charity Movement, the Communist Party (CP), the (communist and nationalist) Agrarian Party (AP), and the (ultra-nationalist) Liberal Democratic Party (LDP). The first multi-party elections were held in December 1993.

Party strength: Russia's Choice 94, LDP 78, CP 64, AP 55, Yabloko 28, Unity 22, others and ind 109.

President: Boris Yeltsin (elected 1991).

THE CABINET
Prime Minister: Viktor Chernomyrdin.

First Deputy Prime Minister: Oleg Soskovets.

Deputy Prime Minister: Aleksander Zaverukha.

Deputy Prime Minister and Chairman of the Committee for the Management of State Property: Anatoly Chubais.

Deputy Prime Minister and Minister for Economics: Aleksandr Shokhin.

Deputy Prime Minister: Yuri Yarov.

Minister of Agriculture and Foodstuffs: Viktor Khlystun.

Minister of Atomic Energy: Viktor Mikhailov.

Minister of Civil Defence and Emergency Situations: Sergei Shoygu.

Minister of Communications: Vladimir Bulgak.

Minister of Culture: Evgeni Sidorov.

Minister of Defence: Pavel Grachev.

Minister of Ecology and Natural Resources: Viktor Danilov-Danilyan.

Minister of Education: Evgeni Tkachenko.

Minister of External Economic Affairs: Oleg Davydov.

Minister of Finance: Sergei Dubinin.

Minister of Foreign Affairs: Andrei Kozyrev.

Minister of Fuel and Power Engineering: Yuri Shafranik.

Minister of Health: Eduard Nechaev.

Minister of Internal Affairs: Viktor Yerin.

Minister of Justice: Uriy Kalmikov.

Minister of Labour: Gennady Melikyan.

Minister of Nationalities and Regional Policy: Nikolai Egorov.

Minister for Railways: Gennady Fadeyev.

Minister of Science, Higher School and Technological Policies: Boris Saltykov.

Minister of Social Protection for the Population: Ludmilla Bezlepkina.

Minister of Transport: Vitaly Yefimov.

REPUBLICS OF THE RUSSIAN FEDERATION
Under the new Russian constitution, republics and other territories are divided into six different types of administrative unit: republics (which have the greatest amount of autonomy), regions (the main administrative divisions of Russia), autonomous regions (which have much the same functions as republics), autonomous cities and autonomous districts.

Adygea (formerly Adygei) Area: 7600 km² (2935 sq mi). Population: 442,000 (1992 est). Capital: Maikop.

Bashkortostan (formerly called Bashkiria).

Area: 143,600 km² (55,430 sq mi). Population: 4,008,000. Capital: Ufa.

Buryatia Area: 351,500 km² (135,630 sq mi). Population: 1,059,000 (1992 est). Capital: Ulan-Ude.

Chechenya (half of the former republic of Checheno-Ingushetia, Chechenya has unilaterally declared its independence from the Russian Federation) Area: 10,300 km² (4000 sq mi). Population: 700,000 (1992 est). Capital: Grozny.

Chuvashia Area: 18,300 km² (7065 sq mi). Population: 1,353,000 (1992 est). Capital: Cheboksary.

Dagestan Area: 50,300 km² (19,415 sq mi). Population: 1,890,000 (1992 est). Capital: Makhachkala.

Gorno-Altay Area: 92,600 km² (35,740 sq mi). Population: 198,000 (1992 est). Capital: Gorno-Altaisk.

Ingushetia Area: 9000 km² (3500 sq mi). Population: 500,000 (1992 est). Capital: Nazran.

Kabardino-Balkaria Area: 12,500 km² (4825 sq mi). Population: 784,000 (1992 est). Capital: Nalchik.

Kalmykia (or Kalmg Tangch) Area: 75,900 km² (29,300 sq mi). Population: 327,000 (1992 est). Capital: Elista.

Karachay-Cherkessia (formerly Karachevo-Cherkess) Area: 14,100 km² (5440 sq mi). Population: 431,000 (1992 est). Capital: Cherkessk.

Karelia Area: 172,400 km² (83,730 sq mi). Population: 800,000. Capital: Petrozavodsk.

Khakassia Area: 61,900 km² (23,900 sq mi). Population: 581,000 (1992 est). Capital: Abakan.

Komi Area: 415,900 km² (160,540 sq mi). Population: 1,255,000 (1992 est). Capital: Syktyvkar.

Mari El Area: 23,200 km² (8955 sq mi). Population: 762,000 (1992 est). Capital: Yoshkar-Ola.

Mordvinia (formerly Mordovia) (a republic) Area: 26,200 km² (10,110 sq mi). Population: 964,000 (1992 est). Capital: Saransk.

North Ossetia (Severo Ossetiya) Area: 8000 km² (3090 sq mi). Population: 695,000 (1992 est). Capital: Vladikavkaz.

Russia Area: 12,198,300 km² (4,709,800 sq mi). Population: 125,115,000 (1992 est). Capital: Moscow. Russia comprises 49 regions, one autonomous region - Yevreyskaya (the Jewish Region), six territories - Altay, Khabarovsk, Krasnodar, Krasnoyarsk, Primorye (the Maritime Territory) and Stavropol, two autonomous cities - Moscow and St Petersburg, and ten autonomous districts - Aga-Buryat, Chukchi, Evenk, Khanty-Mansi, Komi-Peryak, Koryak, Nenets, Taymyr, Ust-Orda Buryat, and Yamalo-Nenets. The unit called Russia (see below) comprises that part of the Russian Federation that is not included within any of the 21 republics. Unlike the other republics it does not have any administrative functions - these are delegated to the 68 units into which Russia is divided.

Sakha (formerly Yakutia) Area: 3,103,200 km² (1,197,760 sq mi). Population: 1,093,000 (1992 est). Capital: Yakutsk.

Tatarstan Area: 68,100 km² (26,650 sq mi). Population: 3,696,000 (1992 est). Capital: Kazan.

Tuva Area: 170,500 km² (65,810 sq mi). Population: 306,000 (1992 est). Capital: Kyzyl-Orda.

Udmurtia Area: 42,100 km² (16,250 sq mi). Population: 1,637,000 (1992 est). Capital: Izhevsk.

GEOGRAPHY

Russia is the largest country in the world and covers over 10% of the total land area of the globe. Most of the land between the Baltic and the Ural Mountains is covered by the North European Plain, south of which the relatively low-lying Central Russian Uplands stretch from the Ukrainian border to north of Moscow. To the east of the Urals is the vast West Siberian Lowland, the greater part of which is occupied by the basin of the River Ob and its tributaries. The Central Siberian Plateau - between the rivers Yenisey and Lena - rises to around 1700 m (5500 ft). Beyond the Lena are the mountains of east Siberia, including the Chersky Mountains and the Kamchatka Peninsula. Much of the south of Siberia is mountainous. The Yablonovy and Stanovoy Mountains rise inland from the Amur Basin, which drains to the Pacific coast. The Altai Mountains lie south of Lake Baikal and along the border with Mongolia. Between the Black

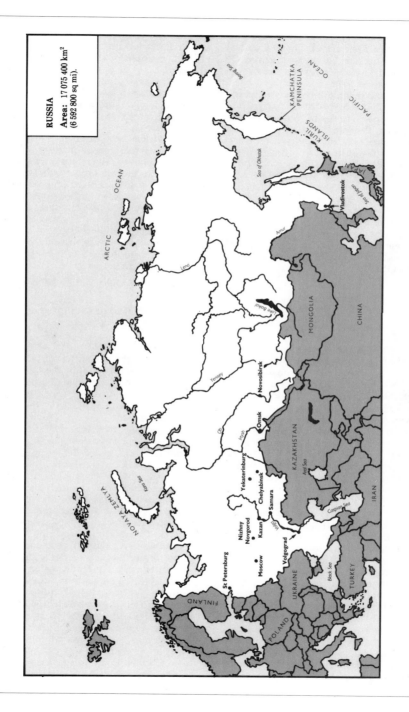

RUSSIA

Area: 17 075 400 km²
(6 592 800 sq mi).

and Caspian Seas are the high Caucasus Mountains on the Georgian border. The Kaliningrad enclave between Poland and Lithuania on the Baltic is a detached part of Russia. Highest point: Elbrus (on the Georgian border) 5642 m (18,510 ft). Principal rivers: Yenisey, Lena, Ob, Amur, Volga, Angara, Irtysh, Dvina, Pechora, Kama. Climate: Russia has a wide range of climatic types, but most of the country is continental and experiences extremes of temperature. The Arctic north is a severe tundra region in which the subsoil is nearly always frozen. The forested taiga zone - to the south - has long hard winters and short summers. The steppes and the Central Russian Uplands have cold winters, but hot, dry summers. Between the Black and Caspian seas conditions become almost Mediterranean. The Kaliningrad enclave has a more temperate climate than the rest of Russia.

ECONOMY

Russia is one of the largest producers of coal, iron ore, steel, petroleum and cement. However, its economy is in crisis and Russia's GNP declined by nearly 20% in 1992 and by over 10% in 1993. The economic reforms (1985-91) of Mikhail Gorbachov introduced decentralization to a centrally-planned economy. Since 1991, reform has been accelerated through the introduction of free market prices and the encouragement of private enterprise. However, there have been widespread calls for slower reform as economic chaos has spread and living standards have fallen. A lack of motivation in the labour force affects all sectors of the economy and poor distribution has resulted in shortages of many basic goods. Inflation became rampant, reaching 2200% in 1992 but Russia's economic decline slowed in 1993 and 1994. Russia continues to look for more Western assistance and investment but a combination of political uncertainty and economic problems means that - with the notable exception of the oil and gas industries - Western investment levels have fallen far short of Russian expectations. Manufacturing involves one third of the labour force and includes the steel, chemical, textile and heavy machinery industries. The production of consumer goods is not highly developed. Russian industry is characterized by a poor infrastructure and out-of-date plant and the country has found very considerable difficulties in competing internationally. Agriculture is large scale and organized either into state-owned farms or collective farms, although the right to own and farm land privately has been introduced. Despite mechanization and the world's largest fertilizer industry, Russia cannot produce enough grain for its needs, in part because of poor harvests, and poor storage and transport facilities. Imports from Ukraine and Kazakhstan have assumed added importance. Major Russian crops include wheat, barley, oats, potatoes, sugar beet and fruit. Natural resources include the world's largest reserves of coal, nearly one third of the world's natural gas reserves, one third of the world's forests, major deposits of manganese, gold, potash, bauxite, nickel, lead, zinc and copper, as well as plentiful sites for hydroelectric power installations. Machinery, petroleum and petroleum products are Russia's major exports. Russia is self-sufficient in energy

Currency: Rouble; 1US$ = 2008.5 roubles (June 1994).

GDP: US$24,100,000,000 (1993 est); US$160 per head.

RECENT HISTORY

Following the revolution of February 1917 - largely brought about by the catastrophic conduct of World War I - Tsar Nicholas II abdicated and a provisional government was established. In November 1917 the Bolsheviks (Communists) - led by Vladymir Ilich Lenin (1870-1924) - overthrew the provisional government in a bloodless coup. Russia withdrew from the war, ceded Poland to Germany and Austria, and recognized the independence of the Baltic states, Finland, and Ukraine. Other parts of the former empire soon declared independence, including the Transcaucasian states and Central Asia. A civil war between the Bolsheviks and the White Russians (led by former Tsarists) lasted until 1922. The Communists gradually reconquered most of the former Russian empire and in December 1922 formed the Union of Soviet Socialist Republics. The economy was reorganized under central control, but shortages and famine were soon experienced. After Lenin's death (1924), a power struggle took place between the supporters of Joseph Stalin (1879-1953) and Leon Trotsky (1879-1940). Stalin expelled Trotsky's supporters from the Communist Party and exiled him. The rapid industrialization of the country began. In 1929-

30 Stalin liquidated the kulaks (richer peasants). Severe repression continued until his death - opponents were subjected to 'show trials' and summary execution, and millions died as a result of starvation or political execution. In World War II - in which up to 20 million Soviet citizens may have died - the USSR at first concluded a pact with Hitler (1939), and invaded Poland, Finland, Romania and the Baltic states, annexing considerable territory. However, in 1941 the Germans invaded the USSR, precipitating the Soviet Union's entry into the war on the Allied side. In victory the Soviet Union was confirmed as a world power, controlling a cordon of satellite states in Eastern Europe and challenging the West in the Cold War. However, the economy stagnated and the country was drained by the burdens of an impoverished and overstretched empire. Leonid Brezhnev (leader 1964-82) reversed the brief thaw that had been experienced under Nikita Khruschev (leader 1956-64), and far-reaching reform had to await the policies of Mikhail Gorbachov (1931-) after 1985. Faced with severe economic reforms, Gorbachov attempted to introduce reconstruction (perestroika) and greater openness (glasnost) by implementing social, economic and industrial reforms. The state of the economy also influenced the desire to reduce military spending by reaching agreements on arms reduction with the West. Dissent was tolerated, a major reform of the constitution led to more open elections, and the Communist Party gave up its leading role. Many hardliners in the Communist Party were defeated by reformers (many of them non-Communists) in elections in 1989. The abandonment of the Brezhnev Doctrine - the right of the USSR to intervene in the affairs of Warsaw Pact countries (as it had done militarily in Hungary in 1956 and Czechoslovakia in 1968) - prompted rapid change in Eastern Europe, where one after another the satellite states renounced Communism and began to implement multi-party rule. From 1989 there were increased nationalistic stirrings within the USSR, particularly in the Baltic republics and the Caucasus. In August 1991, an attempt by a group of Communist hardliners to depose Gorbachov was defeated by the resistance of Russian President Boris Yeltsin (1931-) and by the refusal of the army to take action against unarmed civilian protestors. The opposition of Yeltsin and the Russian parliament to the coup greatly enhanced the status and powers of Russia and the 14 other Union Republics. Fourteen of the 15 republics declared independence and the secession of the three Baltic republics was recognized internationally. The remaining republics began to renegotiate their relationship. Gorbachov suspended the Communist Party and - with Yeltsin - initiated far-reaching political and economic reforms. However, it was too late to save the Soviet Union, whose fate was sealed by the refusal of Ukraine, the second most important of the republics, to participate in the new looser Union proposed by Gorbachov. By the end of 1991 the initiative had passed from Gorbachov to Yeltsin, who was instrumental in establishing the Commonwealth of Independent States (CIS), a military and economic grouping of sovereign states that included most of the former Union republics. After Gorbachov resigned and the Soviet Union was dissolved (December 1991), Russia took over the international responsibilities of the USSR, including its seat on the UN Security Council. Externally, Russia faced disputes concerning the future of CIS forces and potential territorial claims on other former Soviet republics. Internally, Russia faced a severe economic crisis as the command economy is replaced by a market economy. These changes were impeded by the activities of former Communist hardliners in Parliament, who also held up constitutional reform. The contest between Yeltsin and the hardliners came to a head in the autumn of 1993 when a core of hardliners - led by Vice-President Aleksandr Rutskoy and Ruslan Khasbulatov, the speaker of parliament - organized an armed uprising. A two-week siege of the Parliament building ended when the army intervened on Yeltsin's behalf to crush the revolt. Yeltsin has since imposed a new constitution which concentrates power in the hands of the president. In multi-party elections in December 1993 Communists and Vladimir Zhirinovsky's extreme right wing 'Liberal Democrats' gained support. Russian influence grew in 1993 and 1994 in many parts of the former Soviet Union - for example, through brokering a peace agreement between the Georgians and Abkhazians, in attempting to achieve a settlement in the Nagorno Karabakh dispute between Armenia and Azerbaijan, and in a strengthened military presence in Moldova and Tajikistan, both of which had been wracked by civil war.

223

Tajikistan

Official name: Jumhurii Tojikiston (Republic of Tajikistan).

Member of: UN, CIS, CSCE.

Area: 143,100 km² (55,300 sq mi).

Population: 5,587,000 (1992 est).

Capital: Dushanbe 592,000 (1991 census).

Other major city: Khodzhent (Khujand; formerly Leninabad) 165,000 (1991 est).

Language: Tajik (official; 59%), Uzbek (23%), Russian (10%).

Religion: Sunni Islam majority.

Education: Education is compulsory between the ages of seven and 17. There are no figures regarding literacy rate. There is a university and a polytechnic.

Defence: In 1993 the total armed strength was 3000; there were over 4000 CIS (mainly Russian) troops in the country

Transport: There are nearly 14,000 km (8700 mi) of roads and 891 km (554 mi) of railways. Dushanbe has an international airport.

Media: There are over 70 newspapers, some of them published daily. There is a single state-run radio and television service.

TAJIKISTAN

*Area:*143 100 km²
(55 300 sq mi).

GOVERNMENT
The constitution provides for the election of an 80-member Majlis and a President for four years. The 230-member Supreme Soviet retains power. The main political parties are the People's Party, the Communist Party, the People's Democratic Party and the Party of Economic Freedom. All anti-Communist parties were banned in June 1993.

President (acting): Imomali Rakhmanov.

Prime Minister (acting): Abduljalil Samadov.

GEOGRAPHY
The mountainous republic of Tajikistan lies within the Tien Shan range and part of the Pamirs. The most important lowland is the Fergana valley. Highest point: Mount Garmo (formerly known as Pik Kommunizma 7495 m (24,590 ft). Principal rivers: Syrdarya, Amu Darya. Climate: High altitude and the country's position deep in the interior of Asia combine to give most of Tajikistan a harsh continental climate. The Fergana valley is subtropical.

ECONOMY
Cotton is the mainstay of the economy. Other agricultural interests include fruit, vegetables and raising cattle. Major natural resources include coal, natural gas, iron ore, oil, lead, zinc and hydroelectric-power potential. Industries include textiles and carpet-making. The economy remains centrally planned and largely state-owned. The economy has been damaged by civil war. Tajikistan has reentered the rouble zone and is economically dependent upon Russia.

Currency: Tajikistan uses Russian currency.

GDP: US$2,537,000,000 (1992); US$480 per head.

RECENT HISTORY
The area was annexed by Tsarist Russia (1860-68). After the Russian Revolution, the area was reoccupied by the Soviet Red Army (1920), but Tajik revolts simmered from 1922 to 1931. Tajikistan became a Union Republic within the USSR in 1929, declared independence after the abortive coup by Communist hardliners in Moscow (September 1991), and was internationally recognized when the Soviet Union was dissolved (December 1991). Since independence the country has been wracked by civil war between former Communists and Islamic fundamentalists. During 1993-94 the government, with the help of CIS forces, consolidated its position against the rebels.

224

Turkmenistan

Official name: Tiurkmenostan (Turkmenistan).

Member of: UN, CIS, CSCE, ECO.

Area: 488,100 km² (188,500 sq mi).

Population: 3,861,000 (1992 est).

Capital: Ashkabad (Ashgabat) 416,000 (1991 est).

Other main cities: Chardzhou (Charjew) 166,000, Dashhowuz 117,000 (1991 est).

Languages: Turkmen (72%), Russian (9%), Uzbek (9%), Kazakh (3%).

Religion: Sunni Islam majority.

Education: Education is compulsory between the ages of seven and 15. There are no figures regarding the literacy rate. There is a university and a polytechnic.

Defence: In 1993 the total armed strength was 28,000. Military service lasts for 18 months.

Transport: There are 13,400 km (8300 mi) of roads and 2120 km (1317 mi) of railways. Ashkabad has an international airport.

Media: There are several daily newspapers. There is a single state-run radio and TV service.

GOVERNMENT
A 50-member (Majlis) legislature and a President are elected by universal adult suffrage for four years. The main political parties are the (former Communist) Democratic Party (DP) and Agzybirlik (Unity). The Democratic Party has a leading role.

President: Saparmuryad Niyazov (DP).

Prime Minister: Khan Akhmedov (DP).

GEOGRAPHY
The sandy Kara-Kum Desert occupies the centre of the republic, over 90% of which is desert. The Kopet Dag mountains form the border with Iran. Highest point: Firyuza 2942 m (9652 ft). Principal rivers: Amu Darya, Murgah. Climate: Turkmenistan has a continental climate characterized by hot summers, freezing winters and very low precipitation.

ECONOMY
Turkmenistan is rich in oil and natural gas. Industries include engineering, metal processing and textiles. Collective farms grow cotton under irrigation and raise sheep, camels and horses. The economy remains state-owned and centrally planned although reforms began in 1993.

Currency: Manat; in theory, the manat is on a par with the US dollar. It is not yet quoted internationally.

GDP: US$4,898,400,000 (1992); US$1270 per head.

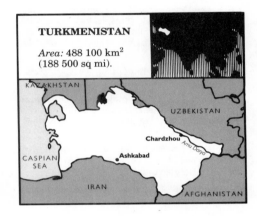

TURKMENISTAN

Area: 488 100 km²
(188 500 sq mi).

RECENT HISTORY
The Turkmens are a nomadic Turkic people who were nominally subject to Persia, or to the khans of Khiva and Bukhara (now both in Uzbekistan), before coming under Russian rule between 1869 and 1881. The Turkmens fiercely resisted the Russians and rose in revolt in 1916. An autonomous Transcaspian government was formed after the Russian Revolution, and the area was not brought under Soviet control until the Red Army invaded in 1919. The Turkmen territories were reorganized as the Republic of Turkmenistan in 1924 and admitted to the USSR as a full Union Republic in 1925. Independence was declared following the abortive coup by Communist hardliners in Moscow (September 1991), and the republic received international recognition when the USSR was dissolved (December 1991). Since independence opposition has been curtailed and Niyazov has been the object of a growing personality cult. Turkmenistan has remained largely aloof from CIS activities.

225

Ukraine

Official name: Ukraina (The Ukraine).

Member of: UN, CIS, CSCE, NATO (partner for peace).

Area: 603,700 km² (233,100 sq mi).

Population: 52,344,000 (1993 est).

Capital: Kiev (Kyiv) 2,616,000 (1990 est).

Other major cities: Kharkov (Kharkiv) 1,618,000, Dnepropetrovsk (Dnipropetrovske) 1,187,000, Donetsk (Donetske) 1,117,000, Odessa (Odesa) 1,106,000, Zaporozhye (Zaporizhia) 891,000, Lvov (Lviv) 798,000 (1990 est).

Languages: Ukrainian (74%), Russian (22%), Belarussian (2%); Romanian (1%), Polish (1%).

Religions: Orthodox (majority) - Ukrainian Autocephalous and Russian; Ukrainian Uniat (Roman Catholic; largest single denomination).

Education: Schooling is compulsory between the ages of seven and 15. In 1993 the literacy rate was over 98%. There are 10 universities and eight polytechnics.

Defence: In 1992 the total armed strength was 230,000. Compulsory military service lasts 18 months.

Transport: There are 247,500 km (154,700 mi) of roads in Ukraine. Ukraine has 22,730 km (14,205 mi) of railway track. Kiev, Kharkov and Dneipropetrovsk have metro systems. The Dnepr is an important inland navigation. The main sea ports are Odessa and Yalta. Kiev, Lvov, Odessa and Chernovtsy have international airports.

Media: There are 12 major daily papers and a state-run radio and television service.

GOVERNMENT

A 450-member legislature (Verkhova Rada) and a President, who appoints a Council of Ministers, are elected for four years by universal adult suffrage. Voting is conducted in three rounds, and to be successful, in either of the first two rounds, candidates must have an overall majority. There are 24 provinces plus the autonomous republic of Crimea. Political parties include the Communist Party (CP), the Socialist Party (SP), the (nationalist) Rukh party, and other nationalist parties. In June 1994 over 100 seats were vacant.

Party strength: Independents 167, CP-SP 113, Rukh 30, other nationalists 27, vacant 112.

President: Leonid Kuchma.

CABINET

includes

Acting Prime Minister: Yukhym Zvyahilsky.

Vice Prime Ministers: Vasyl Yevtukhov, Valentyn Landyk, Volodymyr Demyanov, Valeriy Shmarov, Mykola Zhulynsky.

Minister of Agriculture and Food Supply: Yuriy Karasyk.

Minister of Communication: Oleh Prozhyvalsky.

Minister of Construction: Yuriy Serbin.

Minister of Defence: Vitaliy Radzetsky.

Minister of Economics: Roman Shpek.

Minister of Education: Petro Talanchuk.

Minister of Energy: Vilen Symenyuk.

Minister of Finances: Hryhoriy Pyatachenko.

Minister of Foreign Affairs: Anatoliy Zlenko.

Minister of Industry: Anatoliy Holubchenko.

Minister of Internal Affairs: Andriy Vasylyshyn.

Minister of Justice: Vasyl Onopenko.

Minister of Labour: Mykhailo Kaskevych.

Minister of Social Welfare: Arkadiy Yershov.

Minister of Transport: Orest Klympush.

AUTONOMOUS REPUBLIC

Crimea (Krym) Area: 27,000 km² (10,400 sq mi). Population: 2,550,000 (1991 est). Capital: Simferopol.

GEOGRAPHY

Most of Ukraine - the second largest country in Europe - comprises plains (steppes), interrupted by plateaux and basins. The north includes part of the Pripet Marshes; the south is a lowland beside the Black Sea and Sea of Azov. The centre comprises the Dnepr Lowland and the Dnepr Plateau, the largest upland. The east comprises the Don Valley and part of the Central Russian Upland. The diverse scenery of the west includes an extensive lowland and the Carpathian Mountains. Crimea consists of parallel ridges and fertile valleys. Highest point: Hoverla 2061 m (6762 ft). Principal rivers: Dnepr, Don, Donets, Bug. Climate: Crimea is Mediterranean. The rest of Ukraine is temperate but becomes more extreme further north and east. Winters are milder and summers are cooler in the west. Rainfall is moderate, with a summer maximum.

ECONOMY

Large collectivized farms on the steppes grow cereals, fodder crops and vegetables. Potatoes and flax are important in the north; fruit farming (including grapes and market gardening) is widespread, particularly in Crimea. Natural resources include iron ore, manganese and rock salt, but the vast Donets coalfield is the principal base of Ukraine's industries. Ukraine has a large iron and steel industry but much of the plant is old-fashioned. Other major industries include consumer goods, heavy engineering (railway locomotives, shipbuilding, generators), food processing, and chemicals and chemical equipment. The economy has been almost untouched by reform since the break-up of the USSR. Production of industrial and agricultural goods has fallen, inflation has soared (to over 3000% in 1993) and the GDP fell by over 20% in 1993. The country has suffered the

UKRAINE

Area: 603 700 km² (233 100 sq mi).

loss of cheap electricity from Russia and does not have the funds to purchase supplies or to replace unsafe nuclear power stations (including the remaining sections of Chernobyl). Massive EC assistance is being sought in return for the decommissioning of nuclear

power stations, but political uncertainty is likely to retard recovery and reform.

Currency: Karbovanets; 1US$ = 19,525 karbovanets (June 1994).

GDP: $5,500,000,000 (1993 est); US$105 per head.

RECENT HISTORY

The Ukrainians in Russia took the opportunity afforded by World War I and the Russian Revolutions of 1917 to proclaim independence (January 1918), but a Ukrainian Soviet government was set up in Kharkov, where Russians are in the majority. Ukraine united with Galicia when the Austro-Hungarian Empire collapsed (November 1918). The new state was invaded by Poland and by the Soviet Red Army. The latter prevailed and in 1922 Ukraine became a founding republic of the USSR, but the Lvov area of Galicia remained Polish. From 1928, Soviet leader Joseph Stalin instituted purges in Ukraine and increased Russification. After World War II - when Ukraine was occupied by Nazi Germany - Ukraine gained Lvov (from Poland), Bukovina (from Romania), Ruthenia (from Czechoslovakia), and, finally, Crimea (from Russia) in 1954. Ukrainian nationalism was spurred by the perceived Soviet indifference to Ukraine at the time of the nuclear accident at Chernobyl, north of Kiev, in 1986. Ukrainian politicians responded to the restructuring of the USSR in the late 1980s by seeking increased autonomy. Ukraine's declaration of independence after the abortive coup in Moscow by Communist hardliners (September 1991) hastened the demise of the USSR. Ukraine gained international recognition in December 1991 when the USSR collapsed. Tension remains between Moscow and Kiev over the Black Sea fleet, the former Soviet nuclear weapons based in Ukraine and, above all, about the status of the Crimea, which has a Russian majority and seeks reunion with Russia. In 1994 Crimea assumed near-sovereignty. Ukraine's economic collapse increased the separatist feelings of the Russian majority in the Don valley industrial region in the east. The 1994 elections saw the defeat of President Kravchuk by Leonid Kuchma (who advocates closer ties with Russia), and the emergence of split between the nationalist west and the Communist, ethnic Russian east which threatens the existence of Ukraine as a single country.

227

Uzbekistan

Official name: Ozbekistan Jumhuriyati (Republic of Uzbekistan).

Member of: UN, CIS, CSCE.

Area: 447,400 km² (172,700 sq mi).

Population: 20,995,000 (1992 est).

Capital: Tashkent 2,120,000 (1991 est).

Other major cities: Samarkand (Samarqand) 372,000, Namangan 333,000, Andizhan 302,000 (1991 est).

Languages: Uzbek (official; 71%), Russian (8%), Tajik (4%).

Religion: Sunni Islam majority.

Education: Education is compulsory between the ages of seven and 15. In 1990 the literacy rate was 80%. There are three universities and two polytechnics.

Defence: In 1993 the total armed strength was 40,000. Military service lasts for 18 months.

Transport: There are over 89,210 km (55,433 mi) of roads and 6800 km (4225 mi) of state-run railways. Tashkent has an international airport and a metro.

Media: There are over 200 newspapers, many of which are daily. There is a single state-run radio and television service.

GOVERNMENT
A 500-member legislature and a President are elected for four years by universal adult suffrage. The only legal political party is the (former Communist) People's Democratic Party; the opposition Birlik (Unity) and Erk (Freedom) parties have been banned.

President: Islam A. Karimov.

Prime Minister: Abdulhashim Mutalov.

GEOGRAPHY
The west is flat and mainly desert. The mountainous east includes ridges of the Tien Shan and part of the Fergana valley. Highest point: Bannovka 4488 m (14,724 ft). Principal rivers: Amu Darya, Kara Darya. Climate: Uzbekistan has a warm continental climate characterized by hot summers and low rainfall. Only the mountains receive over 500 mm (20 in) of rain a year.

ECONOMY
Uzbekistan is one of the world's leading producers of cotton, but the extraction of irrigation from the Amu Darya and its tributaries has contributed to the gradual shrinkage of the

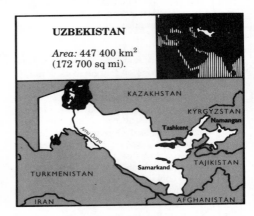

Aral Sea. The republic has important reserves of natural gas and major machine and heavy engineering industries. The economy is still mainly state-owned and centrally planned. Economic reforms have been slowed because of goverment fears of economic and political instability.

Currency: Som; in theory, 1US$ = 3 soms, but the currency is not quoted internationally.

GDP: 18,398,000,000 (1992); US$860 per head.

RECENT HISTORY
The Uzbeks did not finally come under Russian rule until the khans of Bukhara and Khiva became vassals of the Tsar (1868-73). After the Russian Revolution, the Basmachi revolt (1918-22) resisted Soviet rule, but the khans were eventually deposed (1920) and Soviet republics established (1923-4). Uzbekistan was created in 1924 when the boundaries of Soviet Central Asia were reorganized. Independence was declared after the abortive coup in Moscow by Communist hardliners (September 1991) and international recognition was achieved when the USSR was dissolved (December 1991). The lack of human rights in independent Uzbekistan - which occupies an important role in Central Asia - has attracted international criticism.

THE FAR EAST

China, Republic of China (Taiwan), Japan,
Peoples' Democratic Republic of Korea (North Korea)
Republic of Korea (South Korea),
Mongolia, Other territories.

China and the Little Dragons

The developing nations of eastern Asia share social characteristics that arise from a common tradition of values. This area stretches from Korea in the north, through coastal China and off-shore Taiwan, to Hong Kong and Singapore. Historically as well as geographically, Vietnam forms part of this continuum. The prevalence of the general characteristics of respect, frugality and perseverance throughout the region must be balanced against the disparities between its constituent parts. China has a population of over 1,158,000,000 – projected to add another 17,000,000 to that total every year throughout the 1990s. South Korea, with a population of over 42,000,000 ranks with the medium-sized European powers but its capital is one of the ten largest cities in the world. It has already fulfilled its objective of becoming one of the world's ten largest trading nations and aims to join the Organization for Economic Cooperation and Development by the late 1990s. Singapore and Hong Kong, both smaller than Taiwan in both area and population, have average incomes around 50% higher.

The UN Development Progamme's Fourth Annual Report on Human Development (1993) ranks the world's nations according to a 'Quality of Life' index. Japan ranks top, with Canada second, the US sixth and the UK tenth. Of the 'top twenty' developing nations Hong Kong ranks second (24th overall), with South Korea seventh (33rd) and Singapore tenth (43rd); neither Taiwan nor China figure in this list. China's long-term objective is to quadruple the GNP of 1980 by the year 2000. Realization of this objective would require an annual average growth rate of 6%. Economic growth in China in 1992 is estimated to have in fact been between 12% and 14%, the fastest in Asia and probably in the world. But this has been accompanied by lack of coordination between the various economic sectors. Industrial growth is twice as fast as overall GNP growth but agricultural growth is only half as fast. There are alarming signs of monetary and fiscal overheating, with inflation surpassing 30% in some cities. Its uneven incidence is a sign of the growing disparities between city and countryside, and between the coast and the interior.

Disordered public finances and a money-supply running out of control have forced the introduction of several short-lived austerity packages and, in June 1993, the summary dismissal of the Governor of the Central Bank. Colossal projects are still envisaged, however. In 1992 formal approval was given for the construction of the 'Three Gorges' dam project on the Yangtze River. When completed it should produce the equivalent of an eighth of current national electricity output, as well as allowing 10,000-ton ships to penetrate far into the backward interior, linking it to international markets. Foreign participation plays a major role in China's transformation, through the provision of technology, capital and managerial skills. The economic changes of the 1980s raised non-material expectations as well as living-standards, prompting demands for political and economic liberalization. Such demands were literally crushed in the Tiananmen Square massacre of 1989. This damaged links with the West, but in 1992 40,000 new foreign-funded projects were agreed. In May 1994 President Clinton's willingness to de-couple renewal of China's 'Most-Favoured Nation' trading status from previous insistence on changes in human-rights policy signified a recognition that potential losses to American business outranked other considerations.

During a public tour in 1992 Deng Xiaoping praised the 'special enterprise zones' of Zhuhai and Shenzhen and urged Guangdong to emulate the four 'little dragons' (a.k.a. 'little tigers' – South Korea, Taiwan, Hong Kong and Singapore). Each 'little dragon' has made changes in its political system that were bound to induce economic uncertainty. Each has also been preoccupied with corruption scandals and demands for environmental protection. And each has upgraded its skills to maintain competitiveness. Korea's maturation is retarded by the continuing burden of major defence expenditures. Committed to greater liberalization, it accepted opening of the domestic rice market, under direct GATT pressure, in February 1994 – resulting in farmers' riots and the fall of the prime minister. Taiwan, experiencing shortages of both land and labour, has countered by relocating its export-orientated industries on the South-East Asian mainland and in China itself. In 1990 a Foundation for Exchanges Across the Taiwan Strait was established for the discussion of mutual interests.

Far East Trade

China Imports ($ million): 63,791 (1991). Exports ($ million): 71,910 (1991). Main imports: machinery and transport equipment 31.5% (1990), basic manufactures 16.6% (1990), chemicals and related products, food and live animals. Main exports: products of textile industries, rubber and metal products 34% (1990), light industrial products 15.9% (1988), miscellaneous manufactured products, food and live animals, mineral fuels and lubricants, chemicals and related products. Principal trading partners: Hong Kong, Japan, USA, Germany, Singapore, Canada, Australia, UK, Italy, Netherlands, France, Malaysia.

China (Taiwan) Imports (NT$ million): 1,690 (1991). Exports (NT$ million): 2,040 (1991). Main imports: cold cathode and photocathode valves and tubes, diodes, crystals 8.3% (1991), machinery and transport equipment 6% (1991), oil, coal and petroleum 7.4% (1991), maize, soyabeans. Main exports: synthetic and other garments, footwear and cloth 13% (1991), light industrial products 21.8% (1991), calculating machines, plastic articles, dolls and toys. Principal trading partners: Japan, USA, Hong Kong, Germany, South Korea, Singapore, UK, Canada, Thailand, Australia, Indonesia.

Japan Imports ($ million): 236 744 (1991). Exports ($ million): 314 525 (1991). Main imports: petroleum and petroleum products 15.9% (1991), machinery and transport equipment 16.6% (1991), miscellaneous manufactured articles, basic maunufactures, food. Main exports: motor vehicles, parts and passenger cars 31.6% (1991), office machinery 7% (1991), non-electric machinery, iron and steel, basic maunfactures, chemicals and chemical products. Principal trading partners: USA, South Korea, Germany, Taiwan, China, Australia, United Arab Emirates, UK, Canada, France, Malaysia.

Korea (North) Imports ($ million): 2900 (1989). Exports ($ million): 1800 (1989). Main imports: wheat and raw sugar. Main exports: rice and silk. Principal trading partners: Russia, Japan, China.

Korea (South) Imports ($ million): 81,775.3 (1992). Exports ($ million): 76,631.5 (1992). Main imports: machinery and transport equipment 32.7% (1989), manufactured goods 15.7% (1989), crude petroleum, wood, power-generating machinery. Main exports: machinery and transport equipment 37.7% (1989), manufactured goods 22.0% (1989), textiles and fabrics, footwear, thread and yarn, rubber tyres and tubes. Principal trading partners: USA, Japan, Germany, Australia, Canada, Singapore, Saudi Arabia, Hong Kong, UK, France, Malaysia.

Mongolia Imports ($ million): 2030 (1988). Exports ($ million): 812 (1988). Main imports: fuels, minerals and metals 33.5% (1988), machinery and transport equipment 30.2% (1988). Main exports: raw materials and food products 41.7% (1988), minerals and metals 39.0% (1988). Principal trading partners: Japan, China, Russia.

China

Official name: Zhonghua Renmin Gongheguo (The People's Republic of China).

Member of: UN.

Area: 9,571,300 km² (3,695,500 sq mi).

Population: 1,158,230,000 (1991 est).

Capital: Beijing (Peking) 10,819,000 (including suburbs; 1991 est).

Other major cities: Shanghai 13,400,000, Tianjin (Tientsin) 8,430,000, Shenyang 4,450,000, Wuhan 3,750,000, Guangzhou (Canton) 3,580,000, Chongquin 2,980,000, Harbin 2,930,000, Chengdu 2,810,000, Xian 2,760,000, Nanjing (Nanking) 2,500,000, Zibo 2,460,000, Dalian (Darien) 2,400,000, Jinan 2,290,000, Changchun 2,070,000, Qingdao (Tsingtao) 2,040,000, Shenzhen 2,000,000, Taiyuan 1,900,000, Zhengzhou 1,660,000, Kunming 1,500,000, Guiyang (Kweiyang) 1,490,000, Tangshan 1,490,000, Lanzhou (Lanchow) 1,480,000, Anshan 1,370,000, Qiqihar (Tsitsihar) 1,370,000, Fushun 1,330,000, Hangzhou 1,330,000, Nanchang 1,330,000, Changsha 1,300,000, Shijiazhuang (Shihkiachwang) 1,300,000, Fushu (Foochow) 1,270,000, Jilin (Kirin) 1,250,000, Baotou (Paotow) 1,180,000, Huainan 1,170,000, Luoyang 1,160,000, Urümqi 1,110,000, Datong 1,090,000, Handan 1,090,000, Ningbo 1,070,000, Nanning 1,050,000 (1991 est). Twenty-one other municipalities - with overwhelmingly rural populations - have over 1,000,000 inhabitants; these municipalities are Lupanshui, Zhaozhuang, Linyi, Pingxiang, Xintao, Yancheng, Yulin, Chao'an, Dongguang, Xiaogan, Suining, Xintai, Puyang, Bozhou, Zhongshan, Laiwu, Leshan, Heze, Linhai, Macheng, and Changshu.

Languages: Chinese ('Mandarin' dialect in the majority, with local dialects in south and southeast, e.g. Cantonese, Wu), with small Mongol, Tibetan and other minorities.

Religions: Officially atheist but those religions and philosophies practised include Confucianism and Daoism (over 20% together), Buddhism (c. 15%).

Education: In 1990 the literacy rate was estimated to be 73.3%. Schooling is not compulsory but is available between the ages of seven and 17; there are plans to introduce nine years of compulsory schooling by 1995. There are 79 state universities, several private universities plus 45 institutes of university status.

Defence: In 1992 the total armed strength was 3,010,000 - 2,300,000 in the army, 240,000 in the navy (including the marines) and 470,000 in the air force. There was also a paramilitary force of 12,000,000. Military service is selective - three years for the army and marines, four years for the air force and navy.

Transport: There are 1,100,000 km (683,650 mi) of built-up roads. The state-run railways operate 54,000 km (33,560 mi) of track. Beijing and Tianjin have metro systems. Shanghai, Tianjin, Canton and Dalian are the main ports. Beijing and Shanghai have the main international airports.

Media: The state-controlled media publishes some 852 newspapers including a daily paper in every province. The Ministry for Radio, TV and Films censors all broadcasts. There are 510 local television stations and China Central Television Station operates three channels nationwide.

GOVERNMENT

The 2978 deputies of the National People's Congress are elected for a five-year term by the People's Congresses of the 22 provinces, five autonomous provinces and three municipal provinces, and by the People's Liberation Army. The Congress elects a Standing Committee, a President (for a five-year term), a Prime Minister and a State Council (or Cabinet) - all of whom are responsible to the Congress. The only legal party is the Chinese Communist Party, which holds a Congress every five years. The Party Congress elects a Central Committee, which in turn elects a Politburo, and it is these two bodies that hold effective power.

President: Jiang Zemin.

General Secretary of the Communist Party: Jiang Zemin.

THE CABINET

Prime Minister: Li Peng.

Minister of Agriculture: Liu Jiang.

Minister of the Chemical Industry: Gu Xiulian.

Minister of Civil Affairs: Doje Cering.

Minister of the Coal Industry: Wang Senhao.

Minister of Communications: Huang Zhendong.

Minister of Construction: Hou Jie.

Minister of Culture: Liu Zhongde.

Minister of Defence: Chi Haotian.

Minister of the Electronics Industry: Hu Qili.

Minister of Finance: Liu Zhongli.

Minister of Foreign Affairs: Qian Qichen.

Minister of Foreign Trade and Economic Co-operation: Wu Yi.

Minister of Forestry: Xu Youfang.

Minister of Geology and Mineral Resources: Sun Ruixiang.

Minister of Internal Trade: Zhang Haoruo.

Minister of Justice: Xiao Yang.

Minister of Labour: Li Boyong.

Minister of the Machine-Building Industry: He Guangyuan.

Minister of the Metallurgical Industry: Liu Qi.

Minister of the People's Bank of China: Li Guixian.

Minister of Personnel: Song Defu.

Minister of Posts and Telecommunications: Wu Jichuan.

Minister of the Power Industry: Shi Dazhen.

Minister of Public Health: Chen Minzhang.

Minister of Public Security: Tao Siju.

Minister of Radio, Film and Television: Sun Jiazheng.

Minister of the Railways: Han Zhubin.

Minister of the State Auditing Administration: Guo Zhengian.

Minister of the State Commission for Economic Restructuring: Li Tieying.

Minister of the State Economic and Trade Commission: Wang Zhongyu.

Minister of the State Family Planning Commission: Peng Peiyun.

Minister of the State Education Commission: Zhu Kaixuan.

Minister of the State Nationalities Affairs Commission: Ismail Amat.

Minister of the State Physical Culture and Sports Commission: Wu Shaozu.

Minister of the State Planning Commission: Chen Jinhua.

Minister of the State Science and Technology Commission: Song Jian.

Minister of the State Commission for Science, Technology and Industry for National Defence: Ding Henggao.

Minister of State Security: Jia Chunwang.

Minister of Supervision: Cao Qingze.

PROVINCES

Anhui Area: 139,900 km² (54,020 sq mi). Population: 56,180,000 (1990 census). Capital: Hefei.

Beijing (Peking) (municipal province) Area: 17,800 km² (6870 sq mi). Population: 10,819,000 (1991 est). Capital: Beijing.

Fujian Area: 123,100 km² (47,530 sq mi). Population: 30,048,000 (1990 census). Capital: Fushu.

Gansu Area: 530,000 km² (204,600 sq mi). Population: 22,371,000 (1990 census). Capital: Lanzhou.

Guangdong Area: 197,900 km² (76,400 sq mi). Population: 62,829,000 (1990 census). Capital: Guangzhou (Canton).

Guangxi Zhuang (autonomous province) Area: 220,400 km² (85,100 sq mi). Population: 42,246,000. Capital: Nanning.

Guizhou Area: 174,000 km² (67,200 sq mi). Population: 32,391,000 (1990 census). Capital: Guiyang.

Hainan Area: 33,570 km² (12,960 sq mi). Population: 6,557,000 (1990 census). Capital: Haikou.

Hebei Area: 202,700 km² (78,260 sq mi). Population: 61,082,000 (1990 census). Capital: Shijiazhuang (Shihkiachwang).

Heilongjiang Area: 463,600 km² (179,000 sq mi). Population: 35,215,000 (1990 census). Capital: Harbin.

Henan Area: 167,000 km² (64,480 sq mi). Population: 85,510,000 (1990 census). Capital: Zhengzhou.

233

Hubei Area: 187,500 km² (72,400 sq mi). Population: 53,969,000 (1990 census). Capital: Wuhan.

Hunan Area: 210,500 km² (81,270 sq mi). Population: 60,660,000 (1990 census). Capital: Changsha.

Jiangsu Area: 102,200 km² (39,460 sq mi). Population: 67,057,000 (1990 census). Capital: Nanjing (Nanking).

Jiangxi Area: 164,800 km² (63,630 sq mi). Population: 37,710,000 (1990 census). Capital: Nanchang.

Jilin Area: 187,000 km² (72,200 sq mi). Population: 24,659,000 (1990 census). Capital: Changchun.

Liaoning Area: 151,000 km² (58,300 sq mi).

Population: 39,460,000 (1990 census). Capital: Shenyang.

Nei Monggol (Inner Mongolia; autonomous province) Area: 450,000 km² (173,700 sq mi). Population: 21,457,000 (1990 census). Capital: Hohhot (Huhehot).

Ningxia Hui (autonomous province) Area: 170,000 km² (65,600 sq mi). Population: 4,655,000 (1990 census). Capital: Yinchuan.

Qinghai Area: 721,000 km² (278,400 sq mi). Population: 4,457,000 (1990 est). Capital: Xining.

Shaanxi Area: 195,800 km² (75,600 sq mi). Population: 32,882,000 (1990 census). Capital: Xian.

Shandong Area: 153,300 km² (59,190 sq mi).

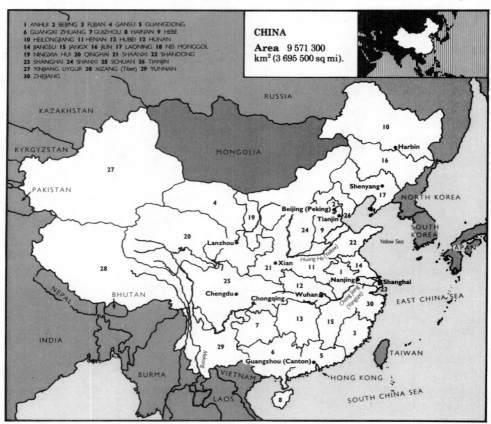

1 ANHUI 2 BEIJING 3 FUJIAN 4 GANSU 5 GUANGDONG
6 GUANGXI ZHUANG 7 GUIZHOU 8 HAINAN 9 HEBE
10 HEILONGJIANG 11 HENAN 12 HUBEI 12 HUNAN
14 JIANGSU 15 JIANGX 16 JILIN 17 LAONING 18 NEI MONGGOL
19 NINGXIA HUI 20 QINGHAI 21 SHAANXI 22 SHANDONG
23 SHANGHAI 24 SHANXI 25 SICHUAN 26 TIANJIN
27 XINJIANG UYGUR 28 XIZANG (Tibet) 29 YUNNAN
30 ZHEJIANG

CHINA

Area 9 571 300 km² (3 695 500 sq mi).

Population: 84,393,000 (1990 census). Capital: Jinan.

Shanghai (municipal province) Area: 5800 km² (2240 sq mi). Population: 13,400,000 (1991 est). Capital: Shanghai.

Shanxi Area: 157,100 km² (60,660 sq mi). Population: 28,759,000 (1990 census). Capital: Taiyuan.

Sichuan Area: 569,000 km² (219,700 sq mi). Population: 107,218,000 (1990 census). Capital: Chengdu.

Tianjin (Tientsin; municipal province) Area: 4000 km² (1540 sq mi). Population: 8,430,000 (1991 est). Capital: Tianjin.

Xinjiang Uygur (Sinkiang) (autonomous province) Area: 1,646,900 km² (635,870 sq mi). Population: 15,156,000 (1990 census). Capital: Urümqi.

Xizang (Tibet) (autonomous province) Area: 1,221,600 km² (471,660 sq mi). Population: 2,196,000 (1990 census). Capital: Lhasa.

Yunnan Area: 436,200 km² (168,420 sq mi). Population: 36,973,000 (1990 census). Capital: Kunming.

Zhejiang Area: 101,800 km² (39,300 sq mi). Population: 41,446,000 (1990 census). Capital: Hangzhou.

GEOGRAPHY

China is the third largest country in the world in area and the largest in population. Almost half of China comprises mountain chains, mainly in the west, including the Altaï and Tien Shan Mountains in Xinjiang Uygur, and the Kun Lun Mountains to the north of Tibet. The Tibetan Plateau - at an altitude of 3000 m (10,000 ft) - is arid. In the south of Tibet is the Himalaya, containing 40 peaks over 7000 m (23,000 ft). In the far south, the Yunnan Plateau rises to nearly 3700 m (12,000 ft), while in the far northeast, ranges of hills and mountains almost enclose the Northeast Plain, more usually known as Manchuria. Crossing central China - and separating the basins of the Yellow (Huang He) and Yangtze (Chang Jiang) rivers - is the Nan Ling Range of hills and mountains. In east and central China, three great lowlands support intensive agriculture and dense populations - the plains of central China, the Sichuan Basin and the flat North China Plain. A vast loess plateau, deeply dissected by

ravines, lies between the Mongolian Plateau - which contains the Gobi Desert - and the deserts of the Tarim and Dzungarian Basins in the northwest. Highest point: Mount Everest 8863 m (29,078 ft). Principal rivers: Yangtze (Chang Jiang), Huang He (Yellow River), Xijiang (Sikiang or Pearl River), Heilongjiang (Amur). Climate: In general, temperatures increase from north to south, and rainfall increases from northwest to southeast. Northeast China has a continental climate with warm and humid summers, long cold winters, and rainfall of less than 750 mm (30 in). The central lowlands contain the hottest areas of China, and have 750 to 1100 mm (30 to 40 in) of rainfall. The south is wetter, while the extreme subtropical south experiences the monsoon. The continental loess plateau is cold in the winter, warm in summer and has under 500 mm (20 in) of rain. The northwest is arid, continental and experiences cold winters. The west - Tibet, Xinjiang Uygur, Gansu and Nei Monggol - experiences an extreme climate owing to its altitude and distance from the sea; rainfall is low and most of Tibet has less than two months free of frost.

ECONOMY

Agriculture occupies approximately 60% of the labour force. All large-scale production is on collective farms, but traditional and inefficient practices remain. Nearly two thirds of the arable land is irrigated, and China is the world's largest producer of rice. Other major crops include wheat, maize, sweet potatoes, sugar cane and soyabeans. Livestock, fruit, vegetables and fishing are also important, but China is still unable to supply all its own food. The country's mineral and fuel resources are considerable and, for the most part, underdeveloped. They include coal, petroleum, natural gas, iron ore, bauxite, tin, antimony and manganese in major reserves, as well as huge hydroelectric power potential. The economy is centrally planned, with all industrial plant owned by the state. Petrochemical products account for nearly one quarter of China's exports. Other major industries include iron and steel, cement, vehicles, fertilizers, food processing, clothing and textiles. The most recent five-year plans have promoted modernization and reform, including an 'open-door' policy under which joint ventures with other countries and foreign loans have been encouraged, together with a degree of small-scale private enterprise. Most of this investment went into light industry and textiles. Special Economic Zones and 'open cities' were designated in the south and central coastal areas to encourage industrial links with the west. Although progress was halted when foreign investment diminished after the 1989 pro-democracy movement was suppressed, sustained economic growth has been achieved in southern China, in particular Guangdong where the new city of Shenzhen (near Hong Kong) is the centre of industrial development, and other coastal areas, for example the huge Pudong development at Shanghai.

Currency: Renminbi (People's currency) or Yuan of 10 jiao and 100 fen; 1US$ = 8.658 Yuan.

GDP: US$435,000,000,000 (1993 est); US$360 per head.

RECENT HISTORY
At the beginning of the 20th century China was in turmoil. The authority of the emperor had been weakened in the 19th century by outside powers greedy for trade and by huge rebellions which had left large areas of the country beyond the control of the central government. In 1911 a revolution, led by the Guomintang (Kuomintang or Nationalists) under Sun Zhong Shan (Sun Yat-sen; 1866-1925), overthrew the last of the Manchu emperors. Strong in the south (where Sun had established a republic in 1916), the Nationalists faced problems in the north, which was ruled by independent warlords. Sun's successor, Jiang Jie Shi (Chiang Kai-shek; 1887-1975), made some inroads in the north, only to be undermined by the emergent Communist Party. After a series of disastrous urban risings, the Communist Mao Zedong (Mao Tse-tung; 1893-1976) concentrated on rural areas. After being forced to retreat from Jiangxi in 1934, Mao led his followers for 12 months on a 9000 km (5600 mi) trek, the 'Long March', to the remote province of Shaanxi. In 1931 the Japanese seized Manchuria and established a puppet regime. After the Japanese occupied Beijing (Peking) and most of coastal China in 1937, Jiang and Mao combined against the invaders but were able to achieve little against superior forces. After World War II, the Soviets tried to ensure that Mao's Communists took over China. In 1946 Mao marched into Manchuria, beginning a civil war that lasted until 1949 when Mao declared a People's Republic in Beijing and Jiang fled to the offshore island of Taiwan, where a Nationalist government was set up (see below). In 1950 Chinese forces invaded Tibet - an independent state since 1916. Repressive Communist rule alienated the Tibetans, who, loyal to their religious leader the Dalai Lama, unsuccessfully rose in revolt in 1959. Chinese 'volunteers' were active in the Korean War on behalf of the Communist North Koreans (1950-53). China has been involved in a number of border disputes and conflicts, including clashes with the USSR in the late 1950s, with India in 1962 and with Vietnam in 1979. Relations with the USSR deteriorated in the 1950s, triggered by ideological clashes over the true nature of Communism. The Sino-Soviet rift led to the acceleration of Chinese research into atomic weapons - the first Chinese bomb was tested in 1964 - and a rapprochement with the USA in the early 1970s. The 'Great Leap Forward', an ambitious programme of radicalization in the 1950s, largely failed. In the 1960s Mao tried again to spread more radical revolutionary ideas in the so-called Cultural Revolution. Militant students formed groups of 'Red Guards' to attack the existing hierarchy. Thousands died as the students went out of control, and the army had to restore order. Since Mao's death (1976), China has effectively been under the leadership of Deng Xiaoping (1904-), although he holds none of the major state or party offices. A more careful path has been followed both at home and abroad; a rapprochement with the USSR was achieved in 1989, and agreement has been reached with the UK for the return of Hong Kong to Chinese rule in 1997. China was opened to foreign technology and investment, together with a degree of free enterprise, but this led to internal pressures for political change, culminating in massive pro-democracy demonstrations by students and workers early in 1989. These were brutally suppressed in the massacre of students in Tiananmen Square (June 1989) and hardline leaders gained in influence. Economic progress has been a priority in the 1990s. Living standards have improved drastically. However, an ageing political leadership continued to deny many basic human rights. Relations with the UK became strained when Britain proposed to widen the suffrage in the British colony of Hong Kong, which is due to revert to China in 1997.

236

Taiwan
(China, Republic of)

Official name: Chung-hua Min Kuo (The Republic of China). The country is popularly known as Taiwan. (For some international purposes, for example sport, Taiwan is known as 'Chinese-Taipei'.)

Member of: Taiwan is not a member of any major international organization.

Area: 35,981 km² (13,893 sq mi), including the small islands of Quemoy and Matsu, which are situated just off the coast of the Chinese mainland province of Fukien.

Population: 20,926,000 (1993 est).

Capital: Taipei 2,720,000 (city 2,680,000; 1993 est).

Other major cities: Kaohsiung 1,406,000, Taichung 802,000, Tainan 697,000, Panchiao 539,000, Chilung 360,000 (1993 est).

Language: Chinese (northern or Amoy dialect, popularly known as Mandarin; official).

Religions: Various Chinese folk religions (over 48%; includes Daoist), Buddhist (over 40%), various Christian Churches (mainly Roman Catholic; over 7%), small Sunni Islam minority.

Education: Education is compulsory between the ages of six and 15. In 1991 the literacy rate was 93%. There are 18 universities including an institute of university status.

Defence: In 1991 the total armed strength was 360,000 - 260,000 in the army, 30,000 in the navy and 70,000 in the air force. Military expenditure is considerably above the world average. Tsoying and Keelung are the main naval bases. Compulsory military service lasts for two years.

Transport: There are 19,490 km (12,113 mi) of roads and 4600 km (2859 mi) of railways. Taipei has a metro/rapid light transit system. Kaohsiung and Keelung are the main commercial shipping ports. Taipei has an international airport.

Media: Sixteen daily newspapers are published in Taipei; a further 10 are published in the provinces. Over 200 radio stations are operated by 33 radio corporations. There are three principal television systems, each operating a number of channels.

GOVERNMENT
The 161-member Parliament (the Legislative Yuan) comprises 125 members elected by universal adult suffrage for six years and additional members indirectly elected. The Yuan is the effective legislature of Taiwan. There is also a National Assembly, which comprises 325 directly-elected members. The Assembly has no legislative powers, other than to elect the President and to amend the constitution. The President appoints a Prime Minister and a Council of Ministers. The main political parties are the (Nationalist) Guomintang (Kuomintang; KMT), the (mainly Taiwanese) National Democratic Progressive Party (DPP) and the Chinese New Party (CNP; a split from the KMT). After the election held in December 1992 the KMT retained power.

Party strength: KMT 94, DPP 52, others and ind 15.

President: Lee Teng-hui (KMT).

THE CABINET
includes

Prime Minister: Lien Chan (KMT).

Vice-Prime Minister: Hsu Li-teh (KMT).

Secretary-General: Li Hou-kao (KMT).

Minister of Defence: Su Chen.

Minister of Economic Affairs: P.K. Chan (KMT).

Minister of Education: Kuo Wei-fan (KMT).

Minister of Foreign Affairs: Frederick Chien Fu (KMT).

Minister of the Interior: Wu Po-hsiung (KMT).

Minister of Justice: Ma Ying-jeou (KMT).

GEOGRAPHY
Taiwan is an island 160 km (100 mi) off the southeast coast of mainland China with a mountainous interior. Most of the inhabitants live on the coastal plain in the west. The Republic of China also includes the small islands of Quemoy and Matsu close to the Chinese mainland. Highest point: Yu Shan 3997 m (13,113 ft). Principal rivers: Hsia-tan-shui Chi, Chosui Chi. Climate: Taiwan - which is subtropical in the north, and tropical in the south - has rainy summers and mild winters. Tropical cyclones (typhoons) may occur between July and September.

ECONOMY

Despite Taiwan's diplomatic isolation, the island is a major international trading nation, exporting machinery, electronics, and textiles. The principal exports are calculating machines, plastic articles, dolls and toys, clothing (including knitted goods), synthetic fabrics, yarn and television sets. These exports have enabled Taiwan to build up impressive trade surpluses and its GDP is 54% of that of its giant neighbour, mainland China. The republic is expected to go into deficit in its budget in 1994-95 owing to high expenditure on improving the infrastructure. Taiwan has achieved high export-led economic growth rates over the past four decades. However, some manufacturers are beginning to relocate from Taiwan to other places in Asia as Taiwanese labour costs rise. A favourite area for this relocation is the neighbouring mainland Chinese province of Fukien, across the Taiwan Straits, where Taiwanese investment has transformed the local economy. Mineral resources include coal, marble and gold, and there are small but significant deposits of petroleum and natural gas. However, Taiwan has to rely upon imported energy sources and petroleum is the main import. Other major imports include the raw materials for the textile and clothing industries, food and wood and wood products. Despite the fertility of the soil, agriculture has declined in relative importance. About 10% of the labour force are employed in farming, mainly on small owner-occupied plots. The principal crops are rice, sugar cane, maize and sweet potatoes.

Currency: New Taiwan dollar of 100 cents; US$ = 26.66 New Taiwan dollars (June 1994).

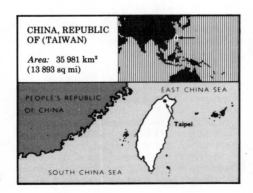

CHINA, REPUBLIC OF (TAIWAN)

Area: 35 981 km² (13 893 sq mi)

PEOPLE'S REPUBLIC OF CHINA

EAST CHINA SEA

Taipei

SOUTH CHINA SEA

GDP: US$251,000,000,000 (1993 est); US$11,900 per head.

RECENT HISTORY

In 1895, the Chinese province of Taiwan - which used to be called Formosa - was taken by the Japanese, who began the modernization of agriculture, transport and education. In 1949, the Nationalist forces of Jiang Jie Shi (Chiang Kai-shek) were driven onto Taiwan by the Communist victory on the mainland (see China above). Under US protection, the resulting authoritarian regime on Taiwan declared itself the Republic of China, and claimed to be the legitimate government of all China. America's rapprochement with the mainland People's Republic of China lost Taiwan its UN seat in 1971 and US recognition in 1978. By the late 1980s Taiwan was moving cautiously towards democracy, although its international status remained problematic. In 1988 a native Taiwanese became president and in 1990 an agreement was reached to speed up the retirement of Guomintang 'life members' from Taiwan's political bodies. (Until then, the majority of the members of the parliament of the Republic of China were KMT 'life members' elected in 1947-48 to represent constituencies on the Chinese mainland.) A new constitution in 1991 marked the transition to a more Taiwanese, less Chinese, identity. At the same time, Taiwan officialy ended four decades of 'civil war' between the 'Republic of China' (Taiwan) and the People's Republic of China, and Taiwan proposed that Taiwan and the People's Republic of China should recognize each other as separate political entities. Mainland China has rejected this suggestion and continues to insist that the island of Taiwan is a Chinese province. In 1993 Taiwan and China entered into 'non-official' level discussions about trade and communications. There are increasing disagreements between the 'One China' conservatives in the KMT and younger independence-minded Taiwanese. The (mainly Taiwanese) opposition DPP has won a number of local elections and now has realistic prospects of gaining national power. Taiwan still has diplomatic relations with a decreasing number of (mainly small) Third World and Latin American countries. The sale of arms to Taiwan - notably by the USA and France - has strained the relations of those countries with Beijing.

Japan

Official name: Nippon or Nihon ('The Land of the Rising Sun').

Member of: UN, G7, OECD.

Area: 377,815 km² (145,874 sq mi).

Population: 124,670,000 (1993 est).

Capital: Tokyo 25,000,000 (city 11,874,000, Yokohama 3,299,000, Kawasaki 1,195,000, Chiba 816,000, Funabashi 533,000; 1992 est).

Other major cities: Osaka 8,735,000 (city 2,603,000, Kobe 1,457,000, Sakai 803,000, Higashiosaka 518,000), Yokohama (see Tokyo, above), Kyoto 2,606,000, Nagoya 2,162,000, Sapporo 1,717,000, Kobe (see Osaka, above), Fukuoka 1,262,000, Kawasaki (see Tokyo, above), Hiroshima 1,097,000, Kitakyushu 1,021,000, Sendai 889,000, Chiba (see Tokyo, above), Sakai (see Osaka, above), Okayama 597,000, Kumamoto 579,000, Kagoshima 537,000, Hamamatsu 535,000, Funabashi (see Tokyo, above), Higashiosaka (see Osaka, above) (1992 est).

Language: Japanese (official).

Religions: Shintoism (40%), Buddhism (38%), various Christian denominations (4%). Shintoism and Buddhism overlap.

Education: Education is compulsory between the ages of six and 15. In 1992 the literacy rate was estimated to be virtually 100%. There are 79 state universities (including the open university) and 69 private universities.

Defence: In 1993 the total armed strength was 238,000 - 150,000 in the army (Ground Self-Defence Force), 43,000 in the navy (Maritime Self-Defence Force) and 45,000 in the air force (Air Self-Defence Force). The principal naval bases are Yokosuka and Sasebo. There is no military service.

Transport: There are 1,112,844 km (691,488 mi) of roads of which 4661 km (2897 mi) are motorways. There are 38,125 km (23,690 mi) of railways operated by seven private companies. Tokyo, Osaka, Fukuoka, Hiroshima, Kobe, Kyoto, Nagoya, Sapporo, Sendai and Yokohama have metro systems. The main commercial shipping ports are Tokyo, Yokohama, Nagoya, Kobe and Osaka. Tokyo has two international airports (including the world's sixth largest airport in terms of passengers). Osaka and Nagoya also have international airports.

Media: Japanese papers enjoy the highest circulations in the world. There are over 100 daily newspapers. The daily press is concentrated in Tokyo, whose papers form a national press. NHK, a non-commercial public corporation, runs two television and three radio stations. There are nearly 400 commercial radio stations and over 6800 commercial television stations.

GOVERNMENT

The head of state is the Emperor who has no executive power. The 252-member House of Councillors - the upper house of the Diet (Parliament) - is elected for six years by universal adult suffrage. One half of the councillors retire every three years. A system of proportional representation is used to elect 100 of the councillors. The 512-member House of Representatives (lower house) is elected for four years, also by universal adult suffrage. The Diet chooses a Prime Minister who commands a majority in the lower house. The PM in turn appoints a Cabinet of Ministers who are responsible to the Diet. There are nine administrative regions, which are further divided into a total of 47 prefectures. The main political parties are the (centre right) Liberal Democratic Party (Jiminto), the Social Democratic Party (Shakaito; SDP), the (mainly Buddhist) Clean Government Party (Komeito), the (centre right) Kaishin bloc - comprising the Japan Renewal Party (Shinseito), the Japan New Party (Nihon Shinto), the Democratic Socialists (Minsha), the Liberal Party (Jiyuto; LDP) and Kyu-Kaikakau no Kai - the (reformist) New Harbinger Party (Sakigake), Shinto Mirai, the (Green) Niin Club and the Communist Party (Kyosanto). Following the election in July 1993, a coalition government was formed. Further party splits in 1993-94 resulted in the formation of further coalitions - most recently a SDP-LDP-Sakigake government in July 1994.

Party strength (House of Representatives): (June 1994) Kaishin 126 (Shinseito 62, Nihon Shinto 33, Minsha 19, Jiyuto 7, Kyu-Kaikakau no Kai 4, others 1), Jiminto 206, Shakaito 74, Komeito 52, Sakigake 22, Kyosanto 15, Shinto Mirai 5, independents 9, vacant 2.

Emperor: HIM the Heisei Emperor - known outside Japan as Emperor Akihito (who succeeded upon the death of his father, 7 January 1989).

239

THE CABINET

Prime Minister: Tomichi Murayama (SDP).

Deputy Prime Minister and Minister for Foreign Affairs: Yohei Kono (LDP).

Minister of Agriculture, Forestry and Fisheries: Taichiro Okawara (LDP).

Minister of Construction: Koken Nosaka (SDP).

Minister of Education: Kaoru Yosano (LDP).

Minister of Finance: Masayoshi Takamura (Sakigake).

Minister of Health and Welfare: Shoichi Ide (Sakigake).

Minister of Home Affairs: Hiromu Nonaka (LDP).

Minister of International Trade and of Industry: Ryutaro Hashimoto (LDP).

Minister of Justice: Isao Maeda (LDP).

Minister of Labour: Manso Hamamoto (SDP).

Minister of Posts and Telecommunications: Shun Oide (SDP).

Minister of Transport: Shizuka Kamei (LDP).

REGIONS

Chubu Area: 66,777 km^2 (25,783 sq mi). Population; 21,162,000 (1992 est). Main centre: Nagoya.

Chugoku Area: 31,789 km^2 (12,273 sq mi). Population: 7,754,000 (1992 est). Main centre: Hiroshima.

Hokkaido Area: 83,520 km^2 (32,247 sq mi). Population: 5,659,000 (1992 est). Main centre: Sapporo.

Kanto Area: 32,383 km^2 (12,503 sq mi). Population: 39,047,000 (1992 est). Main centre: Tokyo.

Kinki Area: 33,074 km^2 (12,770 sq mi). Population: 25,293,000 (1992 est). Main centre: Osaka.

Kyushu Area: 42,164 km^2 (16,278 sq mi). Population: 13,314,000 (1992 est). Main centre: Fukuoka.

Ryukyu Area: 2255 km^2 (871 sq mi). Population; 1,238,000 (1992 est). Main centre: Naha.

Shokoku Area: 18,808 km^2 (7262 sq mi). Population: 4,182,000 (1992 est). Main centre: Matsuyama.

Tohoku Area: 66,912 km^2 (25,834 sq mi). Population: 9,752,000 (1992 est). Main centre: Sendai.

GEOGRAPHY

Japan consists of over 3900 islands, of which Hokkaido in the north occupies 22% of the total land area, and Shikoku and Kyushu in the south respectively occupy 5% and 11% of the area. The central island of Honshu occupies 61% of the total land area and contains 80% of the population. To the south of the four main islands, the Ryukyu Islands - including Okinawa - stretch almost to Taiwan. Nearly three quarters of Japan is mountainous. Coastal plains - where the population is concentrated - are limited. The principal lowlands are Kanto (around Tokyo), Nobi (around Nagoya) and the Sendai Plain in the north of Honshu. There are also over 60 active volcanoes in Japan, and the country is prone to severe earthquakes. Highest point: Fujiyama (Mount Fuji) 3776 m (12,388 ft). Principal rivers: Tone, Ishikarai, Shinano, Kitakami. Climate: Japan experiences great variations in climate. Although the whole country is temperate, the north has long cold snowy winters, while the south has hot summers and mild winters. Rainfall totals are generally high, with heavy rain and typhoons being common in the summer months.

ECONOMY

Despite the generally crowded living conditions in the cities, the Japanese enjoy a high standard of living. The country has the second largest industrial economy in the world, despite having very few natural resources. Japanese industry is heavily dependent on imported raw materials - about 90% of the country's energy requirements come from abroad and petroleum is the single largest import. There is, therefore, considerable interest in offshore petroleum exploration, particularly in the Korean Straits. Japan's economic success is based on manufacturing industry, which - with construction - employs nearly one third of the labour force. Japan is the world's leading manufacturer of motor vehicles, and one of the major producers of ships, steel, synthetic fibres, chemicals, cement, electrical goods and electronic equipment. Rapid advances in Japanese research and technology have helped the expanding export-led economy. The banking and financial sectors have prospered in line with the manufacturing sector, and Tokyo is one of the world's principal stock exchanges and commercial centres. The high growth rates of the 1980s gave way to recession in the early 1990s. Unemployment has increased and the Japanese tradition of a job for life has been seriously challenged. The stock market and the property market both collapsed (1992-93), and Japan's retail boom vanished. Although the economy began to pick up in 1993, political uncertainty has not helped the recovery. Agriculture is labour intensive. Although Japan is self-sufficient in rice, agriculture is not a priority and 30% of its food requirements - particularly cereals and fodder crops - have to be imported. The traditional Japanese diet is sea-based and the fishing industry is a large one, both for export and for domestic consumption.

Currency: Yen; 1US$ = 103.49 yen (June 1994).

GDP: US$4,700,000,000,000 (1993 est); US$37,561 per head.

RECENT HISTORY
At the end of the 19th century, the Meiji Emperor overthrew the last shogun and restored power to the throne. He encouraged Western institutions and a Western-style economy, so that by the beginning of the 20th century Japan was rapidly industrializing and on the brink of becoming a world power. By the

JAPAN

Area: 377 815 km²
(145 874 sq mi).

time of the death of the Meiji Emperor in 1912, the Japanese had established an empire. Japan had defeated China (1894-95) - taking Port Arthur and Taiwan - and startled Europe by beating Russia (1904-5) on land and at sea. Korea was annexed in 1910. Allied with Britain from 1902, Japan entered World War I against Germany in 1914, in part to gain acceptance as an imperial world power. However, Japan gained little except some of the German island territories in the Pacific and became disillusioned that the country did not seem to be treated as an equal by the Great Powers. The rise of militarism and collapse of world trade in the 1930s led to the rise of totalitarianism and a phase of aggressive Japanese expansion. In 1931 the Japanese army seized Chinese Manchuria, and in 1937 mounted an all-out attack on China itself, occupying large areas. Japan became allied to Nazi Germany and in 1941 Japanese aircraft struck Pearl Harbor in Hawaii, bringing the USA into World War II. An initial rapid Japanese military expansion across Southeast Asia and the Pacific was halted, and the war ended for Japan in disastrous defeat and the horrors of atomic warfare. Emperor Hirohito (reigned 1926-89) surrendered in September 1945. Shintoism - which had come to be identified with aggressive nationalism - ceased to be the state religion, and in 1946 the emperor renounced his divinity. The Allied occupation (1945-52) both democratized politics and began an astonishing economic recovery based on an aggressive export policy. The economy was jolted by major rises in petroleum prices in 1973 and 1979, but Japan nevertheless maintained its advance to become a technological front-runner. By 1988 Japan surpassed the USA as the world's largest aid-donor. The Japanese political world was dominated by the Liberal Democrats, who held office from 1955 to 1993 despite a number of financial scandals. Since 1993 coalitions have held power and several parties have split from the Liberal Democrats. Electoral reform and corruption have become issues, and there has been rising public pressure for more open government. Japan has also started to re-examine its role in the world. Japanese neutrality almost prevented the country taking a non-military role in the UN undertaking in Cambodia. A permanent seat for Japan on the UN Security Council has also become an issue.

Korea, Democratic People's Republic of

Official name: Chosun Minchu-chui Inmin Konghwa-guk (Democratic People's Republic of Korea). Popularly known as North Korea.

Member of: UN.

Area: 120,538 km² (46,540 sq mi).

Population: 22,646,000 (1991 est).

Capital: Pyongyang 2,640,000 (1986 est).

Other major cities: Hamhung 775,000, Chongjin 755,000, Chinnamp'o 690,000 (1986 est).

Language: Korean.

Religions: Daoism and Confucianism (14%), Chondism (14%), Buddhism (2%).

Education: Education is compulsory between the ages of five and 16. No figures for the literacy rate are available. There are five universities.

Defence: In 1993 the total armed strength was 1,130,000. There is selective military service.

Transport: There are 23,000 km (14,290 mi) of roads and 5024 km (3122 mi) of railways. Nampo and Wonsam are the main ports; Pyongyang has an international airport.

Media: There are four state-controlled daily newspapers, and a state-run radio and television service.

GOVERNMENT
The Party Congress of the (Communist) Korean Worker's Party elects a Central Committee, which elects a Politburo, the seat of power. Every four years there are unopposed elections for the 615-member Supreme People's Assembly, which elects the President, Prime Minister and Central People's Committee, which nominates Ministers.

President: Kim Jong-Il.

Prime Minister: Yon Hyong Muk.

GEOGRAPHY
Over three quarters of the country consists of mountains. Highest point: Paek-tu 2744 m (9003 ft). Principal rivers: Imjin, Ch'ongch'on, Yalu. Climate: The country has long cold dry winters and hot wet summers.

ECONOMY
Over one third of the labour force works on cooperative farms, mainly growing rice. Natural resources include coal, zinc, magnetite, iron ore and lead. Great emphasis has been placed on industrial development, with the metallurgical, machine-building, chemical and cement industries being the most important. The end of barter deals with the former USSR (1990-91) brought a sharp economic decline.

Currency: Won of 100 chon; 1US$ = 2.149 wons.

GDP: US$23,300,000,000 (1991); US$1100 per head.

RECENT HISTORY
Korea - a Japanese possession from 1910 to 1945 - was divided into zones of occupation in 1945. The USSR established a Communist republic north of the 38th parallel (1948). North Korea launched a surprise attack on the South in 1950, hoping to achieve reunification by force. The Korean War devastated the peninsula. At the ceasefire in 1953 the frontier was re-established close to the 38th parallel. North Korea has the world's first Communist dynasty, whose personality cult has surpassed even that of Stalin. President Kim Il-Sung (1912-94) and his son and successor, Kim Jong-Il, have rejected political reforms. Since the collapse of international Communism, North Korea has become increasingly isolated. Pyongyang's refusal to allow international inspection of suspected nuclear weapons installations increased tension in 1994.

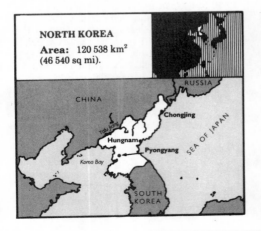

NORTH KOREA
Area: 120 538 km² (46 540 sq mi).

CHINA

RUSSIA

Chongjing

Hungnam

Pyongyang

SEA OF JAPAN

Korea Bay

SOUTH KOREA

Korea, Republic of (South Korea)

Official name: Daehan-Minkuk (Republic of Korea). Popularly known as South Korea.

Member of: UN.

Area: 99,143 km² (38,279 sq mi).

Population: 44,042,000 (1993 est).

Capital: Seoul (Soul) 11,000,000 (city 10,613,000; 1990 census).

Other major cities: Pusan 3,825,000, Taegu 2,248,000, Inchon 1,682,000, Kwangju 1,206,000, Taejon 1,062,000, Ulsan 683,000, Sowon 645,000 (1990 census).

Language: Korean (official).

Religions: Buddhist (24%), various Protestant Churches (16%), Roman Catholic (5%).

Education: Education is compulsory btween the ages of six and 12. In 1990 the literacy rate was 96.3%. There are 39 universities including an open university.

Defence: In 1992 the total armed strength was 633,000 - 520,000 in the army, 60,000 in the navy and 53,000 in the air force. The main naval bases are Chinhae and Inchon. Compulsory military service lasts between 30 and 36 months.

Transport: There are 55,778 km (34,659 mi) of roads and 6586 km (4092 mi) of railways. Seoul and Pusan have metros. There are international airports at Seoul, Pusan and Cheju. The main commercial shipping ports are Pusan and Inchon.

Media: There are 45 daily newspapers, 23 of which have a national circulation. There are eight radio systems operating over 60 radio stations. Three television systems operate over 40 television channels.

GOVERNMENT

The 299-member National Assembly is elected by universal adult suffrage every four years - 237 members are directly elected to represent constituencies; the remaining 62 members are chosen under a system of proportional representation. The President - who appoints a State Council (Cabinet) and a Prime Minister - is directly elected for a single five-year term. There are nine provinces and six cities of provincial status. The main political parties include the Democratic Liberal Party (a merger of the Democratic Justice Party, the Reunification Democratic Party, and the New Democratic Republican Party; DLP), the Democratic Party (DP), the United People's Party (UPP), and the New Political Reform Party (NPRP). After the election held in December 1992 a DLP government was formed.

Party strength: DLP 149, DP 97, UPP 31, NPRP 1, ind 21.

President: Kim Young Sam (DLP).

THE CABINET

Prime Minister: Lee Yung-Duk (DLP).

Deputy Prime Minister and Minister of Economic Planning: Chung Jai-Suk.

Deputy Prime Minister and Minister of National Unification: Lee Hong-Koo.

Minister of Agriculture, Forestry and Fisheries: Kim Yang-Bae.

Minister of Construction: Kim Woo-Suk.

Minister of Culture and Sports: Lee Min-Sup.

Minister of Defence: Lee Pyong-Tae.

Minister of Education: Kim Sook-He.

Minister of the Environment: Park Yun-Heum.

Minister of Finance: Hong Jae-Hyung.

Minister of Foreign Affairs: Han Sung-Joo.

Minister of Government Administration: Hwang Young-Ha.

Minister of Health and Social Affairs: Suh Sang-Mok.

Minister of Home Affairs: Choi Hyung-Woo.

Minister of Justice: Kim Doo-Hee.

Minister of Labour: Nam Jae-Hee.

Minister of Legislation: Hwan Kil-Su.

Minister for Patriots and Veterans' Affairs: Lee Chung-Kil.

Minister of Political Affairs (I): Suh Chong-Won.

Minister of Political Affairs (II): Kwon Young-Ja.

Minister of Science and Technology: Kim Si-Joong.

Minister of Trade, Industry and Energy: Kim Chul-Su.

Minister of Transportation: Oh In-Hwan.

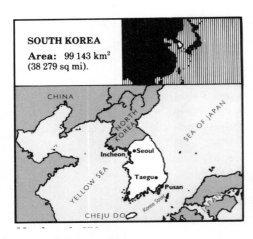

SOUTH KOREA

Area: 99 143 km²
(38 279 sq mi).

GEOGRAPHY
Apart from restricted coastal lowlands and the densely-populated river basins, most of the country is mountainous. Highest point: Halla-san 1950 m (6398 ft) on Cheju Island. Principal rivers: Han, Kum, Naktong, Somjin, Yongsan. Climate: Korea experiences cold dry winters and hot summers during which the monsoon brings heavy rainfall.

ECONOMY
Agriculture involves about 20% of the labour force. The principal crops are rice, wheat and barley. A flourishing manufacturing sector is dominated by a small number of large family conglomerates (chaebol). Moves were taken in 1994 to begin to restrict the power of these conglomerates. The important textile industry was the original manufacturing base, but South Korea is now the world's leading producer of ships and footwear, and a major producer of electronic equipment, electrical goods, steel, petrochemicals, motor vehicles (Hyundai) and toys. Banking and finance are expanding. The

country experienced high economic growth rates throughout the 1980s and early 1990s, and South Korea now has the world's 11th largest economy. The standard of living in, and the GDP of, South Korea are immensely greater than those of North Korea. The costs of having to underwrite the modernization of North Korea if that regime were to collapse is a major concern.

Currency: Won (KRW) of 100 chon; 1US$ = 807.3 KRW (June 1994).

GDP: US$375,000,000,000 (1993 est); US$8440 per head.

RECENT HISTORY
The Yi dynasty (1392-1910) gave Korea a long period of cultural continuity, but in 1910 Korea was annexed by the Japanese, who instituted a harsh colonial rule. After World War II, the peninsula was divided into Soviet and US zones of occupation. In 1948 the Republic of Korea was established in the American (southern) zone. The surprise invasion of the South by the Communist North precipitated the Korean War (1950-53). The war cost a million lives, devastated the cities and industries of the south and ended in stalemate with the division of Korea confirmed. Closely allied to the USA, an astonishing economic transformation took place in South Korea. However, the country has experienced long periods of authoritarian rule including the presidencies of Syngman Rhee and Park Chung-Hee, but the election of ex-General Roh Tae Woo - amid political unrest in 1987 - introduced a more open regime. Much prestige was gained through the successful Seoul Olympic Games, and trading and diplomatic contacts have been established with Russia and all the former Communist countries of Eastern and Central Europe. This has left Communist North Korea increasingly isolated. Tension in the peninsula rose in 1994 when North Korea refused to allow international inspection of suspected nuclear weapons installations and increased following the death of the North Korean dictator Kim Il-Sung. Under President Kim Young Sam, South Korea has been extensively reformed - the last vestiges of the country's authoritarian past have been removed and corruption in politics and business has been tackled. South Korea is concerned about the future of North Korea under Kim Jong-Il.

Mongolia

Official name: Mongol Uls (Mongolian Republic).

Member of: UN.

Area: 1,565,000 km ^{2}(604 250 sq mi).

Population: 2,256,000 (1993 est).

Capital: Ulan Bator (Ulaan Baatar) 575,000 (1991 est)

Other major cities: Darhan 90,000, Erdenet 58,000 (1991 est).

Languages: Khalkh Mongolian (official; 78%), Kazakh (6%).

Religion: Religion was suppressed from 1924 to 1990; there has been a recent revival of Buddhism.

Education: Education is compulsory between the ages of six and 16. In 1989 the literacy rate was over 97%. There are four universities.

Defence: In 1993 the total armed strength was over 21,0000 - 20,000 of whom were in the army. Compulsory military service lasts two years.

Transport: There are 49,200 km (30,600 mi) of roads and 2325 km (1445 km) of state-run railways. Ulan Bator has an international airport.

Media: There are nearly 30 main national newspapars but none is daily. There is a state-run radio and television service.

GOVERNMENT

A 76-member Great Hural (Assembly) and an executive President are elected by universal adult suffrage for four years. The President appoints a Prime Minister and a Council of Ministers. The main political parties are the (Communist) Mongolian People's Revolutionary Party (BDY) and the Mongolian National Democratic Party (DG). Following the election in 1993 a BDY government was formed.

Party strength: BDY 70, DG 6.

President: Punsalmaagiyn Ochirbat (DG).

Prime Minister: Dashin Byambasuren (BDY).

GEOGRAPHY

Mongolia comprises mountains in the north, a series of basins in the centre, and the Gobi Desert and Altai Mountains in the south. Highest point: Mönh Hayrhan Uul 4362 m (14,311 ft). Principal rivers: Selenge, Orhon, Hereleng. Climate: Mongolia has a dry climate with generally mild summers and severely cold winters.

ECONOMY

Mongolia depends on collectivized animal herding (cattle, sheep, goats and camels). Cereals (including fodder crops) are grown on a large scale on state farms. The industrial sector is dominated by food processing, hides and wool. Copper is a major export. The collapse of trade with the former Soviet Union has created severe economic difficulties and Mongolia is increasingly looking to Japan and China for trade and economic assistance. Privatization has advanced since 1993.

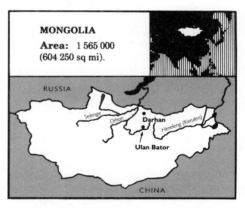

MONGOLIA
Area: 1 565 000 (604 250 sq mi).

Currency: Tugrik of 100 mongo; 1 US$ = 399.7 tugriks (June 1994).

GDP: US$240,700,000 (1990); US$112 per head.

RECENT HISTORY

In 1921, Outer Mongolia broke away from China with Soviet assistance, and in 1924 the Mongolian People's Republic was established. Pro-democracy demonstrations early in 1990 led to a liberalization of the regime. The first multi-party elections were held in July 1990 when the Communists were returned to power. However, when the incumbent Communist President Ochirbat was dropped by his party in the 1993 presidential election, he was adopted by the opposition and won.

245

Other territories

HONG KONG

Status: a British Crown colony with adjoining areas - the New Territories - leased from China.

Area: 1045 km² (403 sq mi) - Hong Kong island 79 km² (30.4 sq mi), Kowloon peninsula 42 km² (16.3 sq mi), New Territories 924 km² (356.5 sq mi).

Population: 6,019,000 (1993 est).

Capital: Victoria.

Government: The British sovereign is represented by a Governor who presides over the Executive Council, which comprises four ex officio and 10 appointed members. The 60-member Legislative Council currently comprises 18 members directly elected by universal adult suffrage, 21 members elected from 'functional constituencies' representing occupational and professional interests, three ex officio members and 18 appointed members. Proposals for constitutional reform, which would increase the number of elected representatives, are opposed by China.

Geography: Hong Kong comprises Hong Kong island, Kowloon peninsula, the hilly New Territories on the Chinese mainland, Lantau Island and 234 other smaller islands. Highest point: Tai Mo Shan 957 m (3140 ft). Climate: The climate is subtropical with monsoon rains between March and May.

Economy: Hong Kong has emerged as one of the economic 'little dragons' of the Far East with a GDP of US$127,000,000,000 (1993 est); US$21,500 per head. The colony grew as the trading 'gateway' to China and became the financial and banking centre for Communist China. Hong Kong is a leading industrial power - originally based upon cheap labour. Principal exports include clothing, textiles, electrical machinery, data-processing and telecommunications equipment, and sound equipment. The economy has been increasingly integrated with that of the neighbouring Chinese province of Guangdong, but confidence has been dented by disputes between China and Britain and the impending return of Hong Kong to China.

Recent History: China ceded Hong Kong

island to Britain in 1842. Kowloon was added to the colony in 1860 and the UK acquired a lease on the New Territories in 1898. Japan occupied Hong Kong from 1941 to 1945. Hong Kong is to return to China on 1 July 1997 when the New Territories lease expires. Under the Basic Law (agreed by the UK and China), Hong Kong will be a Special Administrative Region retaining its present laws and economic system and enjoying considerable autonomy. However, disputes between Britain and China concerning the construction of a new airport and the constitutional reforms proposed by the Governor, Chris Patten, have cast some doubts on the full implementation of the agreement.

MACAU

Status: a Special Territory of Portugal.

Area: 17 km² (6.5 sq mi).

Population: 452,000 (1990 est).

Capital: Macau 452,000 (1990 est).

Government: The President of Portugal is represented by a Governor, who is assisted by up to seven under-secretaries. The 23-member Legislative Assembly comprises seven deputies appointed by the Governor, eight elected by universal adult suffrage for four years and eight indirectly elected.

Geography: The territory comprises the peninsula of Macau on the Chinese mainland and two small adjoining islands. Highest point: an unnamed point 99 m (325 ft). Climate: Macau has a subtropical climate.

Economy: Nearly one half of the labour force is involved in manufacturing industry, in particular textiles and clothing, plastic goods, toys, furniture, electrical goods and electronics, and footwear. The growth of these industries was encouraged by low labour costs and Macau's free port status. Tourism, attracted by casinos, makes a major contribution to the economy.

Recent History: Macau, a Portuguese colony since 1557, has since 1974 been a special territory under Portuguese administration but, in which, China has a leading role. Negotiations between Portugal and China (1987) resulted in an agreement to transfer sovereignty to China in 1999 when the territory will become an autonomous Special Administrative Region of China.

THE MIDDLE EAST AND NORTH AFRICA

Algeria, Bahrain, Egypt, Iran, Iraq, Israel, Jordan, Kuwait, Lebanon, Libya, Morocco, Oman, Qatar, Saudi Arabia, Syria, Tunisia, Turkey, United Arab Emirates, Yemen, Other territories.

Islam and Politics

Political Islam is an explosive compound of fundamentalist Islam and radical politics. The mixture, which is also referred to as 'militant Islam', or 'Islamic fundamentalism', has shaken governments across the Muslim world and beyond. Islam as a political force burst onto the international stage in 1979 with the revolution in Iran. Encouraged by Ayatollah Khomeini, Islamic political groups mushroomed across the Muslim world. In 1994 Islamic militants engaged governments in virtual civil war in Algeria and Tajikistan, assassinated senior politicians and damaged the tourist industry in Egypt, and threatened the fledgling peace between Israel and the PLO. In Turkey, one of the few countries where they are tolerated, Islamic parties did well at the polls. Religious fundamentalism was transformed into a radical political creed by Muslim thinkers appalled by the domination of the Arab world by European powers following the First World War. The latest generation of fundamentalists is more radical still. Many of them call for a jihad, or holy war, to rescue Muslims from the perceived corruption of secular governments. What makes the latest movement explosive is its widespread popularity. Many Muslims support political Islamic groups out of genuine religious sentiment. Others believe that Islamic government and a return to traditional Islamic values can re-create the Golden Age of Islam, and unite the Muslim world from Mauritania to Indonesia. Yet others turn to radical Islam out of a sense of dislocation as they struggle to reconcile traditional beliefs with the onslaught of western culture. Even more Muslims turn to Islamic militant groups for political reasons; in most Muslim states secular political opposition parties are banned or impotent. But overwhelmingly it is economic despair that drives people to militant Islam.

In such states Islamic groups recruit easily from a growing pool of young people frustrated by a widening gap between rich and poor. To this problem the Islamic militants offer a deceptively simple solution: the rejection of western values, the introduction of government based upon Islamic law and the return to traditional Islamic ways. Where Islamic groups have taken control of government – in Iran, Sudan and Afghanistan – they have done so

respectively by revolution, coup and civil war. In other Muslim states secular governments have adopted a range of strategies to prevent radical Islamic groups coming to power. Some, including Iraq, Syria and Libya, ruthlessly repress all Islamic groups. Most, such as Tunisia, Morocco and Tajikistan, attempt to suppress extremists while encouraging 'official' Islam by building mosques and strengthening Muslim family law. Governments in some of these states outlaw Islamic political parties on the ground that they are fundamentally anti-democratic and should therefore not be allowed to use democratic means to win power. But a few, including working democracies like Turkey's or Pakistan's or would-be democracies such as Jordan and Egypt, allow moderate Islamic groups to take part in elections, hoping to contain them by giving them a stake in the status quo. Other governments, such as Algeria, have no consistent policy.

In the 1980s Iran was the powerhouse of militant Islam, attempting to export Islamic revolution to Kuwait, Saudi Arabia, Lebanon, Afghanistan and elsewhere. Saudi Arabia also sponsored its own brand of Islamic fundamentalism throughout the Muslim world. In the 1990s Sudan has emerged as a sponsor of Islamic extremism – and according to some governments, of Islamic terrorism. Islamic mujaheddin fighters from Afghanistan have turned up fighting for anti-government Islamic groups in Tajikistan, Algeria, Eritrea and Kashmir. Some secular governments in the Muslim world, such as Egypt's, claim the existence of an international network of Islamic terrorism centred upon Iran, Sudan and Afghanistan. In most of Central Asia, except Tajikistan, Islam is returning gradually, after the retreat of Soviet rule. In Pakistan's legislative elections in October 1993 the Islamic Alliance was trounced. The government in the Philippines has reached an accommodation with its Muslim separatists. And in Lebanon the Islamic terror groups that flourished in the 1970s and 1980s have been brought under a semblance of government control. But the growth of Islamic militancy has encouraged most governments in the Muslim world to take precautions. For example the government of Malaysia, which faced a rise of Islamic fundamentalism in the 1980s and early 1990s, is trying to promote the country as a progressive Muslim state.

Regional Organizations of the Middle East and North Africa

THE CO-OPERATION COUNCIL FOR THE ARAB STATES OF THE GULF (GCC)

The GCC was established in 1981 to promote economic, cultural and social co-operation between the Arab states of the Gulf. It has since also taken on a security role, notably during the Gulf War of 1991. In March 1991, the members of GCC concluded economic and defence agreements with Egypt and Syria, although the latter two states are not members of the Council.

Headquarters: Riyadh, Saudi Arabia.

Membership: Bahrain, Kuwait, Oman, Qatar, Saudi Arabia, and the United Arab Emirates.

LEAGUE OF ARAB STATES (THE ARAB LEAGUE)

The League of Arab States, which is popularly known as the Arab League, was founded in Cairo, Egypt, in March 1945. It aims to protect the independence and sovereignty of members, to strengthen ties between them, and to encourage co-ordination of their social, economic, political, cultural and legal policies. The League comprises a Council (on which each state has one vote), special committees, over 20 specialized agencies and a Secretariat.

Headquarters: Cairo, Egypt.

Secretary General: Dr Ahmad al-Meguid (Egypt).

Membership: Algeria, Bahrain, Djibouti, Egypt, Iraq, Jordan, Kuwait, Lebanon, Libya, Mauritania, Morocco, Oman, the Palestine Liberation Organization (currently governing Gaza-Jericho), Qatar, Saudi Arabia, Somalia, Sudan, Syria, Tunisia, the United Arab Emirates, and Yemen.

ORGANIZATION OF ARAB PETROLEUM EXPORTING COUNTRIES (OAPEC)

OAPEC was founded in 1968 to encourage co-operation in economic activities, to ensure the flow of oil to consumer markets, and to promote a favourable climate for the investment of capital and expertise. The oil ministers of members form the Ministerial Council, which meets twice a year. The General Secretariat is the executive organ of OAPEC.

Headquarters: Cairo, Egypt.

Membership: Algeria, Bahrain, Egypt, Iraq, Kuwait, Libya, Qatar, Saudi Arabia, Syria, and the United Arab Emirates.

ORGANIZATION OF THE ISLAMIC CONFERENCE (OIC)

The Organization was founded in Rabat, Morocco, in May 1971 to promote Islamic solidarity, to consolidate economic, social and cultural co-operation between members, and to safeguard the Holy Places of Islam and the independence of Muslim people.

Headquarters: Jeddah, Saudi Arabia.

Membership: Afghanistan, Algeria, Bahrain, Bangladesh, Benin, Brunei, Burkina Faso, Cameroon, Chad, Comoros, Djibouti, Egypt, Gabon, The Gambia, Guinea, Guinea-Bissau, Indonesia, Iran, Iraq, Jordan, Kuwait, Lebanon, Libya, Malaysia, Maldives, Mali, Mauritania, Morocco, Niger, Oman, Pakistan, the Palestine Liberation Organization (currently governing Gaza-Jericho), Qatar, Saudi Arabia, Senegal, Sierra Leone, Somalia, Sudan, Syria, Tunisia, Turkey, Uganda, the United Arab Emirates, and Yemen. Mozambique is an associate member.

OTHER ORGANIZATIONS

The following countries of North Africa are members of the Organization of African Unity (OAU): Algeria, Egypt, Libya, and Tunisia.

Turkey belongs to a number of European organizations (see pp. 350-51).

Middle Eastern and North African Trade

Algeria Imports ($ million): 7396 (1988). Exports ($ million): 8164 (1988). Main imports: machinery, transport equipment and industrial equipment 39.0% (1990), food and beverages 22.5% (1990). Main exports: minerals, fuels and lubricants (mainly crude petroleum and natural gas) 96.3% (1990). Principal trading partners: France, Italy, USA, Germany, Belgium-Luxembourg, Netherlands, UK.

Bahrain Imports ($ million): 3711 (1990). Exports ($ million): 3758 (1990). Total imports: crude-petroleum products 54.3% (1990), non-petroleum products 45.7% (1990). Total exports: petroleum products 79.0% (1990), aluminium products 5.6% (1990). Principal trading partners: USA, United Arab Emirates, Saudi Arabia, Japan.

Egypt Imports (E£ million): 25,216.3 (1991). Exports (E£ million): 11,764.7 (1991). Main imports: machinery and transport equipment 23.6% (1991), foodstuffs and live animals 21.7% (1991), basic manufactures, chemicals and chemical products. Main exports: basic manufactures 21.8% (1991), petroleum and petroleum products 49.9% (1991), vegetables and fruit. Principal trading partners: USA, Germany, France, Italy, Netherlands, Saudi Arabia, Russia, UK, Switzerland.

Iran Imports ($ million): 11,989 (1990). Exports ($ million): 13,200 (1986). Main imports: machinery and transport equipment 36.7% (1988/89), iron and steel 18.5% (1988/89), chemicals and chemical products, food and live animals. Main exports: petroleum and products 92.6% (1989), carpets, nuts, fruits and hides 7.4% (1989), agricultural goods, skins and hides. Principal trading partners: Germany, Japan, Turkey, UK, United Arab Emirates, Italy, Switzerland, Belgium-Luxembourg.

Iraq Imports ($ million): 4834 (1990). Exports ($ million): 392 (1990). Main imports: machinery and transport equipment 39.8% (1987), manufactured goods 27.1% (1987). Main exports: fuels and other energy 99.5% (1989), food and agricultural raw materials 0.5% (1989). (The export of petroleum and petroleum products virtually in 1990 under the terms of UN sanctions.) Principal trading partners: Turkey, Germany.

Israel Imports ($ million): 16,906 (1991). Exports ($ million): 11,893 (1991). Main imports: diamonds (rough) 15.1% (1991), machinery and parts 15.4% (1991), crude petroleum, chemicals and chemical products. Main exports: diamonds (worked) 20.7% (1991), machinery and parts 15.3% (1991), chemicals and chemical products. Principal trading partners: USA, UK, Germany, Belgium-Luxembourg, Japan, Switzerland, Italy, France, Netherlands.

Jordan Imports ($ million): 2512 (1991). Exports ($ million): 902 (1991). Main imports: machinery and transport equipment 17.4% (1991), basic manufactures 19% (1991), food and live animals. Main exports: chemicals and chemical products 29.5% (1991), phosphate fertilizers 20.5% (1991), potash. Principal trading partners: Saudi Arabia, Germany, UK, Iraq, USA, Pakistan, India, Saudi Arabia, Turkey.

Kuwait Imports ($ million): 6303 (1989). Exports ($ million): 11 476 (1989). Main imports: transport equipment 31.1% (1987), miscellaneous manufactured articles 24.7% (1987). Main exports: petroleum and products 92.2% (1989). Principal trading partners: Japan, Netherlands, USA, Germany, Italy, France, Taiwan, South Korea.

Lebanon Imports ($ million): 2580 (1989). Exports ($ million): 570 (1989). Main imports: consumer goods 40.0% (1982), machinery and transport equipment 35.0% (1982). Main exports: jewellery 10.2% (1985), clothing 5.2% (1985), metal products, machinery and electrical apparatus, food. Principal trading partners: Saudi Arabia, Italy, France, Germany, Switzerland, Turkey, Belgium-Luxembourg.

Libya Imports ($ million): 5879 (1988). Exports ($ million): 6683 (1988). Main imports: foodstuffs 42.3% (1989), agricultural goods 18.5% (1989), machinery and transport equipment, chemicals and chemical products. Main exports: crude petroleum 96.8% (1989), chemicals and related products. Principal trading partners: Italy, Germany, Spain, France, Turkey, UK, Belgium-Luxembourg.

Morocco Imports ($ million): 6919 (1990). Exports ($ million): 4229 (1990). Main imports: capital goods 26.8% (1990), crude oil 14.3%

(1990), sulphur, chemicals and chemical p[rod-ucts. Main exports: food 24.8% (1990), phosphates 9.7% (1990), fertilizer, clothing. Principal trading partners: France, Spain, USA, Germany, Italy, UK, Belgium-Luxembourg, Japan.

Oman Imports ($ million): 2681 (1990). Exports ($ million): 5215 (1990). Main imports: machinery and transport equipment 36.1% (1990), manufactured goods 18.4% (1990). Main exports: petroleum 91.7% (1990). Principal trading partners: Japan, South Korea, United Arab Emirates, USA.

Qatar Imports (QR million): 6261 (1991). Exports (QR million): 11,467 (1989). Main imports: machinery and transport equipment 37.0% (1989), manufactured goods 23.9% (1989). Main exports: crude petroleum and products 82.0% (1989), liquefied gas chemicals 12.4% (1989). Principal trading partners: Japan, UK, Germany.

Saudi Arabia Imports ($ million): 24,069 (1990). Exports ($ million): 44,417 (1990). Main imports: transport equipment 20.4% (1990), machinery and appliances 16.3% (1990), textiles and textile p[roducts, live animals and food, chemicals and chemical products. Main exports: crude petroleum 74% (1989), refined petroleum 16.2% (1990). Principal trading partners: USA, Japan, UK, France, Netherlands, Australia, South Korea, Switzerland, Singapore, Taiwan, Brazil, Bahrain.

Syria Imports (£S million): 26,936.1 (1990). Exports (£S million): 47,281.6 (1990). Main imports: foods, beverages and tobacco 24.8% (1990), machinery and equipment 19.7% (1990), base metals. Main exports: crude petroleum and products 43.9% (1989), textiles, raw cotton, wool and leather 26% (1990), vegetables. Principal trading partners: France, Italy, Germany, Saudi Arabia, Turkey, Lebanon, Netherlands, Russia.

Tunisia Imports ($ million): 5189 (1991). Exports ($ million): 3713 (1991). Main imports: textiles 8.4% (1989), wheat 4.9% (1989). Main exports: clothing and accessories 26.0% (1989), petroleum and products 20.0% (1989), phosphoric acid, fertilizers. Principal trading partners: France, Italy, Germany, Belgium-Luxembourg, USA, Spain.

Turkey Imports ($ million): 22,872 (1992). Exports ($ million): 14,715 (1992). Main imports: machinery and transport equipment 25.7% (1992), crude petroleum 11.5% (1992). Main exports: textiles 35% (1992), iron and steel 10.5% (1992), tobacco, dried fruit. Principal trading partners: Germany, USA, Italy, Saudi Arabia, France, Japan, Russia, UK, Iran, Netherlands.

United Arab Emirates Imports (UAE dirham million): 12,349 (1991). Exports (UAE dirham million): 81,300 (1991). Main imports: machinery and transport equipment 42.3% (1991), basic manufactures 21.3% (1991). Main exports: crude petroleum 64.8% (1991). Principal trading partners: Japan, UK, USA, France.

Yemen Imports ($ million): 1378 (1987). Exports ($ million): 101 (1987. Main imports: food and live animals 39.5% (1990), machinery and transport equipment 15% (1990). Main exports: petroleum and petroleum products 91.1% (1990). Principal trading partners: USA, Saudi Arabia, Italy, France, UK.

Algeria

Official name: El Djemhouria El Djazaïria Demokratia Echaabia (the Democratic and Popular Republic of Algeria).

Member of: UN, OAU, Arab League, OPEC.

Area: 2,381,741 km² (919,595 sq mi).

Population: 25,888,000 (1991 est).

Capital: Algiers (El Djazaïr or Alger) 1,722,000 (including suburbs; 1989 est).

Other major cities: Oran (Ouahran) 664,000, Constantine (Qacentina) 449,000, Annaba 348,000, Blida (el-Boulaïda) 191,000, Sétif (Stif) 187,000 (all including suburbs; 1989 est).

Languages: Arabic (official; 83%), French, Berber (17%).

Religion: Sunni Islam (official; over 99%), small Roman Catholic and other minorities.

Education: Education is compulsory in theory between the ages of six and 15. In 1990 the literacy rate was estimated to be 58.4%. There are 15 universities including five institutes of university status.

Defence: In 1993 the total armed strength was estimated to be nearly 140,000 - 120,000 in the army, 7000 in the navy and 12,000 in the air force. The navy is based at Algiers. Algerian males are subject to military service of six months at the age of 19.

Transport: There are 82,000 km of roads (50,960 mi) of roads and 3998 km ((2423 mi) of state-run railways. A metro system is under construction in Algiers. Algiers, Annaba and Atzew are the principal commercial shipping ports. Algiers has an international airport.

Media: There are eight daily newspapers, two of which are published in French and two in both Arabic and French. There is a national state-run television network and three state-run radio networks broadcasting in Arabic, French and Berber.

GOVERNMENT

The constitution provides for the election of a President, who is executive head of state, and a 296-member National Assembly by universal adult suffrage every five years. In 1992 the constitution was suspended and a (military) High State Council - whose chairman is President - was appointed. For local government purposes the country is divided into 47wilayat. Political life has virtually ceased - the main political parties before military-backed rule was established in 1992 were the (now banned fundamentalist) Islamic Salvation Front (FIS), the (socialist) National Liberation Front (FLN) and the (largely Berber) Socialist Forces Front (FFS).

President: Lamine Zeroual.

THE CABINET
includes

Prime Minister: Mokdad Sifi.

Minister of Agriculture: Nourredine Bahbouh.

Minister of Commerce: Saci Aziza.

Minister of Education: Amar Sakhri.

Minister of Finance: Ahmed Benbitour.

Minister of Foreign Affairs: Mohamed Salah Dembri.

Minister of Health and Population: Yahia Guidoum.

Minister of Housing: Mohamed Maghlaoui.

Minister of Industry and Energy: Amar Makhloufi.

Minister of the Interior and Local Communities, Minister of the Environment and of Administrative Reform: Abderrahmane Meziane Cherif.

Minister of Justice: Mohamed Teguia.

Minister of Labour and Social Protection: Mohamed Laichoubi.

Minister of Transport: Mohand Arezkli Isli.

GEOGRAPHY

Over 85% of Algeria is covered by the Sahara Desert. To the north lie the Atlas Mountains, which enclose a dry plateau. In the southeast are the Hoggar mountains. Along the Mediterranean coast are plains and lower mountain ranges. Highest point: Mont Tahat 2918 m (9573 ft). Principal river: Chéliff. Climate: There is a Mediterranean climate along the coastline with hot summers, mild winters and adequate rainfall. In the Sahara, it is hot and arid.

ECONOMY

Petroleum and natural gas are the main exports and the basis of important industries. The country faces severe economic problems including high unemployment. Algeria has a massive deficit owing to heavy spending on defence and the state, large subsidies on loss-making state enterprises and unrealistically high wages paid to public sector workers. Food subsidies, which had been another drain on the economy, were removed in 1992. Ambitious privatization plans have yet to be put into

ALGERIA

Area: 2 381 741 km²
(919 595 sq mi)

action - in theory, private and foreign firms may hold up to 49% of shares in the state-owned oil companies. The economy remains in need of considerable reforms. These problems have been added to by the migration of some westernized middle class Algerians, who - alarmed by the rise of fundamentalism - have taken their skills to France. The great imbalance in the population structure is also a problem - nearly 45% of Algerians are under the age of 15. Nevertheless, the country is still experiencing growth - over 3% in 1993 - but the dinar is not yet convertible. Farmers and farm workers account for over 20% of the labour force, but lack of rain and suitable land means that Algeria has to import two thirds of its food. The small amount of arable land main-

ly produces wheat, barley, fruit and vegetables, while arid pasturelands support sheep, goats and cattle. Before the rise of fundamentalism and violence against foreigners, tourism had become an important source of foreign currency, but the tourist industry has since collapsed.

Currency: Algerian dinar (DZD) of 100 centimes; 1US$ = 37.38 DZD (May 1994).

GDP: US$58,000,000,000 (1993 est); US$2090 per head.

RECENT HISTORY

France gradually colonized Algeria between 1830 and 1860. Nationalist riots against French colonial rule were ruthlessly suppressed in 1945, and in 1954 the FLN initiated a revolt that became a bitter war. A rising by French settlers, in favour of the integration of Algeria with France, led to the crisis that returned de Gaulle to power in France (1958). Despite two further risings by the settlers, and the activities of the colonists' terrorist organization, the OAS, Algeria gained independence in 1962. The first president, Ahmed Ben Bella (1916-), was overthrown in 1965 by Colonel Houari Boumédienne (1932-78), who aimed to re-establish the principles of the 1963 socialist constitution. His successor, Colonel Benjedid Chadli (1929-), began to steer Algeria towards democracy in the late 1980s. In 1992 the second round of national multi-party elections was cancelled when the fundamentalist FIS gained a large lead in the first round. The military took power and suspended political activity. Tension increased when the military-appointed head of state, President Boudiaf, was assassinated. The army's domination of the government increased in 1994 when the struggle between the military and the fundamentalists became more violent. The authorities have taken increasingly harsh measures against the fundamentalists who have virtual control of some poor districts of Algiers and other large cities. At the same time fundamentalists have assassinated intellectuals, whom they accuse of favouring Francophone rather than Arabic culture, and foreigners working in Algeria. This has resulted in the withdrawal of personnel by Western companies based in Algeria.

253

Bahrain

Official name: Daulat al-Bahrain (The State of Bahrain).

Member of: UN, Arab League, OPEC, GCC.

Area: 691 km² (267 sq mi).

Population: 516,000 (1991 est).

Capital: Manama 152,000 (1988 est).

Other main city: al-Muharraq 78,000 (1988 est).

Language: Arabic (official; 75% asa a first language), Farsi and Urdu minorities.

Religions: Sunni Islam (33%), Shia Islam (60%).

Education: Education is not compulsory but is available for Bahrainis between the ages of six and 17. In 1990 the literacy rate was estimated to be 77.4%. There are two universities.

Defence: In 1993 the total armed strength was estimated to be 7150. There is no military service.

Transport: There are 2671 km (1660 mi) of roads. Mina Sulman is the main port; al-Muharraq has an international airport.

Media: There are two Arabic- and one English-language daily newspapers. There is a single state-run radio service and two television channels.

GOVERNMENT
Bahrain is ruled directly by an Amir (a hereditary monarch), who appoints a Prime Minister and a Cabinet of Ministers. In 1992 the Amir appointed a 30-member Consultative Council. There are no political parties.

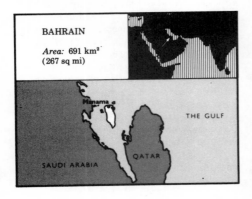

BAHRAIN

Area: 691 km² (267 sq mi)

Manama

THE GULF

SAUDI ARABIA

QATAR

Amir: HH Shaikh Isa II bin Sulman Al-Khalifa (succeeded upon the death of his father, 2 November 1961).

THE CABINET
includes

Prime Minister: Shaikh Khalifa bin Sulman Al-Khalifa.

Minister of Defence: Brig-Gen Khalifa bin Ahmed al-Khalifah.

Minister of Finance and the Economy: Ibrahim Abdul-Karim Mohammed.

Minister of Foreign Affairs: Shaikh Mohammed bin Mubarak al-Khalifah.

Minister of the Interior: Shaikh Mohammed bin Khalifa al-Khalifah.

Minister of Justice and Islamic Affairs: Shaikh Abdullah bin Kahlifa al-Khalifah.

GEOGRAPHY
Bahrain Island, the largest of the 35 small islands in the archipelago, consists mainly of sandy plains and salt marshes, and is linked to Saudi Arabia by causeway. There are no rivers. Highest point: Jabal al-Dukhan 134 m (440 ft).
Climate: The climate is very hot. The annual average rainfall is 75 mm (3 in).

ECONOMY
The wealth of Bahrain is due to its petroleum and natural gas resources, and the oil-refining industry. As reserves began to wane in the 1970s, the government encouraged diversification. As a result, Bahrain is now one of the Gulf's major banking and communication centres.

Currency: Bahraini dinar of 1000 fils; 1US$ = 0.377 dinars (June 1994).

GDP: US$6,910,000,000 (1991); US$6310 per head.

RECENT HISTORY
Bahrain - a British protectorate from the end of the 19th century - was the first state in the region to develop its petroleum industry. Since independence in 1971, there has been tension between the Sunni and Shiite communities. Responding to threats from revolutionary Shiite Iran, Bahrain entered defence agreements with Saudi Arabia and other Gulf states, and joined the coalition forces against Iraq after the invasion of Kuwait (August 1990).

Egypt

Official name: Jumhuriyat Misr al-'Arabiya (Arab Republic of Egypt).

Member of: UN, OAU, Arab League.

Area: 997,739 km² (385,229 sq mi).

Population: 57,110,000 (1993 est).

Capital: Cairo (El-Qahira) 13,300,00 (city 6,663,000; El-Giza 2,156,000; Shubrâ El-Kheima 811,000; 1991 est).

Other major cities: Alexandria (El-Iskandariyah) 3,295,000, Port Said (Bur Sa'id) 449,000, al-Mahallah al-Kubra 385,000, Suez (El Suweis) 376,000 (1991 est).

Language: Arabic (official).

Religions: Sunni Islam (90%), Coptic Christian (7%).

Education: Education is compulsory, in theory, between the ages of six and 15. In 1990 the literacy rate was estimated to be 48.4%. There are 13 universities.

Defence: In 1993 the total armed strength was 430,000 - 310,000 in the army, 20,000 in the navy and 100,000 in the air force. There are 604,000 reservists. Selective military service lasts for three years.

Transport: There are 48,804 km (30,326 mi) of roads and 8831 km (5489 mi) of state-run railways. Cairo has a metro; both Alexandria and Cairo have a rapid light transit system. The Nile is an important inland waterway. About 18,000 vesels per annum use the Suez Canal, which connects the Mediterranean with the Indian Ocean, via the Red Sea. Alexandria is the main port; Suez and Port Said are also major ports. Cairo and Alexandria have international airports.

Media: There are 17 daily newspapers, published in Cairo and Alexandria. Most are published in Arabic, but some are in French, Greek, English and Armenian. The state-run broadcasting system supplies five television channels (some of which are regional) and several radio stations.

GOVERNMENT
Every five years, 454 members are elected by universal adult suffrage to the Majlis ash-Sha'ab (People's Assembly); up to 10 additional members are appointed by the President, who is nominated by the Assembly and confirmed by referendum for a six-year term. The President appoints a Prime Minister, Ministers and Vice-President(s). The main political parties include the (centrist) National Democratic Party (NDP), the (traditional rightist) New Wafd Party (which boycotted the 1990 election), the Socialist Labour Party (which also boycotted the 1990 election), and the National Progressive Unionist Rally (NPU). After the election of November and December 1990 a NDP government retained power.

Party strength: NDP 348, ind 83, NUP 6.

President: Mohammed Hosni Mubarak (NDP).

THE CABINET
includes

Prime Minister: Dr Atef Mohamed Naguib Sedki.

Deputy Prime Minister and Minister of Planning: Dr Kamal Ahmed El-Ganzuri.

Deputy Prime Minister and Minister of Agriculture, Animal and Fishery Wealth and Land Reclamation: Dr Youssef Amin Wali.

Minister of Cabinet Affairs: Ahmed Radwan Gomaa.

Minister of Culture: Farouk Abdel-Aziz Hosni.

Minister of Defence and Military Production: Field Marshal Mohamed Hussein Tantawi.

Minister of the Economy and Foreign Trade: Mohamed Mahmoud Baioumi.

Minister of Education: Dr Hussein Kamel Bahaa-El-Din.

Minister of Electricity and Energy: Mohamed Maher Abaza.

Minister of Finance: Dr Mohamed Ahmed El Razzaz.

Minister of Foreign Affairs: Amr Mahmoud Mousa.

Minister of Health: Dr Ali El-Makhzangi.

Minister of Housing and Public Utilities: Mohamed Salah El-Din Hassb-Allah.

255

Minister of Industry and Mineral Wealth: Dr Ibrahim Fawzi Abdel-Wahed.

Minister of Information: Mohamed Safwat El-Sherif.

Minister of the Interior: Hassan El-Alfy.

Minister of Justice: Farouk Mahmoud Seif-El-Nasr.

Minister of Local Administration: Dr Mahmoud Ahmed Sherief.

Minister of Petroleum: Dr Hamdi El-Banbi.

Minister of the Public Business Sector: Dr Atef Mohamed Ebeid.

Minister of Public Work and Water Resources: Mohamed Abdel-Hadi Radi.

Minister of Supply and Home Trade: Dr Mohamed Galal Abul-Dahab.

Minister of Tourism: Dr Mamdouh El-Beltagi.

Minister of Transport, Communications and Cvil Aviation: Soliman Metwalli Soliman.

GEOGRAPHY
Desert covers more than 90% of Egypt. The Western Desert - which stretches into Libya and Sudan - is low-lying. The Eastern Desert is divided by wadis and ends in the southeast in mountains beside the Red Sea. Most Egyptians live in the Nile River valley and delta, intensively cultivated lands that rely on irrigation by the annual flood of the Nile. East of the Suez Canal is the Sinai Peninsula. Highest point: Mount Catherine (Jabal Katrina) 2642 m (8668 ft). Principal river: Nile. Climate: Egyptian winters are mild and summers are hot and arid. Alexandria has the highest rainfall total - 200 mm (8 in) - while the area beside the Red Sea receives virtually no rain.

ECONOMY
Over a third of the labour force is involved in agriculture, producing maize, wheat, rice and vegetables for the domestic market, and cotton and dates mainly for export. Petroleum reserves (small by Middle Eastern standards), canal tolls and tourism are major foreign-currency earners. However, tourism suffered a major decline in 1993-94 owing to the activities of Muslim fundamentalists.The economy is held back by rapid population growth and by the demands of a large public sector and food subsidies, but there has been a considerable

increase in foreign investment in Egypt in 1993-94.

Currency: Egyptian pound of 100 piastres; 1US$ = 3.38 Egytian pounds (June 994).

GDP: US$47,000,000,000 (1993 est); US$810 per head.

RECENT HISTORY
In the 19th century, Egypt was nominally part of the Ottoman (Turkish) Empire, although it was effectively ruled by a local dynasty. The construction of the Suez Canal bankrupted Egypt, and the UK - a major creditor - occupied Egypt (1882) and established a protectorate (1914-22). The corrupt regime of King Farouk was toppled in a military coup (1952) and a republic was established (1953). The radical Gamal Abdel Nasser (1918-70) became president in 1954. He nationalized the Suez Canal and made Egypt the leader of Arab nationalism. Nasser was twice defeated by Israel in Middle East wars (1967 and 1973), but his successor, President Anwar Sadat, made peace with Israel (1979) and was ostracized by the Arab world. Since Sadat's assassination (1981), Egypt has regained its place in the Arab fold, and the prominent role played by Egypt in the coalition against Saddam Hussein's Iraq (1991)

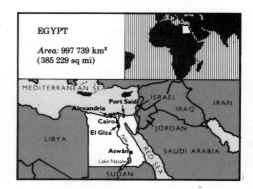

EGYPT

Area: 997 739 km²
(385 229 sq mi)

confirmed Egypt as one of the leaders of the Arab world. The country is faced by severe economic problems. In the early 1990s, there was a growth in Islamic fundamentalism, but the authorities rounded up many militants in 1993-94. However, intermittent attacks by militants upon foreign tourists continue.

Iran

Official name: Jomhori-e-Islami-e-Irân (Islamic Republic of Iran). Until 1935 Iran was known as Persia.

Member of: UN, OPEC.

Area: 1,648,000 km² (636,296 sq mi).

Population: 60,768,000 (1993 est).

Capital: Tehran 7,100,000 (including suburbs; 1991 est).

Other major cities: Mashad 1,464,000, Isfahan 987,000, Tabriz 971,000, Shiraz 848,000, Ahvaz 580,000, Bakhtaran 561,000, Qom 543,000 (all including suburbs; 1986 census).

Languages: Farsi or Persian (official; 45%), Azeri (26%), Kurdish, Luri, Baluchi and Arabic minorities.

Religion: Shia Islam (official; 98%).

Education: Education is compulsory between the ages of six and 10. In 1990 the literacy rate was 54%. There are 29 universities.

Defence: In 1993 the total armed strength was 528,000 - 305,000 in the army, 18,000 in the navy, 35,000 in the air force and 170,000 in the revolutionary guard. Compulsory military service lasts for two years.

Transport: There are 151,488 km (94,130 mi) of roads and 4567 km (2838 mi) of state-run railways. Tehran is constructing a metro. Kharg Island (for oil), Bandar Shahid Rajai and Bandar Khomeini are the principal commercial shipping ports. Tehran has an international airport.

Media: The media are strongly influenced by the state. There are 11 principal daily newspapers and a state-run radio and television service (with two television channels and three radio stations).

GOVERNMENT

A Council of Experts - 83 Shiite clerics - is elected by universal adult suffrage to appoint the Wali Faqih (religious leader), who exercises supreme authority over the executive, legislature, judiciary and military, and is, therefore, a quasi-head of state. There is no fixed term for the Wali Faqih, whose role may be taken by a joint leadership of three or five persons. The 270-member Islamic Consultative Assembly (Majlis) and the President are directly elected for four years. The President - who is head of government - appoints a Cabinet which is responsible to the Majlis. For local government purposes Iran is divided into 24 provinces. Iran is effectively a non-party state. The most recent parliamentary election was held in April and May 1992.

Supreme Religious Leader (Wali Faqih) and Commander-in-Chief of the Armed Forces: Ayatollah Seyed Ali Khamenei.

THE CABINET

includes

President: Hojatolislam Hashemi Ali Akbar Rafsanjani.

Vice-President: Habib Ebrahim Habibi.

Vice-President and Minister for Legal and Majlis Affairs: Seyed Ataollah Mohajerani.

Vice-President and Head of Planning and of Budgetary Organization: Massoud Roehani Zanjani.

Vice-President and Head of the State Atomic and Energy Organization: Reza Amrollahi.

Vice-President and Head of the Organization for State Employment and Administrative Affairs: Mansour Razavi.

Vice-President and Head of the State Environmental Protection Organization: Mehdi Manafi.

Vice-President and Head of the State Physical Education Organization: Hassan Ghafurifard.

Minister of Defence and Minister for the Armed Forces: Mohammad Forouzandry.

Minister of Economic Affairs and Minister of Finance: Morteza Mohammad Khan.

Minister of Foreign Affairs: Ali Akbar Vellayati.

Minister of the Interior: Ali Mohammad Besharati.

Minister of Justice: Hojatoislam Ismail Shostari.

Minister for Oil: Gholamreza Agazadeh.

GEOGRAPHY

Apart from restricted lowlands along the Gulf,

257

the Caspian Sea and the Iraqi border, Iran is a high plateau, surrounded by mountains. The Elburz Mountains lie in the north; the Zagros Mountains form a barrier running parallel to the Gulf. In the east, lower areas of the plateau are covered by salt deserts. Highest point: Demavend 5604 m (18,386 ft). Principal rivers: Kàrùn, Safid, Atrak, Karkheh. Climate: Iran has an extreme climate ranging from very hot on the Gulf to sub-zero temperatures in winter in the northwest. The Caspian Sea coast has a subtropical climate with rainfall totals around 1000 mm (40 in) a year. Most of Iran, however, has little rain.

ECONOMY

Petroleum is Iran's main source of foreign currency. The principal industries are petrochemicals, carpetweaving, textiles, vehicles and cement, but the war with Iraq and the country's international isolation have severely interrupted trade. Over a quarter of the labour force is involved in agriculture, mainly producing cereals (wheat, maize and barley) and keeping livestock, but lack of water, land ownership problems and manpower shortages have

IRAN

Area: 1 648 000 km²
(636 296 sq mi).

restricted yields. In the past decade the economy has been held back by Iran's strained relations with Western powers and the consequent lack of investment. However, commercial ties with Western Europe have developed recently.

The government has placed an emphasis upon rapid growth in the hope of heading off a rising tide of discontent.

Currency: Rial; 1US$ = 1757.5 rials (June 1994).

GDP: US$65,000,000,000 (1993 est); US$1004 per head.

RECENT HISTORY

In the 19th century, Russia and Britain became rivals for influence in the region. In 1921 an Iranian Cossack officer, Reza Khan Pahlavi (1877-1944), took power. Deposing the Qajar dynasty in 1925, he became Shah (emperor) himself as Reza I and modernized and secularized Iran. However, because of his pro-German sentiments, he was forced to abdicate by Britain and the USSR (1941) and was replaced by his son Mohammed Reza (1919-80). The radical nationalist prime minister Muhammad Mussadiq briefly toppled the monarchy (1953). On regaining his throne, the Shah tightened his grip through oppression and sought popularity through land reform and rapid development with US backing.

However, the policy of Westernization offended the clergy, and a combination of students, the bourgeoisie and religious leaders eventually combined against him, overthrowing the monarchy in 1979 and replacing it with a fundamentalist Islamic Republic inspired by the Ayatollah Ruhollah Khomeini (1900-89). The Western-educated classes fled Iran as the clergy tightened control. Radical anti-Western students seized the US embassy and held 66 American hostages (1979-81). In 1980 Iraq invaded Iran, beginning the bitter First Gulf War, which lasted until 1988 and resulted in great losses of manpower for Iran. Following the death of Khomeini in 1989, economic necessity brought about a less militant phase of the Islamic revolution. The new president, Rafsanjani, emphasized pragmatic rather than radical policies and attempted to heal the diplomatic rift with Western powers. After the collapse of the USSR (1991), Iran began to look for closer ties with the Islamic former Soviet republics of Central Asia. Iran continues to sponsor militant Islam abroad but tensions inside the regime have increased as economic discontent has surfaced.

Iraq

Official name: Al-Jumhuriya al-'Iraqiya (The Republic of Iraq).

Member of: UN, Arab League, OPEC.

Area: 441,839 km² (170,595 sq mi).

Population: 19,453,000 (1993 est).

Capital: Baghdad 5,348,000 (including suburbs; 1985 est).

Other major cities: Basrah (Al Basrah) 617,000, Mosul (Al Mawsil) 571,000, Irbil 334,000, As Sulaymaniyah 279,000, An Najaf 243,000 (1985 est).

Languages: Arabic (official; 80%), Kurdish (19%).

Religions: Sunni Islam (41%), Shia Islam (51%), with a small Christian minority.

Education: Education is compulsory between the ages of six and 12. In 1990 the literacy rate was estimated to be nearly 60%. There are eight universities.

Defence: In 1993 the total armed strength was 382,000 - 350,000 in the army, 2000 in the navy and 30,000 in the air force. Compulsory military service lasts between 21 and 24 months.

Transport: There are 45,555 km (28,305 mi) of roads and 2389 km (1484 km) of state-run railways. Before the imposition of international sanctions against Iraq, Basrah and Umm Qasr were the main ports. Baghdad and Basrah have international airports.

Media: The media in Iraq are state-controlled. There are nine daily newspapers and a single radio and television service.

GOVERNMENT
The 250-member National Assembly is elected for a four-year term by universal adult suffrage. The non-elected Revolutionary Command Council appoints the President, who - in turn - appoints the Council of Ministers. The Kurdish provinces of the north have de facto self-government.. The only effective legal party is the Arab Ba'ath Socialist Party, which is part of the National Progressive Front coalition. The most recent election was in 1989.

President: Saddam Hussein.

THE CABINET
includes

Prime Minister: The President (see above).

Vice-President: Taha Mohieddin Maarouf.

Vice-President: Taha Yassin Ramadan.

Deputy Prime Minister: Tariq Aziz.

Minister of Defence: Ali Hasan al-Majid.

Minister of Foreign Affairs: Muhammad Said Kazim al-Sahhaf.

Minister for Industry and for Military Industrialization: Lt-Gen. Hussein Kamil.

Minister of Information and Culture: Hamid Yusuf Hammadi.

Minister of the Interior: Watban Ibrahim al-Hasan.

Minister for Oil: Safa Hadi Jawad.

Minister of Trade: Muhammad Mehdi Saleh.

AUTONOMOUS KURDISH REGION
The provinces of Dahuk, Irbil and as-Sulaymaniyah have effectively ceased to be under Iraqi government control. Protected from Iraqi forces by the air exclusion zone, the region has now its own government.

Kurdish Region Area: 38,650 km² (14,923 sq mi). Population: 2,365,000 (1991 est). Capital: Irbil.

GEOGRAPHY
The basins of the rivers Tigris and Euphrates contain most of the arable land and most of the population. Desert in the southwest occupies nearly one half of Iraq. Highest point: Rawanduz 3658 m (12,001 ft). Principal rivers: Tigris (Dijlah), Euphrates (al Furat). Climate: Summers are hot and dry with high temperatures. Most of the rainfall - ranging from 100 mm (4 in) in the desert to 1000 mm (40 in) in the mountains - comes in winter.

ECONOMY
Agriculture involves one third of the labour force. Irrigated land in the Tigris and Euphrates basins produces cereals, fruit and vegetables for domestic consumption, and dates for export. Iraq traditionally depends upon its substantial reserves of petroleum, but exports were halted by international sanctions (1990). The Iraqi economy was badly damaged

during the First Gulf War against Iran, and devastated by the Second Gulf War. Since then production has slumped and the country has been in a state of almost total economic collapse. Inflation is rampant and there is a shortage of many basic commodities.

Currency: Iraqi dinar of 1000 fils; 1US$ = 0.31 dinars (official rate).

GDP: US$73,000,000,000 (1991); US$4110 per head.

RECENT HISTORY
Iraq was absorbed by the Turkish Ottoman Empire in the 16th century. In World War I the British occupied the area, but Iraqi nationalists were disappointed when Iraq became a British mandate with virtual colonial status (1920). In 1921 the Amir Faisal ibn Husain became King

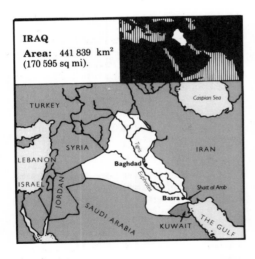

IRAQ
Area: 441 839 km²
(170 595 sq mi).

and in 1932 Iraq became fully independent. Following a military coup that brought pro-German officers to power in 1941, the British occupied Iraq until 1945. The royal family and the premier were murdered in the 'Free Officers' coup in 1958. Differences in the leadership led to a further coup in 1963 and a reign of terror against the left. In 1968 Ba'athist (pan-Arab nationalist) officers carried out another coup. Embittered by the Arabs' humiliation in the 1967 war and by US support for the

Israelis, the regime turned to the Soviets. In 1980 President Saddam Hussein attacked a weakened Iran, responding to Iran's threat to export Islamic revolution. What had been intended as a quick victory became the costly First Gulf War (1980-88), resulting in many casualties and the virtual bankruptcy of the country. In an attempt to restore Iraq's economic fortunes, Saddam Hussein invaded oil-rich Kuwait (1990). UN sanctions against Iraq were imposed. Forces from the USA, the UK and over 20 other countries (including Egypt and Syria) were dispatched to the Gulf to prevent an Iraqi invasion of Saudi Arabia. Following Saddam Hussein's failure to respond to repeated UN demands to withdraw from Kuwait, the Second Gulf War began (January 1991). Coalition forces routed the Iraqi army which sustained heavy casualties. Iraq accepted all the UN resolutions regarding Kuwait and agreed to a ceasefire after a campaign that lasted only 100 hours. During March and April Saddam Hussein suppressed revolts by Shiites in the south and Kurds in the north. International efforts were made to feed and protect over 1,000,000 Shiite and Kurdish refugees who had fled. Despite being forced to accept UN inspection of Iraq's chemical and biological weapons and the country's nuclear capacity, Saddam continued to defy UN demands concerning disarmament and recognition of the Kuwaiti border. The Kurdish provinces have been effectively autonomous since an Allied air exclusion zone was imposed, prohibiting Iraq aircraft from flying over the north of the country. (However, the fate of the Kurdish autonomous area is compromised by serious clashes between the supporters of the rival Kurdish leaders - Massoud Barzani - who leads the Kurdistan Democratic Party - and Jalal Talabani - who leads the Patriotic Union of Kurdistan.) A similar exclsuion zone exists in the south to protect the Shia Muslims and marsh Arabs, although the latter's livelihood is threatened by politically-inspired drainage schemes on the rivers Tigris and Euphrates further north. Saddam's grip on power remains strong, despite continuing coup attempts. In 1994 Saddam assumed the premiership himself and more members of his Takriti clan and of his family were appointed to the administration.

260

Israel

Official name: Medinat Israel (The State of Israel).

Member of: UN.

Area: 21,946 km² (8473 sq mi), including East Jerusalem.

Population: 5,451,000 (1992 est), includes East Jerusalem, Golan and Jewish West Bank localities.

Capital cities: Jerusalem (not recognized internationally as capital) 544,000 (1992 est).

Other major cities: Tel-Aviv 1,132,000 (city 353,000, Holon 162,000, Petach-Tikva 149,000, Bat-Yam 146,000, Rishon LeZiyyon 140,000), Haifa 400,000 (city 246,000), Netanya 132,000, Beersheba (Be'er Sheva) 122,000 (1992 est).

Languages: Hebrew (official; 85%), Arabic (15%).

Religions: Judaism (official; 85%), Sunni Islam (13%), various Christian denominations.

Education: Education is compulsory between the ages of five and 15. In 1990 the literacy rate was 92%. There are eight universities.

Defence: In 1992 the total armed strength was 176,000 - 134,000 in the army, 10,000 in the navy and 32,000 in the air force. There are about 504,000 reserves. Military service is compulsory for Jewish Israeli men and women (who serve for 36 and 24 months respectively) and voluntary for Christian and Arab Israelis.

Transport: There are 13,300 km (8266 mi) of roads and 574 km (357 mi) of state-run railways. Haifa and Ashdod are the main shipping ports. Eilat is the only Israeli port on the Red Sea. Tel-Aviv is the main international airport.

Media: There are 26 daily newspapers, most of which are published in Hebrew. IBA, a state corporation, broadcasts six radio channels. There are two television channels.

GOVERNMENT

The 120-member Knesset (Assembly) is elected by proportional representation for four years by universal adult suffrage. A Prime Minister and Cabinet take office after receiving a vote of confidence from the Knesset. The President is elected for five years by the Knesset. The main political parties are the (centre-left) Labour Party (Lab), the (right wing) Likud Party, the Meretz Party, the (right-wing) Tzomet Party, the (ultra-orthodox) Shas Party, the National Religious Party (NRP), United Tora Judaism Party (UTJP), the (right-wing nationalist) Moledet, the Arab Democratic Party (ADP), and the (left-wing Palestinian) Hadash Party. There is a Labour-Meretz coalition.

Party strength: (June 1992 election) Lab 44, Likud 32, Meretz 12, Tzomet 8, Shas 6, NRP 6, UTJP 4, Moledet 3, ARP 3, Hadash 3.

President: Ezer Weizman.

THE CABINET

Prime Minister, Minister of Religious Affairs and of the Interior: Yitzhak Rabin (Lab).

Minister of Agriculture: Ya'akov Tsur (Lab).

Minister of Communications, Science and Technology: Shulamit Aloni (Meretz).

Minister of Economics: Shimon Shetreet (Lab).

Minister of Education and Culture: Amnon Rubinstein (Meretz).

Minister of the Environment: Yossi Sarid (Meretz).

Minister of Finance: Avraham Shochat (Lab).

ISRAEL

Area: 21 946 km² (8473 sq mi), including East Jerusalem

261

Minister of Foreign Affairs: Shimon Peres (Lab).

Minister of Health: Ephraim Sneh (Lab).

Minister of Housing: Binyamin Ben-Eliezer (Lab).

Minister of Immigrant Absorption: Yair Tsaban (Meretz).

Minister of Industry and Trade: Michael Harish (Lab).

Minister of Justice: David Libai (lab).

Minister of Labour and Social Affairs: Ora Namir (Lab).

Minister of Police and Minister of Energy and Infrastructure: Moshe Shachal (Lab).

Minister of Tourism: Uzi Baram (Lab).

Minister of Transport: Yisrael Kessar (Lab).

GEOGRAPHY
Israel - within the boundaries established by the 1949 cease-fire line - consists of a fertile thin coastal plain beside the Mediterranean, parts of the arid mountains of Judaea in the centre, the Negev Desert in the south, and part of the Jordan Valley in the northeast. Highest point: Har Meron (Mt Atzmon) 1208 m (3963 ft). Principal rivers: Jordan (Yarden), Qishon. Climate: Israel's climate is Mediterranean with hot, dry summers and mild, wetter winters. Most of Israel receives less than 200 mm (8 in) of rain a year.

ECONOMY
Economic problems stem, in part, from Israel's large defence budget and political circumstances, which prevent trade with neighbouring countries. Israel is a major producer and exporter of citrus fruit. Much land is irrigated and over 75% of Israel's arable land is farmed by collectives (kibbutzim) and cooperatives. Mineral resources are few, but processing imported diamonds is a major source of foreign currency. Tourism to biblical sites is important. Qualified immigrants from the former USSR have helped an expansion of the service sector but immigrant unemployment remains a problem.

Currency: Shekel of 100 agorot; 1US$ = 3.06 shekels (June 1994).

262 GDP: US$68,500,000,000 (1993 est); US$12,690 per head.

RECENT HISTORY
The Turkish Ottoman Empire ruled the area from the early 16th century until 1917-18, when Palestine was captured by British forces. The Zionists had hoped to establish a Jewish state, and this hope was intensified following the Balfour Declaration by the British foreign secretary in favour of a homeland (1917). However, Palestine came under British administration and it was not until 1948-9 - after the murder of some 6 million Jews in concentration camps by the Nazis - that an explicitly Jewish state emerged. The establishment of a Jewish state met with hostility from Israel's neighbours and indigenous Palestinians (many of whom left), leading to a series of Arab-Israeli wars. In 1956, while the UK and France were in conflict with Egypt over the Suez Canal, Israel attacked Gaza and Sinai, but later withdrew. When the UN emergency force between Israel and Egypt was expelled in 1967, Egypt imposed a sea blockade on Israel, which responded by invading Sinai. In six days, an Arab coalition of Egypt, Jordan and Syria was defeated, and Israel occupied Sinai, Gaza, the West Bank and Golan. In 1973, Egypt attacked Israel but a ceasefire was arranged within three weeks. In 1979 Israel and Egypt made peace - Egypt recognized Israel's right to exist and Israel withdrew from Sinai in stages. In 1982 Israeli forces invaded Lebanon, intent on destroying bases of the PLO (Palestine Liberation Organization). Eventually Israeli forces withdrew in 1985. In 1987 the intifada (Palestinian uprising) against continued Israeli rule in Gaza and the West Bank began. The harsh reaction of Israeli security forces attracted international condemnation. The intifada continued sporadically and was given extra impetus by the large-scale influx of Soviet Jews into Israel (from 1990) and the encouragement given to the Palestinians and their leader Yasser Arafat by President Saddam Hussein of Iraq. Israeli politics in the 1980s and 1990s was characterized by political instability owing to the electoral system that resulted in the large number of very small parties. Having come under increasing international pressure to achieve an Middle East settlement, Israel reached an agreement with Arafat in 1993 for limited Palestinian self-rule, and an Israeli military withdrawal from Gaza and Jericho.

Jordan

Official name: Al-Mamlaka al-Urduniya al-Hashemiyah (The Hashemite Kingdom of Jordan).

Member of: UN, Arab League.

Area: 89,206 km² (34,443 sq mi) - East Bank only (Jordan cut all legal ties with the Israeli-occupied West Bank in July 1988).

Population: 3,285,000 (1991 est).

Capital: Amman 1,160,000 (1986 est).

Other major cities: Zarqa 318,000, Irbid 168,000, Salt 134,000 (1986 est).

Language: Arabic (official).

Religion: Sunni Islam (over 80%), Shia Islam and various Christian minorities.

Education: Education is compulsory between the ages of five and 14. In 1990 the literacy rate was 80.1%. There are five universities.

Defence: In 1993 the total armed strength was estimated to be nearly 100,000 - 85,000 in the army, 400 in the navy and 14,000 in the air force.

Transport: There are 5625 km (3496 mi) of roads in Jordan and 788 km (490 mi) of railways. Aqaba is the only port.

Media: There are five daily newspapers, one of which is published in English. There is a single government-run radio and television service.

GOVERNMENT

Jordan is a constitutional monarchy. The King appoints the 30 members of the Senate - the upper house of the National Assembly - and names a Prime Minister and Cabinet. The senators serve an eight-year term, with one half of their number retiring every four years. For local government purposes there are eight governates. The 80 members of the House of Representatives are elected every four years by universal adult suffrage. The main political parties include the Islamic Action Front (IAF), the (leftist) Jordanian Arab Democratic Party (JADP), the (centrist) Al-Ahd Party (AAP), the (Communist) Jordanian Social Democratic Party (JSDP), the (left-wing) Hashd Party - People's Democratic Party (PDP), the (centrist) National Alliance Party (NAP), the (centrist) Al-Yakatha Party, and the (left-wing)

Jordanian Arab Ba'ath Socialist Party (JABSP) - the majority of MPs sit as independents.

Party strength: (general election held in November 1993) Independent centrists 44, IAF 16, independent Islamists 6, independent leftists 4, JADP 2, AAP 2, others 6.

King: HM King Hussein I (succeeded upon the deposition of his father, on grounds of illness, 11 August 1952).

THE CABINET

Prime Minister, Minister of Defence and Minister of Foreign Affairs: Dr Abdul Salam Al Majali.

Deputy Prime Minister: Thogan al-Hindawi.

Minister of Agriculture: Mansour bin Tareef.

Minister for the Civil Service: Muhammad Thneibat.

Minister of Communications and Postal Affairs: Hasham Dabbas.

Minister of Culture: Jumaa' Hammad.

Minister of Education: Abdul Raouf al-Rawabdeh.

Minister of Energy and Mineral Resources: Talal Ereikat.

Minister of Finance: Sami Gammouh.

Minister of Health: Aref Batayneh.

Minister of Higher Education: Rateb al-Saoud.

Minister of Information, Minister of State for Prime Ministry Affairs: Dr Jawad Anani.

Minister of Interior Affairs: Salamah Hammad.

Minister of Islamic Affairs: Abdul Salam al-Abbadi.

Minister of Justice: Hisham al-Tal.

Minister of Labour: Khaled al-Ghezawi.

Minister of Municipal and Rural Affairs: Tawfiq Kheishan.

Minister of Planning: Hisham al-Khatib.

Minister of Public Works and Housing: Dr Abdul Razak al-Nsour.

Minister of Social Development: Dr Muhammad al-Sqour.

Minister of State for Foreign Affairs: Talal al-Hassan.

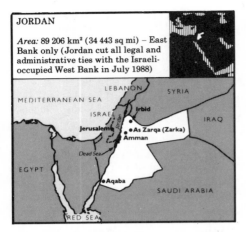

JORDAN

Area: 89 206 km² (34 443 sq mi) – East Bank only (Jordan cut all legal and administrative ties with the Israeli-occupied West Bank in July 1988)

Minister of State for Parliamentary Affairs: Abdul Baqi Gammouh.

Minister of Supply: Abdullah al-Qdah.

Minister of Tourism and Antiquities: Muhammad al-Idwan.

Minister of Trade and Industry: Dr Rima Khalef.

Minister of Transport: Samir Kawar.

Minister of Water and Irrigation: Saleh Irsheidat.

Minister of Youth: Fawaz Abu al-Ghanam.

Ministers of State: Yousef al-Dalabeeh, Abdullah al-Jazi, Muhammad Salem al-Thwayyeb.

GEOGRAPHY

The steep escarpment of the East Bank Uplands borders the Jordan Valley and the Dead Sea. The Jordan Valley is the principal agricultural region of the country. Deserts occupy most of the east and the south and cover over 80% of the kingdom. Highest point: Jabal Ramm 1754 m (5755 ft). Principal river: Jordan (Urdun). Climate: The summers are hot and dry; the winters are cooler and wetter, although much of Jordan experiences very low rainfall.

ECONOMY

Apart from potash – the principal export – Jordan has few resources. Arable land accounts for only about 5% of the total area. Foreign aid and money sent back by Jordanians working

abroad are major sources of foreign currency. The Gulf Crisis (1990-91) severely damaged Jordan's economy - Iraq was Jordan's principal trading partner and the imposition of UN sanctions against Iraq has hurt Jordan. An influx of 350,000 Palestinians from Kuwait into Jordan after the Gulf War placed a strain on the Jordanian economy and added to an unemployment rate that already stood at over 25%. Jordan's sympathy for Iraq lost the country considerable Saudi aid and investment.

Currency: Jordanian dinar (JD) of 1000 fils; 1US$ = 0.7 JD (June 1994).

GDP: US$3,881,000,000 (1991); US$1120 per head.

RECENT HISTORY

In World War I the British aided an Arab revolt against Ottoman rule. The League of Nations awarded the area east of the River Jordan - Transjordan - to Britain as part of Palestine (1920), but in 1923 Transjordan became a separate emirate under Abdullah ibn Hussein, a member of the Hashemite dynasty of Arabia. In 1946 the country gained complete independence as the Kingdom of Jordan with Amir Abdullah (1880-1951) as its sovereign. The Jordanian army fought with distinction in the 1948 Arab-Israeli War, and occupied the West Bank territories, including East Jerusalem, which were formally incorporated into Jordan in April 1950. In 1951 Abdullah was assassinated. Abdullah's grandson, King Hussein (reigned 1952-), was initially threatened by radicals encouraged by Egypt's President Nasser. In the 1967 Arab-Israeli War, Jordan lost the West Bank, including Arab Jerusalem, to the Israelis. In the 1970s the power of the Palestinian guerrillas in Jordan challenged the very existence of the Jordanian state. After a short but bloody civil war in September 1979 the Palestinian leadership fled abroad. King Hussein renounced all responsibility for the West Bank in 1988. The Palestinians - who form the majority of the Jordanian population - supported Iraq in the Gulf Crisis of 1990-91, although King Hussein adopted a position of neutrality. In 1971 Jordan became a single-party state and in 1976 that sole political party was abolished. Multi-party politics were restored in 1991 and multi-party elections were held in 1993 when the majority of successful candidates were independents. Informal peace discussions with Israel began in 1994.

Kuwait

Official name: Daulat al-Kuwait (State of Kuwait).

Member of: UN, Arab League, OPEC, GCC.

Area: 17,818 km² (6880 sq mi).

Population: 1,433,000 (1993).

Capital: Kuwait City 1,375,000 (city 44,000; 1992 unofficial est).

Language: Arabic (official).

Religions: Sunni Islam (official; about 70%), Shia Islam (30%).

Education: Education is compulsory between the ages of six and 14. In 1990 the literacy rate was 73%. There is a single university.

Defence: In 1993 the total armed strength was 13,700. Military service lasts for two years.

Transport: There are 4273 km (2655 mi) of roads. Shuwaikh and Shuiaba are the main ports. Kuwait City has an international airport.

Media: There are seven daily newspapers and a state-run radio and television service.

GOVERNMENT
Kuwait is a monarchy ruled by an Amir, who is chosen from and by the adult male members of the ruling dynasty. The Amir appoints a PM

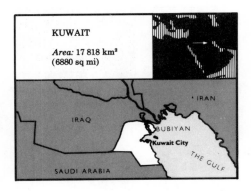

KUWAIT

Area: 17 818 km²
(6880 sq mi)

IRAN

IRAQ

BUBIYAN

Kuwait City

THE GULF

SAUDI ARABIA

and a Council of Ministers. A 50-member National Assembly is elected for four years by literate adult male Kuwaitis whose families fulfil stringent residence qualifications. There are unofficial groups rather than political parties. The most recent election was in October 1992.

Group strength: Government supporters 19, Islamic fundamentalists 19, liberals 12.

Amir: HH Shaikh Jabir III bin Ahmad as-Sabah (succeeded upon the death of his cousin, 31 December 1977).

Prime Minister: HH Shaikh Saad al-Abdullah as-Sabah, Crown Prince of Kuwait.

GEOGRAPHY
Most of Kuwait is desert, relatively flat and low lying. There are no permanent rivers. Highest point: 289 m (951 ft) at Ash Shaqaya. Climate: Kuwait experiences extremely high temperatures in summer. Almost all the annual rainfall of 100 mm (4 in) comes during the cooler winter.

ECONOMY
Kuwait was devastated by the Iraqi invasion and the Second Gulf War, but reconstruction followed rapidly. Large reserves of petroleum and natural gas are the mainstay of Kuwait. Owing to lack of water, little agriculture is possible.

Currency: Kuwait dinar of 1000 fils; 1US$ = 0.29 dinars (June 1994).

RECENT HISTORY
From 1899 to 1961 Kuwait was a British-protected state. Oil was discovered in 1938 and was produced commercially from 1946. Iraq attempted to take over Kuwait in 1961, but the dispatch of British troops to the Gulf discouraged an Iraqi invasion. In August 1990 - despite having recognized the emirate's sovereignty in 1963 - Iraq invaded and annexed Kuwait. Iraq refused to withdraw despite repeated UN demands and in January 1991 the war to remove Iraqi forces from Kuwait - the Gulf War - began. In February, coalition forces entered the emirate, which was freed in a swift campaign during which the Iraqi forces were routed. Kuwait was found to have been devastated by the occupying Iraqi forces. After the liberation, pressure for constitutional reform grew and the constitution - which had been suspended since 1968 - was restored in 1992. Large numbers of Palestinians - who were perceived to have favoured Iraq - were expelled from Kuwait in 1991-92.

Lebanon

Official name: Al-Lubnan (The Lebanon).

Member of: UN, Arab League.

Area: 10,452 km² (4036 sq mi).

Population: 2,760,000 (1992 est.).

Capital: Beirut (Bayrouth) 1,500,000 (including suburbs; 1990 est.).

Other major cities: Tripoli (Tarabulus) 240,000, Zahleh 200,000, Sidon (Saida) 100,000 (all including suburbs; 1990 est.).

Languages: Arabic (official), French, with small Armenian and Kurdish minorities.

Religions: Shia Islam (31%), Sunni Islam (27%), Druze minority; Maronite Christian (22%), other Christian Churches (16% - mainly Armenian, Greek Orthodox, Syrian and various Roman Catholic Uniat Churches).

Education: Education is freely available for Lebanese aged between five and 17, but it is not compulsory. In 1990 the literacy rate was estimated to be 80.1%. There are five universities.

Defence: In 1992 the total armed strength was estimated to be nearly 39,000 - 37,500 in the army, 400 in the navy and 800 in the air force. There are about 9000 paramilitary, and over 35,000 Syrian troops are based in Lebanon. The Israeli-supported 'South Lebanon Army' has 2500 men. There is no military service.

Transport: There are about 7100 km (4413 mi) of roads. Only 222 km (138 mi) of the state-run railway system are still running. Beirut is a major shipping port and has an international airport.

Media: There are nearly 40 daily newspapers, two published in French. The Lebanese press is one of the most influential in the Middle East. The state-run LBS runs radio services. There are nine national and several local television stations.

GOVERNMENT

The constitution was amended in 1990 to provide for the election by universal adult suffrage of a 108-member National Assembly (comprising 54 members elected by Muslims and 54 deputies elected by Christians). The Assembly elects a (Maronite) President, who appoints a (Sunni Muslim) Prime Minister, who, in turn, appoints a Council of Ministers (six Christians and five Muslims). The main political parties include (Shia Islamic) Amal group, (Islamic fundamentalist) Hizbollah (Party of God), the (Maronite) Phalangist Party, the (pro-Syrian) Amal Party, the (mainly Druze) Progressive Socialist Party (PSP), the (Maronite) Bloc national, the Armenian Revolutionary Federation (PT), the (Arab Socialist) Ba'ath Party, the Lebanese Communist Party and the Syrian National Socialist Party. The general election of 1992 was boycotted by the Christian parties and resulted in a large majority of Amal and Hizbollah members and their allies.

President: Elias Hrawi.

THE CABINET

Prime Minister and Minister of Finance: Rafik al-Hariri.

Deputy Prime Minister: Michel El Murr.

Minister of Agriculture: Adel Kortas.

Minister of Defence: Mohsen Dalloul.

Minister of Economy and Trade: Yacob Y. Damarjian.

Minister of Employment: Abdullah Al Amin.

Minister of Foreign Affairs: Fares Boueiz.

Minister of Health and Social Affairs: Marwan Hamade.

Minister of Housing and Co-operatives: Mahmoud Abou Hamdan.

Minister of Industry and Petrol: Dr Asaad Rizk.

Minister of Information: Micehl Samaha.

Minister of Interior Affairs: Bichara Merhej.

Minister of Justice and Administrative Reforms: Dr Bahij Tabbara.

Minister of National Education and Fine Art: Mikhail Al Daher. Minister of Public Works and Transport: Mohammad B. Murtada.

Minister of State for Culture and Higher Education: Michel Eddeh.

Minister of State for Displaced Persons: Walid Joumblat.

Minister of State for the Environment: Samir Mokbel.

Minister of State for Finance: Fouad Siniora.

Minister of State for Immigrants: Dr Rida Wahid.

Minister of State for Municipalities: Suleiman Franjieh.

Minister of State for Professional and Technical Education: Hassan Ezzedine.

Minister of State for Social Welfare and the Handicapped, and Minister of Hydraulics and Electrical Resources: Elias Hobeika.

Minister of State for Transport: Omar Misqawi.

Minister of Telecommunications: Mohammad Ghaziri.

Minister of Tourism: Nicholas Fattoush.

Ministers of State: Shahi Borsoumian, Ali Osseiran, Anwar El Khalil, Jean Obeid.

GEOGRAPHY

A narrow coastal plain is separated from the fertile Beka'a Valley by the mountains of Lebanon. To the east are the Anti-Lebanese range and Hermon Mountains. Highest point: Qurnat as-Sawda 3088 m (10,131 ft). Principal river: Nahr al-Litani. Climate: The lowlands have a Mediterranean climate. The cooler highlands experience heavy snowfall in winter.

ECONOMY

Reconstruction of an economy devastated by civil war began in 1991. The principal agricultural crops are citrus fruit (mainly for export), wheat, barley and olives. The illegal cultivation of opium poppies is economically important. The textile and chemical industries and the financial sector have been reconstructed.

Currency: Lebanese pound (LBP) of 100 piastres; 1US$ = 1682.5 LBP (June 1994).

GDP: US$5,500,000,000 (1993 est); US$2000 per head.

RECENT HISTORY

Intercommunal friction was never far from the surface when the Ottoman Turks ruled Lebanon. A massacre of thousands of Maronites by the Druzes (1860) brought French intervention. After World War I, France received Syria as a League of Nations mandate, and created a separate Lebanese territory to protect Christian interests. The constitution under which Lebanon became independent in 1943 enshrined power-sharing between Christians and Muslims. The relative toleration between the various religious groups in Lebanon began to break down in the late 1950s when Muslim numerical superiority failed to be matched by corresponding constitutional changes. Radical Muslim supporters of the union of Syria and Egypt in 1958 clashed with the pro-Western party of Camille Chamoun (President 1952-58). Civil war ensued, and US marines landed in Beirut to restore order. The 1967 Arab-Israeli war and the exile of the Palestinian leadership to Beirut (1970-71) destabilized Lebanon. Civil war broke out in 1975, with subsequent Syrian and Israeli interventions. The war continued, plunging the country into ungovernable chaos, with Maronites, various Sunni and Shia Lebanese groups (including Iranian-backed fundamentalists), Syrian troops, Druze militia and UN peace-keeping forces all occupying zones of the fragmented country. In 1990, the Christian militia of Michel Aoun was crushed by the Syrians and the Lebanese government was able to reassert its authority over the whole of Beirut. However, Israeli sponsored forces continue to occupy the south and the (Islamic fundamentalist) Hizbollah forces control the Beka'a Valley. A new constitution (1990) enshrines Muslim-Christian equality in government and the continuing presence of Syrian troops have allowed a reconstruction of the Lebanese state.

Libya

Official name: Daulat Libiya al-'Arabiya al-Ëlshtrakiya al-Jumhuriya (The Great Socialist People's Libyan Arab Jamahiriya).

Member of: UN, Arab League, OPEC.

Area: 1,759,540 km² (679,363 sq mi).

Population: 4,573,000 (1993 est).

Capital: Tripoli (Tarabulus) 591,000 (1988 est). In 1988 government functions were decentralized to Sirte (Surt) and Al Jofrah as well as Tripoli and Benghazi.

Other major cities: Benghazi (Banghazi) 446,000 Misurata (Misratah) 122,000, az-Zawiyah 89,000 (1988 est).

Language: Arabic (official).

Religion: Sunni Islam (over 97%), small Christian (mainly Roman Catholic) minority.

Education: Education is compulsory between the ages of six and 15. In 1990 the literacy rate was nearly 94%. There are five universities.

Defence: In 1993 the total armed strength was 70,000 - 40,000 in the army, 8000 in the navy and 22,000 in the air force. There is also a 2500-

LIBYA

Area: 1 759 540 km²
(679 363 sq mi)

member 'Islamic pan-African legion' recruited by Libya. Tripoli and Benghazi are the main naval bases. Compulsory military service lasts for three years in the army, and for four years in the navy and the air force.

Transport: There are 19,300 km (11,992 mi) of

roads in Libya. Tripoli and Benghazi, the main commercial shipping ports, also have international airports. Sebha also has an international airport.

Media: There is a single state-controlled daily newspaper. There is a state-run radio and television service.

GOVERNMENT

Over 1110 delegates from directly elected local Basic People's Congresses, trade unions, 'popular committees' and professional organizations meet as the Great People's Congress, which chooses a Leader of the Revolution, who is effectively the head of state, although he has no formal post in the administration. The Congress also chooses the 22-member General People's Committee (which is equivalent to a Council of Ministers). The appointed General Secretariat assists the Congress. However, effective power remains with the Leader of the Revolution and his colleagues on the former Revolutionary Command Council. For local government purposes Libya is divided into 13 baladiyat. There are no political parties.

Leader of the revolution (the Libyan head of state): Moamar al Gaddafi.

THE CABINET

(THE GENERAL PEOPLE'S COMMITTEE) includes

Head of government (Secretary-General of the General People's Committee - the equivalent of Prime Minister): Abd al-Majid al-Qa'ud.

Senior Adviser (the second most important post in the government - in some respects, the equivalent of Deputy President): Maj. Abdel Salem Jalloud.

Joint Co-ordinator of the General Provisional Committee for Defence: Abu Bakr Jaber Yunes.

Joint Co-ordinator of the General Provisional Committee for Defence: Mustafa Kharrubi.

Joint Co-ordinator of the General Provisional Committee for Defence: Khoueldi

Member of the General People's Committee for Communications and Transport: Izz al-Din al-Hinshari.

Member of the General People's Committee for Education: Madani Ramadhan.

Member of the General People's Committee for

Energy: Abdullah Salem al-Badri.

Member of the General People's Committee for Finance: Mohammad al-Madami.

Member of the General People's Committee for Health: Dr Zaydan Bader Zaydan.

Member of the General People's Committee for Information and Culture: Ali Milad Abu Jaziyah.

Member of the General People's Committee for Foreign Liaison and International Co-operation: Omar Mustafa al-Muntasir.

Member of the General People's Committee for Planning: Mohammad Bait al-Mal.

Member of the General People's Committee for Strategic Industry: Jadullah Azzuzz.

Secretary-General of the General People's Congress: Zentani Mohammad Zentani.

GEOGRAPHY
The Sahara Desert covers most of Libya. In the northwest - the traditional region of Tripolitania - coastal oases and a low plain form the country's main agricultural region. In the northeast (the traditional region of Cyrenaica) a coastal plain and mountain ranges support Mediterranean vegetation. The third (southwestern) region of Libya, Fezzan, consists of a desert plateau with a few scattered oases, rising to the Tibesti Mountains in the far south. Highest point: Bette Peak 2286 m (7500 ft). Principal river: Wadi al-Farigh (which does not flow for all of the year). Although there are no perennial rivers, extensive percolation of water supports artesian wells and springs. Climate: Libya is hot and dry, with lower temperatures and higher rainfall near the Mediterranean coast. Droughts of up to two years are not uncommon.

ECONOMY
Libya is one of the world's largest producers of petroleum. Liquefied gas is also exported. The principal industries are petroleum refining, food processing and the production of cement. Despite a high standard of living, the Libyan economy is beset with many problems. The economy suffers through over dependence upon the export of a single commodity, petroleum. The country's political volatility and international isolation have combined to discourage foreign investment that would broad-

en Libya's economic base and encourage development projects. In 1992-93 UN sanctions - including the freezing of Libyan assets abroad, mandatory air, arms and diplomatic sanctions, and bans of sales of certain types of equipment to Libya (see below) - have added to these problems. However, the impact of these sanctions is difficult to judge as Libya releases so few economic figures. Coastal oases produce wheat, barley, nuts, dates and grapes. Although the agricultural sector employs over 12% of the labour force, Libyan farming produces only a fraction of the country's food needs and much food has to be imported. The imposition of UN sanctions upon Libya has damaged the country's agriculture as the importation of fertilizers and machine parts has been restricted.

Currency: Libyan dinar of 1000 millemes; 1US$ = 0.308 Libyan dinars (June 1994).

GDP: US$28,900,000,000 (1990); US$6,800 per head.

RECENT HISTORY
In 1911 the Italians took Libya, which had been under Ottoman (Turkish) rule since the 16th century. The British Eighth Army defeated the Italians in the Libyan Desert (1942), and after World War II the country was divided between British and French administrations. Libya gained independence in 1951 under King Idris, formerly Amir of Cyrenaica. Although oil revenues made Libya prosperous, the pro-Western monarchy became increasingly unpopular. In 1969 junior army officers led by Col. Moamar al Gaddafi (1942-) took power. Gaddafi nationalized the oil industry, but his various attempts to federate with other Arab countries proved abortive. In the 1970s he began a cultural revolution, dismantled formal government, collectivized economic activity, limited personal wealth and suppressed opposition. Libya's alleged support of international terrorism provoked US air raids on Tripoli and Benghazi in 1986, since when Gaddafi has kept a lower international profile. However, alleged Libyan involvement in the bombing of a US airliner led to the imposition of UN sanctions in 1992. In 1994 the International Court found against Libya in a long-standing territorial dispute with Chad, whose extreme northern border area has been occupied by Libyan forces.

Morocco

Official name: Al-Mamlaka al-Maghribiya (The Kingdom of Morocco).

Member of: UN, Arab League.

Area: 458,730 km² (177,115 sq mi) excluding the disputed Western Sahara; 710,850 km² (274,461 sq mi) including the Western Sahara (see p. 87).

Population: 26,494,000 (1993 est) excluding the Western Sahara (see p. 87).

Capital: Rabat (incl. Salé) 1,545,000 (1992 est).

Other major cities: Casablanca (Dar el Beida) 3,311,000 (city 1,069,000), Marrakech 745,000, Meknès 660,000, Oujda 635,000, Kénitra 610,000, Fez (Fès) 605,000, Tetouan 500,000 (1992 est).

Languages: Arabic (official; 75% as a first language, but universally understood), Berber (about 25%), French.

Religions: Sunni Islam (official; 98%), Roman Catholic (2%).

Education: Education is compulsory, in theory, between the ages of seven and 13. In 1990 the literacy rate was 49.5%. There are seven universities.

Defence: In 1993 the total armed strength was 196,000 - 175,000 in the army, 7000 in the navy and 14,000 in the air force. There are also 10,000 paramilitary 'gendarmerie royale' and 30,000 paramilitary 'force auxiliaire'. Compulsory military service lasts for 18 months.

Transport: There are over 59,500 km (37,000 mi) of roads and 1893 km (1177 mi) of state-run railways. Casablanca and Muhammdia are the main commercial shipping ports, while Tangier is a major ferry port. There are eight international airports of which Casablanca, Rabat, Tangier, Marrakech and Agadir are the most important.

Media: There are 12 daily newspapers printed in either Rabat or Casablanca. There are two radio services (one state-owned, one private) and two television channels (one state-owned, one commercial).

GOVERNMENT

Morocco is a constitutional monarchy. The 333-member Chamber of Representatives consists of 222 members elected by universal adult suffrage for six years and 111 members chosen by an electoral college representing municipal

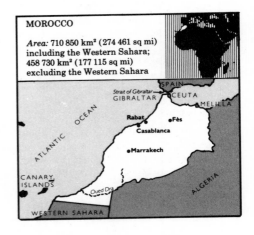

MOROCCO

Area: 710 850 km² (274 461 sq mi) including the Western Sahara; 458 730 km² (177 115 sq mi) excluding the Western Sahara

authorities and professional bodies. The King appoints a Prime Minister and Cabinet and may also dissolve the Chamber. The main political parties include the Constitutional Union (UC), the Popular Movement (MP), the National Popular Movement (MNP), the National Democratic Party (PND), the Socialist Union of Popular Forces (USFP), the Istiqal Party (PI), the Party of Progress and Socialism (PPS), the Organization of Democratic and Popular Action (OADP), the National Rally of Independents (RNI), and the Party of Action (PA). After elections held in September 1993 a non-party government was formed.

Party strength: UC 54, MP 51, MNP 25, PND 24 (UC-MP-MNP-PND form the Entente Nationale), USFP 52, PI 50, PPS 12, OADP 2 (USFP-PI-FPS-OADP form the Bloc Democratique), RNI 41, PA 2, others 11.

King: HM King Hassan II (succeeded upon the death of his father, 26 February 1961).

THE CABINET

Prime Minister and Minister of Foreign Affairs and Cooperation: Abdellatif Filali.

Minister of Agriculture and Agricultural Development: Abdelaziz Meziane Belfkih.

Minister of Cultural Affairs: Mohamed Allai Sinaceur.

Minister of Employment and Social Affairs: Rafiq Haddaoui.

Minister of Energy and Mines: Abdelatif Gurraoui.

Minister of Finance: Mohamed Sagou.

Minister of Foreign Trade, Foreign Investments and Handicraft: Mourad Charif.

Minister of Habous and Islamic Affairs: Abdelkebir M'Daghri Alaoui.

Minister of Housing: Driss Toulali.

Minister of Justice: Moulay Mohamed Idrissi Alami Machichi.

Minister of Maritime Fisheries and the Merchant Navy: Mustapha Sahel.

Minister of National Education: Mohamed Kniidri.

Minister of Posts and Telecommunications: Abdeslam Ahizoune.

Minister of Public Health: Dr Abderrahim Harouchi.

Minister of Public Works, Staff and Vocational Training: Mohamed Hassad.

Minister of State: Moulay Ahmed Alaoui.

Minister of State for the Interior and Information; Driss Basri.

Minister of Tourism: Serge Berdugo.

Minister of Trade and Industry: Driss Jettou.

Minister of Transport: Rachidi Rhezouane.

Minister of Youth and Sports: Driss Alaoui M'Daghri.

Secretary General of the Government: Abdessadek Rabiaa.

GEOGRAPHY
Over one third of Morocco is mountainous. The principal uplands are the Grand, Middle and Anti Atlas Mountains in the west and north and a plateau in the east. Much of the country - including the disputed Western Sahara territory - is desert. Highest point: Jebel Toubkal 4165 m (13,665 ft). Principal rivers: Oued Dra, Oued Moulouya, Sebov. Climate: The north has a Mediterranean climate with hot dry summers and warm wetter winters. The south and much of the interior have semi-arid and tropical desert climates.

ECONOMY
Agriculture employs over 40% of the labour force. The main crops include citrus fruits, grapes (for wine) and vegetables for export, and wheat and barley for domestic consumption. Morocco is the world's leading exporter of phosphates. Other resources include iron ore, lead and zinc. Since independence many important industries and services have come into state ownership. Tourism is growing in importance and over 3,500,000 foreign visitors come to Morocco for their holidays per annum. Economic problems include unemployment and a high rate of population increase (which is partly offset by migration to Europe).

Currency: Dirham of 100 centimes; 1US$ = 9.01 dirhams (June 1994).

GDP: US$27,047,000,000 (1992); US$1030 per head.

RECENT HISTORY
In the 19th century Spain confirmed control of several long-claimed coastal settlements. In the 'Moroccan Crises' (1905-6 and 1911), French interests in Morocco were disputed by Germany. Under the Treaty of Fez in 1912 France established a protectorate over Morocco, although the Spanish enclaves remained. The 1925 Rif rebellion stirred nationalist feelings, but independence was not gained until 1956. King Hassan II (reigned 1961-) has survived left-wing challenges through strong rule and vigorous nationalism - as in his 1975 'Green March' of unarmed peasants into the then-Spanish (Western) Sahara. Morocco continues to hold the Western Sahara despite international pressure and the activities of the Algerian-backed Polisario guerrillas fighting for the territory's independence. A ceasefire was agreed in 1991. Discussions concerning a UN-sponsored referendum in the disputed territory are continuing.

Oman

Official name: Sultanat 'Uman (Sultanate of Oman).

Member of: UN, Arab League, GCC.

Area: 300,000 km² (120,000 sq mi).

Population: 2,210,000 (1991 est).

Capital: Muscat 380,000 (city 85,000; 1990 est).

Other main towns: Sohar 92,000, Rustaq 66,000 (1990 est).

Languages: Arabic (official).

Religions: Ibadi Islam (75%), Sunni Islam (25%).

Education: Education is not compulsory. The literacy rate was 41% in 1990. There is a university.

Defence: The total armed strength in 1993 was 26,500 - 20,000 in the army, 3000 in the navy, 3500 in the air force.

Transport: There are nearly 27,500 km (17,190 mi) of roads. Muscat has an international airport and a commercial shipping port.

Media: There are three daily newspapers (one in English). There are two radio stations and a television station.

GOVERNMENT

Oman is an absolute monarchy in which the Sultan - who rules by decree - is assisted by an appointed Cabinet. The 60-member Majlis (consultative assembly) comprises the Sultan's representative (who presides) and 59 other representatives, one nominated by each provincial governor (who is appointed by the Sultan). There are no political parties.

Sultan: HM Qaboos bin Said (succeeded upon the deposition of his father, 23 July 1970).

Prime Minister: The Sultan.

GEOGRAPHY

A barren range of hills rises sharply behind a narrow coastal plain. Desert extends into the Rub' al Khali (The Empty Quarter). A detached portion of Oman lies north of the United Arab Emirates. Highest point: Jabal ash Sham 3170 m (10,400 ft). Climate: Oman is arid and very hot in the summer, but milder in the winter and in the mountains.

ECONOMY

Oman depends almost entirely upon exports of petroleum and natural gas. The oil and gas industries, and much of the state's modern commercial infrastructure, rely upon almost 400,000 foreign workers. Owing to aridity, less than 1% of Oman is cultivated.

Currency: Omani rial of 1000 baiza. 1US$ = 0.384 RO (May 1994).

GDP: US$9,503,000,000 (1990 est); US$6327 per head.

RECENT HISTORY

Ahmad ibn Sa'id, who became Imam in 1749, founded the dynasty that still rules Oman. His successors built an empire including the Kenyan coast and Zanzibar, but in 1861 Zanzibar and Oman separated. A British pres-

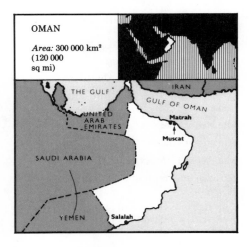

ence was established in the 19th century and Oman did not regain complete independence until 1951. Sultan Qaboos, who came to power in a palace coup in 1970, has modernized and developed Oman. In the 1970s South Yemen supported left-wing guerrillas in the southern region of Dhofar, but the revolt was suppressed with military assistance from the UK.

Qatar

Official name: Dawlat Qatar (State of Qatar).

Member of: UN, Arab League, OPEC, GCC.

Area: 11,437 km² (4416 sq mi).

Population: 456,000 (1991 est).

Capital: Doha 272,000 (city 217,000, ar-Rayyani 42,000, al-Wakrah 13,000; 1986 est).

Other major town: Umm Sa'id 6000 (1986 est).

Language: Arabic.

Religion: Wahhabi Sunni Islam (official; 98%).

Education: Schooling is available but is not compulsory. Most Qatar children attend school at least between the ages of six and 11. In 1986 the literacy rate was estimated to be 75.7%. There is a single university.

Defence: In 1991 the total armed strength was estimated to be 7500 - 6000 in the army, 700 in the navy and 800 in the air force. There is no military service.

Transport: There are over 1600 km (995 mi) of roads and no railways. Doha and Umm Sa'id are shipping ports; Doha has an international airport.

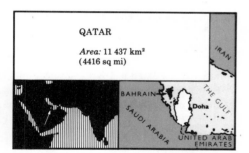

QATAR

Area: 11 437 km²
(4416 sq mi)

IRAN
BAHRAIN
THE GULF
Doha
SAUDI ARABIA
UNITED ARAB EMIRATES

Media: There are four daily newspapers, one of which is published in English. There is a single state-run radio and television service.

GOVERNMENT
Qatar is an absolute monarchy. The Amir - who is head of state and of government - appoints a Council of Ministers. There are neither formal political institutions nor political parties.

Amir and head of government: HH Shaikh Khalifa bin Hamad Al-Thani (succeeded upon the deposition of his cousin, 22 February 1972).

THE CABINET
The Cabinet includes:

Prime Minister: The Amir.

Deputy Prime Minister and Minister of Defence: HH Crown Prince Shaikh Hamad bin Khalifah Al-Thani.

Minister of Finance, the Economy and Trade: Shaikh Mohammad bin Khalifah Al-Thani.

Minister of Foreign Affairs: Shaikh Hamad bin Jassem bin Jabr Al-Thani.

Minister of the Interior: Shaikh Abdulla bin Khalifah Al-Thani.

Minister of Justice: Shaikh Ahmed bin Said Al-Thani.

GEOGRAPHY
Qatar is a low barren peninsula projecting into the Gulf. There are no rivers. Highest point: 73 m (240 ft) in the Dukhan Heights. Climate: Qatar is very hot in summer, but milder in winter. Rainfall averages between 50 and 75 mm (2 to 3 in).

ECONOMY
Qatar's high standard of living is due almost entirely to the export of petroleum and natural gas. The North Field, which is now being actively exploited, is thought to be the largest natural gas field in the world. The steel and cement industries have been developed in an attempt to diversify.

Currency: Qatari riyal (QAR) of 100 dirhams; 1US$ = 3.63 QAR (June 1994).

GDP: US$6,968,000,000 (1991); US$16,000 per head.

RECENT HISTORY
In the 1860s Britain intervened in a dispute between Qatar and its Bahraini rulers, installing a member of the Qatari Al-Thani family as shaikh. Qatar was part of the Ottoman Empire from 1872 until 1914. Its ruler signed protection treaties with Britain in 1916 and 1934, and did not regain complete independence until 1971. Qatar joined the coalition forces against Saddam Hussein's Iraq in the Second Gulf War (1991).

273

Saudi Arabia

Official name: Al-Mamlaka al-'Arabiya as-Sa'udiya (The Kingdom of Saudi Arabia).

Member of: UN, Arab League, OPEC, GCC.

Area: 2,240,000 km² (864,869 sq mi).

Population: 15,267,000 (1992 est).

Capital: Riyadh (Ar Riyad) 2,000,000 (including suburbs; 1986 est).

Other major cities: Jeddah (Jiddah) 1,400,000, Mecca (Makkah) 620,000, Medina (Al-Madinah) 500,000, Taif 205,000, Buraida 185,000, Abha 155,000 (all including suburbs; 1986 est).

Language: Arabic (official).

Religion: Islam (official) - Sunni (92%; mainly Wahhabi), Shia (8%).

Education: Education is available free of charge but is not compulsory. In 1990 the literacy rate was estimated to be 62.4% (73.1% for males; 48.1% for females). There are seven universities.

Defence: In 1992 the total armed strength was 191,500 - 73,000 in the army, 10,500 in the frontier force, 11,000 in the navy, 18,000 in the air force, 4000 in the air defence force, 75,000 in the national guard.

Transport: There are over 93,000 km (58,100 mi) of roads. Damaman and Jiddah are the main commercial shipping ports. There are major international airports at Jiddah, Riyadh and Dhahran.

Media: There are seven Arabic-language and three English-language daily newspapers. There is a state-run radio and television service.

GOVERNMENT

Saudi Arabia is an absolute monarchy with neither formal political institutions nor parties. The King - whose official title in Saudi Arabia is 'Custodian of the Two Holy Mosques' - appoints a Council of Ministers. Succession to the throne passes from brother to brother according to seniority. The King appoints a 60-member consultative Council to hold office for four years.

King: HM King Fahd ibn Abdul Aziz Al Saud (succeeded upon the death of his brother, 13 May 1982).

THE COUNCIL OF MINISTERS (CABINET)
Prime Minister: The King.

First Deputy Prime Minister and Commander of the Natiional Guard: HRH Crown Prince Abdullah ibn Abdul Aziz.

Second Deputy Prime Minister, Minister of Defence and Aviation and Inspector General: HRH Prince Sultan ibn Abdul Aziz.

Minister of Agriculture and Water: Dr Abdul Rahman ibn Abdul Aziz ibn Hasan al Shaikh.

Minister of Commerce: Dr Sulaiman Abdul Aziz al Sulmain.

Minister of Communications: Hussein Ibrahim al Mansouri.

Minister of Education: Dr Abdul Aziz al Abdullah al Khuwaiter.

Minister of Finance and the National Economy: Muhammad Ali Aba'l Khail.

Minister of Foreign Affairs: HRH Prince Saud al Faisal.

Minister of Health: Faisal ibn Abdul Aziz al Hejailan.

Minister of Higher Education: Khalid al Angari.

Minister of Industry and Electricity: Dr Abdul Aziz al Zamil.

Minister of Information: Ali ibn Hasan al Shaer.

Minister of the Interior: HRH Prince Naif ibn Abdul Aziz.

Minister of Justice: Abdallah bin al Shaikh Muhammad.

Minister of Labour and Social Affairs: Muhammad al Ali al Fayiz.

Minister of Municipal and Rural Affairs: Muhammad al Shaikh.

Minister of Petroleum and Mineral Resources: Hisham Nazer.

Minister of Pilgrimage Affairs (Haj): Abdul Wahhab Ahmad Abdul Wasi.

Minister of Planning: Abdel Wahhab al Attar.

Minister of Posts and Telecommunications: Dr Alawi Darwish Kayyal.

SAUDI ARABIA

Area: 2 240 000 km²
(864 869 sq mi)

Minister of Public Works and Housing: HRH Prince Miteb ibn Abdul Aziz.

PROVINCES

(The areas of the provinces are estimates.)

Central Province (al-Wusta; formerly Nejd) Area: 1,332,000 km² (514,200 sq mi). Population: 3,632,000 (1985 est). Main administrative centre: Riyadh.

Eastern Province (ash-Sharqiyah; formerly al-Hasa) Area: 106,700 km² (41,200 sq mi). Population: 3,031,000 (1985 est). Main administrative centre: Damman.

Northern Province (ash-Shamaliyah) Area: 364,700 km² (128,500 sq mi). Population: 680,000 (1985 est). Main administrative centre: Sakakah.

Southern Province (al-Janubiyah; formerly Asir) Area: 100,000 km² (40,000 sq mi). Population: 625,000 (1985 est). Main administrative centre: Abha.

Western Province (al-Gharbiyah; formerly Hejaz) Area: 332,800 km² (128,500 sq mi). Population: 3,043,000 (1985 est). Main administrative centre: Mecca.

GEOGRAPHY

Over 95% of the country is desert, including the Rub 'al-Khali ('The Empty Quarter') - the largest expanse of sand in the world. The Arabian plateau ends in the west in a steep escarpment overlooking a coastal plain beside the Red Sea. There are no permanent streams. Highest point: Jebel Razikh 3658 m (12,002 ft). Climate: The country is very hot - with temperatures up to 54 C (129 F). The average rainfall is 100 mm (4 in), but many areas receive far less and may not experience any precipitation for years.

ECONOMY

Saudi Arabia's spectacular development and present prosperity are based almost entirely upon exploiting vast reserves of petroleum and natural gas. Industries include petroleum refining, petrochemicals and fertilizers. The country has developed major banking and commercial interests. Less than 1% of the land can be cultivated. Under the current five-year plan efforts are being made to encourage the private sector. Oil revenues are being maximized to pay for improved social services.

Currency: Rial (SAR) of 100 halalas; 1US$ = 3.75 SAR (May 1994).

GDP: US$125,000,000,000 (1993 est); US$7006 per head.

RECENT HISTORY

In the 20th century the Wahhabis - a Sunni Islamic sect - united most of Arabia under Ibn Saud (1882-1953). In 1902 Ibn Saud took Riyadh and in 1906 defeated his rivals to control central Arabia (Nejd). Between 1912 and 1927 he added the east, the southwest (Asir) and the area around Mecca (Hejaz). In 1932 these lands became the kingdom of Saudi Arabia. Although the country has been pro-Western, after the 1973 Arab-Israeli War, Saudi Arabia put pressure on the USA to encourage Israel to withdraw from the occupied territories by cutting oil production. Saudi Arabia has not escaped problems caused by religious fundamentalism and the rivalry between Sunni and Shia Islam. In 1980 Saudi Arabia found itself bound to support Iraq in its war with Shiite Iran. Influenced by the Iranian revolution and the First Gulf War, Saudi Arabia formed the defensive Gulf Cooperation Council (GCC) with its neighbouring emirates. Saudi Arabia was threatened by Iraq following the invasion of Kuwait (August 1990), and played a major role in the coalition against Saddam Hussein in the Second Gulf War (1991). The Basic Law (1992), which established the consultative Council, reflects the growing expectations of the middle classes.

275

Syria

Official name: Al-Jumhuriya al-'Arabiya as-Suriya (The Syrian Arab Republic).

Member of: UN, Arab League.

Area: 185,180 km² (71,498 sq mi) - including the Israeli-occupied Golan Heights.

Population: 12,958,000 (1992 est).

Capital: Damascus (Dimashq) 1,451,000 (1992 est).

Other major cities: Halab (formerly Aleppo) 1,445,000, Homs 518,000, Latakia 284,000, Hama 254,000 (1992 est).

Languages: Arabic (89%; official), Kurdish (6%), Armenian (3%).

Religions: Islam (official; Sunni 90%, Shia and Druze minorities), with various Orthodox and Roman Catholic minorities.

Education: Education is compulsory between the ages of six and 12. In 1990 the literacy rate was estimated to be 64.5%. There are four universities.

Defence: In 1993 the total armed strength was estimated to be 408,000 - 300,000 in the army, 8200 in the navy and 100,000 in the air force. There are also about 400,000 reserves and 8000 paramilitary gendarmes. Some 35,000 Syrian troops were based in Lebanon in mid-1993. Syrian males are subject to compulsory military service of 30 months.

Transport: There are over 29,750 km (18,490 mi) of roads and 1766 km (1098 mi) of state-run railways. Latakia is the principal commercial shipping port. Damascus has an international airport.

Media: The media are government-controlled. There are nine daily newspapers. There is a single state-run radio and television service.

GOVERNMENT

The 250-member National People's Assembly is elected by universal adult suffrage for four years. The President - who is directly elected for seven years - appoints a Prime Minister (to assist him in government) and a Council of Ministers. The National Progressive Front - including the ruling Ba'ath Arab Socialist Party, the Arab Socialist Union Party, the Syrian Arab Socialist Party, the Arab Socialist Party and the Communist Party - has a leading role.

President: Hafez al-Assad.

THE CABINET

Prime Minister: Mahmoud Zubi.

Deputy Prime Minister and Minister of Defence: Lt-Gen Mustafa Tlaas.

Deputy Prime Minister for Economic Affairs: Dr Salim Yasin.

Deputy Prime Minister for Social Affairs: Rashid Akhtarini.

Minister of Building and Construction: Majed Ezzo Rehebani.

Minister of Communication: Radwan Martini.

Minister of Culture: Dr Najah Al-Attar.

Minister of the Economy and Foreign Trade: Dr Muhamed Al-Imadi.

Minister of Education: Muhamed Ghassan Al-Halabi.

Minister of Electricity: Mounib Sa'em Aldahen.

Minister of Finance: Dr Muhamed Khaled Al-Mahayni.

Minister of Foreign Affairs: Farouq Al-Sharaa.

Minister of Health: Dr Muhamed Iyad Al-Shatti.

Minister of Higher Education: Dr Salha Sankar.

Minister of Housing and Utilities:Hussam El-Safadi.

Minister of Industry: Dr Ahmad Nizam El-Din.

Minister of Information:Dr Muhamed Salman.

Minister of Irrigation: Abdel Rahman Madani.

Minister of the Interior: Dr Muhamed Harba.

Minister of Justice:Dr Abdallah Talaba.

Minister of Local Administration: Yahya Abou-Assali.

Minister of Oil and Mineral Wealth: Dr Nader Nabulsi.

Minister for Presidency Affairs: Wahib Fadel.

Minister of Religious Trusts: Dr Abdel-Majid Trabulsi.

Minister of Social Affairs and Labour: Ali Khalil.

Minister of Supply and Internal Trade: Nadim Akkash.

Minister of Tourism: Amin Abou Al-Shamat.

Minister of Transport: Dr Mufid Abdel-Karim.

Ministers of State: Yusuf Al Ahmad, Hussein Hassoun, Nabil Mallah, Hanna Murad.

Minister of State for the Environment: Abdel-Hamid Munajed.

Minister of State for Foreign Affairs: Nasser Qaddur.

Minister of State for Planning: Dr Abdel-Rahim Al-Sbei'i.

Minister of State for the Prime Minister's Office: Danho Dawood.

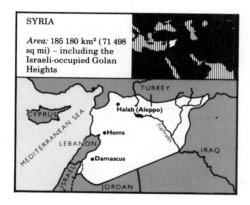

SYRIA

Area: 185 180 km² (71 498 sq mi) – including the Israeli-occupied Golan Heights

GEOGRAPHY
Behind a well-watered coastal plain, mountains run from north to south. Inland, much of the country is occupied by the Syrian Desert. Highest point: Jabal ash Shaik (Mount Hermon) 2814 m (9232 ft). Principal rivers: Euphrates (Al Furat), Asi (Orontes) Climate: The coast has a Mediterranean climate. The arid interior has hot summers and cool winters.

ECONOMY
Petroleum is the main export although Syria's petroleum reserves are small by Middle Eastern standards. Agriculture involves nearly one quarter of the labour force, with cultivation concentrated in the coastal plain and irrigated land in the Euphrates Valley. Major crops include cotton, wheat and barley. The country has benefited from increased investment from the West since 1991, but the economy is burdened by a large and inefficient state-owned sector.

Currency: Syrian pound (SYP) of 100 piastres; 1US$ = 20,466 SYP (June 1994).

GDP: US$14,234,000,000 (1991); US$1110 per head.

RECENT HISTORY
Ottoman rule in Syria lasted from 1516 until 1917, when a combined British-Arab army was led into Damascus by Prince Faisal ibn Husain. In 1920 independence was declared with Faisal as king, but the victors of World War I handed Syria to France (1920) as a trust territory. From independence in 1946 until 1970 Syria suffered political instability - between December 1946 and December 1951 Syria had no fewer than 20 Prime Ministers. The pan-Arab, secular, socialist Ba'ath Party engineered Syria's unsuccessful union with Egypt (1958-61). Syria fought wars with Israel in 1948-49, 1967 and 1973, and in the 1967 Arab-Israeli War Israel captured the strategic Golan Heights from Syria. A pragmatic Ba'athist leader Hafiz al-Assad came to power in 1970 and allied Syria to the USSR. Assad's popularity has been challenged by Syria's increasing involvement in Lebanese affairs since 1976 and by Shiite fundamentalism. In 1990 Syria defeated the Lebanese Christian militia of Michel Aoun and restored the authority of the Lebanese government to the whole of Beirut. After 1989-90, economic pressures lessened Syria's dependence upon the USSR and the collapse of the Soviet Union in 1991 brought a more pragmatic phase to Syria's foreign relations. Syria's participation in the coalition against its old rival Iraq in 1990-91 gained greater international acceptance for Syria, which had attracted criticism for its sponsorship of terrorism. In 1993-94 Syria tentatively began to enter the Middle East peace process with the object of recovering the Golan Heights from Israel.

Tunisia

Official name: Al-Jumhuriya at-Tunisiya (Republic of Tunisia).

Member of: UN, Arab League, OAU.

Area: 163,610 km² (63,170 sq mi).

Population: 8,530,000 (1993 est).

Capital: Tunis 1,420,000 (city 620,000; Aryanah 131,000; Ettadhamen 112,000; 1989 est).

Other major cities: Sfax (Safaqis) 222,000, Sousse (Susah) 102,000, Bizerta (Banzart) 95,000, Djerba 93,000, Gabes (Qabis) 93,000, Kairouan (Qayrawan) 75,000 (all including suburbs; 1989 est).

Languages: Arabic (official), Berber minority. The use of the French language is still relatively widespread.

Religion: Sunni Islam (official; 99%), small Christian (mainly Roman Catholic) and Jewish minorities.

Education: Education is freely available for six years for primary schooling (and an additional seven years for secondary schooling) from the age of six but it is not compulsory. In 1990 the literacy rate was 65.3%. There are five universities.

Defence: In 1993 the total armed strength was 35,000 - 27,000 in the army, 4500 in the navy, and 3500 in the air force. There is also a 3500-member paramilitary Public Order Brigade and a 10,000-member National Guard. Bizerta is the principal naval base. Compulsory conscription varies in length with the service.

Transport: There are 29,183 km (18,133 mi) of roads and 2162 km (1343 mi) of state-run railways. Tunis has a metro/rapid light transit system. Tunis La Goulette and Bizerta are the main commercial shipping ports. There are international airports at Tunis, Sfax, Djerba, Monastir, Tabarka and Tozeur. Apart from Tunis, most of these are primarilty concerned with holiday charter flights.

Media: There are six daily newspapers - four published in Arabic and two published in French. There is a state-run radio and television service, with two television channels.

GOVERNMENT

The President and the 141-member National Assembly are elected by universal adult suffrage for a five-year term. The President appoints a Cabinet, headed by a Prime Minister. For local government purposes Tunisia is divided into 23 governates. The main political parties are the (socialist former monopoly) Democratic Constitutional Rally (formerly called the Destour Socialist Party; RCD), the Movement of Democratic Socialists (MDS), the (former Communist) Renovation Movement (MR), and the (banned Islamic) Renaissance Party (al-Nahda). After the election held in May 1994 the RCD retained power.

Party strength: RCD 141.

President: Zine el-Abidine Ben Ali (RCD).

THE CABINET

includes

Prime Minister: Hamed Karoui (RCD).

Minister of Defence: Abdelaziz Ben Dhia (RCD).

Minister of Economic Affairs: Sadok Rabah (RCD).

Minister of Education, Higher Education and Scientific Research: Mohammed Charfi (RCD).

Minister of Equipment and Housing: Ahmed Friaa (RCD).

Minister of Finance: Nouri Zorgati (RCD).

Minister of Foreign Affairs: Habib Ben Yahia (RCD).

Minister of Infrastructure and Minister of Territorial Management: Salah Jebali (RCD).

Minister of the Interior: Abdullah Kallal (RCD).

Minister of International Co-operation and Foreign Investment: Mohammed Gannouchi (RCD).

Minister of Justice: Sadouk Chaabane (RCD).

Minister of the National Economy: Sadok Rabah (RCD).

Minister of Planning and Regional Development: Nabli Mustapha Kamel (RCD).

Minister of Professional Training and Minister of Employment: Taoufik Cheikhrouhou (RCD).

Minister of Social Affairs: Ahmed Smaoui (RCD).

Minister of Tourism and Handicrafts: Mohammed Jegham (RCD).

Minister of Youth Affairs and Minister for Children: Mohammed Saad (RCD).

Secretary General for the Presidency: Mohammed Jeri (RCD).

GEOGRAPHY
The north part of Tunisia is occupied by the Northern Tell mountains and the High Tell mountains. Wide plateaux cover central Tunisia. The Sahara Desert lies south of a zone of shallow salt lakes. Highest point: Jabal ash-Shanabi 1544 m (5066 ft). Principal river: Medjerda. Climate: The north of the country experiences a temperate Mediterranean climate with warm winters, hot summers and adequate rainfall. The south has a hot dry climate.

ECONOMY
Phosphates and petroleum are the mainstay of the economy, normally providing over 40% of Tunisia's exports. The principal crops are wheat, barley and vegetables, as well as olives and citrus fruit for export. Tourism (particularly from Germany and France) is a major foreign-currency earner. The continuation of heavy subsidies, now confined to basic commodities, is a major drain upon the economy. Government reform policies in the early 1990s have included the privatization of many state-owned companies. Reforms have also stimulated economic growth, helped to control inflation and reduced Tunisia's debts. However, there is still a large, and growing, budget deficit. Unemployment remains a major problem and large numbers of Tunisians seek work in Europe, in particular in France and Italy.

Currency: Tunisian dinar of 1000 millimes; 1US$ = 0.994 Tunisian dinars (June 1994).

GDP: US$12,417,000,000 (1991); US$1450 per head.

RECENT HISTORY
In 1881 France established a protectorate, although the bey (monarch) remained the nominal ruler of Tunisia throughout the colonial period. Nationalist sentiments grew in the 20th century. Tunisia was occupied by the Germans from 1942 to 1943, but French rule was then restored until 1956, when independence was gained under the premiership of Habib Bourguiba (1903-). In 1957 the monarchy was abolished and Bourguiba became president. From 1979 until the early 1990s, the presence of the headquareters of the Arab League and of

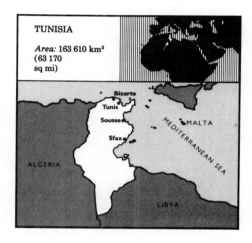

TUNISIA

Area: 163 610 km² (63 170 sq mi)

the Palestine Liberation Organization (PLO) in Tunis allowed Tunisia to exercise an influence in the Arab world that was quite out of proportion to its size. However, the Arab League returned to Cairo in 1990 and the PLO was able to transfer its headquarters to Gaza City in 1994. In the late 1980s the regime became increasingly unpopular and intolerant of opposition. Relations with the USA were severely strained in 1985 when Israeli planes bombed the headquarters of the Palestinian Liberation Organization near Tunis. In 1987 President Bourguiba was deposed in a bloodless coup by his Prime Minister and was declared 'mentally and physically unfit' for office. Since then multi-party politics have been permitted, but opposition is restricted. Although opposition parties are now legally permitted to enter parliament, the 1994 general election again returned only RCD members. However, not all Tunisian political parties took part in these elections. There has recently been a growth in Islamic fundamentalism, but this is unable to find political expression owing to the ban upon the Renaissance Party (al-Nahda).

279

Turkey

Official name: Türkiye Cumhuriyeti (Republic of Turkey).

Member of: UN, NATO, OECD, CSCE, Council of Europe.

Area: 779,452 km² (300,948 sq mi).

Population: 59,869,000 (1993 est).

Capital: Ankara 3,022,000 (city 2,560,000; 1990 census).

Other major cities: Istanbul 6,620,000 (city 6,293,000), Izmir 2,665,000 (city 2,319,000), Adana 1,430,000 (city 972,000), Bursa 1,031,000 (city 775,000), Konya 1,015,000 (city 543,000), Gaziantep 760,000 (city 574,000), Mersin (Icel) 701,000 (city 414,000), Kayseri 588,000 (city 461,000), Diyarbakir 560,000 (city 371,000), Manisa 557,000 (city 158,000), Sanliurfa 521,000 (city 240,000) (1990 census).

Languages: Turkish (86%; official); Kurdish (10% plus). There is no agreement regarding the size of the Kurdish population in Turkey; some sources quote estimates as large as 20%.

Religion: Sunni Islam (67%), Shia Islam (30%), various Christian Churches (3%).

Education: Between the ages of six and 14 all Turkish children must attend six years of schooling. There are 29 universities.

Defence: All male Turks are subject to 18 months' conscription at the age of 20. The army has 450,000 personnel, the navy has 52,000 and the air force 58,000. Turkey is an important element within NATO.

Transport: There are over 365,000 km (228,000 mi) of roads. There are 8439 km (5274 mi) of state-owned railway. The main ports are Istanbul, Bandirma and Iskenderun. Istanbul, Ankara, Izmir, Adana, Dalaman and Antalya have international airports.

Media: There are five TV channels and four radio networks run by the state-owned company TRT. Turkey has over 50 daily newspapers.

GOVERNMENT

The 450-member National Assembly is elected by universal adult suffrage for five years. The President - who is elected by the Assembly for seven years - appoints a Prime Minister and a Cabinet with a majority in the Assembly.

Political parties include the (conservative) Motherland Party (ANAP), the Social Democratic Populist Party (SHP), the True Path Party (DYP), the Welfare Party (RP) and the Democratic Left (DSP). The last general election was held in October 1991. A new DYP-SHP coalition government was formed in 1993.

Party strength: DYP 178, ANAP 115, SHP and allies 88, RP and allies 62, DSP 7.

President: Suleyman Demirel (DYP).

THE CABINET

Prime Minister: Prof. Dr. Tansu Ciller (DYP).

Deputy Prime Minister: Murat Karayalçin (SHP).

Minister of Agriculture and Rural Affairs: Refaiddin Sahin (DYP).

Minister of Communications: Mehmet Köstepen (DYP).

Minister of Culture: D. Fikri Saglar (SHP).

Minister of Defence: Mehmet Gölhan (DYP).

Minister of Education: Nevzat Ayaz (DYP).

Minister of Energy and Natural Resources: Veysel Ataso (DYP).

Minister for the Environment: Riza Akçali (DYP).

Minister of Finance and Customs: Ismet Atilla (DYP).

Minister of Forestry: Hasan Ekinci (DYP).

Minister of Foreign Affairs: Hikmet Cetin (SHP).

Minister of Health: Kazim Dinc (DYP).

Minister of the Interior: Nahit Mentese (DYP).

Minister of Justice: M. Seyfi Oktay (SHP).

Minister of Labour and Social Security: Mehmet Mogultay (SHP).

Minister of Public Works and Housing: Onur Kumbaracibasi (SHP).

Minister of Tourism: Abdulkadir Ates (SHP).

Minister of Trade and Industry: M. Tahir Köse (SHP).

GEOGRAPHY

Turkey west of the Dardanelles - 5% of the total area - is part of Europe and the city of

Istanbul is partly in Europe and partly in Asia. Asiatic Turkey comprises the central Anatolian Plateau and its basins, bordered to the north by the Pontic Mountains (which adjoin the Black Sea), to the south by the Taurus Mountains (which adjoin the Mediterranean Sea), and to the east in high ranges bordering the Caucasus. Few of the east Aegean islands are in Turkish waters. Highest point: Büyük Aguridaguı (Mount Ararat) 5185 m (17,011 ft). Principal rivers: Euphrates (Firat), Tigris (Dicle), Kizilirmak (Halys), Sakarya. Climate: The coastal regions of Turkey have a Mediterranean climate. The interior is continental with hot, dry summers and cold, snowy winters.

ECONOMY

Agriculture involves just under one half of the labour force. Major crops include wheat, rice, tobacco and cotton. Both tobacco and cotton have given rise to important processing industries, and textiles (including clothing and carpets) account for about one third of Turkey's exports. Manufacturing - in particular the chemical and steel industries - has grown rapidly. Natural resources include copper, coal and chromium. Unemployment is severe, inflation is high and the demands of a large public sector add to severe economic problems. Money sent back by the large number of Turks working in Western Europe - particularly in Germany - is a major source of foreign currency. Tourism is important and efforts have been made to promote Turkish Mediterranean resorts. However, the future of tourism is overshadowed by attacks by Kurdish terrorists.

Currency: Turkish lira (TRL); 1US$ = 32,400

TURKEY

Area 779 452 km²
(300 948 sq mi).

TRL (June 1994).

GDP: US$143,000,000,000 (1993 est); US$2340 per head.

RECENT HISTORY

In 1908 the Young Turks revolt attempted to stop the decline of the once-powerful Turkish Ottoman Empire, but defeat in the Balkan Wars (1912-13) virtually expelled Turkey from Europe. Alliance with Germany in World War I ended in defeat and the loss of all non-Turkish areas. The future of Turkey in Asia itself seemed in doubt when Greece took the area around Izmir and the Allies defined zones of influence. General Mustafa Kemal (1881-1938) - later known as Atatürk ('father of the Turks') - led forces of resistance in a civil war and went on to defeat Greece. Turkey's present boundaries were established in 1923 by the Treaty of Lausanne. With the abolition of the sultanate (1922) Turkey became a republic, which Atatürk transformed into a secular Westernized state. Islam was disestablished, Arabic script was replaced by the Latin alphabet, the Turkish language was revived, and women's veils were banned. Soviet claims on Turkish territory in 1945 encouraged a pro-Western outlook, and in 1952 Turkey joined NATO. PM Adnan Menderes was overthrown by a military coup (1960) and hanged on charges of corruption and unconstitutional rule. Civilian government was restored in 1961, but a pattern of violence and ineffective government led to a further army takeover in 1980. In 1974, after President Makarios was overthrown in Cyprus by a Greek-sponsored coup, Turkey invaded the island and set up a Turkish administration in the north (1975). Differences with Greece over Cyprus have damaged the country's attempts to join the EC, as has the country's record on human rights. In 1983 civilian rule was restored. Since then Turkey has drawn as close as possible to Western Europe. Since the dissolution of the USSR (1991), Turkey has forged links with the (mainly Turkic) former Soviet republics of Central Asia. However, relations with Armenia have been, at best, difficult. Unrest among Turkey's ethnic Kurds - in the southeast - has increased. A Kurdish terrorist movement has been active not only in Turkey but also in Europe, where Turkish diplomatic and other offices have been targets. There has been international criticism of the actions of Turkish forces in containing this violence.

United Arab Emirates

Official name: Al-Imarat Al'Arabiya Al-Muttahida (The United Arab Emirates).

Member of: UN, Arab League, OPEC, GCC.

Area: 77,700 km² (30,000 sq mi).

Population: 1,945,000 (1992 est).

Capital: Abu Dhabi 243,000 (1985 census).

Other major cities: Dubai 266,000, Sharjah 125,000, al'Ayn 102,000 (1985 census).

Languages: Arabic (official; 20-25%); various Indian languages (70%), Iranian.

Religion: Sunni Islam (official; majority).

Education: Education is compulsory between six and 12. In 1990 the literacy rate was over 76%. There is a university.

Defence: In 1992 the total armed strength was 55,000. Military service is voluntary.

Transport: There are over 2700 km (1680 mi) of roads. Abu Dhabi, Dubai, Sharjah, Fujairah and Ras al-Khaimah have commercial shipping ports and international airports.

Media: There are nine daily newspapers. There are seven radio and five television services.

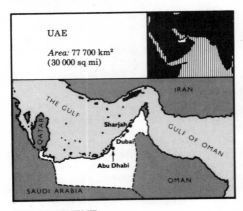

UAE

Area: 77 700 km²
(30 000 sq mi)

GOVERNMENT
The hereditary rulers of the seven emirates form the Supreme Council which elects one of its members as President, who appoints a Premier, Council of Ministers, and a 40-member advisory Federal National Council.

President: HH Shaikh Zayid bin Sultan Al Nihayyan.

Prime Minister: HH Shaikh Maktum bin Rashid Al Maktum.

EMIRATES
Population figures are from the 1985 census.

Abu Dhabi Area: 67,350 km² (26,000 sq mi). Population: 67, 000. Capital: Abu Dhabi.

Ajman Area: 250 km² (100 sq mi). Population: 64,000. Capital: Ajman.

Dubai Area: 3900 km² (1510 sq mi). Population: 419,000. Capital: Dubai.

Fujairah Area: 1150 km² (440 sq mi). Population: 54,000. Capital: Fujairah.

Ras al-Khaimah Area: 1700 km² (660 sq mi). Population: 116,000. Capital: Ras al-Khaimah.

Sharjah Area: 2600 km² (1000 sq mi). Population: 269,000. Capital: Sharjah.

Umm al-Qaiwain Area: 750 km² (290 sq mi). Population: 29,000. Capital: Umm al-Qaiwain.

GEOGRAPHY
The country is a low-lying desert except in the Jajar Mountains in the east. Highest point: Al-Hajar 1189 m (3901 ft). Climate: Summer temperatures are very high; winter temperatures are milder. Rainfall totals are very low.

ECONOMY
Based upon the export of offshore and onshore reserves of petroleum and natural gas, the country has a high standard of living. Dry docks, fertilizer factories, commercial banking interests, international airports and an entrepôt trade have been developed. Most of the labour force are from the Indian subcontinent .

Curency: Dirham of 100 fils; 1US$ = 3.67 dirhams (May 1994).

GDP: US$31,613,000,000 (1990); US$16,614 per head.

RECENT HISTORY
Britain signed treaties with local rulers during the 19th century, bringing the emirates under British protection. In 1958 oil was discovered. When Britain withdrew in 1971 the states formed the UAE, which joined the coalition against Saddam Hussein's Iraq (1990-91).

Yemen

Official name: Al-Jamhuriya al-Yamaniya (The Republic of Yemen).

Member of: UN, Arab League.

Area: 531,870 km² (205,360 sq mi) - includes the island of Socotra, which lies off the coast of

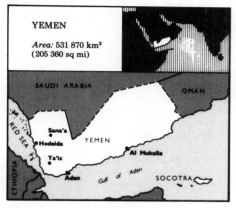

YEMEN

Area: 531 870 km²
(205 360 sq mi)

SAUDI ARABIA

OMAN

RED SEA

Sana'a
Hodeida
YEMEN
Ta'iz
Al Mukalla
Aden

ETHIOPIA

Gulf of Aden

SOCOTRA

Somalia and is usually considered to be physically part of the African continent.

Population: 12,460,000 (1993 est).

Capital: Sana'a 427,000 (including suburbs; 1986 est).

Other main cities: Aden 318,000, Taiz 178,000, Hodeida (al-Hudaydah) 155,000, Mukalla (al-Mukalla) 154,000 (all including suburbs; 1986 est). (The population of Aden fell during the 1994 civil war, which also saw an exodus from the southern city of Mukalla.)

Language: Arabic (official).

Religions: Islam (official) - Sunni Islam (54%), Zaidist Shia Islam (46%).

Education: Education is not compulsory in the former North Yemen but is freely available between the ages of six and 12 (at primary level) and between the ages of 12 and 18 (at secondary level). In the former South Yemen schooling is compulsory, in theory, between the ages of seven and 15. In 1990 the literacy rate was estimated to be 38.8%. There are two universities.

Defence: In 1992 the total armed strength was nearly 65,000 - 60,500 in the army, 1500 in the navy and 3000 in the air force. There is also a 20,000-member paramilitary force. Since the civil war in 1994, the size of the forces has been reduced through the disbanding of some southern-based units. Military service is, in theory, compulsory and lasts for three years in the former North Yemen, and for two years in the former South Yemen.

Transport: There are 39,200 km (24,363 mi) of roads. The main commercial shipping port is Aden, which was badly damaged during the 1994 civil war. The other main port is Hodeida. Sana'a, Aden, Hodeida and Taiz have international airports.

Media: There are four daily newspapers, all of which have regional rather than national readerships. There are three state-run radio stations and a government-run television service.

GOVERNMENT

The first elections by universal adult suffrage for a new 301-member House of Representatives for a united Yemen were held in April 1993. This replaced a transitional House formed by merging the former North Yemeni Consultative Council and the former South Yemeni Supreme People's Council. Pending presidential elections, the President of former North Yemen remains President. A Prime Minister and a Council of Ministers are appointed by the President. For local government purposes the country is divided into 17 governates. The main political parties include the General People's Congress (GPC), the (right-wing fundamentalist) Yemeni Alliance for Reform (YAR), the Islah Islamic Party, the (Communist) Yemeni Socialist Party (YSP), and the (liberal) Yemeni Unionist Party. After the election held in April 1993 the parties held the following numbers of seats.

Party strength: GPC 122, YAR 62, YSP 56, others 12, ind 49. (Since the 1994 civil war there are many vacant seats in the House of Representatives, in particular seats formerly occupied by YSP members.)

President: Col. Ali Abdullah Saleh.

Acting Prime Minister: Muhammed Said el-Attar.

GEOGRAPHY

In the west, the Yemen Highlands rise from a

283

narrow coastal plain. In the south, an arid plateau - 3200 m (10,500 ft) high - extends from the coastal plain into the Arabian Desert that occupies most of the north and east. The island of Socotra, which lies off the coast of Somalia, is rugged and arid. Highest point: Jebel Hadhar 3760 m (12,336 ft). Principal river: Bana, which is almost the only significant permanent river. Climate: Most of the highlands in the north and west have a temperate climate. The rest of the country is very hot and dry, although the mountains are cooler in winter.

ECONOMY

Cereal crops, coffee and citrus fruit are grown under irrigation in the fertile highlands in the north and west. In the south, subsistence agriculture and fishing occupy the majority of the labour force. Petroleum (from the south) is becoming a major export, although the reserves are small by Middle Eastern standards. Money sent back by Yemenis working in Saudi Arabia was one of the most important source of revenue until many Yemenis were expelled from Saudi Arabia during the 1991 Gulf War, when the Yemeni goverment adopted a pro-Iraqi stance. However, remittances still make a significant contribution to the economy. Much of the Aden area was badly damaged during the 1994 civil war and will take time, and considerable foreign aid, to repair.

Currency: There are two official currencies - in the former North Yemen, the Riyal of 1000 fils; in the former South Yemen, the Dinar of 1000 fils. 1US$ = 36.22 Riyals (June 1994); 1US$ = 0.282 Dinars (official rate; June 1994).

GDP: US$6,746,000,000 (1991); US$540 per head.

RECENT HISTORY

The Ottoman Turks first occupied the north and west in the 16th century and were not finally expelled until 1911, when Imam Yahya secured (North) Yemen's independence. In the south, Britain took Aden as a staging post to India (1839) and gradually established a protectorate over the 20 sultanates inland. Tension grew in the Aden Protectorate in 1959 when Britain created a federation of the feudal sultanates and the city of Aden. In 1963 an armed rebellion began against British rule. After much bloodshed - and a civil war between two rival liberation movements - independence

was gained in 1967 as South Yemen. In (North) Yemen, a republican revolution broke out in 1962, and from 1963 until 1970 a bloody civil war was fought, with President Nasser's Egypt supporting the victorious republicans and Saudi Arabia supporting the royalists. Marxist South Yemen became an ally of the USSR and was frequently in conflict with North Yemen, although eventual union of the two Yemens was the objective of both states. The collapse of the Communist regimes in Eastern Europe and the end of considerable Soviet aid (1989-90) hastened the collapse of South Yemen's weak economy, and the two countries merged in May 1990. The union was, however, more apparent than real. There was no integration of the economies of north and south, and the currencies of both continued in circulation. Although Yemen successfully held the first free multi-party elections in the Arabian peninsula in 1993, the parties taking part in that election were almost all regional, that is, confined to either the north or the south. The economy of the north advanced more than that of the south, and the benefit that the north gained from oil revenues from the south was much resented in Aden. In May 1994 the strains pulling the nominal union apart increased when President Saleh concluded a pact with a northern Isamic party. This angered southern Socialist politicans, whose influence was greatly reduced. Southern leaders feared their total exclusion from power and tension exploded in a short civil war. Fighting erupted along the former border between the two halves of the country. The Prime Minister of Yemen (and former President of South Yemen), Hayder Abu Bakr al-Attas, declared the former South Yemen to be an independent state, the Democratic Republic of Yemen. The secession seemed to win popular approval in the south, but the self-proclaimed state failed to win any international recognition. The north refused to accept the situation and began a military campaign to thwart the secessionist ambitions of the south. The UN called for a ceasefire, but the north viewed the secession as a revolt and a purely internal matter. Despite some initial successes, including rocket attacks on northern cities, the south was defeated after a siege of Aden, its capital city. In June 1994 Aden fell and the leaders of the southern breakaway state fled abroad.

Other territories

GAZA AND JERICHO (PALESTINE)

Area: 412 km² (159 sq mi) - Gaza 352 km² (136 sq mi), Jericho 60 km² (23 sq mi).

Population: 780,000 (1992 est) - Gaza 755,000, Jericho 25,000.

'Capital': Gaza (Ghazzah) 60,000 (1992 est).

Other main town: Jericho 25,000 (1992 est).

Government: A 24-member Palestinian authority has been appointed by the PLO (see below) to legislate in matters designated in the 1993-94 Israeli-PLO agreement.

Geography: The area governed by the Palestinian authority comprises the arid low-lying Gaza Strip and the small enclave around Jericho, in the Jordan valley, which is relatively fertile and well-watered. Highest point: an unnamed point 100 m (328ft) near Gaza City. Climate: The climate is Mediterranean.

Economy: The Gaza Strip relies upon agriculture, producing citrus fruit, wheat and vegetables, but the area is overpopulated and unemployment is high in the overcrowded region. There is some industry including textiles and clothing. Jericho produces fruit and vegetables, but relies on tourism as the major employer.

Recent History: See West Bank (below).

GOLAN HEIGHTS

Status: part of Syria under Israeli occupation and formally annexed by Israel in 1981.

Area: 378 km² (146 sq mi).

Population: 26,000 (1990 est).

Main town: al-Qunaytirah 5000 (1990 est).

Geography: The mountainous Golan Heights are fertile in the south. Highest point: on the upper slopes of Mt Hermon 2224 m (7297 ft). Climate: The area has a dry Mediterranean climate with relatively cool winters.

Economy: Golan has been settled by Israelis who have established kibbutzim and large vineyards.

Recent History: The Golan Heights were part of Syria until taken by Israeli forces during the Arab-Israeli War of 1967. A UN buffer zone between the Syrian and Israeli armistice lines was established in 1973. The annexation of

Golan by Israel (1981) is not recognized by the international community. In 1994 the Israeli government indicated that it was willing to discuss Golan with Syria as part of an overall peace settlement.

WEST BANK

Status: under Israeli occupation.

Area: 5819 km² (2247 sq mi) - excludes Jericho and East Jerusalem.

Population: 930,000 (1990 est) - excludes Jericho and East Jerusalem.

Main towns: Nablus (Nabulus) 106,000, Hebron (Al-Khalil) 87,000 (1990 est).

Government: The occupied West Bank is under Israeli administration.

Geography: The West Bank is a mountainous arid area between the Israeli border to the west and the River Jordan and the Dead Sea in the east. The enclave of Jericho has autonomy (see Gaza-Jericho). Highest point: an unnamed point north of Hebron 1013 m (3323 ft). Climate: The West Bank has a dry Mediterranean climate.

Economy: The Jordan Valley supports farming, mainly for fruit and vegetables. The area relies heavily upon foreign (largely Arab) aid and money sent back by Palestinians working abroad. The intifada (see below) has retarded recent development.

Recent History: The West Bank was part of Palestine within the (Turkish) Ottoman Empire and then, after 1920, included within the British League of Nations mandate of Palestine. After 1948-49, the area was incorporated into Jordan and received a large influx of Palestinian refugees from districts now within the borders of Israel. Israel took the West Bank during the Arab-Israeli War of 1967. In 1964 the Palestine Liberation Organization (PLO) was formed by exiled Palestinians with the objective of overthrowing Israel. In 1988 Jordan severed all legal ties with the West Bank. Beginning in 1988, an uprising (intifada) by Palestinians living in Gaza and the West Bank increased tensions in the area. In the same year, the PLO issued a declaration of Palestinian independence. International efforts to secure a Middle East peace accord accelerated in 1991 and a Norwegian-sponsored Israeli-PLO agreement (1993-94) secured limited Palestinian autonomy in Gaza and Jericho (see above).

NORTH AMERICA

Canada, Mexico, the United States of America
Other territories.

The North American Free Trade Agreement (NAFTA)

NAFTA is a regional free-trade area established in 1989 to promote increased trade and investment between the USA and Canada. It was extended to include Mexico in 1994 and must be seen in the context of a wider movement in the world economy aimed at trade liberalization both generally through the auspices of the General Agreement on Tariffs and Trade (see pp. 10-11) and through various regional alliances, such as the European Union and the European Free Trade Association. The initial 1989 free-trade agreement between Canada and the USA formally recognized the substantial economic interdependence between them. Canadian external trade is closely tied in with the USA – in 1992 the USA accounted for 76% of total Canadian merchandise exports and for 69% of its merchandise imports. Canadian fears of growing protectionist sentiment in the USA, and American and Canadian concerns with exclusion from European markets in the wake of the Single European Act, 1986, gave added impetus to the establishment of a North American trading bloc. The NAFTA is seen as providing greater opportunities for businesses to expand sales while promoting greater economic efficiency and lower prices. It also establishes North America as a powerful third force in the trading bloc triad of Europe and Japan/South-East Asia.

The main provisions of the 1989 agreement were the elimination of all tariffs, the reduction of non-tariff barriers to trade and the liberalization of investment flows. A number of areas, however, are not covered by the agreement, for example transport, the beer industry and government subsidies to industry in general, while a number of sectors continue to be subjected to restrictions limiting trade. Studies have estimated the likely gains from free trade between the USA and Canada to be equivalent to around 2.5-3.5% of 1990 GNP levels, mainly occurring through cost savings from the elimination of duplication, more centralized production and greater cross-frontier competition. However, 'free' trade is not necessarily 'fair'

trade and trade frictions may well persist. For example, the USA Commerce Department ruled in 1992 that Canada was unfairly subsidizing its lumber industry and imposed import duties of up to 15% on Canadian lumber products sold in the USA.

Mexico originally approached the USA (with which it conducts the bulk of its export trade) in 1990 to secure a free-trade pact. Unlike in the case of a common market such as the European Union, individual members of a free-trade area can make their own trade arrangements with non-members. A separate bilateral trade agreement between the USA and Mexico running alongside the Canadian-USA agreement (a so-called 'hub and spoke' system) would have created a situation whereby only the USA would have tariff-free access to both markets, giving the USA greater bargaining power. But, Canada became involved in the negotiations on an extended NAFTA arrangement that gave equal access to the markets of all participants; this was duly agreed and Mexico joined NAFTA in January 1994. The NAFTA-Mexico pact provides for the removal of most duties and restrictions on trade in manufactured goods and agricultural produce over a phased 10-15-year period. Mexico is to gradually open up its banking, insurance etc. sectors to USA and Canadian investment, eliminating all barriers by the year 2007. In the car sector, the original 1989 50% 'locally-made content' stipulation has been increased to 62.5% North American content to be free of tariffs.

Mexico's inclusion in the NAFTA has been strongly opposed by some groups in the USA since it involves two prosperous industrial economies linking themselves with a newly industrializing country characterized by relatively low wages. Fears have been expressed that low Mexican wages could induce many US and Canadian firms to close down their local plants and set up new plants in Mexico. But looked at 'in the round' advocates of the NAFTA remain optimistic that a commitment to free trade will yield substantial long-term benefits to all three participants. Major initiatives under the NAFTA are approved at the Ministerial level; the day-to-day administration of the NAFTA is relatively informal – each member country has a small secretariat that deals with the implementation of NAFTA provisions, and organizes ad hoc arbitration panels to settle particular inter-country disputes.

The USA: The Only Remaining Superpower

It is sobering to reflect on how far international affairs have moved in the few years since the end of the Cold War. Possible conflict between Moscow and Washington has been swept away. Gone is the sense of terror underpinning international relations, but gone too is the clearcut sense of balance superpower rivalry produced. After the fall of Communism the possibilities for US world leadership seemed almost limitless. Visions of a new world order in which the USA could ensure stability and peace based on democracy and consensus carried enormous appeal. The US-led victory in the Gulf War appeared to reinforce this vision. However, harsh reality has reasserted itself; crises persist in Bosnia, Rwanda, Haiti and elsewhere and the American role in dealing with them is widely perceived to have been weak and vacillating, with the Clinton administration unable to show the will, skill or consistency befitting the only remaining superpower. The result is a vacuum in world affairs that is filled by a sense of drift and a fear of more instability. Is this emphasis on US failings justified? Or is the criticism based on unrealistic expectations of what the USA – as the only remaining superpower – could achieve? A major reason suggested for the alleged failures of the Clinton administration is its pre-occupation with domestic affairs, to the detriment of a coherent foreign policy. Prior to the collapse of Communism it was commonly argued that America was in a state of steady and inevitable decline from the result of what became known as imperial overstretch, the phenomenon whereby the diversion of resources into maintaining a world role is so great as to fatally compromise the productivity of the domestic economy. Domestic weakness then becomes a brake on the capacity to perform a world role.

ECONOMIC RENEWAL

There is little doubt that the American economy had become grossly imbalanced or that Clinton was elected to reverse these trends. America's role in international affairs helped to create the domestic crisis and its resolution is the essential requirement of an effective foreign policy, and of any aspirations to continuing world leadership. This is all the more true because the new international order will depend more on economic factors than the Cold War era. This puts a premium on economic competitiveness. The new order will be united around a consensus which puts economic prosperity, achieved through some variant of the market system, above all else. The common goal provides a discipline to international relations and potential for co-operation; but in a race for competitiveness the potential for nationalist rivalry and hence for massive instability is equally apparent. There is no way to predict which aspect will take precedence. In this context the principle which must govern American foreign policy is clear; it must improve its own competitiveness, not as an alternative to world leadership, but as a precondition of fulfilling its potential as the only power capable of ensuring that harmony prevails over discord.

It is this imperative which has led the Clinton administration to focus on issues of international trade. Here the passage of the North American Free Trade Agreement (NAFTA), the successful completion of the Uruguay Round of GATT and the creation of the World Trade Organization (WTO) are evidence of successful policy. Similarly American influence in the economic reconstruction of the former Soviet Union republics and maintaining a degree of balance in the emerging economic powerhouse of the Pacific Rim has been constructive. Seen in this light the US record looks better than when judged against the handling of crises such as those in Bosnia and Haiti. If we avoid the unrealism of the claims for US omnipotence and focus on the essence of US interests in a changing world the impression we gain is that of an administration that has its sights firmly fixed on the essentials. The fruits of such a policy will not be evident immediately and may never be spectacular. In the meantime the focus of attention tends to be on immediate crises where criticism is still based on a conception of US power that is far fetched. In the uncertain post-Cold War world it is perhaps natural that many should look to the USA to solve all the problems. That can never be its role. In defining its interest more narrowly than before the USA is bringing a new realism to what leadership requires, its own economic renewal, and what it can aspire to; less the only superpower and more the first among equals in the common pursuit of security through prosperity.

Regional Organizations of North America

NORTH AMERICA FREE TRADE AGREEMENT (NAFTA)

NAFTA was founded in 1992 to eliminate tariffs, quotas and import licences between states in membership. The Agreement has no formal secretariat. See p. 287 for details of the aims and operation of NAFTA.

Membership: Canada, Mexico, and the United States of America.

OTHER ORGANIZATIONS

Canada and the USA are members of NATO (see pp. 350-51). Canada, Mexico and the USA are members of the OAS (see p. 175).

NAFTA Trade

Canada Imports ($ million): 118,119 (1991). Exports ($ million): 126,883 (1991). Main imports: road motor vehicles and parts 17.6% (1991), chemicals 6.1% (1991), miscellaneous fabricated materials, miscellaneous inedible end products, food, animal feed, beverages, inedible crude materials. .Main exports: road motor vehicles and parts 16.5% (1991), crude materials 13.6% (1991), miscellaneous inedible end products, miscellaneous fabricated materials, inedible crude materials, foodstuffs, animal feed, beverages. Principal trading partners: USA, Japan, UK, Germany, France, China, South Korea, Netherlands, Italy, Taiwan, Hong Kong.

Mexico Imports ($ million): 29,993 (1991). Exports ($ million): 26,524 (1991). Main imports: metallic products, machinery and equipment 41% (1991), food, beverages and tobacco 8.6% (1991). Main exports: crude petroleum 33% (1991), metallic products, machinery and equipment 18% (1991), raw coffee, frozen shrimps and prawns, tomatoes, copper. Principal trading partner: USA, Japan, Germany, Spain, Canada, France, Italy, Brazil, UK.

United States of America Imports ($ million): 532,352 (1992). Exports ($ million): 447,471 (1992). Main imports: machinery and transport equipment 43.5% (1992), basic and miscellaneous manufactures 17.8% (1992), mineral fuels and lubricants, chemicals and related products. Main exports: machinery and transport equipment 48% (1992), basic and miscellaneous manufactures 11.4% (1992), chermicals and related products, crude materials (inedible). Principal trading partners: Canada, Japan, Mexico, Germany, UK, Taiwan, France, China, Italy, Singapore, Netherlands, Hong Kong, Belgium-Luxembourg, Saudi Arabia, Venezuela, Brazil.

Canada

Member of: UN, Commonwealth, OAS, NATO, CSCE, G7, NAFTA.

Area: 9,970,610 km² (3,849,674 sq mi).

Population: 28,149,000 (1993 est).

Capital: Ottawa 921,000 (city 301,000; 1991 census).

Other major cities: Toronto 3,893,000 (city 612,000), Montréal 3,127,000 (city 1,015,000), Vancouver 1,603,000 (city 431,000), Edmonton 840,000 (city 574,000), Calgary 754,000 (city 636,000), Winnipeg 652,000 (city 595,000), Québec 646,000 (city 165,000), Hamilton 600,000 (city 307,000), London 382,000 (city 269,000), St Catharine's-Niagara 365,000 (St Catharine's city 123,000), Kitchener 356,000 (city 151,000), Halifax 321,000 (city 114,000), Victoria 288,000 (city 66,000), Windsor 262,000 (city 193,000), Oshawa 240,000 (city 124,000), Saskatoon 210,000 (city 178,000), Regina 192,000 (city 175,000), St John's 172,000 (city 69,000) (1991 census).

Languages: English (62% as a first language; official), French (25% as a first language; official), bilingual English-French (10%).

Religions: Roman Catholic (45%), United Church of Canada (15%), Anglican (10%).

Education: Years of compulsory schooling vary between provinces, but education is generally compulsory from five to 16. In 1990 the literacy rate was virtually 99%. There are 66 universities.

Defence: In 1993 the total armed strength was 78,000 - 20,000 in the army, 12,500 in the navy, 20,500 in the air force and 25,000 others.

Transport: There are 849,404 km (527,794 mi) of roads of which 14,796 km (9188 mi) are motorways. There are 86,880 km (53,985 mi) of railways. Toronto, Montreal, Calgary and Vancouver have metros. The Great Lakes system-St Lawrence Seaway is a major inland waterway. The main commercial ports are Vancouver, Sept-Iles, Montréal, Thunder Bay, Toronto and Québec. The main airports are Toronto, Vancouver, Montréal (two airports), Calgary, Ottawa, Halifax, Winnipeg and Edmonton.

Media: The Canadian press remains regional.

There are 106 daily papers, with those in Québec province published in French. CBC is a national state-owned broadcasting service operating over 760 radio outlets as well as television services. There are four main private television networks.

GOVERNMENT
The Canadian Federal Parliament has two houses - a 118-member Senate appointed by the Governor General to represent the provinces, and the House of Commons, whose 295 members are elected for five years by universal adult suffrage. A Prime Minister, commanding a majority in the House of Commons, is appointed by the Governor General, who is the representative of the British Queen as sovereign of Canada. The PM, in turn, appoints a Cabinet of Ministers which is responsible to the House. Each province has its own government and legislature. The main political parties are the Liberal Party (Lib), the (radical) Reform Party (Reform), the (nationalist Francophone) Bloc Québecois (BQ), the (social democrat) New Democratic Party (NDP) and the Progressive Conservative Party (PC). After the election in October 1993 a Liberal government was formed.

Party strength: Lib 178, BQ 54, Reform 52, NDP 8, PC 2, ind 1.

THE CABINET
All Cabinet members are Liberals.

Prime Minister: Jean Chrétien.

Deputy Prime Minister and Minister of the Environment: Sheila Copps.

Minister of Agriculture and of Agri-Food: Ralph Goodale.

Minister of Canadian Heritage: Michel Dupuy.

Minister of Citizenship and Immigration: Sergio Marchi.

Minister of Defence and for Veterans Affairs: David Collenette.

Minister of Finance and for the Federal Office of Regional Development - Québec: Paul Martin.

Minister of Fisheries and Oceans: Brian Tobin.

Minister of Foreign Affairs: André Oullet.

Minister of Health: Diane Marleau.

CANADA

Area: 9 970 610 km²
(3 849 674 sq mi).

Minister of Human Resources and of Western Economic Diversification: Lloyd Axworthy.

Minister of Indian Affairs and Northern Development: Ron Irwin.

Minister of Industry: John Manley.

Minister of International Trade: Roy MacLaren.

Minister of Justice and Attorney General: Fernand Robichaud.

Minister of National Resources: Anne McLellan.

Minister of National Revenue: David Anderson.

Minister of Public Security and Government House Leader: Herbert Gray.

Minister of Public Works and Government Services and for the Atlantic Canada Opportunities Agencies: David Dingwall.

Minister of Transport: Doug Young.

President of the Treasury Board and Minister responsible for Infrastructure: Arthur Eggleton.

Government Senate Leader and Minister with special responsibility for Literacy: Joyce Fairbairn.

President of the Queen's Privy Council and Minister of Intergovernmental Affairs and Public Service Renewal: Marcel Massé.

PROVINCES AND TERRITORIES
Population figures are 1992 estimates.

Alberta Area: 661,199 km² (255,285 sq mi). Population: 2,628,000. Capital: Edmonton.

British Columbia Area: 948,596 km² (366,255 sq mi). Population: 3,448,000. Capital: Victoria.

Manitoba Area: 650,087 km² (251,000 sq mi). Population: 1,112,000. Capital: Winnipeg.

New Brunswick Area: 73,437 km² (28,354 sq mi). Population: 749,000. Capital: Fredericton.

Newfoundland and Labrador Area: 404,517 km² (156,185 sq mi). Population: 581,000. Capital: St John's.

Nova Scotia Area: 55,490 km² (21,425 sq mi). Population: 921,000. Capital: Halifax.

Ontario Area: 1,068,582 km² (412,582 sq mi). Population: 10,593,000. Capital: Toronto.

Prince Edward Island Area: 5657 km² (2184 sq mi). Population: 130,000. Capital: Charlottetown.

Québec Area: 1,540,680 km² (594,860 sq mi). Population: 7,143,000. Capital: Québec.

Saskatchewan Area: 651,900 km² (251,700 sq mi). Population: 1,004,000. Capital: Regina.

Northwest Territories Area: 1,178,000 km² (454,900 sq mi). Population: 36,000. Capital: Yellowknife.

Nunavut Area: 2,201,400 km² (850,000 sq mi). Population: 22,000. Capital: Iqaluit.

Yukon Territory Area: 482,515 km² (186,299 sq mi). Population: 28,000. Capital: Whitehorse.

GEOGRAPHY
Nearly one half of Canada is covered by the Laurentian (or Canadian) Shield, a relatively flat region of hard rocks stretching round Hudson's Bay and penetrating deep into the interior. Inland, the Shield ends in a scarp that is pronounced in the east, beside the lowlands around the St Lawrence River and the Great Lakes. To the west, a line of major lakes (including Lake Winnipeg) marks the boundary with the interior plains, the Prairies. A broad belt of mountains - over 800 km (500 mi) wide - lies west of the plains. This western cordillera comprises the Rocky, Mackenzie, Coast and St Elias Mountains - which include Canada's highest point. A lower, more discontinuous, chain of highlands borders the east of Canada, running from Baffin Island, through Labrador and into New Brunswick and Nova Scotia. Highest point: Mount Logan 5951 m (19,524 ft). Principal rivers: Mackenzie, Slave, Peace, St Lawrence, Yukon, Nisutlin, Nelson, Saskatchewan. Climate: Much of Canada experiences extreme temperatures, with mild summers and long, cold winters. The climate in the far north is polar. Average winter temperatures only remain above freezing point on the Pacific coast. In most of British Columbia precipitation is heavy. In the rest of the country, rainfall totals are moderate or light. Nearly all of Canada experiences heavy winter snowfalls.

ECONOMY
Canada enjoys one of the highest standards of living in the world, due, in part, to great mineral resources. There are substantial deposits of zinc, nickel, gold, silver, iron ore, uranium, copper, cobalt and lead, as well as major reserves of petroleum and natural gas, and enormous hydroelectric-power potential. These resources are the basis of such industries as petroleum refining, motor vehicles, metal refining, chemicals, and iron and steel. Canada is one of the world's leading exporters of cereals - in particular, wheat from the Prairie provinces. Other agricultural interests include fruit (mainly apples), beef cattle and potatoes. Vast coniferous forests have given rise to large lumber, wood-pulp and paper industries. Rich Atlantic and Pacific fishing grounds have made Canada the world's leading exporter of fish and seafood. The country has an important banking and insurance sector, and the economy is closely linked with that of the USA within NAFTA.

Currency: Canadian Dollar of 100 cents: 1US$ = 1.381 Canadian dollars (June 1994).

GDP: US$603,000,000,000 (1993 est); US$21,318 per head.

RECENT HISTORY
In 1867 Ontario, Québec, New Brunswick and Nova Scotia formed the Dominion of Canada. Other provinces joined between 1870 and 1905, but Newfoundland did not join until 1949. The late 19th century saw major mineral finds, such as the Klondike gold rush, and the western provinces developed rapidly. The nation was linked by the Canadian Pacific Railway. In World War I, Canadian forces distinguished themselves at Vimy Ridge, and Canada won itself a place as a separate nation at the peace conferences after the war. The Statute of Westminster (1931) recognized Canadian independence. The Depression of the 1930s had a severe impact on Canada - Newfoundland, for example, went bankrupt. Canada played an important role in World War II and the Korean War, and was a founder member of NATO. In the 1970s and 1980s, there was friction over the use and status of French, and separatism became an issue in Québec. The constitution was redefined in 1982, but Québec refused to ratify it. A series of constitutional amendments was formulated to persuade Québec to adhere to the constitution, but some English-speaking provinces would not agree to Québec being declared 'a distinct society' with additional powers. The failure of the Accord (1990) encouraged Québec nationalists to call for 'sovereignty association' (a politically independent Québec in economic association with Canada).

Mexico

Official name: Estados Unidos Mexicanos (United Mexican States).

Member of:UN, OAS, OECD,NAFTA, ALADI.

Area: 1,958,201 km² (756,066 sq mi).

Population: 89,955,000 (1993 est).

Capital: Mexico City 19,480,000 (city 9,816,000; Greater Mexico City 13,636,000; Nezahualcoyotl 1,255,000; 1990 census).

Other major cities: Guadalajara 3,187,000 (city 1,650,000), Monterrey 2,859,000 (city 1,069,000), Puebla 1,707,000 (city 1,007,000), León 1,081,000 (city 758,000), Ciudad Juárez 798,000, Tijuana 743,000 (city 699,000), Mexicali 602,000, Acapulco 592,000 (all including suburbs; 1990 census).

Languages: Spanish (92%; official), various Indian languages.

Religion: Roman Catholic (91%), various Protestant Evangelical Churches (5%).

Education: Education is compulsory between the ages of six and 12. In 1990 the literacy rate was 87.3%. There are 54 universities.

Defence: In 1993 the total armed strength was 175,000 - 130,000 in the army, 37,000 in the navy and 8000 in the air force, There is also a rural defence militia of 14,000. Military service of one year is decided by lottery.

Transport: There are 243,509 km (151,309 mi) of roads, of which 1231 km (765 mi) are motorways. FNM, the state railway company, runs 26,334 km (16,363 mi) of railways. Mexico City has a metro. The principal ports are Coatzacoalcos and Guaymas. Mexico City has an important international airport. There are 30 other international airports.

Media: There are 65 daily newspapers, over 125 television stations and over 930 radio stations.

GOVERNMENT
The 64-member Senate and the President - who may serve only once - are elected by universal adult suffrage for six years. The 500-member Chamber of Deputies is directly elected for three years - 200 of the members are elected under a system of proportional representation; the remaining 300 represent single-member constituencies. The President appoints a Cabinet. Each of the 31 states has its own Chamber of Deputies. The main political parties are the Institutional Revolutionary Party (PRI), the (reformist) National Action Party (PAN), the (reformist) Democratic Revolutionary Party (PRD), the (Marxist) Cardenista Front of National Reconstruction (PFCRN), and the Authentic Party of the Mexican Revolution. After the election held in 1991 the PRI continued in office.

Party strength: PRI 320, PAN 89, PRD and allies 91.

President: Carlos Salinas de Gortari (PRI).

THE CABINET

Minister of Agrarian Reform: Victor Cervera Pacheco (PRI).

Minister of Agriculture and Water Resources: Prof. Carlos Hank Gonzalez (PRI).

Minister of Communication and Transport: Emilio Gamboa Patron (PRI).

Minister for the Coordination of National Security: Arsenio Farell Cubillas (PRI).

Minister of Defence: Gen. Antonio Riviello Bazan (PRI).

Minister of Education: Jose Angel Pescador Osuna (PRI).

Minister of Energy, Mining and State Industries: Emilio Lozoya Thalmann (PRI).

Minister of Finance and Public Credit: Dr Pedro Aspe Armella (PRI).

Minister of Fishing: Guillermo Jimenez Morales (PRI).

Minister of Foreign Affairs: Manuel Tello Macias (PRI).

Minister of Health: Dr Jesus Kumate Rodriguez (PRI).

Minister of the Interior: Dr Jorge Carpizo McGregor (PRI).

Minister of Labour and Social Welfare: Manuel Gomezperalta Damiron (PRI).

Minister of Naval Affairs: Admiral Luis Carlo Ruano Angulo (PRI).

Minister of Tourism: Jesus Silva Herzog (PRI).

Minister of Social Development: Carlos Rojas Gutierrez (PRI).

Minister of Trade and Industry: Dr Jaime Serra Puche (PRI).

Attorney General: Humberto Benitez Trevino (PRI).

Attorney of Justice for Mexico City: Ernesto Santillana Santillana (a full cabinet member; PRI).

Comptroller General: Maria Elena Vasquez Nava (PRI).

Mayor of Mexico City: Manuel Aguilera Gomez (a full cabinet member; PRI).

STATES
Population figures are from the 1990 census.

Aguascalientes Area: 5471 km² (2112 sq mi). Population: 720,000. Capital: Aguascalientes.

Baja California Norte Area: 69,921 km² (26,996 sq mi). Population: 1,658,000. Capital: Mexicali.

Baja California Sur Area: 73,475 km² (28,369 sq mi). Population: 317,000. Capital: La Paz.

Campeche Area: 50,812 km² (19,619 sq mi). Population: 529,000. Capital: Campeche.

Chiapas Area: 74,211 km² (28,653 sq mi). Population: 3,204,000. Capital: Tuxtla Gutiérrez.

Chihuahua Area: 244,938 km² (94,571 sq mi). Population: 2,440,000. Capital: Ciudad Juárez.

Coahuila Area: 149,982 km² (57,908 sq mi). Population: 1,971,000. Capital: Saltillo.

Colima Area: 5191 km² (2004 sq mi). Population: 425,000. Capital: Colima.

Durango Area: 123,181 km² (47,560 sq mi). Population: 1,352,000. Capital: (Victoria de) Durango.

Guanajuato Area: 30,491 km² (11,773 sq mi). Population: 3,980,000. Capital: Guanajuato.

Guerrero Area: 64,281 km² (24,819 sq mi). Population: 2,622,000. Capital: Chilpancingo.

Hidalgo Area: 20,813 km² (8036 sq mi). Population: 1,881,000. Capital: Pachuca de Soto.

Jalisco Area: 80,836 km² (31,211 sq mi). Population: 5,279,000. Capital: Guadalajara.

México Area: 21,355 km² (8245 sq mi). Population: 9,816,000. Capital: Toluca de Lerdo.

Michoacán Area: 59,928 km² (23,138 sq mi). Population: 3,534,000. Capital: Morelia.

Morelos Area: 4950 km² (1911 sq mi). Population: 1,195,000. Capital: Cuernavaca.

Nayarit Area: 26,979 km² (10,417 sq mi). Population: 816,000. Capital: Tepic.

Nuevo León Area: 64,924 km² (25,067 sq mi). Population: 3,086,000. Capital: Monterrey.

Oaxaca Area: 93,952 km² (36,275 sq mi). Population: 3,022,000. Capital: Oaxaca.

Puebla Area: 33,902 km² (11,493 sq mi). Population: 4,118,000. Capital: Puebla.

Querétaro Area: 11,449 km² (4420 sq mi). Population: 1,044,000. Capital: Querétaro.

Quintana Roo Area: 50,212 km² (19,387 sq mi). Population: 493, 000. Capital: Chetumal.

San Luis Potosí Area: 63,068 km² (24,351 sq mi). Population: 2,002,000. Capital: San Luis Potosí.

Sinaloa Area: 58,328 km² (22,520 sq mi). Population: 2,211,000. Capital: Culiacán Rosales.

Sonora Area: 182,052 km² (70,290 sq mi). Population: 1,822,000. Capital: Hermosillo.

Tabasco Area: 25,267 km² (9756 sq mi). Population: 1,501,000. Capital: Villahermosa.

Tamaulipas Area: 79,304 km² (30,619 sq mi). Population: 2,244,000. Capital: Ciudad Victoria.

MEXICO

Area: 1 958 201 km²
(756 066 sq mi)

Tlaxcala Area: 4016 km² (1551 sq mi). Population: 764,000. Capital: Apizaco.

Veracruz Area: 71,699 km² (27,683 sq mi). Population: 6,215,000. Capital: Jalapa Enrique.

Yucatán Area: 38,402 km² (14,827 sq mi). Population: 1,364,000. Capital: Mérida.

Zacatecas Area: 73,252 km² (28,283 sq mi). Population: 1,278,000. Capital: Zacatecas.

Federal District Area: 1479 km² (570 sq mi). Population: 8,237,000. Capital: Mexico City.

GEOGRAPHY

Between the Sierra Madre Oriental mountains in the east and the Sierra Madre Occidental in the west is a large high central plateau with several volcanoes. The coastal plains are generally narrow in the west, but wider in the east. The Yucatán Peninsula in the southeast is a broad limestone lowland; Baja California in the northwest is a long narrow mountainous peninsula. Mexico is prone to earthquakes. Highest point: Volcán Citlaltepetl (Pico de Orizaba) 5610 m (18,405 ft). Principal rivers: Río Bravo de Norte (Rio Grande), Balsas, Grijalva, Pánuco. Climate: There is considerable climatic variation, in part reflecting the complexity of the relief. In general, the south and the coastal lowlands are tropical, while the central plateau and the mountains are cooler and drier.

ECONOMY

One quarter of the labour force is involved in agriculture and many Mexicans are still subsistence farmers growing maize, wheat, kidney beans and rice. Coffee, cotton, fruit and vegetables are the most important export crops. Mexico is the world's leading producer of silver. The exploitation of large reserves of natural gas and petroleum enabled the country's spectacular economic development in the 1970s and 1980s. An expanding industrial base includes important petrochemical, textile, motor-vehicle and food-processing industries. In the early 1990s major US companies were encouraged by a combination of government policy, the new NAFTA trade agreement and low labour costs to set up factories in Mexico. The result has been a spectacular growth in the Mexican economy which is now the 12th largest in the world. Economic problems remain, and high unemployment has stimulated immigration - often illegal - to the USA.

Curency: Mexican peso of 100 centavos: 1US$ = 3.366 pesos (June 1994).

GDP: US$372,000,000,000 (1993 est); US$4040 per head.

RECENT HISTORY

The first revolt against Spanish rule broke out in 1810, but Mexican independence was not gained until 1821 after a guerrilla war led by Vicente Guerrero. Initially an empire - under Agustin Itúrbide - Mexico became a republic in 1823, but conflict between federalists and centralists erupted, developing into civil war. In 1836 Texas rebelled against Mexico, declaring independence. When the USA annexed Texas in 1845, war broke out, resulting in the loss of half Mexico's territory - Texas, New Mexico and California. A period of reform began in 1857, with a new liberal constitution. A civil war (1858-61) between reformists and conservatives was won by the reformists under Benito Juárez (1806-72), but the economy was shattered. After Mexico failed to repay debts, Spain, Britain and France invaded in 1863. Although Spain and Britain soon withdrew, France remained, appointing Archduke Maximilian of Austria (1832-67) as Emperor (1864). Under US pressure and Mexican resistance, the French withdrew in 1867. Maximilian remained in Mexico City and was captured and executed. Juárez re-established the republic. The authoritarian rule of General Porfirio Díaz (President 1876-80 and 1888-1910) brought peace, but wealth was concentrated into a few hands. Revolution against the power of the landowners erupted in 1910. The reformist policies of President Francisco Madero (1873-1913) were supported by the outlaw Pancho Villa (1877-1923), but revolutionary violence continued, and in 1916-17 a US expeditionary force was sent against Villa. From 1924 the revolution became anticlerical and the Church was persecuted. Order was restored when the Institutional Revolutionary Party came to power in 1929. In the 1930s the large estates were divided and much of the economy was nationalized. Political opposition has been tolerated, although the ruling party is virtually guaranteed perpetual power. In 1989, the first non-PRI state governor was elected, but opposition claims of electoral fraud have continued. A more liberal economic and political climate has emerged since 1990, and Mexico's adherence to the NAFTA agreement seemed to mark the country's 'coming of age'. However, in 1994 the assassination of the PRI presidential candidate and a peasant uprising in Chiapas state increased tension and raised doubts about the country's stability.

United States of America

Member of: UN, NATO, OAS, CSCE, G7, NAFTA, ANZUS.

Area: 9,372,614 km² (3,618,770 sq mi).

Population: 256,561,000 (1993 census est).

Capital: Washington, D.C. 3,924,000 (city 598,000; 1990 census; 578,000 - 1993 est).

Other major cities: New York 18,087,000 (city 7,323,000, Newark 275,000), Los Angeles 14,532,000 (city 3,485,000, Long Beach 429,000, Anaheim 266,000), Chicago 8,066,000 (city 2,784,000), San Francisco 6,253,000, (city 724,000, San Jose 782,000, Oakland 372,000), Philadelphia 5,899,000 (city 1,586,000), Detroit 4,665,000 (city 1,028,000), Boston 4,172,000 (city 574,000), Dallas 3,885,000 (city 1,007,000; Fort Worth 478,000), Houston 3,711,000 (city 1,631,000), Miami 3,193,000 (city 359,000), Atlanta 2,834,000 (city 394,000), Cleveland 2,760,000 (city 506,000), Seattle 2,559,000 (city 516,000), San Diego 2,498,000 (city 1,111,000), Minneapolis - St Paul 2,464,000 (city 368,000; St Paul 272,000), St Louis 2,444,000 (city 397,000), Baltimore 2,382,000 (city 736,000), Pittsburgh 2,243,000 (city 370,000), Phoenix 2,122,000 (city 983,000), Tampa 2,068,000 (city 280,000), Denver 1,848,000 (city 468,000), Cincinnati 1,744,000 (city 364,000), Milwaukee 1,607,000 (city 628,000), Kansas City 1,566,000 (city 435,000), Sacramento 1,481,000 (city 369,000), Portland 1,478,000 (city 437,000), Norfolk 1,396,000 (city 261,000), Columbus 1,377,000 (city 633,000), San Antonio 1,302,000 (city 936,000), Indianapolis 1,250,000 (city 742,000), New Orleans 1,239,000 (city 497,000), Buffalo 1,189,000 (city 328,000), Charlotte 1,162,000 (city 396,000), Providence 1,142,000 (city 161,000), Hartford 1,086,000 (city 140,000), Orlando 1,073,000 (city 165,000), Salt Lake City 1,072,000 (city 160,000), Rochester 1,002,000 (city 232,000), Nashville 985,000 (city 511,000), Memphis 982,000 (city 610,000), Oklahoma City 959,000 (city 445,000), Louisville 953,000 (city 269,000), Dayton 951,000 (city 182,000), Greensboro 942,000 (city 184,000), Birmingham 908,000 (city 266,000), Jacksonville 907,000 (city 673,000), Albany 874,000 (city 101,000), Richmond 866,000 (city 203,000), West Palm Beach 864,000 (city 365,000), Honolulu 836,000 (city 365,000), Austin 782,000 (city 466,000), Las Vegas 741,000 (city 258,000), Raleigh 735,000 (city 208,000), Scranton 734,000 (city 82,000), Tulsa 709,000 (city 367,000) (all including suburbs; 1990 census).

Languages: English (official), Spanish (6%, as a first language).

Religions: Roman Catholic (23%), Baptist (10%), Methodist (5%), Lutheran (3%), Judaism (2%), Orthodox (2%), Presbyterian (2%), Mormons (2%).

Education: Education is compulsory in all states, on average between the ages of seven and 16. In 1990 the literacy rate was 97%. There are 658 universities and 980 other colleges of university status.

Defence: In 1993 the total armed strength was 1,730,000 - 587,000 in the army, 510,000 in the navy, and 633,000 in the air force. The US Navy's main bases are at San Diego, Orlando and Norfolk. The US forces can call upon about 1,720,000 reservists. There is no military service although there is a selective call-up in time of war.

Transport: There are 6,257,882 km (3,888,460 mi) of roads, of which over 83,964 km (52,142 mi) are motorways. There are 225,000 km (140,000 mi) of railways. New York, Chicago, Washington, DC, San Francisco, Philadelphia, Atlanta, Baltimore, Buffalo, Detroit, Los Angeles and Miami have metros. The main commercial shipping ports are Long Beach, Philadelphia, Los Angeles, New Orleans, and Hampton-Roads. The principal international airports: Anchorage, Atlanta, Baltimore, Boston, Chicago, Cincinnati, Cleveland, Dallas/Fort Worth, Denver, Detroit, Honolulu, Houston, Kansas City, Las Vegas, Los Angeles, Miami, Minneapolis, New Orleans, New York (three airports), Orlando, Philadelphia, Phoenix, Pittsburgh, Portland, St Louis, Salt Lake City, San Diego, San Francisco, Seattle, Tampa and Washington, DC (two airports).

Media: There are over 1600 daily newspapers in the USA. The size of the country means that there is no national press, although about five or six papers - the Wall Street Journal and the New York Times (both of which are printed at several locations), and the Washington Post, the Los Angeles Times, and the (Boston) Christian Science Monitor - enjoy a near-

GDP: US$6,710,000,000,000,000 (1993 est);
US$25,687 per head.

RECENT HISTORY

At the beginning of the 19th century, the USA doubled in size with the Louisiana Purchase (1803). This acquisition took the US frontier deep into the Central Lowlands. The expansion of the USA to the west was part of the transformation of the country from an underdeveloped rural nation into a world power stretching from the Atlantic to the Pacific. As a result of wars against Mexico in the 1840s vast new territories were added to the Union - Texas, California, Arizona and New Mexico. Strains appeared between the increasingly industrial North and the plantation South over the issue of slavery. This led to the Civil War under the presidency of Abraham Lincoln (1809-65). The North was victorious, but after federal troops were withdrawn from the South in 1877 racial segregation returned to the South until after World War II. Between 1880 and 1900 the USA emerged as an industrial giant. At the same time, the population increased dramatically, as immigrants flocked to the New World, in particular from Germany, Eastern Europe and Russia. Interest in world trade increased American involvement abroad. The Cuban revolt against Spanish rule led the USA into a war against Spain (1898) and brought US rule to the Philippines, Puerto Rico and Guam. American participation in World War I from 1917 hastened the Allied victory, but the idealistic principles favoured by President Woodrow Wilson (1856-1924) were compromised in the post-war settlement. After the war the USA retreated into isolationism and protectionism in trade. The imposition of Prohibition (1919-33) increased smuggling and the activities of criminal gangs, but the 1920s were prosperous until the Depression began in 1929 with the collapse of the stock market. Federal investment and intervention brought relief through the New Deal programme of President Franklin Roosevelt (1882-1945). The Japanese attack on Pearl Harbor brought the USA into World War II (1941). American involvement in the European and Pacific theatres of war was decisive and committed the USA to a world role as a superpower in 1945. US assistance was instrumental in rebuilding Europe (through the Marshall Plan) and Japan. From the late 1940s to the end of the 1980s, the USA confronted the Soviet Union's perceived global threat in the Cold War. As the leader of the Western alliance, the USA established bases in Europe, the Far East and the Indian and Pacific Oceans, so encircling the Soviet bloc. The USA was involved in the Korean War (1950-53) against Chinese and North Korean forces, and in direct military intervention in Guatemala (1954), Lebanon (1958 and 1983-85), the Dominican Republic (1965), Panama (1968 and 1989) and Grenada (1983). The greatest commitment, however, was in Vietnam, where from 1964 to 1973 US forces attempted to hold back a Communist takeover of Indochina, but a growing disenchantment with the war forced an American withdrawal. From the 1950s the civil rights movement - led by Martin Luther King (1929-68) - campaigned for full political rights for blacks and for desegregation of schools, hospitals, buses, etc. In the early 1960s President John F. Kennedy (1917-63) made racial discrimination illegal. Kennedy supported the unsuccessful invasion of Cuba by right-wing exiles (1961), successfully pressured the USSR to withdraw its missiles from Cuba (1962), and was assassinated in 1963. Growing economic problems in the 1970s led to the election of a monetarist President, Ronald Reagan (1911-), in 1981. The USA continued to support movements and governments perceived as being in the Western interest - for example, backing Israel in the Middle East and providing weapons to the UNITA guerrillas in Angola and the Contra guerrillas in Nicaragua. However, the increasing economic challenge from Japan, and the collapse of Soviet power in Eastern Europe in 1989, raised questions about the USA's future world role. Early in 1990 President George Bush (1924-) announced plans to close certain overseas bases, but later in the same year he organized the international coalition against Iraq after the invasion of Kuwait (1990). American forces played a major role in the massive but short air and ground war (1991) that liberated Kuwait. In 1992 the USA played a major role in the (largely unsuccessful) UN intervention in Somalia. Since 1993, under President Bill Clinton, domestic issues have taken priority over foreign affairs.

301

Other territories

BERMUDA

Status: a British Crown colony.

Area: 54 km² (21 sq mi).

Population: 60,500 (1991 est).

Capital: Hamilton 6000 (1991 est).

Government: The British sovereign is represented by a Governor. The legislature comprises the 11-member appointed Senate, the upper house, and the 40-member House of Assembly, the lower house. The Governor appoints a Premier and a Cabinet of Ministers. The House of Assembly is elected for five years by universal adult suffrage. Premier: Sir John Swan.

Geography: Bermuda comprises over 100 small islands in the western Atlantic. Seven islands are linked together by causeways and bridges. Highest point: Gibb's Hill 78 m (256 ft). Climate: Bermuda has a humid subtropical climate.

Economy: Tourism dominates the economy, supplying over 60% of foreign-currency earnings and accounting for 65% of all employment, both directly and indirectly. There has been an important recent growth in 'offshore' financial services.

Recent History: Although settled by the English in 1609, Bermuda did not formally become a Crown colony until 1684. Its parliament - founded in 1620 - is the oldest in the Americas. Bermuda received internal self-government in 1968. In the 1960s and 1970s there was racial tension between the majority of African origin and the minority of European origin.

GREENLAND

Status: an internally self-governing part of the Kingdom of Denmark.

Area: 2,175,600 km² (839,800 sq mi).

Population: 55,500 (1991 est).

Capital: Nuuk (formerly Godthab) 12,200 (1991 est).

Government: Denmark is represented by a Governor. The 27-member Parliament (Landsting) is elected for four years by universal adult suffrage under a system of proportional representation. Parliament elects a seven-member government including a Prime Minister. Prime Minister: Lars Emil Johansen.

Geography: Greenland, the largest island in the world, has a highly indented fjord coastline. Over four-fifths of the island are covered by a permanent ice cap. The ice-free land is largely mountainous with a tundra vegetation. Highest point: Gunnbjoerns Fjeld 3733 m (12,247 ft). The climate is arctic although average summer temperatures in the southwest reach 7C (45F).

Economy: The economy is dominated by fishing and fish-processing. The harsh environment restricts agriculture to 1% of the country in the southwest where hay and vegetables are grown and sheep are kept.

Recent History: The original Norse settlement in Greenland disppeared in the 15th century and the island was not resettled from Europe until 1721 when it became a Danish colony. In 1953 Greenland became a part of Denmark. In 1979 Greenland gained home rule, retaining its status as part of Denmark. It is not part of the EU/EC.

ST PIERRE AND MIQUELON

Status: a French territorial collectivity.

Area: 242 km² (93 sq mi) - St Pierre group 26 km² (9 sq mi), Miquelon-Langlade 216 km² (83 sq mi).

Population: 6400 (1990 census).

Capital: St Pierre 5700 (1990 census).

Government: The 19-member General Council is elected by universal adult suffrage for six years. St Pierre-Miquelon is represented in the French National Assembly by a deputy and in the Senate by a senator.

Geography: The territory comprises two main islands and six islets 25 km (16 mi) off the coast of Newfoundland. Highest point: an unnamed point 240 m (787 ft). The climate is wet and windy, and cold in winter and fresh in summer.

Economy: Fishing, fish-freezing and tourism are - apart from government service - almost the only sources of employment.

Recent History: The only remains of the once-large French possessions in North America, the islands were settled from France in the 17th century. During Prohibition (1920-33), the islands were involved in supplying illicit alcohol into the USA. Since 1976 St Pierre-Miquelon has been an integral part of the French Republic.

SOUTH ASIA

Afghanistan, Bangladesh, Bhutan, India, Maldives, Myanmar
(Burma), Nepal, Pakistan, Sri Lanka.

Population trends in South Asia

The countries of South Asia are characterized by low GDPs and rapid increases in population. India, Pakistan and Bangladesh have high birth rates compared with the countries of the developed world - the population of India, for example, is increasing by 2% per annum - but that rate of increase is low compared with the states of eastern and central Africa.

The countries of the Indian sub-continent depend upon subsistence agriculture as their principal economic activity, and, compared with the countries of the developed world, have only limited social services and lack most forms of advanced agricultural technology. Under these conditions, rural families tend to be large, ensuring a degree of labour as well as support for members of the family in their old age. Hence, large families - as was formerly the case in the developed world - continue to be an essential norm for the poor, who represent the majority of the population in the Indian sub-continent.

Ironically, the emphasis placed upon eliminating disease among the young - for example, through mass immunization programmes - has lowered the levels of infant mortality in India, Pakistan and Bangladesh. Immunization has increased the population in all three countries, often leaving members of families without prospects of work. Many Indians, Pakistanis and Bangladeshis are still rural - indeed, four of the countries of the region (Bangladesh, Bhutan, Afghanistan and Nepal) are listed among the ten states with the lowest percentage of urban population in the world. To the large, rural populations of the Indian sub-continent, the towns and cities are seen as havens for alternative employment, although they offer limited job opportunities, and migration to towns and cities has done little to break the poverty cycle.

The combination of a rush by the rural poor to the cities and a high rate of population increase is reflected in the astounding growth of the major urban areas of India, Pakistan and Bangladesh. The sub-continent already contains 10 cities with over 3,000,000 inhabitants. Bombay, the largest, has over 12,000,000 people in its urban area and, at its present rate of growth, by the year 2010 will have almost 25,000,000 inhabitants. Dacca, the capital of Bangladesh, has an even faster growth rate as large numbers of the unemployed flock from the overcrowded countryside of the flood-prone republic into the city. From an estimated population of over 6,000,000 today, Dacca will have grown to a sprawling metropolis of nearly 18,000,000 in only 15 years' time.

This pattern is being repeated across the Indian sub-continent, although the pull of the larger urban areas is greater than that of the smaller cities. Although the economies of all the countries of the region are advancing, none of these states is in a position to expand and improve its urban infrastructure in order to cope with such a great influx of people. The problem of rural poverty in India, Pakistan and Bangladesh is being replaced by the problem of urban squalor and overcrowding. The present provision of water, electricity, housing, roads and public transport, schools and health care are all inadequate to cope with the demands of the current citizens of cities such as Bombay, Dacca, Karachi, Delhi, Madras and Calcutta. None of these centres has the resources nor aid to be able to cope with the increased demands that will be made by an expanding urban population. Housing, in particular, is a major concern and already many of the inhabitants of Calcutta and Bombay are homeless and hungry.

In addition, regional instability, characterized by the continuing rivalry between India and Pakistan and their dispute over Kashmir, means that too great a proportion of their national wealth is spent on armaments. Large-scale visible projects such as dams also eat up revenue. International efforts have sought to play a greater role in relieving the crisis of hunger and urban squalor; international organizations such as the UN World Food Programme, the Food and Agriculture Organization, the UN Children's Fund and the UN Development Programme have all attempted to assist developing countries, including those of the Indian sub-continent, where threats of hunger and deprivation are rife. These international organizations are supported by the efforts of donor governments and by voluntary non-governmental organizations working in these countries. But it is only the governments of the region, with their local knowledge, that have the ability to focus assistance directly where it is most needed.

Regional Organizations of South Asia

COLOMBO PLAN

The Colombo Plan for Co-operative Economic and Social Development in Asia and the Pacific was founded in 1950 to promote economic and social development within the region and to encourage training programmes, capital and technical co-operation.

Headquarters: Colombo, Sri Lanka.

Membership: Afghanistan, Australia, Bangladesh, Bhutan, Cambodia, Canada, Fiji, Indonesia, Iran, Japan, South Korea, Laos, Malaysia, Maldives, Myanmar (Burma), Nepal, New Zealand, Pakistan, Papua New Guinea, the Philippines, Singapore, Sri Lanka, Thailand, the United Kingdom, and the United States of America.

SOUTH ASIAN ASSOCIATION FOR ECONOMIC CO-OPERATION (SAARC)

The Association was founded in December 1985. It aims to encourage trade and economic development in South Asia.

Headquarters: Delhi, India.

Membership: Bangladesh, Bhutan, India, Maldives, Nepal, Pakistan, and Sri Lanka.

OTHER ORGANIZATIONS

The following countries of South Asia are members of the Commonwealth: Bangladesh, India, Maldives, Pakistan, and Sri Lanka.

South Asian Trade

Bangladesh Imports ($ million): 3405 (1990). Exports ($ million): 1690 (1991). Main imports: machinery and transport equipment 11.5% (1989/90), textile, yarn, fabrics and made-up articles 10.6% (1989/90). Main exports: ready-made garments 39.8% (1989/90), hides, skins and leather 11.2% (1989/90). Principal trading partners: Japan, USA, Singapore, India.

Bhutan Imports ($ million): 48 (1986). Exports ($ million): 22 (1986). Main imports: road vehicles 14.4% (1987), iron and steel 10.9% (1987). Main exports: electricity 39.3% (1987), wood and wood manufactures 17.7% (1987). Principal trading partner: India.

India Imports (rupee million): 43,928.6 (1990/91). Exports (rupee million): 325,533.4 (1990/91). Main imports: mineral fuels and lubricants 25% (1990/91), pearls and stones 8.6% (1990/91), non-electric machinery 15.7% (1990/91). Main exports: pearls, stones and jewellery 16.7% (1990/91), ready made garments 12.3% (1990/91). Principal trading partners: USA, Japan, Germany, UK, Belgium, Saudi Arabia.

Maldives Imports ($ million): 150.9 (1991). Exports ($ million): 53.7 (1991). Main imports: consumer goods 49.2% (1991), intermediate and capital goods 36.2% (1991). Main exports: apparel and clothing accessories 36.2% (1991), dried and frozen skipjack tuna 31.3% (1991). Principal trading partners: Thailand, Japan, Sri Lanka.

Myanmar (Burma) Imports ($ million): 616 (1991). Exports ($ million): 412 (1991). Main imports: machinery and equipment 51.4% (1989), raw materials for industry 31.4% (1989). Main exports: agricultural products 31.5% (1989), forest products 23.8% (1989). Principal trading partners: Japan, India, Germany, China.

Nepal Imports ($ million): 673 (1992). Exports ($ million): 287 (1992). Main imports: machinery and transport equipment 23.5% (1992), basic manufactured goods 17% (1992). Main exports: basic manufactures 80% (1992), food and live animals 14.3% (1992). Principal trading partners: India, China, Bangladesh.

Pakistan Imports (rupee million): 231,325 (1991/92). Exports (rupee million): 172,810 (1991/92). Main imports: non-electric machinery and electrical goods 26.9% (1991/92), mineral oils 9% (1991/92). Main exports: cotton yarn 17% (1991/92), cotton fabrics 11.8% (1991/92). Principal trading partners: USA, Japan, Germany, UK, Saudi Arabia.

Sri Lanka Imports ($ million): 3083 (1991). Exports ($ million): 1965 (1990). Main imports: machinery and transport equipment 15.4% (1990), petroleum products 13.3% (1990). Main exports: tea 24.9% (1990), rubber 3.9% (1990). Principal trading partner: USA, Japan, UK, Iran.

Afghanistan

Official name: Jamhuria Afghanistan (Republic of Afghanistan).

Member of: UN.

Area: 652,225 km² (251,773 sq mi).

Population: 18,052,000 (1992 est).

Capital: Kabul 2,000,000 (1993 est).

Other major cities: Kandahar (Qandahar) 226,000, Herat 177,000, Mazar-i-Sharif 131,000, Qonduz 108,000, Charikar 100,000 (1988 est).

Languages: Pushto (52%), Dari (Persian; 30%) - both official; Nuristani, Turkmen, Uzbek.

Religions: Sunni Islam (74%), Shia Islam (25%).

Education: Education is compulsory in theory between the ages of seven and 15. In 1990 the literacy rate was 29.4%. There are four universities.

Defence: In 1991 the total strength of government forces was estimated at 40,000.

Transport: There are over 22,000 km (13,750) mi of roads. Kabul has an international airport.

Media: There are five (irregular) daily newspapers and a state-run radio and television service.

GOVERNMENT

The constitution provides for a two-chamber National Assembly, elected by universal adult suffrage. The Loya Jirgha (supreme state body), comprising the National Assembly, the Cabinet, provincial, legal and tribal representatives, elects a President, who appoints a Prime Minister and other Ministers. The President and PM of the provisional government lead opposing military factions and constitutional government has ceased to exist.

President: Burhanuddin Rabbani.

Prime Minister: Gulbuddin Hekmatyar.

GEOGRAPHY

The central mountains, dominated by the Hindu Kush, cover over 75% of the state. Plains in the north form the main farming region. The southwest is desert and semidesert. Highest point: Noshaq 7499 m (24,581 ft). Principal rivers: Helmand, Amu Darya (Oxus).

AFGHANISTAN
Area: 652 225 km² (251 773 sq mi).

Climate: The highlands are cold with adequate rainfall; the dry plains have cold winters and hot summers.

ECONOMY

Farmers and herders account for over 60% of the labour force. Most of the usable land is pasture, mainly for sheep. Cereals, mainly wheat and maize, are also important. Exports include fresh and dried fruit, wool, cotton and natural gas. The economy has been damaged by civil war, and much of the infrastructure destroyed.

Currency: Afghani of 100 puls; 1US$ = 1702.6 Afghanis (May 1994).

GDP: US$3,100,000,000 (1988); US$220 per head.

RECENT HISTORY

Afghan independence was secured in 1921 after three wars with the British. Unrest followed until the reign of King Muhammad Zahir Shah (1933-73), which ended in a coup. Close relations with the USSR followed the 1978 Saur Revolution, but the Soviet invasion (1979) led to civil war. The Soviet withdrawal (1989) left the cities in government hands and Muslim fundamentalists controlling the countryside. In 1992 fundamentalists took Kabul, forming a provisional government. Factional, largely ethnic, fighting continues. By 1994 the government controlled few regions.

Bangladesh

Official name: Gana Praja Tantri Bangla Desh (People's Republic of Bangladesh).

Member of: UN, Commonwealth, SAARC.

Area: 143,998 km² (55,598 sq mi).

Population: 115,075,000 (1993 est).

Capital: Dhaka 6,105,000 (including suburbs; 1991 census).

Other major cities: Chittagong 2,133,000, Khulna 1,029,000, Rajshahi 427,000, Mymensingh 191,000, Comilla 185,000, Sylhet 169,000, Barisal 159,000 (1991 census).

Languages: Bengali (official; 97%), tribal dialects.

Religion: Sunni Islam (over 85%); Hindu (12%).

Education: Education is compulsory between the ages of five and ten. In 1990 the literacy rate was estimated to be 35%. There are six universities.

Defence: In 1993 the total armed strength was estimated to be 107,000 - 93,000 in the army, 7500 in the navy, 6500 in the air force. Chittagong is the principal naval base. There is no military service.

Transport: There are 193,283 km (120,100 mi) of roads and 2746 km (1706 mi) of state-run railways. Inland waterways are important communications routes. Dhaka is the chief river port; Chittagong is the principal seaport. Dhaka has an international airport.

Media: There are 40 daily newspapers, of which eight are published in English. There is a state-run radio service (wih six regional stations) and a state-run television service.

GOVERNMENT

The Parliament (Jatiya Sangsad) comprises 300 members elected for five years by universal adult suffrage and 30 women chosen by the elected members. Parliament elects a President - who is largely ceremonial and who serves for five years - and a Prime Minister who appoints a Council of Ministers. There are four divisions and 64 districts. The main political parties include the (centre right) Bangladesh National Party (BNP), the (nationalist) Bangladesh Awami League (Awami), the (left-wing) Jatiya Party (JP), the (Islamic fundamentalist) Jamit-i-Islami (JI) and the Communist Party of Bangladesh (CPB). Following the election in 1991 a BNP government was formed.

Party strength: BNP 171, Awami 93, JP 35, JI 20, CPB 3, others 8.

President: Abdur Rahman Biswas.

THE CABINET

Prime Minister: Begum Khaleda Zia (BNP).

Minister of Agriculture, Irrigation, Flood Control and Water Development: M. Mazid-Ul-Haq (BNP).

Minister of Commerce: M. Shamsul Islam (BNP).

Minister of Communications: Col. Oli Ahmed (BNP).

Minister of Education: Jamiruddin Sircar (BNP).

Minister of the Environment and Forests: Col. Akbar Hossain (BNP).

Minister of Finance: M. Saifur Rahman (BNP).

Minister of Fisheries and Livestock: Abdullah Al-Noman (BNP).

Minister of Food: Lt-Gen. Mir Shawkat Ali (BNP).

Minister of Foreign Affairs: A.S.M. MosLafizur Rahman (BNP).

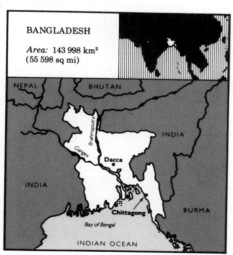

BANGLADESH

Area: 143 998 km² (55 598 sq mi)

NEPAL
BHUTAN
INDIA
Brahmaputra
Ganges
Dacca
INDIA
BURMA
Chittagong
Bay of Bengal
INDIAN OCEAN

Minister of Health and Family Welfare: Chowdhury Kamal Ibne Yusuf (BNP).

Minister of Home Affairs: Abdul Matin Chowdhury (BNP).

Minister of Industries: A.M. Zahiruddin Khan (BNP).

Minister of Information: Nazmul Huda (BNP).

Minister of Jute: A.S.M. Hannan Shah (BNP).

Minister of Labour and Manpower: Abdul Mannan Bhuiyan (BNP).

Minister of Law, Justice and Parliamentary Affairs: Mirza Golam Hafiz (BNP).

Minister of Local Government, Rural Development and Co-operatives: Abdus Salam Talukdar (BNP).

Minister of Posts and Telecommunications: Tariqul Islam (BNP).

Minister of Power, Energy and Mineral Resources: Dr Khandaker Mosherrat Hossain (BNP).

Minister of Religious Affairs: M. Keramat Ali (BNP).

Minister of Shipping: M.K. Anwar (BNP).

Minister of Works: M. Rafiqul Islam Mia (BNP).

DIVISIONS

Chittagong Area: 47,016 km² (18,153 sq mi). Population: 27,097,000 (1991 census). Capital: Chittagong.

Dhaka Area: 31,178 km² (12,038 sq mi). Population: 32,271,000 (1991 census). Capital: Dhaka.

Khulna Area: 35,742 km² (13,800 sq mi). Population: 19,967,000 (1991 census). Capital: Khulna.

Rajshahi Area: 34,457 km² (13,304 sq mi). Population: 25,432,000 (1991 census). Capital: Rajshahi.

GEOGRAPHY

Most of Bangladesh comprises alluvial plains in the deltas of the rivers Ganges and Brahmaputra, which combine as the Padma. The swampy plains - generally less than 9 m (30 ft) above sea level - are dissected by rivers dividing into numerous distributaries with raised banks. The south and southeast coastal regions contain mangrove forests (the Sundarbans). The only uplands are the Sylhet Hills in the northeast and the Chittagong hill country in the east. Principal rivers: Ganges, Brahmaputra. Highest point: Keokradong 1230 m (4034 ft). Climate: The climate is tropical with the highest temperatures between April and September. Most of the country's rainfall comes during the annual monsoon (June to October) when intense storms accompanied by high winds bring serious flooding. Rainfall totals reach 5000 mm (200 in) in the Sylhet Hills.

ECONOMY

With a rapidly increasing population, Bangladesh is among the world's poorest countries and is heavily dependent on foreign aid. Agriculture involves over 70% of the population. Rice is produced on over 75% of the cultivated land, but although the land is fertile, crops are often destroyed by floods and cyclones. The Flood Action Plan will alter the river courses and raise embankments. The main cash crops are jute and tea. Industries include processing jute, cotton and sugar. Mineral resources are few, but there are reserves of natural gas.

Currency: Taka of 100 paisas; 1US$ = 39.5 takas (June 1994).

GDP: US$24,805,000,000 (1992); US$220 per head.

RECENT HISTORY

On the partition of British India in 1947, as the majority of its inhabitants were Muslim, the area became the eastern province of an independent Pakistan. Separated by 1600 km (1000 mi) from the Urdu-speaking, politically dominant western province, East Pakistan saw itself as a victim of economic and ethnic injustice. Resentment led to civil war in 1971 when Indian aid to Bengali irregulars gave birth to an independent People's Republic of Bangladesh ('Free Bengal') under Sheik Mujib-urRahman. The Sheik's assassination in 1975 led eventually to a takeover by General Zia-ur-Rahman, who amended the constitution to create an 'Islamic state'. The General in turn was assassinated in 1981, and General Ershad took power in 1982. Martial law was lifted in 1986 when the constitution was amended and a civilian government took office. Following a period of unrest, President Ershad was deposed in 1990. In 1991, the BNP, led by Zia's widow, won multi-party elections. Bangladesh has since switched from a presidential to a parliamentary system of government.

Bhutan

Official name: Druk-yul (Realm of the Dragon).

Member of: UN, SAARC.

Area: 46,500 km² (17,954 sq mi).

Population: 1,442,000 (1990 UN est; a 1992 Bhutanese government estimate gives a population of over 850,000).

Capital: Thimpu 27,000 (1991 est).

Other main towns: Phuntsoling 10,000, Paro 8,000 (1990 est).

Languages: Dzongkha (Tibetan; official; 70%), Nepali (30%).

Religions: Buddhist (70%), Hindu (25%).

Education: Education is free but is not compulsory. The literacy rate was 15% in 1988. There is a university and a polytechnic.

Defence: The total armed strength in 1992 was 5500. There is selective conscription of between three and 12 weeks.

Transport: There are about 2500 km (1560 mi) of roads. Paro has a small international airport.

Media: There is a weekly newspaper. A single state-run radio service broadcasts in four languages

GOVERNMENT
Bhutan is an hereditary monarchy without a formal constitution. The King shares power with a Council of Ministers, the Tshogdu (National Assembly) and the head abbot of Bhutan's 3000-4000 Buddhist monks. Of the 151 members of the National Assembly, 106 are elected for three years by universal adult suffrage; the remainder include the Royal Advisory Council, the Ministers and 10 religious representatives. There are no political parties but there are two outlawed mainly Nepali groups - the Bhutan People's Party and the United Liberation People's Front .

King: HM the Druk Gyalpo Jigme Singhye Wangchuk, King of Bhutan (succeeded 24 July 1972 on the death of his father).

Prime Minister: The King.

GEOGRAPHY
The Himalaya make up most of the country. The valleys of central Bhutan are wide and fertile. The narrow Duars Plain - a subtropical jungle - lies along the Indian border. Principal rivers: Amo-chu, Wang-chu. Highest point: Khula Kangri 7554 m (24,784 ft). Climate: The Duars Plain is hot and wet. Temperatures get progressively lower with altitude resulting in glaciers and permanent snow cover in the north. Precipitation is heavy.

ECONOMY
Bhutan is one of the poorest and least developed countries in the world. Farm workers producing food crops account for about 90% of the labour force. The country's HEP potential is being developed.

Currency: Ngultrum of 100 Chetrum. 1US$ = 31.37 ngultrums (May 1994). The ngultrum is on a par with the Indian rupee which is also legal tender.

GDP: US$273,000,000 (1990 est); US$190 per head.

RECENT HISTORY
In 1907 the governor of Tongsa was elected as the first king of Bhutan. By a treaty of 1910 the Bhutanese government agreed to be guided by the British government in its external relations. In 1949 India returned to Bhutan territory that had been annexed by British India in 1865. At the same time, India assumed influence formerly exercised by Britain over Bhutan's external affairs. Bhutan remains largely closed to external influences and measures taken in the 1990s discriminate against the Nepalese minority, which forms the majority in the south of Bhutan.

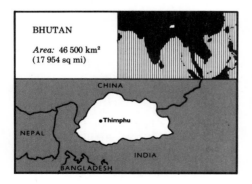

BHUTAN

Area: 46 500 km²
(17 954 sq mi)

CHINA

NEPAL

●Thimphu

INDIA

BANGLADESH

309

India

Official name: Bharat (Republic of India).

Member of: UN, Commonwealth, SAARC.

Area: (de facto) 3,287,263 km² (1,269,212 sq mi) including the Indian-held part of Jammu and Kashmir.

Population: 897,567,000 (1993 est) - including the Indian-held part of Jammu and Kashmir.

Capital: Delhi 8,419,000 (city 7,207,000, New Delhi 294,000; 1991 census).

Other major cities: Bombay 12,596,000 (city 9,926,000, Kalyan 1,014,000, Thane, formerly Thana, 797,000) Calcutta 11,022,000 (city 4,388,000, Hoara, formerly Howrah, 946,000), Madras 5,422,000 (city 3,841,000), Hyderabad 4,254,000 (city 3,146,000), Bangalore 4,130,000 (city 3,303,000), Ahmedabad 3,298,000 (city 2,873,000), Pune (formerly Poona) 2,485,000 (city 1,560,000), Kanpur 2,111,000 (city 1,958,000), Nagpur 1,661,000 (city 1,622,000), Lucknow 1,642,000 (city 1,592,000), Surat 1,517,000 (city 1,497,000), Jaipur 1,514,000 (city 1,455,000), Kochi (formerly Cochin) 1,140,000 (city 564,000), Coimbatore 1,136,000 (city 853,000), Vadodara (formerly Baroda) 1,115,000 (city 1,021,000), Indore 1,104,000 (city 1,087,000), Patna 1,099,000 (city 917,000), Madurai 1,094,000 (city 952,000), Bhopal 1,064,000, Visakhapatnam 1,052,000 (city 750,000), Varanasi (formerly Banaras or Benares) 1,026,000, Ludhiana 1,012,000, Agra 956,000 (city 899,000), Jabalpur 887,000 (city 740,000), Allahabad 858,000 (city 806,000), Meerut 847,000 (city 752,000), Vijaywada 845,000 (city 701,000), Jamshedpur 835,000 (city 461,000), Thiruvananthapuram (formerly Trivandrum) 826,000 (city 524,000), Dhanbad 818,000, Kozhikode (formerly Calicut) 801,000 (city 420,000), (1991 census).

Languages: Hindi (30%; official), English (official), Bengali (8%), Telugu (8%), Marathi (8%), Tamil (7%), Urdu (5%), Gujarati (5%), with over 1600 other languages.

Religions: Hindu (83%), Sunni Islam (11%), Christian (mainly Roman Catholic) (nearly 3%).

Education: Education is compulsory (in theory) between the ages of six and 14, except in Nagaland and Himachal Pradesh. In 1991 the literacy rate was 52.1%. There are 157 universities including the open university and institutes of university status.

Defence: In 1993 the total armed strength was 1,265,000 - 1,101,000 in the army, 54,000 in the navy and 11,000 in the air force.The The main naval bases are Bombay, Goa, Calcutta and Vishakhapatnam. There is no military service but it is the legal duty of every citizen to perform national service if called upon.

Transport: There are 2,037,000 km (1,266,000 mi) of roads and 62,660 km (38,662 mi) of state-run railways. Calcutta has a metro. Nearly 15,600 km (9700 mi) of inland waterways are navigable - the most important are the rivers Ganges, Brahmaputra, Godavari and Natmada. The principal commercial shipping ports are Bombay and Calcutta. The airports at Bombay, Calcutta, Delhi, Goa, Madras, Hyderabad, Ahmedabad and Thiruvananthapuram handle international flights.

Media: The size of India, and its many social, religious and linguistic barriers, have prevented the development of a national press, although a small number of English-language papers enjoy a wide circulation. All India Radio (AIR) runs 104 radio stations, operating in 81 languages. Television India runs 18 channels. Both organizations are government-financed and controlled. Satellite television is now widely received and has become an important influence.

GOVERNMENT

India is a federal republic in which each of the 25 states has its own legislature. The upper house of the federal parliament - the 250-member Council of States (Rajya Sabha) - consists of 12 members nominated by the President and 238 members elected by the assemblies of individual states. One third of the Council retires every two years. The lower house - the House of the People (Lok Sabha) - consists of 542 members elected for a five-year term by universal adult suffrage, plus two nominated members. The President - who serves for five years - is chosen by an electoral college consisting of the federal parliament and the state assemblies. The President appoints a Prime Minister - who commands a majority in the House - and a Council of Ministers, who are responsible to the House. The main political parties include the Congress (I) Party (Cong I), the Janata Dal (People's Party) (JD), the (right-wing Hindu) Bharatiya Janata Party (Indian People's Party; NJP), the Communist Party of India - Marxist (CPIM), the Communist Party of India (CPI), the All India Anna Dravida Munnetra Kazagam (AIADMK), Telegu Desam (TD), the Revolutionary Socialist Party (RSP), and a number of regional groupings. After the election held in June 1991 a Cong I-JD-CPIM-AIDMK coalition (which includes over 12 other smaller parties) took office.

Party strength: (Lok Sabha): (June 1994) Cong I 269, BJP 117, CPIM36, JD 35, CPI 14, AIDMK 12, TD 7, RSP4, others 37, plus vacant seats.

President: Ramaswamy Venkataraman.

THE CABINET
Prime Minister: P.V. Narasimha Rao.

Minister of Agriculture: Bajram Jakhar.

Minister for Chemicals and Fertilizers: Ram Lakhan Singh Yadav.

Minister of Civil Aviation and Tourism: Ghulam Nabi Azad.

Minister of Civil Supplies, Consumer Affairs and Public Distribution: A.K. Antony.

Minister of Commerce: Franab Mukherjee.

Minister of External Affairs: Dinesh Singh.

Minister of Finance: Manmohan Singh.

Minister of Health and Family Development: B. Shankaranand.

Minister of Home Affairs: S.B. Chavan.

Minister of Human Resource Development: Arjun Singh.

Minister of Power: N.K.P. Salve.

Minister of Railways: C.K. Jaffer Sharief.

Minister of Urban Development: Sheila Kail.

Minister of Water Resources and Minister of Parliamentary Affairs: Vidyacharan Shukla.

Minister of Welfare: Sitaram Kesri.

(There are, in addition, 27 Ministers of State.)

INDIAN STATES
The population figures are from the 1991 census.

Andhra Pradesh Area: 276,814 km² (106,878 sq mi). Population: 66,355,000. Capital: Hyderabad.

Arunachal Pradesh Area: 83,587 km² (32,269 sq mi). Population: 858,000. Capital: Itanagar.

Assam Area: 78,523 km² (30,310 sq mi). Population: 22,295,000. Capital: Gauhati.

Bihar Area: 173,876 km² (67,134 sq mi). Population: 86,339,000. Capital: Patna.

Goa Area: 3701 km² (1429 sq mi). Population: 1,169,000. Capital: Panaji.

Gujarat Area: 195,984 km² (75,669 sq mi). Population: 41,310, 000. Capital: Gandhinagar.

Haryana Area: 44,222 km² (17,074 sq mi). Population: 16,318,000. Capital: Chandigarh (a separate Union territory, see below).

Himachal Pradesh Area: 55,673 km² (21,495 sq mi). Population: 5,111,000. Capital: Simla.

Jammu and Kashmir Area: 101,283 km² (39,105 sq mi) - the Indian-held part of the state only. Population: 7,719,000. Capital (summer only): Srinagar. Capital (winter only): Jammu.

Karnataka Area: 191,773 km² (74,044 sq mi). Population: 44,806,000. Capital: Bangalore.

Kerala Area: 38,864 km² (15,005 sq mi). Population: 29,033,000. Capital: Thiruvanan-thapuram (formerly Trivandrum).

Madhya Pradesh Area: 442,841 km² (170,981 sq mi). Population: 66,136,000. Capital: Bhopal.

Maharashtra Area: 307,762 km² (118,827 sq mi). Population: 78,748,000. Capital: Bombay.

Manipur Area: 22,356 km² (8632 sq mi). Population: 1,847,000. Capital: Imphal.

Meghalaya Area: 22,429 km² (8660 sq mi). Population: 1,761,000. Capital: Shillong.

Mizoram Area: 21,090 km² (8143 sq mi). Population: 690, 000. Capital: Aizawl.

Nagaland Area: 16,527 km² (6381 sq mi). Population: 1,216,000. Capital: Kohima.

Orissa Area: 155,707 km² (60,118 sq mi). Population: 31,512,000. Capital: Bhubaneshwar.

Punjab Area: 50,376 km² (19,450 sq mi). Population: 20,191,000. Capital: Chandigarh (a separate Union territory, see below).

Rajasthan Area: 342,239 km² (132,138 sq mi). Population: 43,881,000. Capital: Jaipur.

Sikkim Area: 7298 km² (2818 sq mi). Population: 406,000. Capital: Gangtok.

Tamil Nadu Area: 130,357 km² (50,331 sq mi). Population: 55,638,000. Capital: Madras.

Tripura Area: 10,477 km² (4045 sq mi). Population: 2,745,000. Capital: Agartala.

Uttar Pradesh Area: 294,413 km² (113,673 sq mi). Population: 139,031,000. Capital: Lucknow.

West Bengal Area: 87,853 km² (33,920 sq mi). Population: 68,078,000 Capital: Calcutta.

UNION TERRITORIES
Andaman and Nicobar Islands (territory) Area: 8293 km² (3202 sq mi). Population: 279,000. Capital: Port Blair.

Chandigarh Area: 114 km² (44 sq mi). Population: 641,000. Capital: Chandigarh (which is capital of two states; see above).

Dadra and Nagar Haveli Area: 491 km² (190 sq mi). Population: 138,000. Capital: Silvassa.

Daman and Diu Area: 112 km² (43 sq mi). Population: 101,000. Capital: Daman.

Delhi Area: 1485 km² (573 sq mi). Population: 9,370,000. Capital: Delhi.

Lakshadweep Area: 32 km² (12 sq mi). Population: 52,000. Capital: Kavaratti.

Pondicherry Area: 492 km² (190 sq mi). Population: 807,000. Capital: Pondicherry.

GEOGRAPHY
The Himalaya cut the Indian subcontinent off from the rest of Asia. Several Himalayan peaks in India rise to over 7000 m (23,000 ft). South of the Himalaya, the basins of the Rivers Ganges and Brahmaputra and their tributaries are intensively farmed and densely populated. The Thar Desert stretches along the border with Pakistan. In south India, the Deccan - a large plateau of hard rocks - is bordered in the east and west by the Ghats, discontinuous ranges of hills descending in steps to coastal plains. Natural vegetation ranges from tropical rain forest on the west coast and monsoon forest in the northeast and far south, through dry tropical scrub and thorn forest in much of the Deccan to Alpine and temperate vegetation in the Himalaya. Highest point: Kangchenjunga 8598 m (28,208 ft). Principal rivers: Ganges (Ganga), Brahmaputra, Sutlej, Yamuna, Tapti,

Godavari, Krishna .Climate: India has three distinct seasons: the hot season from March to June, the wet season - when the southwest monsoon brings heavy rain - from June to October, and a cooler drier season from November to March. Temperatures range from the cool of the Himalaya to the tropical heat of the southern states.

ECONOMY
Two thirds of the labour force are involved in subsistence farming, with rice and wheat as the principal crops. Cash crops tend to come from large plantations and include tea, cotton, jute and sugar cane - all grown for export. The monsoon rains and irrigation make cultivation possible in many areas, but drought and floods are common. India is a major industrial power and is beginning to import more consumer goods rather than relying upon her own industries to supply all her needs. Major coal reserves provide the power base for industry. Other mineral deposits include diamonds, bauxite, and titanium, copper and iron ore, as well as substantial reserves of natural gas and petroleum. The textile, vehicle, iron and steel, pharmaceutical and electrical industries make important contributions to the economy, but India has balance-of-payment difficulties and relies upon foreign aid for development. Privatization of some state enterprises began in the early 1990s and intensified in 1993-94. The Indian economy, which had in many ways been remarkably self-sufficient, began to rejoin the world economy. Economic and social problems include a population growth of over 2% per annum, a considerable government deficit, poor infrastructure in rural areas, inefficient tax collection and the massive problem of poverty - over one third of the population is below the official poverty line. India has, however, maintained economic growth throughout the early 1990s.

Currency: Rupee of 100 paise; 1US$ = 31.367 rupees (June 1994).

GDP: US$269,000,000,000 (1993 est); US$298 per head.

RECENT HISTORY
The British Indian Empire included present-day Pakistan and Bangladesh, and comprised the Crown Territories of British India and over

620 Indian protected states. The Indian states covered about 40% of India, and enjoyed varying degrees of autonomy under the rule of their traditional princes. From the middle of the 19th century the British cautiously encouraged Indian participation in the administration of British India. British institutions, the rail-

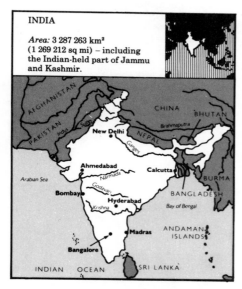

INDIA

Area: 3 287 263 km²
(1 269 212 sq mi) – including
the Indian-held part of Jammu
and Kashmir.

ways and the English language - all imposed upon India by a modernizing imperial power - fostered the growth of an Indian sense of identity beyond the divisions of caste and language. However, ultimately the divisions of religion proved stronger. The Indian National Congress - the forerunner of the Congress Party - was first convened in 1885, and the Muslim League first met in 1906. Political and nationalist demands grew after British troops fired without warning on a nationalist protest meeting - the Amritsar Massacre (1919). The India Acts (1919 and 1935) granted limited autonomy and created an Indian federation, but the pace of reform did not satisfy Indian expectations. In 1920 Congress - led by Mohandas (Mahatma) Karamchand Gandhi (1869-1948) - began a campaign of non-violence and non-cooperation with the British authorities. However relations between Hindus and Muslims steadily deteriorated, and by 1940 the Muslim League was demanding a separate sovereign state. By 1945, war-weary Britain had accepted the inevitability of Indian independence. However, religious discord forced the partition of the subcontinent in 1947 into predominantly Hindu India - under Jawaharlal (Pandit) Nehru (1889-1964) of the Congress Party - and Muslim Pakistan (including what is now Bangladesh) - under Mohammed Ali Jinnah (1876-1948) of the Muslim League. Over 70 million Hindus and Muslims became refugees and crossed the new boundaries, and thousands were killed in communal violence. The frontiers remained disputed. India and Pakistan fought border wars in 1947-49, 1965 (over Kashmir) and again in 1971 - when Bangladesh gained independence from Pakistan with Indian assistance. Kashmir is still divided along a cease-fire line. There were also border clashes with China in 1962. Under Nehru (PM 1947-64) India became one of the leaders of the nonaligned movement of Third World states. Under the premiership (1966-77 and 1980-84) of his daughter Indira Gandhi (1917-84) India continued to assert itself as the dominant regional power. Although India remained the world's largest democracy - despite Mrs Gandhi's brief imposition of emergency rule (1975-77) - local separatism and communal unrest have threatened unity. The Sikhs have conducted an often violent campaign for an independent homeland - Khalistan - in the Punjab. In 1984 Mrs Gandhi ordered the storming of the Golden Temple of Amritsar, a Sikh holy place that extremists had turned into an arsenal. In the same year Mrs Gandhi was assassinated by her Sikh bodyguard and was succeeded as PM by her son Rajiv Gandhi (PM 1984-89), who was assassinated during the 1991 election campaign. The once dominant Congress party has split and a plethora of opposition parties, many of them regional in nature, has flourished. Coalition government is now the norm in India. Tension and violence between Hindus and Muslims has increased since a campaign to build a Hindu temple on the site of a mosque in the holy city of Ayodhya. The destruction of the mosque by Hindu fundamentalists (1992) led to widespread disorders. Sectarian violence remains just below the surface, while the conflict with Pakistan in Kashmir, where separatism has become an issue, continues to smoulder.

313

The Maldives

Official name: Dhivehi Raajjeyge Jumhooriyyaa (The Republic of the Maldives).

Member of: UN, SAARC, Commonwealth.

Area: 298 km² (115 sq mi).

Population: 237,000 (1993 est).

Capital: Malé 55,000 (1990 census).

Languages: Dhivehi (Maldivian; official).

Religions: Sunni Islam (official; almost 100%).

Education: Education normally lasts from the age of six to the age of 11, but is not compulsory. Secondary education, which begins at 11, can last up to seven years. The literacy rate was 98.2% in 1991. Although there is no university, there are several tertiary education institutions.

Defence: There are no armed forces. The 800-member police force is responsible for national security.

Transport: There are no figures for the total length of roads. Malé has an international airport and a commercial shipping port. The former RAF base at Gan is now also an international airport.

Media: There are four daily newspapers. There is a radio service and a television service.

GOVERNMENT
The 48-member Majlis (Assembly) comprises eight members nominated by the President and 40 elected for five years by universal adult suffrage - two members are elected by Malé and two members are elected by each of the 19 administrative units into which the republic is divided. The President, who is also directly elected for five years, appoints a Cabinet of Ministers. (The post of Prime Minister was abolished in 1975.) There are no political parties.

President (Head of state and head of government): Maumoon Abdul Gayoom.

GEOGRAPHY
The country is a chain of over 1190 small low-lying coral islands, which lie about 675 km (420 mi) to the southwest of Sri Lanka. Only 203 of the islands are inhabited. The Maldive Islands are grouped into 19 main atolls (which form the administrative divisions of the country). There are no significant rivers. Highest point: 3 m (10 ft). Climate: The Maldives have a tropical climate with heavy rainfall brought by the monsoon between May and August.

ECONOMY
The growing tourist industry has displaced fishing as the mainstay of the economy. The government has encouraged industry but development has been held back by the shortage of labour. Almost all the principal staple foods have to be imported. The greatest problem facing the low-lying Maldives is flooding from violent monsoon storms and tidal waves - in 1991 large areas of Malé were inundated by sea water.

Currency: Rufiyaa of 100 laari. 1US$ = 11.2 Rufiyaa (May 1994).

GDP: US$114,000,000 (1992); US$500 per head.

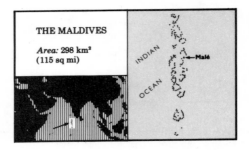

THE MALDIVES

Area: 298 km²
(115 sq mi)

INDIAN OCEAN

Malé

RECENT HISTORY
From 1887, until independence in 1965, the Maldives were an internally self-governing British protectorate. From 1956 to 1975 there was an important RAF base on the island of Gan. In 1968 the ad-Din sultanate, which had been established in the 14th century, was abolished in favour of a republican system. In recent years, the low-lying Maldives have played a leading role in raising international concern over the possible effects of a rise in sea level as a result of global warming - it has been suggested that the entire country would be one of the first land masses to disappear beneath the waves if sea level were to rise.

Myanmar (Burma)

Official name: Myanmar Naingngandaw (The Union of Myanmar). The name Burma was officially dropped in May 1989 but remains in widespread use internationally and is still used by the opposition in the country.

Member of: UN.

Area: 676,552 km² (261,218 sq mi).

Population: 44,613,000 (1993 est).

Capital: Rangoon (Yangon) 2,513,000 (1983 census).

Other major cities: Mandalay 533,000, Moulmein (Mawlamyine) 220,000, Pegu (Bago) 151,000, Bassein (Pathein) 144,000, Taunggyi 108,000 (1983 census).

Languages: Burmese (official; 80%), Karen, Mon, Shan, Kachin, and other minorities.

Religion: Buddhist (88%), various Christian Churches (5%), Sunni Islam and animist minorities.

Education: Education is compulsory, in theory, between the ages of five and 10. In 1990 the literacy rate was 80.6%. There are three universities.

Defence: In 1993 the total armed strength was 286,000 - 250,000 in the army, 12,000 in the navy and 24,000 in the air force. There is also a 50,000-member paramilitary People's Police Force and a 35,000-member People's Militia. There is no military service.

Transport: There are 23,463 km (14,579 mi) of road and 3137 km (1949 mi) of railways. Rangoon, the main port, has an international airport.

Media: There are two daily newspapers and a state-run radio and television service.

GOVERNMENT

Power is held by a 19-member State Law-and-Order Restoration Council whose Chairman is head of state. There is constitutional provision for a 489-member Assembly which is empowered to elect a Council of Ministers and a Council of State, whose Chairman is head of state. The country is divided into seven divisions (provinces) and seven states. The states are, in theory, autonomous. Multi-party elections were held in May 1990 but the Military

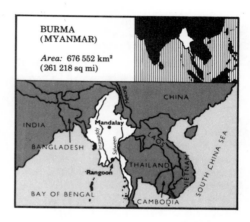

BURMA
(MYANMAR)

Area: 676 552 km²
(261 218 sq mi)

State Law-and-Order Restoration Council refused to transfer power to the National League for Democracy, which had won a clear majority in the election. The other main political parties are the (military-backed) National Unity Party and the Democratic Allaince of Burma (which is an umbrella organization for some 20 opposition, ethnic and other pro-democracy groups). The Assembly is suspended.

Head of state and head of government: (Chair of the ruling junta, Chair of the State Law and Order Restoration Council, Prime Minister and Minister of Defence) Gen. Than Shwe.

THE CABINET
includes

Prime Minister and Minister of Defence: see above.

Deputy Prime Minister: Vice-Admiral Maung Khin.

Deputy Prime Minister: Lt-Gen. Tin Tun.

Minister of Foreign Affairs: U Ohn Gyaw.

Minister of Home Affairs: Lt-Gen. Phone Myint.

Minister of Trade: Maj-Gen. Tun Kyi.

STATES
Population figures are from the 1983 census.

Chin Area: 36,019 km² (13,907 sq mi). Population: 369,000. Capital: Hakha.

Kachin Area: 89,041 km² (34,379 sq mi). Population: 905,000. Capital: Myitkyina.

Karen Area: 30,383 km² (11,731 sq mi). Population: 1,055,000. Capital: Pa-an (Hpa-an).

Kayah Area: 11,733 km² (4530 sq mi). Population: 168,000. Capital: Loi-kaw.

Mon Area: 12,297 km² (4748 sq mi). Population: 1,680,000. Capital: Moulmein (Mawlamyine).

Rakhine (formerly Arakan) Area: 36,778 km² (14,200 sq mi). Population: 2,046,000. Capital: Sittwe (Akyab).

Shan Area: 155,801 km² (60,155 sq mi). Population: 3,717,000. Capital: Taunggyi.

DIVISIONS
Irrawaddy (Ayeyarwady) Area: 35,138 km² (13,567 sq mi). Population: 4,994,000. Capital: Bassein (Pathein).

Magwe Area: 44,820 km² (17,305 sq mi). Population: 3,243,000. Capital: Magwe.

Mandalay Area: 37,024 km² (14,295 sq mi). Population: 4,578,000. Capital: Mandalay.

Pegu (Bago) Area: 39,404 km² (15,214 sq mi). Population: 3,800,000. Capital: Pegu.

Rangoon (Yangon) Area: 10,171 km² (3927 sq mi). Population: 3,966,000. Capital: Rangoon (Yangon).

Sagaing Area: 94,625 km² (36,535 sq mi). Population: 3,862,000. Capital: Sagaing.

Tenasserim (Tanintharyi) Area: 43,343 km² (16,735 sq mi). Population: 917,000. Capital: Tavoy (Dawei).

GEOGRAPHY
The north and west of Burma are mountainous. In the east is the Shan Plateau along the Thai border. Central and south Burma consists of tropical lowlands. Highest point: Hkakado Razi 5881 m (19,296 ft). Principal rivers: Irrawaddy, Sittang, Mekong. Climate: Burma is tropical, experiencing monsoon rains - up to 5000 mm (200 in) in the south - from May to October.

ECONOMY
Burma is rich in agriculture, timber, and minerals, but because of poor communications, lack of development and serious rebellions by a number of ethnic minorities, the country has been unable to realize its potential. Subsistence farming involves about 80% of the labour force, with rice as the staple crop. In some years there is enough rice for export. Other crops include sugar cane, maize, groundnuts, tobacco and rubber. The illegal cultivation of opium in the north is a cause of international concern. For several decades the economy has been restricted through official policies of self-sufficiency, international isolation and public ownership. In the early 1990s attempts have been made to open up the country to foreign investment and liberalization measures to encourage a market economy began in 1990.

Currency: Kyat of 100 pyas; 1US$ = 5.81 kyats (June 1994).

GDP: US$16,330,000,000 (1990); US$400 per head.

RECENT HISTORY
Separated from British India in 1937, Burma became a battleground for British and Japanese forces in World War II. In 1948, Burma left the Commonwealth as an independent republic, keeping outside contacts to a minimum, particularly following the coup of General Ne Win in 1962. Continuing armed attempts to gain autonomy by non-Burman minorities have strengthened the army's role. In 1988-89, demonstrations for democracy appeared to threaten military rule, but were repressed. The military retained power following multi-party elections in 1990, and detained or restricted the principal members of the National League for Democracy, including the party leader, Aung San Suu Kyi. The military successfully increased their activities against separatists in the 1990s and by 1993 had secured cease-fire agreements with the Shan and Kachin guerrilla movements. The most active rebelllion in 1993-94 was the Karen movement. International pressure upon the military government to respect human rights, introduce democratic reforms and to free Aung San Suu Kyi from detention intensified.

Nepal

Official name: Nepal Adhirajya (Kingdom of Nepal).

Member of: UN, SAARC.

Area: 147,181 km² (56,827 sq mi).

Population: 19,379,000 (1991 est).

Capital: Kathmandu 420,000 (city 235,000; 1987 est)

Other main towns: Biratnagar 120,000, Lalitpur 100,000 (1987 est).

Languages: Nepali (official; 58%), Bihari (19%), Maithir (12%).

Religions: Hindu (official; 90%), Buddhist (5%), Sunni Islam (3%).

Education: Education is compulsory in theory between the ages of six and 11. In 1990 the literacy rate was 25.6%. There are two universities.

Defence: In 1993 the total armed strength was 36,000 (plus 28,000 paramilitary).

Transport: There are over 6300 km (3940 mi) of roads and two short stretches of railway - 101 km (63 mi) - entering Nepal from India. Kathmandu has an international airport.

Media: There are 12 daily newspapers (of which three are in English). There is a state-run radio and television service.

GOVERNMENT
Nepal is a constitutional monarchy with a two-chamber Parliament. The Lower House consists of 205 members elected for five years by universal adult suffrage. The Upper House consists of 60 appointed and indirectly elected members, including six members appointed by the King. The main political parties are the Nepali Congress Party (NCP) and the Communist Party-United Leninist Party Alliance (UCPN).

Party strength: (Lower House) NCP 110, UCPN 69, others 26.

King: HM King Birendra (succeeded upon the death of his father, 31 January 1972).

Prime Minister: Girija Prasad Koirala (NCP).

GEOGRAPHY
In the south are densely populated subtropical lowlands. A hilly central belt is divided by fertile valleys. The Himalaya dominate the north. Highest point: Mount Everest 8863 m (29,078 ft). Principal rivers: Karnali, Naryani, Kosi. Climate: The climate varies between the subtropical south and the glacial Himalayan peaks. All of Nepal experiences the monsoon.

ECONOMY
Nepal is one of the least developed countries in the world, with most of the labour force involved in subsistence farming, mainly growing rice, beans and maize. Forestry is important, but the increased clearing of land for agriculture has led to serious deforestation. Tourism is an important foreign-currency earner.

Currency: Nepalese rupee (NPR) of 100 paisa; 1US$= 49.18 NPR (June 1994).

GDP: US$3,289,000,000 (1990); US$170 per head.

RECENT HISTORY
In 1768 the ruler of the principality of Gurkha in the west conquered the Kathmandu valley, and began a phase of expansion that ended in defeat by the Chinese in Tibet (1792) and the British in India (1816). From 1846 to 1950 the Rana family held sway as hereditary chief ministers of a powerless monarchy. Their isolationist policy preserved Nepal's independence at the expense of its development. A brief experiment with democracy was followed by a reassertion of royal autocracy (1960) by King Mahendra (reigned 1952-72). Violent pro-democracy demonstrations in 1990 forced the King to concede a democratic constitution.

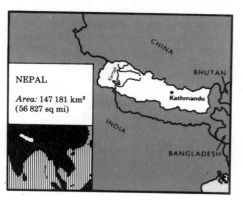

NEPAL

Area: 147 181 km²
(56 827 sq mi)

CHINA

BHUTAN

Kathmandu

INDIA

BANGLADESH

Pakistan

Official name: Islami Jamhuria-e-Pakistan (Islamic Republic of Pakistan).

Member of: UN, Commonwealth, SAARC.

Area: 803,943 km² (310,403 sq mi) or (de facto) 888,102 km² (333,897 sq mi) including the Pakistani-held areas of Kashmir (known as Azad Kashmir) and the disputed Northern Areas (Gilgit, Baltistan and Diamir).

Population: 127,962,000 (1993 est; including the Pakistani-held areas of Kashmir - Azad Kashmir and the disputed Northern Areas - Gilgit, Baltistan and Diamir).

Capital: Islamabad 266,000 (including suburbs; 1992 est).

Other major cities: Karachi 6,771,000, Lahore 3,850,000, Faisalabad 1,435,000, Rawalpindi 1,100,000, Hyderabad 1,041,000, Multan 999,000, Gujranwala 912,000, Peshawar 770,000, Sialkot 418,000 (all including suburbs; 1992 est).

Languages: Urdu (national; 20%), Punjabi (60%), Sindhi (12%), English, Pushto, Baluchi.

Religions: Sunni Islam (official; 92%), Shia Islam (5%), with small Ismaili Muslim and Ahmadi minorities.

Education: Education is not compulsory but is available, at primary level, between the ages of five and 10. In 1990 the literacy rate was 34.8%. There are 22 universities including an open university.

Defence: In 1992 the total armed strength was 580,000 - 515,000 in the army, just under 20,000 in the navy and 45,000 in the air force. There is also a 238,000-member paramilitary force. Karachi is the principal naval base. There is no military service.

Transport: There are 140,080 km ((87,060 mi) of roads and 8775 km (5453 mi) of state-run railways. The principal commercial shipping port is Karachi. There are international airports at Karachi, Lahore, Rawalpindi, Peshawar and Quetta.

Media: There are nearly 60 daily newspapers, 11 of which are published in English. Karachi and Lahore are the main centres of publishing, but there are other regional presses. The government-owned PBC and PTC respectively broadcast radio and television programmes from 22 regional centres. There is also a private television company.

GOVERNMENT

The 87-member Senate (the upper house of the Federal Legislature) comprises 19 senators elected for six years by each of the four provinces, plus 8 senators elected from the fed-

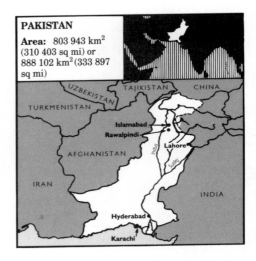

PAKISTAN

Area: 803 943 km² (310 403 sq mi) or 888 102 km² (333 897 sq mi)

erally administered Tribal Areas and 3 senators chosen to represent the federal capital. The 237-member National Assembly comprises 207 members elected by universal adult suffrage for five years, 20 seats reserved for women, and 10 members representing non-Islamic minorities. The President - who is chosen by the Federal Legislature - appoints a Prime Minister who commands a majority in the National Assembly. The PM, in turn, appoints a Cabinet of Ministers, responsible to the Assembly. The President has the power to dismiss the current government and dissolve the national and provincial assemblies. The four provinces, Azad Kashmir and the Northern Areas have their own legislatures. The main political parties include the Pakistan People's Party (PPP), the Pakistan Muslim League (Nawaz Group; PMLNG), the Pakistan Muslim

League (Junejo Group; PMLJG), the Awami National Party (ANP), the Islami Jamhoori Mahaz (IJM), the Pakhtoon Khwa Milli Awami Party (PKMAP), the Pakistan Islami Front (PIF), and various regional parties. After the election held in 1993 a PPP-led coalition government took office.

Party strength: PPP 91, PMLNG 72, PMLJG 6, ANP 3, IJM 3, PKMAP 3, PIF 3, others 9, independents 17.

President: Farooq Ahmad Khan Leghari.

THE CABINET
Prime Minister: Benazir Bhutto.

Minister of Commerce: Chaudhry Ahmad Mukhtar.

Minister of Defence:Aftab Shahban Mirani.

Minister of Education: Khurshid Ahmad Shah.

Minister of Food, Agriculture and Livestock: Nawab Muhammad Yousif Talpur.

Minister of Foreign Affairs: Sardar Aseff Ahmad Ali.

Minister of Industries and Production: Brig. Muhammad Asghar.

Minister of the Interior: Maj-Gen. Nasirullah Khan Babar.

Minister of Kashmir Affairs and Northern Affairs: Muhammad Afzal Khan.

Minister of Law, Justice and Parliamentary Affairs: Sayed Iqbal Haider.

Minister of Petroleum and Natural Resources: Anwar Saifullah Khan.

Minister of Population Welfare: Julius Salik.

Minister of Social Welfare and Special Education: Dr Sher Afghan Khan Kharal.

Minister of Water and Power: Ghulam Mustafa Khar.

Minister of Works: Makhdoom Muhammad Amin Fahim.

Minister of State for Finance: Makhdoom Shahabuddin.

Minister of State for Labour and Manpower: Ghulam Akbar Lasi.

Minister of State for States and Frontier Regions: Abdul Qayyum Khan.

PAKISTANI PROVINCES AND FEDERAL TERRITORIES
Baluchistan Area: 347,188 km^2 (134,050 sq mi). Population: 5,670,000 (1990 est). Capital: Quetta.

North-West Frontier Area: 74,522 km^2 (28,773 sq mi). Population: 14,340,000 (1990 est). Capital: Peshawar.

Punjab Area: 205,345 km^2 (79,284 sq mi). Population: 62,060,000 (1990 est). Capital: Lahore.

Sind Area: 140,913 km^2 (54,407 sq mi). Population: 24,980,000 (1990 est). Capital: Karachi.

Federal Capital Territory Area: 907 km^2 (350 sq mi). Population: 266,000 (1990-91 est). Capital: Islamabad.

DISPUTED TERRITORIES
Azad Kashmir (that part of the state of Jammu and Kashmir held by Pakistan) Area: 11,639 km^2 (4494 sq mi). Population: 2,580,000 (1990 est). Capital: Muzaffarabad.

Northern Areas (Baltistan, Diamir and Gilgit) (administered by Pakistan but disputed by India.) Combined area: 72,520 km^2 (28,000 sq mi). Combined population: 730,000 (1990 est). Capital: (of Baltistan) Skardu, (of Diamir) Chilas, (of Gilgit) Gilgit.

GEOGRAPHY
The Indus Valley divides Pakistan into a highland region in the west and a lowland region in the east. In Baluchistan - in the south - the highlands consist of ridges of hills and low mountains running northeast to southwest. In the north - in the North-West Frontier Province and the disputed territories - the mountain chains rise to over 7000 m (21,300 ft) and include the Karakoram, and parts of the Himalaya and Hindu Kush. The Indus Valley - and the valleys of its tributaries - form a major agricultural region and contain the majority of Pakistan's population. A continuation of the Indian Thar Desert occupies the east. Highest point:K2 (Mount Godwin Austen) 8607 m (28,238 ft). Principal rivers: Indus, Sutlej, Chenab, Ravi, Jhelum. Climate: The north and west of Pakistan are arid; the south and much of the east experience a form of the tropical monsoon. Temperatures vary dramatically by season and with altitude, from the hot tropical coast to the cold mountains of the far north.

ECONOMY

Nearly one half of the labour force is involved in subsistence farming, with wheat and rice as the main crops. Cotton is the main foreign-currency earner. The government is encouraging irrigation schemes, but over one half of the cultivated land is subject to either waterlogging or salinity. Although there is a wide range of mineral reserves - including coal, gold, graphite, copper and manganese - these resources have not been extensively developed. Manufacturing is dominated by food processing, textiles and consumer goods. Unemployment and underemployment are major problems, and the country relies heavily upon foreign aid and money sent back by Pakistanis working abroad. Tax collection remains a problem and government tax receipts are way below budget estimates. Pakistan runs a large government deficit. The Pakistani government has placed a priority upon encouraging the development of manufacturing industries, particularly in the private sector.

Currency: Pakistan rupee of 100 paisas; 1US$ = 30.62 rupees (June 1994).

GDP: US$56,600,000,000 (1993 est); US$446 per head.

RECENT HISTORY

From the 18th century the region came under British rule. Pakistan as a nation was born in August 1947 when British India was partitioned as a result of demands by the Muslim League for an Islamic state in which Hindus would not be in a majority. Large numbers of Muslims moved to the new state and up to 1,000,000 people died in the bloodshed that accompanied partition. Pakistan had two 'wings' - West Pakistan (the present country) and East Pakistan (now Bangladesh) - separated by 1600 km (1000 mi) of Indian territory. A number of areas were disputed with India. Kashmir - the principal bone of contention - was effectively partitioned between the two nations, and in 1947-49 and 1965 tension over Kashmir led to war between India and Pakistan. The problem of Kashmir remains unsolved, with fighting continuing intermittently along parts of the ceasefire line. The Muslim League leader Muhammad Ali Jinnah (1876-1949) was the first Governor General, but

Jinnah, who was regarded as 'father of the nation', died soon after independence. Pakistan - which became a republic in 1956 - suffered political instability and periods of military rule, including the administrations of General Muhammad Ayub Khan (from 1958 to 1969) and General Muhammad Yahya Khan (from 1969 to 1971). Although East Pakistan contained the majority of the population, from the beginning West Pakistan held political and military dominance. In elections in 1970, Shaikh Mujibur Rahman's Awami League won an overwhelming majority in East Pakistan, while the Pakistan People's Party (PPP) won most of the seats in West Pakistan. Mujibur Rahman seemed less interested in leading a new Pakistani government than in winning autonomy for the East. In March 1971, after abortive negotiations, the Pakistani army was sent from the West to East Pakistan, which promptly declared its independence as Bangladesh. Civil war broke out and India supported the new state, forcing the Pakistani army to surrender by the end of the year. The leader of the PPP, Zulfiqar Ali Bhutto (PM 1972-77), was deposed in a military coup led by the Army Chief of Staff, Muhammad Zia al-Haq. Bhutto was imprisoned (1977) for allegedly ordering the murder of the father of a former political opponent, sentenced to death (1978) and, despite international protests, hanged (1979). In 1985 Zia lifted martial law and began to return Pakistan to civilian life. In 1988 Zia was killed in a plane crash. In elections a few months later the PPP - led by Bhutto's daughter, Benazir - became the largest party, and Benazir Bhutto became the first woman prime minister of an Islamic state. Since 1991 two premiers have been dismissed by the president, partly as a result of a trial of strength between the presidency and the government. Benazir Bhutto was accused of nepotism and corruption and dismissed. Following a general election, won by a coalition led by the Pakistan Muslim League, the new premier, Nawaz Sharif, was also dismissed, but was reinstated by the Supreme Court. At subsequent elections, the PPP was returned to office. The armed forces remain influential behind the scenes and have been supportive in recent reforms designed to root out corruption and tax defaulting.

Sri Lanka

Official name: Sri Lanka Prajatantrika Samajawadi Janarajaya (Democratic Socialist Republic of Sri Lanka). Formerly called Ceylon.

Member of: UN, Commonwealth, SAARC.

Area: 65,610 km² (25,332 sq mi).

Population: 17,616,000 (1993 est).

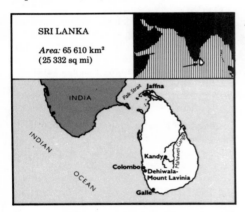

Capital: Colombo 1,459,000 (city 615,000, Dehiwala-Lavinia 191,000, Moratuwa 170,000, Sri Jayawardenepura Kotte - legislative capital and capital designate - 109,000; 1989 est).

Other major cities: Jaffna 143,000, Kandy 102,000, Galle 82,000 (1989 est).

Languages: Sinhala (official; 72%), Tamil (official; 21%), English (official).

Religions: Buddhist (69%), Hindu (15%), Sunni Islam (8%), various Christian Churches (7%; mainly Roman Catholic).

Education: Education is compulsory between the ages of five and 15. In 1990 the literacy rate was 88.4%. There are nine universities.

Defence: The total armed strength in 1993 was 110,800 - 90,000 in the army, 10,000 in the navy and 10,700 in the air force.

Transport: There are 25,952 km (16,130 mi) of roads and 1423 km (884) mi of railways. Colombo, one of the main ports of southern Asia, has an international airport.

Media: There are 15 daily newspapers. There is a single radio service, a state corporation, and two television services (one independent).

GOVERNMENT

The 225-member Parliament is elected for six years under a system of proportional representation by universal adult suffrage. The executive President - who is also directly elected for six years - appoints a Cabinet and a Prime Minister who are responsible to Parliament. The main political parties are the (social democratic) United National Party (UNP), the (socialist) Sri Lanka Freedom Party (SLFP), the (Tamil) Eeelavar Democratic Front (EDF), the (coalition) Tamil United Liberation Front (TULF), the (Buddhist) Mahajana Eksath Peramuna (MEP), the Sri Lankan Muslim Congress (SLMC) and the (Communist) United Socialist Alliance (USA). After the election in February 1989 a UNP government was formed.

Party strength: UNP 125, SLFP 67, EDF 13, TULF 10, SLMC 4, MEP 3, USA 3.

President: (also Minister of Finance, of Defence, of Policy Planning and Implementation and of Buddha Sasana) Dingiri Banda Wijetunga (UNP).

THE CABINET

Prime Minister, Minister of Industries and Minister of Science and Technology: Ranil Wickremasinghe (UNP).

Minister of Agricultural Development and Research: R.M. Dharmadasa Banda (UNP).

Minister of Constitutional and State Affairs: K.N. Choksy (UNP).

Minister of Education and Cultural Affairs: W.J.M. Lokubandara (UNP).

Minister of the Environment and Parliamentary Affairs: Dr Wimal Wickremasinghe (UNP).

Minister of Fisheries and Aquatic Resources: Festus Perera (UNP).

Minister of Food, Co-operatives and Janasaviya: Weerasinghe Mallimarachchi (UNP).

321

Minister of Forestry and Irrigation: Gamini Athukorale (UNP).

Minister of Foreign Affairs: A.C.S. Hameed (UNP).

Minister of Handlooms and Textile Industries: U.B. Wijekoon (UNP).

Minister of Health and Minister of Women's Affairs: Renuka Ranaweera (UNP).

Minister of Home Affairs and Provincial Councils: John Amaratunga (UNP).

Minister of Information and Broadcasting: Tyronne Fernando (UNP).

Minister of Housing and Construction: B. Sirisena Coorey (UNP).

Minister of Justice: Harold Herat (UNP).

Minister of Labour and Vocational Training: M.L.M. Aboosally (UNP).

Minister of Lands: E.P. Paul Perera (UNP).

Minister of the Mahaweli Development: Gamini Dissanayake (UNP).

Minister of Peoplization and Public Enterprises: Joseph Michael Perera (UNP).

Minister of Plantation Industries: Rupa Karunatilleke (UNP).

Minister of Ports and Shipping: Ronnie de Mel (UNP).

Minister of Posts and Telecommunications: A.M.S. Adikari (UNP).

Minister of Public Administration: Alick Aluvihare (UNP).

Minister of Reconstruction, Rehabilitation and Social Welfare: P. Dayaratne (UNP).

Minister of Regional Development: Jayawickrema Perera (UNP).

Minister of Tourism and Rural Industrial Development: S. Thondaman (UNP).

Minister of Transport and Highways: Wijayapala Mendis (UNP).

Minister of Youth Affairs and Sport: C. Nanda Mathew (UNP).

GEOGRAPHY
Central Sri Lanka is occupied by highlands.

Most of the rest of the island consists of forested lowlands, which in the north are flat and fertile. Highest point: Pidurutalagala 2527 m (8292 ft). Principal rivers: Mahaweli Ganga, Kelani Ganga. Climate: The island has a tropical climate modified by the monsoon. Rainfall totals vary between 5000 mm (20 in) in the southwest and 1000 mm (40 in) in the northeast.

ECONOMY
About one half of the labour force is involved in agriculture, growing rice for domestic consumption, and rubber, tea and coconuts for export. Major irrigation and hydroelectric installations on the Mahaweli Ganga River are being constructed. Industries include food processing, cement, textiles and petroleum refining. Tourism is increasingly important.

Currency: Sri Lankan rupee of 100 cents; 1US$ = 49.02 rupees (June 1994).

GDP: US$9,400,000,000 (1992); US$540 per head.

RECENT HISTORY
From 1796 British rule replaced the Dutch in Ceylon, uniting the entire island for the first time. Nationalist feeling grew from the beginning of the 20th century, leading to independence in 1948, and a republican constitution in 1972. The country has been bedevilled by Tamil-Sinhalese ethnic rivalry, which led to major disorders in 1958, 1961 and since 1977. In 1971 a Marxist rebellion was crushed after heavy fighting. Sri Lanka elected the world's first woman Prime Minister, Sirimavo Bandaranaike (1916- ; PM 1960-65 and 1970-77). In the 1980s separatist Tamil guerrillas fought for an independent homeland (Eelam). Fighting between rival Tamil guerrilla groups, Sinhalese extremists and government forces reduced the northeast to near civil war. An Indian 'peace-keeping' force intervened (1987), but this aggravated an already complex situation. Indian forces were completely withdrawn in 1990. The Tamils are scheduled to achieve a degree of autonomy. The Tamil Tigers guerrillas registered as a political party in 1989 but Tamil guerrilla activity continues in the northeast. Tension increased in 1993 following the assassination of President Premasada.

SOUTHEAST ASIA

Brunei, Cambodia, Indonesia, Laos, Malaysia, Philippines, Singapore,
Thailand, Vietnam, Other territories.

Crises in waiting?

During the early 1990s the countries of Southeast Asia have achieved remarkable economic growth rates. However, a number of potential international disputes and internal crises threaten to disturb the region's economic growth. The most important factor in this equation is the rise of China as an economic and military giant. By the year 2000, China, and not Japan, is likely to dominate the East.

China is already an active player in the region and has territorial disputes with several Southeast Asian nations. The most likely scenes of conflict are the Paracel Islands, which are to the east of Vietnam, and the Spratly Islands, between Vietnam and the Philippines. Both island groups, inherited by the Vietnamese from the French, were largely ignored until the prospect of offshore oil and natural gas turned them into desirable properties. In 1974 China invaded and occupied the Paracels. It has also occupied one of the Spratly Islands and built a military base. Vietnam, Malaysia and the Philippines are also active in the islands while Brunei and Taiwan claim the Spratly group. In the late 1980s isolated clashes occurred in the islands and further conflict is possible if China, or any of the other regional players, decides to pursue its claim.

The potential for internal conflicts also casts shadows over the region. In the Philippines rebellions by Communists and by Muslim separatists in the south have never been completely quashed. The Khmer Rouge in Cambodia may have been contained early in 1994 but are not totally defeated. The Vietnamese minority in Cambodia is increasingly restless and the possibility of disputes between Phnom-Penh and Hanoi are growing. Vietnam's territorial argument along the border with China is also never far below the surface.

Unrest, including banditry, remains endemic in the so-called 'Golden Triangle' on the borders of Thailand, Laos and Myanmar (Burma). This is one the principal drug-producing areas in the world. Opium smugglers and related criminal activity are a threat to the stability of all three nations. Piracy, particularly in the South China Sea, is also a very real problem.

As a response to possible external and internal threats the majority of countries in Southeast Asia have increased spending on military equipment. The regional arms race has only added to the tension although the regional economic pact, ASEAN, might become involved in cooperation in defence matters.

The settlement of people from overpopulated Java in other islands of Indonesia has been greatly resented by the original inhabitants. Separatism in Aceh (northern Sumatra) is a long-running problem. In West Irian (Irian Jaya) there is also continuing resistance to integration into Indonesia, but the main threat to national stability, and to Indonesia's international reputation, is East Timor. East Timor was briefly independent in 1975 when Indonesia invaded, claiming to have been invited to intervene, and formally annexed the area. This action has never been recognized internationally, and Timorese resistance has been fierce. A combination of famine and Indonesian military activity has led to the death of over a quarter of a million Timorese. Strong international protests followed the killing of unarmed Timorese demonstrators in 1991.

In Malaysia and Singapore living standards have risen sharply, but have been accompanied by growing demands for more liberal government. In Malaysia there has been tension between the federal government in Kuala Lumpur and the opposition-controlled local government in Sabah. Restrictions and censorship in Singapore have received wide international publicity and their tough attitude towards crime and 'non-conformism' has attracted condemnation. Laos is gradually opening up to Western trade but the Communist government could collapse as economic and political pressure increase. The resulting confusion and instability could provoke Vietnamese intervention in the affairs of a neighbour once more.

ASEAN may be the best hope for avoiding conflict in the region even though there is little precedent for cooperation between the states of Southeast Asia. However, there are some doubts that members are willing to put regional interests before national concerns. Unless the Southeast Asian nations agree to cooperate to prevent or contain local conflicts it seems likely that China may impose its own solutions.

Regional Organizations of Southeast Asia

ASSOCIATION OF SOUTH EAST ASIAN NATIONS (ASEAN)

The Association of South East Asian Nations was founded in Bangkok, Thailand, in 1967. It aims to accelerate the economic, social and cultural development of members, to maintain stability in the region, and to encourage co-operation between members.

Secretary General: Rusli Noor (Indonesia).

Membership: Brunei, Indonesia, Malaysia, the Philippines, Singapore and Thailand.

ASSOCIATION OF SOUTH EAST ASIAN NATIONS REGIONAL FORUM (ARF)

Founded in Manila, the Philippines, in 1994 ARF is a conference, without a formal organization, that brings together the main economic and military powers of the Far East and Southeast Asia.

Headquarters: Djakarta, Indonesia.

Membership: Australia, Brunei, Cambodia, China, Indonesia, Japan, South Korea, Laos, Malaysia, New Zealand, Papua New Guinea, the Philippines, Russia, Singapore, Thailand, the United States of America, and Vietnam. The EU also has membership as an organization rather than membership for each country of the Union.

OTHER ORGANIZATIONS

The following countries in Southeast Asia are members of the Commonwealth: Brunei, Malaysia and Singapore.

Southeast Asian Trade

Brunei Imports ($ million): 883 (1989). Exports ($ million): 1894 (1989). Main imports: machinery and transport equipment 38.0% (1986), manufactured goods 21.1% (1986). Main exports: natural gas 52.9% (1986), crude oil 40.6% (1986). Principal trading partners: Japan, Thailand, South Korea, USA.

Cambodia Imports ($ million): 118 (1985 est). Exports ($ million): 12 (1985 est). Main imports: machinery and transport equipment 36.9% (1985), petroleum and petroleum products 30.2% (1985). Main exports: rubber 82.9% (1985), basic manufactures 5.1% (1985). Principal trading partners: Thailand, Singapore.

Indonesia Imports ($ million): 25,869 (1991). Exports ($ million): 29,142 (1991). Main imports: machinery and transport equipment 44.8% (1991), chemical and related products 13% (1991). Main exports: crude petroleum and petroleum products 42.5% (1991), natural and manufactured gas 14.3% (1991). Principal trading partners: Japan, USA, Singapore, Germany.

Laos Imports ($ million): 162 (1988). Exports ($ million): 81 (1988). Main imports: machinery and transport equipment. Main exports: wood 47.6 (1988), electricity 17.5 (1988). Principal trading partners: Thailand, Japan, China.

Malaysia Imports ($ million): 36,699 (1991). Exports ($ million): 34,375 (1991). Main imports: machinery and transport equipment 53.9% (1991), basic manufactures 15.8% (1991). Main exports: thermionic valves and tubes 15.0% (1989), machinery and transport equipment 41% (1991), crude petroleum 10.7% (1989). Principal trading partners: Japan, Singapore, USA, UK, Germany.

Philippines Imports ($ million): 13,042 (1990). Exports ($ million): 8186 (1990). Main imports: petroleum and petroleum products 14.3% (1990), iron and steel 4.6% (1990). Main exports: electrical machinery and parts 7.8% (1990), clothing 8.3% (1990). Principal trading partners: USA, Japan, Taiwan, Germany.

Singapore Imports (S$ million): 114,194.9 (1991). Exports (S$ million): 101,879.5 (1991). Main imports: machinery and transport equipment 46.7 (1991), petroleum and petroleum products 14% (1991). Main exports: office machines 24% (1991), petroleum products 13.9% (1991). Principal trading partners: USA, Japan, Malaysia, Thailand, Hong Kong.

Thailand Imports ($ million): 33,379 (1990). Exports ($ million): 23,068 (1990). Main imports: electrical power equipment and machinery 31.2% (1990), transport equipment 10.2% (1990). Main exports: electrical power equipment and machinery 21.1% (1990), textiles and apparel 12.1% (1990). Principal trading partners: USA, Japan, Singapore, Germany.

Vietnam Imports ($ million): 3050 (1989). Exports ($ million): 1502 (1989). *Main imports*: fuel and raw materials 44.7% (1985), machinery 23.2% (1985). Main exports: raw materials 46.0% (1985), handicrafts 24.1% (1985). Principal trading partners: Singapore, Japan, Hong Kong, France.

Brunei

Official name: Negara Brunei Darussalam (Sultanate of Brunei).

Member of: UN, Commonwealth, ASEAN.

Area: 5765 km² (2226 sq mi).

Population: 264,000 (1991 est)

Capital: Bandar Seri Begawan (formerly Brunei Town) 52,000 (1988 est).

Other main towns: Seria 23,400, Kuala Belait 19,300 (1988 est).

Languages: Malay (official; over 50%), Chinese (mainly Hokkien dialect; 26%), English.

Religions: Sunni Islam (official; over 50%), Buddhist (12%), various Christian Churches (9%).

Education: Primary and secondary education are free and are practically universal, but are not compulsory. The literacy rate was estimated to be 86.8% in 1990. There is a single university but many Bruneians attend tertiary courses at universities abroad.

Defence: In 1993 the total armed strength was 4450 - 3600 in the army, 550 in the navy and 300 in the air force.

Transport: There are 2250 km (1406 mi) of roads. Brunei has no public railways although there are 19 km (12 mi) of freight light railways. Muara, which is 27 km (17 mi) north of Bandar Seri Begawan, is the main commercial shipping port. There is an international airport near Bandar Seri Begawan.

Media: There is a daily English-language paper and a weekly Malay paper. The state-run broadcasting service runs two radio networks (one in Malay; the other in English and Chinese) and a television network (in Malay and English).

GOVERNMENT

The Sultan, a hereditary monarch, rules by decree, assisted by a Council of Ministers whom he appoints. The constitution granted in 1959 has been largely in abeyance since 1962. There are no political parties.

Sultan: HM Haji Hassanal Bolkiah, Sultan of Brunei (succeeded upon the abdication of his father, 5 October 1967).

Prime Minister: The Sultan.

GEOGRAPHY

Brunei consists of two coastal enclaves. The (larger) western part is hilly; the eastern enclave is more mountainous and forested. Highest point: Bukit Pagon (on the border with Malaysia) 1850 m (6070 ft). Principal river: Brunei River. Climate: Brunei has a tropical monsoon climate with rainfall totals in excess of 2500 mm (100 in).

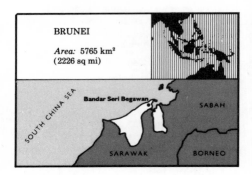

BRUNEI

Area: 5765 km² (2226 sq mi)

SOUTH CHINA SEA

Bandar Seri Begawan

SABAH

SARAWAK

BORNEO

ECONOMY

The economy is dominated by exploitation of substantial deposits of petroleum and natural gas. Much of Brunei's private commercial sector is controlled by the state's Chinese population. Most of the country's food has to be imported.

Currency: Brunei dollar (or ringit; BND) of 100 cents; 1US$ = 1.54 BND (May 1994).

GDP: US$3,302,000,000 (1990 est); US$13,290 per head.

RECENT HISTORY

By the 19th century the sultans of Brunei ruled a fraction of their former territory. The British restored order to what had become a pirates' paradise and established a protectorate from 1888 to 1971. Oil was discovered in 1929. During World War II Brunei was under Japanese occupation from 1941 to 1945. A rebellion in 1962 was partly sparked by the prospect of Brunei of joining the new federation of Malaysia. Full independence was restored in 1984 under the absolute rule of Sultan Hassanal Bolkiah, allegedly the world's richest man. All political parties were banned in 1988.

Cambodia

Official name: Roat Kampuchea (The State of Cambodia) - previously known as the Khmer Republic and Kampuchea.

Member of: UN.

Area: 181,035 km² (69,898 sq mi).

Population: 9,280,000 (1993 est).

Capital: Phnom-Penh 900,000 (1991 est).

Other major cities: Battambang (Batdambang) 45,000, Kampong Cham 32,000 (1987 est).

Languages: Khmer (official), French, Vietnamese and Chinese minorities.

Religion: Buddhist (official; majority), small Roman Catholic minority.

Education: Education is compulsory, in theory, between the ages of five and 14. In 1991 the literacy rate was estimated to be 87.5%. There is a single university.

Defence: In 1993 the total armed strength was estimated to be 103,000 (excluding various local militias and paramilitary forces) - 50,500 in the army, 50,500 in provincial forces, 1000 in the navy, and 1000 in the army. Military service is selective and varies in length.

Transport: The infrastructure of Cambodia was severely damaged by civil war. There are 14,800 km (9200 mi) of roads and 649 km (403 mi) of (intermittently working) railways. Kompong Som is the main seaport. Inland navigation - on the River Mekong and on the Tonle Sap (Great Lake) - are important and Phnom-Penh is a river port. Phnom-Penh has an international airport.

Media: The press was reestablished in 1993-94 and several daily newspapers have reappeared and new titles have been founded. There is a state-run radio and television service.

GOVERNMENT

Internationally supervised multi-party elections were held in May 1993 for a 123-member National Assembly, which is drafting a new constitution. The monarchy was restored in May 1993. The King appoints a Prime Minister who enjoys a majority in the Assembly. The Prime Minister, in turn, appoints a Council of Ministers. For local government administration there are 23 provinces. The main political parties are the (monarchist) United National Front for an Independent, Neutral, Peaceful and Co-operative Cambodia (FUNCINPEC), the (left-wing) National Liberation Front of Kampuchea (KPNLF), the (former Communist) Cambodian People's Party (CPP), and the (Buddhist) Liberal Democratic Party (PLD). The (Khmer Rouge) Party of Democratic Kampuchea refused to participate in the elections in 1993 and was banned in July 1994. After the election held in May 1993 a coalition FUNCINPEC-CPP government of national unity was formed.

Party strength: FUNCINPEC 58, CPP 51, LDP 10, KPNLF 1.

King: HM King Norodom Sihanouk (who was restored to the throne on 24 September 1993, having abdicated on 2 March 1955. He originally came to the throne on 16 April 1941).

THE CABINET
includes

First Prime Minister and Co-Minister of Defence and Public Security: HRH Prince Norodom Ranariddh (FUNCINPEC).

Second Prime Minister: Hun Sen (CPP).

Deputy Prime Minister and Minister for Foreign Affairs and International Administration: N. Sereivut (FUNCINPEC).

Deputy Prime Minister and Minister of the Interior: Sar Kheng (CPP).

State Minister and Minister of Economic Affairs and for Finance: Sam Rangsi.

Minister of National Defence: Gen. Tea Banh (CPP).

GEOGRAPHY

Central Cambodia consists of fertile plains in the Mekong River valley and surrounding the Tonle Sap (Great Lake). To the north and east are plateaux covered by forests and savannah. The southern Phnom Kravanh mountains run parallel to the coast. Highest point: Phnum Aoral 1813 m (5947 ft). Principal river: Mekong. Climate: Cambodia is tropical and humid. The monsoon season (June-November) brings heavy rain to the whole country, with annual totals as high as 5000 mm (200 in) in the mountains.

ECONOMY

Invasion, civil wars, massacres of the civilian population (1976-79) and the (temporary) abolition of currency (in 1978) all but destroyed the economy. Aided by the Vietnamese since 1979, agriculture and - to a lesser extent - industry have been slowly rebuilt, but Cambodia remains one of the world's poorest nations. Rice yields - formerly exported - still fall short of Cambodia's own basic needs. The infrastructure was slowly reconstructed in the early 1990s, but the country is still not attracting nearly enough investment owing to its continuing instability and the activities of the Khmer Rouge. Chronic inflation hinders recovery.

Currency: Riel of 100 sen; 1US$ = 2498.7 riels (June 1994).

GDP: US$930,000,000 (1991); US$130 per head.

RECENT HISTORY

A French protectorate was established in 1863 and continued, apart from a period of Japanese occupation during World War II, until independence was regained in 1953. Throughout the colonial period, Cambodia's monarchy remained in nominal control. In 1955, King Norodom Sihanouk abdicated to lead a broad coalition government, but he could not prevent Cambodia's involvement in the Vietnam War or allay US fears of his sympathies for the Communists. A republic was declared when he was overthrown in 1968. A pro-US military coup toppled the government in 1970. The military regime was attacked by Communist Khmer Rouge guerrillas, who sought to create a self-sufficient workers' utopia. The Khmer Rouge were finally victorious in 1975. Under Pol Pot, they forcibly evacuated the towns and massacred up to 2,000,000 of their compatriots. In 1978 Vietnam - Cambodia's traditional foe - invaded, overthrowing the Khmer Rouge. After Vietnamese troops withdrew in 1989, resistance forces of the exiled tripartite coalition government - led by Prince Sihanouk and including the Khmer Rouge - became active in much of western and southern Cambodia. In 1991 the country's warring factions agreed a peace plan that included free elections and UN supervision, and the reduction of all Cambodian forces. A large UN peace keeping force was deployed in 1992 and UN participation in the administration of Cambodia was agreed. Sovereignty was temporarily vested in the hands of a 12-member Supreme National Council, which originally included the Khmer Rouge. The membership of the Council was reduced to 10 when the Khmer Rouge withdrew. The Council was a unique example of the United Nations assuming responsibilities in the internal affairs of a sovereign country. The UN operation was backed by a multinational force, largely drawn from Asian and Pacific countries, and, when multi-party elections were held and a new government was formed, the operation was considered to be an important success for the world body and an encouraging sign of a 'new world order'. However, violence resumed when the Khmer Rouge effectively withdrew from the peace plan and refused to take part in multi-party elections in May 1993. A government of national unity - led by Prince Norodom Ranariddh, the son of Prince Norodom Sihanouk, and by Hun Sen, the former Communist ruler of Cambodia - took office. In September 1993 Prince Norodom Sihanouk was restored as King of Cambodia. UN forces gradually withdrew after the end of 1993, but unrest and instability persists. The Khmer Rouge received major setbacks in 1994 but rebounded to take control of several parts of the country and, having proclaimed a secessionist regime, were officially banned. An attempted coup in 1994 by Prince Norodom Chakrapong, a rival of his half-brother Prince Norodom Ranariddh, illustrates the country's deteriorating security situation. The rival militias that fought two decades of civil wars remain armed, and law and order has broken down in much of the country.

CAMBODIA

Area: 181 035 km² (69 898 sq mi)

THAILAND

LAOS

Mekong

VIETNAM

Phnom-Penh

SOUTH CHINA SEA

Gulf of Thailand

Indonesia

Official name: Republik Indonesia (Republic of Indonesia).

Member of: UN, OPEC, ASEAN.

Area: 1,919,443 km² (741,101 sq mi) - including East Timor which has an area of 14,874 km² (5743 sq mi), or 1,904,569 km² (735,358 sq mi) excluding East Timor (see p. 342).

Population: 188,216,000 (1993 est).

Capital: Jakarta 7,836,000 (including suburbs; 1990 est).

Other major cities: Surabaya 2,421,000, Bandung 2,027,000, Medan 1,686,000, Semarang 1,005,000, Palembang 874,000, Ujung Pandang (Makassar) 842,000 (all including suburbs; 1985 est).

Languages: Bahasa Indonesia (official), Javanese (34%), Madurese (6%), Sundanese (14%) and about 25 other main languages.

Religions: Sunni Islam (80%), Roman Catholic (3%), other Christians (7%), Hindu (2%).

Education: Education is compulsory, in theory, between the ages of six and 13. In 1990 the literacy rate was 77%. There are 35 state universities and 26 private universities.

Defence: In 1992 the total armed strength was 283,000 - 215,000 in the army, 44,000 in the navy and 24,000 in the air force. There is also a 180,000-member paramilitary police; there are 1,500,000 trainees in the KAMRA (People's Security). Selective military service lasts for two years.

Transport: There are 266,326 km (165,523 mi) of roads and 6583 km ((4090 mi) of railways. The main ports are Tanjung Priok (Jakarta), Tanjung Perak (Surabaya) and Belawan (Medan). There are seven international airports of which the most important are Jakarta, Bali, Medan and Surabaya.

Media: There are over 35 daily newspapers, most of which are published in Jakarta. There is a state-controlled radio service. There are three television services - one state-controlled and two commercial.

GOVERNMENT

Every five years elections are held by universal adult suffrage for 400 members of the House of Representatives; the remaining 100 members are chosen by the President. The People's Consultative Assembly - which consists of the members of the House plus 500 representatives of provincial governments, occupational and special interests - meets once every five years to oversee broad principles of state policy and to elect the President, who appoints a Cabinet. Indonesia is divided into 23 provinces (24, if East Timor is included), a metropolitan district (Jakarta) and two special autonomous districts (see below). The main political parties are (the government alliance) Golkar, the (Islamic) United Development Party (PPP), and the (mainly Christian and nationalist) Indonesian Democratic Party (PDI). After the election held in June 1992 Golkar retained power.

Party strength: Golkar 281, PPP 63, PDI 56.

President: Gen. T.N.I. Suharto (Golkar).

THE CABINET

includes the following (who are all members of Golkar):

Minister of Agriculture: Syarifuddin Baharsjah.

Minister of Communications: Haryanto Dhanutirto.

Minister of Co-operatives and Small-Scale Enterprises: Subiakto Tjakrawerdaja.

Minister of Defence and Security: Gen. Edi Sudradjat.

Minister of Education and Culture: Wardiman Djojonegoro.

Minister of Finance: Mar'ie Mohammad.

Minister of Foreign Affairs: Ali Alatas.

Minister of Forestry: Djamaloedin Soeryohadi Koesoemo.

Minister of Health: Suyudi.

Minister of Home Affairs: Yogie S. Memet.

Minister of Industry: T. Ariwibowo.

Minister of Information: Harmoko.

Minister of Justice: Oetojo Oesman.

Minister of Manpower: Abdul Latief.

Minister of Mining and Energy: I.B. Sudjana.

Minister of Public Works: Radinal Mochtar.

Minister of Religious Affairs: Tarmizi Tahir.

Minister/Secretary of State: Moerdiono.

Minister/Secretary of the Cabinet: Saadilah Mursjid.

Minister of Social Affairs: Endang Kusuma Inten Soeweno.

Minister of Tourism, Posts and Telecommunication: Yoop Ave.

Minister of Trade: Satrio Budiardjo Yudono.

Minister of Transmigration and Human Settlement: Siswondo Yudohusodo.

Minister of State for National Development Planning: Ginandjar Kartasasmita.

Minister of State for Foods: Ibrahim Hasan.

Minister of State for Research and Technology: B.J. Habibie.

Minster of State for Population Affairs: Haryono Suyono.

Minister of State for Investment: Sanyoto Sastrowardoyo.

Minister of State for Agrarian Reform: Soni Harsono.

Minister of State for Public Housing: Akbar Tanjung.

Minister of State for the Environment: Sarwono Kusumaatmadja.

Minister of State for the Role of Women: Mien Sughand.

Minister of State for Youth Affairs and Sport: Hayono Isman.

Minister of State for Administrative Reforms: T.B. Silalahi.

Attorney General: Singgih.

AUTONOMOUS DISTRICTS
Population figures are from the 1990 census.

Aceh Area: 55,392 km² (21,387 sq mi). Population: 3,416,000. Capital: Banda Aceh.

Yogyakarta Area: 3169 km² (1224 sq mi). Population: 2,913,000. Capital: Yogyakarta.

PROVINCES
Bali Area: 5561 km² (2147 sq mi). Population: 2,778,000. Capital: Denpasar.

Bengkulu Area: 21,168 km² (8173 sq mi). Population: 1,179,000. Capital: Bengkulu.

Irian Jaya Area: 421,981 km² (162,928 sq mi). Population: 1,649,000. Capital: Jayapura.

Jakarta Raya Area: 590 km² (228 sq mi). Population: 8,259,000. Capital: Jakarta.

Jambi Area: 44,800 km² (17,297 sq mi). Population: 2,021,000. Capital: Jambi.

Jawa Barat Area: 46,300 km² (17,877 sq mi). Population: 35,384,000. Capital: Bandung.

Jawa Tengah Area: 34,206 km² (13,207 sq mi). Population: 28,521,000. Capital: Semarang.

Jawa Timur Area: 47,921 km² (18,502 sq mi). Population: 32,504,000. Capital: Surabaya.

Kalimantan Barat Area: 146,760 km² (56,664 sq mi). Population: 3,229,000. Capital: Pontianak.

Kalimantan Selatan Area: 37,660 km² (14,541 sq mi). Population: 2,598,000. Capital: Banjarmasin.

Kalimantan Tengah Area: 152,600 km² (58,919 sq mi). Population: 1,396,000. Capital: Palangkaraya.

Kalimantan Timur Area: 202,440 km² (78,162 sq mi). Population: 1,877,000. Capital: Samarinda.

Lampung Area: 33,307 km² (12,860 sq mi). Population: 6,018,000. Capital: Tanjung Karang.

Maluku Area: 74,505 km² (28,767 sq mi). Population: 1,858,000. Capital: Ambon.

Nusa Tenggara Barat Area: 20,177 km² (7790

sq mi). Population: 3,370,000. Capital: Mataram.

Nusa Tenggara Timur Area: 47,876 km² (18,485 sq mi). Population: 3,269,000. Capital: Kupang.

Riau Area: 94,561 km² (36,510 sq mi). Population: 3,304,000. Capital: Pakanbaru.

Sulawesi Selatan Area: 72,781 km² (28,101 sq mi). Population: 6,982,000. Capital: Ujung Padang.

Sulawesi Tengah Area: 69,726 km² (26,921 sq mi). Population: 1,711,000. Capital: Palu.

Sulawesi Tenggara Area: 27,686 km² (10,690 sq mi). Population: 1,350,000. Capital: Kendari.

Sulawesi Utara Area: 19,023 km² (7345 sq mi). Population: 2,478,000. Capital: Menado.

Sumatera Barat Area: 49,778 km² (19,219 sq mi). Population: 4,000,000. Capital: Padang.

Sumatera Selatan Area: 103,688 km² (40,034 sq mi). Population: 6,313,000. Capital: Palembang.

Sumatera Utara Area: 70,787 km² (27,331 sq mi). Population: 10,256,000. Capital: Medan.

GEOGRAPHY

Indonesia consists of nearly 3700 islands, of which about 3000 are inhabited. The southern chain of mountainous, volcanic islands comprises Sumatra, Java with Madura, Bali, and the Lesser Sunda Islands (including Lombok, Flores and Timor). Java and its smaller neighbour Madura are fertile and densely populated, containing nearly two thirds of Indonesia's people. The northern chain comprises Kalimantan (the Indonesian sector of Borneo), the irregular mountainous island of Sulawesi (Celebes), the Moluccas group, and Irian Jaya (the western half of New Guinea). Over two thirds of the country is covered by tropical rain forests. Highest point: Ngga Pulu (Carstenz Pyramid) 5030 m (16,503 ft) (on Irian Jaya). Principal rivers: Kapuas, Digul, Barito. Climate: The climate is tropical with heavy rainfall throughout the year.

ECONOMY

Indonesia has great mineral wealth - petroleum, natural gas, tin, nickel, coal, bauxite and copper - but is relatively poor because of its great population. Over 50% of Indonesians are subsistence farmers with rice being the major crop, but both estate and peasant farmers produce important quantities of rubber, tea, coffee, tobacco and spices for export. Industry is largely concerned with processing mineral and agricultural products. Indonesia achieved high economic growth rates throughout the 1980s and early 1990s, and has become one of the emerging economic powers of Asia.

Currency: Rupiah of 100 sen; 1US$ = 49.23 rupiahs.

GDP: US$156,000,000,000 (1993 est); US$803 per head.

RECENT HISTORY

From the 17th century, the East Indies became the major and most profitable part of the Dutch Empire. The Netherlands retained control until 1942 when the Japanese invaded and were welcomed by most Indonesians as liberators from colonial rule. Upon Japan's surrender in 1945, Achmed Sukarno (1901-70) - the founder of the nationalist party in 1927 - declared the Dutch East Indies to be the independent republic of Indonesia. Under international pressure, the Dutch accepted Indonesian independence (1949) after four years of intermittent but brutal fighting. Sukarno's rule became increasingly authoritarian and the country sank into economic chaos. In 1962 he seized Netherlands New Guinea, which was formally annexed as Irian Jaya in 1969, although a separatist movement persists. Between 1963 and 1966 Sukarno tried to destabilize the newly-created Federation of Malaysia by armed incursions into north Borneo. General T.N.I. Suharto's suppression of a Communist uprising in 1965-66 enabled him to reverse Sukarno's anti-Americanism and eventually to displace him with both student and army support. Around 80,000 members of the Communist Party were killed in this period. The annexation of Portuguese East Timor by Indonesia in 1976 is unrecognized by the international community, and guerrilla action by local nationalists continues. International protests followed the killing of unarmed Timorese demonstrators by Indonesian troops in 1991. An ambitious programme of resettlement has been attempted to relieve overcrowded Java, but the Javanese settlers have been resented in the outlying, underdeveloped islands.

Laos

Official name: Saathiaranagroat Prachhathippatay Prachhachhon Lao (The Lao People's Democratic Republic).

Member of: UN.

Area: 236,800 km² (91,400 sq mi).

Population: 4,533,000 (1993 est).

Capital: Vientiane (Viengchane) 442,000 (1990 est).

Other major cities: Savannakhet 97,000, Luang Prabang (Louangphrabang) 68,000, Pakse 47,000 (1985 est).

Language: Lao (official; 96%).

Religions: Buddhism (57%), various traditional local religions (over 30%).

Education: Education is compulsory between the ages of seven and 15. In 1985 the literacy rate was estimated to be 83.9%. There is a university and eight other institutions that offer degree level courses.

Defence: In 1992 the total armed strength was 37,000, of whom 33,000 were in the army. Military service of 18 months is compulsory.

Transport: There are 14,093 km (8757 mi) of roads. Inland navigation on the Mekong River is important. Vientiane has an international airport.

Media: The media are state-run. There are three daily newspapers, a radio service and two television channels.

GOVERNMENT
Effective power is exercised by the Central Committee of the (Communist) Lao People's Revolutionary Party. Pending the implementation of a new constitution, representatives of directly elected local authorities have met as the National Congress to appoint the President, the Prime Minister and the Council of Ministers. There is constitutional provision for a 79-member Supreme People's Assembly to be elected for five years by universal adult suffrage.

President: Nouhak Phoumsavan.

Prime Minister: Khamtay Siphandone.

GEOGRAPHY
Except for the Plain of Jars in the north and the Mekong Valley and low plateaux in the south, Laos is largely mountainous. Highest point: Phou Bia 2820 m (9252 ft). Principal river: Mekong. Climate: Laos has a tropical climate with heavy monsoon rains between May and October.

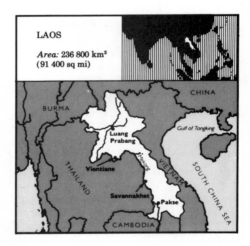

ECONOMY
War, floods and drought have retarded the development of Laos, one of the poorest countries in the world. The majority of Laotians work on collective farms, mainly growing rice. Since 1990, the Laotian government has attempted to encourage Western investment.

Currency: Kip; 1US$ = 719.53 kips (June 1994).

GDP: US$965,000,000 (1991); US$230 per head.

RECENT HISTORY
A French protectorate was established in 1893. Japanese occupation in World War II led to a declaration of independence, which the French finally accepted in 1954. However, the kingdom was wracked by civil war, with royalist forces fighting the Communist Pathet Lao. The Viet Cong used Laos as a supply route in the Vietnam War, and US withdrawal from Vietnam allowed the Pathet Lao to take over Laos (1975). Since 1990, the government has begun to introduce reforms, but there is no suggestion that a multi-party system will be tolerated.

Malaysia

Official name: Persekutuan Tanah Melaysiu (The Federation of Malaysia).

Member of: UN, Commonwealth, ASEAN.

Area: 329,758 km² (127,320 sq mi).

Population: 19,077,000 (1993 est).

Capital: Kuala Lumpur 1,233,000 (including suburbs; 1991 census).

Other major cities: Ipoh 390,000, George Town 325,000, Johor Baharu 325,000, Petaling Jaya 270,000, Kelang (Klang) 250,000, Kuala Trengganu (Kuala Terengganu) 235,000, Kota Baharu 220,000, Taiping 190,000, Seramban 175,000, Kuantan 170,000, Kota Kinabalu 140,000, Malacca (Melaka) 115,000 (1990 est).

Languages: Bahasa Malaysia (Malay; official; over 58%), English, Chinese (32%), Tamil.

Religions: Sunni Islam (official; over 55%), with Buddhist, Daoist and various Christian minorities.

Education: Education is freely available between the ages of six and 18 but is not compulsory. In 1990 the literacy rate was 78.4%. There are seven universities.

Defence: In 1992 the total armed strength was 127,500 - 105,000 in the army, 10,500 in the navy and 12,000 in the air force. There is no military service.

Transport: There are 52,500 km (32,622 mi) of roads and 2222 km (1381 mi) of railways. The main port is Klang; other ports include Penang, Johore and Kota Kinabalu. Kuala Lumpur has an international airport.

Media: There are 35 daily newspapers, published in Bahasa Malaysia, English, Tamil and Chinese. State corporations provide six radio and two television networks. There is a subscription radio and a commercial television channel.

GOVERNMENT

The Yang di-Pertuan Agong (the King of Malaysia) holds office for five years. He is elected - from their own number - by the hereditary sultans who reign in 9 of the 13 states. The 70-member Senate (upper house) comprises 40 members appointed by the King and two members elected by each of the state and territorial assemblies for a three-year term. The 180-member House of Representatives is elected by universal adult suffrage for five years. The King appoints a Prime Minister and a Cabinet commanding a majority in the House, to which they are responsible. The main political parties include the Barisan Nasional (National Front - a coalition of parties including the United Malays National Organization; BN), the (democratic socialist) Democratic Action Party (DAP), the Spirit of '46 Party (S46), and the Sabah United Party (PBS). After the election held in October 1990 a BN government retained power.

Party strength: BN 127, DAP 20, PBS 14, S46 8, others 7, ind 4.

King of Malaysia: HM Ja'afar ibni Al-Marhum, Sultan of Negeri Sembilan, inaugurated 26 April 1994.

Prime Minister: Prime Minister and Minister of Home Affairs: Dato' Dr Mohamad Mahathir (BN).

MALAYSIAN STATES AND TERRITORIES

Population figures are from the 1991 census.

Johore (Johor) (sultanate) Area: 18,985 km² (7330 sq mi). Population: 2,107,000. Capital: Johor Baharu.

Kedah (sultanate) Area: 9425 km² (3639 sq mi). Population: 1,413,000. Capital: Alor Star (Alur Setar).

Kelantan (sultanate) Area: 14,931 km² (5765 sq mi). Population: 1,220,000. Capital: Kota Baharu.

Malacca Area: 1650 km² (637 sq mi). Population: 584,000. Capital: Malacca.

Negeri Sembilan (sultanate) Area: 6643 km² (2565 sq mi). Population: 724,000. Capital: Seremban.

Pahang (sultanate) Area: 35,965 km² (13,886 sq mi). Population: 1,055,000. Capital: Kuantan.

Penang (Pinang) Area: 1033 km² (399 sq mi). Population: 1,142,000. Capital: George Town.

Perak (sultanate) Area: 21,005 km² (8110 sq mi). Population: 2,220,000. Capital: Ipoh.

Perlis (sultanate) Area: 795 km² (307 sq mi). Population: 188,000. Capital: Kangar.

Sabah Area: 80,429 km² (29,353 sq mi). Population: 1,470,000. Capital: Kota Kinabalu.

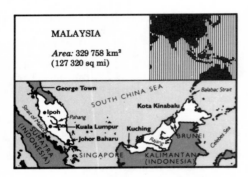

MALAYSIA

Area: 329 758 km²
(127 320 sq mi)

Sarawak Area: 121,449 km² (48,250 sq mi). Population: 1,669,000. Capital: Kuching.

Selangor (sultanate) Area: 7962 km² (3074 sq mi). Population: 1,978,000. Capital: Shah Alam.

Trengganu (Terengganu) (sultanate) Area: 12,955 km² (5002 sq mi). Population: 752,000. Capital: Kuala Trengganu.

Federal Territory Area: 243 km² (94 sq mi). Population: 1,233,000. Capital: Kuala Lumpur.

Labuan (territory) Area: 91 km² (35 sq mi). Population: 26,000. Capital: Victoria.

GEOGRAPHY
Western (peninsular) Malaysia comprises mountain ranges - including the Trengganu Highlands and Cameron Highlands - running north to south and bordered by densely populated coastal lowlands. Tropical rainforest covers the hills and mountains of Eastern Malaysia - Sabah and Sarawak, the north of Borneo. Highest point: Kinabalu (in Sabah) 4101 m (13,455 ft). Principal rivers: Pahang, Kelantan. Climate: Malaysia has a tropical climate with heavy rainfall (up to 2500 mm/100 in in the west). There is more seasonal variation in precipitation than temperature, with the northeast monsoon (from October to February) and the southwest monsoon (from May to September) bringing increased rainfall, particularly to peninsular Malaysia.

ECONOMY
Rubber, petroleum and tin are the traditional mainstays of the economy, but all three suffered drops in price on the world market in the 1980s. Pepper (from Sarawak), cocoa and timber are also important. Over one quarter of the labour force farms, with large numbers of Malays growing rice as a subsistence crop.

Manufacturing industry is now the largest exporter; major industries include rubber, tin, timber, textiles, machinery and cement. The government has greatly encouraged industrialization, investment and a more active role for the Malay population in industry, which, along with commerce and finance, has been largely the preserve of Chinese Malaysians. Malaysia has experienced high economic growth rates since the early 1980s. A growing tourist industry is being promoted.

Currency: Ringgit of 100 sen; 1US$ = 2.59 ringgits (June 1994).

GDP: US$73,000,000,000 (1993 est); US$3713 per head.

RECENT HISTORY
Malaysia's ethnic diversity reflects its complex history and the lure of its natural wealth and prime trading position. The British established themselves on the island of Penang in 1786, founded Singapore in 1819, and in 1867 established an administration for the Straits Settlements - Malacca, Penang and Singapore. Ignoring Thai claims to overlordship in the peninsula, the British took over the small sultanates as protected states. The British suppressed piracy, developed tin mining with Chinese labour and rubber plantations with Indian workers. Sarawak became a separate state under Sir James Brooke - the 'White Raja' - and his family from 1841, and was ceded to the British Crown in 1946. Sabah became British - as British North Borneo - from 1881. The Japanese occupied the whole of Malaysia during World War II. A Federation of Malaya - the peninsula - was established in 1948, but was threatened by Communist insurgency until 1960. Malaya became independent in 1957 with a constitution protecting the interests of the Malays, who were fearful of the energy and acumen of the Chinese. Sabah, Sarawak and Singapore joined the Federation - renamed Malaysia - in 1963. Singapore left in 1965, but the unity of the Federation was maintained, with British armed support, in the face of an Indonesian 'confrontation' in Borneo (1965-66). Tension between Chinese and Malays led to riots and the suspension of parliamentary government (1969-71), but scarcely hindered the rapid development of a resource-rich economy. During the 1980s and early 1990s, the growth of Islamic fundamentalism led to a defensive re-assertion of Islamic values and practices among the Muslim Malay ruling elite.

The Philippines

Official name: República ñg Pilipinas (Republic of the Philippines).

Member of: UN, ASEAN.

Area: 300,000 km² (115,831 sq mi).

Population: 64,955,000 (1993 est).

Capital: Manila 7,832,000 (city 1,599,000; Quezon City 1,667,000, Caloocan City 761,000, Pasay City 367,000 (1990 census).

Other major cities: Davao City 850,000, Cebu City 610,000, Zamboango City 442,000, Bacolod City 364,000 (1990 census).

Languages: Filipino (based on Tagalog; national; 55%), Tagalog (over 20%), Cebuano (24%), Ilocano (11%), English, Spanish.

Religions: Roman Catholic (84%), Aglipayan Church (4%), Sunni Islam (5%).

Education: Education is compulsory between the ages of seven and 13. In 1990 the literacy rate was over 90%. There are 55 universities.

Defence: In 1992 the total armed strength was 117,000 - 68,000 in the army, 23,000 in the navy, 15,600 in the air force.

Transport: There are 160,633 km (99,813 mi) of roads and 1059 km (658 mi) of railways. Manila has a rapid light transit system. Manila and Cebu City, the main ports, have international airports.

Media: There are 30 daily newspapers, published in Filipino, English and Chinese. There are over 270 radio stations and five principal television networks (with over 25 stations).

GOVERNMENT

The President and the 24-member Senate - the upper House of Congress - are elected by universal adult suffrage for six years. The House of Representatives - the lower House of Congress - comprises 201 directly elected members (plus up to 50 appointed members). The President appoints a Cabinet. Part of Mindanao island and the Sulu Archipelago form an autonomous region (see below). Political parties include the Liberal Party (LP), the (right-wing) National People's Coalition (NPC), the National Union of Christian Democrats (NUCD), and the Democratic Filipino Struggle (DFS). After the election held in May 1992 a non-party government took office.

Party strength: DFS 87, NUCD 51, NPC 48, LP 15.

President: Fidel Ramos (ind).

THE CABINET

Executive Secretary: Teofisto T. Guingona Jr.

Cabinet Secretary for Agrarian Reform: Ernesto G. Garilao.

Cabinet Secretary for Agriculture: Roberto S. Sebastian.

Cabinet Secretary for the Budget and Management: Salvador M. Enriquez II.

Cabinet Secretary for Education, Culture and Sports: Ricardo T. Gloria.

Cabinet Secretary for Energy: Delfin L. Lazaro.

Cabinet Secretary for the Environment and Natural Resources: Angel C. Alcala.

Cabinet Secretary for Finance: Roberto de Ocampo.

Cabinet Secretary for Foreign Affairs: Roberto R. Romulo.

Cabinet Secretary for Health: Juan M. Flavier.

Cabinet Secretary for the Interior and Local Government: Rafael M. Alunan III.

Cabinet Secretary for Justice: Franklin M. Drilon.

Cabinet Secretary for Labour and Employment: Nieves R. Confesor.

Cabinet Secretary for National Defence: Renato S. de Villa.

Cabinet Secretary for Science and Technology: William Padolina.

Cabinet Secretary for Social Welfare and Development: Corazon A.G. de Leon.

Cabinet Secretary for Tourism: Vicente J. Carlos.

Cabinet Secretary for Trade and Industry: Rizalino S. Navarro.

Cabinet Secretary for Transportation and Communication: Jesus B. Garcia Jr.

335

AUTONOMOUS REGION
Muslim Mindanao Area: 13,122 km² (5698 sq mi). Population: 1,830,000 (1990 est). Capital: Cotabato City.

GEOGRAPHY
Some 2770 of the Philippines' 7000 islands are named. The two largest islands, Luzon and Mindanao, make up over 65% of the country's area. Most islands are mountainous with restricted coastal plains, although Luzon has a large, densely populated central plain. Highest point: Mount Apo 2954 m (9692 ft). Principal rivers: Cagayan, Pampanga, Abra, Agusan, Magat, Laoang, Agno. Climate: The climate is tropical maritime with high humidity, high temperatures and heavy rainfall. Typhoons are frequent.

ECONOMY
Almost one half of the labour force is involved in agriculture. Rice and maize are the principal subsistence crops, while coconuts, sugar cane,

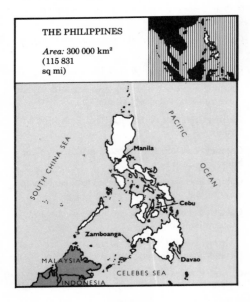

THE PHILIPPINES

Area: 300 000 km²
(115 831 sq mi)

pineapples and bananas are grown for export. The timber industry is important, but deforestation is a problem as land is cleared for cultivation. Major industries include textiles, food processing, chemicals and electrical engineering. Mineral resources include copper (a major export), gold, petroleum and nickel. Money sent back by Filipinos working abroad is an important source of foreign currency.

Currency: Philippine peso of 100 centavos; 1US$ = 26.45 pesos (June 1994).

GDP: US$61,000,000,000 (1993 est); US$913 per head.

RECENT HISTORY
Following an unsuccessful revolt (1896) against Spanish rule, the islands were ceded to the USA after the Spanish-American War (1898), but local resistance continued until 1906. A powerful American presence had a profound effect on Filipino society, which bears the triple imprint of Asian culture, Spanish Catholicism and American capitalism. US policy wavered between accelerating and delaying Filipino self-rule. In 1935 the nationalist leader Manuel Quezon became president of the semi-independent 'Commonwealth' of the Philippines. After the surprise Japanese invasion of 1941, Japan set up a puppet 'Philippine Republic', but, after the American recapture of the archipelago, a fully independent Republic of the Philippines was established in 1946. Between 1953 and 1957 the charismatic President Ramon Magsaysay crushed and conciliated Communist-dominated Hukbalahap guerrillas, but his death ended a programme of land reforms. Coming to power in 1965, Ferdinand Marcos (1917-89) inaugurated flamboyant development projects, but his administration presided over corruption on an unprecedented scale. Marcos used the continuing guerrilla activity as a justification for his increasingly repressive rule. When he attempted to rig the result of presidential elections in 1986, Marcos was overthrown in a popular revolution in favour of Corazon Aquino, the widow of a leading opposition politician who had allegedly been murdered on Marcos' orders. Her government faced several attempted military coups, but she was succeeded by the democratically elected President Ramos in 1992. Insurgency by groups including the (Islamic) Moro National Liberation Front and the (Communist) New People's Army remains a problem.

Singapore

Official name: Hsing-chia p'o Kung-ho Kuo (Chinese) or Republik Singapura (Malay) or Republic of Singapore.

Member of: UN, ASEAN, Commonwealth.

Area: 623 km² (240 sq mi).

Population: 2,876,000 (1993 est).

Capital: Singapore 2,876,000 (1992 est).

Languages: Chinese (77%), Malay (14%), Tamil (5%) and English - all official.

Religions: Buddhist and Daoist (54%), Sunni Islam (15%), various Christian Churches (13%), Hindu (4%).

Education: Education is not compulsory but is freely available for nine years at primary and secondary level. In 1990 the literacy rate was nearly 91%. There are five universities and three institutes of university status.

Defence: In 1993 the total armed strength was 55,000. Military service lasts for 30 months for enlisted men, and 24 months for officers.

Transport: There are 2924 km (1817 mi) of roads and 26 km (16 mi) of railways. There is a metro. Singapore has an important international airport. The shipping port handles over 190,000,000 tonnes a year and is the world's second largest.

Media: There are nine daily newspapers, including three in English and three in Chinese. There are two radio services (one state-run, one commercial) and a state-run television service.

GOVERNMENT

The 81 members of Parliament are elected from single- and multi-member constituencies by universal adult suffrage for five years. The President - who is elected by Parliament for four years - appoints a Prime Minister who commands a parliamentary majority. The PM, in turn, appoints a Cabinet which is responsible to Parliament. The constitution is to be revised to create an executive presidency in 1995. The main political parties are the People's Action Party (PAP), the Singapore Democratic Party (SDP) and the Workers' Party (WP). After the election held in August 1991, the PAP retained power.

Party strength: PAP 77, SDP 3, WP 1.

President: Ong Teng Cheong (PAP).

Prime Minister: Goh Chok Tong (PAP).

GEOGRAPHY

Singapore is a low-lying island - with 56 islets - joined to the Malay peninsula by causeway. Highest point: Bukit Timah 177 m (581 ft). Principal river: Sungei Seletar. Climate: The climate is tropical with monsoon rains from December to March.

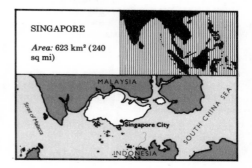

SINGAPORE

Area: 623 km² (240 sq mi)

ECONOMY

Singapore relies on imports for its flourishing manufacturing industries and entrepôt trade. Finance and tourism are important. Singapore has the second highest standard of living in Asia, after Japan.

Currency: Singaporean dollar of 100 cents; 1US$ = 1.52 dollars (June 1994).

GDP: US$39,250,000,000 (1991); US$12,890 per head.

RECENT HISTORY

Singapore was revived by Sir Stamford Raffles for the British East India Company (1819), and developed rapidly as a port for shipping Malaya's tin and rubber. It acquired a cosmopolitan population and became a strategic British base. Occupied by the Japanese (1942-45), it achieved self-government (1959), and joined (1963) and left (1965) the Federation of Malaysia. Since independence it has become wealthy under the strong rule of Prime Minister Lee Kuan Yew (1923- ; PM 1965-91). There has been criticism of Singapore's strict law and order policies and the government's attitude to opposition.

Thailand

Official name: Prathet Thai (Kingdom of Thailand). Muang-Thai is an alternative Thai name for the country. Before 1939 Thailand was known as Siam.

Member of: UN, ASEAN.

Area: 513,115 km² (198,115 sq mi).

Population: 57,829,000 (1993 est).

Capital: Bangkok 5,876,000 (including suburbs; 1990 census). The Thai government has approved a site for a new capital near Chachoengsao, which is located 120 km (75 mi) east of Bangkok. The new city is expected to be constructed by 2010.

Other major cities: Nakhon Ratchasima (Khorat) 207,000, Songkhla 173,000, Chiang Mai 150,000, Chon Buri 164,000 (all including suburbs; 1990 census).

Language: Thai (official); Lao, Chinese and Khmer minorities.

Religions: Buddhism (95%), Sunni Islam (4%).

Education: Education is compulsory for a total of six years between the ages of seven and 15. In 1990 the literacy rate was 93%. There are 19 universities including an open university and institutes of university status.

Defence: In 1993 the total armed strength was 280,000 - 173,000 in the army, 50,000 in the navy and 57,000 in the air force. Bangkok is the main naval base. Part of the Thai navy is based on the River Mekong, which forms the border with Laos. Compulsory military service lasts for two years.

Transport: There are 72,170 km (44,844 mi) of roads and 3861 km (2399 mi) of state-run railways. Bangkok is planning the construction of a metro. The main commercial shipping port is Bangkok. There are international airports at Bangkok, Chiang Mai and Phuket.

Media: There are over 20 daily newspapers, which are published in Thai, Chinese and English. There are three radio services, including the government-owned service which runs nearly 100 stations. There are six television channels.

GOVERNMENT
Thailand is a constitutional monarchy. The constitution provides for a National Assembly, which comprises a non-political Senate - whose 270 members are appointed by the National Peacekeeping Council (which is dominated by the military) - and a 360-member House of

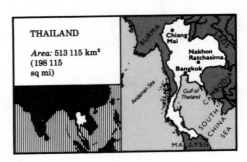

THAILAND

Area: 513 115 km² (198 115 sq mi)

Representatives elected by universal adult suffrage for four years. The King appoints a Prime Minister who commands a majority in the House. The PM in turn appoints a Cabinet of Ministers responsible to the House. Thailand is divided into 73 provinces. The main political parties include the (conservative) Thai Nation Party (TNP), the (right-wing) National Development Party (NDP), the (reformist) New Aspiration Party (NAP), the (liberal) Democrat Party (DP), Palang Dharma (Righteous) Party (RP), and the (reformist) Solidarity Party (SP). Of these parties, the Thai Nation Party and the National Development Party may be categorized as pro-military parties, while the other political parties listed above may be categorized as pro-democracy. The most recent election was in September 1992. A new NAP-DP-RP-SP government took office in 1993.

Party strength: DP 79, TNP 77, NDP 60, NAP 51, RP 47, SP 8, others 4.

King: HM King Bhumibol Adulyadej (Rama IX) (succeeded upon the death of his brother, 9 June 1946).

THE CABINET
Includes

Prime Minister: Chuan Leekpai (DP).

Deputy Prime Minister: Banyat Bantadtan (DP).

Deputy Prime Minister: Amnuay Viravan (NAP).

Deputy Prime Minister: Boonchu Rojanastien (RP).

Deputy Prime Minister: Supachai Panitchpakdi (DP).

Minister of Agriculture and Cooperation: Niphon Promphan (DP).

Minister of Commerce: Uthai Pimchaichon (SP).

Minister of Defence: Gen. Vijit Sookmark (DP).

Minister of Education: Samphan Thongsamak (DP).

Minister of Finance: Tarrin Nimmanahahaemin (DP).

Minister of Foreign Affairs: Squadron Leader Prasong Soonsiri (DP).

Minister of Industry: Maj-Gen. Sanan Kajornprasart (DP).

Minister of the Interior: Gen. Chavalit Yongchaiyudh (NAP).

Minister of Justice: Sawai Patano (DP).

Minister of Labour and Social Affairs: Phaithoon Kaeothong (NAP).

Minister of Public Health: Arthit Urairat (ind).

Minister of Science, Technology and the Environment: Phisan Moolasartsathorn (NAP).

Minister of Transport and Communications: Col. Winai Sompong.

Minister of University Affairs: Suthep Atthakor (RP).

GEOGRAPHY

Central Thailand is a densely populated fertile plain. The north is mountainous. The infertile Khorat Plateau occupies the northeast, while the mountainous Isthmus of Kra joins southern Thailand to Malaysia. Highest point: Doi Inthanon 2595 m (8514 ft). Principal rivers: Mekong, Chao Pyha, Mae Nam Mun. Climate: Thailand has a subtropical climate with heavy monsoon rains from June to October, a cool season from October to March, and a hot season from March to June. Rainfall totals are greatest in the south of the country and least near the Laotian border.

ECONOMY

Agriculture occupies two thirds of the labour force, mainly growing rice - Thailand is the world's largest exporter of rice. Other important crops include tapioca and rubber. Tin and natural gas are the main natural resources. Manufacturing - based on cheap labour - is expanding and includes textiles, clothes, electrical and electronic engineering, and food processing. Thailand achieved high economic growth rates throughout the 1980s and early 1990s. An expanding middle class is leading to the development of more service industries. The economic boom has created major problems in Bangkok which has become overcrowded, congested with traffic and spoiled by pollution. The government is actively encouraging developments in the provinces, particularly in the underdeveloped north. Tourism has become a major foreign-currency earner and resorts such as Phuket have been developed on the southern coast.

Currency: Baht of 100 satang; 1US$ = 24.99 bahts.

GDP: US$128,000,000,000 (1993 est); US$2134 per head.

RECENT HISTORY

Thailand was known as Siam before 1939. During the 19th century Thai kings were forced to cede their claims over neighbouring lands to Britain and France. A constitutional monarchy was established by a bloodless coup (1932), whose Westernized leaders - Pibul Songgram and Pridi Phanomyang - struggled for political dominance for the next quarter of a century. During World War II Thailand was forced into an alliance with Japan. Since then Thailand has made a decisive commitment to the US political camp, which has brought major benefits in military and technical aid. Despite continuing army interventions in politics - in 1991 the military took over the government for the 17th time in 50 years - Thailand has prospered. However, the stability of the country was compromised by the wars in Vietnam and by the continuing Cambodian conflict (until 1991). Constitutional rule was restored in 1992. Thailand is coming under increasing international pressure to restrain the Khmer Rouge movement, which is operating from Thai territory into Cambodia. In 1993-94 Thailand cut supply routes to insurgent armies, in particular, the Karen in the east of Myanmar (Burma).

Vietnam

Official name: Cộng hoa xâ hôi chu nghia Viêt (The Socialist Republic of Vietnam).

Member of: UN.

Area: 329,566 km² (127,246 sq mi).

Population: 70,902,000 (1993 est).

Capital: Hanoi 2,095,000 (1992 est).

Other major cities: Ho Chi Minh City (formerly Saigon) 4,076,000, Haiphong 1,517,000, Da Nang 371,000, Long Xuyen 217,000 (1991-92 est).

Language: Vietnamese (official; 84%), Tay, Khmer, Thai, Muong.

Religions: Buddhist (55%), Roman Catholic (7%), Cao Dai (3%), Daoist.

Education: Education is compulsory between the ages of six and 11. In 1990 the literacy rate was 87.6%. There are six universities.

Defence: In 1993 the total armed strength was 857,000 - 700,000 in the army, 43,000 in the navy 114,000 in the air force. Compulsory military service lasts three years.

Transport: There are 88,000 km (54,670 mi) of roads and 3220 km (2000 mi) of railways. Ho

VIETNAM

Area: 329 566 km²
(127 246 sq mi)

Chi Minh City and Haiphong, the principal ports, also have international airports.

Media: There are six daily state-controlled newspapers and a single state-run radio and television service.

GOVERNMENT

The 496-member National Assembly is elected by universal adult suffrage for five years. The Assembly elects, from its own members, a Council of State - whose Chairman is President - and a Council of Ministers, headed by a Prime Minister. Effective power is in the hands of the Communist Party, which is the only legal party.

President: Le Duc Anh.

THE CABINET

Prime Minister: Vo Van Klet.

Vice Premiers: Phan Van Khai, Nguyen Khanh, Tran Duc Luong.

Minister of Agriculture and the Food Industry: Nguyen Cong Tan.

Minister of Culture and Information: Tran Hoan.

Minister of Commerce: Le Van Triet.

Minister of Communication and Transport: Bui Danh Luu.

Minister of Construction: Ngo Xuan Loc.

Minister of Defence: Lt-Gen. Doan Khue.

Minister of Education and Training: Tran Hong Quan.

Minister of Energy: Thai Phung Ne.

Minister of Finance: Ho Te.

Minister of Forestry: Nguyen Quang Ha.

Minister of Foreign Affairs: Nguyen Manh Cam.

Minister of Heavy Industry: Tran Lum.

Minister of the Interior: Bui Thien Ngo.

Minister of Justice: Nguyen Dinh Loc.

Minister of Labour, War Veterans and Social Affairs: Tran Dinh Hoan.

Minister of Light Industry: Dang Vu Chu.

Minister of Marine Products: Nguyen Tan Trinh.

Minister of Public Health: Nguyen Trong Nhan.

Minister of Science, Technology and the Environment: Dang Huu,

Minister of Water Conservancy: Nguyen Canh Dinh.

GEOGRAPHY

Plateaux, hill country and chains of mountains in Annam (central Vietnam) lie between the Mekong River delta in the south and the Red River (Hongha) delta in the north. Highest point: Fan si Pan 3142 m (10,308 ft). Principal rivers: Mekong, Songkoi, Songbo, Hongha. Climate: Vietnam has a hot humid climate, although winters are cool in the north. Heavy rainfall comes in the monsoon season from April to October.

ECONOMY

Agriculture involves over three quarters of the labour force, mainly cultivating rice. Other crops include cassava, maize and sweet potatoes for domestic consumption, and rubber, tea and coffee for export. Natural resources include coal, phosphates and tin, which are the basis of industries in the north. The wars in Vietnam, involvement in Cambodia and the loss of skilled workers through emigration have all had a serious effect on the economy. Vietnam received aid from the USSR and East European countries in the 1980s. Nevertheless, Vietnam remains underdeveloped, and lacks the investment to overcome basic problems such as food shortages. Overpopulation is a problem, and official sanctions are taken against couples that have more than two children. The virtual end of aid from former Communist countries in the 1990s has added to Vietnam's economic problems, and attempts have been made to encourage Western investment.

Currency: Dong; 1US$ = 10,976.8 dongs (June 1994).

GDP: US$15,200,000,000 (1990); US$210 per head.

RECENT HISTORY

The French intervened in the area from the 1860s, established a protectorate in Vietnam in 1883 and formed the Union of Indochina - including Cambodia and Laos - in 1887. Revolts against colonial rule in the 1930s marked the start of a period of war and occupation that lasted for over 40 years. The Japanese occupied Vietnam in 1940 and eventually set up a puppet government under the Emperor Bao Dai. In 1941 the Communist leader Ho Chi Minh established the Viet Minh as a nationalist guerrilla army to fight the Japanese. In the closing months of the war, the Viet Minh received US aid, and - after the Japanese surrender - a Democratic Republic of Vietnam was established in Hanoi with Ho as president. French rule was not re-established until 1946, with Ho's republic initially recognized as a 'free state' within French Indochina. After clashes between the Hanoi government and the French, Ho left Hanoi and began a guerrilla war against the colonial authorities and the restored Emperor Bao Dai. The Viet Minh gradually gained all of Tonkin and in 1954 forced the French to surrender at Dien Bien Phu after a siege of 55 days. The Geneva Peace Agreement (July 1954) partitioned Vietnam between a Communist zone in the north and a zone ruled by Boa Dai in the south. Elections for the entire country were scheduled for 1956, but the north refused to participate. In 1955 Bao Din was deposed and Ngo Dinh Diem proclaimed a republic in South Vietnam. Diem's oppressive regime encouraged Communist guerrilla activity in the south and in 1960 the (Communist) Viet Cong was formed in South Vietnam with the aim of overthrowing the pro-Western government. In 1961 US President John F. Kennedy sent American military advisers to help South Vietnam. By 1964 the 'advisers' had grown into an army of regular US troops. After the North Vietnamese allegedly attacked US naval patrols (1964), the Americans began regular aerial bombardment of the north. By the end of 1964 nearly 200,000 US combat troops were in action in Vietnam. The 1968 (Communist) Tet offensive was withstood but the weakness of South Vietnam became evident. Opposition to the war increased in the USA. Peace talks began in 1969 but in 1970 US forces were active against the Viet Cong in both Laos and Cambodia. The war was formally ended by the Paris Peace Agreements (1973), but continued after the withdrawal of US troops. Since the Communist takeover of the south (1975) and the reunification of Vietnam, reconstruction has been hindered by a border war with China (1979) and the occupation of Cambodia (1979-89) by Vietnamese forces. Lack of Western aid and investment has hindered economic development, and this, combined with political repression, has led to large numbers of refugees (the 'Boat People') fleeing the country. Since 1989-90 more pragmatic policies have been adopted in an attempt to attract Western capital. Although the liberalization of the economy is being pursued, there is no indication that political reforms will follow.

Other territories

CHRISTMAS ISLAND

Status: an Australian external territory.

Area: 135 km² (52 sq mi).

Population: 1275 (1991 census).

Capital: Flying Fish Cove.

Geography: Christmas Island is an isolated tropical mountain with abrupt cliffs rising from the sea. It lies 360 km (200 mi) south of Java.

Economy: The island depends upon phosphate workings.

Recent History: The island was claimed by Britain in 1888 and Malay and Chinese workers were imported to mine phosphate. It was annexed to Singapore in 1900. After occupation by Japan (1942-45) during World War II, the island was ceded by Britain to Australia in 1958.

COCOS (KEELING) ISLANDS

Status: an Australian external territory.

Area: 14 km² (5.5 sq mi).

Population: 650 (1991 census).

Capital: Bantam Village 480 (1991 census).

Geography: Situated about 2225 km (1390 mi) southwest of Sri Lanka, the Cocos form two atolls comprising 27 small coral tropical islands.

Economy: Large stands of coconut palms produce copra, the only export.

Recent History: The Cocos were settled in the 1830s when John Clunies-Ross imported Malays to work the coconut palms. Britain annexed the Cocos (1857), granting them to the Clunies-Ross family, who ruled until 1978 when Australia bought out their interests. The islands were ceded to Australia by the UK in 1955.

EAST TIMOR

Status: disputed territory.

Area: 14,874 km² (5743 sq mi).

Population: 748,000 (1990 census).

Capital: Dili (Oekussi) 60,000 (1990 est).

Geography: East Timor comprises the mountainous tropical eastern half of the island of Timor plus an enclave in the western half of the island.

Economy: The economy, which formerly depend upon coffee, has been devastated by violence associated with Indonesia's annexation of East Timor. Much of the population has been uprooted; many villages have been destroyed.

Recent History: East Timor - Portuguese since the 16th century - was proclaimed independent by the local nationalist movement Fretilin in 1975. Indonesian forces invaded immediately. In 1976 East Timor was annexed to Indonesia but this action is not recognized by the UN. Up to 200,000 people died during Indonesia's conquest of the territory. International protests followed the killing of unarmed Timorese demonstrators by Indonesian troops in 1991.

PARACEL ISLANDS

Status: a disputed territory.

Area: 160 km² (62 sq mi).

Population: no figures are available; Chinese forces are stationed in the islands.

Geography: The islands comprise over 130 small low-lying arid coral reefs in the South China Sea.

Recent History: The islands were annexed to French Indochina in 1932. In the late 1940s the islands were claimed by both North and South Vietnam, and by both Communist China and Taiwan. The discovery of oil in nearby waters prompted a Chinese occupation of the Paracels.

SPRATLY ISLANDS

Status: a disputed territory.

Area: not defined.

Population: no permanent population.

Geography: The islands comprise a number of very small, rocky islets in the South China Sea.

Recent History: The Spratly Islands, which are thought to contain valuable mineral resources, were claimed by France as part of French Indochina in the 1930s, and are now claimed by Vietnam, China, Taiwan, Malaysia, the Philippines and Brunei.

▶ ▶ ▶ ▶ ▶ ▶ ▶ ▶ ▶ ▶ ▶ ▶ ▶

SOUTHERN AND ANTARCTIC TERRITORIES

Dependent territories and territorial claims in Antarctica and the
Antarctic Ocean.

▶ ▶ ▶ ▶ ▶ ▶ ▶ ▶ ▶ ▶ ▶ ▶ ▶ ▶

Other territories

All territorial claims south of latitude 60S are in abeyance under the terms of the Antarctic Treaty (1959).

ARGENTINE ANTARCTIC TERRITORY

Status: an Argentine territorial claim.

Area: see Geography, below.

Geography: Argentina claims that part of Antarctica between 74W and 25W, a claim that overlaps with the British territorial claim.

AUSTRALIAN ANTARCTIC TERRITORY
Status: an Australian territorial claim.

Area: 6,043,700 km² (2,333,500 sq mi).

Geography: Australia claims that part of Antarctica between 160E and 142E and that part between 136E and 45E.

BOUVET ISLAND
Status: a Norwegian dependency. As Bouvet Island lies north of the area covered by the Antarctic Treaty (1959), Norway's claim to the island is uncontested.

Area: 59 km² (23 sq mi).

Geography: Bouvet Island is a bleak volcanic glaciated island 1600 km (1000 mi) north of the Antarctic mainland.

BRITISH ANTARCTIC TERRITORY
Status: a British territorial claim in the Antarctic.

Area: 1,800,000 km² (700,000 sq mi).

Geography: Britain claims that part of Antarctica between 20W and 80W, extending to the South Pole. This claim overlaps with those Chile and Argentina.

CHILEAN ANTARCTIC TERRITORY
Status: a Chilean territorial claim.

Area: see Geography, below.

Geography: Chile claims that part of Antarctica between 90W and 53W, a claim that overlaps with British and Argentine claims.

FRENCH SOUTHERN AND ANTARCTIC TERRITORIES

Status: French dependencies (Kerguelen and the other islands) with the French territorial claim in the Antarctic (Adélie Land).

Area: 439,797 km² (169,806 sq mi) - of which Adélie Land 432,000 km² (166,800 sq mi).

Geography: The territory comprises that part of Antarctica between 136E and 142E (Adélie Land) plus two archipelagos (Kerguelen and Crozet) and two small islands (Amsterdam and St Paul) in the extreme south of the Indian Ocean.

HEARD AND MCDONALD ISLANDS
Status: an Australian external territory.

Area: 417 km² (161 sq mi).

Geography: The islands, which lie about 4000 km (2500 mi) southwest of Australia, are almost entirely covered in ice.

PETER I ISLAND
Status: a Norwegian territorial claim.

Area: 180 km² (69 sq mi).

Geography: Peter I Island is an ice-covered island 450 km (280 mi) north of Antarctica.

QUEEN MAUD LAND
Status: a Norwegian territorial claim.

Area: as no inland limit to the claim has been made, no estimate of the area can be given.

Geography: Norway claims that part of Antarctica between 20W and 45E.

ROSS DEPENDENCY
Status: a New Zealand territorial claim.

Area: 730,000 km² (282,000 sq mi).

Geography: New Zealand claims that part of Antarctica between 160E amd 150W.

▶ ▶ ▶ ▶ ▶ ▶ ▶ ▶ ▶ ▶ ▶ ▶

WESTERN EUROPE

Andorra, Austria, Belgium, Cyprus, Denmark, Finland, France, Germany, Greece, Iceland, Ireland, Italy, Liechtenstein, Luxembourg, Malta, Monaco, The Netherlands, Norway, Portugal, San Marino, Spain, Sweden, Switzerland, United Kingdom of Great Britain and Northern Ireland, The Vatican City, Other territories.

The Maastricht Treaty

The Maastricht Treaty was drawn up by the 12 members of the European Community in 1991. By August 1993 all EC member countries had ratified the Treaty. The UK negotiated a separate 'protocol', reserving its position on the third stage of European Monetary Union (EMU), and an agreement to opt out of the Social Chapter. The Treaty marks the decisive step from 'common market' status to a much closer and deeper unification of the economic, political and social systems of member countries.

A central feature of the Treaty is the proposal to establish monetary union. It was hoped that this could be achieved in a three-stage plan for the irrevocable change to a single currency, the European Currency Unit (ECU). In the first stage all countries were expected to participate in the 'Exchange Rate Mechanism' (ERM) of the European Monetary System, which requires members to keep the exchange value of their currency at a 'fixed' rate against other members' currencies. Keeping exchange rates fixed, however, can be difficult as evidenced by the withdrawal of the UK and Italy from the ERM in 1992 following speculative pressures on their currencies. In August 1993 pressure on the French franc and other currencies by speculators, coupled with high German interest rates, forced the D-mark artificially high against the French franc, the Spanish peseta and Portuguese escudo. EC governments were forced to effectively suspend the ERM by allowing member currencies to move by 15% on either side of their central rate. This enabled member states to pursue their own exchange policies but at the cost of at least postponing the goal of economic union and single currency. However, other measures of the Treaty can still be implemented as planned.

SUBSIDIARITY

The main authorities of the EC (the European Council in particular) have only limited powers to formulate and implement common policies across the whole of the Community. Some EC countries hoped that Maastricht would help establish a 'federalist' EC with strong central direction involving the ceding of policy-making from national governments to the EC authorities. This has been resisted for the time being. The Treaty affirms that, wherever possible, decisions should be 'taken as closely as possible to the citizens'. This principle, referred to as subsidiarity (Article 3b of the Treaty) requires that the Community confines itself to doing what cannot be sufficiently achieved by member states acting alone and can therefore be better achieved at Community level. This opens up the problem, of course, as to where the dividing line is between issues that can be resolved at the individual state level and those that can only be tackled at the Community-wide level.

PILLARS

Under Maastricht, cooperation in certain fields is to be channelled through new inter-governmental bodies rather than through existing institutions of the EC. In some areas, most notably in foreign policy and defence, the Treaty provides for greater 'inter-governmental cooperation' with a view to establishing a common approach to matters of mutual concern. Points emphasized by the Treaty include a stronger commitment to joint actions where all members agree and a stronger EC voice in defence through NATO. Maastricht defined a European Union resting upon three 'pillars'. The first pillar is the EC, which was to have assumed additional monetary responsibilities. The second pillar, concerning foreign and security matters, and the third pillar, concerning cooperation in a wide variety of areas such as immigration, political asylum and law enforcement, were defined as inter-governmental bodies representing the 12 states. With the postponement of monetary union, the Treaty represents a major widening of cooperation between the EC states without adding substantially to the powers of the EC itself.

To sum up, a union of countries such as the EC obviously needs some common policies if it is to function effectively. A customs union built on 'free trade' can produce economic benefits but these can be considerably enhanced by a deeper integration of members' economies. The EC, of course, is more than just a matter of economics; it represents a social and political movement aimed at creating something resembling a new 'super-state'. There are those in the European movement who would like to see the EC itself assuming the role of the nation state. The Maastricht Treaty is a further, albeit very limited, move in this direction.

The European Community

In 1950 the governments of Belgium, France, the Federal Republic of Germany (West Germany), Italy, Luxembourg and the Netherlands began negotiations to integrate their interests in specific fields. The result was the Treaty of Paris (1951) under which the European Coal and Steel Community was created. Attempts to establish a community concerned with cooperation in foreign affairs and defence proved abortive, but in 1957 the European Economic Community (the EEC) and the European Atomic Energy Community (Euratom) - with memberships identical to the European Coal and Steel Community - came into being under the terms of the Treaty of Rome.

The three Communities were distinct entities until 1967 when - for all practical purposes - they merged their executives and decision-making bodies into a single European Community (the EC). The Community has been enlarged through the accession of Denmark, Greece, Ireland, Portugal, Spain and the UK. *Membership* (with year of accession, an * indicates founder member): Belgium*, Denmark 1973, France*, Germany*, Greece 1981, Ireland 1973, Italy*, Luxembourg*, Netherlands*, Portugal 1986, Spain 1986, UK 1973.

Austria, Finland, Norway and Sweden have completed negotiations for EC membership and are expected to become full EC members in 1995. Turkey, Cyprus, Malta and Switzerland have also applied for membership. Morocco's application was rejected. Associate agreements have been concluded with Poland, Hungary, the Czech Republic and Slovakia, who also have applied for full membership.

In 1992 the EC achieved a Single European Market in which all duties, tariffs and quotas have been removed on trade between member states and many obstacles to the free movement of people, money and goods have been abolished within the Community.

FINANCE

Since 1975 the EC has had its own revenue independent of national contributions. The general budget of the EC covers all the expenditure of the Community. Member states are required to supply funds appropriate to these needs.

EC INSTITUTIONS

The Commission of the European Community

The European Commission consists of 17 members appointed by their national governments for a term of four years. The Commissioners elect from their number a President and six Vice-Presidents. The Commission - which acts independently of national governments - makes proposals to the Council of Ministers (see below) and executes the decisions of the Council.

Headquarters: Brussels, Belgium.

Composition of the European Commission: Belgium is represented by 1 Commissioner, Denmark 1, France 2, Germany 2, Greece 1, Ireland 1, Italy 2, Luxembourg 1, the Netherlands 1, Portugal 1, Spain 2, and the UK 2.

The Council of Ministers

The Council of Ministers is the main decision-making body of the EC. It consists of the foreign ministers of each of the 12 member states. Specialist councils - for example, of the 12 ministers of agriculture - also meet, while heads of government meet three times a year as the *European Council*. Ministers represent national interests. The decisions of the Council are normally unanimous although there is provision for majority voting in certain areas. The *Presidency of the Council of Ministers* rotates, with each member state taking the chair for a period of six months. Council meetings are normally held in the country that currently holds the Presidency, but are also held in Brussels, Belgium.

The European Parliament

The European Parliament consists of 567 members directly elected for five years by universal adult suffrage according to the local practice of each member state. Members (MEPs) have the right to be consulted on legislative proposals submitted by the Council of Ministers or the Commission and the power to reject or amend the budget of the EC. The Parliament also has the power to dismiss the Commission in a vote of censure.

Headquarters: The Parliament meets in Strasbourg (France), its committees meet in Brussels (Belgium) and its Secretariat is based in Luxembourg City.

Composition of the European Parliament: Elections for the European Parliament are held every five years. After the 1994 elections the composition of the Parliament was: Belgium 25, Denmark 16, France 87, Germany 99, Greece 25, Ireland 15, Italy 87, Luxembourg 6, Netherlands 31, Portugal 25, Spain 64, UK 87.

There are 19 parliamentary Standing Committees specializing in matters ranging from foreign affairs and security to women's rights. Parliament is run by a bureau consisting of a President and 14 Vice-Presidents elected by MEPs from among their number.

The European Court of Justice

The European Court of Justice consists of 13 judges and six advocates-general appointed for six years by the governments of member states acting in concert. At least one representative is appointed from each state. The Court is responsible for deciding upon the legality of the decisions of the Council of Ministers and the Commission and for adjudicating between states in the event of disputes.

Headquarters: Luxembourg City.

Court of Auditors of the European Community

The Court - established in 1977 - is responsible for the external audit of the resources managed by the EC. It consists of 12 members elected for six years by the Council of Ministers.

European Investment Bank

The Bank - which works on a non-profit basis - makes or guarantees loans for investment projects in member states. Priority is given to regional development. The capital is subscribed by EC members.

CONSULTATIVE BODIES
Economic and Social Committee

The Committee is an advisory body consulted by the Commission and the Council of Ministers on issues such as free movement of workers, agriculture, transport and harmonization of laws.

European Coal and Steel Community

Consultative Committee

The Committee - which advises the Commission - is appointed by the Council of Ministers for two years. Its members comprise coal and steel producers, works, consumers and dealers in these fields.

Agricultural Advisory Committees

There are four agricultural committees - one dealing with the organization of the market, one dealing with structures and two concerned with social matters in agriculture.

Committee of the Regions

The Maastricht Treaty (see p. 346) provided for a new Committee of the Regions, an advisory body that would represent local and regional governments within member states.

COMMUNITY ACTIVITIES
Agriculture EC cooperation in agriculture is highly developed. Expenditure on agriculture (through the European Agricultural Guidance and Guarantee Fund/EAGGF) is the EC's single largest item of expenditure. The Common Agricultural Policy (CAP) contains the agricultural operations and objectives of the EC.

Consumer Policy The EC has implemented two Consumer Protection Programmes which have standardized health and safety measures, and introduced rules on food additives, packaging, machines and equipment, measures for monitoring the quality and durability of products, the improvement of after-sales service and legal redress concerning faulty goods. Consumer associations have also been encouraged.

Economic and Monetary Union The aim of monetary union and the adoption of a single common currency throughout the Community (the ECU) was detailed in the Maastricht Treaty (see p. 346), but these goals have now been postponed following the collapse of the ERM.

Education Education was excluded from the Treaty of Rome but recent efforts at harmonization have been taken, in particular moves to define equivalent standards in professional qualifications.

Energy The EC has developed overall energy policies within the EEC, Euratom and the European Coal and Steel Community.

Environment The EC's environmental action programmes have laid down various principles for action concerning pollution and environmental protection.

Financial Services Various directives on banking, insurance and capital movement have been implemented.

Fisheries The Common Fisheries Policy (CFP) came into force in 1983.

Industry Industrial cooperation between members began with the establishment of the European Coal and Steel Community.

Overseas Aid - the Lomé Convention The principal channel for EC aid to developing countries is the Lomé Convention, which provides a framework for cooperation with developing countries in Africa, the Caribbean and the Pacific.

Social Policy In 1987 measures were added to the Treaty of Rome to emphasize the need for 'economic and social cohesion' in particular the need to reduce the disparities between regions. In 1989 the Commission produced a Charter of Fundamental Social Rights of Workers - now better known as the Social Chapter. The UK has negotiated an opt out from the protocol.

Transport The establishment of a Community transport policy - to allow the free movement of traffic throughout the EC - is one of the objectives of the Treaty of Rome.

THE SINGLE EUROPEAN MARKET

A key objective of the European Community (EC) is to secure the economic benefits of free trade through the creation of a 'common market' providing for the unrestricted movement of goods, services, capital and labour. Under the founding legislation of the EC - the Treaty of Rome (1957) - attention centred on the elimination of various visible restrictions on interstate trade such as tariffs, quotas and cartels. More recently, under the Single European Act, 1986, and the Maastricht Treaty, 1991, the intent has been to create a more unified EC bloc providing not only greater trading opportunities but also paving the way for a deeper integration of the member states of the EC economically, monetarily, politically and socially.

The Single European Act itself is concerned specifically with sweeping away a large number of less visible obstacles to trade arising from historical differences in the policies and practices of individual EC states. The intention is to end the fragmentation of the EC into 'national' markets and to create a 'level playing field' so that businesses can produce and sell their products throughout the EC bloc of some 350 million people without discrimination. (This free trade area has been extended to the European Free Trade Association bloc, creating what is known as the European Economic Area.)

The Single European Act committed the 12 EC States to remove various impediments to the movement of goods, services, capital and people through the progressive introduction of various practices and regulations. Hitherto, trade has been obstructed and costs and prices increased in many ways: by different national bureaucratic requirements and technical standards, different national taxation structures, and restrictive government procurement practices and subsidies given to local firms.

The Act was introduced in 1992 at a time when intra-Community trade already accounted for over 50% of members' total external trade and it helped boost that total to over 60% in the immediate run-up to 1992. Significant increases in intra-Community trade have occurred (as expected) in the case of the EC's newest members, Greece, Spain and Portugal, but sizeable increases have also been recorded by France, Italy, Denmark and the UK.

The immediate benefits of the single market initiative are primarily economic. Consumers benefit from a wider choice of goods and services, and from lower prices resulting from greater economies of scale and increased competition.

THE EUROPEAN UNION

The new European body, the European Union (EU), came into being on 1 November 1993 following the ratification of the Maastricht Treaty. The European Union is an expression of 'an ever closer union among the people of Europe'. The governments of the 12 member-states that ratified the Maastricht Treaty agreed to a series of objectives that include (eventually) a single currency and a commitment that the European Union should 'assert its identity on the international scene'. The European Union has not replaced the European Community. The EC, its bodies and structure now form one of the three 'pillars' that comprise the European Union (see p. 346).

Other Organizations in Western Europe

CONFERENCE ON SECURITY AND CO-OPERATION IN EUROPE (CSCE)

Members of the CSCE - which was founded in 1975 and reformed in 1990 - affirm 'a commitment to settle disputes by peaceful means' and a 'common adherence to democratic values and to human rights and fundamental freedoms'. CSCE foreign ministers meet at least once a year.

Headquarters (and Secretariat): Prague, the Czech Republic.

CSCE Conflict Prevention Centre: Vienna, Austria.

CSCE Office of Free Elections: Warsaw, Poland.

Membership: Albania, Andorra, Armenia, Austria, Azerbaijan, Belarus, Belgium, Bosnia-Herzegovina, Bulgaria, Canada, Croatia, Cyprus, the Czech Republic, Denmark, Estonia, Finland, France, Georgia, Germany, Greece, Hungary, Iceland, Ireland, Italy, Kazakhstan, Kyrgyzstan, Latvia, Liechtenstein, Lithuania, Luxembourg, Macedonia (The Former Yugoslav Republic of), Malta, Moldova, Monaco, the Netherlands, Norway, Poland, Portugal, Romania, Russia, San Marino, Slovakia, Slovenia, Spain, Sweden, Switzerland, Tajikistan, Turkey, Turkmenistan, Ukraine, the United Kingdom, the United States of America, Uzbekistan, and the Vatican City. Yugoslavia (Serbia and Montenegro) was suspended in 1992.

COUNCIL OF EUROPE

The Council of Europe, which was founded in 1949, aims to achieve a greater European unity, to safeguard members' common European heritage and to facilitate economic and social progress. Membership is restricted to European democracies. The Council of Ministers, comprising the foreign ministers of member states, meets twice a year. Agreements by members are either formalized as European Conventions or recommendations to governments. The Parliamentary Assembly of the Council - which meets three times a year - comprises parliamentary delegates from member states. Delegations range in size from 18 members (from France, Germany, Italy and the United Kingdom) to two members (from Liechtenstein and San Marino). The Council has achieved over 140 conventions and agreements including the European Convention of Human Rights (1950).

Headquarters: Strasbourg, France.

Membership: Austria, Belgium, Bulgaria, Cyprus, the Czech Republic, Denmark, Estonia, Finland, France, Germany, Greece, Hungary, Iceland, Ireland, Italy, Liechtenstein, Lithuania, Luxembourg, Malta, the Netherlands, Norway, Poland, Portugal, San Marino, Slovakia, Slovenia, Spain, Sweden, Switzerland, Turkey, and the United Kingdom.

THE EUROPEAN ECONOMIC AREA (EEA)

The EEA is a free-trade alliance between the members of the EU/EC and most of the members of EFTA (see below). The EEA should have come into force on 1 January 1993. However, Switzerland - an EFTA member - decided in a referendum in December 1992 not to participate in the EEA. The EEA's main aim is to extend the EU/EC's four 'single market freedoms' in the movement of goods, of services, of capital and of labour to create a unified market of approaching 400 million people. All members have adopted the harmonization measures that have been, or are being, implemented by EC countries under the Single European Act (1986). The objective of the EEA is thus to widen the gains to be achieved by the formation of a 'common market' in which goods and services are free to circulate unencumbered by differences in national product requirements, technical specifications and standards, differences in labelling and packaging stipulations, differences in taxation structures, and so on. When the EU expands to take in four EFTA members, with the exceptions of Iceland and Liechtenstein the membership of the two organizations will be the same. It is, therefore, doubtful whether the EEA, and its institutions, will exist for long as a separate body.

Membership: Austria, Belgium, Denmark, Finland, France, Germany, Greece, Iceland, Ireland, Italy, Liechtenstein, Luxembourg, the Netherlands, Norway, Portugal, Spain, Sweden, and the United Kingdom.

EUROPEAN FREE TRADE AREA (EFTA)

EFTA was founded in 1960 by a group of West European countries that felt unable to accept the political and economic consequences of joining the EC. EFTA aims to achieve free trade in industrial goods between members, to help create a single West European market and to encourage an expansion of world trade. The first aim was achieved in 1966 when nearly all internal tariffs on internal goods were abolished. Considerable progress was made towards the second aim in 1984 when trade agreements with the EC abolished tariffs on industrial goods between the EC and EFTA.

Closer integration between the EC and EFTA is being achieved through the EEA (see above). The United Kingdom, Portugal and Denmark have all been EFTA members but withdrew upon joining the EC. Of the current EFTA membership, Austria will join the EU/EC in January 1995, and Sweden, Finland and Norway will also do so if their electorates approve in referenda to be held in the autumn of 1994. Unless it expands through the admission of CEFTA countries, the continued useful existence of EFTA beyond 1995 is in very considerable doubt.

Headquarters: Geneva, Switzerland.

Membership: Austria (will withdraw in January 1995), Finland (will withdraw in January 1995 if Finnish membership of the EU is approved), Iceland, Liechtenstein, Norway (will withdraw in January 1995 if Norwegian membership of the EU is approved), Sweden (will withdraw in January 1995 if Swedish membership of the EU is approved), and Switzerland.

NORTH ATLANTIC TREATY ORGANIZATION (NATO)

The North Atlantic Treaty Organization came unto being in August 1949. NATO is a collective defence organization whose members agree to treat an armed attack on any one of them as an attack against all. The North Atlantic Council is the highest authority of the alliance. It comprises 16 permanent representatives - one from each member - plus observers from signatories of NATO's Partnership for Peace (see below). The Council is chaired by the Secretary General of NATO. The foreign ministers of members meet at least twice a year. The defence of the NATO area is the responsibility of the Defence Planning Committee (DPC). Neither France nor the signatories of the Partnership for Peace are members of the DPC, which meets regularly at ambassadorial level and twice a year at ministerial level.

Headquarters: Brussels, Belgium.

Secretary General: Manfred Wörner (Germany).

Membership: Belgium, Canada, Denmark, France, Germany, Greece, Iceland, Italy, Luxembourg, the Netherlands, Norway, Portugal, Spain, Turkey, the United Kingdom, and the United States of America.

NATO PARTNERSHIP FOR PEACE (PFP)

NATO's Partnership for Peace was first proposed in 1993 and finally adopted in January 1994. It aims to provide former Warsaw Pact countries, CIS members and neutral states with an agreement that will bring them closer to NATO without formal membership. PFP is flexible, offering each partner a different relationship with NATO. Partners open up their defence plans to NATO scrutiny and advice, and share training with NATO. They will also move towards common military doctrines. Through PFP some members will eventually move towards full NATO membership.

Membership: Albania, Azerbaijan, Bulgaria, the Czech Republic, Estonia, Finland, Georgia, Hungary, Latvia, Lithuania, Moldova, Poland, Romania, Russia, Slovakia, Slovenia, Sweden, and Ukraine.

WEST EUROPEAN UNION (WEU)

The WEU, which was refounded in 1955, seeks to harmonize the security and defence of Western European countries. The Union was reactivated in 1984 to strengthen NATO and has virtually taken on the role of the EU/EC's defence arm.

Headquarters: Brussels, Belgium.

Membership: Belgium, Denmark (observer member), France, Germany, Greece, Iceland (associate member), Ireland (observer member), Italy, Luxembourg, the Netherlands, Norway (associate member), Portugal, Spain, Turkey (associate member), and the United Kingdom.

West European Trade

Andorra Imports ($ million): 700.4 (1987). Exports ($ million): 24.6 (1987). Main imports: wearing apparel 52.1% (1990), food and live animals 25.1% (1990). Main exports: machinery and transport equipment 26.8% (1990), food and live animals 25.1% (1990). Principal trading partners: France, Spain.

Austria Imports (Schillings million): 591,898.4 (1991). Exports (Schillings million): 479,029.1 (1991). Main imports: machinery and transport equipment 39% (1991), chemicals and related products 9.7% (1991). Main exports: machinery and transport equipment 34.4% (1991), basic manufactures 30% (1991). Principal trading partners: Germany, Italy, France, Switzerland, Japan.

Belgium Imports (Belgian francs million): 4,119,587 (1991). Exports (Belgian francs million): 4,024,039 (1991). Main imports: machinery and transport equipment 26% (1991), vehicles and vehicle parts 17.9% (1991). Main exports: vehicles and parts 28.3% (1991), chemicals and chemical products 14% (1991). Principal trading partners: France, Germany, Netherlands, UK, Italy.

Cyprus Imports ($ million): 2621 (1991). Exports ($ million): 960 (1991). Main imports: consumer goods 14.9% (1990), transport equipment 12.6% (1990). Main exports: clothing 16.1% (1990), potatoes 6.7% (1990). Principal trading partners: UK, Italy, Germany, Japan.

Denmark Imports ($ million): 32,257 (1991). Exports ($ million): 35,812 (1991). Main imports: machinery and transport equipment 31.4% (1991), consumer goods 17.2% (1991). Main exports: foodstuffs 34.4% (1991), specialized machinery 4.1%. Principal trading partners: Germany, Sweden, UK, USA, Netherlands.

Finland Imports ($ million): 21,711 (1991). Exports ($ million): 23,111 (1991). Main imports: raw materials and produced goods 53.8% (1991), consumer goods 23.2% (1991). Main exports: paper and paper products 36% (1991), machinery and transport equipment 27.4% (1991). Principal trading partners: Germany, Sweden, UK, France, Russia.

France Imports (francs million): 1,263,963.8 (1992). Exports ($ million): 1,228,241.1 (1992). Main imports: machinery and transport equipment 34.4% (1992), chemicals 11% (1991), crude petroleum. Main exports: machinery and transport equipment 39.3% (1992), chemicals and related products 13.5% (1992), food and live animals (particularly cereals), basic manufactures (including iron and steel). Principal trading partners: Germany, Italy, Belgium-Luxembourg, UK, Netherlands, USA, Spain, Switzerland, Japan, Sweden, Algeria.

Germany Imports ($ million): 382,050 (1991). Exports ($ million): 391,295 (1991). Main imports: machinery and transport equipment 35.0% (1991), chemicals and chemical products 8.4% (1991), food and live animals, crude materials (particularly petroleum). Main exports: machinery and transport equipment 48.9% (1991), chemicals and chemical products 12.8% (1991), miscellaneous manufactured articles. Principal trading partners: France, Italy, Netherlands, UK, Belgium, USA, Japan, Spain, Austria, Switzerland, Sweden, Denmark.

Greece Imports ($ million): 21,582 (1991). Exports ($ million): 8653 (1991). Main imports: machinery and transport equipment 32.8% (1991), food and live animals 10.9% (1991). Main exports: food, beverages and tobacco 25.8% (1991), textiles and footwear 21.6% (1991). Principal trading partners: Germany, Italy, France, Netherlands, Japan, Libya.

Iceland Imports ($ million): 1765 (1991). Exports ($ million): 1552 (1991). Main imports: machinery and transport equipment 35.7% (1991), chemicals and chemical products 8% (1991). Main exports: frozen and salted fish, crustaceans and molluscs 79.3% (1991). Principal trading partners: Germany, UK, USA, Japan.

Ireland Imports (IR£ thousand): 12,853,384 (1991). Exports (IR£ thousand): 15,024,639 (1991). Main imports: machinery and transport equipment 324.7% (1991), basic manufactures 15% (1991). Main exports: machinery and transport equipment 29.3% (1991), food 20.2% (1991). Principal trading partners: UK, Germany, USA, France, Netherlands.

Italy Imports ($ million): 182,554 (1991). Exports ($ million): 169,399 (1991). Main imports: machinery and transport equipment 31% (1991), chemicals and chemical products

11% (1991). Main exports: machinery and transport equipment 37.6% (1991), basic manufactures 21.4% (1991), chemical and chemical products, food and live animals, miscellaneous manufactured articles. Principal trading partners: Germany, France, USA, UK, Switzerland, Netherlands, Japan, Belgium-Luxembourg, Greece, Spain.

Liechtenstein Imports ($ million): 535 (1990). Exports ($ million): 989 (1990). Main imports: machinery and transport equipment 31.2% (1991), metal products 13.6% (1991). Main exports: food and food products 20.1% (1991). Principal trading partners: Switzerland, Austria.

Luxembourg Imports (Lux francs million): 277,110 (1991). Exports (Lux francs million): 214,353 (1991). Main imports: machinery and transport equipment 32.7% (1991), mineral products 11.9% (1991). Main exports: metal products, machinery and transport equipment 48% (1991), plastic materials and rubber manufactures 12.6% (1991). Principal trading partners: Germany, France, Belgium.

Malta Imports (LM thousand): 683,164 (1991). Exports (LM thousand): 405,409 (1991). Main imports: machinery and transport equipment 46.9% (1991), basic manufactures 18.3% (1991). Main exports: machinery and transport equipment 29.3% (1991), clothing 13% (1991). Principal trading partners: Italy, Germany, France, UK.

Monaco Imports and Exports: n/a. Monegasque figures are included in the French total. Principal trading partners: France, Italy.

Netherlands Imports ($ million): 125,906 (1991). Exports ($ million): 133,554 (1991). Main imports: machinery and transport equipment 31.9% (1991), chemicals and chemical products 10.4% (1991). Main exports: machinery and transport equipment 23.6% (1991), food and live animals 17.2% (1991). Principal trading partners: Germany, Belgium, France, UK, USA, Italy.

Norway Imports ($ million): 25,244 (1991). Exports ($ million): 33,999 (1991). Main imports: basic manufactures 16.4% (1991), machinery and transport equipment 14.7% (1991). Main exports: mineral fuels and lubricants 48.7% (1991). Principal trading partners: UK, Sweden, Germany, France, Denmark.

Portugal Imports ($ million): 26,113 (1991). Exports ($ million): 16,281 (1991). Main imports: machinery and transport equipment 35.6% (1991), chemicals and chemical products 8.9% (1991). Main exports: textiles and clothing 30.3% (1991), machinery and transport equipment 19.8% (1991). Principal trading partners: Germany, Spain, France, UK, Italy.

San Marino Imports and Exports: n/a. Figures included in the Italian total. Principal trading partner: Italy.

Spain Imports ($ million): 93,314 (1991). Exports ($ million): 60,182 (1991). Main imports: machinery and transport equipment 14% (1991), energy products 11.6% (1991). Main exports: transport equipment 18.1% (1991), agricultural products 13.9% (1991), chemicals and chemical products. Principal trading partners: France, Germany, Italy, UK, USA, Netherlands, Portugal, Japan.

Sweden Imports (kronor million): 289,923 (1991). Exports (kronor million): 326,008 (1991). Main imports: machinery and transport equipment 35.9% (1992), miscellaneous articles 17.3% (1992). Main exports: machinery and transport equipment 42.7% (1992), paper products 25% (1992). Principal trading partners: Germany, UK, USA, Norway, Denmark.

Switzerland Imports ($ million): 66,517 (1991). Exports ($ million): 61,537 (1991). Main imports: machinery and electronics 19.8% (1991), automobiles 6.4% (1991). Main exports: industrial machinery 28.6% (1991), pharmaceuticals 10% (1991). Principal trading partners: Germany, France, Italy, USA, UK.

United Kingdom Imports (£ million): 118,786 (1991). Exports (£ million): 104,877 (1991). Main imports: machinery and transport equipment 36.2% (1991), chemicals and chemical products 9.2% (1991), food (particularly meat and fruit), crude petroleum, chemicals and chemical products, miscellaneous manufactured articles. Main exports: machinery and transport equipment 41.5% (1991), basic manufactures (particularly office machines and equipment) 14.8% (1991), chemicals and related products. Principal trading partners: Germany, USA, France, Netherlands, Italy, Belgium-Luxembourg, Ireland, Switzerland, Canada, Norway, Denmark, Australia.

Vatican City has no 'economy' as such. (Its economic data is included with that of Italy.)

Andorra

Official name: Les Valls d'Andorrà (The Valleys of Andorra).

Member of: UN, CSCE.

Area: 467 km² (180 sq mi).

Population: 61,900 (1993 est).

Capital: Andorra la Vella 35,600 (town 22,400, Les Escaldes 13,200, 1990 est).

Other main towns: Ordino 13,200, Encamp 11,800 (1990 est).

Languages: Catalan (30%; official), Spanish (59%), French (6%).

Religion: Roman Catholic (90%).

Education: Education is compulsory between the ages of six and 14. In 1990 the literacy rate was 100%. There are no institutes of higher education.

Defence: Andorra has neither armed forces nor a defence budget.

Transport: Andorra has neither railways nor an airport. There are 220 km (138 mi) of roads.

Media: There is a single daily newspaper and a commercial radio station.

GOVERNMENT
Andorra has joint heads of state (co-princes) - the president of France and the Spanish bishop

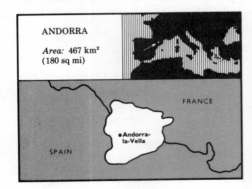

ANDORRA

Area: 467 km²
(180 sq mi)

FRANCE

Andorra-
la-Vella

SPAIN

of Urgel - who delegate their powers to permanent representatives who retain certain rights of veto under the new constitution approved

by a referendum in 1993. A 28-member Parliament is elected for four years by universal adult suffrage. The Parliament comprises 14 members elected by parish constituencies and 14 members elected on a national list. The only political party is the (centre-right) National Democratic Group (AND). After the first modern parliamentary election was held in December 1993 a coalition government of AND members and independents was formed.

Party strength: AND 8, independents 20.

Heads of state (co-Princes): Dr Juan Martí Alansis, Bishop of Urgel, and François Mitterrand, President of the French Republic.

Head of government (President of the Executive Council): Oscar Ribas Reig (AND).

GEOGRAPHY
Situated in the eastern Pyrenees, Andorra comprises two principal river valleys and is surrounded by mountains. Highest point: Pla del'Estany 3011 m (9678 ft). Principal river: Valira. Climate: Andorra is mild in spring and summer, but cold for six months, with snow in winter.

ECONOMY
The economy used to be based mainly on sheep and timber. Tourism has been encouraged by the development of ski resorts and by the duty-free status of consumer goods, and the country receives over 10,000,000 tourists a year, many of them on day visits to the co-principality. The principal imports are various consumer goods imported for sale in duty-free shops.

Currency: Andorra uses both French and Spanish currencies.

GDP: US$1,602,000,000 (1990); US$20,160 per head.

RECENT HISTORY
The country's joint allegiance to French and Spanish co-princes made difficulties for Andorra in obtaining international recognition until major constitutional changes came into force in 1993. The reforms of 1993 included a new constitution, the legalization of political parties and trade unions, a separate judiciary, independent diplomatic representation and UN membership.

Austria

Official name: Republik Osterreich (Republic of Austria)

Member of: UN, EFTA, OECD, CSCE, Council of Europe.

Area: 83,855 km² (32,367 sq mi).

Population: 7,812,000 (1991 census).

Capital: Vienna (Wien) 2,045,000 (city 1,533,000) (1991 census).

Other major cities: Linz 434,000 (city 203,000), Graz 395,000 (city 232,000), Salzburg 267,000 (city 144,000), Innsbruck 235,000 (city 115,000), Klagenfurt 135,000 (city 90,000), Villach 55,000, Wels 53,000, Sankt Pölten 50,000, Dornbirn 41,000, Steyr 40,000, Wiener Neustadt 35,000 (1991 census).

Language: German (official; 96%); Slovene (under 2%), Croat (1.8%), Magyar (Hungarian) small minority.

Religion: Roman Catholic (84%); Lutheran (6%); non-religious (8%).

Education: Education is compulsory between the ages of six and 15. In 1990 the literacy rate was virtually 100%. There are 18 institutions of university status including technical universities, art academies, etc.

Defence: In 1993 the total armed strength was 52,000 - 46,000 in the army and 6000 in the air force. Austria is neutral. All Austrian males are subject to military service of six months and are liable for 60 days of refresher courses.

Transport: There are 107,180 km (66,598 mi) of roads including 1532 km (952 mi) of motorways. State-run OBB operates 90% of the railway services - OBB runs 5623 km (3494 mi) of track; private companies operate 562 km (349 mi) of track. The Danube is used by barge traffic in Austria. Vienna, Graz, Klagenfurt, Innsbruck, Linz and Salzburg have international airports.

Media: The six daily newspapers published in Vienna and one of the titles published in Salzburg comprise Austria's national press. Twelve other daily newspapers are published. ORF, an autonomous state corporation, is the sole provider of radio and television programmes, operating two television channels, three national and 10 regional radio stations.

GOVERNMENT

Executive power is shared by the Federal President - who is elected by universal adult suffrage for a six-year term - and the Council of Ministers (Cabinet), led by the Federal Chancellor. The President appoints a Chancellor who commands a majority in the Federal Assembly's lower chamber, the Nationalrat, whose 183 members are elected by universal adult suffrage according to proportional representation for a term of four years. The 63 members of the upper chamber - the Bundesrat - are elected by the assemblies of the nine provinces of the Federal Republic. The nine provinces (Länder) have considerable autonomy. The main political parties are the (socialist) Social Democratic Party (SPO), (conservative) People's Party (OVP), (right-wing) Freedom Party (FPO), the Liberal Forum (LF) and the Greens (VGO). Following the election held in October 1990 a coalition of OVP and SPO members was formed. (Elections are scheduled for October 1994.)

Party strength: SPO 80, OVP 60, FPO 28, VGO 10, LF 5.

Federal President: Thomas Klestil (OVP).

THE CABINET

Federal Chancellor: Dr Franz Vranitzky (SPO).

Deputy Chancellor and Minister for Science: Dr Erhard Busek (OVP).

Minister of Agriculture and Forestry: Dr Franz Fischler (OVP).

Minister of Defence: Dr Werner Fasslabend (OVP).

Minister of Economic Affairs: Dr Wolfgang Schüssel (OVP).

Minister of Education and the Arts: Dr Rudolf Scholten (SPO).

Minister of Employment and Social Affairs: Josef Hesoun (SPO).

Minister for the Environment and for Youth and Family Affairs: Maria Rauch-Kallat (OVP).

Minister of Federal Affairs: Jürgen Weiss (OVP).

Austrian Provinces

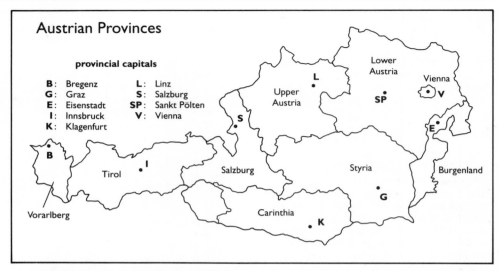

provincial capitals

B: Bregenz   **L**: Linz
G: Graz   **S**: Salzburg
E: Eisenstadt   **SP**: Sankt Pölten
I: Innsbruck   **V**: Vienna
K: Klagenfurt

Lower Austria
Vienna
Upper Austria
SP
V
S
E
B
Tirol I
Salzburg
Styria
Burgenland
Vorarlberg
Carinthia
G
K

Minister of Finance: Ferdinand Lacina (SPO).

Minister of Foreign Affairs: Dr Alois Mock (OVP).

Minister of Health, Consumer Protection and Sport: Dr Crista Krammer (SPO).

Minister of the Interior: Dr Franz Löschnak (SPO).

Minister of Justice: Dr Nikolaus Michalek (ind).

Minister of Public Economy and Transport: Dr Viktor Klima (SPO).

Minister for Women's Affairs: Johanna Dohnal (SPO).

PROVINCES (LÄNDER)

Burgenland Area: 3966 km² (1531 sq mi). Population: 274,000 (1991 census). Capital: Eisenstadt.

Carinthia (Kärnten) Area: 9533 km² (3681 sq mi). Population: 552,000 (1991 census). Capital: Klagenfurt.

Lower Austria (Niederösterreich) Area: 19,171 km² (7402 sq mi). Population: 1,481,000 (1991 census). Capital: Sankt Pölten

Salzburg Area: 7154 km² (2762 sq mi). Population: 484,000 (1991 census). Capital: Salzburg.

Styria (Steiermark) Area: 16,387 km² (6327 sq

mi). Population: 1,185,000 (1991 census). Capital: Graz.

Tirol Area: 12,647 km² (4883 sq mi). Population: 630,000 (1991 census). Capital: Innsbruck.

Upper Austria (Oberösterreich) Area: 11,979 km² (4625 sq mi). Population: 1,340,000 (1991 census). Capital: Linz.

Vienna (Wien) Area: 415 km² (160 sq mi). Population: 1,533,000 (1991 census). Capital: Vienna.

Vorarlberg Area: 2601 km² (1004 sq mi). Population: 333,000 (1991 census). Capital: Dornbirn.

GEOGRAPHY

The Alps - much of which are covered by pastures and forests - occupy nearly two thirds of Austria. Lowland Austria - in the east - consists of low hills, the Vienna Basin and a flat marshy area beside the Neusiedler See on the Hungarian border. Along the Czech border is a forested massif rising to 1200 m (4000 ft). Highest point: Grossglockner 3798 m (12,462 ft). Principal rivers: Danube (Donau), Inn, Mur. Climate: There are many local variations in climate owing to altitude and aspect. The east is drier than the west, and is, in general, colder than the Alpine region in the winter and hotter, but more humid, in the summer. Areas over 3000 m (10,000 ft) are snow-covered all year.

ECONOMY

Although Austria produces about 90% of its own food requirements, agriculture employs only 7% of the labour force. The arable land in the east has fertile soils producing good yields of cereals (wheat, barley and maize), as well as sugar beet and grapes for wine. Dairy produce is an important export from the pasturelands in the east and in the Alps. The mainstay of the economy is manufacturing industry, including machinery and transport equipment, iron and steel products, refined petroleum products, cement and paper. Austrian industry has been characterized by a high proportion of state-ownership, but privatization has been adopted in recent years. Natural resources include magnesite and iron ore, as well as important hydro-electric power potential - about three-quarters

AUSTRIA

Area: 83 855 km² (32 367 sq mi).

of Austria's electricity is supplied by HEP. Austria also has the most considerable forests in central Europe. The Alps attract both winter and summer visitors, making tourism a major earner of foreign currency. Austria retains economic links with countries in Central Europe that were once part of the Habsburg empire. However, Austria's main trading partners are Germany, Italy, France and Switzerland.

Currency: Schilling (ATS) of 100 groschen; 1US$ = 11.592 ATS (May 1994).

GDP: US$182,000,000,000 (1993 est); US$23,380 per head.

RECENT HISTORY

Before World War I, the (Habsburg) Austro-Hungarian Empire - ruled by the Emperor Franz Joseph I (reigned 1848-1916) - comprised not only modern Austria and Hungary but also Slovenia, Croatia, Bosnia-Herzegovina, the Czech Republic, Slovakia and parts of Italy, Poland, Ukraine, Romania and Serbia. The war began as an Austro-Serbian conflict but soon spread to most of the continent and Austria's aims soon became subordinate to those of Germany. By 1917 various nationalities within the Habsburg Empire were demanding indep-ndence and in 1918-19, after Austria's defeat, the Austro-Hungarian Habsburg empire was dismembered and the Emperor Karl I (reigned 1916-18) was deposed. A provisional govern-ment was formed under Dr Karl Renner. An Austrian republic was established as a separate state, despite support for union with Germany, which was forbidden by the post-war treaties that were imposed upon Austria. Austria was unstable throughout the 1920s and 1930s, and in 1933 Chancellor Dollfuss effectively became a dictator, ruling by decree. After Dollfuss was kidnapped and murdered by Nazis (1934), Kurt von Schuschnigg became Chancellor. Pan-German sentiments grew in Austria and, despite Germany's pledge to respect to Austria's sovereignty, Austria was invaded and annexed by Germany in 1938 (the Anschluss). (Adolf Hitler, the leader of the German Nazi Party and ruler of the German Third Reich, was an Austrian by birth.) Austria was liberated in 1945, but Allied occupation forces remained until 1955 when the independence of a neutral Austrian republic was recognized. The new Austrian federal republic has been characterized by coalition governments that link the two major political parties, the OVP and SPO (see above). The upheavals in Central Europe in 1989-90 encouraged Austria to renew links with Hungary, the Czech Republic, Slovenia, Croatia and Slovakia (all once Habsburg territories). In May 1994 the Austrian electorate voted in favour of joining the European Union/European Community - Austria will join the EU/EC on 1 January 1995.

Belgium

Official name: Royaume de Belgique (French) or Koninkrijk België (Flemish) (Kingdom of Belgium).

Member of: UN, NATO, EU/EC, WEU, CSCE, Council of Europe, OECD.

Area: 30,519 km² (11,783 sq mi).

Population: 10,022,000 (1992 est).

Capital: Brussels (Brussel or Bruxelles) 951,000 (1992 est).

Other major cities: Antwerp (Antwerpen or Anvers) 917,000 (city 465,000), Liège (Luik) 601,000 (city 196,000), Ghent (Gent or Gand) 485,000 (city 230,000), Malines (Mechelen) 293,000 (city 76,000), Courtrai (Kortrijk) 275,000 (city 76,000), Namur (Namen) 264,000 (city 104,000), Bruges (Brugge) 260,000 (city 117,000), Mons (Bergen) 92,000, La Louvière 77,000, Aalst (Alost) 77,000, Ostend (Oostende or Ostende) 69,000, St Niklaas (St Nicolas) 68,000, Tournai (Doornik) 68,000, Hasselt 67,000 (1992 est).

Languages: Flemish (a dialect of Dutch; nearly 58% as a first language), French (42%), German (under 1%). About 10% of the population is officially bilingual.

Religion: Roman Catholic (86%).

Education: Education is compulsory between the ages of six and 16, and voluntary full-time or compulsory part-time between the ages of 16 and 18. There are 15 institutions of university status.

Defence: Belgium is part of NATO and houses the organization's headquarters. Belgian males were subject to conscription for eight months until 1994 when compulsory military service was abolished The armed strength in 1993 was 54,100 (army), 4400 (navy) and 17,300 (air force). The Belgian navy is based at Ostend.

Transport: There are 137,876 km (85,672 mi) of roads including 1631 km (1014 mi) of motorways. There are 3466 km (2154 mi) of railways. Brussels has a metro and an international airport. The airports at Antwerp, Charleroi and Liège also receive international flights. Antwerp is the second largest commercial shipping port in Europe; Ostend is a major ferry port.

Media: There are 18 French-language daily newspapers, 15 Flemish-language dailies and one German. Three radio and television networks - one operating in each language - provide programmes. There are also many local radio stations.

GOVERNMENT

Belgium is a constitutional monarchy. The Chamber of Deputies (the lower house) comprises 212 members elected by universal adult suffrage for four years under a system of proportional representation. The Senate (the upper house) has 182 members: 106 directly elected, 50 chosen by provincial councils, 25 co-opted, plus the heir to the throne. The King appoints a Prime Minister, who commands a majority in the Chamber; the PM, in turn, appoints a Cabinet of Ministers responsible to the Chamber. The three regions have their own administrations and ministers. Local government is in the hands of nine provincial councils and 589 communes. Political parties include the (conservative) CVP (Flemish Christian Democrats), the (conservative) PSC (Francophone Christian Democrats), the SP (Flemish Socialist Party), the PS (Francophone Socialist Party), the (Flemish) PVV (Liberal Freedom and Progress Party), the (Francophone) PRL (Liberal Reform Party), the (Green Flemish) Agalev, the (Green Francophone) Ecolo, the (Flemish nationalist) Vlaams Blok and Volksunie parties, and the (Francophone) FDF (Democratic Front). A coalition of CVP, SP, PSC and PS members was formed after the last general election held in November 1991.

Party strength: CVP 39, PS 35, SP 28, PW 26, PRL 20, PSC 18, Vlaams Blok 12, Volksunie 10, Ecolo 10, Agalev 7, FDF 3, others 4.

King: His Majesty Albert II, King of the Belgians (succeeded 9 August 1993, following the death of his brother, 31 July 1993).

THE FEDERAL CABINET

Prime Minister: Jean-Luc Dehaene (CVP).

Deputy Prime Minister and Minister of Transport and Public Enterprises: Elio di Rupo (PS).

Deputy Prime Minister and Minister of Foreign Affairs: Willy Claes (SP).

Deputy Prime Minister, Minister of Justice and

BELGIUM

Area: 30 519 km²
(11 783 sq mi)

NORTH SEA

NETHERLANDS

Bruges
●Ghent
●Antwerp
●Brussels
Liège ●
Maas

GERMANY

FRANCE

LUXEMBOURG

Minister of Economic Affairs: Melchior Wathelet (PSC).

Minister of the Budget: Herman van Rompuy (CVP).

Minister of Defence: Leo Delcroix (CVP).

Minister of Employment: Miet Smet (CVP).

Minister of Finance: Philippe Maystadt (PSC).

Minister of Foreign Trade and European Affairs: Robert Urbain (PS).

Minister of Internal Affairs and the Civil Service: Louis Tobback (SP).

Minister of Pensions: Freddy Willockx (SP).

Minister of Scientific Policy: Jean-Maurice Dehousse (PS).

Minister of Small- and Medium-Sized Enterprises and Minister of Agriculture: André Bourgeois (CVP).

Minister of Social Affairs: Magda de Galan (PS).

Minister of Social Integration and Public Health and Minister for the Environment: Jacques Santkin (PS).

Secretary of State for Development: Eric Derycke (SP).

(Education, transport, culture, tourism, industry, etc., are the concern of the regional governments.)

REGIONS

Brussels (Brussel or Bruxelles) Area: 162 km² (63 sq mi). Population: 951,000 (1992 est). Administrative centre: Brussels.

Flanders (Vlaanderen) Area: 13,512 km² (5217 sq mi). Population: 5,725,000 (1991 census). Administrative centre: Ghent.

Wallonia (Wallonie) Area: 16,844 km² (6503 sq mi). Population: 3,165,000 (1991 census). Administrative centre: Namur.

PROVINCES

Antwerp (Antwerpen or Anvers) Area: 2867 km² (1107 sq mi). Population: 1,611,000 (1992 est). Capital: Antwerp.

Brabant Area: 3358 km² (1297 sq mi). Population: 2,254,000 (1992 est). Capital: Brussels.

East Flanders (Oost Vlaanderen or Flandre orientale) Area: 2982 km² (1151 sq mi). Population: 1,340,000 (1992 est). Capital: Ghent.

Hainaut Area: 3787 km² (1462 sq mi). Population: 1,283,000 (1992 est). Capital: Tournai.

Liège (Luik) Area: 3862 km² (1491 sq mi). Population: 1,006,000 (1992 est). Capital: Liège.

Limburg (Limbourg) Area: 2422 km² (935 sq mi). Population: 756,000 (1992 est). Capital: Hasselt.

Luxembourg (province) Area: 4441 km² (1715 sq mi). Population: 235,000 (1992 est). Capital: Arlon.

Namur (Namen) Area: 3665 km² (1415 sq mi). Population: 426,000 (1992 est). Capital: Namur.

West Flanders (West Vlaanderen or Flandre occidentale) Area: 3134 km² (1211 sq mi). Population: 1,112,000 (1992 est). Capital: Bruges.

GEOGRAPHY

The forested Ardennes plateau occupies the southeast. of the country The plains of central Belgium, an important agricultural region, are covered in fertile loess. The flat, low-lying north contains the sandy Kempenland plateau in the east and the plains of Flanders in the west. Enclosed by dykes behind coastal dunes are polders - former marshes and lagoons reclaimed from the sea. Highest point: Botrange 694 m (2272 ft). Principal rivers:

359

Belgian Regions and Provinces

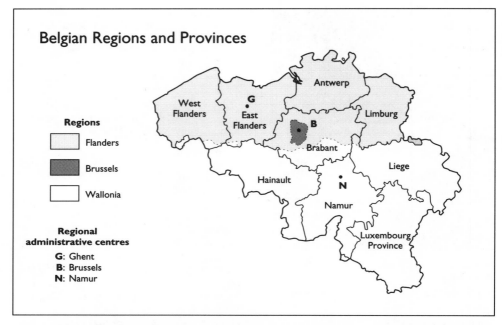

Regions

☐ Flanders

▨ Brussels

☐ Wallonia

Regional administrative centres

G: Ghent
B: Brussels
N: Namur

Scheldt (Schelde or Escaut), Meuse (Maas), Sambre. Climate: Coastal Belgium experiences relatively cool summers and mild winters. Summers are warmer and winters are colder inland.

ECONOMY

Belgium is a densely populated country in which over 96% of the population lives in towns. In the centre and the north soils are generally fertile and the climate encourages high yields of wheat, sugar beet, grass and fodder crops. Metalworking is a major industry, originally using local ores. Textiles, chemicals, ceramics, glass and rubber are also important, but almost all industrial raw materials have to be imported. Belgium is reliant upon foreign trade and is susceptible to fluctuations in the prices of raw materials and the demand for its goods and services. Belgium's economic problems since the 1970s have mirrored the country's linguistic divide with high unemployment - nearly 14% in February 1994 - concentrated in the Francophone (Walloon) south, while the industries of the Flemish north, in particular the Antwerp region, have prospered. Banking, commerce, other financial interests and administration employ increasing num-

bers, and Brussels has benefited as the unofficial capital of the EU/EC.

Currency: Belgian franc of 100 centimes. US$1 = 33.96 Belgian francs (May 1994).

GDP: US$210,000,000,000 (1993 est); US$21,000 per head.

RECENT HISTORY

Belgium's neutrality was broken by the German invasion in 1914 (leading to Britain's declaration of war against Germany). The brave resistance of King Albert I in 1914-18 earned international praise; the capitulation of Leopold III when Belgium was again occupied by Germany (1940-45) was criticized. The Belgian Congo (Zaïre), acquired as a personal possession by Leopold II (1879), was relinquished amidst scenes of chaos in 1960. Belgium is now the main centre of administration of the EU/EC and of NATO and has been an enthusiastic advocate of European integration. However, the country is troubled by the rivalry between its Flemish and French speakers, which has led to a number of violent demonstrations. A federal system, based upon linguistic regions, has gradually evolved, although the status of bilingual Brussels was problematic.

Cyprus

Official name: Kypriaki Dimokratia (Greek) or Kibris Cumhuriyeti (Turkish) (The Republic of Cyprus).

Member of: UN, Commonwealth, CSCE, Council of Europe.

Area: 9251 km² (3572 sq mi) - of which 3355 km² (1295 sq mi) are in the Turkish-controlled zone in the north. In southern Cyprus there are two sovereign British bases - Akrotiri-Episkopi and Dhekelia - which cover a total area of 256 km² (99 sq mi).

Population: 756,000 (1992 est) - 570,000 in the Greek Cypriot zone; 186,000 in the Turkish-controlled zone in the north. The population of the British sovereign bases - Akrotiri-Episkopi and Dhekelia - was estimated to be 4200 in 1993.

Capital: Nicosia (Levkosia) 209,000 (169,000 in the government-controlled zone and 40,000 in the Turkish-controlled zone) (1990-91 est).

Other major cities: Limassol (Lemesos) 135,000, Larnaca (Larnax) 63,000, Paphos (Pafos) 31,000 (1990-91 est) - in the government-controlled zone. The largest towns in the Turkish-controlled zone are Famagusta (Gazimagosa) 21,000, Kyrenia (Girne) 8000 (1990 est).

Languages: Greek (74%), Turkish (24%; including settlers from mainland Turkey).

Religions: Greek Orthodox (75%), Sunni Islam (over 20%; including settlers from the Turkish mainland); Roman Catholic (under 1%).

Education: Education is compulsory between the ages of five and a half and 12 in the government-controlled zone, and between the ages of seven and 15 in the Turkish zone). There is a university.

Defence: In 1993 the National Guard had a total strength of 10,000; Greek Cypriots are liable to 26 months' conscription. In the Turkish-controlled zone there is a Turkish Cypriot regular force of 4000. In 1993 about 30,000 troops of the regular forces of Turkey were based in the north. In the two sovereign British bases (see above) there are about 4200 personnel (1993).

Transport: There are 10,134 km (6334 mi) of roads in the government-controlled zone and 5530 km (3456 mi) of roads in the Turkish-controlled zone. In the government-controlled zone Paphos and Larnaca have international airports; an airport in the Turkish-controlled zone only receives flights from mainland Turkey.

Media: There are 10 Greek-language and one English-language daily newspapers in the government-controlled zone. Eight Turkish-language daily papers (including Cypriot editions of mainland Turkish papers) are published in the Turkish-controlled zone. CBC, a statutory corporation, broadcasts radio and television programmes in the government-controlled zone, which also has eight local radio stations and access to Greek television. In the Turkish-controlled zone a single corporation broadcasts radio and television programmes, and two television channels are received from the Turkish mainland. In the British sovereign bases radio and television services are supplied by the BFBS.

GOVERNMENT

A 56-member House of Representatives is elected by universal adult suffrage in the Greek Cypriot community for five years - an additional 24 seats for the Turkish Cypriot community remain unfilled. An executive President - who appoints a Council of Ministers - is elected from the Greek Cypriot community by universal adult suffrage for a five-year term. There is provision in the constitution for a Vice-President to be similarly elected from the Turkish Cypriot community. The British sovereign bases of Akrotiri-Episkopi and Dhekelia are governed by a British Administrator who is responsible to the British Secretary of State for Defence. In 1975, the administration of the

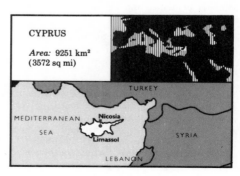

CYPRUS

Area: 9251 km² (3572 sq mi)

TURKEY

MEDITERRANEAN SEA

Nicosia

Limassol

SYRIA

LEBANON

361

Turkish Cypriot community unilaterally established the 'Turkish Republic of Northern Cyprus', which is unrecognized internationally except by Turkey. The main political parties in the Greek Cypriot zone are the (conservative) Democratic Rally (DISY) which is in an electoral alliance with the Liberal Party, the Progressive Party of Working People (the Communist Party, which is known as AKEL), the Democratic Party (DIKO) and the Socialist Party (EDEK). Following elections in the government-controlled zone in May 1991 a DISY and DIKO coalition government was formed.

Party strength: DISY 20, AKEL 18, DIKO 11. EDEK 8.

President: Glafcos Clerides (DISY).

THE CABINET
Minister of Agriculture and the Environment: Kostas Petrides (DISY).

Minister of Commerce and Industry: Stelios Kiliaris (DIKO).

Minister of Communications and Works: Adamos Adamides (DISY).

Minister of Defence: Kostas Eliades (DIKO).

Minister of Education and Culture: Kleri Angelidou (DISY).

Minister of Finance: Phaedros Ekonomides (DISY).

Minister of Foreign Affairs: Alekos Michaelides (DIKO).

Minister of Health: Manolis Christophides (DISY).

Minister of the Interior: Dinos Michaelides (DIKO).

Minister of Justice and Public Order: Alekos Evangelou (DISY).

Minister of Labour and Social Insurance: Andreas Mousioutas (DIKO).

GEOGRAPHY
The south of the island is covered by the Troodos Mountains. Running east to west across the centre of Cyprus is a fertile plain, north of which are the Kyrenian Mountains and the rugged Karpas Peninsula. Highest point: Mount Olympus 1951 m (6399 ft). Principal rivers: Seranhis, Pedieas - all rivers in Cyprus dry up for part of the year. Climate:

Cyprus has a Mediterranean climate with an average of 480 mm (19 in) of rainfall, most of which falls in winter. The Troodos Mountains receive snow during the winter months.

ECONOMY
Potatoes, fruit, wine, clothing and textiles are exported from the government-controlled zone, in which ports, resorts and international airports have been constructed to replace facilities lost since Turkey invaded the north, and over 200,000 refugees, displaced from their homes in the north by the invasion, have been resettled. The government-controlled zone has experienced very high economic growth rates, particularly in the tourist sector, which is the largest foreign-currency earner. The Turkish-controlled zone, which exports fruit and vegetables, is sparsely populated despite an influx of settlers from mainland Turkey. Although tourism is being developed, the Turkish-controlled zone relies heavily on aid from Turkey.

Currency: Cyprus pound (CYP) of 100 cents; 1US\$ =0.499 CYP (May 1994). The Turkish lira is used in the Turkish-controlled zone.

GDP: US\$5,633,000,000 (government-controlled zone only; 1990); US\$8040 per head.

RECENT HISTORY
British administration in Cyprus was established in 1878. During the 1950s, Greek Cypriots - led by Archbishop (later President) Makarios III (1913-77) - campaigned for Enosis (union with Greece). The Turkish Cypriots advocated partition, but following a terrorist campaign by the Greek Cypriot EOKA movement, a compromise was agreed. In 1960 Cyprus became an independent republic. Power was shared by the two communities, but the agreement broke down in 1963, and UN forces intervened to stop intercommunal fighting. The Turkish Cypriots set up their own administration. When pro-Enosis officers staged a coup in 1974, Turkey invaded the north. Cyprus was effectively partitioned and the Turkish Cypriots established the (internationally-unrecognized) 'Turkish Republic of Northern Cyprus'. Over 200,000 Greek Cypriots were displaced from the north, into which settlers arrived from Turkey. Since then, UN forces have manned the 'Attila Line' between the Greek south and Turkish north, but attempts to reunite Cyprus as a federal state have been unsuccessful.

Denmark

(Both the Faeroes and Greenland are part of the Kingdom of Denmark – only 'metropolitan Denmark' is dealt with here. For information on the Faeroes see pp. 424-25; for information on Greenland see p. 302.)

Official name: Kongeriget Danmark (Kingdom of Denmark).

Member of: UN, EC/EU, NATO, Council of Europe, CSCE, OECD, WEU (associate).

Area: 43,092 km² (16,638 sq mi) - metropolitan Denmark, excluding the Faeroes.

Population: 5,162,000 - metropolitan Denmark, excluding the Faeroes (1992 est).

Capital: Copenhagen (Kobenhavn) 1,337,000 (city 465,000; Frederiksberg 86,000) (1992 est).

Other major cities: Aarhus (Århus) 268,000, Odense 179,000, Aalborg (Ålborg) 157,000, Esbjerg 82,000, Randers 61,000, Kolding 58,000, Helsingor 57,000, Horsens 55,000, Vejle 52,000, Roskilde 50,000 (all including suburbs; 1992 est).

Language: Danish (99%; official), German (small minority in South Jutland).

Religion: Lutheran (89%); non-religious (9%).

Education: Education is compulsory between the ages of six and 16. In 1990 the literacy rate was virtually 100%. There are seven institutions of university status (universities, technical universities and university centres).

Defence: The Danish armed forces are raised in part from voluntary enlistment and in part from conscription. Male conscripts are selected at the age of 18-19 and are called up at about the age of 20. They are liable for service of between four and 12 months. In 1993 the armed forces comprised 17,100 in the army, 18,000 in the local defence force, 6900 in the navy, 8800 in the air force and 69,200 in the home guard. The main naval base is at Frederikshavn.

Transport: There are 71,063 km (44,156 mi) of roads, of which 653 km (408 mi) are motorways. State-run Danish railways, DSB, operate 2476 km (1539 mi) of track. Construction of a 17.7 km (11 mi) rail link under the Great Belt linking Denmark and Sweden began in 1988. Copenhagen has a metro system. Copenhagen,

Aarhus, Aalborg and Esbjerg are the main commercial shipping ports. Copenhagen has an important international airport.

Media: There are nearly 30 daily papers. Danmarks Radio-TV is a public corporation which operates a television channel and three national and 10 local radio stations. There is also a national commercial television channel. Over 350 local and community radio stations operate.

GOVERNMENT

Denmark is a constitutional monarchy. The 179 members of Parliament (Folketing) are elected

DENMARK

Area: 43 092 km² (16 638 sq mi) – 'metropolitan' Denmark, excluding dependencies

by universal adult suffrage under a system of proportional representation for four years. Two members are elected from both of the autonomous dependencies (Greenland and the Faeroes). The autonomous dependencies also have their own governments (see pp. 302 and 424-25). Metropolitan Denmark is divided into 14 counties (amstkommuner), the city of Copenhagen and the neighbouring borough of Frederiksberg. The Monarch appoints a Prime Minister, who commands a majority in the Folketing. The PM, in turn, appoints a State Council (Cabinet), which is responsible to the Folketing. The main political parties are the Social Democratic Party (SDP), the Conservative People's Party (KF), the Liberal Party (Venstre), the Socialist People's Party

363

(SFP), the (anti-tax, anti-state bureaucracy) Progress Party (FP), the Centre Democrats (CD), the Christian People's Party (KF), and the Radical Liberals (RV). In 1993 at the general election held on 12 December 1990 these parties obtained the following number of seats and in January 1993 a new SDP, CD, KF and RV coalition was formed.

Party strength: (election December 1990) SDP 69, KF 30, Venstre 29, SFP 15, FP 12, CD 9, RV 7, KF 4, Faeroese and Greenland members 4.

Queen: HM Queen Margrethe II (succeeded upon the death of her father, 14 January 1972).

THE CABINET
Prime Minister: Poul Nyrup Rasmussen (SDP).

Minister of Agriculture and Fisheries: Bjorn Westh (SDP).

Minister for Church Affairs: Arne Oluf Andersen (CD).

Minister for Communications and Tourism: Helge Mortensen (SDP).

Minister of Culture: Jytte Hilden (SDP).

Minister of Defence: Hans Haekkerup (SDP).

Minister of Development Cooperation: Helle Degn (SDP).

Minister for Economic Affairs: Marianne Jelved (RV).

Minister of Education: Ole Vig Jensen (RV).

Minister of Energy: Jann Sjursen (KF).

Minister for the Environment: Svend Auken (SDP).

Minister of Finance: Mogens Lykketoft (SDP).

Minister of Foreign Affairs: Niels Helveg Petersen (RV).

Minister of Health: Torben Lund (SDP).

Minister of Housing and Minister of Nordic and Baltic Affairs: Flemming Kofod Svendsen (KF).

Minister of Industry and Coordination: Mimi Jakobsen (CD).

Minister of the Interior: Birte Weiss (SDP).

Minister of Justice: Erling Olsen (SDP).

Minister of Labour: Jytte Andersen (SDP).

Minister of Research and Ecclesiastical Affairs: Arne Oluf Andersen (CD).

Minister for Social Affairs: Yvonne Herlov Andersen (CD).

Minister of Taxation: Ole Stavad (SDP).

Minister of Transport: Jan Troberg (SDP).

COUNTIES
Aarhus (Århus) Area: 4561 km² (1761 sq mi). Population: 605,000 (1992 est). Capital: Aarhus.

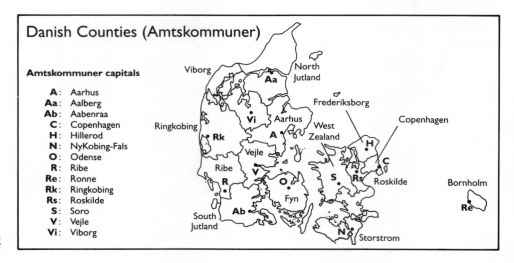

Danish Counties (Amtskommuner)

Amtskommuner capitals

- **A**: Aarhus
- **Aa**: Aalberg
- **Ab**: Aabenraa
- **C**: Copenhagen
- **H**: Hillerod
- **N**: NyKobing-Fals
- **O**: Odense
- **R**: Ribe
- **Re**: Ronne
- **Rk**: Ringkobing
- **Rs**: Roskilde
- **S**: Soro
- **V**: Vejle
- **Vi**: Viborg

Bornholm Area: 588 km² (215 sq mi). Population: 46,000 (1992 est). Capital: Ronne.

Copenhagen (Kobenhavn) (city) Area: 88 km² (34 sq mi). Population: 465,000 (1992 est). Capital: Copenhagen.

Copenhagen (Kobenhavn) (county) Area: 526 km² (203 sq mi). Population: 603,000 (1992 est). Capital: Copenhagen.

Frederiksberg (municipality) Area: 9 km² (3.5 sq mi). Population: 86,000 (1992 est). Capital: Frederiksberg.

Frederiksborg Area: 1347 km² (520 sq mi). Population: 345,000 (1992 est). Capital: Hillerod.

Fyn Area: 3486 km² (1346 sq mi). Population: 433,000 (1992 est). Capital: Odense.

North Jutland (Nordjylland) Area: 6173 km² (2383 sq mi). Population: 485,000 (1992 est). Capital: Aalberg (Årlberg).

Ribe Area: 3131 km² (1209 sq mi). Population: 220,000 (1992 est). Capital: Ribe.

Ringkobing Area: 4853 km² (1874 sq mi). Population: 268,000 (1992 est). Capital: Ringkobing.

Roskilde Area: 891 km² (344 sq mi). Population: 220,000 (1992 est). Capital: Roskilde.

South Jutland (Sonderjylland) Area: 3938 km² (1520 sq mi). Population: 251,000 (1992 est). Capital: Aabenraa (Åbenra).

Storstrom Area: 3398 km² (1312 sq mi). Population: 257,000 (1992 est). Capital: NyKobing-Fals.

Vejle Area: 2997 km² (1157 sq mi). Population: 333,000 (1992 est). Capital: Vejle.

Viborg Area: 4123 km² (1592 sq mi). Population: 230,000 (1992 est). Capital: Viborg.

West Zealand (Vestsjaelland) Area: 2984 km² (1152 sq mi). Population: 285,000 (1992 est). Capital: Soro.

GEOGRAPHY

Denmark is a lowland of glacial moraine - only the island of Bornholm has ancient hard surface rocks. The country comprises the Jutland peninsula - which occupies about two thirds of the total area of Denmark - and, to the east of Jutland, a series of over 400 islands, of which 97 are inhabited. The largest islands are Zealand (Sjaelland), Fyn and Lolland. The island of Bornholm lies to the east in the Baltic Sea. Highest point: Yding Skovhêj 173 m (568 ft). Principal river: Gudená. Climate: The climate is temperate and moist with mild summers and cold winters. Bornholm – an island in the Baltic Sea to the east of the rest of Denmark – is more extreme.

ECONOMY

Denmark has a high standard of living, but few natural resources. Danish agriculture, which is famous for its efficiency, is organized on a cooperative basis, and produces cheese and other dairy products, bacon and beef - all mainly for export. About one fifth of the labour force is involved in manufacturing, with iron- and metal-working, food processing and brewing, engineering and chemicals as the most important industries. The high cost of imported fuel has been a problem, but this has been partly alleviated by petroleum and natural gas from the North Sea. In 1994 Denmark had high interest rates and unemployment stood at nearly 12%.

Currency: Danish krone (DKK) of 100 ore; 1US$ = 6.44 DKK (May 1994).

GDP: US$140,000,000,000 (1993 est); US$ 26,900 per head.

RECENT HISTORY

In the 20th century, Denmark's last colonial possessions were either sold (Virgin Islands) or given independence (Iceland) or autonomy (Greenland and the Faeroe Islands). In 1920 northern Schleswig - surrendered to Germany in 1864 - was returned to Denmark. The country was occupied by Nazi Germany (1940-45), and has since been a member of the Western Alliance. From the 1960s, Denmark has developed economic and political ties with Germany, the United Kingdom and the Netherlands rather than the traditional links with other Scandinavian countries, particularly Norway and Sweden. In 1973 Denmark joined the EC, but the political consequence of joining the Common Market has been a further fragmentation of the country's political parties, which has made the formation of coalition and minority governments a protracted and difficult process. The rejection of the terms of the Maastrict Treaty by the Danish electorate in 1992 temporarily halted moves towards European integration.

Finland

Official name: Suomen Tasavalta (Republic of Finland).

Member of: UN, EFTA, CSCE, Council of Europe, OECD, NATO (partner for peace).

Area: 338,145 km² (130,557 sq mi).

Population: 5,029,000 (1992 est).

Capital: Helsinki (Helsingfors) 1,005,000 (city 498,000; Espoo (Esbo) 176,000; Vantaa (Vanda) 157,000) (1992 est).

Other major cities: Turku (Åbo) 265,000 (city 159,000), Tampere (Tammerfors) 262,000 (city 174,000), Oulu (Uleaborg) 102,000, Lahti 93,000, Kuopio 82,000, Pori (Björneborg) 76,000, Jyväskylä 67,000, Kotka 57,000, Lappeenranta (Villmanstrand) 55,000, Vaasa (Vasa) 54,000, Joensuu 48,000, Hämeenlinna (Tavastehus) 40,000, Kajaani 37,000, Kokkola (Karleby) 35,000 (1992 est).

Languages: Finnish (94%), Swedish (6%), Lapp (small minority).

Religion: Lutheran (88%), Finnish Orthodox, non-religious (11%).

Education: Education is compulsory between the ages of seven and 16. In 1990 the literacy rate was estimated to be virtually 100%. There are 19 institutions of university status - Finnish- and Swedish-language universities, schools of economics, social work, etc.

Defence: Finland has joined NATO's Partnership for Peace. All Finnish males are subject to military conscription of 240, 285 or 330 days and, following this initial training, are liable to recall to refresher courses of 40-100 days. In 1993 the total armed strength was 32,600, including 27,800 in the army, 1800 in the navy and 3000 in the air force. There were over 665,000 reserves. The main naval bases are at Upinniemi (near Helsinki) and at Turku.

Transport: There are 77,980 km (48,738 mi) of roads, of which 225 km (140 mi) are motorways. The state-run railway company VR operates 5863 km (3643 mi) of railways. Helsinki has a metro system and a rapid light transit system. The main commercial shipping ports are Kotka, Helsinki and Turku. Helsinki has an international airport.

Media: There are 65 daily newspapers - 53 in Finnish and 12 in Swedish. The YLE network, a public corporation, broadcasts three television channels, two national radio stations and various regional stations. There are over 30 local radio stations. Broadcasting is in both Finnish and Swedish.

FINLAND
Area: 338 145 km² (130 557 sq mi).

GOVERNMENT

The 200-member Eduskunta (Parliament) is elected for four years under a system of proportional representation by universal adult suffrage. Executive power is vested in a President elected for six years by direct popular vote. The President appoints a Council of State (Cabinet) - headed by a Prime Minister - responsible to the Parliament. There are 12 provinces (laani), one of which, the Åland Islands, has a considerable degree of self-government. The main political parties include the Centre Party (Kesk), the Social Democratic Party (SDP), the (conservative) National Coalition Party (Kok), the Left-Wing Alliance (Vasemmistoliitto), the Green Union (VL), the Swedish People's Party (SFP), the Liberal People's Party (LKP), the Rural Party (SMP), the Finnish Christian Union (SKL) and the Communist Workers' Party. Following the election held in March 1991 a coalition government of members of Kesk, Kok, SFP and SKL was formed; the coalition government has since been reshuffled.

Party strength: (at the general election in March 1991) Kesk 55, SDP 48, Kok 40, Vasemmistoliitto 19, SFP 12, VL 10, SKL 8, SMP 7, LKP 1.

President: Martti Ahtisaari.

THE CABINET

Prime Minister: Esko Aho (Kesk).

Deputy Prime Minister and Minister of Foreign Trade: Pertti Salolainen (Kok).

Minister of Agriculture and Forestry: Mikko Pesala (Kesk).

Minister for Cultural Affairs: Tytti Isohookana-Asunmaa (Kesk).

Minister of Defence: Elisabeth Rehn (SFP).

Minister of Development and Cooperation: Toimi Kankaanniemi (SKL).

Minister of Education: Olli-Pekka Heinonen (Kok).

Minister for the Environment: Sirpa Pietikäinen (Kok).

Minister of Finance: Iiro Viinanen (Kok).

Minister of Foreign Affairs: Heikki Haavisto (Kesk).

Minister of Justice: Anneli Jaatteenmaki (Kesk).

Minister of Housing: Pirjo Rusanen (Kok).

Minister of the Interior: Mauri Pekkarinen (Kesk).

Minister of Labour: Ilkka Kanerva (Kok).

Minister of Social Affairs and Health: Jorma Huuhtanen (Kesk).

Minister of Trade and Industry: Seppo Kaariainen (Kesk).

Minister of Transport and Communications: Ole Norrback (SFP).

AUTONOMOUS PROVINCE

Åland Islands (Ahvenanmaa) Area: 1527 km² (590 sq mi). Population: 24,800 (1992 est). Capital: Mariehamn.

PROVINCES

Hame (Tavastehus) Area: 16,341 km² (6309 sq mi). Population: 685,000 (1992 est). Capital: Hameenlinna

Keski-Suomi (Mellersta Finland) Area: 16,251 km² (6275 sq mi). Population: 255,000 (1992 est). Capital: Jyväskylä.

Kuopio Area: 16,510 km² (6375 sq mi). Population: 24,800 (1992 est). Capital: Kuopio.

Kymi (Kymmene) Area: 10,783 km² (4163 sq

Finnish Provinces (Laani)

Laani capitals

H: Hameenlinna
He: Helsinki
J: Jyvaskyla
Jo: Joensuu
K: Kouvola
Ku: Kuopio
M: Mikkeli
Ma: Mariehamn
O: Oulu
R: Rovaniemi
T: Turku
V: Vaasa

mi). Population: 335,000 (1992 est). Capital: Kouvola.

Lappi (Lappland) Area: 93,057 km² (35,929 sq mi). Population: 202,000 (1992 est). Capital: Rovaniemi.

Mikkeli (St Michel) Area: 16,321 km² (6302 sq mi). Population: 208,000 (1992 est). Capital: Mikkeli.

Oulu (Uleaborg) Area: 56,868 km² (21,957 sq mi). Population: 443,000 (1992 est). Capital: Oulu.

Pohjois-Karjala (Norra Karelen) Area: 17,782 km² (6866 sq mi). Population: 177,000 (1992 est). Capital: Joensuu.

Turku-Pori (Abo-Bjorneborg) Area: 22,839 km² (8818 sq mi). Population: 730,000 (1992 est). Capital: Turku.

Uusimaa (Nyland) Area: 9898 km² (3822 sq mi). Population: 1,264,000 (1992 est). Capital: Helsinki.

Vaasa (Vasa) Area: 26,412 km² (10,198 sq mi). Population: 447,000 (1992 est). Capital: Vaasa.

GEOGRAPHY
Nearly one third of Finland lies north of the Arctic Circle and one tenth of the country is covered by lakes, some 50,000 in all. Saimaa - the largest lake - has an area of over 4400 km² (1700 sq mi). During the winter months the Gulfs of Bothnia (to the west) and of Finland (to the south) freeze, and ports have to be kept open by icebreakers. The land has been heavily glaciated, and except for mountains in the northwest most of the country is lowland. Highest point: Haltiatunturi 1342 m (4344 ft). Principal rivers: Paatsjoki, Torniojoki, Kemijoki, Kokemäenjoki. Climate: Finland's climate is characterized by warm summers and long, extremely cold winters (particularly in the north).

ECONOMY
Forests cover about two thirds of the country and wood products are one of the most important sources of Finland's foreign earnings. Metalworking and engineering - in particular shipbuilding - are among the most important of Finland's industries, which have a reputation for quality and good design. Finland enjoys a high standard of living, although - apart from forests, copper and rivers suitable for hydroelectric power - the country has few natural resources. There is a large fishing industry, and the agricultural sector produces enough cereals and dairy products for export. (There is some concern about the future of Finland's subsidized agriculture within an enlarged EU/EC.) The collapse of trade with Russia - traditionally a major trading partner - brought severe economic difficulties to Finland since 1991. Unemployment peaked at 20% in 1993 and cuts in the welfare state have had to be made as tax returns have slumped.

Currency: Markka of 100 pennis; 1US$ = 5.375 markka (May 1994).

GDP: US$85,000,000,000 (1993 est); US$16,830 per head.

RECENT HISTORY
After the Russian Revolution of 1917, civil war broke out in Russian-ruled Finland. The left-wing forces were eventually defeated at the Battle of Tampere by right-wing forces led by General Carl Gustaf Mannerheim. In 1919 Finland adopted an independent republican constitution, which is still in force today. A Russian Red Army invasion in 1920 was repulsed. The demands of the Swedish-speaking inhabitants of the Åland Islands for union with Sweden were rejected but the islands gained considerable autonomy (1921). Finland's territorial integrity lasted until 1939 when a Soviet invasion followed Finland's refusal to make territorial concessions to the USSR. Despite fierce resistance Finland was defeated (1940) and was forced to cede the Karelian isthmus, the shores of Lake Ladoga and Viipuri (Vyborg) - which was then Finland's second city - to the Soviet Union. In 1941 the transit of German troops across Finnish soil was allowed and, when Germany attacked the USSR, Finland was drawn into a second war against the Soviet Union. Finnish forces made initial advances but, upon Germany's retreat (1944), Finland had to make peace with the USSR. As well as previous territorial losses Finland had to cede her only access to the Arctic Ocean, the port of Petsamo, and was burdened with heavy reparation payments to the USSR. The Soviet Union also gained a long-term lease on the Porkkala peninsula near Helsinki. The term 'Finlandization' was coined to describe this curtailment of sovereignty and independent action of a small nation by a powerful neighbour. Finland has, since 1945, retained its neutrality and independence. Despite having to resettle over 300,000 refugees from areas ceded to the USSR and repaying war reparations, Finland recovered quickly. The country has achieved some influence through the careful exercise of its neutrality, for example, hosting the initial sessions of CSCE (the 'Helsinki accords'). Government in Finland is characterized by multi-party coalitions, and since 1987 parties of the left have lost favour. Economically, Finland is integrated into Western Europe through membership of EFTA, OECD, and NATO's Partnership for Peace and is scheduled to join the EC/EU. A referndum is to be held in autumn 1994 concerning Finnish membership of the EC/EU. If the Finnish electors approve, Finland will join the Community in January 1995.

France

Official name: La République Française (The French Republic).

Member of: UN, EC/EU, NATO, WEU, G7, OECD, CSCE, Council of Europe.

Area: 543,965 km² (210,026 sq mi).

Population: 57,456,000 (1992 est).

Capital: Paris 9,063,000 (city 2,175,000).

Other major cities: Lyon 1,262,000 (city 422,000), Marseille 1,087,000 (city 808,000), Lille 950,000 (city 178,000), Bordeaux 686,000 (city 213,000), Toulouse 608,000 (city 366,000), Nantes 492,000 (city 252,000), Nice 476,000 (city 346,000), Toulon 438,000 (city 170,000), Grenoble 400,000 (city 154,000), Strasbourg 388,000 (city 256,000), Rouen 380,000 (city 105,000), Valenciennes 336,000 (town 39,000), Cannes 336,000 (city 69,000), Lens 323,000 (town 35,000), Saint-Etienne 313,000 (city 202,000), Nancy 311,000 (city 102,000), Tours 272,000 (city 133,000), Béthune 260,000 (town 26,000), Clermont-Ferrand 254,000 (city 140,000), Le Havre 254,000 (city 197,000), Rennes 245,000 (city 204,000), Orléans 243,000 (city 108,000), Montpellier 235,000 (city 211,000), Dijon 226,000 (city 152,000), Mulhouse 224,000 (city 110,000), Reims 206,000 (city 185,000), Angers 206,000 (city 146,000), Brest 201,000 (city 153,000), Douai 200,000 (city 44,000), Dunkerque 193,000 (town 71,000), Metz 193,000 (city 124,000), Le Mans 189,000 (city 148,000), Caen 189,000 (city 116,000), Mantes-la-Jolie 189,000 (town 45,000), Avignon

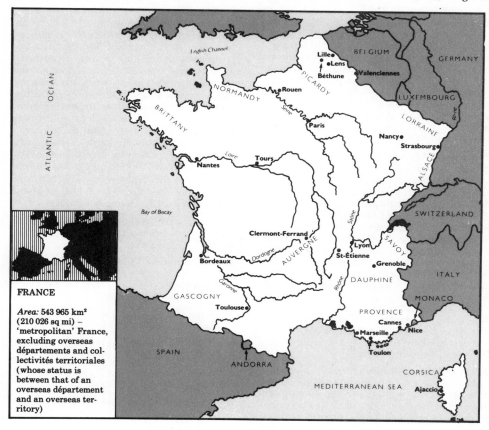

FRANCE

Area: 543 965 km² (210 026 sq mi) – 'metropolitan' France, excluding overseas départements and collectivités territoriales (whose status is between that of an overseas département and an overseas territory)

181,000 (city 89,000), Limoges 170,000 (city 136,000) (1990 census).

Languages: French (over 93% as a first language), Arabic (2.5%% as a first language), German (Alsatian; 2%), Portuguese (1%), Breton (under 1%); plus Catalan, Basque, Flemish and Corsican minorities.

Religions: Roman Catholic (74%), non-religious (18%), various Protestant Churches (4%), Sunni Islam (2%).

Education: Education is compulsory between the ages of six and 16. In 1990 the literacy rate was estimated to be nearly 99%. There are 75 universities including polytechnics of university.

Defence: In 1993 the total armed strength was 545,800 - 285,000 in the army, 8,500 in the Foreign Legion, 95,700 in the paramilitary Gendarmerie, 64,900 in the navy and 91,700 in the air force. This total includes 48,000 stationed in Germany and 15,000 elsewhere abroad. Brest and Toulon are the main naval bases. France is a NATO member although it does not formally come under the NATO command structure. France is a nuclear power with an estimated 426 nuclear warheads. Frenchmen are subject to conscription, normally from the age of 18-19. The period of military service is now 10 months.

Transport: There are 805,600 km (500,576 mi) of roads of which 7100 km (4412 mi) are motorways. The state-run SNCF operates 34,322 km (21,327 mi) of railway. Paris, Lille, Lyon and Marseille have metro systems; Lille, Nantes, St Etienne and Toulouse have rapid light transit systems. The largest port in France is Marseille which handles over 90,300,000 tonnes of goods a year. Le Havre handles over 50,000,000 tonnes of goods a year and Dunkerque handles over 30,000,000 tonnes. Other major commercial shipping ports include Rouen, Nantes-St Nazaire and Bordeaux. Paris Orly and Paris Charles de Gaulle are Europe's third and fourth largest airports. The third Parisian airport is Le Bourget. Other international French airports are Bordeaux, Lille, Lyon, Marseille, Nice, Strasbourg and Toulouse.

Media: Although 16 daily newspapers are published in Paris, France has a regional rather than a national press. The 55 provincial daily papers dominate regional sales. Radio France broadcasts seven channels through 47 local

radio stations. There are over 1700 local commercial radio stations and three commercial stations that are almost national in coverage. Two state-run and three commercial television channels compete.

GOVERNMENT
Executive power is vested in the President, who is directly elected for seven years. The President appoints a Prime Minister and a Council of Ministers - both responsible to Parliament - but it is the President, rather than the PM, who presides over the Council. The Senate (upper house) has 321 members - 296 representing individual départements and 13 representing overseas départements and territories - elected by members of local councils. The remaining 12 senators are elected by French citizens resident abroad. Senators serve for nine years, with one third of the Senate retiring every three years. The National Assembly (lower house) has 577 deputies - including 22 for overseas départements and territories - elected for five years by universal adult suffrage from constituencies, with a second ballot for the leading candidates if no candidate obtains an absolute majority in the first round. The 96 metropolitan départements are grouped into 22 regions which have increasing powers. Political parties include the (conservative Gaullist) RPR (Rally for the Republic), the (centrist) UDF (Union for French Democracy), the PS (Socialist Party), the PCF (Communist Party), and the (right-wing) FN (National Front). Following the election held in March 1993, an RPR-UDF government was formed.

Party strength (Assembly): RPR and RPR allies 257, UDF and UDF allies 215, PS and allies 57, PCF and allies 23, independents 25.

President: François Mitterrand (PS).

THE CABINET
Prime Minister: Edouard Balladur (RPR).

Minister of Agriculture and Fisheries: Jean Puech (UDF allies).

Minister for the Budget and Government Spokesman: Nicolas Sarkozy (RPR).

Minister of Business and Economic Development: Alain Madelin (UDF).

Minister for the Civil Service: André Rossinot (UDF).

Minister of Communications: Alain Carignon (RPR).

Minister for Co-operation: Michel Poussin (RPR).

Minister of Culture and the French Language: Jacques Toubon (RPR).

Minister of State, Minister for Defence: François Léotard (UDF).

Minister of the Economy: Edmond Alphandéry (UDF).

Minister of Education: François Bayrou (UDF).

Minister for the Environment: Michel Barnier (RPR).

Minister of Foreign Affairs: Alain Juppé (RPR).

Minister of Higher Education and Research: François Fillon (RPR).

Minister of Housing: Hervé de Charette (UDF).

Minister for Industry, Posts, Telecommunications and Foreign Trade: Gérard Longuet (UDF).

Minister of State for the Interior and Town and Country Planning: Charles Pasqua (RPR).

Minister of Justice, Minister of State, Keeper of the Seals: Pierre Méhaignerie (UDF allies).

Minister of Labour, Employment and Vocational Training: Michel Giraud (RPR).

Minister for Overseas Départements and Territories: Dominique Perben (RPR).

Minister of Public Works, Transport and Tourism: Bernard Bosson (UDF allies).

Minister of State for Social Affairs, Health and Urban Affairs: Simone Veil (UDF).

Minister for Veterans and War Victims: Philippe Mestre (UDF).

Minister for Youth and Sport: Michèle Alliot-Marie (RPR).

REGIONS

Alsace Area: 8280 km² (3197 sq mi). Population: 1,632,000 (1991 est). Administrative centre: Strasbourg.

Aquitaine Area: 41,308 km² (15,949 sq mi). Population: 2,813,000 (1991 est). Administrative centre: Bordeaux.

Auvergne Area: 26,013 km² (10,044 sq mi).

Population: 1,321,000 (1991 est). Administrative centre:

Brittany (Bretagne) Area: 27,208 km² (10,505 sq mi). Population: 2,805,000 (1991 est). Administrative centre: Rennes.

Burgundy (Bourgogne) Area: 31,582 km² (12,194 sq mi). Population: 1,613,000 (1991 est). Administrative centre: Dijon.

Centre Area: 39,151 km² (15,116 sq mi). Population: 2,384,000 (1991 est). Administrative centre: Orléans.

Champagne-Ardenne Area: 25,606 km² (9886 sq mi). Population: 1,348,000 (1991 est). Administrative centre: Reims.

Corsica (Corse) Area: 8680 km² (3351 sq mi). Population: 250,000 (1991 est). Administrative centre: Ajaccio.

Franche-Comté Area: 16,202 km² (6256 sq mi). Population: 1,098,000 (1991 est). Administrative centre: Besançon.

Ile-de-France Area: 12,012 km² (4638 sq mi). Population: 10,735,000 (1991 est). Administrative centre: Paris.

Languedoc-Roussillon Area: 27,376 km² (10,570 sq mi). Population: 2,139,000 (1991 est). Administrative centre: Montpellier.

Limousin Area: 16,942 km² (6541 sq mi). Population: 723,000 (1991 est). Administrative centre: Limoges.

Lorraine Area: 23,547 km² (9091 sq mi). Population: 2,304,000 (1991 est). Administrative centre: Nancy.

Lower Normandy (Basse Normandie) Area: 17,589 km² (6791 sq mi). Population: 1,395,000 (1991 est). Administrative centre: Caen.

Midi-Pyrénées Area: 45,348 km² (17,509 sq mi). Population: 2,445,000 (1991 est). Administrative centre: Toulouse.

Nord-Pas-de-Calais Area: 12,414 km² (4793 sq mi). Population: 3,968,000 (1991 est). Administrative centre: Lille.

Pays de la Loire Area: 32,082 km² (12,387 sq mi). Population: 3,073,000 (1991 est). Administrative centre: Nantes.

Picardy (Picardie) Area: 19,399 km² (7490 sq mi). Population: 1,819,000 (1991 est).

Administrative centre: Amiens.

Poitou-Charentes Area: 25,810 km² (9965 sq mi). Population: 1,598,000 (1991 est). Administrative centre: Poitiers.

Provence-Côte d'Azur Area: 31,400 km² (12,124 sq mi). Population: 4,294,000 (1991 est). Administrative centre: Marseille.

Rhône-Alpes Area: 43,698 km² (16,872 sq mi). Population: 5,391,000 (1991 est). Administrative centre: Lyon.

Upper Normandy (Haute-Normandie) Area: 12,317 km² (4756 sq mi). Population: 1,746,000 (1991 est). Administrative centre: Rouen.

GEOGRAPHY

The Massif Central, a plateau of old hard rocks, rising to almost 2000 m (6500 ft), occupies central France. The Massif is surrounded by four major lowlands, which together make up almost two thirds of the total area of France. The Paris Basin - the largest of these lowlands - is divided by low ridges, fertile plains and plateaux, but is united by the river system of the Seine and its tributaries. East of the Massif Central is the long narrow Rhône-Saône Valley, while to the west the Loire Valley stretches to the Atlantic. Southwest of the Massif Central lies the Aquitaine Basin, a large fertile region drained by the River Garonne and its tributaries. A discontinuous ring of highlands surrounds France. In the northwest the Armorican Massif (Brittany) rises to 411 m (1350 ft). In the southwest the Pyrenees form a high natural boundary with Spain. The Alps in the southeast divide France from Italy and contain the highest peak in Europe. The lower Jura - in the east - form a barrier between France and Switzerland, while the Vosges Mountains separate the Paris Basin from the Rhine Valley. In the northeast, the Ardennes extend into France from Belgium. The Mediterranean island of Corsica is an ancient massif rising to 2710 m (8891 ft). Highest point: Mont Blanc 4807 m (15,771 ft). Principal rivers: Rhine (Rhin), Loire, Rhône, Seine, Garonne, Saône. Climate: The Mediterranean south has warm summers and mild winters. The rest of France has a temperate climate, although the more continental east experiences warmer summers and colder winters. Rainfall is moderate, with highest falls in the mountains and lowest falls around Paris.

ECONOMY

Over 60% of France is farmed. The principal products include cereals (wheat, maize, barley and even rice), meat and dairy products, sugar beet, and grapes for wine. France is remarkably self-sufficient in agriculture, with tropical fruit and animal feeds being the only major imports. However, the small size of land holdings remains a problem, despite consolidation and the efforts of cooperatives. Reafforestation is helping to safeguard the future of the important timber industry. Natural resources include coal, iron ore, copper, bauxite, tungsten, petroleum, natural gas, and plentiful sites for hydroelectric power plants. Major French industries include: textiles, chemicals, steel, food processing, motor vehicles, aircraft, and mechanical and electrical engineering. Traditionally French firms have been small, but mergers have resulted in larger corporations able to compete internationally. France is now the world's fourth industrial power after the USA, Japan and Germany. Since the late 1980s many state-owned corporations were privatized. Over one half of the labour force is involved in service industries, in particular administration, banking, finance, and tourism. Unemployment stood at over 12% in February 1994.

Currency: Franc of 100 centimes; 1US$ = 5.685 (June 1994).

GDP: US$1,240,000,000,000 (1993 est); US$22,670 per head.

RECENT HISTORY

Between 1919 and 1939 French government was characterized by instability and frequent changes of administration. In World War II (1939-45), Germany rapidly defeated the French in 1940 and completely occupied the country in 1942. Marshal Philippe Pétain (1856-1951) led a collaborationist regime in the city of Vichy, while General Charles de Gaulle (1890-1970) headed the Free French in exile in London from 1940. France was liberated following the Allied landings in Normandy in 1944. After the war, the Fourth Republic (1946-58) was marked by instability and the Suez Crisis of 1956 - when France and the UK sought to prevent Egypt's nationalization of the canal. The end of the colonial era was marked by nationalist revolts in some of the colonies, notably Vietnam - where the Communists defeated French colonial forces at

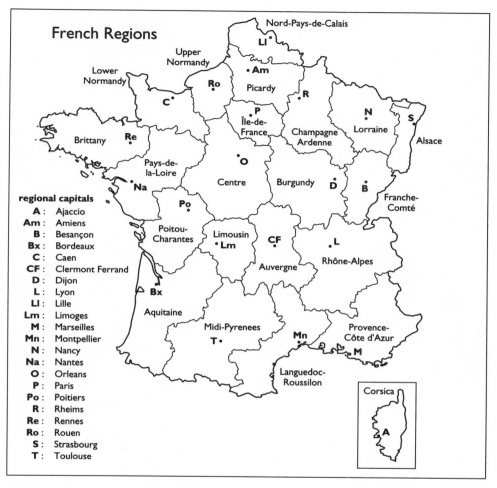

French Regions

Nord-Pays-de-Calais

LI

Upper Normandy

Am

Lower Normandy

Ro

Picardy

R

Île-de-France

P

N

Lorraine

S

Brittany

Re

Pays-de-la-Loire

Champagne Ardenne

Alsace

Na

O

Centre

Burgundy

D

B

Franche-Comté

Po

regional capitals
- **A** : Ajaccio
- **Am** : Amiens
- **B** : Besançon
- **Bx** : Bordeaux
- **C** : Caen
- **CF** : Clermont Ferrand
- **D** : Dijon
- **L** : Lyon
- **LI** : Lille
- **Lm** : Limoges
- **M** : Marseilles
- **Mn** : Montpellier
- **N** : Nancy
- **Na** : Nantes
- **O** : Orleans
- **P** : Paris
- **Po** : Poitiers
- **R** : Rheims
- **Re** : Rennes
- **Ro** : Rouen
- **S** : Strasbourg
- **T** : Toulouse

Poitou-Charentes

Limousin

Lm

CF

L

Auvergne

Rhône-Alpes

Bx

Aquitaine

Midi-Pyrenees

T

Mn

Provence-Côte d'Azur

M

Languedoc-Roussilon

Corsica

A

Dien Bien Phu in 1954 - and Algeria. The troubles in Algeria - including the revolt of the French colonists and the campaign of their terrorist organization, the OAS - led to the end of the Fourth Republic and to the accession to power of General de Gaulle in 1959. As first president of the Fifth Republic, de Gaulle granted Algerian independence in 1962. The French colonial empire - with a few minor exceptions - was disbanded. France's position within Western Europe was strengthened by vigorous participation in the EC. De Gaulle also sought to pursue a foreign policy independent of the USA, building up France's nuclear capability and withdrawing French forces from NATO's integrated command structure. Although restoring political and economic stability to France, domestic dissatisfaction - including the student revolt of May 1968 - led de Gaulle to resign in 1969. De Gaulle's policies were broadly pursued by his successors as president, Georges Pompidou (in office 1969-74) and Valéry Giscard d'Estaing (1974-81). The modernization of France continued apace under the first French Socialist president, François Mitterrand (1916-), who was elected in 1981.

373

Germany

Official name: Bundesrepublik Deutschland (The Federal Republic of Germany).

Member of: UN, EC/EU, NATO, CSCE, WEU, G7, OECD, Council of Europe.

Area: 357,050 km² (137,857 sq mi).

Population: 79,754,000 (1991 est).

Capital: Berlin (capital in name only) 3,590,000 (city 3,446,000), Bonn (administrative capital) 542,000 (city 296,000).

Other major cities: Essen 4,700,000 (Essen/Ruhr agglomeration; Essen city 627,000, Dortmund 601,000 Duisburg 537,000, Bochum 399,000, Gelsenkirchen 294,000, Oberhausen 225,000, Herne 179,000, Mülheim 177,000), Hamburg 1,924,000 (city 1,669,000), Munich (München) 1,465,000 (city 1,229,000), Cologne (Köln) 1,419,000 (city 960,000, Leverkusen 161,000), Frankfurt 1,268,000 (city 654,000), Stuttgart 1,091,000 (city 592,000), Düsseldorf 913,000 (city 578,000), Hannover 680,000 (city 518,000), Bremen 622,000 (city 553,000), Nuremberg (Nürnberg) 617,000 (city 498,000), Dresden 580,000 (city 485,000), Mannheim 539,000 (city 315,000, Ludwigshafen 165,000),Leipzig 532,000 (city 503,000), Wuppertal 485,000 (city 386,000), Solingen 357,000 (city 166,000), Hagen 342,000 (city 216,000), Mönchengladbach 341,000 (city 263,000), Bielefeld 322,000, Chemnitz 306,000 (city 288,000), Halle 303,000, Augsburg 281,000 (city 260,000), Karlsruhe 279,000, Magdeburg 275,000, Münster 264,000, Wiesbaden 264,000, Brunswick (Braunschweig) 259,000, Kiel 259,000 (city 247,000), Krefeld 246,000, Aachen 244,000, Rostock 244,000, Saarbrücken 236,000 (city 192,000), Lübeck 230,000 (city 216,000), Erfurt 205,000, Kassel 197,000, Freiburg 194,000, Mainz 183,000, Hamm 180,000, Osnabrück 165,000, ,Ulm 160,000 (city 112,000) (1990-91 est).

Language: German (official; over 97% as a first language), Turkish (2.1% as a first language), plus small minorities speaking Frisian and Sorb.

Religions: Lutheran and Churches of the Lutheran tradition (43%), Roman Catholic (36%), non-religious (18%), Sunni Islam (2%).

Education: Education is compulsory full time between the ages of six and 16 and is compulsory on a part-time basis up to the age of 18. In 1991 the literacy rate was estimated to be virtually 100%. There are 78 universities including technical, medical and postgraduate universities.

Defence: In 1993 the total armed strength was 447,000 - 316,000 in the army (including 64,000 in the territorial army), 35,000 in the navy, 96,000 in the air force. The main naval bases are at Wilhelmshaven, Bremerhaven, Kiel and Rostock. US, British and French troops are based in Germany; the last Russian troops were withdrawn from the former GDR in 1994. Germany is a NATO member. German males are subject to compulsory military service of 12 months.

Transport: There are 621,267 km (386,037 mi) of roads of which 11,714 km (7279 mi) are motorways. The state-run DB railway system operates 42,000 km (26,098 mi) of track. Berlin, Frankfurt, Munich, Essen, Duisburg and Nuremberg have metros; Wuppertal, Nuremberg, Stuttgart, Karlsruhe, Hamburg, Hannover, Essen, Dortmund, Duisburg and Cologne have rapid light transit systems. The main shipping ports are Hamburg, which handles over 57,000,000 tones of goods a year, and Duisburg, on the Rhine (over 40,000,000 tonnes a year). Other major ports include Bremen with Bremerhaven, Rostock and Wilhelmshaven. There are over 7541 km (4686 mi) of inland waterways of which the most important are the rivers Rhine, Danube, Main and Elbe and the Main-Danube Canal. Frankfurt is a major international airport. Other international airports are Berlin (two airports), Cologne-Bonn, Dresden, Düsseldorf, Hamburg, Hannover, Munich, and Stuttgart.

Media: Nearly 400 daily newspapers are published in Germany but only some Frankfurt, Berlin and Hamburg papers have national circulations. ARD is a national coordinating body for German radio and television networks. Five radio networks, each broadcasting up to five channels, operate in Germany. There are 15 regional broadcasting organizations and three television channels.

GOVERNMENT

Each of the 16 states (Länder; singular Länd) is represented in the 79-member upper house of Parliament - the Federal Council (Bundesrat) - by three, four or six members (depending on population). The lower house - the Federal Assembly (Bundestag) - has 662 members elected for four years by universal adult suffrage under a mixed system of single-member constituencies and proportional representation. Executive power rests with the Federal Government, led by the Chancellor who is elected by the Bundestag. The Federal President is elected for five years by the Bundesrat and an equal number of representatives of the states. Each state has its own government. The main political parties are the (conservative) CDU (Christian Democratic Union) and CSU (Christian Social Union, its Bavarian equivalent), the (socialist) SPD (Social Democratic Party), the (liberal) FDP (Free Democratic Party), Die Grünen (the Green Party), and the PDS (Party of Democratic Socialism; the former East German Communist Party). Following the election held in 1990 a coalition of CDU/CSU and FDP members was formed.

Party strength: CDU/CSU 319, SPD 239, FDP 79, PDS 17, Die Grunen 8.

GERMANY

Area: 357 050 km² (137 857 sq mi).

Federal President: Roman Hertzog (CDU).

THE CABINET

Federal Chancellor: Dr Helmut Kohl (CDU).

Deputy Federal Chancellor: Dr Klaus Kinkel (FDP).

Minister at the Chancellery: Friedrich Bohl (CDU).

Minister of Defence: Volker Rühe (CDU).

Minister of Economic Co-operation and Development: Carl-Dieter Spranger (CSU).

Minister for the Economy: Dr Günter Rexrodt (FDP).

Minister of Education and Science: Dr Karl-Hans Laermann (FDP).

Minister for the Environment, Nature Conservation and Nuclear Safety: Dr Klaus Töpfer (CDU).

Minister for the Family and Senior Citizens: Hannelore Rönsch (CDU).

Minister of Finance: Dr Theo (Theodor) Waigel (CSU).

Minister of Food, Agriculture and Forestry: Jochen Borchert (CDU).

Minister of Foreign Affairs: Dr Klaus Kinkel (FDP).

Minister of Health: Horst Seehofer (CSU).

Minister of the Interior: Manfred Kanther (CDU).

Minister of Justice: Sabine Leutheusser-Schnarrenberger (FDP).

Minister of Labour and Social Affairs: Dr Norbert Blüm (CDU).

Minister of Posts and Telecommunications: Dr Wolfgang Bötsch (CSU).

Minister for Regional Planning, Building and Urban Development: Dr Irmgard Schwaetzer (FDP).

Minister of Research and Technology: Dr Paul Kruger (CDU).

Minister of Transport: Matthias Wissmann (CDU).

Minister for Women and Youth: Angela Merkel (CDU).

375

LANDER

Baden-Württemberg Area: 35,752 km² (13,803 sq mi). Population: 9,822,000 (1991 est). Capital: Stuttgart.

Bavaria (Bayern) Area: 70,546 km² (27,238 sq mi). Population: 11,449,000 (1991 est). Capital: Munich (München)

Berlin Area: 883 km² (341 sq mi). Population: 3,446,000 (1991 est). Capital: Berlin.

Brandenburg Area: 28,016 km² (10,817 sq mi). Population: 2,578,000 (1991 est). Capital: Potsdam.

Bremen Area: 404 km² (156 sq mi). Population: 682 000 (1991 est). Capital: Bremen.

Hamburg Area: 755 km² (292 sq mi). Population: 1 669 000 (1991 est). Capital: Hamburg.

Hesse (Hessen) Area: 21,114 km² (8152 sq mi). Population: 5,763,000 (1991 est). Capital: Wiesbaden.

Lower Saxony (Niedersachsen) Area: 47,431 km² (18,313 sq mi). Population: 7,387,000 (1991 est). Capital: Hannover.

Mecklenburg-West Pomerania (Mecklenburg-Vorpommern) Area: 26,694 km² (10,307 sq mi). Population: 1,924,000 (1991 est). Capital: Schwerin.

North Rhine-Westphalia (Nordrhein-Westfalen) Area: 34,066 km² (13,153 sq mi). Population: 17,350,000 (1991 est). Capital: Düsseldorf.

Rhineland-Palatinate (Rheinland-Pfalz) Area: 19,848 km² (7663 sq mi). Population: 3,764,000 (1991 est). Capital: Mainz.

Saarland Area: 2571 km² (993 sq mi). Population: 1,073, 000 (1991 est). Capital: Saarbrücken.

Saxony (Sachsen) Area: 17,713 km² (6839 sq mi). Population: 4,764,000 (1991 est). Capital: Dresden.

Saxony-Anhalt (Sachsen-Anhalt) Area: 20,297 km² (7837 sq mi). Population: 2,874,000 (1991 est). Capital: Magdeburg.

Schleswig-Holstein Area: 15,720 km² (6069 sq mi). Population: 2,626,000 (1991 est). Capital: Kiel.

Thuringia (Thüringen) Area: 15,209 km² (5872 sq mi). Population: 2,611,000 (1991 est). Capital: Erfurt.

GEOGRAPHY

The North German Plain - a region of fertile farmlands and sandy heaths - is drained by the Rivers Elbe and Weser and their tributaries. In the west, the plain merges with the North Rhine lowlands which contain the Ruhr coalfield and over 20% of Germany's population. A belt of plateaux crosses Germany from east to west and includes the Hunsrück and Eifel highlands in the Rhineland, the Taunus and Westerwald uplands in Hesse, and extends into the Harz and Erz Mountains in Thuringia. The Rhine cuts through these central plateaux in a deep gorge. In southern Germany, the Black Forest (Schwarzwald) separates the Rhine valley from the fertile valleys and scarplands of Swabia. The forested edge of the Bohemian uplands marks the Czech border, while the Bavarian Alps form the frontier with Austria. Highest point: Zugspitze 2963 m (9721 ft). Principal rivers: Rhine (Rhein), Elbe, Danube (Donau), Oder, Moselle (Mosel), Neckar, Havel, Leine, Weser. Climate: The climate of Germany is temperate, but with considerable variations between the generally mild northern coastal plain and the Bavarian Alps in the south, which have cool summers and cold winters. Local relief leads to significant climatic variations. The east has has warm summers and cold winters.

ECONOMY

Germany is the world's third industrial power after the USA and Japan. The country's recovery after World War II has been called the 'German economic miracle'. The principal industries include mechanical and electrical engineering, chemicals, textiles, food processing and vehicles, with heavy industry and engineering concentrated in the Ruhr, chemicals in cities on the Rhine, and motor vehicles in large provincial centres such as Stuttgart. From the 1980s, there has been a spectacular growth in high-technology industries. Apart from coal and brown coal, and small deposits of iron ore, potash and salt, Germany has few natural resources and relies upon imports. Labour has also been in short supply. Large numbers of 'guest workers' (Gastarbeiter), particularly from Turkey and former Yugoslavia, have been recruited. Since 1990 the labour shortage in western Germany has also been met by migration from the east. The service sector is well developed. Banking and finance are major foreign-currency earners, and Frankfurt is one of the world's leading financial and business centres. German economic policy and interest rates have a profound effect upon the economies of the other members of the EU. The unification of Germany in October 1990 presented a major problem for the German economy and, coupled with the effects of international recession, the costs of reunification have resulted in an economic downturn.

The GDR's economy had previously been the most successful in Soviet-controlled Eastern Europe but, compared with West Germany, it lagged in production, quality, design, profitability and standards of living. A trust - the Treuhandanstalt (THA) - was established to oversee the privatization of the state-run firms in eastern Germany. These were broken up into firms and recast as joint-stock companies owned by the THA. In early 1994 unemployment in the former GDR stood at over 20%. The main German agricultural products

German Länder

Länder capitals

B:	Berlin
Br:	Bremen
D:	Düsseldorf
Dr:	Dresden
E:	Erfurt
H:	Hamburg
Hv:	Hannover
K:	Kiel
M:	Munich
Mg:	Magdeburg
Mz:	Mainz
P:	Potsdam
S:	Stuttgart
Sa:	Saarbrücken
Sw:	Schwerin
W:	Wiesbaden

include hops (for beer), grapes (for wine), sugar beet, wheat, barley, and dairy products. The collectivized farms of the former GDR were privatized in 1990-91. Forests, covering over 30% of Germany, support a flourishing timber industry.

Currency: Deutsche Mark (DM) of 100 pfennig; 1US$ = 1.644 DM.

GDP: US$1,910,00,000,000 (1993 est); US$23,520 per head.

RECENT HISTORY
Defeat in World War I led to the loss of much territory in Europe, the end of the German monarchies, the imposition of reparations, and the occupation of the Rhineland by Allied forces until 1930. The liberal Weimar republic (1919-33) did not bring economic or political stability. In the early 1930s the Nazi Party grew, urging the establishment of a strong centralized government, an aggressive foreign policy, and the overturn of the postwar settlement. In 1933, the Nazi leader Adolf Hitler (1889-1945) became Chancellor and in 1934 President. His Third Reich annexed Austria (1938), dismembered Czechoslovakia (1939), and embarked on the extermination of the Jews and others that the Nazis regarded as 'inferior'. In 1939 Hitler concluded the Nazi-Soviet Non-Aggression Pact, which allowed the USSR to annex the Baltic states and agreed to divide Poland between the USSRand Germany. Hitler invaded Poland in September 1939. Britain and France declared war on Germany but were unable to help the Poles. In 1940 Hitler invaded Denmark, Norway, the Low Countries and France. The German invasion of the USSR (1941) opened the Eastern Front. At the height of Axis power (1942), Germany controlled, directly or through allies, most of Europe except the British Isles, Switzerland, Sweden, Spain and Portugal. The tide against the Axis countries turned in North Africa late in 1942. In 1943, Soviet forces started to push back the Germans. In 1944 the Allied landings in Normandy began the liberation of Western Europe. After massive Allied bombing, the end came swiftly for Germany. Hitler committed suicide (April 1945) and Berlin fell to the Soviets (May 1945). Germany lost territory to Poland, and was divided - as was its capital, Berlin - into four zones of occupation by the UK, France, the USA and the USSR. Cooperation between the Allies rapidly broke

down, and in 1948-49 the USSR blockaded West Berlin. The western zones of Germany merged to form the Federal Republic of Germany and the German Democratic Republic was proclaimed in the Soviet zone (1949). Food shortages and repressive Communist rule in the GDR led to an uprising in 1953. West Germany gained sovereignty in 1955. Relations between East and West Germany were soured as large numbers of East Germans fled to the West - this outflow was stemmed only when Walter Ulbricht (GDR Communist Party leader 1950-71) ordered the building of the Berlin Wall (1961). Chancellor Konrad Adenauer (1876-1967) strove to gain the acceptance of West Germany back into Western Europe through reconciliation with France and participation in the EC. The economic revival of Germany begun by Adenauer continued under his Christian Democrat (conservative) successors as Chancellor - Ludwig Erhard (1963-66) and Georg Kiesinger (1966-69). Under the Social Democrat Chancellors - Willy Brandt (1969-74) and Helmut Schmidt (1974-82) - treaties were signed with the Soviet Union (1970) and Poland (recognizing the Oder-Neisse line as Poland's western frontier), and relations with the GDR were normalized (1972). In the late 1980s, West Germany - under Helmut Kohl (Christian Democrat Chancellor from 1982) - acted as an economic and cultural magnet for much of Eastern Europe. The root causes of the GDR's problems remained, however, and resurfaced in the late 1980s. The ageing Communist leadership led by Erich Honecker proved unresponsive to the mood of greater freedom emanating from Gorbachov's USSR. In 1989 fresh floods of East Germans left the GDR for the West by way of Poland, Czechoslovakia and Hungary. Massive public demonstrations in favour of reform led to the appointment of a new East German leadership. The Berlin Wall was reopened (November 1989) allowing free movement between East and West. A government including members of opposition groups was appointed. Free elections were held in the GDR in March 1990 and the Communists were reduced to a minority. When the East German economy collapsed, the call for German reunification became unstoppable - reunification took place on 3 October 1990 but its costs have been far greater than anticipated, bringing recession, unemployment, cuts in government spending and tax increases.

Greece

Official name: Ellenikí Dimokrátia (Hellenic Republic) or Ellás (Greece).

Member of: UN, EC/EU, NATO, Council of Europe, CSCE, OECD, WEU.

Area: 131,957 km² (50,949 sq mi).

Population: 10,269,000 (1991 census).

Capital: Athens (Athínai) 3,097,000 (including Piraeus (Piraiévs) 196,000; 1991 census).

Other major cities: Thessaloníki (Salonika) 706,000, Patras (Pátrai) 155,000, Volos 107,000, Lárisa 102,000, Heraklion (Iráklion) 102,000, Kavalla 57,000, Canea (Khania) 48,000 (all including suburbs; 1991 census).

Language: Greek (official; over 96%), Macedonian (which is recognized by the Greek government as a dialect of Bulgarian; 1.5% - the official figure is smaller); plus small minorities of Turkish-, Albanian- and Vlach-speakers.

Religion: Orthodox (98%; official), Islam (1%).

Education: Education is compulsory between the ages of six and 15. In 1990 the literacy rate was estimated to be 93.2%. There are 16 universities.

GREECE

Area: 131 957 km²
(50 949 sq mi).

Defence: Greece is a NATO member. In 1993 the total armed strength stood at 186,000 - 113,000 in the army, 26,500 in the paramilitary gendarmerie, 19,500 in the navy and 26,800 in the air force. Conscription is compulsory for Greek males, normally without exemptions. Training lasts for 19 months for the army, 21 months for the air force, and 24 months for the navy.

Transport: There are 130,000 km (80,800 mi) of roads of which 116 km (72 mi) are motorways. State-run Greek railways, OSE, operate 2479 km (1540 mi) of track. Athens has a metro system. Athens, Corfu, Heraklion, Rhodes and Thessaloniki are the main international airports.

Media: There are over 130 daily newspapers most with small regional circulations. State-owned ERT provides a national network of radio and television programmes (three channels). There are two commercial television channels.

GOVERNMENT

The 300-member Parliament is elected for four years by universal adult suffrage under a system of proportional representation. The President - who is elected for a five-year term by Parliament - appoints a Prime Minister (who commands a majority in Parliament) and other Ministers. There are 13 regions, which are further subdivided into departments, plus Mount Athos, which has a special status (see below). The main political parties include PASOK (the Pan-Hellenic Socialist Party), the (conservative) NDP (New Democracy Party), the (centre-right) Political Spring (PS), and the (Communist-led) Left Alliance (KKE). Folowing the election held in October 1993 a PASOK government was formed.

Party strength: PASOK 170, NDP 111, PS 10, KKE 9

President: Konstantinos Karamanlis (NDP).

THE CABINET
(all members of PASOK)

Prime Minister: Andreas Papandreou.

Minister for the Aegean: Konstantinos Skandalides.

Minister of Agriculture: Giorgios Moraitis.

Minister of Culture: Athanassios Mikroutsicos.

Minister of Defence: Gerasimos Arsenis.

Minister of Education and Religious Affairs: Dimitri Fatouros.

Minister of the Environment, Town Planning and Public Works: Costas Laliotis; (alternate) Ioannis Souladakis.

Minister of Finance: Alexandros Papadopoulos.

Minister of Finance (National Debt): Nikolaos Kypiazidis.

Minister of Foreign Affairs: Karolos Papoulias; (EC) Theodoros Pangalos.

Minister of Health, Welfare and Social Services: Dimitri Kremastinos.

Minister of Industry, Energy and Technology, and Minister of Commerce: Konstantinos Simitis.

Minister of the Interior: Apostolos Tsohatzopoulos.

Minister of Justice: Giorgios Kouvelakis.

Minister of Labour: Evangelos Yiannopoulos.

Minister for Macedonia and Thrace: Konstantinos Triarides.

Minister for the Merchant Marine: Giorgios Katsifaras.

Minister of the National Economy: Yiannis Papantoniou; (alternate) Giorgios Romaios; (Tourism) Dionysis Livanos.

Minister to the PM's Office: Anastasios Peponis.

Minister of Public Order: Stelios Papathemelis.

Minister of Transport and Communications: Ioannis Haralambous.

REGIONS (DHIAMERISMA)

Attica (Attiki) Area: 3808 km² (1470 sq mi). Population: 3,523,000 (1991 census). Capital: Athens.

Central Greece (Sterea Ellas) Area: 15,549 km² (6004 sq mi). Population: 579,000 (1991 census). Capital: Lamia.

Central Macedonia (Kedriki Makedhonia) Area: 19,147 km² (7393 sq mi). Population: 1,738,000 (1991 census). Capital: Thessaloniki.

Crete (Kriti) Area: 8336 km² (3218 sq mi). Population: 537,000 (1991 census). Capital: Heraklion.

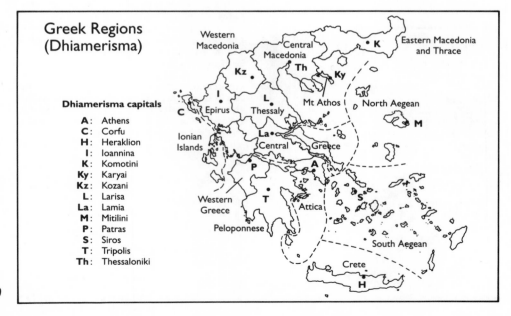

Greek Regions (Dhiamerisma)

Dhiamerisma capitals

A: Athens
C: Corfu
H: Heraklion
I: Ioannina
K: Komotini
Ky: Karyai
Kz: Kozani
L: Larisa
La: Lamia
M: Mitilini
P: Patras
S: Siros
T: Tripolis
Th: Thessaloniki

Eastern Macedonia and Thrace (Anatoliki Makedhonia kai Thraki) Area: 14,157 km² (5466 sq mi). Population: 570,000 (1991 census). Capital: Komotini.

Epirus (Ipiros) Area: 9203 km² (3553 sq mi). Population: 339,000 (1991 census). Capital: Ioannina.

Ionian Islands (Ionioi Nisoi) Area: 2307 km² (891 sq mi). Population: 191,000 (1991 census). Capital: Corfu.

North Aegean (Voreion Aiyaion) Area: 3836 km² (1481 sq mi). Population: 198,000 (1991 census). Capital: Mitilini.

Peloponnese (Peloponnisos) Area: 15,490 km² (5981 sq mi). Population: 606,000 (1991 census). Capital: Tripolis.

South Aegean (Notion Aiyaion) Area: 5286 km² (2041 sq mi). Population: 258,000 (1991census). Capital: Siros.

Thessaly (Thessalia) Area: 14,037 km² (5420 sq mi). Population: 731,000 (1991 census). Capital: Larisa.

Western Greece (Dhytiki Ellas) Area: 11,350 km² (4382 sq mi). Population: 702,000 (1991 census). Capital: Patras.

Western Macedonia (Dhytiki Makedhonia) Area: 9451 km² (3649 sq mi). Population: 293,000 (1991 census). Capital: Kozani.

Mount Athos (Ayion Oros) (an autonomous monks' republic) Area: 336 km² (130 sq mi). Population: 1400 (1990 est). Capital: Karyai.

GEOGRAPHY
Over 80% of Greece is mountainous. The mainland is dominated by the Pindus Mountains, which extend from Albania south into the Peloponnese Peninsula. The Rhodope Mountains lie along the Bulgarian border. Greece has some 2000 islands, of which only 154 are inhabited. Highest point: Mount Olympus 2911 m (9550 ft). Principal rivers: Aliákmon, Piniós, Akhelóös. Climate: Greece has a Mediterranean climate with hot dry summers and mild wet winters. The north and the mountains are colder.

ECONOMY
Agriculture involves about one quarter of the labour force. Much of the land is marginal - in particular the extensive sheep pastures. Greece is largely self-sufficient in wheat, barley, maize, sugar beet, fruit, vegetables and cheese, and produces enough wine, olives (and olive oil) and tobacco for export. The industrial sector is expanding rapidly and includes the processing of natural resources such as petroleum and natural gas, lignite, uranium and bauxite. Tourism, the large merchant fleet, and money sent back by Greeks working abroad are all important foreign-currency earners. Greece receives special economic aid from the EC.

Currency: Drachma; 1US$ = 246.6 drachma (May 1994).

GDP: US$80,000,000,000 (1993 est); US$7700 per head.

RECENT HISTORY
Greece in the 20th century has been marked by great instability. Eleuthérios Venizélos (1864-1936) dominated Greek politics from 1910 to 1935, a period of rivalry between republicans and royalists. An attempt by his rival King Constantine I to seize Anatolia from Turkey (1921-22) ended in military defeat and the establishment of a republic in 1924. The monarchy was restored in 1935, but it depended upon a military leader, General Ioannis Metaxas (1871-1941), who, claiming the threat from Communism as justification, ruled as virtual dictator. The nation was deeply divided. The German invasion of 1941 was met by rival resistance groups of Communists and monarchists, and the subsequent civil war between these factions lasted from 1945 to 1949, when, with British and US aid, the monarchists emerged victorious. Continued instability in the 1960s led to a military coup in 1967. King Constantine II, who had not initially opposed the coup, unsuccessfully appealed for the overthrow of the junta and went into exile. The dictatorship of the colonels ended in 1974 when their encouragement of a Greek Cypriot coup brought Greece to the verge of war with Turkey. Civilian government was restored, and a new republican constitution was adopted in 1975. Greece has since forged closer links with Western Europe, in particular through membership of the EC (1981). Greek opposition delayed international recognition of the former Yugoslav republic of Macedonia in 1992-93 and in 1994 Greece defied the European Community by imposing an economic blockade upon Macedonia. This move strained relations with the rest of the EU .

Iceland

Official name: Lydveldid Island (The Republic of Iceland).

Member of: UN, NATO, EFTA, Council of Europe, CSCE, OECD.

Area: 103,001 km² (39,769 sq mi).

Population: 264,000 (1993 est).

Capital: Reykjavik 154,000 (city 101,000; Kópavogur 17,000; Hafnarfjördhur 16,000) (1992 est).

Other major towns: Akureyri 15,000, Keflavik 7500 (1992 est).

Language: Icelandic (official; 100%).

Religion: Evangelical Lutheran Church (nearly 93%), non-religious (7%), Roman Catholic (under 1%).

Education: Education is compulsory between the ages of six and 16. In 1990 the literacy rate was 100%. There is a single university.

Defence: There is a coast guard service of 130 personnel. US forces based in Iceland form the 3000-strong Iceland Defence Force. Iceland is a NATO member.

Transport: There are 11,460 km (7121 mi) of roads. Iceland has no railways. Coastal ferries are important. Reykjavik is the principal commercial shipping port. Keflavik has an international airport.

Media: Despite a very small domestic market, Iceland has six daily newspapers. There are two television channels - one state-owned, the other commercial. There are two state-owned radio stations and one commercial radio station.

GOVERNMENT

The 63-member Althing (Parliament) is elected under a system of proportional representation by universal adult suffrage for a four-year term. The Althing elects 20 of its members to sit as the Upper House and the remaining 43 members to sit as the Lower House. The President - who is directly elected for four years - appoints a Prime Minister and a Cabinet who are responsible to the Althing. For purposes of local government Iceland is divided into eight municipalities (main towns) and (in the countryside) districts which are grouped into provinces. These units are grouped into eight regions. The main political parties include the (conservative) Independence Party (IP), the Progressive Party (PP), the Social Democratic Party (SDP), the (socialist) People's Alliance (PA), and the Women's Alliance (WA). As a result of elections held in April 1991, a coalition of IP and SDP members was formed.

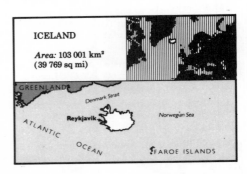

ICELAND

Area: 103 001 km² (39 769 sq mi)

GREENLAND

Denmark Strait

ATLANTIC OCEAN

Reykjavik

Norwegian Sea

FAROE ISLANDS

Party strength: IP 26, PP 13, SDP 10, PA 9, WA 5.

President: Vigdis Finnbogadottir.

THE CABINET

Prime Minister and Minister for the Statistical Bureau of Iceland: David Oddsson (IP).

Minister of Agriculture and Minister of Communications: Halldór Blöndal (IP).

Minister of Commerce and Minister of Industry: Sighvatur Björnvinsson (SDP).

Minister of Finance: Fridrik Sophusson (IP).

Minister of Education and Culture: Olafur G. Einarsson (IP).

Minister of the Environment: Ossur Skarphedinsson (SDP).

Minister for Fisheries, Minister of Justice and Ecclesiatical Affairs: Thorsteinn Pálsson (IP).

Minister of Foreign Affairs and Foreign Trade: Jón Baldvin Hannibalsson (SDP).

Minister of Health and Social Security: Gudmundur Arni Stefansson (SDP).

Minister of Social Affairs: Jóhanna Sigurdardóttir (SDP).

REGIONS

Capital area (Hofudhborgarsvaedhi) Area: 30 km² (12 sq mi). Population: 152,000 (1992 est). Administrative centre: Reykjavik.

East region (Austurland) Area: 21,991 km² (8491 sq mi). Population: 13,000 (1992 est). Administrative centre: Egilsstadhir.

Northland East region (Nordhurland eystra). Area: 22,368 km² (8636 sq mi). Population: 26,700 (1992 est). Administrative centre: Akureyri.

Northland West region (Nordhurland vestra) Area: 13,093 km² (5055 sq mi). Population: 10,400 (1992 est). Administrative centre: Saudharkrokur.

South region (Sudhurland) Area: 25,214 km² (9735 sq mi). Population: 20,700 (1992 est). Administrative centre: Selfoss.

Southwest Peninsula (Sudhurnes) Area: 1952 km² (754 sq mi). Population: 15,500 (1992 est). Administrative centre: Keflavik.

Western Peninsula (Vestfirdhir) Area: 9470 km² (3657 sq mi). Population: 9700. Administrative centre: Isafjordhur.

West region (Vesturland) Area: 8701 km² (3360 sq mi). Population: 14,500 (1992 est). Administrative centre: Borgarnes.

GEOGRAPHY

The greater part of Iceland has a volcanic landscape with hot springs, geysers and some 200 volcanoes - some of them active. Much of the country is tundra. The south and centre are covered by glacial icefields. Nearly 60% of the Icelandic population is concentrated into a small area in and around Reykjavik. Highest point: Hvannadalshnúkur 2119 m (6952 ft). Principal rivers: Thjórsá, Skjalfanda Fljót. Climate: The cool temperate climate is warmed by the Gulf Stream, which keeps Iceland milder than most places at the same latitude.

ECONOMY

The fishing industry normally provides about 75% of Iceland's exports. A drop in the export price of fish and declining fish stocks signalled a downturn in the economy at the end of the 1980s and in the early 1990s. Whaling was formerly important and Iceland continues to catch a number of whales annually 'for scientific purposes'. This action led to problems in Iceland's relations with the USA and to Iceland's withdrawal from the IWC (International Whaling Commission) in 1992. Hydroelectric power is used in the aluminium-smelting, fertilizer and ferro-silicon industries, while geothermal power warms extensive greenhouses. Ample grazing land makes the country self-sufficient in meat and dairy products. Economic problems include high inflation, a shortage of labour and over dependence upon a single export.

Currency: Krona of 100 aurar; 1US$ = 70.19 kronar (June 1994).

GDP: US$5,814,000,000 (1991); US$22,580 per head.

RECENT HISTORY

Icelandic nationalism grew in the 19th century. The Althing (the ancient Icelandic parliament) was restored in 1845 and in 1841 the Icelandic independence movement was founded by Jon Sigurdsson (1811-79). Large-scale emigration, mainly to Canada, at the end of the 19th century held up the island's progress towards self-rule. However, the country gained autonomy in 1903 and in 1918 Iceland gained independence from Denmark. However, the two countries remained linked by their shared monarchy. In World War II the Danish link was severed and a republic was declared (1944). After the German occupation of Denmark, British, and later American, forces occupied Iceland in order to prevent a German invasion of the island. The importance of the fishing industry to the Icelandic economy caused Iceland to extend its territorial waters in 1964 and again in 1972. On both occasions British opposition to the extensions resulted in clashes between British coastal vessels and Icelandic coastal patrols - the so-called 'cod wars'. More recently Iceland's determination to protect an exclusive right to these waters threatened to derail talks between the EC and the EFTA upon setting up the EEA trade bloc. Iceland's stance concerning fishing rights could prevent her from eventually joining the EU/EC, although opinion polls in 1994 suggested that Icelandic public support for EC membership was growing. During the Cold War, the continuing presence of US forces at Keflavik gave rise to some difficulties both in relations with the USA and in internal politics. In 1994 Iceland became involved in a fishing dispute with Norway.

Ireland

Official name: Poblacht na h'Eireann (Republic of Ireland).

Member of: UN, EC/EU, CSCE, Council of Europe, OECD, WEU (associate).

Area: 70,282 km² (27,136 sq mi).

Population: 3,523,000 (1991 census).

Capital: Dublin 921,000 (city 478,000; Dún Laoghaire 55,000) (1991 census).

Other major cities and towns: Cork 174,000 (city 127,000), Limerick 77,000 (city 52,000), Galway 51,000, Waterford 41,000, Dundalk 29,000 (town 27,000), Bray 25,000, Drogheda 24,000, Sligo 18,000 (1991 census).

IRELAND

Area: 70 282 km² (27 136 sq mi)

Languages: Irish (official; 5% as a first language); English (over 94% as a first language).

Religion: Roman Catholic (93%), non-religious (3%), Anglican (3%).

Education: Education is compulsory between the ages of six and 15. In 1990 the literacy rate was estimated to be virtually 100%. There are seven universities and university colleges.

Defence: In 1993 the total armed strength was 13,000 - 10,900 in the army, 1000 in the navy and 1000 in the air force. Service is voluntary.

Transport: There are 92,303 km (57,354 mi) of roads of which 24 km (15 mi) are motorways. State-run CIE operates over 1967 km (1222 mi) of railways. Dublin, Dun Laoghaire and Cork are the main commercial ports. Dublin, Shannon, Cork and Knock have international airports.

Media: There are seven Irish daily newspapers. RTE, an autonomous corporation, operates two national television and radio channels. There are over 20 local and one national commercial radio stations.

GOVERNMENT

The Seanad (Senate) has 60 members - 11 nominated by the Taoiseach (PM), six elected by the universities and 43 indirectly elected for a five-year term to represent vocational and special interests. The Dáil (House) comprises 166 members elected by proportional representation for five years by universal adult suffrage. The President is directly elected for seven years. The Taoiseach and a Cabinet of Ministers are responsible to the Dáil. The main political parties are the (centre-right) Fianna Fáil (FF), (centre-right) Fine Gael (FG), the (social democratic) Labour Party (Lab), (centre-right) Progressive Democrats (PD) and the Democratic Left (DL). After elections in November 1992 a FF-Lab coalition was formed.

Party strength: FF 68, FG 45, Lab 33, PD 18, DL 4, others 6.

President: Mary Robinson.

THE CABINET

Prime Minister (Taoiseach) : Albert Reynolds (FF).

Deputy Prime Minister (Tánaiste) and Foreign Minister: Dick Spring (Lab).

Minister of Agriculture, Fisheries and Food: Joe Walsh (FF).

Minister of Arts, Culture and the Gaeltacht: Michael Higgins (Lab).

Minister of Defence and the Marine: David Andrews (FF).

Minister of Education: Niamh Bhreathnach (Lab).

Minister of Enterprise and Employment: Ruairi Quinn (Lab).

Minister for the Environment: Michael Smith (FF).

Minister for Equality and Law Reform: Mervyn Taylor (Lab).

Minister of Finance: Bertie Ahern (FF).

Minister of Health: Brendan Howlin (Lab).

Minister of Justice: Maire Geoghegan-Quinn (FF).

Minister of Social Welfare: Michael Woods (FF).

Minister of Trade and Tourism: Charlie McCreevy (FF).

Minister of Transport, Energy and Communications: Brian Cowan (FF).

Attorney General: Harold A. Whelehan (ind.).

Chief Whip and Minister in the Department of the Taoiseach: Noel Dempsey (FF).

COUNTIES

Carlow Area: 896 km² (346 sq mi). Population: 41,000 (1991 census). County town: Carlow.

Cavan Area: 1891 km² (730 sq mi). Population: 53,000 (1991 census). County town: Cavan.

Clare Area: 3188 km² (1231 sq mi). Population: 91,000 (1991 census). County town: Ennis.

Cork Area: 7460 km² (2880 sq mi). Population: 410,000 (1991 census). County town: Cork.

Donegal Area: 4830 km² (1865 sq mi). Population: 128,000 (1991 census). County town: Lifford.

Dublin Area: 922 km² (356 sq mi). Population: 1,024,000 (1991 census). County town: Dublin.

Galway Area: 5940 km² (2293 sq mi). Population: 180,000 (1991 census). County town: Galway.

Kerry Area: 4701 km² (1815 sq mi). Population: 122,000 (1991 census). County town: Tralee.

Kildare Area: 1694 km² (654 sq mi). Population: 123,000 (1991 census). County town: Kildare.

Kilkenny Area: 2062 km² (796 sq mi). Population: 74,000 (1991 census). County town: Kilkenny.

Laoighis Area: 1719 km² (664 sq mi). Population: 52,000 (1991 census). County town: Portlaoise.

Leitrim Area: 1525 km² (581 sq mi). Population: 25,000 (1991 census). County town: Carrick on Shannon.

Limerick Area: 2686 km² (1037 sq mi). Population: 162,000 (1991 census). County town: Limerick.

Longford Area: 1044 km² (403 sq mi). Population: 30,000 (1991 census). County town: Longford.

Louth Area: 823 km² (318 sq mi). Population: 91,000 (1991 census). County town: Dundalk.

Mayo Area: 5398 km² (2084 sq mi). Population: 111,000 (1991 census). County town: Castlebar.

Meath Area: 2336 km² (902 sq mi). Population: 106,000 (1991 census). County town: Navan.

Monaghan Area: 1291 km² (498 sq mi). Population: 51,000 (1991 census). County town: Monaghan.

Offaly Area: 1998 km² (771 sq mi). Population: 58,000 (1991 census). County town: Tullamore.

Roscommon Area: 2463 km² (951 sq mi). Population: 52,000 (1991 census). County town: Roscommon.

Sligo Area: 1796 km² (693 sq mi). Population: 55,000 (1991 census). County town: Sligo.

Tipperary Area: 4254 km² (1643 sq mi) - North Riding 1996 km² (771 sq mi); South Riding 2258 km² (872 sq mi). Population: 133,000 - North Riding 58,000; South Riding 75,000 (1991 census). County towns: Nenagh (North Tipperary), Clonmel (South Tipperary).

Waterford Area: 1838 km² (710 sq mi). Population: 92,000 (1991 census). County town: Waterford.

Westmeath Area: 1763 km² (681 sq mi). Population: 41,000 (1991 census). County town: Mullingar.

Wexford Area: 2351 km² (908 sq mi). Population: 102,000 (1991 census). County town: Wexford.

Wicklow Area: 2025 km² (782 sq mi). Population: 97,000 (1991 census). County town: Wicklow.

GEOGRAPHY

Central Ireland is a lowland crossed by slight ridges and broad valleys, bogs and lakes. Except on the east coast north of Dublin, the lowland is surrounded by coastal hills and mountains including the Wicklow Mountains, the hills of Connemara and Donegal, and the Macgillicuddy's Reeks. Highest point:

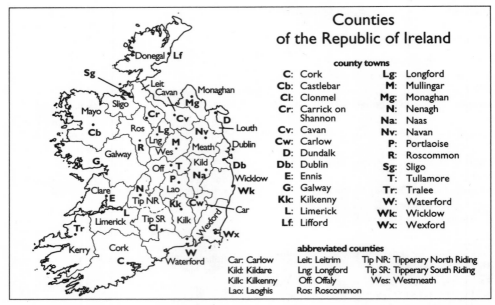

Counties of the Republic of Ireland

county towns

C:	Cork	**Lg**:	Longford
Cb:	Castlebar	**M**:	Mullingar
Cl:	Clonmel	**Mg**:	Monaghan
Cr:	Carrick on Shannon	**N**:	Nenagh
Cv:	Cavan	**Na**:	Naas
Cw:	Carlow	**Nv**:	Navan
D:	Dundalk	**P**:	Portlaoise
Db:	Dublin	**R**:	Roscommon
E:	Ennis	**Sg**:	Sligo
G:	Galway	**T**:	Tullamore
Kk:	Kilkenny	**Tr**:	Tralee
L:	Limerick	**W**:	Waterford
Lf:	Lifford	**Wk**:	Wicklow
		Wx:	Wexford

abbreviated counties

Car: Carlow	Leit: Leitrim	Tip NR: Tipperary North Riding
Kild: Kildare	Lng: Longford	Tip SR: Tipperary South Riding
Kilk: Kilkenny	Off: Offaly	Wes: Westmeath
Lao: Laoghis	Ros: Roscommon	

Carrauntuohill 1041 m (3414 ft). Principal rivers: Shannon, Suir, Boyle, Barrow. Climate: Ireland has a mild temperate climate. Rainfall is high.

ECONOMY
Manufactured goods - in particular machinery, metals and engineering, electronics and chemical products - make a major contribution to Ireland's exports. Agriculture concentrates upon the production of livestock, meat and dairy products. Food processing and brewing are major industries. Natural resources include lead-zinc, offshore petroleum and natural gas, and hydroelectric power sites. Ireland suffers high rates of unemployment and emigration.

Currency: Punt (Irish pound) of 100 pennies; 1US$ = 0.68 punt (June 1994).

GDP: US$45,500,000,000 (1993 est); US$12,660 per head.

RECENT HISTORY
In the 19th century Ireland campaigned for reform and later independence from the British Parliament. After Home Rule Bills were rejected by Parliament (1883 and 1893), more revolutionary nationalist groups gained support. Fearing Catholic domination, Protestant Unionists in Ulster strongly opposed the Third Home Rule Bill (1912). Nationalists declared an independent Irish state in the Dublin Easter Rising of 1916, which was put down by the British. After World War I, Irish nationalist MPs formed a provisional government in Dublin led by Eamon de Valera (later PM and President; 1882-1975). Except in the northeast, British administration in Ireland crumbled. Fighting broke out between nationalists and British troops and police, and by 1919 Ireland had collapsed into violence. In response the UK offered Ireland two Parliaments - one in Protestant Ulster, another in the Catholic south. Partition was initially rejected by the south, but by the Anglo-Irish Treaty (1921) dominion status was granted, although six (mainly Protestant) counties in Ulster - Northern Ireland - opted to remain British. The Irish Free State was proclaimed in 1922 but de Valera and the Republicans refused to accept it and civil war (1922-23) broke out between the provisional government - led by Arthur Griffith and Michael Collins - and the Republicans. In 1937 the Irish Free State became a republic. The country remained neutral in World War II. Relations between south and north - and between the Republic and the UK - have often been tense during the 'troubles' in Northern Ireland (1968-).

Italy

Official name: Repubblica Italiana (Republic of Italy).

Member of: UN, EC/EU, NATO, WEU, G7, Council of Europe, OECD, CSCE.

Area: 301,277 km² (116,324 sq mi).

Population: 57,104,000 (1991 est).

Capital: Rome (Roma) 2,985,000 (city 2,791,000; 1990 census).

Other major cities: Milan (Milano) 3,670,000 (city 1,432,000), Naples (Napoli) 2,905,000 (city 1,206,000), Turin (Torino) 1,114,000 (city 992, 000), Genoa (Genova) 786,000 (city 701,000), Palermo 755,000 (city 734,000), Florence (Firenze) 433,000 (city 408,000), Bologna 412,000, Catania 384,000 (city 364,000), Bari 373,000 (city 353,000), Venice (Venezia) 318,000, Messina 275,000, Verona 257,000, Trieste 252,000 (city 230,000), Taranto 244,000, Padua (Padova) 218,000, Cagliari 212,000, Salerno 206,000 (city 151,000), Brescia 202,000 (city 196,000), Reggio di Calabria 179,000, Modena 178,000, Parma 173,000, Livorno 171,000, Prato 166,000, Foggia 159,000, Perugia 151,000, Ferrara 141,000 (1990 census).

Languages: Italian (official; over 94% as a first language), Sardinian (2.7%), Rhaetic languages (1.2%), German (0.5%), French (under 0.5%), plus Catalan-, Slovene- and Albanian-speakers.

Religion: Roman Catholic (83%); non-religious (16%).

Education: Education is compulsory between the ages of six and 14. In 1990 the literacy rate was estimated to be 97.1%. There are 55 universities.

Defence: Italy is a NATO member. In 1992 the total armed strength was 465,600 - 230,000 in the army, 111,400 paramilitary Carabinieri, 48,000 navy, and 76,200 air force. The main Italian naval bases are Spezia, Taranto, Naples and Ancona. Italian males are subject to compulsory military service of 12 months.

Transport: There are 302,403 km (187,904 mi) of roads of which 6695 km (4160 mi) are motorways. State-run Italian railways operate 15,983 km (9931 mi) of track; private companies operate 3000 km (1860 mi) of track. Milan, Naples and Rome have metro systems. The largest commercial shipping port is Genoa; other ports include Venice, Trieste, Naples and Palermo. Fiumicino (Rome) is one of Europe's biggest airports. Milan (two airports), Catania, Florence, Genoa, Naples and Turin also receive international flights.

Media: The Italian press is concentrated in Milan and Rome. There are 80 daily papers, most with regional circulations. Television stations include RAI (the national network with three channels), a Roman Catholic network, and seven national and over 450 local commercial stations. As well as RAI's stations, there are over 1000 local commercial radio stations.

GOVERNMENT

The two houses of Parliament are elected for a five-year term by universal adult suffrage. Elections to both the 315-member Senate (upper house) and the 630-member Chamber of Deputies (lower house) are by the first-past-the-post system for the majority of seats with a minority elected by proportional representation. The Senate is elected by citizens aged over 25 to represent the regions, plus former Presidents and five life senators chosen by the President. The Chamber of Deputies is elected by citizens aged over 18. The President is elected for seven years by an electoral college comprising Parliament and 58 regional representatives. The President appoints a PM (who commands a majority in Parliament) and a Council of Ministers who are responsible to Parliament. The 20 regions of Italy have their own governments. Political parties include the (conservative) Forza Italia Party (Forza), the (federalist conservative) Northern League (LN), the (right-wing) National Alliance (AN, which includes the neo-fascist MSI Party), the (former Communist) Democratic Party of the Left (PDS), the (southern anti-Mafia) La Rete (Rete), the Greens (Verdi), the (Marxist) Communist Refoundation (RC), the Socialist Party (PSI), the (centrist) Pact for Italy (PI; an electoral alliance of the Popular Party, which was formerly the Christian Democratic Party, and the Segni Pact), and the Social Democratic Party (SD). After the election in 1994 a government of Forza, LN, AN and PI members was formed.

Party strength (Chamber of Deputies): Forza-LN 205, AN 160, Progressives (PDS-RC-Rete-Verdi-PSI) 213, PI 46, others 4.

President: Oscar Luigi Scalfaro.

THE CABINET
Prime Minister: Silvio Berlusconi (Forza).

Deputy Prime Minister: Giuseppe Tatarella (AN).

Deputy Prime Minister: Roberto Maroni (LN).

Minister of Agriculture: Adriana Poli Bortone (AN).

Minister for the Budget: Giancarlo Pagliarini (LN).

Minister of Cultural Affairs: Domenico Fisichella (AN).

Minister of Defence: Cesare Previti (Forza).

Minister of Education: Francesco D'Onofrio (PI).

Minister for the Environment: Altero Matteoli (AN).

Minister for the European Union and Regional Affairs: Domenico Comino (LN).

Minister for Family Affairs: Antonio Guidi (Forza).

Minister of Finance: Giulio Tremonti (ind.).

Minister of Foreign Affairs: Antonio Martino (Forza).

Minister of Foreign Trade: Giorgio Bernini (Forza).

Minister of Health: Raffaele Costa (PI).

Minister of Industry: Vito Gnutti (LN).

Minister for Institutional Reform: Francesco Enrico Speroni (LN).

Minister of the Interior: Roberto Maroni (LN).

Minister for Italians resident abroad: Sergio Berlinguer (ind.).

Minister of Justice: Alfredo Biondi (Forza).

Minister of Labour: Clemente Mastella (PI).

Minister of Posts and Telecommunications: Giuseppe Tatarella (AN).

Minister of Public Administration: Giuliano Urbani (Forza).

Minister of Public Works: Roberto Radice (Forza).

Minister for Relations with Parliament: Giuliano Ferrara (Forza).

Minister of Transport: Publio Fiori (AN).

Minister for the Treasury: Lamberto Dini (ind.).

Minister for Universities and Science: Stefano Podesta (LN).

REGIONS
Abruzzi Area: 10,794 km^2 (4168 sq mi). Population: 1,249,000 (1991 census). Capital: L'Aquila; Pescara shares some of the functions of capital with L'Aquila.

Basilicata Area: 9992 km^2 (3858 sq mi). Population: 592,000 (1991 census). Capital: Potenza.

Calabria Area: 15,080 km^2 (5822 sq mi). Population: 2,010,000 (1991 census). Capital: Catanzaro.

Campania Area: 13,595 km^2 (5249 sq mi). Population: 5,626,000 (1991 census). Capital: Naples.

Emilia Romagna Area: 22,123 km^2 (8542 sq mi). Population: 3,984,000 (1991 census). Capital: Bologna.

Friuli-Venezia Giulia Area: 7846 km^2 (3029 sq mi). Population: 1,216,000 (1991 census). Capital: Trieste.

Lazio Area: 17,203 km^2 (6642 sq mi). Population: 5,146,000 (1991 census). Capital: Rome.

Liguria Area: 5413 km^2 (2090 sq mi). Population: 1,702,000 (1991 census). Capital: Genoa.

Lombardy (Lombardia) Area: 23,834 km^2 (9202 sq mi). Population: 8,941,000 (1991 census). Capital: Milan.

Marche Area: 9692 km^2 (3742 sq mi). Population: 1,447,000 (1991 census). Capital: Ancona.

Molise Area: 4438 km^2 (1714 sq mi). Population: 321,000 (1991 census). Capital: Campobasso.

Piedmont (Piemonte) Area: 25,399 km^2 (9807 sq mi). Population: 4,338,000 (1991 census). Capital: Turin.

Puglia Area: 19,347 km^2 (7470 sq mi). Population: 3,970,000 (1991 census). Capital: Bari.

Sardinia (Sardegna) Area: 24,090 km^2 (9301 sq

ITALY

Area: 301 277 km²
(116 324 sq mi).

Apennines in the south, the Alps in the west and the Adriatic Sea in the east. The narrow ridge of the Ligurian Alps joins the Maritime Alps to the Apennines, which form a backbone down the entire length of the Italian peninsula. The restricted coastal lowlands include the Arno Basin in Tuscany, the Tiber Basin around Rome, the Campania lowlands around Naples, and plains beside the Gulf of Taranto and in Puglia. The islands of Sardinia and Sicily are both largely mountainous. Italy has four active volcanoes, including Etna on Sicily and Vesuvius near Naples. Highest point: just below the summit of Monte Bianco (Mont Blanc) 4760 m (15 616 ft). Principal rivers: Po, Tiber (Tevere), Arno, Volturno. Climate: Italy enjoys a Mediterranean climate with warm, dry summers and mild winters. Northern Italy is cooler and wetter. Sicily and Sardinia tend to be warmer and drier than the mainland.

ECONOMY

Northern Italy, with its easy access to the rest of Europe, is the main centre of Italian industry. The south, in contrast, remains mainly agricultural, producing grapes, sugar beet, wheat, maize, and tomatoes. Most farms are small and many southern farmers have resisted change; incomes in southern Italy (the 'Mezzogiorno') are on average much lower than in the north. Agriculture in the north is more mechanized; major crops include wheat, maize, rice, grapes (for wine), fruit and fodder crops for dairy herds. Industry in the south has been promoted. The well-developed industries of the north include electrical and electronic goods, cars and bicycles, textiles, clothing, leather goods, cement, glass, china and ceramics, as well as finance and banking - Milan is Italy's commercial capital. Apart from Alpine rivers that are harnessed for HEP, Italy has few natural resources. Tourism and money sent back by Italians living abroad are important sources of foreign currency. Recession and a crippling public deficit have added to Italy's economic problems. Unemployment increased sharply in the 1990s and in February 1994 stood at 11.2%. Large-scale privatization of the large state-sector began in the early 1990s.

Currency: Lira; 1US$ = 11590.82 lire (June 1994).

GDP: US$1,010,000,000,000 (1993 est); US$17,600 per head.

mi). Population: 1,645,000 (1991 census). Capital: Cagliari.

Sicily (Sicilia) Area: 25,708 km² (9926 sq mi). Population: 4,990,000 (1991 census). Capital: Palermo.

Trentino-Alto Adige Area: 13,613 km² (5256 sq mi). Population: 935,000 (1991 census). Capitals: Trento and Bolzano.

Tuscany (Toscana) Area: 22,992 km² (8877 sq mi). Population: 3,599,000 (1991 census). Capital: Florence.

Umbria Area: 8456 km² (3265 sq mi). Population: 823,000 (1991 census). Capital: Perugia.

Valle d'Aosta Area: 3262 km² (1259 sq mi). Population: 117,000 (1991 census). Capital: Aosta.

Veneto Area: 18,368 km² (7092 sq mi). Population: 4,453,000 (1991 census). Capital: Venice.

GEOGRAPHY

The Alps form a natural boundary between Italy and its neighbours. A string of lakes where the mountains meet the foothills includes Lakes Maggiore, Lugano and Como. The fertile Po Valley - the great lowland of northern Italy - lies between the Alpine foothills in the north, the foothills of the

Italian Regions

Trentino Alto Adige
Bz
Valle d'Aosta
Tr
Friuli Venezia Giulia
Ao
Lombardy
Ts
M
Veneto
T
V
Piedmont
Emilia Romagna
Bg
G
Liguria
F
A
Tuscany
Pg
Marche
Umbria
Abruzzi
Molise
L'A
Lazio
R
Cm
Puglia
N
B
Sardinia
Campania
Pt
C
Calabria
Cz
P
Sicily

regional capitals

- **A:** Ancona
- **Ao:** Aosta
- **B:** Bari
- **Bg:** Bologna
- **Bz:** Bolzano
- **C:** Cagliari
- **Cm:** Campobasso
- **Cz:** Catanzaro
- **F:** Florence
- **G:** Genoa
- **L'A:** L'Aquila
- **M:** Milan
- **N:** Naples
- **P:** Palermo
- **Pg:** Perugia
- **Pt:** Potenza
- **R:** Rome
- **T:** Turin
- **Tr:** Trento
- **Ts:** Trieste
- **V:** Venice

RECENT HISTORY

After World War I fear of Communist revolution led to an upsurge of Fascism and the Fascist Benito Mussolini (1883-1945) became PM in 1922 with a programme of extensive domestic modernization and an aggressive foreign policy. In 1936 Italy allied with Germany in the Rome-Berlin Axis, and declared war on Britain and France in 1940. When Italy was invaded by Allied troops in 1943, Mussolini was dismissed by the king and Italy joined the Allies. In 1946 a republic was proclaimed. Communist influence increased and Communists gained control of many large city councils. However, the dominance of the (conservative) Christian Democrat Party kept the Communists out of the succeeding coalitions that ruled Italy. Particularly in the 1970s, terrorist movements (both left- and right-wing) were active, kidnapping and assassinating politicians and industrialists, including the former PM Aldo Moro (1978). The political structure of Italy remained unstable and coalitions were often short-lived - between 1945 and 1993 over 50 governments came to and fell from power. In the 1990s, public disillusion with state institutions grew and Italy was weakened by corruption, the activities of the Mafia and the growth of regional separatism in the North. The traditional political parties collapsed and an interim government was formed (1993) to effect constitutional changes. The new political movements that emerged dominated the 1994 election.

Liechtenstein

Official name: Fürstentum Liechtenstein (The Principality of Liechtenstein).

Member of: UN, Council of Europe, CSCE, EFTA.

Area: 160 km² (62 sq mi).

Population: 29,400 (1991 est).

Capital: Vaduz 4900 (1991 est).

Other major town: Schaan 5000 (1991 est).

Language: German (official).

Religion: Roman Catholic (87%), Lutheran (8%).

Education: Education is compulsory between the ages of six and 15. In 1990 the literacy rate was virtually 100%.

Defence: Liechtenstein has no armed forces.

Transport: There are 323 km (201 mi) of roads. There are 18.5 km (11.5 mi) of railways.

Media: There are two daily newspapers. Swiss radio and television are received.

GOVERNMENT

The country is a constitutional monarchy ruled by a Prince. The 25-member Landstag (Parliament) is elected by universal adult suffrage by proportional representation for four years. The Landstag elects a 5-member National Committee (Cabinet) including a Prime Minister, who is then appointed by the Prince. Political parties include the VU (Fatherland Union), the FBP (Progressive Citizens' Party) and the (Green) Free List. A VU-FBP coalition was formed after the general election held in October 1993.

Party strength: VU 13 seats, FBP 10, Free List 1

Prince: HSH Prince Hans Adam II (succeeded upon the death of his father, 13 November 1989).

THE CABINET

Prime Minister, Minister of Finance and Justice: Dr Mario Frick (VU).

Minister of Education, Environmental Protection, Agriculture and Forestry, and the Interior: Thomas Buchel (FBP).

Minister for Foreign Relations, Culture, Youth

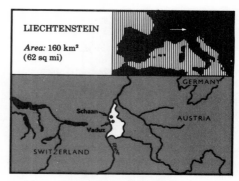

LIECHTENSTEIN
Area: 160 km²
(62 sq mi)

GERMANY
Schaan
Vaduz
AUSTRIA
SWITZERLAND

and Sport: Dr Andrea Willi (VU).

Minister of the Economy, the Family, Social Affairs and Health: Dr Michael Ritter (VU).

Minister of Construction and Transport: Dr Cornelia Gassner-Matt (FBP).

GEOGRAPHY

The Alps stand in the east of the principality. The west comprises the floodplain of the River Rhine. Principal rivers: Rhine (Rhein), Samina. Highest point: Grauspitze 2599 m (8326 ft). Climate: The country has an Alpine climate.

ECONOMY

Liechtenstein has one of the highest standards of living in the world. Tourism, insurance and manufacturing (precision goods) and, in particular, banking are all important foreign-currency earners. Tourism is represented by both summer visitors on day trips to the principality and winter visitors attracted by skiing.

Currency: Liechtenstein uses Swiss currency (see pp. 414-16).

GDP: US$940,000,000 (1990 est); US$32,790 per head).

RECENT HISTORY

Liechtenstein was the only German principality not to join the German Empire in 1871. Before World War I (1914-18) the Princes of Liechtenstein resided on their Austrian estates rather than within the principality. Since 1924 the country has enjoyed a customs and monetary union with Switzerland, which also represents Liechtenstein diplomatically. However, since 1989 the country has taken a more active role on the international stage, for instance, joining EFTA and the UN.

Luxembourg

Official names: Grand-Duché de Luxembourg (in French), Groussherzogtum Letzebuerg (in Letzeburgish) and Grossherzogtum Luxemburg (in German) (Grand Duchy of Luxembourg).

Member of: UN, EC/EU, NATO, WEU, CSCE, OECD, Council of Europe.

Area: 2586 km² (999 sq mi).

Population: 392,000 (1993 est).

Capital: Luxembourg 117,000 (city 78,000; 1991 census).

Other main towns: Esch-sur-Alzette 24,000, Differdange 16,000, Dudelange 15,000, Pétange 12,000, Sanem 12,000 (1991 census).

Languages: Letzeburgish (official; a German-Frankish dialect; 72.5% as a first language), German (official; 10% as a first language, but universally understood); French (official; 6% as a first language, but universally understood), Portuguese (9% as a first language).

Religions: Roman Catholic (95%); non-religious (4%), various Protestant Churches (1%).

Education: Education is compulsory between the ages of six and 15. In 1993 the literacy rate was estimated to be virtually 100%. There is a university centre.

Defence: In 1993 the total armed strength was 800, all in the army. There are 1600 reserves. Military service is voluntary.

Transport: There are 5091 km (3163 mi) of roads, of which 118 km (73 mi) are motorways. SNCFL, the state-run railway company, operates 271 km (168 mi) of railways. Barge traffic uses the canalized River Moselle upon which Grevenmacher is a port. Luxembourg City has an international airport.

Media: There are five daily newspapers - four national papers published in French and German, and one local edition of a French paper. RTL, a private company, operates television and radio programmes both inside and outside the Grand Duchy. Two other stations broadcast seven television channels and a satellite network.

GOVERNMENT

Luxembourg is a constitutional monarchy with a Grand Duke or Duchess as sovereign. The 60-member Chamber of Deputies is elected by proportional representation by universal adult suffrage for five years. A Council of Ministers and a President of the Council (Premier) are appointed by the sovereign. There are three local government districts, which are subdivided into a total of 13 cantons. The main political parties are the (centre-right) Social Christian Party (PCS), the Socialist Party (POSL), the (liberal) Democratic Party (PD), Green Alternative and Green Ecologists, and the (pension rights) 5/6 Action Committee (CA). Following the election held in May 1994 the PCS-PS coalition continued in office.

Party strength: PCS 21, POSL 17, PD 12, Greens 5, CA 5.

Grand Duke: HRH Grand Duke Jean I (succeeded upon the abdication of his mother, 12 November 1964).

THE CABINET

Prime Minister: (Minister for the Exchequer and Minister for Cultural Affairs) Jacques Santer (PCS) - to be EC Commission President Jan. 1995.

Deputy Prime Minister, Minister for Foreign Affairs and Foreign Trade, Minister for the Armed Forces: Jacques Poos (POSL).

Minister of Agriculture, Viticulture, Country Planning: Marie-Josee Jacobs (PCS).

Minister for the Economy, Minister of Public Works and Transport: Robert Goebbels (PCS).

Minister of Education, Minister of Justice, Minister for Sport: Marc Fischbach (PCS).

Minister for Family Affairs, Social Solidarity, the Middle Classes, Minister of Tourism: Fernand Boden (PCS).

Minister of Finance, Minister of Labour: Jean-Claude Juncker (PCS).

Minister of Health and Social Security, Minister of Sport: Johny Lahure (POSL).

Minister of the Interior, Housing and Town Planning: Jean Spautz: (PCS).

Minister of Land Planning, the Environment, Energy and Communications: Alex Bodry (POSL).

Secretaries of State: Georges Wohlfart (POSL), Mady Delvaux-Stehres (POSL).

DISTRICTS

Diekirch   Area: 1157 km² (447 sq mi). Population: 57,000 (1991 census). District centre: Diekirch.

Grevenmacher Area: 525 km² (203 sq mi). Population: 43,000 (1991 census). District centre: Grevenmacher.

Luxembourg Area: 904 km² (349 sq mi). Population: 284,000 (1991 census). District centre: Luxembourg.

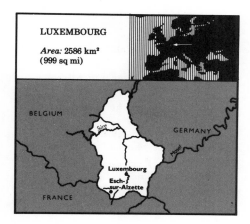

GEOGRAPHY

The Oesling - the northern one-third of the country - is a wooded plateau (part of the Ardennes), which is deeply dissected by river valleys. The Gutland (or the Bon Pays) in the south is a lowland region of valleys and ridges. Physically a continuation of the Paris Basin, the Gutland contained one of the richest deposits of iron ore in Europe. Highest point: Huldange 550 m (1804 ft). Principal rivers: Moselle, Sûre, Our, Alzette. Climate: Luxembourg has relatively warm summers and mild winters.There is winter snow in the Ardennes in the north.

ECONOMY

The north of the Grand Duchy grows potatoes and fodder crops; the south produces wheat and fruit, including grapes for wine. The iron and steel industry - once based on local ore in the Gutland - is the main manufacturing interest, but has declined in relative importance as the financial sector has expanded. However, the steel firm ARBED is still the Grand Duchy's largest employer. Luxembourg has become a major banking centre - nearly 200 banks have branches in Luxembourg City. Luxembourg is also a major centre for stock exchange dealings in Eurobonds and for insurance. The government is encouraging the development of the data-processing and audio-visual industries. The population of the Grand Duchy has grown very little in the last three decades and a labour shortage has attracted immigrants, particularly from Portugal.

Currency: Luxembourg franc; 1US$ = 33.559 Luxembourg francs (June 1994).

GDP: US$11,761,000,000 (1991); US$31,080 per head (one of the highest GDP per capita figures in the world).

RECENT HISTORY

After centuries of incorporation in other states, Luxembourg was revived as an independent country in 1815 when the Dutch king also became sovereign of Luxembourg. In 1831 the western (French-speaking) part of the country became a province of Belgium, when that country's boundaries were defined following its war of independence against the Netherlands. The Luxembourg crisis (1867) concerned the refusal of the Prussian garrison to evacuate the fortress of Luxembourg City after the dissolution of the German Confederation (1866). The crisis was resolved by the Treaty of London (1867), which confirmed Luxembourg's independence, neutrality and territorial integrity. When the Dutch royal family died out in the male line in 1890, Luxembourg was inherited by a junior branch of the House of Orange, which later had to change the laws of succession when it too became extinct in the male line. Luxembourg was occupied by, and annexed to, Germany from 1914 to 1918. Luxembourg concluded an economic union with Belgium in 1922. The Grand Duchy was occupied and annexed by Germany again from 1940 to 1945, during which time large-scale deportations occurred following a strike against the country's Nazi occupiers. Since 1945 Luxembourg has enthusiastically supported European unity and, despite its small size, has been an active member of NATO and the EU/EC. Luxembourg City has become one of the European Community's three centres of administration.

393

Malta

Official names: Repubblika Ta'Malta and Republic of Malta.

Member of: UN, Commonwealth, CSCE, Council of Europe.

Area: 316 km² (122 sq mi) - the island of Malta 246 km² (95 sq mi), Gozo 67 km² (26 sq mi), Comino 3 km² (1 sq mi).

Population: 360,000 (1992 est) - the island of Malta 334,000, Gozo 24,000, Comino 2000.

Capital: Valletta 205,000 (city 9200; 1991 est for the combined Inner Harbour and Outer Harbour regions).

Other main towns: Birkirkara 21,000, Qormi 20,000, Hamrun 14,000, Sliema 14,000 and Zabbar 13,000 are all part of the Valletta, or Inner and Outer Harbour, agglomeration (1991 est). The largest town on Gozo is Victoria 6000 (1991 est).

Languages: Maltese and English (both official).

Religion: Roman Catholic (official; 98%).

Education: Education is compulsory between the ages of five and 16. The literacy rate in 1990 was estimated to be over 98%. There is a single university.

Defence: The total armed strength in 1993 was 1650. Military service is voluntary.

Transport: There are 1553 km (965 mi) of roads. Malta has no railways. There is an international airport at Luqa near Valletta. Grand Harbour is a commercial shipping port.

Media: There are three daily newspapers - two published in Maltese, one in English. The Malta Broadcasting Authority, an independent statutory authority, operates radio and television services; there are over 10 private radio stations and a cable television service.

GOVERNMENT
The 65-member House of Representatives is elected by universal adult suffrage under a system of proportional representation for five years. The President - whose role is largely ceremonial - is elected for five years by the House. The President appoints a Prime Minister and a Cabinet who command a majority in the House. There are no local government units

although the island of Gozo is administered separately. The main political parties are the (conservative) National Party (Partit Nazzjonalista; PN), the (social democratic) Malta Labour Party (Partit tal-Haddiema; MLP) and the (environmentalist) Democratic Alternative (Alternattiva Demokratika). After the general election held in February 1992 a government of National Party members was formed.

Party strength: PN 34, MLP 31.

President: Hugo Mifsud Bonnici.

THE CABINET
Prime Minister: Edward (Eddie) Fenech-Adami (PN).

Deputy Prime Minister and Minister for Foreign Affairs: Prof. Guido de Marco (PN).

Minister of Economic Services: Dr George Bonello du Puis (PN).

Minister of Education and the Development of Human Resources: Michael Falzon (PN).

Minister of the Environment: Dr Francis Zammit Dimech (PN).

Minister of Finance: John Dalli (PN).

Minister of Food, Agriculture and Fisheries: Lawrence Gatt (PN).

Minister for Gozo: Anton Tabone (PN).

Minister of Home Affairs and for Social Development: Dr Louis Galea (PN).

Minister of Justice: Dr Josef (Joe) Fenech (PN).

Minister of Social Security: Dr George Hyzler (PN).

Minister of Transport and Communications: Dr Michael Frendo (PN).

Minister of Youth, Sport and the Arts: Dr Michael Refalo (PN).

REGIONS
(Except in the case of Gozo and Comino, the regions have no administrative functions.)

Gozo and Comino Area: 70 km² (27 sq mi). Population: 26,000 (1991 est). Capital: Victoria. (No other Maltese region has an administrative centre.)

Inner Harbour Region Area: 15 km² (6 sq mi). Population: 102,000 (1991 est).

Northern Region Area: 78 km² (30 sq mi). Population: 34,000 (1991 est).

Outer Harbour Region Area: 32 km² (12 sq mi). Population: 103,000 (1991 est).

South Eastern Region Area: 53 km² (20 sq mi). Population: 45,000 (1991 est).

Western Region Area: 69 km² (27 sq mi). Population: 46,000 (1991 est).

GEOGRAPHY

The republic, which is situated about 100 km (60 mi) south of Sicily, comprises the three inhabited islands of Malta, Gozo and Comino (Kemmuna) plus Cominotto (Kemmunett) and two other small unihabited islets. The islands consist of low limestone plateaux with little surface water. There are no significant rivers. Highest point: an unnamed point 249 m (816 ft). Climate: Malta has a pleasant Mediterranean climate with hot dry summers and mild win-

MALTA

Area: 316 km²
(122 sq mi)

GOZO

COMINO

MEDITERRANEAN SEA

MEDITERRANEAN SEA

Sliema
Valletta

ters during which most of the annual precipitation falls. The climate has encouraged the growth of tourism, particularly in the winter.

ECONOMY

The main industries are footwear and clothing, food processing and beverages, ship repairing, machinery and transport equipment. Tourism (mainly from the UK) is the main foreign-currency earner, and the tourist industry employs about one third of the islands' labour force. Although soils are poor and natural vegetation is sparse, Malta is virtually self-sufficient in

agricultural products. Potatoes, flowers, tomatoes and onions are exported. There are no natural resources in Malta and the republic relies upon imported petroleum, natural gas and coal to satisfy its energy needs. However, reserves of petroleum have been found in Maltese offshore waters and exploration for oil and natural gas continues. Malta has an older population profile as many younger people have left the islands to find work elsewhere, particularly in the UK and Australia. In some years in the 1980s the population of Malta declined.

Currency: Maltese Lira (formerly called the pound) of 100 cents and 1000 mils; 1US$ = 0.389 Maltese lira (May 1994).

GDP: US$2,342,000,000 (1990), US$6630 per head.

RECENT HISTORY

Maltese history reflects the struggles for control of this strategically-placed island group in the narrow seas between the eastern and western Mediterranean. As a British colony (from 1814), Malta became a vital naval base, and its economy was bound to the fortunes of the British naval dockyard. Malta received the George Cross for its valour in World War II when it suffered an Italian aerial bombardment. Malta's political development under British rule was characterized by a series of constitutions granting self-government. Each of these constitutions was eventually revoked or suspended. In 1956 a referendum supported by the Malta Labour Party (MLP) resulted in a majority in favour of the integration of Malta in the UK. However, the plebiscite was boycotted by the National Party and the MLP rejected Britain's final proposals. Malta gained independence in 1964 and became a republic in 1974. The last British forces were withdrawn in 1979 and Malta's alliance with the UK ended. Malta has since pursued a policy of non-alignment. Maltese political life has been polarized between the National Party and the Maltese Labour Party. Dom Mintoff - Labour PM (1971-84) - developed close links with Communist and Arab states, notably Libya. Malta has an association agreement with the European Community and applied for full membership of the Community in 1990. However, negotiations for Maltese entry to the EU/EC did not accompany those for Austria and the Scandinavian countries in 1993-94.

Monaco

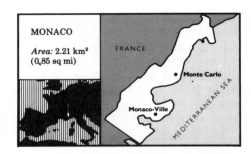

MONACO

Area: 2.21 km² (0,85 sq mi)

FRANCE

Monte Carlo

Monaco-Ville

MEDITERRANEAN SEA

Official name: Principauté de Monaco (Principality of Monaco).

Member of: UN, CSCE.

Area: 2.21 km² (0.85 sq mi).

Population: 29,900 (1990 census) - only about 15% of these residents are Monegasques; the majority are either French or Italians.

Capital: Monaco 1200 (1990 census).

Other major towns: Monte-Carlo 13,200, La Condamine 12,700, Fontvieille 2800 (1990 census).

Languages: French (official), Monegasque.

Religion: Roman Catholic (90%).

Education: Education is compulsory between the ages of six and 16. In 1990 the literacy rate was estimated to be virtually 100%. There are no higher education institutions.

Defence: There is a small palace guard.

Transport: There are 50 km (31 mi) of roads and 1.7 km (1 mi) of railway track. There is a heliport at Fontvieille.

Media: There is a Monegasque edition of a French daily newspaper. There are commercial radio and television stations.

GOVERNMENT
Monaco is a constitutional monarchy. Legislative power is jointly held by the Prince and the 18-member National Council, which is elected by universal adult suffrage for five years. Executive power is held by the Prince, who appoints a four-member Council of Government headed by the Minister of State, a French civil servant chosen by the sovereign. There are no political parties, but political groups include the Liste Campora and the Liste Médicin. The last election was held in January 1993.

Group strength: Liste Campora 15, Liste Médecin 2, independent 1.

Prince: HSH Prince Rainier III (succeeded upon the death of his grandfather, 9 May 1949).

THE CABINET
Minister of State: Jacques Dupont.

Chief of the Cabinet: Denis Ravera.

Councillor of Finance and Economic Affairs: Jean Pastorelli.

Councillor of the Interior: Michel Eon.

Councillor of Public Works and Social Affairs: Bernard Fautrier.

GEOGRAPHY
Monaco consists of a rocky peninsula and a narrow stretch of coast. Since 1958 the area of the principality has increased by one fifth through reclamation of land from the sea. Highest point: on Chemin de Révoirés 162 m (533 ft). Principal river: Vésubie. Climate: Monaco enjoys a pleasant Mediterranean climate.

ECONOMY
Monaco depends upon real estate, banking, insurance, light industry and tourism. Light industry is largely based upon the reclaimed zone of Fontvieille.

Currency: Monaco uses French currency.

GDP: No figures are available; Monegasque GDP is included in the French total.

RECENT HISTORY
The towns of Menton and Roquebrune, which formed the greater part of the principality, seceded in 1848 and were annexed by France in 1861, when Monaco came under French protection. The principality was occupied by the Italians (1941-43) and then by the Germans (1943-45) during World War II. In 1962 Monaco was involved in a serious dispute with France over the principality's refusal to levy taxes on foreign residents and companies. Prince Rainier III granted a liberal constitution in 1962.

The Netherlands

Official name: Koninkrijk der Nederlanden (The Kingdom of the Netherlands).

Member of: UN, EC/EU, NATO, CSCE, WEU, Council of Europe, OECD.

Area: 41,785 km² (16,140 sq mi).

Population: 15,302,000 (1993 est).

Capital: Amsterdam - capital in name only - 1,080,000 (city 713,000), The Hague ('s Gravenhage) - capital de facto; the seat of government and administration - 693,000 (city 445,000) (1992 est).

Other major cities: Rotterdam 1,060,000 (city 590,000), Utrecht 540,000 (city 233,000), Eindhoven 388,000 (city 194,000), Arnhem 306,000 (city 133,000), Heerlen-Kerkrade 269,000 (Heerlen city 95,000), Enschede 253,000 (city 147,000), Nijmegen 246,000 (city 146,000), Tilburg 234,000 (city 161,000), Haarlem 214,000 (city 150,000), Dordrecht 210,000 (city 112,000), Groningen 208,000 (city 169,000), 's Hertogenbosch 200,000 (city 93,000), Leiden 191,000 (city 113,000), Geleen-Sittard 183,000 (Sittard town 46,000), Maastricht 164,000 (city 118,000), Breda 163,000 (city 127,000) (1992 est).

Languages: Dutch (official; over 96% as a first language), plus small Frisian, Ambonese, and Turkish minorities.

Religions: Roman Catholic (36%), Reformed and Calvinist (27%); non-religious (33%), Sunni Islam (2%).

Education: Education is compulsory between the ages of five and 16. In 1991 the literacy rate was virtually 100%. There are 22 universities and specialized (mainly religious) institutes of university status.

Defence: In 1993 the total armed strength was nearly 75,000 - 43,500 in the army, 15,000 in the navy and 16,500 in the air force. Den Helder is the main naval base. Conscription was abolished in 1994. There are plans to amalgamate the navies of Belgium and the Netherlands. Dutch forces are also based in the Netherlands Antilles.

Transport: There are 118,214 km (73,470 mi) of roads including 2094 km (1301 mi) of motorways. There are 2798 km (1739 mi) of railways.

Rotterdam and Amsterdam have metros. Rotterdam is the world's largest port, handling over 288,000,000 tonnes of goods a year. Other ports include Amsterdam and IJmuiden. Dutch inland waterways - both canals and canalized rivers - carry about 30% of all freight moved in the Netherlands. Schiphol (Amsterdam) is one of Europe's main airports. Rotterdam, Groningen and Maastricht also have international airports.

Media: The Dutch national press comprises eight titles published in the three main cities. There are over 70 regional daily papers. NOS/NOB - a state corporation - operates three television channels. There are five national, 10 regional and over 140 local radio stations.

GOVERNMENT

The Netherlands is a constitutional monarchy. The 75-member First Chamber of the States-General is elected for six years by the 12 provincial councils - with one half of the members retiring every three years. The 150-member Second Chamber is elected for four years by universal adult suffrage by proportional representation. The monarch appoints a Prime Minister who commands a majority in the

THE NETHERLANDS

Area: 41 785 km² (16 140 sq mi), or 33 937 km² (13 103 sq mi) excluding freshwater

States-General. The PM, in turn, appoints a Council of Ministers (Cabinet) who are responsible to the States-General. There are 12 provinces. The main political parties include the (conservative) CDA (Christian Democratic Appeal Party), PvdA (the Labour Party), the (liberal) VVD (People's Party for Freedom and Democracy), D66 (Democracy 66), the (Calvinist) SGP (Political Reformed Party), the PPR (Reformed Political Federation), the (Calvinist) Evangelical Political Federation (RPF), the Green Left, the Socialist Party (PS), the Communist Party (PC), the Association for the Elderly (Elderly), Union 55+ (U), and the (right-wing) Centre Democrats (CD). After the election held in May 1994, the previous CDA-PvdA coalition remained in office while protracted negotiations continued to form a new government.

Party strength: PdvA 37, CDA34, VVD 31, D66 24, Elderly 6, Green Left 5, RPF 3, CD 3, others 7.

Queen: HM Queen Beatrix (succeeded on the abdication of her mother, 30 April 1980).

THE CABINET
(The following list of Ministers is to be replaced when a new coalition government takes office sometime in the summer or autumn of 1994.)

Prime Minister: Ruud F.M. Lubbers (CDA).

Deputy Prime Minister and Minister of Finance: Wim Kok (PvdA).

Minister of Agriculture, Nature Management and Fisheries: Piet Bukman (CDA).

Minister of Defence: A.L. ter Beek (PvdA).

Minister of Development Cooperation: Jan P. Pronk (PvdA).

Minister of Economic Affairs: Dr J.E. Andriessen (CDA).

Minister of Education and Science: Dr. Jo M.M. Ritzen (PvdA).

Minister of Foreign Affairs: Dr P.H. Kooijmans (CDA).

Minister of Foreign Trade: Y.M.C.T. van Rooy (CDA).

Minister of Home Affairs: D.IJ.W. de Graaf-Nauta (CDA).

Minister of Housing, Planning and the Environment: J. (Hans) G.M. Alders (PdvA).

Minister of Justice and Minister of Netherlands Antillean and Aruban Affairs: A. Kosto (PvdA).

Minister for Social Affairs and Employment: Dr. Bert de Vries (CDA).

Minister of Transport and Public Works: J.R. Hanja Maij-Weggen (CDA).

Minister of Welfare, Health and Cultural Affairs: Hedy d'Ancona (PvdA).

Minister Plenipotentiary of the Netherlands Antilles: E.A.V. Jesrun.

Minister Plenipotentiary of Aruba: R.H. Laclé.

PROVINCES
Population figures are 1992 estimates.

Drenthe Area: 2654 km^2 (1025 sq mi). Population: 446,000. Capital: Assen.

Flevoland Area: 1422 km^2 (549 sq mi). Population: 233,000. Capital: Lelystad.

Friesland Area: 3353 km^2 (1295 sq mi). Population: 602,000. Capital: Leeuwarden.

Gelderland Area: 5011 km^2 (1935 sq mi). Population: 1,829,000. Capital: Arnhem.

Groningen Area: 2346 km^2 (906 sq mi). Population: 555,000. Capital: Groningen.

Limburg Area: 2170 km^2 (838 sq mi). Population: 1,116,000. Capital: Maastricht.

North Brabant (Noord-Brabant) Area: 4946 km^2 (1910 sq mi). Population: 2,225,000. Capital: 's Hertogenbosch.

North Holland (Noord-Holland) Area: 2665 km^2 (1029 sq mi). Population: 2,422,000. Capital: Haarlem.

Overijssel Area: 3339 km^2 (1289 sq mi). Population: 1,032,000. Capital: Zwolle.

South Holland (Zuid-Holland) Area: 2908 km^2 (11234 sq mi). Capital: The Hague.

Utrecht Area: 1331 km^2 (514 sq mi). Population: 1,037,000. Capital: Utrecht.

Zeeland Area: 1792 km^2 (692 sq mi). Population: 359,000. Capital: Middelburg.

GEOGRAPHY
Over one quarter of the Netherlands - one of the world's most densely populated countries - lies below sea level. A network of canals and canalized rivers cross the west of the country where sand dunes and man-made dykes protect low-lying areas and polders (land reclaimed from the sea). The polders reclaimed

during the 20th century include the large Northeast Polder and the entire province of Flevoland. The coast has been straightened by sea walls protecting Zeeland in the southwest and enclosing a freshwater lake, the IJsselmeer, in the north. The east comprises low sandy plains. Highest point: Vaalserberg 321 m (1053 ft). Principal rivers: Rhine (Rijn) - dividing into branches including the Lek, Waal and Oude

Western Europe. Banking and finance are well developed.

Currency: Gulden (known in English as the guilder) 100 cents: 1US$ = 1.788 gulden (June 1994).

GDP: US$315,000,000,000 (1993 est); US$20,410 per head.

Provinces of the Netherlands

provincial capitals

A: Arnhem
As: Assen
G: Groningen
H: The Hague
Ha: Haarlem
L: Lelystad
Le: Leeuwarden
M: Middelburg
Ma: Maastricht
's-H: 's-Hertogenbosch
U: Utrecht
Z: Zwolle

Rijn, Maas (Meuse). Climate: The country has a maritime temperate climate, with cool to warm summers and relatively mild winters.

ECONOMY

Despite having few natural resources - except natural gas - the Netherlands has a high standard of living. Agriculture and horticulture are highly mechanized with a concentration on dairying and glasshouse crops, particularly flowers. Food processing is a major industry, and the country is a leading exporter of cheese. Manufacturing includes chemical, machinery, petroleum refining, metallurgical and electrical engineering industries. Raw materials are imported through Rotterdam, which is the largest port in the world and serves much of

RECENT HISTORY

The Dutch were neutral in World War I, but suffered occupation by the Germans 1940 to 1945. Following a bitter colonial war, the Dutch accepted that they could not reassert control over Indonesia after World War II. The Netherlands has shown enthusiasm for European unity, and, with the other Low Countries (Belgium and Luxembourg), founded Benelux, the core of the EC. Dutch politics has been characterized by a large number of small parties, some of a confessional nature, and a system of proportional representation has prevented any of these parties attaining a parliamentary majority. The formation of a new coalition government after each general election has often been difficult and time-consuming.

Norway

Official name: Kongeriket Norge (Kingdom of Norway).

Member of: UN, EFTA, NATO, CSCE, Council of Europe, OECD.

Area: 323,878 km² (125,050 sq mi) or 386,958 km² (149,469 sq mi) including Svalbard and Jan Mayen.

Population: 4,274,000 (1992 est).

Capital: Oslo 467,000 (1992 est).

Other major cities: Bergen 213,000, Trondheim 138,000, Stavanger 98,000, Kristiansand 66,000, Drammen 52,000, Tromso 51,000, Skien 48,000, Sandnes 45,000, Asker 42,000, Bodo 37,000, Sandefjord 36,000, Alesund 36,000 (1990 census).

Languages: Two official forms of Norwegian - Bokmaal and Nynorsk; Lapp (small minority).

Religion: Lutheran (official; 88%). non-religious (9%), various Protestant Churches (2%).

Education: Education is compulsory between the ages of six and 16. In 1990 the literacy rate was estimated to be virtually 100%. There are 14 universities including university centres and colleges and academies of university status.

Defence: In 1993 the total armed strength was 33,500 - 15,900 in the army, 7,300 navy, 700 coast guard service, 9,500 air force. The home guard had a total strength of 80,000. The Norwegian navy is based at Bergen. Norway is a NATO member. Conscription is compulsory for all Norwegian males. Initial training lasts 12 months for the army and air force and 15 months in the navy. Recruits are liable to recall for regular refresher courses.

Transport: There are 88,922 km (55,253 mi) of roads of which 437 km (272 mi) are motorways. State-run NSB operates 4027 km (2502 mi) of railway track. Oslo has a metro and a rapid light transit system. The main commercial shipping ports are Narvik and Oslo. Oslo, Bergen and Stavanger have international airports.

Media: Norway has over 60 daily (mainly regional) newspapers. A few Oslo titles have a national readership. NRK, an autonomous state corporation, has a monopoly on broadcasting, but operates regional as well as national stations.

GOVERNMENT

Norway is a constitutional monarchy. The 165-member Parliament (Storting) is elected under a system of proportional representation by universal adult suffrage for a four-year term. In order to legislate, the Storting divides itself into two houses - the Lagting (containing one quarter of the members) and the Odelsting (containing the remaining members). The King appoints a Prime Minister who commands a majority in the Storting. The PM, in turn, appoints a Council of Ministers who are responsible to the Storting. Norway is divided into 19 counties (fylker). Political parties include the Labour Party (DnA), the Conservative Party (H), the Progress Party (FP), the Socialist Left Party (SVP), the Christian Democratic Party (KrF), the Centre Party (SP), the Red Electoral Alliance and the Liberal Party (Venstre). Following the election held in September 1993 a DnA government was formed in October 1993.

Party strength: DnA 67, SP 32, H 28, KrF 13, SVP 13, FP 10, Venstre 1, others 1.

King: HM King Harald V (succeeded upon the death of his father, 17 January 1991).

THE CABINET

(all members of the DnA)

Prime Minister: Gro Harlem Brundtland.

Minister of Agriculture: Gunnhild Oeyangen.

Minister for Children and Family Affairs: Grete Berget.

Minister of Cultural Affairs: Ase Kleveland.

Minister of Defence: Joergen Kosmo.

Minister of Development Cooperation: Kari Nordheim-Larsen.

Minister of Education and Research, and Minister of Church Affairs: Gudmund Hernes .

Minister for the Environment: Thorbjoern Berntsen.

Minister of Finance: Sigbjoern Johnsen.

Minister of Fisheries: Jan Henry T. Olsen.

Minister of Foreign Affairs: Bjorn Tore Godal.

Minister of Government Administration: Nils Olav Totland.

Minister of Health: Werner Christie.

Minister of Industry and Energy: Jens Stoltenberg.

Minister of Justice: Grete Faremo.

Minister of Local Government and Labour: Gunnar Berge.

Minister of Social Affairs: Hill-Marta Solberg.

Minister of Trade and Shipping: Grete Knudsen.

Minister of Transport and Communications: Kjell Opseth.

COUNTIES

Akershus Area: 4917 km² (1898 sq mi). Population: 422,000 (1992 est). Capital: Oslo.

Buskerud Area: 14,927 km² (5763 sq mi). Population: 226,000 (1992 est). Capital: Drammen.

East Agder (Aust-Agder) Area: 9212 km² (3557 sq mi). Population: 98,000 (1992 est). Capital: Arendal.

Finnmark Area: 48,637 km² (18,779 sq mi). Population: 75,000 (1992 est). Capital: Vadso.

Hedmark Area: 27,388 km² (10,575 sq mi). Population: 188,000 (1992 est). Capital: Hamar.

Hordaland Area: 15,634 km² (6036 sq mi). Population: 414,000 (1992 est). Capital: Bergen.

More and Romsdal (More og Romsdal) Area: 15,104 km² (5832 sq mi). Population: 239,000 (1992 est). Capital: Molde.

Nordland Area: 38,327 km² (14,798 sq mi). Population: 240,000 (1992 est). Capital: Bodo.

North Trondelag (Nord-Trondelag) Area: 22,463 km² (8673 sq mi). Population: 127,000 (1992 est). Capital: Steinkjer.

Oppland Area: 25,260 km² (9753 sq mi). Population: 182,000 (1992 est). Capital: Lillehammer.

Oslo Area: 454 km² (175 sq mi). Population: 467,000 (1992 est). Capital: Oslo.

Ostfold Area: 4183 km² (1615 sq mi). Population: 238,000 (1992 est). Capital: Moss.

Rogaland Area: 9141 km² (3529 sq mi). Population: 342,000 (1992 est). Capital: Stavanger.

Sogn and Fjordane (Sogn og Fjordane) Area: 18,634 km² (7195 sq mi). Population: 107,000 (1992 est). Capital: Leikanger.

South Trondelag (Sor-Trondelag) Area: 18,831 km² (7271 sq mi). Population: 253,000 (1992 est). Capital: Trondheim.

Telemark Area: 15,315 km² (5913 sq mi). Population: 163,000 (1992 est). Capital: Skien.

Troms Area: 25,954 km² (10,021 sq mi). Population: 148,000 (1992 est). Capital: Tromso.

Vestfold Area: 2216 km² (856 sq mi). Population: 200,000 (1992 est). Capital: Tonsberg.

West Agder (Vest-Agder) Area: 7281 km² (2811 sq mi). Population: 146,000 (1992 est). Capital: Kristiansand.

DEPENDENCIES

Jan Mayen Area: 380 km² (147 sq mi). Population: uninhabited.

Svalbard Area: 62,924 km² (24,295 sq mi). Population: 3700 (1992 est).

GEOGRAPHY

Norway's coastline is characterized by fjords, a series of long, deep, narrow inlets formed by glacial action. The greater part of Norway comprises highlands of hard rock. Permanent glaciers occur in the southwest. Svalbard (formerly known as Spitsbergen) is a bleak archipelago in the Arctic. Jan Mayen is an active volcanic island situated between Norway and Greenland. The principal lowlands in Norway are along the Skagerrak coast and around

NORWAY

Area: 323 878 km² (125 050 sq mi) or 386 958 km² (149 469 sq mi) including the Arctic island territories of Svalbard and Jan Mayen.

Oslofjord and Trondheimsfjord. Highest point: Galdhopiggen 2469 m (8098 ft). Principal rivers: Glomma (Glama), Lågen, Tanaelv. Climate: Norway's temperate climate is the result of the warming Gulf Stream. Summers are remarkably mild for the latitude, while winters are long and very cold. Precipitation is heavy - over 2000 mm (80 in) in the west, with marked rain shadows inland.

ECONOMY

Norway enjoys a high standard of living. Only a small proportion of the land can be cultivated, and agriculture - which is heavily subsidized - is chiefly concerned with dairying and fodder crops. Timber is a major export of Norway, over one half of which is forested. The fishing industry is an important foreign-currency earner, and fish farming - which has been encouraged by government development schemes - is taking the place of whaling and deep-sea fishing. (Whaling has recommenced despite widespread international condemnation.) Manufacturing - which has traditionally been concerned with processing fish, timber and iron ore - is now dominated by petrochemicals and allied industries, based upon large reserves of petroleum and natural gas in Norway's sector of the North Sea. Petroleum and natural gas supply over one third of the country's export earnings. The development of industries such as electrical engineering has been helped by cheap hydroelectric power.The island of Spitsbergen is exploited for its coal.

Currency: Norwegian krone of 100 ore; 1US$ = 7.22 krone (May 1994).

GDP: US$110,000,000,000 (1993 est); US$25,410 per head.

RECENT HISTORY

Norway came under the rule of the kings of Sweden after the Napoleonic Wars, although a separate Norwegian Parliament was allowed a considerable degree of independence. Growing nationalism in Norway placed great strains upon the union with Sweden, and in 1905 - following a vote by the Norwegians to repeal the union - King Oscar II of Sweden gave up his claims to the Norwegian crown to allow a peaceful separation of the two countries. After a Swedish prince declined the Norwegian throne, Prince Carl of Denmark was confirmed as King of Norway - as Haakon VII - by a plebiscite. Norway was neutral in World War I,

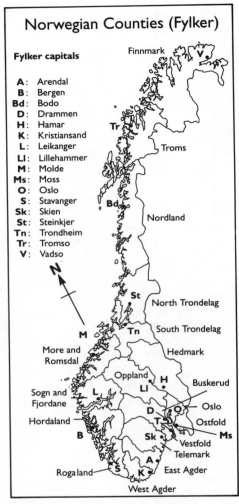

Norwegian Counties (Fylker)

Fylker capitals

A: Arendal
B: Bergen
Bd: Bodo
D: Drammen
H: Hamar
K: Kristiansand
L: Leikanger
Ll: Lillehammer
M: Molde
Ms: Moss
O: Oslo
S: Stavanger
Sk: Skien
St: Steinkjer
Tn: Trondheim
Tr: Tromso
V: Vadso

Finnmark

Troms

Nordland

North Trondelag

South Trondelag

Hedmark

Buskerud

Oslo

Ostfold

Ms

Vestfold

Telemark

East Agder

West Agder

More and Romsdal

Sogn and Fjordane

Hordaland

Rogaland

and declared neutrality in World War II, but was occupied by German forces (1940) who set up a puppet government under Vidkun Quisling. After the war, Norway joined NATO and agreed in 1972 to enter the EC, but a national referendum rejected membership. In 1992, Norway reapplied to join the EC. A referendum on EU/EC membership is scheduled for the autumn of 1994. In the 1990s Norwegian diplomacy has been notably active, for example in bringing about the Israeli-Palestinian peace accord.

Portugal

Official name: A República Portuguesa (The Portuguese Republic).

Member of: UN, EC/EU, NATO, Council of Europe, CSCE, WEU, OECD.

Area: 92,072 km² (33,549 sq mi) including Madeira and the Azores.

Population: 10,421,000 (1991 est).

Capital: Lisbon (Lisboa) 2,131,000 (city 950,000; Amadora 100,000; Barreiro 55,000; Almada 45,000; Queluz 45,000) (1990 est).

Other major cities: Oporto (Porto) 1,695,000 (city 450,000; Vila Nova de Gaia 65,000), Setúbal 80,000, Coímbra 75,000, Braga 67,000, Funchal 47,000 (all with suburbs; 1990 est).

Language: Portuguese (official; 100%).

Religion: Roman Catholic (94%).

Education: Education is compulsory between the ages of six and 15. In 1990 the literacy rate was estimated to be 86.8%. There are 16 universities.

Defence: In 1993 the total armed strength was 108,100 - 32,700 in the army, 20,900 National Republican Guard, 8900 border guard, 20,000 paramilitary police, 15,300 navy and 10,300 air force. Lisbon is the main naval base. The USA has a base in the Azores. Portuguese males are subject to compulsory military service which is to be reduced to four months in 1994-95.

Transport: There are 70,176 km (43,605 mi) of roads of which 318 km (198 mi) are motorways. CP runs the state-owned railways which operate 3588 km (2229 mi). Lisbon has a metro; Lisbon and Oporto have light transit systems. The main international airport is at Lisbon.

PORTUGAL

Area: 92 072 km²
(33 549 sq mi) including Madeira and the Azores

International flights also serve Funchal (Madeira), Faro, Oporto and Santa Maria and San Miguel (both in the Azores). Lisbon, Leixoes (Oporto), Setubal and Funchal are the main commercial shipping ports.

Media: There are 30 daily newspapers. TP, a state corporation, operates two television channels and three regional stations. Two commercial stations offer competition. There are four national and five regional RDP (state corporation) radio stations as well as one national commercial and over 300 local radio stations.

GOVERNMENT

An executive President is elected for five years by universal adult suffrage. The 230-member Assembly is directly elected for four years. The President appoints a Prime Minister who commands a majority in the Assembly. The PM, in turn, appoints a Council of Ministers (Cabinet), responsible to the Assembly. There are 18 districts and two autonomous regions. The main political parties include PSD (the Social Democratic Party), PS (the Socialist Party), the (centre-left) Centre Democratic Party (CDS), the Communist alliance (CDU) and the (pensioners') National Solidarity Party (PSN). After the election held in October 1991 a PSD government was formed.

Party strength: PSD 135, PS 72, CDU 17, CDS 5, PSN 1.

President: Mario Alberto Soares (PSD).

THE CABINET

Prime Minister: Annibal Cavaço Silva (PSD).

Deputy Prime Minister (and Minister of Defence): Joaquim Fernando Nogueira (PSD).

Minister of Agriculture, Fisheries and Food: Antonio Duarte Silva (PSD).

Minister of Commerce and Tourism: Fernando Faria de Oliveira (PSD).

Minister of Education: Manuela Ferreira Leite (PSD).

Minister of Employment and Social Security: José Falcao e Cunha (PSD).

Minister for the Environment and National Resources: Teresa Gouveia (PSD).

Minister of Finance: Eduardo Catroga (PSD).

Minister of Foreign Affairs: Jose Miguel Durão Barroso (PSD).

Minister of Health: Paulo Mendo (PSD).

Minister of Industry and Energy: Luis Mira Amaral (PSD).

Minister of the Interior: Manuel Dias Loureiro (PSD).

Minister of Justice: Dr Alvaro Laborinho Lucio (PSD).

Minister for Parliamentary Affairs: Luis Marques Mendes (SP).

Minister of Planning and Territorial Administration: Luis Valente de Oliveira (PSD).

Minister of Public Works, Transport and Communications: Joaquim Ferreira do Amaral (PSD).

Minister for the Sea: Eduardo de Azevedo Soares (PSD).

AUTONOMOUS REGIONS

Azores (Açores) Area: 2247 km² (868 sq mi). Population: 253,000 (1991 est). Capital: Ponta Delgada.

Madeira (includes Porto Santo) Area: 794 km² (306 sq mi). Population: 273,000 (1991 est). Capital: Funchal.

DISTRICTS

Aveiro Area: 2808 km² (1084 sq mi). Population: 656,000 (1991 est). Capital: Aveiro.

Beja Area: 10,225 km² (3948 sq mi). Population: 168,000 (1991 est). Capital: Beja.

Braga Area: 2673 km² (1032 sq mi). Population: 746,000 (1991 est). Capital: Braga.

Braganca Area: 6608 km² (2551 sq mi). Population: 158,000 (1991 est). Capital: Braganca.

Castelo Branco Area: 6675 km² (2577 sq mi). Population: 215,000 (1991 est). Capital: Castelo Branco.

Coimbra Area: 3947 km² (1524 sq mi). Population: 428,000 (1991 est). Capital: Coimbra.

Evora Area: 7393 km² (2854 sq mi). Population: 174,000 (1991 est). Capital: Evora.

Faro Area: 4960 km² (1915 sq mi). Population: 340,000 (1991 est). Capital: Faro.

Guarda Area: 5518 km² (2131 sq mi). Population: 188,000 (1991 est). Capital: Guarda.

Leiria Area: 3515 km² (1357 sq mi). Population: 428,000 (1991 est). Capital: Leiria.

Lisbon (Lisboa) Area: 2761 km² (1066 sq mi). Population: 2,064,000 (1991 est). Capital: Lisbon.

Oporto (Porto) Area: 2395 km² (925 sq mi). Population: 1,622,000 (1991 est). Capital: Oporto.

Portalegre Area: 6065 km² (2342 sq mi). Population: 134,000 (1991 est). Capital: Portalegre.

Santarem Area: 6747 km² (2605 sq mi). Population: 443,000 (1991 est). Capital: Santarem.

Setubal Area: 5064 km² (1955 sq mi). Population: 714,000 (1991 est). Capital: Setubal.

Viana do Castelo Area: 2255 km² (871 sq mi). Population: 249,000 (1991 est). Capital: Viana do Castelo.

Vila Real Area: 4328 km² (1671 sq mi). Population: 237,000 (1991 est). Capital: Vila Real.

Viseu Area: 5007 km² (1933 sq mi). Population: 401,000 (1991 est). Capital: Viseu.

GEOGRAPHY

Behind a coastal plain, Portugal north of the River Tagus is a highland region, at the centre of which is the country's principal mountain range, the Serra da Estrela. A wide plateau in the northeast is a continuation of the Spanish Meseta. Portugal south of the Tagus is mainly an undulating lowland. The Atlantic islands of Madeira and the Azores are respectively nearly 1000 km (620 mi) and 1200 km (745 mi) southwest of the mainland.The Azores comprise nine main islands and many much smaller islets. The mountainous islands, which include volcanic craters, are in three groups. The island of São Miguel contains over 50% of the population. Madeira is a tropical island group comprising Madeira island, Porto Santo and seven other tiny uninhabited islets. Highest point: Punta do Pico 2315 m (7713 ft) in the Azores. Malhao de Estrela, 1993 m (6537 ft), is the highest mainland point. Principal rivers: Tagus (Rio Tejo), Douro, Guadiana. Climate: Portugal has a mild and temperate climate which is wetter and more Atlantic in the north, and drier, hotter and more Mediterranean in the south.

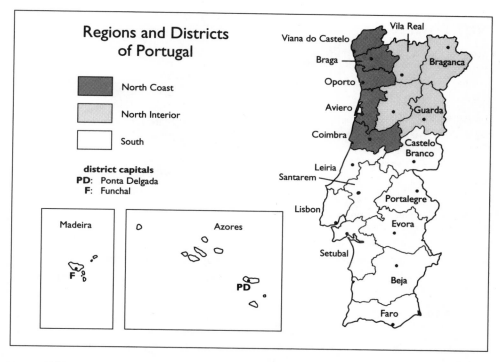

Regions and Districts of Portugal

- ■ North Coast
- ▨ North Interior
- ☐ South

district capitals
PD: Ponta Delgada
F: Funchal

Madeira

Azores

Vila Real
Viana do Castelo
Braga
Braganca
Oporto
Aviero
Guarda
Coimbra
Castelo Branco
Leiria
Santarem
Portalegre
Lisbon
Evora
Setubal
Beja
Faro

ECONOMY

Agriculture involves about 15% of the labour force, but lacks investment following land reforms in the 1970s, since when production has fallen. The principal crops include wheat and maize, as well as grapes (for wines such as port and Madeira), tomatoes, potatoes and cork trees. The country lacks natural resources. Manufacturing industry includes textiles and clothing (major exports), footwear, food processing, cork products, and, increasingly, electrical appliances and petrochemicals. Tourism and money sent back by Portuguese working abroad are major foreign-currency earners. Despite recent impressive economic development - following severe disruption during and immediately after the 1974 revolution - Portugal remains Western Europe's poorest country.

Currency: Escudo (PTE); 1US$ = 164.2 escudos (June 1994).

GDP: US$80,000,000,000 (1993 et); US$6320 per head.

RECENT HISTORY

Portugal experienced political instability for much of the 19th century. The monarchy was violently overthrown in 1910, but the Portuguese republic proved unstable and the military took power in 1926. From 1932 to 1968, under the dictatorship of Premier Antonio Salazar (1889-1970), stability was achieved but at great cost. Portugal became a one-party state, and expensive colonial wars dragged on as Portugal attempted to check independence movements in Angola and Mozambique. In 1974 there was a left-wing military coup whose leaders granted independence to the African colonies (1974-75), and initially attempted to impose a Marxist system on the country. However, elections in 1976 decisively rejected the far left. Civilian rule was restored as Portugal effected a transition from dictatorship to democracy, and simultaneously - through the loss of empire and membership of the EC (from 1986) - became more closely integrated with the rest of Europe.

405

San Marino

Official name: Serenissima Repubblica di San Marino (Most Serene Republic of San Marino).

Member of: UN, CSCE, Council of Europe.

Area: 61 km² (23 sq mi).

Population: 23,700 (1992 est).

Capital: San Marino 9000 (city 4200; Borgo Maggiore 4200; 1991 est).

Other main town: Seravalle 7300 (1991 est).

Language: Italian.

Religion: Roman Catholic (official; 95%).

Education: Education is compulsory from six to 14. There is no university.

Defence: There is a Voluntary Military Force.

Transport: There are 237 km (147 mi) of roads.

Media: Italian papers circulate. There are commercial radio and television stations.

GOVERNMENT
The 60-member Great and General Council - elected by universal adult suffrage for five years - elects two of its members as Captains-Regent, who are joint heads of state for six months. The Captains-Regent chair a 10-member Congress of State (Cabinet), which is elected by the Council for five years. Political parties include the (conservative) Christian Democratic Party (PDCS), the Socialist Party (PSS), the (former Communist) Democratic Progressive Party (PDP), the Popular Democratic Alliance (PDA), the Democratic Movement (MD) and the Reformed Communist Party (RC). After the election in May 1993 a PDCS-PSS coalition was formed.

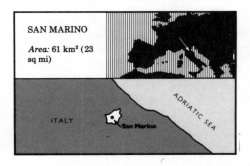

SAN MARINO

Area: 61 km² (23 sq mi)

ITALY

San Marino

ADRIATIC SEA

Party strength: PDCS 26, PSS 14, PDP 11, PDA 4, MD 3, RC 2.

THE CABINET (CONGRESS OF STATE)
Secretary of State for Finance and the Budget: Clelio Galassi (PDCS).

Secretary of State for Foreign and Political Affairs: Gabriele Gatti (PDCS).

Secretary of State for Internal Affairs, Civil Protection and Justice: Antonio Volpinari (PSS).

Minister of State for Labour and Cooperation: Sante Canducci (PDCS).

Minister of State for Commerce: Ottaviano Rossi (PDCS).

Minister of State for Education and Culture: Emma Rossi (PSS).

Minister of State for the Environment: Piernatalino Mularoni (PDCS).

Minister of State for Health and Social Security: Renzo Ghiotti (PDCS).

Minister of State for Industry and Handicrafts: Fiorenzo Stolfi (PSS).

Minister of State for Transport, Communications, Tourism and Sport: Augusto Casali (PSS).

GEOGRAPHY
The country is dominated by the triple limestone peaks of Monte Titano, the highest point at 739 m (2424 ft). There are no significant rivers. Climate: San Marino has a Mediterranean climate with warm summers, mild winters and moderate rainfall.

ECONOMY
Tourism, in particular visitors on excursions, is the mainstay of the economy. Manufacturing - particularly leather, footwear, textiles and ceramics - has been encouraged.

Currency: San Marino uses Italian currency.

GDP: US$188,000,000 (1987); US$8500 per head.

RECENT HISTORY
San Marino's independence was recognized by the new Kingdom of Italy (1862). In 1957 a bloodless 'revolution' replaced the Communist-Socialist administration that had been in power since 1945.

Spain

Official name: Reino de España (Kingdom of Spain).

Member of: UN, NATO, EC/EU, WEU, CSCE, Council of Europe, OECD.

Area: 504,782 km² (194,897 sq mi) including the Canary Islands, Ceuta and Melilla.

Population: 39,952,000 (1991 census) including the Canary Islands, Ceuta and Melilla.

Capital: Madrid 4,846,000 (city 3,121,000; Móstoles 193,000; Leganés 173,000; Alcalá de Henares 159,000; Fuenlabrada 145,000; Alcorcon 140,000; Getafe 139,000; 1991 census).

Other major cities: Barcelona 3,400,000 (city 1,707,000; L'Hospitalet 269,000; Badalona 206,000; Sabadell 184,000; Santa Coloma de Gramanet 132,000), Valencia 1,060,000 (city 777,000), Seville (Sevilla) 754,000 (city 684,000), Zaragoza 614,000, Málaga 525,000, Bilbao 477,000 (city 372,000), Las Palmas de Gran Canaria 348,000, Valladolid 345,000, Murcia 329,000, Córdoba 309,000, Palma de Mallorca 309,000, Granada 287,000, Vigo 277,000, Alicante 271,000, Gijón 260,000, La Coruña 251,000, Cádiz 240,000 (city 157,000), Vitoria 209,000, Oviedo 203,000, Santander 194,000, Santa Cruz de Tenerife 192,000, Pamplona 191,000, Salamanca 186,000, Jérez de la Frontera 184,000, Elche 181,000, Donostia-San Sebastián 174,000, Cartagena 172,000, Burgos 169,000, Salamanca 163,000, Tarrasa 154,000, Alméria 153,000, León 144,000, Huelva 141,000 (all including suburbs; 1991 census).

Languages: Spanish or Castilian (official; as a first language over 70%), Catalan (as a first language over 20%), Basque (3%), Galician (4%).

Religion: Roman Catholic (95%).

Education: Education is compulsory between the ages of six and 16. In 1991 the literacy rate was almost 86%. There are 36 universities and institutes of university status.

Defence: In 1993 the total armed strength was 201,000 - 139,000 in the army, 30,000 in the navy and 32,000 in the air force. There are over 75,000 paramilitary. Compulsory military service lasts for nine months.

Transport: There are 331,961 km (206,315 mi) of roads including 2700 km (1678 mi) of motor-ways. State-owned RENFE runs 12,560 km (7804 mi) of railways. Other companies run 1854 km (1152 mi) of track. Madrid and Barcelona have metros; Bilbao and Valencia are building metros. The main commercial ports are Barcelona, Santa Cruz, Gijon, Las Palmas and Seville. Barajas (Madrid) is one of Europe's principal airports. Other international airports include Barcelona, Bilbao, Malaga, Palma, Seville, Valencia and two airports in the Canaries.

Media: Strong regional identity and the lack of a single language have prevented the emergence of a national press. There are 120 daily newspapers. RTVE, a state corporation, controls broadcasting. There are seven regional television companies, five national and three regional radio stations, and over 300 local radio stations.

GOVERNMENT

Spain is a constitutional monarchy. The Cortes (Parliament) comprises a Senate (Upper House) and a Chamber of Deputies (Lower House). The Senate consists of 208 senators - 4 from each province, 5 from the Balearic Islands, 6 from the Canary Islands and 2 each from Ceuta and Melilla - elected by universal adult suffrage for four years, plus 49 senators indirectly elected by the autonomous communities. The Congress of Deputies has 350 members directly elected for four years under a system of proportional representation. The King appoints a Prime Minister (President of the Council) who commands a majority in the Cortes. The PM, in turn, appoints a Council of Ministers (Cabinet) responsible to the Chamber of Deputies. Each of the 17 regions has its own legislature. The main political parties include the PSOE (Socialist Workers' Party), the (conservative) PP (Partido Popular), the (left-wing) coalition) Izquierda Unida (United Left, which includes the Communist Party; IU), the (Catalan) Convergencia i Unio (CIU) and PNV (the Basque Nationalist Party). After the election held in June 1993 a coalition of PSOE members and independents was formed.

Party strength: PSOE 159, PP 141, UI 18, CIU 17, PNV 5, others 10.

King: HM King Juan Carlos I (succeeded upon the restoration of the monarchy, 22 November 1975).

THE CABINET

Prime Minister: Felipe González Marquez (PSOE).

Deputy Prime Minister: Narcis Serra y Serra (PSOE).

Minister of Agriculture: Luiz Maria Atienza.

Minister of Commerce and Tourism: Javier Gomez Navarro (ind).

SPAIN

Area: 504 782 km² (194 897 sq mi) including the Canary Islands, Ceuta and Melilla

Minister of Culture: Carmen Alborch Bataller (ind).

Minister of Defence: Julián Garcia Vargas (PSOE).

Minister of Economic Affairs and Finance: Pedro Solbes Mira (ind).

Minister of Education and Science: Gustavo Suarez Pertierra (PSOE).

Minister of Foreign Affairs: Javier Solana Madariaga (PSOE).

Minister of Health and Consumer Affairs: Angeles Amador Millán (ind).

Minister of Industry: Juan Eguiagaray Ucelay (PSOE).

Minister of Justice and the Interior: Juan Belloch Julve (ind).

Minister of Labour and Social Security: José Antonio Griñan Martinez (PSOE).

Minister for Parliamentary Relations: Alfredo Pérez Rubalcaba (PSOE).

Minister of Public Administration: Jerónimo Saavedra Acevedo (PSOE).

Minister of Public Works, Transportation and the Environment: José Borrell Fontellas (PSOE).

Minister of Social Affairs: Cristina Alberdi Alonso (ind).

AUTONOMOUS COMMUNITIES

Andalusia (Andalucia) Area: 87,268 km² (33,694 sq mi). Population: 6,860,000 (1991 census). Capital: Seville.

Aragón Area: 47,669 km² (18,405 sq mi). Population: 1,179,000 (1991 census). Capital: Zaragoza.

Asturias Area: 10,565 km² (4079 sq mi). Population: 1,091,000 (1991 census). Capital: Oviedo.

Balearic Islands (Islas Baleares) Area: 5014 km² (1936 sq mi). Population: 703,000 (1991 census). Capital: Palma de Mallorca.

Basque Country (Euzkadi or Pais Vasco) Area: 7261 km² (2803 sq mi). Population: 2,093,000 (1991 census). Capital: Vitoria.

Canary Islands (Islas Canarias) Area: 7273 km² (2808 sq mi). Population: 1,456,000 (1991 census). Equal and alternative capitals: Las Palmas and Santa Cruz de Tenerife.

Cantabria Area: 5289 km² (2042 sq mi). Population: 524,000 (1991 census). Capital: Santander.

Castile-La Mancha (Castilla-La Mancha) Area: 79,226 km² (30,589 sq mi). Population: 1,650,000 (1991 census). Capital: Toledo.

Castile and León (Castilla y León) Area: 94,147 km² (36,350 sq mi). Population: 2,538,000 (1991 census). Capital: Valladolid.

Catalonia (Catalunya or Cataluña) Area: 31,930 km² (12,328 sq mi). Population: 5,960,000 (1991 census). Capital: Barcelona.

Extremadura Area: 41,602 km² (16,063 sq mi). Population: 1,050,000 (1991 census). Capital: Mérida.

Galicia (Galiza) Area: 29,434 km² (11,364 sq mi). Population: 2,710,000 (1991 census). Capital: Santiago de Compostela.

Madrid Area: 7995 km² (3087 sq mi). Population: 4,846,000 (1991 census). Capital: Madrid.

Murcia Area: 11,317 km² (4369 sq mi). Population: 1,032,000 (1991 census). Capital: Murcia (although the regional parliament meets at Cartagena).

Ceuta-Melilla (North African enclaves) Area: Ceuta - 19 km² (7 sq mi); Melilla - 14 km² (5.5 sq mi). Population: 125,000 (1991 census). Capitals: Ceuta and Melilla.

Spanish Autonomous Communities

O: Oviedo
P: Pamplona
Pm: Palma de Mallorca
S: Seville
SC: Santa Cruz de Tenerife
Sg: Santiago de Compostela
St: Santander
T: Toledo
V: Valladolid
VI: Valencia
Vt: Vitoria
Z: Zaragoza

community capitals

B: Barcelona
L: Logroño
LP: Las Palmas
M: Madrid
Me: Merida
Mr: Murcia

Navarre (Navarra) Area: 10,421 km² (4024 sq mi). Population: 516,000 (1991 census). Capital: Pamplona.

La Rioja Area: 5034 km² (1853 sq mi). Population: 262,000 (1991 census). Capital: Logroño.

Valencia Area: 23,305 km² (8998 sq mi). Population: 3,831,000 (1991 census). Capital: Valencia.

GEOGRAPHY

In the north of Spain a mountainous region stretches from the Pyrenees - dividing Spain from France - through the Cantabrian mountains to Galicia on the Atlantic coast. Much of the country is occupied by the central plateau, the Meseta. This is around 600 m (2000 ft) high, but rises to the higher Sistema Central in Castile, and ends in the south at the Sierra Morena. The Sierra Nevada range in Andalusia

409

in the south contains Mulhacén, mainland Spain's highest peak at 3478 m (11,411 ft). The principal lowlands include the Ebro Valley in the northeast, a coastal plain around Valencia in the east, and the valley of the Guadalquivir River in the south. The Balearic Islands in the Mediterranean comprise four main islands - Mallorca (Majorca), Menorca (Minorca), Ibiza and Formentera - with seven much smaller islands. The Canary Islands, off the coast of Morocco and the Western Sahara, comprise five large islands - Tenerife, Fuerteventura, Gran Canaria, Lanzarote and La Palma - plus two smaller islands and six islets. The cities of Ceuta and Melilla are enclaves on the north coast of Morocco. Highest point: Pico del Tiede 3716 m (12,192 ft) in the Canaries. Principal rivers: Tagus (Tajo), Ebro, Douro (Duero), Guadiana, Guadalquivir. Climate: The southeast has a Mediterranean climate with hot summers and mild winters. The dry interior is continental with hot summers and cold winters. The high Pyrenees have a cold Alpine climate, while the northwest (Galicia) has a wet Atlantic climate with cool summers.

ECONOMY

Over 10% of the labour force is involved in agriculture. The principal crops include barley, wheat, sugar beet, potatoes, citrus fruit and grapes (for wine). Pastures for livestock occupy some 20% of the land. Manufacturing developed rapidly from the 1960s, and there are now major motor-vehicle, textile, plastics, metallurgical, shipbuilding, chemical and engineering industries, as well as growing interests in telecommunications and electronics. Foreign investors have been encouraged to promote new industry, but unemployment remains high. Banking and commerce are important, and tourism is a major foreign-currency earner with around 53,000,000 foreign visitors a year, mainly staying at beach resorts on the Mediterranean, Balearic Islands and the Canaries. After the G7 countries, Spain has the largest gross national product in the world.

Currency: Peseta; 1US$ = 131.55 pesetas (June 1994).

GDP: US$477,000,000,000 (1993 est); US$12,180 per head.

RECENT HISTORY
When Cuba, the Philippines, Guam and Puerto

Rico were lost after the Spanish-American War (1898), doubts grew as to whether Alfonso XIII's constitutional monarchy was capable of delivering the dynamic leadership that Spain was thought to require. Spain remained neutral in World War I. Social tensions increased and a growing disillusionment with parliamentary government and political parties led to a military coup (1923) led by General Miguel Primo de Rivera (1870-1930). Primo was supported by Alfonso XIII until 1930 when the King withdrew support. However, the range of forces arrayed against the monarchy and the threat of civil war led Alfonso to abdicate (1931). The peace of the succeeding republic was short-lived. Neither of the political extremes - left nor right - was prepared to tolerate the perceived inefficiency and lack of authority of the Second Spanish Republic. In 1936, nationalist army generals rose against a new republican government. Led by General Francisco Franco (1892-1975) and supported by Germany and Italy, the nationalists fought the republicans in the bitter Spanish Civil War. Franco triumphed in 1939 to become ruler - Caudillo - of the neo-Fascist Spanish State. Political expression was restricted, and from 1942 to 1967 the Cortes (Parliament) was not directly elected. Spain remained neutral in World War II, although it was beholden to Germany. After 1945, Franco emphasized Spain's anti-Communism - a policy that brought his regime some international acceptance from the West during the Cold War. In 1969, Franco named Alfonso XIII's grandson Juan Carlos (1938-) as his successor. The monarchy was restored on Franco's death (1975) and the King eased the transition to democracy through the establishment of a new liberal constitution in 1978. In 1981 Juan Carlos played an important role in putting down an attempted army coup. In 1982 Spain joined NATO and elected a socialist government, and since 1986 the country has been a member of the EC. Despite the granting of some regional autonomy since 1978, Spain continues to be troubled by campaigns for provincial independence - for example in Catalonia - and by the violence of the Basque separatist movement ETA.

Sweden

Official name: Konungariket Sverige (Kingdom of Sweden).

Member of: UN, EFTA, CSCE, Council of Europe, OECD, NATO (partner for peace).

Area: 449,964 km² (173,732 sq mi).

Population: 8,644,000 (1992 est).

Capital: Stockholm 1,471,000 (city 679,000; 1992 est).

Other major cities: Göteborg (Gothenburg) 720,000 (city 432,000), Malmö 466,000 (city 235,000, Lund 90,000), Uppsala 171,000, Linköping 124,000, Orebro 122,000, Norrköping 121,000, Västeras 120,000, Jönköping 112,000, Helsingborg 110,000, Boras 102,000, Sundsvall 94,000 (all including suburbs; 1992 est).

Languages: Swedish (official; nearly 100%); small Lapp minority.

Religion: Lutheran (85% - of whom over one half are nominal Lutherans); non-religious (12%).

Education: Education is compulsory between the ages of six and 16. In 1990 the literacy rate was virtually 100%. There are 20 institutions of university status.

Defence: Military service lasts between seven and a half and 15 months depending upon the force. In 1993 the total armed strength ws 60,500 - 43,500 in the army, 9500 in the navy and 7500 in the air force.

Transport: There are 133,673 km (83,060 mi) of roads of which 936 km (582 mi) were motorways. There are 9846 km (6118 mi) of state-run railways. Stockholm has a metro. The largest ports are Gothenburg, Helsingborg, Stockholm and Malmo. Stockholm, Gothenburg and Malmo have international airports.

Media: There are about 65 daily newspapers. SR, an autononous state corporation, operates two television channels and four national radio stations. There are two commercial television channels and over 35 local and community radio stations.

GOVERNMENT

Sweden is a constitutional monarchy in which the King has no executive role. The 349-member Riksdag (Parliament) is elected for three years by universal adult suffrage by proportional representation. The Speaker of the Riksdag nominates a Prime Minister who commands a parliamentary majority. The PM, in turn, appoints a Cabinet of Ministers who are responsible to the Riksdag. There are 24 counties (lan). The main political parties are the Social Democratic Labour Party (SDAP), the (conservative) Moderate Party (MS), the Liberal Party (FP), the Centre Party (CP), the Christian Democratic Party (KdS), the (rightwing) New Democracy Party (ND) and the (former Communist) Left Party (VP). After the election held in September 1991 a coalition of MS, FP, CP and KdS members was formed.

Party strength: SDAP 138, MS 80, FP 33, CP 31, Kd) 26, ND 25, VP 16.

King: HM King Carl XVI Gustaf (succeeded upon the death of his grandfather, 15 September 1973).

SWEDEN

Area: 449 964 km² (173 732 sq mi)

THE CABINET

Prime Minister: Carl Bildt (MS)

Deputy Prime Minister and Minister of Social Affairs: Bengt Westerberg (FP).

Minister of Agriculture: Karl Erik Olsson (CP).

Minister of Aid and Human Rights: Alf Svenssen (KdS).

Minister for the Civil Service (Public Administration): Inger Davidsson (KdS).

Minister of Constitutional and Civil Law: Reidunn Laurén (ind.).

Minister of Defence: Anders Björck (MS).

Minister of Education: Per Unckel (MS).

411

Minister for the Environment: Olof Johansson (CP).

Minister for European Affairs and Foreign Trade: Ulf Dinkenspiel (ind).

Minister of Finance: Anne Wibble (FP).

Minister of Fiscal Affairs and Financial Markets: Bo Lundgren (FP).

Minister of Foreign Affairs: Baroness Margaretha af Ugglas (MS).

Minister of Health and Social Security: Bo Konberg (FP).

Minister of Immigration and Cultural Affairs: Birgit Friggebo (FP).

Minister of Industry and Commerce: Per Westerberg (MS).

Minister of Justice: Gun Hellsvik (MS).

Minister of Labour: Borje Hornlund (CP).

Minister of Physical Planning: Görel Thurdin (KdS).

Minister for Schools and Adult Education: Beatrice Ask (MS).

Minister of Transport and Communications: Mats Odell (KdS).

COUNTIES (LAN)

Population figures are 1992 estimates.

Alvsborg Area: 11,395 km² (4400 sq mi). Population: 444,000. Capital: Vanersborg.

Blekinge Area: 2941 km² (1136 sq mi). Population: 151,000. Capital: Karlskrona.

Gavleborg Area: 18,191 km² (7024 sq mi). Population: 289,000. Capital: Gavle.

Gothenburg and Bochus (Göteborg och Bohus) Area: 5141 km² (1985 sq mi). Population: 743,000. Capital: Gothenburg.

Gotland Area: 3140 km² (1212 sq mi). Population: 58,000. Capital: Visby.

Halland Area: 5454 km² (2106 sq mi). Population: 258,000. Capital: Halmstad.

Jamtland Area: 9,443 km² (19,090 sq mi). Population: 136,000. Capital: Ostersund.

Jönköping Area: 9944 km² (3839 sq mi). Population: 310,000. Capital: Jönköping.

Kalmar Area: 11,170 km² (4313 sq mi). Population: 241,000. Capital: Kalmar.

Kopparberg Area: 28,194 km² (10,886 sq mi). Population: 290,000. Capital: Falun.

Kristianstad Area: 6087 km² (2350 sq mi). Population: 292,000. Capital: Kristianstad.

Kronoberg Area: 8458 km² (3266 sq mi). Population: 179,000. Capital: Växjö .

Malmöhus Area: 4938 km² (1907 sq mi). Population: 787,000. Capital: Malmö.

Norrbotten Area: 98,913 km² (38,191 sq mi). Population: 265,000. Capital: Lulea.

Orebro Area: 8519 km² (3289 sq mi). Population: 274,000. Capital: Orebro.

Swedish Counties (Lan)

Lan capitals

F:	Falun	M:	Mariestad
G:	Gavle	Ml:	Malmo
Gb:	Gothenburg	N:	Nykoping
H:	Harnosand	O:	Ostersund
Hm:	Halmstad	Or:	Orebro
J:	Jonkoping	S:	Stockholm
K:	Karlstad	U:	Umea
Kk:	Karlskrona	Up:	Uppsala
Km:	Kalmar	V:	Vanersborg
Kr:	Kristianstad	Vs:	Visby
L:	Lulea	Vt:	Vasteras
Lk:	Linkoping	Vx:	Vaxjo

Ostergotland Area: 10,562 km² (4078 sq mi). Population: 406,000. Capital; Linköpi.

Skaraborg Area: 7937 km² (3065 sq mi). Population: 278,000. Capital: Mariestad.

Sodermanland Area: 6060 km² (2340 sq mi). Population: 257,000. Capital: Nyköping.

Stockholm Area: 6488 km² (2505 sq mi). Population: 1,655,000. Capital: Stockholm.

Uppsala Area: 6989 km² (2698 sq mi). Population: 274,000. Capital: Uppsala.

Varmland Area: 17,584 km² (6789 sq mi). Population: 284,000. Capital: Karlstad.

Vasterbotten Area: 55,401 km² (21,390 sq mi). Population: 254,000. Capital: Umea.

Vasternorrland Area: 21,678 km² (8370 sq mi). Population: 261,000. Capital: Harnosand.

Vastmanland Area: 6302 km² (2433 sq mi). Population: 259,000. Capital: Västeras.

GEOGRAPHY

The mountains of Norrland - in the north and along the border with Norway - cover 70% of Sweden. Norrland is characterized by fast-flowing rivers with many falls and rapids which have been utilized for hydroelectric power. There are about 90,000 lakes in Sweden, the largest being Vänern, Vättern and Malaren in central Sweden, Svealand. In the south are the low Smaland Highlands and the fertile lowland of Skane, Sweden's most important agricultural region. Sweden's Baltic coastline is rocky and indented with many hundreds of small wooded islands. All of Sweden shows the results of either glacial erosion or glacial deposition. Highest point: Kebnekaise 2123 m (6965 ft). Principal rivers: Göta, Ume, Torne, Angerman, Klar, Dal. Climate: Sweden experiences long cold winters and warm summers, although the north - where snow remains on the mountains for eight months - is more severe than the south, where Skane has a relatively mild winter.

ECONOMY

Sweden's high standard of living has been based upon its neutrality in the two World Wars, its cheap and plentiful hydroelectric power, and its mineral riches - large uranium deposits, and reserves of iron ore. Agriculture - like the bulk of the population - is concentrated in the south. The principal products include dairy produce, meat (including reindeer), barley, sugar beet and potatoes. Vast coniferous forests are the basis of the paper, board and furniture industries, and large exports of timber. Heavy industries include motor vehicles,

aerospace and machinery, although the shipbuilding industry - once the world's second largest - has ceased to exist. Rising labour costs, relatively high inflation and industrial unrest added to growing economic problems, and Sweden has been badly hit by the recession in the early 1990s. The government has been forced to abandon the state commitment to full employment, to make cuts in the welfare state, to reduce taxation and public spending, and to privatize some of the many state-run enterprises.

Currency: Krona of 100 ore; 1US$ = 7.716 krona (May 1994).

GDP: US$198,000,000,000 (1993 est); US$22,660 per head.

RECENT HISTORY

The union of Norway and Sweden - which resulted from the Vienna Congress of 1814-15 - was dissolved in 1905, when the King Oscar II (reigned 1872-1907) gave up the Norwegian throne upon Norway's vote for separation. During and after World War I (1914-18) there was a sudden worldwide demand for many of the industrial products of neutral Sweden, which experienced an unprecedented boom. The result was a dramatic increase in Sweden's industrial output and capacity, and a corresponding change from a rural agricultural society to an urban industrial society. During the Great Depression in the early 1930s, Sweden began to develop what was to become a comprehensive welfare state under successive social democratic governments, which ruled Sweden from 1932 until 1976. (In the period 1945-50 in particular, Sweden underwent a programme of intense social reform.) Sweden was neutral in World War II, but was forced to allow the transit of German troops across Swedish soil after the fall of Norway (1940). Sweden has assumed a moral leadership on world, social and environmental issues but was jolted by the (unclaimed) assassination of PM Olof Palme (1986). Sweden has been an enthusiastic supporter of the UN and has participated in many UN humanitarian operations. In the 1990s economic necessity has obliged Sweden to dismantle certain aspects of the welfare system. The country is to vote on joining the EU/EC in the autumn of 1994, and - if the Swedish electorate approves - Sweden will become an EU member on 1 January 1995.

Switzerland

Official name: Schweizerische Eidgenossenschaft (German) or Confédération suisse (French) or Confederazione Svizzera (Italian) or Confederaziun Helvetica (Romansch); (Swiss Confederation).

Member of: EFTA, CSCE, OECD, Council of Europe.

Area: 41,293 km² (15,943 sq mi).

Population: 6,870,000 (1992 est).

Capital: Berne (Bern) 299,000 (city 134,000; 1990 est).

Other major cities: Zürich 839,000 (city 343,000), Geneva (Genève) 389,000 (city 165,000), Basel 359,000 (city 170,000), Lausanne 263,000 (city 123,000), Lucerne (Luzern) 161,000 (city 59,000), St Gallen 126,000 (city 73,000), Winterthur 108,000 (city 86,000), Biel/Bienne 83,000 (city 53,000), Thun 78,000 (city 38,000), Lugano 69,000 (city 25,000), Neuchâtel 66,000 (city 33,000), Fribourg (Freiburg) 57,000 (city 34,000) (1990 est).

Languages: German (65% as a first language), French (18% as a first language), Italian (10% as a first language), Romansch (under 1%), others (including Croat, Serb and Turkish workers; 6%).

Religions: Roman Catholic (47%), Reformed Churches (Federation of Swiss Protestant Churches; 43%).

Education: Education is compulsory between the ages of six and 16. Literacy is virtually 100%. There are 10 universities and institutions of university status.

Defence: Switzerland is neutral. All Swiss males are subject to compulsory military service comprising 17 weeks at the age of 20, refresher courses between the ages of 21 and 32, then 39 days' training between the ages of 33 and 42 for the Landwehr (militia) and a further 13 days' training between the ages of 43 and 50 for the Landsturm (home guard). In 1992 the total armed strength was 676,000 (including about 615,000 conscripts serving for a period of army training, about 60,000 conscripts in the air force and about 1600 full-time personnel).

Transport: There are 71,099 km (44,179 mi) of roads (including 1515 km/941 mi of motorways). SBB, the state railway company, operate 2998 km (1863 mi) of railways; 120 private companies operate an additional 2210 km (1373 mi) of track. Basel is an important inland port on the River Rhine. The principal international airport is Zürich; international flights also operate from Geneva and Basel airports.

Media: Four national languages and a strong local identity have encouraged the existence of many (107) daily newspapers. RTSR broadcasts radio and television programmes in French, DRS in German and RTSI in Italian. There are also private commercial stations.

GOVERNMENT

Switzerland is a federal republic in which the governments of the 20 cantons and 6 half cantons have considerable powers. The Federal Assembly comprises the 46-member Council of States and the 200-member National Council. The former is directly elected for three or four years with two members from each canton and one from each half canton; the latter is elected for four years by universal adult suffrage by proportional representation. The Federal Assembly elects a seven-member Federal Council (Cabinet) for four years. The Council appoints one of its members to be President for one year. Political parties include the (liberal) Radical Democratic Party (FDP), the Social Democratic Party (SP), the (conservative) Christian Democratic Party (CVP), the (centre) Swiss People's Party (SVP), the Environmentalists (GPS), the Liberal-Democrats (LPS), the Independent Alliance (LDU), the Automobile Party (APS), the (right-wing) Swiss Democrats (SD), the Evangelical People's Party (EVP), the Ticino League (Lega) and the (former Communist) Workers' Party (PdA). Following the election held in October 1991 an SD, FDP, CDVS and SVP coalition was formed.

Party strength: FDP 44, SP 43, CVP 37, SVP 25, GPS 14, LPS 10, LDU6, APS 8, SD 5, Lega 2, PdA 2, others 1.

President: (for 1994) Otto Stich (SP) (see below).

THE FEDERAL COUNCIL (CABINET)

Minister of Finance: Otto Stich (SP); also President for 1994.

Minister of Foreign Affairs: Flavio Cotti (CVP).

Minister of Home Affairs: Ruth Dreifuss (SP).

Minister of Justice and for the Police: Arnold Koller (CVP).

Minister for the Public Economy: Jean-Pascal Delamuraz (FDP).

Minister of Transport, Communications and Energy: Adolf Ogi (SVP).

Minister of Defence: Kaspar Villiger (FDP); also Vice-President for 1994 - by convention, the Vice-President usually succeeds as President in the following year.

CANTONS

Aargau Area: 1404 km² (542 sq mi). Population: 490,000 (1990 est). Capital: Aarau.

Appenzell Ausser Rhoden (half canton) Area: 243 km² (94 sq mi). Population: 51,000 (1990 est). Capital: Herisau.

Appenzell Inner Rhoden (half canton) Area: 172 km² (66 sq mi). Population: 14,000 (1990 est). Capital: Appenzell.

Basel-Land (half canton) Area: 428 km² (165 sq mi). Population: 229,000 (1990 est). Capital: Liestal.

Basel-Stadt (half canton) Area: 37 km² (14 sq mi). Population: 190,000 (1990 est). Capital: Basel.

Berne (Bern) Area: 6049 km² (2336 sq mi). Population: 937,000 (1990 est). Capital: Berne.

Fribourg (Freiburg) Area: 1670 km² (645 sq mi). Population: 204,000 (1990 est). Capital: Fribourg.

Geneva (Genève) Area: 282 km² (109 sq mi). Population: 373,000 (1990 est). Capital: Geneva.

Glarus Area: 684 km² (264 sq mi). Population: 37,000 (1990 est). Capital: Glarus.

Graubünden (Grisons) Area: 7109 km² (2745 sq mi). Population: 169,000 (1990 est). Capital: Chur.

Jura Area: 838 km² (324 sq mi). Population: 65,000 (1990 est). Capital: Delémont.

Lucerne (Luzern) Area: 1494 km² (577 sq mi). Population: 315,000 (1990 est). Capital: Lucerne.

Neuchâtel Area: 797 km² (308 sq mi). Population: 159,000 (1990 est). Capital: Neuchâtel.

St Gallen Area: 2016 km² (778 sq mi). Population: 415,000 (1990 est) Capital: St Gallen.

Schaffhausen Area: 298 km² (115 sq mi). Population: 71,000 (1990 est). Capital: Schaffhausen.

Schwyz Area: 908 km² (351 sq mi). Population: 108,000 (1990 est). Capital: Schwyz.

Solothurn Area: 791 km² (305 sq mi). Population: 224,000 (1990 est). Capital: Solothurn.

Thurgau Area: 1006 km² (388 sq mi). Population: 202,000 (1990 est). Capital: Frauenfeld.

Ticino Area: 2811 km² (1085 sq mi). Population: 283,000 (1990 est). Capital: Bellinzona.

Unterwalden Nidwalden (half canton) Area: 274 km² (106 sq mi). Population: 32,000 (1990 est). Capital: Stans.

Unterwalden Obwalden (half canton) Area: 492 km² (190 sq mi). Population: 28,000 (1990 est). Capital: Sarnen.

Uri Area: 1075 km² (415 sq mi). Population: 34,000 (1990 est). Capital: Altdorf.

Valais (Wallis) Area: 5231 km² (2020 sq mi). Population: 244,000 (1990 est). Capital: Sion.

Vaud Area: 3211 km² (1240 sq mi). Population: 572,000. Capital: Lausanne.

Zug Area: 239 km² (92 sq mi). Population: 84,000 (1990 est). Capital: Zug.

Zürich Area: 1729 km² (668 sq mi). Population: 1,145,000 (1990 est). Capital: Zürich.

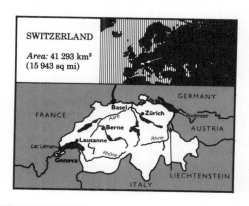

SWITZERLAND

Area: 41 293 km² (15 943 sq mi)

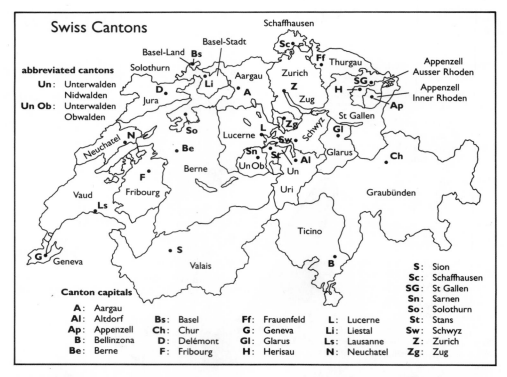

Swiss Cantons

abbreviated cantons

Un: Unterwalden
Nidwalden
Un Ob: Unterwalden
Obwalden

Canton capitals

A:	Aargau					S:	Sion
Al:	Altdorf	Bs:	Basel	Ff:	Frauenfeld	Sc:	Schaffhausen
Ap:	Appenzell	Ch:	Chur	G:	Geneva	SG:	St Gallen
B:	Bellinzona	D:	Delémont	Gl:	Glarus	Sn:	Sarnen
Be:	Berne	F:	Fribourg	H:	Herisau	So:	Solothurn

L:	Lucerne
Li:	Liestal
Ls:	Lausanne
N:	Neuchatel

St:	Stans
Sw:	Schwyz
Z:	Zurich
Zg:	Zug

GEOGRAPHY

The parallel ridges of the Jura Mountains lie in the northwest on the French border. The south of the country is occupied by the Alps. Between the two mountain ranges is a central plateau that contains the greater part of Switzerland's population, agriculture and industry. Highest point: Dufourspitze (Monte Rosa) 4634 m (15,203 ft). Principal rivers: Rhine (Rhein), Rhône, Aare, Inn, Ticino. Climate: Altitude and aspect modify Switzerland's temperate climate. Considerable differences in temperature and rainfall are experienced over relatively short distances.

ECONOMY

Switzerland's neutrality has allowed it to build a reputation as a secure financial centre. Zürich is one of the world's leading banking and commercial cities. The country enjoys one of the world's highest standards of living. Industry - in part based upon cheap hydroelectric power - includes engineering (from turbines to watches), textiles, food processing (including cheese and chocolate), pharmaceuticals and chemicals. Dairying is important in the agricultural sector, and there is a significant timber industry. Tourism and the international organizations based in Switzerland are major foreign-currency earners. Foreign workers - in particular Italians - help alleviate the country's labour shortage.

Currency: Swiss Franc of 100 centimes; 1US$ = 1.35 Swiss Francs (June 1994).

GDP: US$236,000,000,000 (1993 est); US$34,610 per head.

RECENT HISTORY

Neutrality enabled Switzerland to escape involvement in the two World Wars and made it the ideal base for the Red Cross (1863), the League of Nations (1920), etc. Switzerland avoids membership of any body it considers might compromise its neutrality - a referendum in 1992 confirmed that Switzerland should not join the EEA.

United Kingdom

Official name: The United Kingdom of Great Britain and Northern Ireland.

Member of: UN, EC/EU, NATO, Commonwealth, G7, OECD, CSCE, Council of Europe.

Area: 244,103 km² (94,249 sq mi).

Population: 58,080,000 (1993 est).

Capital: London (see below).

Languages: English (over 98% as a first language), various languages of the Indian subcontinent (under 2% as a first language), Welsh (0.05%), Gaelic (0.014%).

Religions: Anglican (55% nominal, 4% practising), Roman Catholic (9%), Presbyterian (3%, including Church of Scotland), Methodist (2%), other Christian Churches (4%), Islam (2%), non-religious (24%).

Education: Education is compulsory between the ages of five and 16. In 1992 the literacy rate was virtually 100%. There are 93 universities, including the autonomous university colleges of the University of Wales and the Open University.

Defence: In 1993 the total armed strength was 293,500 - 145,300 in the army, 62,200 in the navy, 86,000 in the air force. Over 53,000 British troops are based in northern Germany; other British forces are based in Belize, Brunei, Cyprus, the Falkland Islands, and Hong Kong. The main naval bases are Portsmouth and Devonport.

Transport: There are 358,034 km (222,472 mi) of roads of which over 3150 km (1958 mi) are motorways. There are 37,849 km (23,518 mi) of railways, which are scheduled to be privatized. London, Glasgow, Newcastle, Sheffield and Mnachester have metros and/or rapid light transit systems. The main commercial ports are Immingham-Grimsby, London, Milford Haven, Tees-Hartlepool, Southampton and Grangemouth-Leith. London Heathrow and London Gatwick are, respectively, the largest and fifth largest airports in Europe. Other international airports include Belfast, Birmingham, Bristol, Cardiff, Edinburgh, Glasgow, Leeds/Bradford, Liverpool, London City, London Stansted, Luton, Norwich, and Manchester.

Media: There are 12 national British daily newspapers and 88 other daily regional newspapers, including national Scottish and Northern Irish titles. The BBC runs five national and over 50 local and regional radio services, and two television channels. There are three national, and over 80 local and community independent radio stations. There are two national commercial television channels with programmes supplied by regional and other contractors.

ENGLAND

Area: 130,441 km² (50,363 sq mi).

Population: 47,378,300 (1992 est).

Capital: London 7,926,000 (London Urban Area - Greater London 6,803,100).

Other major cities: Birmingham 2,360,000 (West Midlands Urban Area; city 1,009,000; Dudley 305,000; Walsall 263,000; Wolverhampton 248,000; Solihull 201,000; West Bromwich 153,000), Manchester 2,337,000 (Greater Manchester Urban Area; city 435,000; Stockport 289,000; Bolton 264,000; Salford 230,000; Oldham 220,000; Rochdale 206,000), Leeds-Bradford 1,581,000 (West Yorkshire Urban Area; Leeds city 722,000, Bradford city 478,000; Huddersfield 147,000), Newcastle-upon-Tyne 797,000 (Tyneside Urban Area; city 282,000; Gateshead 203,000), Liverpool 690,000 (Urban Area; city 479,000), Sheffield 673,000 (Urban Area; city 531,000; Rotherham 122,000), Nottingham 631,000 (Urban Area; city 283,000), Bristol 568,000 (Urban Area; city 397,000), Brighton 495,000 (Brighton-Worthing Urban Area; Brighton town 155,000; Worthing 97,000), Portsmouth 476,000 (Urban Area; city 190,000; Havant 119,000; Fareham 100,000), Leicester 423,000 (Urban Area; city 285,000), Stoke-on-Trent 389,000 (The Potteries Urban Area; city 253,000; Newcastle-under-Lyme 123,000), Middlesbrough 380,000 (Teesside Urban Area; town 146,000; Stockton-on-Tees 177,000), Bournemouth 376,000 (Urban Area; town 159,000; Poole 136,000), Coventry 348,000 (Coventry-Bedworth Urban Area; city 305,000), Hull 331,000 (Kingston-upon-Hull Urban Area; city 269,000), Southampton 322,000 (Southampton-Eastleigh Urban Area; Southampton city 208,000), Preston 320,000 (Urban Area; town 131,000), Southend 299,000 (Urban Area; town 165,000), Blackpool 293,000 (Urban Area; town 152,000), Birkenhead

417

279,000 (Urban Area; town 93,000), Plymouth 258,000, Rochester 247,000 (Medway Towns Urban Area; city 148,000; Gillingham 96,000), Aldershot 244,000 (Urban Area; Aldershot with Farnborough 88,000), Luton 227,000 (Luton-Dunstable Urban Area; Luton town 176,000), Derby 227,000, Reading 220,000 (Urban Area; town 137,000), Sunderland 202,000 (Urban Area; the city has a population of 297,000 and covers a wider area than the Urban Area), Norwich 195,0000 (Urban Area; city 128,000),

England was divided for administrative purposes into 39 administrative counties, 36 metropolitan districts, 32 Greater London Boroughs, the City of London, and one 'most-purpose' authority (the Isles of Scilly). From 1995, most of the administrative counties will be replaced by unitary authorities; the metropolitan districts and Greater London Boroughs will remain. For geographical purposes, the 40 traditional counties of England will be reinstated.

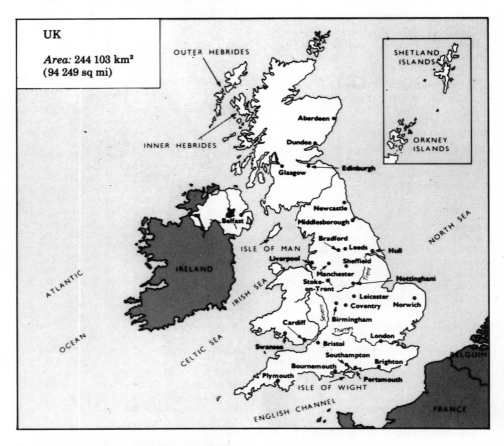

UK

Area: 244 103 km² (94 249 sq mi)

Northampton 186,000, Milton Keynes 181,000. (The population figures for the Urban Areas - the cities and their agglomerations; 1992 est.)

Counties: The local government system of England is currently under review. In 1994

NORTHERN IRELAND
Area: 14,120 km² (5452 sq mi).

Population: 1,610,000 (1992 est).

Capital: Belfast 437,000 (Urban Area; city

288,000; Newtownabbey 75,000; Castlereagh 62,000).

Other major towns and cities: Derry 96,000, Craigavon-Portadown-Lurgan 77,000 (Portadown 24,000, Lurgan 22,000), Bangor 35,000, Lisburn 28,000, Ballymena 20,000 (town 17,000). (The population figures for the Urban Areas - the cities and their agglomerations; 1992 est.)

Districts: For local goverment purposes Northern Ireland is divided into 26 districts, which, for education and some other services, are grouped into areas. See the map on page 421. For geographical purposes, the six traditional counties of Northern Ireland are used.

SCOTLAND
Area: 78,775 km² (30,415 sq mi).

Population: 5,111,000 (1992 est).

Capital: Edinburgh 527,000 (Urban Area; city 439,000).

Other major cities and towns: Glasgow 1,648,000 (Central Clydeside Urban Area; city 684,000; Motherwell 144,000; Paisley 84,000; Hamilton 52,000; Clydebank 46,000), Aberdeen 231,000 (Urban Area; city 217,000), Dundee 172,000, Greenock 91,000 (Urban Area; town 58,000), Falkirk 74,000 (Urban Area; 36,000), Ayr 62,000 (Urban Area; town 49,000), Dunfermline 58,000 (Urban Area; town 52,000), Irvine 56,000, Kilmarnock 55,000 (town 52,000), Cumbernauld 50,000. (The population figures for the Urban Areas - the cities and their agglomerations; 1992 est.)

Districts: Local government in Scotland is being restructured. The present arrangement of nine regional authorities, three all-purpose authorities and 53 district councils will be replaced by 32 all-purpose unitary authorities. See the map on page 421. For geographical purposes the 33 traditional Scottish counties are to be reinstated.

WALES
Area: 20,768 km² (8019 sq mi).

Population: 2,899,000 (1992 est).

Capital: Cardiff 326,000 (Urban Area; city 296,000).

Other major cities and towns: Swansea 289,0000 (Urban Area; city 188,00; Neath 48,000; Port Talbot 40,000), Newport 137,000,

Rhondda-Pontypool 128,000 (Urban Area; Rhondda 79,000; Pontypool 36,000); Wrexham 80,000 (Urban Area; town 40,000), Merthyr Tydfil 60,000, Aberdare 55,000 (Urban Area; town 32,000), Pontypool 50,000 (Urban Area; town 36,000), Bridgend 50,000 (Urban Area; town 31,000). (The population figures for the Urban Areas - the cities and their agglomerations; 1992 est.)

Counties: Local government in Wales is being restructured. The present arrangement of eight administrative counties and 37 district councils will be replaced by 21 all-purpose unitary authorities. See the map on page 421. For geographical purposes the 13 traditional Welsh counties are to be reinstated.

GOVERNMENT
The UK is a constitutional monarchy without a written constitution. The UK comprises four countries - England, Scotland, Wales and Northern Ireland; there is (suspended) constitutional provision for devolved government for the latter. The House of Lords - the Upper (non-elected) House of Parliament - comprises over 750 hereditary peers and peeresses, over 20 Lords of Appeal (non-hereditary peers), over 370 life peers, and 2 archbishops and 24 bishops of the Church of England. The House of Commons consists of 651 members elected for five years by universal adult suffrage. The sovereign appoints a Prime Minister who commands a majority in the Commons. The PM, in turn, appoints a Cabinet of Ministers. The main political parties include the Conservative Party (C), the Labour Party (Lab), the Liberal Democrats (L), and regional parties including the Scottish National Party (SNP), the (Welsh Nationalist) Plaid Cymru (PC), the Ulster Unionists (UU), the Democratic Unionist Party (DUP), and the (Northern Ireland) Social Democratic and Labour Party (SDLP). After the election held in April 1992 a Conservative government was formed.

Party strength: C 333, Lab 270, L 23, UU 9, PC 4, SDLP 4, SNP 3, DUP 3, others 2.

Queen: HM Queen Elizabeth II (succeeded upon the death of her father, 6 February 1952).

THE CABINET
Prime Minister: John Major.

Minister of Agriculture, Fisheries and Food: William Waldegrave.

Secretary of State for Defence: Malcolm Rifkind.

Secretary of State for Education and Science: Gillian Shephard.

Secretary of State for Employment: Michael Portillo.

Secretary of State for the Environment: John Selwyn Gummer.

Chancellor of the Exchequer: Kenneth Clarke.

Foreign Secretary: Douglas Hurd.

Secretary of State for Health: Virginia Bottomley.

Home Secretary: Michael Howard.

Leader of the House of Commons (and Lord President of the Council): Tony Newton.

Leader of the House of Lords (Lord Privy Seal): Viscount Cranborne.

Lord Chancellor: Lord Mackay of Clashfern.

Secretary of State for National Heritage: Stephen Dorrell.

Secretary of State for Northern Ireland: Sir Patrick Mayhew.

(Chancellor of the Duchy of Lancaster) and Minister of Public Service and Science: David Hunt.

Secretary of State for Scotland: Ian Lang.

Secretary of State for Social Security: Peter Lilley.

Secretary of State for Trade and Industry and President of the Board of Trade: Michael Heseltine.

Secretary of State for Transport: Dr Brian Mawhinney.

Chief Secretary to the Treasury: Jonathan Aitken.

Secretary of State for Wales: John Redwood.

Minister without Portfolio (and Chairman of the Conservative Party): Jeremy Hanley.

GEOGRAPHY

The UK comprises the island of Great Britain, the northeast part of Ireland plus over 4000 other islands. Lowland Britain occupies the south, east and centre of England. Clay valleys and river basins - including those of the Thames and the Trent - separate relatively low ridges of hills, including the limestone Cotswolds and Cleveland Hills, and the chalk North and South Downs and the Yorkshire and Lincolnshire Wolds. In the east, low-lying Fenland is largely reclaimed marshland. The flat landscape of East Anglia is covered by glacial soils. The northwest coastal plain of Lancashire and Cheshire is the only other major lowland in England. A peninsula in the southwest - Devon and Cornwall - contains granitic uplands, including Dartmoor and Exmoor. The limestone Pennines form a moorland backbone running through northern England. The Lake District (Cumbria) is an isolated mountainous dome rising to Scafell Pike, the highest point in England at 978 m (3210 ft). Wales is a highland block, formed by a series of plateaux above which rise the Brecon Beacons in the south, Cader Idris and the Berwyn range in the centre, and Snowdonia in the north, where Snowdon reaches 1085 m (3560 ft). In Scotland, the Highlands in the north and the Southern Uplands are separated by the rift valley of the Central Lowlands, where the majority of Scotland's population, agriculture and industry are to be found. The Highlands are divided by the Great Glen in which lies Loch Ness. Although Ben Nevis is the highest point, the most prominent range of the Highlands is the Cairngorm Mountains. The Southern Uplands lie below 853 m (2800 ft). Other Scottish lowlands include Buchan in the northeast, Caithness in the north, and a coastal plain around the Moray Firth. To the west of Scotland are the many islands of the Inner and Outer Hebrides, while to the north are the Orkney and Shetland Islands. Northern Ireland includes several hilly areas, including the Sperrin Mountains in the northwest, the uplands in County Antrim, and the Mourne Mountains rising to Slieve Donard at 852 m (2796 ft). Lough Neagh - at the centre of Northern Ireland - is the UK's largest lake. Highest point: Ben Nevis 1392 m (4406 ft) in Scotland. Principal rivers: Severn, Thames (with Churn), Trent-Humber, Aire (with Ouse), (Great or Bedford) Ouse, Wye, Tay (with Tummel), Nene, Clyde. The temperate climate of the UK is warmed by the North Atlantic Drift. There is considerable local variety, particularly in rainfall totals, which range from just over 500 mm (20 in) in the southeast to 5000 mm (200 in) in northwest Scotland.

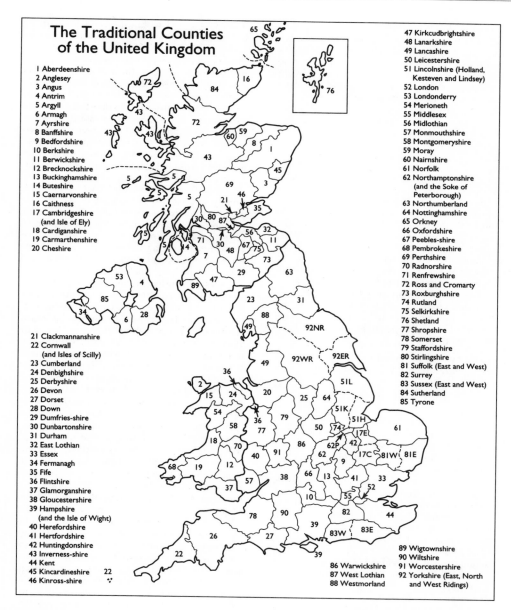

The Traditional Counties of the United Kingdom

1 Aberdeenshire
2 Anglesey
3 Angus
4 Antrim
5 Argyll
6 Armagh
7 Ayrshire
8 Banffshire
9 Bedfordshire
10 Berkshire
11 Berwickshire
12 Brecknockshire
13 Buckinghamshire
14 Buteshire
15 Caernarvonshire
16 Caithness
17 Cambridgeshire
   (and Isle of Ely)
18 Cardiganshire
19 Carmarthenshire
20 Cheshire

21 Clackmannanshire
22 Cornwall
   (and Isles of Scilly)
23 Cumberland
24 Denbighshire
25 Derbyshire
26 Devon
27 Dorset
28 Down
29 Dumfries-shire
30 Dunbartonshire
31 Durham
32 East Lothian
33 Essex
34 Fermanagh
35 Fife
36 Flintshire
37 Glamorganshire
38 Gloucestershire
39 Hampshire
   (and the Isle of Wight)
40 Herefordshire
41 Hertfordshire
42 Huntingdonshire
43 Inverness-shire
44 Kent
45 Kincardineshire
46 Kinross-shire

47 Kirkcudbrightshire
48 Lanarkshire
49 Lancashire
50 Leicestershire
51 Lincolnshire (Holland,
   Kesteven and Lindsey)
52 London
53 Londonderry
54 Merioneth
55 Middlesex
56 Midlothian
57 Monmouthshire
58 Montgomeryshire
59 Moray
60 Nairnshire
61 Norfolk
62 Northamptonshire
   (and the Soke of
   Peterborough)
63 Northumberland
64 Nottinghamshire
65 Orkney
66 Oxfordshire
67 Peebles-shire
68 Pembrokeshire
69 Perthshire
70 Radnorshire
71 Renfrewshire
72 Ross and Cromarty
73 Roxburghshire
74 Rutland
75 Selkirkshire
76 Shetland
77 Shropshire
78 Somerset
79 Staffordshire
80 Stirlingshire
81 Suffolk (East and West)
82 Surrey
83 Sussex (East and West)
84 Sutherland
85 Tyrone

86 Warwickshire
87 West Lothian
88 Westmorland

89 Wigtownshire
90 Wiltshire
91 Worcestershire
92 Yorkshire (East, North
   and West Ridings)

ECONOMY

Over one sixth of the British labour force is involved in manufacturing. The principal industries include iron and steel, motor vehicles, electronics and electrical engineering, textiles and clothing, aircraft, and consumer goods. British industry relies heavily upon imports of raw materials. The country is self-sufficient in petroleum (from the North Sea) and has important reserves of natural gas and coal - although the coal industry is declining as seams in traditional mining areas become uneconomic. As Britain is a major trading nation, London is one of the world's leading banking, financial and insurance centres, and the 'invisible earnings' from these services make an important contribution to exports. Tourism is another major foreign-currency earner and is now generally considered to be Britain's second biggest industry. Agriculture (with forestry) involves about 1% of the labour force and is principally concerned with raising sheep and cattle. Arable farming is widespread in the east, where the main crops are barley, wheat, potatoes and sugar beet. In the 1970s and 1980s the UK did not experience the same rate of economic growth as most other West European states. Economic problems have included repeated crises of confidence in the value of the pound, credit squeezes and high (regional) rates of unemployment. However, in 1993-94 the UK experienced a very tentative economic recovery while most of the rest of Western Europe remained in recession. Since 1980 most major nationalized industries have been privatized.

Currency: Pound sterling (£) of 100 pence (sing. penny); 1US$ = £0.642 (June 1994).

GDP: US$947,000,000,000 (1993 est); US$16,300 per head.

RECENT HISTORY
By the end of the 19th century the economic dominance Britain had enjoyed since the industrial revolution was beginning to be challenged by the USA and, more particularly, by Germany. Rivalry with Imperial Germany was but one factor contributing to the causes of World War I. PM Herbert Asquith (1852-1928) led a reforming Liberal Government from 1908 to 1916 but - after criticism of his conduct of the war - he was replaced by David Lloyd George (1863-1945), who as Chancellor of the Exchequer had introduced health and unemployment insurance. The 'old dominions' - Canada, Australia, New Zealand and South Africa - emerged from the war as autonomous countries, and their independent status was confirmed by the Statute of Westminster (1931). The Easter Rising in Ireland (1916) led to the partition of the island in 1922. Only Northern Ireland - the area with a Protestant

majority - stayed within the United Kingdom, but since the 1970s bitter conflict has resurfaced in the province as Roman Catholic republicans - seeking unity with the Republic of Ireland - clashed with Protestant Loyalists intent upon preserving the link with Britain. British troops were stationed in Northern Ireland to keep order and to defeat the terrorist violence of the IRA and (Protestant) Loyalist illegal organizations. In 1994 a peace initiative – the Downing Street Declaration (which was concluded with the government of the Irish Republic) – did not fulfil its initial expectations. In World War II Britain - led by PM Sir Winston Churchill (1874-1965), who had strenuously opposed appeasement in the 1930s - played a major role in the defeat of the Axis powers, and from 1940 to 1941 the UK stood alone against an apparently invincible Germany. Following the war, the Labour government of Clement Attlee (1883-1967) established the 'welfare state' and nationalized public utilities including water, gas, electricity and the railways. At the same time, the British Empire began its transformation into a Commonwealth of some 50 independent states, starting with the independence of India in 1947. By the late 1980s decolonization was practically complete and Britain was no longer a world power, although a British nuclear deterrent was retained. By the 1970s the United Kingdom was involved in restructuring its domestic economy and, consequently, its welfare state - from 1979 to 1990 under the Conservative premiership of Margaret Thatcher (1925-). During this period most of the public utilities were privatized. In 1982 Argentina invaded the Falkland Islands and its dependencies, which had long been claimed by the Argentines. A British task force recaptured the islands within three months. Under John Major (1943-) - Prime Minister since 1990 - the UK participated in the coalition against Iraq in the Second Gulf War (1991). The country has also joined (1973) and has attempted to come to terms with the European Community. Britain has resisted federalist measures, obtaining an opt-out from the moves to introduce a single European currency. Continued opposition to measures such as the Social Charter, and the use of the veto to block the appointment of a perceived federalist as President of the EC Commission (1994), have raised questions about the UK's commitment to Europe.

Vatican City

Official name: Stato della Cittá del Vaticano (State of the Vatican City). Also known as the Holy See.

Member of: CSCE, UN (observer).

Area: 0.44 km² (0.17 sq mi).

Population: 750 (1989 est).

Languages: Italian and Latin (both official).

Religion: The Vatican is the headquarters of the Roman Catholic Church.

Education: There are five pontifical universities and 11 pontifical colleges.

Defence: There is a 100-member papal defence force, the Swiss Guards.

Transport: The Vatican has its own (little-used) freight railway station. There is also a heliport. There are no figures for the length of roads within the small territories belonging to the Holy See.

Media: A daily newspaper is published in the Vatican, with weekly editions in English, French, German, Italian, Portuguese and Spanish, and monthly in Polish. Vatican Radio broadcasts daily in 35 languages; the Vatican Television Centre produces religious television programmes.

GOVERNMENT
The Pope is elected Bishop of Rome and head of the Roman Catholic Church for life by the Sacred College of Cardinals (who are appointed by the Pope). The Vatican City is administered by a Pontifical Commission appointed by the Pope.

Pope: HH (His Holiness) Pope John Paul II (born Karol Wojtlya), elected 16 October 1978.

GEOGRAPHY
The state comprises the Vatican City, a walled enclave in Rome, plus a number of Roman churches (including St John Lateran, St Mary Major, St Paul without the Walls), the papal villa at Castelgandolfo (beside Lake Albano to the south of Rome) and the Vatican Radio station at Santa Maria di Galeria (20 km/12 mi northwest of the Vatican). Climate: The Vatican has a Mediterranean climate with hot summers and mild winters. Most of the rainfall comes during the winter.

ECONOMY
The income of the Vatican is derived from interest on investments, from voluntary contributions (Peter's Pence), and from the Instituto per le Opere di Religione, popularly known as the Vatican Bank, which distributes funds for religious works. The inhabitants of the Vatican, over one third of whom have Vatican nationality, are mainly clerics. Many pilgrims and tourists visit St Peter's Basilica and the Vatican galleries and museums.

Currency: The Vatican Ciy uses Italian currency (see pp. 387-90).

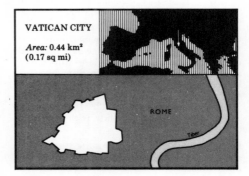

VATICAN CITY

Area: 0.44 km²
(0.17 sq mi)

ROME

Tiber

RECENT HISTORY
The Vatican City is all that remains of the once extensive Papal States, which, at the start of the 19th century, comprised Lazio, Umbria, Marche and much of Emilia Romagna. In 1860 all of these territories except Lazio were annexed by the new kingdom of Italy. When the French troops protecting the Pope were withdrawn in 1870, Italian forces entered Rome, which became the capital of Italy. Pope Pius IX (reigned 1846-78) retreated into the Vatican, from which no Pope emerged until 1929, when the Lateran Treaties provided for Italian recognition of the Vatican City as an independent neutral state. Since the 1960s the Papacy has again played an important role in international diplomacy, particularly under Popes Paul VI (reigned 1963-78) and John Paul II (1978-), whose encouragement of democratic movements in Eastern Europe, particularly in his native Poland, played a part in the fall of Communism in that region.

Other territories

FAEROE ISLANDS

Status: an internally self-governing part of the Kingdom of Denmark.

Area: 1399 km² (540 sq mi).

Population: 48,400 (1991 est).

Capital: Tórshavn 16,200 (1990 est).

Government: Denmark is represented by a High Commissioner. The 32-member Parliament (Logting) is elected for four years by universal adult suffrage. A Cabinet - comprising a Prime Minister and six Ministers - is responsible to the Logting. The Faeroes also elect two members to the Danish Parliament in Copenhagen. Prime Minister: Jogvan Sundstein.

Geography: Lying between Scotland and Iceland, the Faeroes comprise 17 inhabited islands, one uninhabited island and many rocky islets, all with high cliffs. Streymoy, the largest island, contains Tórshavn and nearly 40% of the population. Highest point: Slaettaratindur cliffs 882 m (2894 ft). Climate: The climate is wet and windy with cold winters and cool summers.

Economy: Farming is dominated by sheep rearing. Fishing, the main industry, has contracted recently owing to declining stocks. The Faeroese economy relies heavily upon considerable subsidies from Denmark. The islands - although part of Denmark for most purposes - are not part of the EU/EC.

Recent History: The Faeroes were not finally separated from Danish-ruled Norway administratively until 1709 when they became a Danish royal trade monopoly. Represented in the Danish parliament since 1851, the Faeroes have had their own local assembly since 1852 and have enjoyed internal self-government since 1948.

GIBRALTAR

Status: a British Crown colony.

Area: 2.5 km² (6.5 sq mi).

Population: 31,300 (1991 est).

Capital: Gibraltar 31,300 (1991 est).

Government: The British sovereign is represented by a Governor who is the executive authority. The Governor is advised by the Gibraltar Council which is composed of four ex-officio members and five members elected by the House of Assembly. The House comprises the Speaker (who is appointed by the Governor), two ex-officio members and 15 members who are elected by universal adult suffrage for four years. Under the terms of the constitution, no party may win more than eight seats. The Gibraltarian political parties are the Gibraltar Socialist Labour Party (GSLP), the Gibraltar Social Democrats (GSD) and the Gibraltar National Party (GNP). At the general election held in January 1992 the GSLP gained eight seats and the GND gained seven seats. A GSLP government was formed. Chief Minister: Joe Bossano.

Geography: Gibraltar is a small rocky peninsula connected to the south coast of Spain by a narrow isthmus. It commands the north side of the Atlantic entrance to the Mediterranean sea. Highest point: The Rock 428 m (1396 ft). Climate: Gibraltar has a Mediterranean climate.

Economy: Gibraltar depends on tourism, ship repairing, banking and finance - the Rock has become an 'offshore' banking centre - and the re-export trade (for example, fuel for visiting ships). Owing to lack of space there is no agriculture.

Recent History: The strategic importance of Gibraltar - a British colony since 1713 - has greatly diminished with the decline of the British Empire since World War II. Spain continues to claim the Rock and blockaded Gibraltar from 1969 to 1982-84. Gibraltar has enjoyed self-government since 1964 and became part of the EC when the UK joined that organization in 1973.

GUERNSEY AND DEPENDENCIES

Status: internally self-governing state associated with, but not part of, the UK.

Area: 78.5 km² (30 sq mi) - Guernsey 65 km² (25 sq mi), Alderney 8 km² (3 sq mi), Sark 5.5 km² (2 sq mi).

Population: 61,600 (1991) - Guernsey 58,900 (1991 census), Alderney 2100 (1991 est), Sark 550 (1991 est).

Capital: St Peter Port 19,000 (1986 est) on Guernsey. The capital of Alderney is St Anne's (1800 1986 est); Sark has no capital as settlement is scattered on the island.

Government: The British sovereign is represented by a Lieutenant-Governor. The 60-member States of Deliberation comprises the appointed Bailiff (who is President of the States), 33 People's Deputies (elected by universal adult suffrage), 10 Douzaine Representatives (indirectly elected from parish councils), 12 Conseillers (elected by the States of Election, an electoral college), two ex-officio members and two representatives of Alderney. Bailiff of Guernsey: Graham Dorey. Alderney's 13-member States comprises a President and 12 members elected by universal adult suffrage for three years. President of Alderney: J. Kay-Mouat. The Seigneur of Sark, the hereditary civic head of the island, appoints a Seneschal to preside over the Chief Pleas, which comprises 40 tenants and 12 directly elected members. Seigneur of Sark: Michael Beaumont.

Geography: Guernsey, a plateau surrounded by coastal cliffs, is 48 km (30 mi) west of Normandy. Its smaller dependencies of Alderney and Sark lie respectively to the north and east. Highest point: an unnamed point 90 m (295 ft). Climate: Guernsey has a mild temperate climate.

Economy: The economy is dominated by tourism. Tomatoes and flowers are the principal exports. Guernsey has become an 'offshore' banking centre although it does not yet rival Jersey in this respect.

Recent History: Guernsey, along with the other Channel Islands, is the only remaining part of the Duchy of Normandy attached to the British Crown. The islands were occupied by Germany from 1940-45.

ISLE OF MAN
Status: internally self-governing state associated with, but not part of, the UK.

Area: 572 km² (221 sq mi).

Population: 69,800 (1991 census).

Capital: Douglas 30,700 (town 22,200; Onchan 8500; 1991 census).

Government: The British sovereign - as Lord of Mann - is represented by a Lieutenant-Governor. The parliament, the Tynwald, comprises two houses: the Legislative Council (the upper house) and the House of Keys (the lower house). The Council comprises a President, two ex-officio members (including the Bishop of Sodor and Man), and eight members elected by the House of Keys. The 24-member House is elected by universal adult suffrage for five years. A Council of Ministers, headed by a Chief Minister, is responsible to the House. Chief Minister: Miles Walker.

Geography: The island, which has a rocky indented coast, lies in the Irish Sea between the northwest coast of England and Northern Ireland. Highest point: Snaefell 620 m (2034 ft). Climate: Man has a temperate climate with moderate rainfall.

Economy: The economy largely depends upon tourism, although 'offshore banking' and other financial interests are growing in importance.

Recent History: The Isle of Man was held by a succession of English and Scottish overlords before being sold to the British Crown in 1765. The island became a Crown Dependency but not a part of the United Kingdom. In recent years Man has exercised increasing independence from the United Kingdom.

JERSEY
Status: internally self-governing state associated with, but not part of, the UK.

Area: 116.2 km² (44.8 sq mi).

Population: 84,000 (1991 census).

Capital: St Helier 32,000 (1991 census).

Government: The British sovereign is represented by a Lieutenant-Governor. The Assembly of the States comprises the appointed Bailiff (who is President of the States), 12 Senators elected by universal adult suffrage for six years, 12 Constables elected for three years and 29 Deputies elected for three years, plus three non-voting ex-officio members. Bailiff: Sir Peter Crill.

Geography: The island of Jersey - which is 19 km (12 mi) west of the Cotentin peninsula - is surrounded by cliffs and deeply incised by valleys. Highest point: an unnamed cliff 148 m (485 ft). Climate: Jersey has a pleasant temperate climate with few frosts.

Economy: The economy of Jersey is based upon tourism, farming (which concentrates upon dairying and the breeding of Jersey cattle for export, early potatoes and tomatoes) and, increasingly, upon 'offshore banking'.

Recent History: Jersey, along with the other Channel Islands, is the only remaining part of the Duchy of Normandy attached to the British Crown. The island was occupied by Germany from 1940 to 1945.

WORLD POLITICAL FIGURES

Biographies of heads of state, heads of government and other major political figures.

Abacha, Sanni, Nigerian military leader and politician. Head of State (1994–). He overthrew the military dictator General Babangida, under whom he had served previously.

Abiola, Moshood, Nigerian politician. He is thought to have won the 1993 presidential elections, the results of which were cancelled by General Babangida. In 1994 he declared himself president but was imprisoned.

Advani, Lal Krishna (1927–), Indian politician. Minister of Information and Broadcasting (1977–79), President of the Bharatiya Janata Party (1986–).

Afwerki, Issaias, Eritrean politician. Leader of the Eritrean People's Liberation Front, President of independent Eritrea (1993–).

Ahtisaari, Martti (1937–). Finnish politician and diplomat. Minister for Foreign Affairs (1984–86), Undersecretary-General of the UN (1987–91), Secretary of State for Foreign Affairs (1991–94), President of Finland (1994–).

Ahu, Esko (1954–), Finnish politician. Leader of the Centre Party (Kesk; 1990–). PM (1991–).

Aidid, Farah Muhammad, Somalian general and politician. Head of government (1992–) and leader of one of the major factional groups involved in the Somalian civil war.

Akayev, Askar (1944–), Kyrgyz politician. President (1990–).

Akihito (1933–), Emperor of Japan (1990–). He succeeded on the death of his father, Hirohito.

Albert II (1934–), King of the Belgians (1993–). He succeeded his brother Baudouin I.

Alfonsin (Foulkes), Raul (1927–), Argentinian politician of the Radical Union Party (UCR). He became President of Argentina (1983–89) after the end of the military dictatorship. His economic policies, although initially successful, failed to bring prosperity to Argentina and he was replaced by Carlos Menem.

Aliyev, Geidar, Azeri (former Communist) politician. President of Azerbaijan (1993–).

Arafat, Yasser (1929–), Egyptian-Palestinian politician. Chairman of the Palestine Liberation Organization (PLO; 1969–). Despite challenges to his authority from radical Palestinian factions in the late 1980s and early 1990s, he was a signatory to the Israeli-Palestinian Peace Accord (1993) and has chaired the Palestine Authority in Gaza-Jericho since 1994..

Aristide, Jean-Bertrand (1953–), Haitian priest and politician. President of Haiti (1990–91). A left-wing Catholic priest, he represented a loose coalition of peasants, trade unionists and clerics while in office. He was overthrown by a military coup in 1991.

Ashdown, Paddy (Jeremy) (1941–), British Liberal Democrat politician. Leader of the Liberal Democrat Party (1988–).

Assad, Hafez al- (1928–), Syrian air force officer and politician. Leader of the Baath Party. PM (1970–71), President of Syria (1971–). His 23 years of rule have been repressive. In the early 1990s he attempted to improve relations with the West, aligning Syria with the US-dominated coalition during the Gulf War (1991).

Aung San Suu Kyi (1945–), Burmese politician. With the National League for Democracy she won the 1990 elections but was kept under house arrest and prevented from taking office. She received the Nobel Peace Prize in 1991 for her stand against the military regime.

Aylwin, Patricio (1915–), Chilean Christian Democrat politician. President of Chile (1990–94). His election ended the military rule of General Pinochet.

Aznar, Jose Maria (1953–), Spanish politician. Leader of the (conservative) Popular Party.

Balaguer, Joaquin (1907–), Dominican Republic politician of the Partido Reformista. Minister of Foreign Affairs (1954–55), of Education and Arts (1955–57), Vice-President (1957–60), President (1960, 1966–78, 1986–).

Balladur, Edouard (1929–), French Gaullist politician. Minister of the Economy, of Finance and Privatization (1986–88). PM (1993–).

Banda, Hastings (c. 1902–), Malawian politician of the Malawi Congress Party (MCP), PM (1963–66), President (1966–94). Banda's long authoritarian rule ended after defeat in the 1994 multiparty elections.

Bandaranaike, Sirimavo (1916–), Sri Lankan politician. President of Sri Lanka Freedom Party (1960–), PM, Minister of Defence and External Affairs (1960–65), PM, Minister of Defence and Foreign Affairs, Planning, Economic Affairs and Plan Implementation (1970–77). The widow of former prime minister, S.W.R.D. Bandaranaike, she became the world's first woman PM.

Bashir, Omar Hassan Ahmed al- , Sudanese army officer. PM, Minister of Defence, Culture and Information (1989–). He came to power following a military coup in 1989.

Beatrix (1938–), Queen of the Netherlands (1980–). She succeeded on the abdication of her mother Juliana.

Ben Ali, Zine el-Abidine (1936–), Tunisian politician of the Democratic Constitutional Rally (RCD). President of Tunisia (1987–). He came to power after forcing his predecessor, Habib Bourghiba, to resign.

Bentsen, Lloyd (1921–), US Democrat politician. US Senator from Texas (1971–92) and Secretary of the Treasury (1993–).

Berisha, Sali (1945–), Albanian politician from the Albanian Democratic Party. President

(1992–). He became the first non-Communist president of Albania since World War II when he succeeded President Ramiz Alia.

Berlusconi, Silvio (1936–), Italian businessman and politician. Leader and founder of the Forza Italia Party (1994–). PM (1994–).

Berov, Lyuben (1925–), Bulgarian politician of the Movement for Rights and Freedom (MRF; Turkish). PM (1993–).

Bhumipol (1927–), King of Thailand (1946–). He succeeded his brother Ananda.

Bhutto, Benazir (1953–), Pakistani politician. Leader in exile of the Pakistan People's Party (PPP; 1984–86), leader of the PPP in Pakistan (1986–). PM (1988–90 and 1993-).

Bildt, Carl (1949–), Swedish politician. Leader of the Moderate Party (MS; 1986–), PM (1991–).

Birendra (1945–), King of Nepal (1972–). He succeeded his father Mahendra.

Birkavs, Valdis (1942–), Latvian politician. PM (1993–).

Biya, Paul (1933–), Cameroon politician. Minister of State, Secretary-General to President (1968–75), PM (1975–82), President (1982–).

Blair, Tony (Anthony) (1953–), British Labour politician. Member of the Shadow Cabinet (1984–), leader of the Labour Party (1994–).

Bolger, Jim (1935–), New Zealand politician. Minister of Fisheries and Associated Minister of Agriculture (1977), Minister of Labour (1978–84), Minister of Immigration (1978–81), leader of the National Party (1985–90), PM (1990–).

Bongo, (Albert-Bernard) Omar (1935–), Gabonese politician of the Gabonese Democratic Party (PDG). Vice-President (1966–67), President (1967–), and minister of many other portfolios.

Boross, Peter (1928–), Hungarian Independent politician. Minister of State for the Office of Information and the Office of National Security (1990), Minister of Home Affairs (1990–94), PM (1994).

Borowski, Marek (1946–), Polish politician of the Democratic Left Alliance. Deputy PM and Finance Minister (1993–94).

Bossi, Umberto (1941–), Italian politician. Leader of the Northern League (1987–).

Bouchard, Lucien (1938–), Canadian politician. Minister of the Environment (1988–90). Originally a Conservative, he left the Party in 1990 and established the Bloc Québecois.

Bourassa, Robert (1933–), Canadian politician. Leader of Liberal Party of Quebec (1970–77 and 1983–), PM of Quebec (1970–76 and 1985–).

Boutros Ghali, Boutros (1922–), Egyptian politician and international civil servant. Minister of State for Foreign Affairs (1977–91).

Secretary-General of the United Nations (1992–).

Brazauskas, Mykolas Algirdas (1932–), Lithuanian politician. Leader of the Lithuanian Communist Party (1988–90), leader of the Democratic Labour Party (1990–), deputy PM (1990–91), President of Lithuania (1993–).

Brinkman, Elco (1948–), Dutch politician. Minister for Welfare, Health and Cultural Affairs (1982–89), leader of the Christian Democrat Appeal Party (CDA; 1994–).

Brown, Gordon (1951–), British Labour politician. Member of the Shadow Cabinet (1987–).

Brundtland, Gro Harlem (1939–), Norwegian politician. Environment Minister (1974–79), leader of the Labour Party (1981–) and PM (1981, 1986-89 and 1990–).

Bruton, John (1947–), Irish politician of the Fine Gael Party. Minister of Finance (1981–82), of Industry, Trade, Commerce and Tourism (1982–86), of Finance (1986–87), leader of Fine Gael (1990–).

Busek, Erhard (1941–), Austrian politician for the Austrian People's Party (ÖVP; 1975–78), Deputy Chancellor (1983–).

Bush, George (1924–), US Republican politician. Vice-President (under Ronald Reagan) (1981–89) and 41st President of the USA (1989–93). The Allied victory in the Gulf War won him many plaudits, but he came under increasing criticism for paying insufficient attention to domestic issues. He was defeated by Bill Clinton in the presidential elections of 1992.

Buthelezi, Mangosuthu Gatsha (1928–), South African Zulu politician. PM of the 'non-independent' Zulu homeland of KwaZulu (1972–94), leader of the Inkatha cultural movement for Zulu revival (1989–), Minister of the Interior (1994–). Despite the factional fighting between Inkatha and ANC supporters, Chief Buthelezi participated in the 1994 elections and joined Nelson Mandela's cabinet.

Caldera, Rafael (1916–), Venezuelan politician of the Social Christian Party (COPEI). President of Venezuela (1969–74 and 1994–).

Campbell, Kim (1947–), Canadian Conservative politician. Justice Minister (1990–93), Minister of Defence (1993), leader of the Progressive Conservative Party (1993) and PM (1993). She succeeded Brian Mulroney as leader of the Conservative Party and as PM until the Party's annihilation at the 1993 elections.

Cardenas, Cuauhtemoc (1935–), Mexican politician. Founder of the Democratic Revolutionary Party (PRD) in 1988.

Carl XVI Gustaf (1946–), King of Sweden (1973–). He succeeded on the death of his grandfather Gustaf VI Adolf.

Carlsson, Ingvar (1934–), Swedish politician.

Minister of Education (1969–73), of Housing and Physical Planning (1973–79), Deputy PM (1982–86), leader of the Social Democratic Labour Party (SDAP; 1986–), Minister of the Environment (1985–86), PM (1986–91).

Castro (Ruz), Fidel (1927–), Cuban Communist politician. PM (1959–76), President (1976–). He led the revolutionary forces that ousted Fulgencio Batista and declared the Cuban revolution. Opposed by the USA, he increasingly established diplomatic, economic and military links with the USSR. His defeat of the abortive Bay of Pigs invasion (1961), and survival of the Cuban Missile Crisis (1962), increased his popularity. However, the collapse of the Soviet Union has left his Communist regime isolated.

Cavaco Silva, Anibal (1939–), Portuguese politician. Minister of Finance and Planning (1980–81), leader of Social Democrat Party (PSD), PM (1985–).

Cedras, Raul, Haitian army officer and politician. Effective ruler (1991–). He came to power following a military coup that ousted the cleric Jean-Bertrand Aristide.

Chamorro, Violeta Barrios de (c. 1939–), Nicaraguan politician of the National Opposition Union. President of Nicaragua (1990–). She beat Daniel Ortega in the presidential elections, ending Sandanista rule.

Chernomyrdin, Viktor (1938–), Russian politician. PM (1991–).

Chiluba, Frederick (1943–), Zambian politician of the Movement for Multiparty Democracy (MMD). President of Zambia (1991–). He defeated the long-standing president, Kenneth Kaunda, in the first free elections since 1973.

Chirac, Jacques (1932–), French Gaullist politician. Secretary of State for Employment Problems (1967–68), Secretary of State for Economy and Finance (1968–71), Minister for Parliamentary Relations (1971–72), for Agriculture and Rural Development (1972–74), of the Interior (1974), PM (1974–76 and 1986–88).

Chissano, Joaquim Alberto (1939–), Mozambique politician of FRELIMO. PM (1974–75), Minister of Foreign Affairs (1975–86), President of Mozambique (1986–).

Chretien, Jean (1934–), Canadian politician. Secretary of State for External Affairs, deputy PM (1984), leader of the National Liberal Party (1990–), PM (1993–).

Christopher, Warren (1925–), US diplomat and Democrat politician. Deputy Secretary of State (under Jimmy Carter) (1977–81) and Secretary of State (1993–).

Ciller, Tansu (1946–), Turkish politician. Leader of the True Path Party (DYP) and PM

(1993–).

Claes, Willy (1938–), Belgian Socialist politician. Minister of Education (Flemish) (1972–73), of Economic Affairs (1973–74 and 1977–81), Deputy PM (1979–81 and 1988–), Minister of Economic Affairs, Planning and Education (Flemish) (1988–92), Foreign Minister (1992–).

Clark, Helen (1950–), New Zealand politician of the Labour Party. Minister of Housing and Minister of Conservation (1987–89), of Health (1989–90), of Labour (1989–90), deputy PM (1989–90), leader of the Labour Party (1994–).

Clarke, Kenneth (1940–), British Conservative politician. Secretary of State for Health (1988–90), for Education and Science (1990–92), for the Home Office (1992–93) and Chancellor of the Exchequer (1993–).

Clerides, Glafcos (1920–), Greek Cypriot politician of the Democratic Rally. Minister of Justice (1959–60), Acting President (1974), President (1993–).

Clinton, Bill (William Jefferson) (1946–), US Democratic politician. Governor of Arkansas (1979–81 and 1983–93) and 42nd President of the USA (1993–). He won a liberal and progressive reputation as Governor of Arkansas and defeated George Bush to become the first Democrat in the White House for 13 years. His administration has attempted to push through legislation for health care and gun control.

Collor de Mello, Fernando (1949–), Brazilian politician. Governor of Alagoas (1986), Founder of National Reconstruction Party (1989), President of Brazil (1990–92). He resigned from office following corruption allegations and impeachment proceedings.

Compoaré, Blaise, politician and army officer of Burkina Faso. President of Burkina Faso (1987–). He came to power after overthrowing the former military leader, Captain Thomas Sankara.

Conte, Lansana Guinean politician. President of Guinea (1984–), PM, Minister of Defence, Security, Planning and Co-operation, and Information (1984–). He took office following a military coup.

Crvenkovski, Branko, Macedonian politician of the Social Democratic League (SDLM). PM (1991–).

D'Alema, Massimo, Italian politician. Leader of the Democratic Left (PDS; 1994–).

da Silva, Luis Inacio (Lula) (1946–), Brazilian trade unionist and politician. Leader of the Partido dos Trabalhadores (PT).

Dawkins, John (1947–), Australian politician for the Australian Labor Party. Minister for Trade and Youth Affairs (1984–87), for Employment, Education and Training (1987–91), Treasurer (1991–).

Dehaene, Jean-Luc (1940–), Belgian Christian Democrat politician. Minister of Social Affairs and Institutional Reforms (1981–88), Deputy PM and Minister of Communications and Institutional Reforms (1988–92), PM (1992–).

De Klerk, Frederik Willem (1936–), South African National Party politician. President of South Africa (1989–94), Second Deputy President (1994–). He negotiated peace with the ANC, released Nelson Mandela from prison, and initiated constitutional negotiations for a non-racial 'New South Africa'. He lost the presidency to Mandela in the 1994 elections.

Delors, Jacques (1925–), French Socialist politician and EC official. French Minister for the Economy and Finance (1981–83), for the Economy, Finance and Budget (1983–84), President of the European Commission since 1985 - his term of office ends on 1 January 1995.

Demirel, Suleyman (1924–), Turkish politician of the True Path Party (DYP). PM (1965–71, 1975–77, 1979–80 and 1991–93), President (1993–).

Deng Xiaoping (1904–), Chinese Communist politician. General Secretary of the Chinese Communist Party (1956–67). He was denounced during the Cultural Revolution (1967) and in 1976, but was rehabilitated both times. He remains effective leader of China although he holds no official post. Although he has encouraged modernization, and international trade and relations, he was responsible for the violent repression of the pro-democracy demonstration at Tiananmen Square in 1989.

Denktash, Rauf (1924–), Turkish Cypriot politician.

Diouf, Abdou (1935–), Senegalese politician of the Senagalese Progressive Union (UPS). Minister of Planning and Industry (1968–70), PM (1970–80), President of Senegal (1981–).

Dole, Robert (1923–), US Republican politician. Kansas senator (1968–). Effective leader of the opposition since the election of Bill Clinton.

dos Santos, Jose Eduardo (1942–), Angolan politician of the MPLA. Foreign Minister (1975), First Deputy PM, Minister of Planning and Head of National Planning (1978–79), President (1979–). He came to power on the death of his predecessor Agostinho Neto. In 1991 he helped negotiate a ceasefire between the MPLA and the South African-backed UNITA guerrillas.

Downer, Alexander (1952–), Australian politician. Leader of the Conservative Party (1994–).

Duran Ballen, Sixto (1922–), Ecuadorian politician of the United Republican Party. President (1992–).

Ecevit, Bulent (1925–), Turkish politician. Minister of Labour (1961–65), PM (1974, 1977 and 1978–79), leader of the Democratic Left Party (1989–).

Elchibey, Albulfaz (1938–), Azeri politician of the Popular Front Party. President of Azerbaijan (1992–93).

Elizabeth II (1926–), Queen of Great Britain and Northern Ireland (1952–). She succeeded her father, George VI.

Engholm, Björn (1939–), German politician. Minister for Education and Science (1981–82), State Premier of Schleswig-Holstein (1988–), Leader of the Social Democrat Party (SPD: 1990–93).

Fabius, Laurent (1946–), French Socialist politician. Minister-Delegate for the Budget (1981–83), Minister of Industry and Research (1983–84), PM (1984–86).

Fahd (1923–), King of Saudi Arabia (1982–). Minister of Education (1953), Minister of the Interior (1962–75), deputy PM (1975–82), PM (1982–). He succeeded to the throne on the death of his brother, Khaled.

Fenech Adami, Eddie (1934–), Maltese politician. Leader of the National Party (1977–), PM (1987–).

Fini, Gianfranco (1952–), Italian politician. Leader of the (neo-fascist) National Alliance (1991–).

Finnbogadottir, Vigdis (1930–), Icelandic politician. President of Iceland (1980–).

Five, Kaci Kullman (1951–), Norwegian politician. Minister of Trade and Shipping (1989–90). Leader of the Conservative Party.

Franco, Itamar (1931–), Brazilian independent politician. Senator (1976–92), President of Brazil (1992–). He took over as acting president after impeachment proceedings began against Fernando Collor de Mello and was formally elected in 1992.

Frei Ruiz-Tagle, Eduardo (1943–), Chilean Christian Democrat politician. President of Chile (1994–). He is the son of the former president, Eduardo Frei Montalva (1964–70).

Fujimori, Alberto (1938–), Peruvian politician and founder of the Change '90 Movement. President (1990–).

Gadaffi, Moamar al (1942–), Libyan politician. Leader of the Revolution and effective head of state of Libya (1971–). He led a military coup to overthrow King Idris I in 1969. Allegations of international terrorism have left him isolated and at odds with the USA.

Gaidar, Yegor, Russian politician. Deputy PM (1991–92), PM (1992), leader of the Democratic Choice of Russia party (1994–).

Gaviria, César, Colombian politician. Minister of Finance and Public Credit (1986), of the Interior (1988), President of Colombia (1990–94).

Gligorov, Kiro (1918–). Macedonian politician

of the Social Democratic League (SDLM). President of Macedonia (1991–).

Goh Chok Tong (1941–), Singaporean politician. Minister of State for Finance (1977–79), Minister for Trade and Industry (1979–81), for Health and Second Minister for Defence (1981–82), for Defence and Second Minister for Health (1982–84), PM (1990–).

Goncz, Arpad (1922–), Hungarian politician. Acting President of Hungary (1989), President of Hungary (1990–).

Gonzalez, Felipe (1942–), Spanish politician. Leader of the Spanish Socialist Party (PSOE; 1980–), PM (1982–). He took Spain into the EC and modernized the economy.

Gorbachov, Mikhail (1931–), Soviet statesman. General Secretary of the Communist Party (1985–91), President of the Soviet Union (1989–91). His liberal reforms of glasnost and later perestroika led to far-reaching changes in the economic and political life in the USSR. His liberal credentials, however, were undermined by his harsh suppppression of the nationalist movements in the Baltic republics, but he moved back towards the reformers during 1991. Gorbachov resigned in 1991 following the failure of a coup by Communist hardliners and international recognition of the independence of the former Soviet republics.

Gore, Al(bert) (1948–), US Democratic politician. Senator of Tennessee (1985–92) and Vice-President (1992–).

Gryb, Mechislav, Belarussian politician. Head of state of Belarus (1993-94).

Haider, Joerg (1950–), Austrian politician and leader of the Freedom Party.

Hans Adam II (1945–), Prince of Liechtenstein (1989–). He succeeded his father, Franz Joseph II.

Harald V (1937–), King of Norway (1990–). He succeeded his father, Olav V.

Hassan II (1929–), King of Morocco (1961–). Minister of Defence (1960–61), deputy PM (1960–61), PM (1961–63 and 1965–67), Minister of Defence (1972–73).

Hassanal Bolkiah (1946–), Sultan of Brunei (1967–), PM of Brunei (1984–), Minister of Finance and Home Affairs (1984–86), of Defence (1986–).

Hata, Tsutomu (1936–), Japanese politician. Deputy PM and Minister of Foreign Affairs (1993–94), PM (1994). A disaffected Liberal Democrat, he helped bring down the Miyazawa government, joined the coalition government under Hosakawa, and briefly became PM himself in 1994 with the Japanese Renewal Party (JRP).

Havel, Vaclav (1935–), Czech playwright, writer and politician. Founder and leader of Civic Forum (1989–), President of Czechoslovakia (1989–93), President of the Czech Republic (1993–). A human rights activist, he led peaceful demonstrations against the Communist regime in 1989, and after the fall of the Communist government became president of Czechoslovakia. He became president of the Czech Republic after its split from Slovakia in 1993.

Herzog, Roman (1934–), German Christian Democrat politician. President (1994–).

Horn, Gyula (1932–), Hungarian politician. (Communist) Minister of Foreign Affairs (1989–90), leader of the Hungarian Socialist Party (HSP; 1990–), PM (1994–).

Hosakawa, Morihiro (1938–), Japanese politician. Founder and leader of the Japan New Party (JNP; 1992–), PM (1993–94). A disaffected Liberal Democrat, he founded the new party and headed a coalition government.

Howe, Brian (1936–), Australian politician for the Australian Labor Party, Minister for Defence Support (1983–84), for Social Security (1984–90), for Community Services and Health (1990–), Deputy PM (1991–).

Hrawi, Elias (1930–), Lebanese politician. President of Lebanon (1989–).

Hurd, Douglas (1930–), British Conservative politician. Secretary of State for Northern Ireland (1984–85), for the Home Office (1985–89), for Foreign and Commonwealth Affairs (1989–).

Hussein (1935–), King of Jordan (1952–). He has pursued moderate, pragmatic policies in the face of politicial upheavals within and outside his country, maintaining friendly relations with Western powers and at the same time pacifying Arab nationalist opinion.

Iliescu, Ion (1930–), Romanian politician. President of the National Salvation Front (1989–90), President of Provisional Council for National Unity (1990), President of Romania (1990–).

Inonu, Erdal (1926–), Turkish politician and leader of the Social Democratic Populist Party (1989–). Deputy PM (1991–).

Izetbegovic, Alija (1925–), Bosnian politician of the Moslem Democratic Action. President of Bosnia-Herzegovina (1992–).

Jabir III (1928–), Amir of Kuwait. PM (1965–67), Crown Prince (1966–77), Amir (1978–). In 1986 he suspended the national assembly and resumed feudal rule. He fled to Saudi Arabia during the Iraqi invasion of Kuwait (1990–91).

Jagan, Cheddi (1918–), Guyanese politician of the Progressive People's Party (PPP). Minister of Agriculture, Lands and Mines and Leader of the House of Assembly (1953), Minister of Trade and Industry (1957–61), PM (1957–64), Minister of Development and Planning

431

(1961–64), Leader of the Opposition (1964–73), General Secretary of PPP (1970–), PM (1992–).

Jaruzelski, Wojciech (1923–), Polish soldier and politician. PM (1981–85), President (1989–90). Faced with economic problems and the increasing influence of solidarity, he imposed martial law (1981–82). The success of Solidarity in the 1989 elections forced him to speed up democratic reforms, and he resigned in 1990.

Jean I (1925–), Grand Duke of Luxembourg (1964–). He succeeded on the abdication of his mother, Charlotte.

Jiang Zemin (1926–), Chinese Communist politician. General Secretary of the Chinese Communist Party (CCP; 1987–93), President of China (1993–).

John Paul II (Karol Wojtyla; 1920–), Pope (1978–). He is the first non-Italian Pope since 1522.

Jonassaint, Emil (1912–), Haitian politician and judge. Provisional President and PM (1994–).

Juan Carlos I (1938–), King of Spain (1975–). Grandson of Alfonso XIII, he was named heir by General Franco upon the restoration of the Spanish monarchy. He has eased the transition to democracy through the establishment of a liberal constitution in 1978. Juan Carlos played an important role in putting down an attempted coup in 1981.

Juppé, Alain (1945–), French politician of the Rally for the Republic Party (RPR). Foreign Minister (1993–).

Kafi, Ali (1928-), Algerian politician. President of Algeria (1992-).

Karadzic, Radovan. Bosnian politician of the Serbian Democratic Party. President of the self-proclaimed Republika Srpska.

Karamanlis, Konstantinos (1907–), Greek politician. Minister of Labour (1940), of Transport (1947), of Social Welfare (1948–50), of National Defence (1950–52), of Public Works (1952–54), of Communications and Public Works (1954–55). Founder of the National Radical Union (1956), PM (1955–63), leader (and founder) of New Democracy Party (1974–80), PM (1974–80), President (1990–).

Karim-Lamrani, Mohammad (1919–), Moroccan politician. Minister of Finance (1971), PM (1971–72, 1983–84 and 1984–86 and 1992–).

Karimov, Islam (1938–), Uzbek politician. Head of the Communist Party in Uzbekistan (1990–), President of Uzbekistan (1991–).

Kaunda, Kenneth (1924–), Zambian politician. President of the United National Independence Party (UNIP; 1960–), Minister of Local Government and Social Welfare, N. Rhodesia (1962–64), PM of N. Rhodesia (1964),

President of Zambia (1964–91).

Keating, Paul (1944–), Australian politician. Treasurer and deputy leader of the Australian Labor Party (1983–91) and PM (1991–) after the resignation of Bob Hawke. He has led the campaign to make Australia a republic.

Khamenei, Ayatollah Ali (1940–), Iranian religious leader and politician. Wali Faqih (Religious Leader; 1989–). He succeeded the Ayatollah Khomeini.

Kim Jong Il (1942–), North Korean politician. The eldest son of Kim Il-Sun, he took over from his father as President of North Korea in 1994.

Kim Young Sam (1927–), South Korean politician. Founder and leader of the centrist Reunification Democratic Party (RDP; 1974–90). President of South Korea (1992–). In 1990 he merged the RDP with the ruling Democratic Justice Party and the New Democratic Republican Party to form the Democratic Liberal Party (DLP).

Kinkel, Klaus (1936–), German politician. Leader of the Free Democrats (1993–). Foreign Minister (1992–), Vice-Chancellor (1993–).

Klaus, Vaclav (1941–), Czech politician. Finance Minister (1989–92), deputy PM (1991–92), Chair of the Civic Democratic Party, PM (1992–).

Klestil, Thomas (1933–), Austrian diplomat. President of Austria (1992–).

Kohl, Helmut (1930–), German politician. Leader of the German Christian Democrat Party (CDU; 1973–), Leader of the Opposition in the Bundestag (1976–82), Chancellor of West Germany (1982–91), of a united Germany (1991–). Since reunification he has had to contend with problems arising from the integration of the former GDR (East Germany) into the West German market economy.

Koivisto, Mauno (1923–), Finnish politician. Minister of Finance (1966–67), PM (1968–70, 1979–82), Minister of Finance and deputy PM (1972), President (1982–94).

Kok, Wim (1938–), Dutch politician. Leader of the Labour Party (PvdA; 1986–), Deputy PM and Finance Minister (1989–).

Konan-Bedie, Henri (1934–), politician of Côte d'Ivoire. Minister of Finance (1966–77), President of Cote d'Ivoire (1993–). Leader of the Democratic Party (1994–).

Konari, Alpha Oumar (1946–), Mali politician and leader of the Alliance for Democracy in Mali (ADEMA). President (1992–).

Kono, Yohei (1937–), Japanese politician. Leader of the Liberal Democratic Party (1993–).

Kovac, Michal (1931–), Slovakian politician of the Movement for a Democratic Slovakia (HZDS). President of Slovakia (1993–).

Kozyrev, Andrei (1951–), Russian politician.

Minister of Foreign Affairs (1990–).

Kravchuk, Leonid (1934–), Ukrainian Communist politician. President of Ukraine (1990–94).

Kucan, Milan (1941–), Slovenian independent politician. President (1990–).

Kuchma, Leonid (1938–), Ukrainian politician. PM (1992), President (1994–).

Kuncze, Gabor (1950–), Hungarian politician. Parliamentary leader of the Alliance of Free Democrats (AFD; 1993–).

Laar, Mart (1960–), Estonian politician of the Isamaa coalition. PM (1992–).

Lacalle, Luis Alberto (1941–), Uruguayan politician of the Blanco Party. President of Uruguay (1990–).

Lafontaine, Oskar (1943–), German politician. State Premier of Saarland (1985–), deputy leader of the Social Democratic Party (SPD; 1987–90).

Landsbergis, Vytautas (1932–), Lithuanian music professor and politician of the Sajudis Movement. Leader of Lithuania's campaign for independence in the late 1980s. President of Lithuania (1990–92).

Le Duc Anh (1920–), Vietnamese Communist politician and general. President (1992–).

Le Pen, Jean-Marie (1928–), French right-wing politician. President of the National Front (1972–).

Lee Kuan Yew (1923–), Singaporean politician and founder of the People's Action Party (PAP). PM (1959–90). He has overseen a successful programme of economic development.

Lee Teng-hui (1923–), Taiwanese politician. Governor Taiwan Province (1981–84), Vice-President (1984–88), President (1988–).

Leghair, Farooq Ahmad Khan (1940–), Pakistani politician of the Pakistan People's Party (PPP). Minister of Water and Power (1989–90), Minister of Finance (1993), Minister for Foreign Affairs (1993), President (1993–).

Leon, Ramiro de (1942–), Guatemalan politician. President (1993–). A human-rights campaigner, he took over following a crisis over the presidential succession.

Letsie III (1963–), King of Lesotho (1990–). He succeeded upon the deposition of his father.

Li Peng (1928–), Chinese Communist politician. PM (1987–). He has maintained firm central and party control over the economy.

Lilic, Zoran (1953–), Yugoslavian politician of the Socialist Party of Serbia. President of Yugoslavia (1993–).

Lubbers, Ruud (Rudolphus) (1939–), Dutch politician. Parliamentary leader of the Christian Democrat Appeal Party (CDA; 1978–94), PM (1982–94).

Lubys, Bronislovas (1938–), Lithuanian independent politician. Deputy PM (1990–92), PM (1992–).

Lukashenko, Alexander (1955–), Belarussian populist politician. President (1994–).

Mahdi, Ali, Somalian politician. President (1991–93). Head of the major factional groups involved in the Somalian civil war.

Major, John (1943–), British Conservative politician. Chief Secretary to Treasury (1987–89), Secretary of State for Foreign and Commonweath Affairs (1989), Chancellor of Exchequer (1989–90). Leader of the Conservative Party and PM (1990–). He came to power following the resignation of Margaret Thatcher.

Mandela, Nelson (1918–), South African politician. President of the African National Congress (1991–). President of South Africa (1994–). An ANC activist from the 1940s, he became the symbolic leader of most Black South Africans during his imprisonment from 1962. He was freed by de Klerk in 1991 and headed ANC negotiations with the government before becoming President.

Manning, Patrick (1946–), Trinidadian politician. Minister of Information, and of Industry and Commerce (1981), of Energy (1981–86), leader of the People's National Movement Party (1987–), PM of Trinidad and Tobago (1991–).

Manning, Preston (1942–), Canadian politician. Founder and leader of the Reform Party (1987–).

Margrethe II (1940–), Queen of Denmark (1972–). She succeeded her father, Frederik IX.

Maroni, Roberto (1955–), Italian politician of the Northern League. Deputy PM and Interior Minister (1994–).

Martens, Wilfried (1936–), Belgian Social Christian (CVP) politician. PM (1979–92). He headed a series of coalition governments before being replaced as prime minister by Jean-Luc Dehaene.

Martino, Antonio (1943–), Italian politician of Forza Italia. Foreign Minister (1994–).

Masire, Quett (1925–), Botswanan politician for the Botswana Democratic Party (BDP). Deputy PM (1965–66), Vice-President and Minister of Finance (1966–80), Minister of Development Planning (1967–80), President (1980–).

Mazowiecki, Tadeusz (1927–), Polish politician and founder member of solidarity. PM (1989–90).

McKinnon, Donald (1939–), New Zealand politician of the National Party. Minister of External Relations and Trade, Minister of Foreign Affairs, Deputy PM (1990–).

McLaughlin, Audrey (1936–), Canadian politician. Leader of the New Democratic Party (NDP; 1989–).

Meciar, Vladimir (1931–), Slovakian politician of the Movement for a Democratic Slovakia (HZDS). PM (1992–94). He was influential in the campaign for Slovakian independence.

Meksi, Aleksandr (1939–), politician of the Albanian Democratic Party. PM (1992–).

Menem, Carlos (1935–), Argentinian politician. President of the Peronist (Justice) Party in La Rioja (1968–), Governor of La Rioja (1983–89) and President of Argentina (1989–). He has introduced widespread privatization and public spending cuts.

Meri, Lennart (1929–), Estonian politician of the nationalist Fatherland Party and member of the Isamaa coalition. Minister of Foreign Affairs (1991–92), President of Estonia (1992–).

Mifsud Bonnici, Hugo (1932–), Maltese politician of the National Party. Minister of Education (1987–94), President of Malta (1994–).

Milosevic, Slobodan (1941–), Nationalist socialist Serbian politician. President of Serbia (1988–). An advocate of a 'Greater Serbia', he encouraged ethnic Serbs in their wars of secession in the former Yugoslavian republics of Croatia and Bosnia-Herzegovina.

Mitterrand, François (1916–), French Socialist politician. Minister for Ex-Servicemen, Secretary of State to Presidency of the Council, Minister of State (1947–54), Minister of the Interior (1954–55), Minister for State for Justice (1956–57), First Secretary of the Socialist Party (1971–81), President of France (1981–). A strong advocate of the French nuclear bomb and European union, he weathered economic and political crises and profited from disunity on the right to secure a second term in 1988.

Miyazawa, Kiichi (1919–), Japanese politician of the Liberal Democrat Party (LDP). Minister of State, Director-General of Economic Planning Agency (1962–64, 1966–68, 1977–78), Minister of International Trade and Industry (1970–71), of Foreign Affairs (1974–76), of Finance (1986–88), deputy PM and Minister of Finance (1987–88), Minister of State, Chief Cabinet Secretary (1980–82), PM (1991–93).

Mobuto Sese Seko (1930–), Zairean politician. Secretary of State for National Defence (1960), President of Zaire (1965–), President of Cabinet (1966–), Minister of Foreign Affairs (1966–72). He seized power in a military coup at the end of the Congo Crisis, and maintained order by imposing harsh policies. Allegations of corruption, violent opposition and rebel activities have undermined his long rule, and law and order have broken down in much of the country.

Mohammad Mahathir (1925–), Malaysian politician. Minister of Education (1974–77), of Trade and Industry (1977–81), of Defence (1981–86), of Home Affairs (1986–87), Deputy PM (1976–81), PM (1981–).

Moi, Daniel arap (1924–), Kenyan politician and leader of KANU (Kenyan African National Union). Minister of Education (1961–62), of Local Government (1962–64), Home Affairs (1964–67), Vice-President of Kenya (1967–68), Minister of Home Affairs and President of Kenya (1978–). He has continued the pro-capitalist policies of his predecessor, Jomo Kenyatta, but imposed restrictions on political activities after an attempted coup in 1990. In multiparty elections in 1993 he was returned to power.

Moravcik, Jozef (1945–), Slovakian politician. Foreign Minister (1993–94), PM (1994–). Originally a member of the Movement for a Democratic Slovakia (HZDS), he resigned from the Foreign Affairs Ministry in 1994 and founded the Democratic Union.

Mswati III (1968–), King of Swaziland (1986–). He has supreme powers as the 1968 constitution was suspended in 1973.

Mubarak, Mohammed Hosni (1928–), Egyptian politician. Leader of the National Democratic Party (NDP; 1982–), President of Egypt (1981–), PM (1981–82). He succeeded to the presidency on the assassination of Sadat, whose moderate policies he has continued. In the 1990s he has attempted to contain the rise of radical Islamic fundamentalism.

Mugabe, Robert (1924–), Zimbabwean politician. PM of Zimbabwe (1980–88), President (1988–). As leader of the Zimbabwe African National Union (ZANU; 1963–), he fought with Joshua Nkomo's Zimbabwe African People's Union (ZAPU) against the white government of Rhodesia until independence (as Zimbabwe) in 1980. He won the fierce power struggle with Nkomo, and the two parties agreed an alliance in 1976 and finally merged in 1986.

Mulroney, (Martin) Brian (1939–), Canadian Conservative politician. Leader of the Progressive Conservative Party of Canada (1983–93), PM (1984–93).

Muluzi, Bakili (1943–), Malawian politician of the United Democratic Front (UDF). President of Malawi (1994–).

Murayama, Tomiichi (1924–), Japanese trade unionist and Socialist politician. PM (1994–).

Museveni, Yoweri (1944–), Ugandan politician. President of Uganda and Minister of Defence (1986–). He came to power following a military coup.

Mwinyi, Ali Hassan (1925–), Tanzanian politician. Minister of Natural Resources and Tourism (1982–83), President of Zanzibar (1984), Vice-President of Tanzania (1984–85), President (1985–), Minister of Defence and National Service (1990–).

Narasimha Rao, P. V. (1921–), Indian politician of the Congress (I) Party. Chief Minister of Andhra Pradesh (1971–73), Minister of External Affairs (1980–85), of Defence and Acting Minister of Planning (1985), of Human Resources Development and Health and Family Welfare (1985–88), of External Affairs (1988–90). Leader of Congress (I) and PM (1991–). He took over the Party leadership after the assassination of Rajiv Gandhi, and went on to win the general election. His government has faced the growth of the militant Hindu fundamentalism and increasing ethnic fighting.

Nazarbayev, Nursultan (1940–), Kazakh politician. President of Kazakh Republic before independence, President of independent Kazakhstan (1991–). A Communist politician in the Kazakh Republic in the USSR, he retained power in Kazakhstan after independence.

Netanyahu, Benjamin (1949–), Israeli politician. Deputy Minister of Foreign Affairs (1988–92), Leader of the Likud Party (1993–).

Niyazov, Saparmuryad (1940–), Turkmen politician. PM (1985), Head of the Communist Party in Turkmenistan (1985–90), President of (independent) Turkmenistan (1990–).

Nuhayyan, Sheikh Sultan Zayid bin Al (1918–), Ruler of Emirate of Abu Dhabi. President of United Arab Emirates (1971–).

Nujoma, Sam (1929–), Namibian politician. President of SWAPO (1959–), President of Namibia (1990–). Nujoma was arrested in 1959 and forced into exile in 1960. He returned to Namibia in 1966 and took up the armed struggle against South Africa. On Namibian independence he became president.

Nyerere, Julius (1922–), Tanzanian politician and founder of the Tanganyika African National Union (TANU). Chief Minister (1960–61), PM (1961–62), President of Tanganyika (1962–64).

Nzo, Alfred (1925–), South African politician of the African National Congress. Minister of Foreign Affairs (1994–).

Occhetto, Achille (1936–), Italian politician of the Democratic Left (PDS) formerly the Communist Party (PCI). Deputy leader of the PDS (1987–88), leader of the PDS (1991–94).

Ochirbat, Punsalmaagiyn (1942–), Mongolian politician formerly of the Mongolian People's Revolutionary Party (MPRP), Minister of Fuel and Power Industry and Geology (1976), Minister of External Economic Relations (1985), President of Mongolia (1990–), since 1993 as a member of the opposition Mongolian National Democratic Party.

Oddsson, David (1948–), Icelandic politician. Leader of the Independence Party (1991–), PM and Minister for the Statistical Bureau (1991–).

Ortega, Daniel (1945–). Nicaraguan Socialist politician. President of Nicaragua (1981–90). As part of the Sandinista Liberation Front (FSLN), he helped overthrow the corrupt regime of Anastasio Somoza in 1979. As president he organized the war against Contra guerrillas. He was succeeded by Violeta Chamorro.

Ozawa, Ichiro (1942–), Japanese politician. Minister of Home Affairs (1985–87). A powerful figure in Japanese politics, he helped bring down the government of Kiichi Miyazawa. Originally of the Liberal Democrat Party, he left to head the new Japanese Renewal Party (JRP).

Panyarachun, Anand (1932–), Thai politician. PM (1991–).

Papandreou, Andreas (1919–), Greek politician. Minister of Economic Co-ordination (1965), Leader of the Pan-Hellenic Socialist Party (PASOK; 1974–), Leader of Opposition in Parliament (1977–81), PM (1981–89 and 1993–), Minister of Defence (1981–86).

Papoulias, Karolos (1929–), Greek politician of the Pan-Hellenic Socialist Party (PASOK). Minister of Foreign Affairs (1985–89, and since 1993).

Patterson, P. (Percival) J. (1935–), Jamaican politician. Deputy PM and Minister of Development, Planning and Production (1989–92), Finance Minister (1990–91), leader of the People's National Party (PNP) and PM (1992–). He came to power after the resignation of Michael Manley due to ill health.

Pawlak, Waldemar (1959–), Polish politician of the Polish Peasant Party. PM (1993–).

Peres, Shimon (1923–), Israeli politician of the Labour Party. Minister for Economic Development in the Administered Areas and for Immigrant Absorption (1969–70), of Transport and Communications (1970–74), of Information (1974), of Defence (1974–77), Acting PM (1977), Leader of the Opposition (1974–84), PM (1984–86), Minister of the Interior and of Religious Affairs (1984–85), Deputy PM and Finance Minister (1988–90), Minister of Foreign Affairs (1992–).

Perez Balladres, Ernesto (1946–), Panamanian politician. President (1994–).

Perez, Carlos (1922–), Venezuelan politician. Minister of the Interior (1963–64), President of Venezuela (1974–79, 1989–93). He was suspended from office on charges of corruption.

Perry, William (1927–), US Democrat politician. Deputy Secretary of State for Defense (1993–94) and Secretary of State for Defense (1994–).

Peterson, Niels Helveg (1939–), Danish politician of the Radical Liberal Party. Minister for Economic Affairs (1988–90), Foreign Minister (1993–).

Phoumsavanh, Nouhak (1914–), Laotian Communist politician. President of Laos (1992–).

Pinochet, Augusto (1915–), Chilean general and politician. Commander-in-Chief of Armed Forces (1973–), President (1974–90). He overthrew President Salvador Allende in a military coup in 1973, becoming president the following year. After 16 years of repressive rule, he allowed elections to be held in 1989, handing over to Patricio Aylwin.

Pol Pot (1925–). Cambodian Communist politician. Leader of the Khmer Rouge (1962–85), PM (1976–79). His attempt to create a self-sufficient workers' utopia resulted in the massacre of up to 2,000,000 of his compatriots. He was overthrown by the Vietnamese in 1978, and although no longer the military leader of the Khmer Rouge he remains an influential figure within the organization.

Qaboos Bin Said (1940–), Sultan of Oman, PM, Minister of Foreign Affairs, Defence and Finance (1970–).

Rabbini, Burhanuddin (1943–), Afghan politician. President of Afghanistan (1992–).

Rabin, Yitshak (1922–), Israeli Labour politician. Minister of Labour (1974), Leader of the Labour Party (1974–77), PM (1974–77 and 1992–). His second term of office saw the signing of the Israeli-Palestinian Peace Accord.

Rabuka, Sitiveni (1948–), Fijian army officer and politician. Head of State (1987), Minister of Home Affairs (1987–90), deputy PM and Minister of Home Affairs (1991–92), PM (1992–). Following the election of an Indian-dominated government in 1987, Rabuka staged two successive military coups and temporarily became head of state. He helped introduce a constitution (1990) that guaranteed political power for the Melanese (Fijian) population.

Rafsanjani, Hashemi (1934–), Iranian politician. President of Iran (1989–). His rule has seen a more pragmatic phase of the Iranian revolution.

Rainier III (1923–), Prince of Monaco (1949–). He succeeded on the death of his grandfather.

Ramaphosa, Cyril (1953–), South African politician.

Ramos, Fidel (1928–), Filippino politician and army officer. Secretary of National Defence (1988–92), President (1992–).

Rannariddh, Prince Norodom, leader of the royalist FUNCINPEC (United National Front for an Independent, Neutral, Peaceful and Cooperative Cambodia), PM (1993–).

Rasmussen, Poul Nyrup (1944–), Danish politician. Leader of the Social Democratic Party (1992–), PM (1993–). He succeeded Poul Schluter.

Rau, Johannes (1931–), German politician of the Social DEmocratic Party. State Premier of North Rhine-Westphalia (1978–).

Rawlings, Flight Lt. Jerry (1947–), Ghanaian politician. Head of the Armed Forces Revolutionary Council (1979), Head of State (1982–), Chairman of the Provisional National Defence Council (1981–), Chief of Defence (1982–). Rawlings took power in 1979 following his first coup but returned power to an elected government the same year. After his second coup in 1981, however, he remained head of a military government. In 1992 he was returned to power after multiparty elections.

Reno, Janet (1938–), US Democrat politician. State Attorney for Florida (1978–93), Attorney General of the USA (1993–).

Reynolds, Albert (1935–), Irish politician of the Fianna Faíl Party. Minister for Posts and Telegraphs and Transport (1979–81), for Industry and Energy (1982), for Industry and Commerce (1987–88), for Finance and the Public Service (1988–89), of Finance (1989–), Taoiseach (PM; 1992–). He came to power after the resignation of his predecessor, Charles Haughey.

Robinson, Mary (1944–), Irish politician. President of Ireland (1990–).

Rocard, Michel (1930–), French Socialist politician. Minister of State, Minister of Planning and Regional Development (1981–83), of Agriculture (1983–85), PM (1988–91).

Saddam Hussein (1937–), Iraqi politician of the Ba'ath Party. Vice-President of the Revolutionary Command Council (1969–79), President of the Revolutionary Command Council (1979–), President of Iraq (1979–), PM (1994–). He has ruled repressively and embroiled his country in two disastrous wars, the Iran–Iraq War (1980–88) and the Gulf War of 1991, which followed the Iraqi invasion and annexation of Kuwait (1990). Saddam has faced numerous attempted coups. Although still in power, he faces rebellions from the Kurds in the north (where the Iraqi central government no longer exercises authority), unrest in the Shiite south of Iraq and the threat of UN economic sanctions.

Saleh, Ali Abdullah (c. 1942–), Yemeni politician and army officer. President of Yemen Arab Republic (North Yemen; 1978–90), of the (united) Republic of Yemen (1990–).

Salinas, Carlos (1948–), Mexican politician of the Institutional Revolutionary Party (PRI). Minister of Planning and Federal Budget (1982–87), President of Mexico (1988–). His term of office expires in 1994.

Samper, Ernesto (1951–), Colombian politician of the Liberal Party. President (1994–).

Sanchez de Lozada, Gonzalo (1930–), Bolivian politician of the Revolutionary Nationalist Movement (MNR). President of Bolivia (1993–).

Sandiford, Lloyd Erskine (1937–), Barbados politician for the Democratic Labour Party. Member of Senate (1967–71), Minister for Education (1967–71), for Education, Youth Affairs, Community Development and Sport (1971–75), of Health and Welfare (1975–76), Deputy PM and Minister of Education and Culture (1986–87), PM and Minister of Economic Affairs (1987–).

Santer, Jacques (1937–), Luxembourg politician of the Social Christian Party. Minister of Finance, of Labour and of Social Security (1979–84), PM (1984–). President-designate of the EC Commission (1994) - his term of office begins on 1 January 1995.

Savimbi, Jonas (1934–), Angolan military leader and politician. Initially associated with the FNLA Party, he broke away to form UNITA and fought first against the Portuguese for independence and then against the MPLA government. However, he refused to accept the results of the 1992 free elections and has resumed the military struggle.

Scalfaro, Luigi (1918–), Italian politician. Minister of Transport and Civil Aviation in the Moro, Leone and Andreotti governments of the 1960s and 1970s, Minister of Education in Andreotti's 1976–79 government, Minister of the Interior (1983–87), President (1992–).

Scharping, Rudolf (1948–), German politician. State Premier of Rhineland-Palatinate (1991–), leader of the Social Democratic Party (SPD; 1993–).

Schlüter, Poul (1929–), Danish Conservative politician. Leader of the Conservative People's Party (KF; 1974–93), PM (1982–93).

Sedki, Atef (1930–), Egyptian politician of the National Democratic Party (NDP). PM (1986–).

Shamir, Yitzhak (1915–), Israeli politician of the Likud Party. Minister of foreign Affairs (1980–83), PM (1983–84 and 1986–92), Minister of Foreign Affairs (1984–86), Acting Minister of the Interior (1987–88). While in office he refused to negotiate with the PLO.

Sharif, Nawaz (1949–), Pakistani politician of the Islamic Democratic Alliance. Chief Minister of Punjab (1988–90), PM of Pakistan (1990–93).

Sharma, Shankar (1918–), Indian politician.

Chief Minister of Bhopal (1952–56), Minister of Communications (1974–77), Vice-President of India (1987–92), President of India (1992–).

Shevardnadze, Eduard (1928–), Georgian politician. Soviet Foreign Minister (1985–90), President of Georgia (1992–). As Foreign Minister under Gorbachov he revolutionized Soviet foreign policy. Relations with the West were improved, a number of arms reduction treaties agreed with the USA and its NATO allied, and the Soviet Union abandoned its commitment to intervene in the affairs of Warsaw Pact countries. In 1991 he resigned from the Communist Party and as Foreign Minister. The following year he became President of Georgia.

Sihanouk, Norodom (1922–), King of Cambodia (1941–55; abdicated), PM and Minister of Foreign Affairs (1955–60), Head of State (1960–70 and 1975–76), self-styled President of a National Government of Cambodia (while in exile) (1982–90), restored as King of Cambodia (1993–). After his abdication in 1955 he dominated Cambodian political life until 1970, when he was overthrown in a US-backed military coup. He was nominal head of state (1975–76) following the victory of the Khmer Rouge in the civil war, but was finally forced into exile. He returned to Cambodia in 1989 to help broker a UN-sponsored peace settlement. He regained the throne in 1993 following multiparty elections.

Silajdzic, Haris, Bosnian politician. PM of Bosnia-Herzegovina (1994–).

Siphandon, Khamtay, General (1923–), Laotian Communist politician. PM (1993–).

Snegur, Mireca (1940–), Moldovan politician. President of Moldova (1990–).

Soares, Mario (1924–), Portuguese Socialist politician. PM (1976–78 and 1983–85), President (1986–). He became Portugal's first civilian president for 60 years.

Soglo, Nicéphore (1934–), Benin politician. PM of Benin (1990–91) and President (1991–).

Solana, Javier (1942–), Spanish politician. Minister of Education (1988–92), Minister of Foreign Affairs (1992–).

Spring, Dick (1950–), Irish politician. Leader of the Labour Party (1982–), Deputy PM (1982–87), Minister for the Environment (1982–83), for Energy (1983–87), Tánaiste (Deputy PM), Minister for Foreign Affairs (1993–).

Stoltenberg, Thorvald (1931–), Norwegian politician of the Labour Party. Minister of Defence (1979–81), of Foreign Affairs (1987–89 and 1990–).

Strasser, Valentine (1965–), Sierra Leone soldier and politician. Head of State and

Chairman of the National Ruling Council (NPRC) (1992–).

Streibl, Max (1932–), German politician. Leader of the Christian Social Union (CSU; 1967–71), State Premier of Bavaria (1988–94).

Suharto, T.N.I. (1921–), Indonesian army officer and politician. President (1967–). He came to power after the overthrow of his predecessor, Achmed Sukarno. During the coup tens of thousands of supposedly Communist sympathizers were killed. His invasion of East Timor in 1975 has been internationally condemned.

Tatarella, Giuseppe (1936–), Italian politician of the (neo-fascist) National Alliance. Deputy PM and Minister for Telecommunications (1994–).

Taya, Maaouiya Ould (1943–), Mauritanian military officer and politician. PM and Minister of Defence (1981–84), Minister of Defence and President (1984–). Taya ruled as head of a military government until 1992 when he was returned to power in multiparty elections.

Ter-Petrosyan, Levon (1945–), Armenian politician and leader of the Armenian National Movement. President (1991–).

Than Shwe, Burmese politician. Head of military junta (State Law and Order Restoration Council; SLORC) (1992–).

Treurnicht, Andries (1921–), South African politician. Minister of Public Works, Statistics and Tourism (1979–80), of Administration and Statistics (1980–82), leader of the Conservative Party (1982–).

Tudjman, Franjo (1922–), Croatian politician of the Croat Democratic Union. President of Croatia (1990–).

Ulmanis, Guntis (1939–), Latvian politician President (1993–).

Vacaroiou, Nicolae (1943–), Romanian independent politician. PM (1992–).

Vranitzky, Franz (1937–), Austrian politician of the Social Democratic Party (SPL). Federal Minister of Finance (1984–86), Federal Chancellor (1986–).

Waigel, Theo (1939–), German politician. Leader of the Christian Social Union (CSU; 1988–), Minister of Finance (1989–).

Waldheim, Kurt (1918–), Austrian politician and diplomat. Minister for Foreign Affairs (1968–70), UN Secretary-General (1972–81) and President of Austria (1986–92).

Walesa, Lech (1943–), Polish politician. President of Poland (1990–). As an underground trade union organizer in Gdansk in the 1970s, he helped create the free trade union Solidarity. He was imprisoned after the declaration of martial law in 1981, but in 1989 he negotiated the agreement that ended Communist rule in Poland. He split from Solidarity in 1993.

Wasmosy, Juan Carlos (1939–), Paraguayan politician of the Colorado Party. President (1993–).

Weizman, Ezer (1924–), Israeli politician, originally Likud Party but later Labour Party. Minister of Transport (1969–70), of Defence (1977–80), of Communications (1984–88), of Science (1988–93), President (1993–).

Westerberg, Bengt (1943–), Swedish politician. Leader of the Liberal Party (1984–), deputy PM and Minister of Social Welfare (1991–).

Wijetunga, Dingiri Banda (1922–), Sri Lankan politician of the United National Party. Minister of Information and Broadcasting (1978–79), of Power and Highways (1979–80), of Power, Energy, Posts and Telecommunications (1980–82), of Posts and Finance and Planning (1989–), PM (1989–).

Yeltsin, Boris (1931–), Russian politician. President of the Russian Federation (within the Soviet Union) (1990–91), President of the independent Russian Federation (1991–). The dominant statesman of post-Communist Russia, he led the opposition to the attempted coup by Communist hardliners in 1991 and was instrumental in the establishment of the Commonwealth of Independent States (CIS). He introduced deregulation and privatization to Russia, but has been beset by economic problems and political crises.

Zafy, Albert , Madagascan politician. President of Madagascar (1993–).

Zenawi, Meles, Ethiopian politician of the Ethiopian People's Revolutionary Democratic Front (EPRDF). President of Ethiopia (1991–).

Zhelev, Zhelo (1936–), Bulgarian politician of the Union of Democratic Forces. President (1990–).

Zhirinovsky, Vladimir (1947–), Russian populist nationalist politician. Leader of the Liberal Democratic Party.

Zhivkov, Todor (1911–), Bulgarian Communist politician. First Secretary of Central Committee (1954–81), PM (1962–71), General Secretary of the Bulgarian Communist Party (1981–89), Head of State (1971–89). His effective rule over Bulgaria from 1954 came to an end in 1989 when he was replaced by reformers. He was tried and convicted on corruption charges in 1992.

Zhu Rongji (1929–), Chinese Communist politician. Chairman of the Economic and Trade Office (1992–).

Zia, Begum Khalida, Bangladeshi politician (widow of the former President General Ziaur Rahman). Leader of the Bangladesh Nationalist Party (BNP; 1982–), PM (1991–).

Index

441

446